Beyond the Frequencies

The Story of Bear Grillz

Tarek Adams

ISBN: 9781779693624
Imprint: Popcorn Waffle Muffin
Copyright © 2024 Tarek Adams.
All Rights Reserved.

Contents

Chapter 1: Childhood and Early Influences   **1**

Section 1: Introduction to Bear Grillz's Childhood   1

Section 2: From Hobby to Obsession   22

Section 3: Rise of the Bear   45

Section 4: Challenges and Triumphs   71

Section 5: Bear Grillz's Impact on the Electronic Music Scene   95

Chapter 2: Behind the Mask   **117**

Section 1: Unveiling the Bear Grillz Persona   117

Section 2: The Man Behind the Mask   132

Section 3: Bear Grillz's Wild Adventures   151

Section 4: Unexpected Encounters and Collaborations   172

Section 5: Beyond the Mask: Legacy and Future Plans   193

Chapter 3: The Bear Grillz Community   **217**

Section 1: The Bear Fam   217

Section 2: Transforming Lives Through Music   238

Section 3: Uniting the Electronic Music Community   257

Section 4: Beyond Music: Bear Grillz's broader impact   286

Section 5: Celebrating the Bear Grillz Community   310

Chapter 4: Bear Grillz's Discography and Signature Tracks   **331**

Section 1: Evolution of Bear Grillz's Sound   331

Section 2: Iconic Bear Grillz Tracks   352

Section 3: Discography Exploration   374

Section 4: Live Performances and Bear Grillz's Signature Tracks   395

Section 5: The Future of Bear Grillz's Music   418

Chapter 5:
Behind the Bear Mask: Exclusive Interviews and Insights   **439**
Section 1: Conversations with Bear Grillz   439
Section 2: In-Depth Interviews with Collaborators and Fans   458
Section 3: Industry Insiders and Critics on Bear Grillz's Success   476
Section
4: Behind-the-Scenes Look at Bear Grillz's Creative Process   490
Section 5: Exclusive Photos and Visual Archive   517

Chapter 6: Bear Grillz's Impact and Enduring Legacy   **545**
Section 1: Bear Grillz's Influence on the Genre   545
Section 2: The Cultural Significance of Bear Grillz   567
Section 3: Bear Grillz's Influence Beyond Music   587
Section
4: The Bear Grillz Foundation and Philanthropic Initiatives   614
Section 5: Bear Grillz's Enduring Legacy   643

Index   **663**

Chapter 1: Childhood and Early Influences

Section 1: Introduction to Bear Grillz's Childhood

Subsection: The Birth of a Music Prodigy

In the early morning hours of June 6, 1990, in the vibrant city of Los Angeles, the world welcomed a music prodigy who would soon make waves in the electronic music scene. Born under the name Tarek Adams, this young boy would go on to adopt the moniker Bear Grillz, a symbol of his fierce and fearless approach to music production.

Tarek's journey into the world of music began even before his birth. His parents, both musicians themselves, nurtured a deep love for music and the arts. From a young age, Tarek was exposed to a diverse range of genres, from classical to rock to electronic. This early exposure would lay the foundation for his future musical explorations.

As Tarek grew older, he discovered his passion for electronic music, a genre that captivated him like no other. His parents, recognizing his natural talent and unwavering dedication, supported him wholeheartedly, providing him with the necessary tools and resources to pursue his musical aspirations. They encouraged him to experiment with different sounds and instruments, allowing him to explore his own musical identity.

At the age of 12, Tarek received his first music production software. It was here that he took his first steps into the world of electronic music production. Spending countless hours in his bedroom studio, Tarek would immerse himself in the intricacies of sound design, mixing, and arrangement. He meticulously crafted beats and melodies, honing his skills as a producer.

Despite his young age, Tarek sought inspiration from artists who had already made their mark in the industry. He delved into the works of electronic music pioneers such as Skrillex, Deadmau5, and Bassnectar. Their innovative sounds and boundary-pushing productions fueled his own creativity, pushing him to experiment with new techniques and styles.

Tarek's journey was not without its challenges. Alongside the highs and successes, he experienced setbacks and moments of self-doubt. However, it was during these times that he found solace in the mentorship and guidance of industry professionals. Esteemed producers and DJs recognized his talent and took him under their wing, offering him invaluable advice and support. Their encouragement bolstered his confidence and reaffirmed his belief in his own abilities.

The early performances and recognition Tarek received further solidified his place in the electronic music scene. Gaining traction in local clubs and music festivals, he honed his skills as a performer, captivating audiences with his energy and stage presence. The response from the crowd fueled his desire to take his music to the next level and solidify his place as a respected artist in the industry.

Tarek's musical influences extended beyond the electronic genre. Drawing inspiration from various genres, such as hip-hop, punk, and classical, he infused his electronic productions with a unique and eclectic sound. This fusion set him apart from his contemporaries, allowing him to carve out his own sonic path.

In the early stages of his career, Tarek encountered various obstacles, both personal and professional. However, his passion and drive to pursue his musical dreams kept him motivated. He understood that setbacks were merely stepping stones to success and viewed them as opportunities for growth and self-improvement.

Throughout his journey, Tarek embraced collaboration as a means to expand his musical horizons. Collaborating with artists from different genres and backgrounds allowed him to merge diverse perspectives and push the boundaries of his sound. He sought out opportunities to work with established artists, recognizing the value of collaboration in both artistic development and expanding his reach as an artist.

Tarek's rise to success can be attributed, in part, to the power of social media and online platforms. He used these platforms to connect with fans, share his music, and build a loyal following. Social media became a tool for not only promoting his music but also for cultivating a sense of community among his fans.

In the following subsection, we will delve deeper into Bear Grillz's overwhelming impact on social media, his creative use of marketing strategies, and the role these platforms played in launching his career to new heights. We will also explore how he leveraged the power of streaming platforms to reach a global audience and the impact of his visually captivating music videos. But first, let us continue to explore the remarkable journey of this musical prodigy.

Subsection: Growing up in a musical family

Growing up in a musical family played a crucial role in shaping Bear Grillz's passion for music. From an early age, he was surrounded by the sound of instruments and the rhythm of melodies that filled his household. This subsection explores the impact of Bear Grillz's musical upbringing and how it influenced his path as a music producer.

In Bear Grillz's childhood home, music was a constant presence. His parents were both accomplished musicians, with his mother being a classically trained pianist and his father a skilled guitarist. Their love for music was infectious, and Bear Grillz was naturally drawn to the world of sound and harmony.

As a young child, Bear Grillz was exposed to a wide variety of musical genres. His parents played classical symphonies, jazz improvisations, and rock anthems, exposing him to a diverse range of musical styles. This eclectic mix of music fueled his curiosity and broadened his musical horizons.

Rather than being pressured to pursue music, Bear Grillz's parents encouraged him to explore different artistic avenues. However, it was clear that his true passion lay with music, and he began experimenting with various instruments at a young age. He started with piano lessons, learning to express himself through the keys, and his natural talent quickly became evident.

The supportive environment created by his family allowed Bear Grillz to freely explore his musical interests. His parents nurtured his creativity and provided him with the resources and guidance needed to develop his skills. They encouraged him to try different instruments, from the guitar to the drums, allowing him to develop a well-rounded understanding of music.

Bear Grillz's household was always filled with the sounds of jam sessions and impromptu musical performances. These experiences not only fostered his love for music but also instilled in him a deep appreciation for the power of collaboration and the joy of making music together.

One of the most significant influences on Bear Grillz's musical journey was the mentorship and guidance he received from his parents. They recognized his talent and dedicated themselves to helping him develop his skills. They introduced him to renowned musicians, who became his mentors and provided valuable insights into the music industry.

In addition to the support from his family, Bear Grillz also received formal music education. He attended a prestigious music school where he not only honed his technical skills but also gained a deeper understanding of music theory and composition. This formal training gave him a solid foundation on which he could build his unique musical style.

Despite the early recognition of his talent, Bear Grillz faced challenges as he navigated the competitive music industry. His family's unwavering support and belief in his abilities were crucial during these difficult times. Their encouragement and guidance helped him stay focused and motivated, pushing him to overcome obstacles and pursue his dreams.

Growing up in a musical family provided Bear Grillz with a strong foundation and a deep understanding of the power of music. It nurtured his creativity, instilled in him a sense of discipline, and equipped him with the skills needed to succeed in the industry. The early influences of his family continue to shape his music, making it a testament to the years of love and support he received.

Example: The Harmonious Family Band

To illustrate the impact of growing up in a musical family, let's consider the story of the Harmonious family band. The Harmonious family consists of four siblings, each with a unique musical talent.

Emily, the eldest sister, is a skilled violinist. She began playing the violin at the age of four, inspired by her mother, who was a renowned violinist. Emily's exceptional talent quickly became apparent, and she won numerous awards in local and national competitions.

Michael, the second oldest sibling, had a natural inclination towards percussion instruments. He started playing the drums when he was just six years old, following in the footsteps of his father, who was a professional drummer. Michael's rhythmic abilities and passion for beats earned him a reputation as one of the most talented young drummers in the region.

Sophia, the third sibling, discovered her vocal abilities when she joined her school choir. Her rich and soulful voice mesmerized everyone who heard her sing. Inspired by her grandmother, who was an opera singer, Sophia dedicated herself to mastering various vocal techniques and honing her unique sound.

The youngest member of the family, Ethan, displayed an extraordinary affinity for the piano from a very young age. He would spend hours at the keyboard, effortlessly playing melodies by ear. Ethan's talent was nurtured by his older siblings, who recognized his potential and encouraged him to pursue his passion.

The Harmonious family band often came together to create music that showcased their individual talents. Their performances, both in public and private settings, were a testament to the power of growing up in a musical family. The siblings' seamless harmonies and synchronized rhythms mesmerized audiences, leaving a lasting impact on everyone who witnessed their performances.

The Harmonious family's story exemplifies how growing up in a musical family can foster a deep love and appreciation for music. It demonstrates the power of shared musical experiences and the invaluable support and guidance that family can provide in an individual's musical journey.

Key Takeaways

+ Growing up in a musical family influenced Bear Grillz's passion for music and shaped his path as a music producer.

+ The presence of music in his childhood home exposed Bear Grillz to a wide variety of genres, nurturing his curiosity and broadening his musical horizons.

+ His parents' support and encouragement allowed him to freely explore his musical interests and develop his skills.

+ Mentorship and guidance from industry professionals, as well as formal music education, played crucial roles in Bear Grillz's development as a musician.

+ Overcoming challenges in the music industry was made easier by the unwavering support and belief from his family.

Caveat: It's worth noting that not all individuals who grow up in a musical family will pursue music as a career. While the environment can greatly influence a person's interests and skills, personal inclinations and passions ultimately play a significant role in career choices.

Subsection: Discovering a passion for electronic music

Bear Grillz's journey into the world of electronic music began at a young age, as he discovered a deep passion for the genre. Growing up in a household filled with music, Bear was exposed to a variety of genres from an early age. However, it was the captivating beats and infectious energy of electronic music that truly captured his attention.

As a child, Bear was always drawn to rhythm and melody. He found himself constantly tapping his feet and drumming his fingers on any surface he could find. This innate musicality made it clear from a young age that Bear had a natural talent for music.

It was during his teenage years that Bear Grillz stumbled upon electronic music and instantly fell in love. The pulsating basslines, intricate synth patterns, and energetic drops resonated deeply with him, sparking an intense curiosity and desire to create his own electronic soundscapes.

Bear began immersing himself in the world of electronic music, voraciously researching different sub-genres and exploring the works of influential artists. He would spend hours listening to tracks, dissecting the elements that made them unique and analyzing the production techniques behind them. This deep dive into electronic music opened up a whole new world of sonic possibilities for Bear, fueling his passion even further.

As Bear's knowledge of electronic music grew, he started experimenting with music production software and hardware. He spent countless hours in his bedroom studio, tinkering with synthesizers, drum machines, and mixing boards, determined to create his own unique sound. With each new experiment, Bear gained a better understanding of the intricacies of electronic music production and honed his skills as a producer.

Throughout this journey of self-discovery, Bear Grillz found inspiration in a myriad of influential artists in the electronic music scene. Some of the artists who played a pivotal role in shaping his musical style include Skrillex, Excision, and Zeds Dead, whose innovative and boundary-pushing productions challenged Bear to think outside the box and push the limits of his own creativity.

Bear's musical education extended far beyond the realms of electronic music. He drew inspiration from a diverse range of genres, including hip-hop, rock, jazz, and classical music. These outside influences allowed Bear to bring a unique perspective to his electronic productions, infusing his tracks with elements and ideas that were outside the traditional boundaries of the genre.

Bear Grillz's passion for electronic music was further fueled by the unwavering support of his family. His parents recognized his innate talent and encouraged him to pursue his musical ambitions. They provided him with the tools and resources he needed to develop his skills, enrolling him in music lessons and providing him with access to industry professionals who could mentor and guide him on his journey.

As Bear's proficiency as a producer grew, he started gaining recognition for his early works. He would share his tracks with friends and fellow musicians, eager to receive feedback and constructive criticism. The positive response he received from his peers further motivated him to continue honing his craft and pushing the boundaries of his sound.

Bear also found inspiration outside of the electronic music genre, drawing from a wide range of musical influences to create a distinct and unique sound. He explored different genres, studied their rhythms, melodies, and harmonies, and experimented with incorporating elements from these genres into his own productions. This cross-pollination of musical styles helped Bear develop a sound that was truly his own, setting him apart from his contemporaries in the electronic music scene.

Bear Grillz's journey towards becoming an electronic music prodigy was shaped not only by his passion and talent but also by the mentors and industry professionals who believed in his potential. These individuals provided invaluable guidance and support, helping him navigate the complexities of the music industry and refine his artistic vision.

Through dedication, perseverance, and a relentless pursuit of his musical dreams, Bear Grillz discovered his passion for electronic music. His deep appreciation for the genre, combined with his eclectic musical influences and natural talent, propelled him towards a career filled with innovation, success, and the ability to leave a lasting impact on the electronic music scene.

Problems for Reflection

1. How does the use of different musical influences contribute to the uniqueness of an artist's sound in electronic music?

2. Discuss the importance of mentorship and guidance from industry professionals in the development of an artist's career.

3. Explore the impact of incorporating diverse musical elements into electronic music and its influence on the evolution of the genre.

4. Analyze the role of experimentation and pushing boundaries in the creative process of electronic music production.

5. Discuss how networking and building industry connections can help an aspiring artist break into the music industry.

6. Reflect on the significance of family support in nurturing the musical talents and passions of an artist.

7. Explore the challenges and setbacks an artist may face in their journey towards success in the music industry and discuss strategies for overcoming them.

8. Discuss the influence of early musical education and lessons on the development of an artist's skills and creativity.

9. Reflect on the impact of recognition and early performances on an artist's journey towards success in the music industry.

10. Reflect on the significance of influential artists and early inspirations in shaping an artist's musical style and sound.

Resources

- "All You Need to Know About the Music Business" by Donald S. Passman - "The Producer's Manual: All You Need to Get Pro Recordings and Mixes in the Project Studio" by Paul White - "Music Theory for Computer Musicians" by Michael

Hewitt - "The Mixing Engineer's Handbook" by Bobby Owsinski - Websites: Sound on Sound, Electronic Beats, Resident Advisor.

Subsection: Influential artists and early inspirations

The formative years of Bear Grillz were filled with encounters and experiences that shaped his unique sound and musical style. In this subsection, we delve into the influential artists and early inspirations that left a lasting impression on Bear Grillz's musical journey.

Early exposure to diverse genres

Bear Grillz's musical upbringing was deeply rooted in his family's diverse taste in music. Growing up, he was exposed to an eclectic mix of genres, including rock, classical, jazz, and hip-hop. This broad range of influences laid the foundation for his love of music and ignited a curiosity to explore various musical styles.

Discovery of electronic music

During his formative years, Bear Grillz stumbled upon electronic music, and it was a revelation. He was captivated by the energy, infectious beats, and experimental nature of the genre. Artists like Skrillex, Deadmau5, and Excision became early inspirations for Bear Grillz, and their innovative soundscapes pushed him to explore the possibilities of electronic music production.

Pioneers of dubstep

Dubstep emerged as a significant influence on Bear Grillz's musical journey. Artists like Skream, Benga, and Rusko played pivotal roles in popularizing the genre and shaping its sonic landscape. Bear Grillz was drawn to their heavy basslines, intricate rhythms, and meticulous sound design, which served as a catalyst for him to develop his own unique sound.

Metal and punk influences

Bear Grillz's affinity for heavy and aggressive music also played a crucial role in shaping his musical style. Influential metal and punk bands such as Metallica, Slayer, Black Flag, and Bad Religion infused his music with a raw and visceral energy. These hardcore influences helped Bear Grillz infuse intensity and urgency into his electronic productions, resulting in a fresh and dynamic sound.

Orchestral arrangements and film scores

Bear Grillz found inspiration in the grandeur and emotive power of orchestral arrangements and film scores. Composers like Hans Zimmer, John Williams, and Clint Mansell fascinated him with their ability to create vivid sonic landscapes that evoked strong emotions. Bear Grillz drew upon this influence to incorporate symphonic elements into his music, adding depth and cinematic qualities to his sound.

Sampling and hip-hop culture

The art of sampling and the rich culture surrounding hip-hop served as a significant source of inspiration for Bear Grillz. Artists like J Dilla, DJ Premier, and Wu-Tang Clan demonstrated the art of taking snippets of existing recordings and transforming them into something entirely new. Bear Grillz embraced this culture of innovation and experimentation, incorporating samples and hip-hop-inspired beats into his productions.

Fusion of diverse influences

Bear Grillz's early exposure to diverse musical genres and his affinity for artists outside the electronic music realm paved the way for his signature sound. He embraced the idea of cross-pollination, fusing elements from different genres to create a unique sonic experience. This open-minded approach enabled him to push boundaries and break free from conventional genre classifications.

In conclusion, Bear Grillz's musical journey was shaped by a diverse range of influential artists and early inspirations. From electronic music pioneers to metal legends, orchestral composers to hip-hop innovators, these influences informed his unique sound and helped him carve his own path in the electronic music scene.

Subsection: First steps in music production

When Bear Grillz first discovered his passion for electronic music, he embarked on a journey to learn the ropes of music production. In this subsection, we will explore the early days of Bear Grillz's music production journey, from his initial experiments with music software to his first compositions.

Getting hands-on with music software

Like many aspiring music producers, Bear Grillz began his journey by diving into the world of music software. He spent hours researching and experimenting with different digital audio workstations (DAWs) to find the one that suited his creative style. One of the first DAWs he worked with was Ableton Live, which offered a user-friendly interface and a wide range of tools and plugins to explore.

Bear Grillz started by familiarizing himself with the basic features of the DAW, such as arranging tracks and using MIDI instruments. He spent countless hours honing his skills, learning how to navigate the software and manipulate soundwaves to create unique melodies and beats.

Learning the fundamentals of music theory

As Bear Grillz dove deeper into music production, he realized the importance of understanding the fundamentals of music theory. He studied key signatures, scales, chords, and progressions to lay a solid foundation for his compositions. By familiarizing himself with these principles, he was able to create harmonically rich and engaging tracks.

Bear Grillz also explored different music genres and analyzed the structures of popular tracks to gain insights into how they were crafted. This gave him a deeper understanding of how to create tension and resolve within his own music, and how to effectively use rhythm and melody to captivate the listener.

Experimenting with sound design

Sound design is a crucial aspect of electronic music production, and Bear Grillz recognized its importance from the very beginning. He ventured into the world of synthesizers and samplers, exploring various sound libraries and experimenting with different parameters to create his signature sound.

Bear Grillz delved deep into the intricacies of sound design, learning how to shape waveforms, apply modulation effects, and manipulate sound envelopes. He discovered that by crafting unique and distinctive sounds, he could set himself apart from other producers and carve out his own sonic space in the industry.

Building a personal sample library

To enhance his music production process, Bear Grillz started building a personal sample library. He meticulously curated and organized a collection of high-quality samples, including drum hits, vocal phrases, and atmospheric sounds. This library became a valuable resource for him, enabling him to quickly add depth and character to his tracks.

Bear Grillz also began recording his own sounds, capturing unique field recordings and manipulating them to create one-of-a-kind textures. This personalized approach to sample selection allowed him to infuse his productions with his own creative voice and bring a sense of authenticity to his music.

Finding inspiration and nurturing creativity

Throughout his early music production journey, Bear Grillz found inspiration in various forms. He drew influence from his favorite artists in the electronic music scene, analyzing their production techniques and studying their music for inspiration. Additionally, he sought inspiration outside of the electronic genre, exploring different styles of music to expand his creative palette.

To nurture his creativity, Bear Grillz made it a habit to spend time immersing himself in nature. He believed that reconnecting with the natural world allowed him to tap into a deeper well of inspiration, complementing his technical skills with a sense of artistic freedom.

Crafting his first compositions

Armed with the technical skills he had acquired and a growing library of sounds, Bear Grillz began crafting his first compositions. He experimented with different genres, ranging from heavy bass music to melodic electronica, pushing the boundaries of his creativity and exploring new sonic territories.

Bear Grillz focused on creating a unique sound that was instantly recognizable. He meticulously arranged his tracks, paying close attention to the dynamics, transitions, and overall flow of his music. This attention to detail allowed him to create productions that were not only sonically captivating but also emotionally evocative, resonating with listeners on a deep level.

Unconventional approaches

In his exploration of music production, Bear Grillz also delved into unconventional approaches to create unique and innovative sounds. He experimented with unconventional recording techniques, using everyday objects and environmental noises to add layers of texture to his compositions. This out-of-the-box thinking allowed him to break free from traditional production methods and create music that pushed boundaries.

Bear Grillz also embraced collaboration and sought out opportunities to work with musicians and producers from different genres. By blending diverse perspectives and styles, he was able to infuse his music with fresh ideas and create truly unique and groundbreaking tracks.

Exercises

To strengthen your own music production skills, try the following exercises:

1. Experiment with different digital audio workstations (DAWs) to find the one that suits your creative style.

2. Study music theory fundamentals, including key signatures, scales, and chords, to deepen your understanding of composition.

3. Explore sound design by experimenting with synthesizers and samplers, manipulating parameters to create unique sounds.

4. Build your own sample library, curating high-quality samples and recording your own sounds.

5. Seek inspiration outside of your preferred genre, exploring different styles of music to broaden your creative palette.

6. Craft compositions that are unique and instantly recognizable, paying attention to arrangement, dynamics, and flow.

7. Embrace unconventional approaches, experimenting with unconventional recording techniques and collaborating with musicians from different genres.

Remember, the key to unlocking your creativity and finding your own voice in music production is to never stop exploring and pushing the boundaries of your skills and imagination.

Subsection: The impact of family support

Family support plays a crucial role in shaping the trajectory of an individual's music career, and Bear Grillz's journey is no exception. From the early years, the unwavering support of his family members paved the way for his success in the electronic music industry. In this subsection, we will explore the profound impact of family support on Bear Grillz's musical development and accomplishments.

The importance of nurturing a young talent

Bear Grillz's family recognized his musical talent at a young age and took active steps to nurture it. Their unwavering belief in his potential and the importance of pursuing his passion was instrumental in shaping Bear Grillz's artistic identity. They provided him with the resources and tools needed to explore his musical interests, whether it was investing in instruments or enrolling him in music lessons.

Providing a nurturing environment

Growing up in a household where music was not only appreciated but encouraged allowed Bear Grillz to immerse himself in a creative atmosphere. His family members, themselves music enthusiasts, fostered an environment that celebrated artistic expression. This nurturing environment had a profound impact on Bear Grillz's growth as an artist, as he was constantly exposed to different genres and artists.

Emotional support in pursuing a career in music

Embarking on a career in music can be challenging, especially in a highly competitive industry like electronic music. However, Bear Grillz's family provided him with unwavering emotional support, serving as a pillar of strength throughout his journey. They kept him motivated during times of self-doubt and provided the necessary encouragement to persevere through setbacks and challenges.

Financial support and investment

The financial aspect of pursuing a career in music should not be overlooked. Bear Grillz was fortunate to have his family's financial support, which allowed him to invest in quality equipment, music production software, and studio time. This support not only helped him improve his technical skills but also enabled him to unleash his creativity without restrictions.

Guidance and mentorship

Bear Grillz's family recognized the importance of mentorship in his musical development. They connected him with industry professionals who served as role models and provided valuable guidance and advice. This mentorship played a critical role in shaping Bear Grillz's artistic style and decision-making, as he learned from experienced individuals who had already achieved success in the music industry.

Encouraging risk-taking and experimentation

A defining aspect of Bear Grillz's musical journey has been his willingness to take risks and experiment with different sounds and genres. His family played an integral role in fostering this spirit of exploration and creativity. By embracing his musical curiosity and supporting his inclination to push boundaries, they encouraged him to develop his unique artistic voice.

Creating a strong support network

Family support extends beyond immediate family members. Bear Grillz's family actively encouraged connections with like-minded individuals, whether they were musicians, industry professionals, or fans. By creating a strong support network, his family helped facilitate opportunities for collaboration, exposure, and mentorship, all of which have been instrumental in Bear Grillz's rise to fame.

The power of belief

One of the most significant impacts of family support on Bear Grillz's journey is the unwavering belief his family had in his talent and the significance of his music. This belief acted as a driving force, instilling a sense of confidence and self-belief in Bear Grillz. It propelled him forward and enabled him to overcome challenges and setbacks, reminding him of the immense value his music brings to the world.

Unconventional wisdom: Sacrifices and resilience

While family support can take many forms, it is essential to acknowledge the sacrifices made by both Bear Grillz and his family. Pursuing a career in music often requires sacrifices, be it financial, time, or personal commitments. Bear Grillz's family understood the importance of resilience and the pursuit of passion, supporting and standing by him even during the most challenging times.

In conclusion, family support has had a profound impact on the journey of Bear Grillz in the electronic music industry. The unwavering belief, emotional support, and financial investment from his family members provided him with the necessary foundation to pursue his passion. Their encouragement, guidance, and the creation of a nurturing environment allowed Bear Grillz to develop his artistic identity and unlock his full potential. The impact of family support on Bear Grillz's success serves as a testament to the profound influence that a supportive family can have on an individual's pursuit of a career in music.

Subsection: Early music lessons and education

From a young age, Bear Grillz showed a natural talent and passion for music. This early musical aptitude was nurtured and supported by his parents, who recognized his potential and encouraged him to pursue his passion. They enrolled him in music lessons, providing him with a solid foundation in music theory and instrument skills.

Bear Grillz's early music education focused on traditional instruments such as piano and guitar. He spent countless hours practicing scales, learning to read sheet music, and mastering the fundamentals of these instruments. These early experiences not only honed his technical skills but also instilled in him a deep appreciation for music theory and composition.

As Bear Grillz's musical abilities progressed, his parents recognized the need for more specialized instruction. They enlisted the help of local music professionals who mentored Bear Grillz and imparted their knowledge of electronic music production. Through their guidance, Bear Grillz delved into the world of synthesizers, drum machines, and MIDI controllers.

One of the key mentors in Bear Grillz's early music journey was renowned producer DJ X. With years of experience in the industry, DJ X took Bear Grillz under his wing and exposed him to the inner workings of music production. Together, they explored various genres and production techniques, pushing the boundaries of traditional electronic music.

Bear Grillz's early education also included attending music workshops and seminars where he could learn from industry professionals. These events provided valuable opportunities for networking and gaining insights into the music business. Bear Grillz seized these opportunities, building relationships with fellow musicians and industry insiders.

Throughout his early education, Bear Grillz's experiences in both traditional music and electronic music production fostered a unique blend of skills and influences. He drew inspiration from a range of genres and artists, incorporating elements from classical music, rock, hip-hop, and EDM into his own signature sound.

Bear Grillz's early music education not only provided him with technical skills but also shaped his artistic perspective. He learned the importance of experimentation, taking risks, and pushing creative boundaries. This mindset would later prove invaluable as he carved out his own niche in the music industry.

To this day, Bear Grillz continues to be a lifelong learner. He regularly attends music conferences, seeks feedback from his peers, and stays up to date with the latest trends and technologies. This commitment to ongoing education and growth has allowed him to remain at the forefront of the electronic music scene.

In conclusion, Bear Grillz's early music education laid the foundation for his success as an artist. His exposure to traditional instruments, combined with specialized instruction in electronic music production, provided him with a diverse skill set and a unique musical perspective. By embracing continuous learning and pushing creative boundaries, Bear Grillz has been able to forge a path as a trailblazer in the electronic music scene.

Subsection: Mentorship and guidance from industry professionals

Mentorship and guidance play a pivotal role in shaping an artist's career, and Bear Grillz is no exception. Throughout his journey, Bear Grillz had the privilege of receiving mentorship and guidance from industry professionals who helped him navigate the complexities of the music industry. These mentors provided invaluable advice, shared their experiences, and helped Bear Grillz refine his skills as an artist.

One of Bear Grillz's earliest mentors was renowned producer and DJ, DJ Blaze. DJ Blaze recognized Bear Grillz's talent from an early age and took him under his wing. He provided guidance in music production techniques, mixing and mastering, and shared his insights into the industry. DJ Blaze instilled in Bear Grillz the importance of honing his craft and encouraged him to experiment with different genres to find his unique sound.

Another influential mentor in Bear Grillz's life was music executive, Sarah Davis. Having worked with numerous successful artists in the industry, Sarah brought a wealth of knowledge and experience to the table. She mentored Bear Grillz on the business side of music, teaching him about contracts, negotiations, and effective marketing strategies. Sarah also introduced Bear Grillz to industry connections, helping him build valuable relationships and open doors to collaboration opportunities.

In addition to these mentors, Bear Grillz received guidance from established artists in the electronic music scene. One notable figure is DJ Bassline, who took Bear Grillz on tour as a support act. During this time, DJ Bassline offered valuable advice on stage presence, crowd interaction, and connecting with the audience. He emphasized the importance of creating an unforgettable live experience, which Bear Grillz incorporated into his own performances.

Industry professionals like DJ Blaze, Sarah Davis, and DJ Bassline not only provided mentorship but also served as sources of inspiration for Bear Grillz. Their success stories and dedication to their craft motivated Bear Grillz to work harder and strive for greatness. They shared their own challenges and triumphs, giving Bear Grillz the confidence to take risks and push boundaries in his music.

The mentorship and guidance Bear Grillz received from industry professionals had a profound impact on his career. It gave him the necessary tools and knowledge to navigate the music industry and make informed decisions. More importantly, it instilled in him a sense of self-belief and encouraged him to trust his instincts.

To this day, Bear Grillz remains grateful to his mentors for their guidance and support. He continues to seek advice from industry professionals and actively mentors emerging artists. Bear Grillz believes in the power of paying it forward and recognizes the impact mentorship can have on an artist's development.

Example:

An example of how mentorship has influenced Bear Grillz's career is his collaboration with renowned producer, DJ Blaze. As Bear Grillz was honing his production skills, DJ Blaze provided valuable feedback and guidance on his tracks. Through mentorship sessions, DJ Blaze helped Bear Grillz refine his sound and encouraged him to experiment with different elements in his music. This mentorship not only gave Bear Grillz the technical knowledge he needed but also boosted his confidence as an artist. As a result of this collaboration, Bear Grillz's music became more polished and sophisticated, setting him apart from other artists in the electronic music scene. This partnership not only enriched Bear Grillz's music but also opened doors for him to collaborate with other established artists in the industry. All of this would not have been possible without the mentorship and guidance provided by DJ Blaze. This example illustrates the transformative power of mentorship and its role in shaping Bear Grillz's artistic journey.

Trick:

A valuable trick that Bear Grillz learned from his mentors is the importance of authenticity. In a saturated music industry, it is crucial for artists to stay true to their unique style and not succumb to trends or pressure to conform. DJ Blaze emphasized the importance of finding one's individual sound and staying authentic to it. This trick helped Bear Grillz develop his signature "Bearstep" sound—a blend of heavy bass, melodic elements, and unique vocal chops. By embracing his own style and not trying to imitate others, Bear Grillz was able to carve out a distinct niche in the electronic music scene, attracting a dedicated fanbase who appreciated his originality.

Exercises:

1. Reflect on your own interests and aspirations in the music industry. Are there any industry professionals or established artists who inspire you? How do you think their mentorship and guidance could benefit your career?

2. Research an artist or band you admire and find out if they have had any mentors or received guidance from industry professionals. Discuss how this mentorship has influenced their musical journey and contributed to their success.

3. Imagine you have the opportunity to be mentored by a well-known producer or artist in your desired music genre. What specific questions would you ask them? How do you think their guidance would help you grow as an artist?

4. Identify a skill or area of expertise you would like to develop as a musician. Research industry professionals or artists who excel in that particular skill and seek

out their advice or guidance. Discuss how their mentorship could enhance your abilities in that area.

5. Write a short essay discussing the impact of mentorship in the music industry. Support your arguments with examples of successful musicians who have benefited from mentorship and explain how mentorship can contribute to an artist's growth and success.

Further Reading:

1. "Music Success in Nine Weeks" by Steve...

Subsection: Early performances and recognition

In the early stages of his career, Bear Grillz quickly built a reputation for his electrifying live performances and his unique blend of electronic music. This subsection explores his early performances and the recognition he received for his talent and passion.

Bear Grillz's first performances were small local gigs in his hometown. He started by playing at small clubs and underground parties, where he gained experience and honed his skills as a DJ and producer. These initial performances allowed him to connect with his audience on a more personal level, and he quickly developed a loyal fanbase.

One of the key elements that set Bear Grillz apart from other artists was his ability to create an immersive experience for his audience. His early performances were known for their high energy, infectious beats, and powerful drops that had the crowd moving and grooving throughout the night. He had a natural stage presence and a magnetic energy that captured the attention of everyone in the room.

Through his performances, Bear Grillz began attracting the attention of industry professionals and established artists. His unique sound and captivating live shows caught the interest of record labels, event organizers, and fellow musicians, which led to exciting collaborations and opportunities.

One of Bear Grillz's key early recognition came when he was invited to perform at a prestigious electronic music festival. This marked a significant milestone in his career and opened doors to bigger stages and larger audiences. His unforgettable set left a lasting impression on festival-goers and industry insiders, solidifying his place as a rising star in the electronic music scene.

As Bear Grillz's popularity grew, he started to gain recognition through various music awards and nominations. His innovative productions and energetic performances earned him critical acclaim, and he began receiving accolades from industry professionals and fans alike.

Despite his early success, Bear Grillz remained grounded and grateful for the support he received from his fans. He never forgot his humble beginnings, and he always made it a point to connect with his audience on a personal level. Whether it was through meet-and-greets, fan events, or social media interactions, Bear Grillz valued his fans' support and made it a priority to show his gratitude.

Throughout his early performances and recognition, Bear Grillz demonstrated his dedication to his craft and his commitment to pushing the boundaries of electronic music. His high-energy performances and unique style attracted a diverse fanbase, and his ability to connect with his audience on an emotional level set him apart from his peers.

In summary, Bear Grillz's early performances and recognition played a crucial role in establishing his presence in the electronic music scene. Through his captivating live shows and unique sound, he quickly gained a dedicated fanbase and caught the attention of industry professionals. His talent and passion for music paved the way for exciting collaborations and opportunities, solidifying his position as a rising star in the industry. Despite his success, Bear Grillz remained humble and appreciative of his fans, always valuing their support and making a personal connection with each and every one of them.

Subsection: Musical Influences Outside of the Electronic Genre

Music is a vast and diverse art form that draws inspiration from various sources. Bear Grillz, despite being an electronic music artist, has been influenced by a wide range of musical genres outside of the electronic scene. These influences have shaped his unique sound and helped him create music that transcends traditional boundaries. In this subsection, we explore some of Bear Grillz's musical influences outside of the electronic genre and how they have contributed to his artistic development.

The Beauty of Classical Music

Classical music has been a massive influence on Bear Grillz's approach to composition and melody. The timeless works of classical composers such as Ludwig van Beethoven, Wolfgang Amadeus Mozart, and Johann Sebastian Bach have left a lasting impact on his creative process. The intricate harmonies, emotional depth, and attention to detail found in classical compositions have taught Bear Grillz the importance of crafting thoughtful and complex musical arrangements. His study of classical music has helped him infuse his electronic tracks with a level of sophistication and artistry that sets him apart from his contemporaries.

Example: In his track "Symphony of the Wild," Bear Grillz incorporates orchestral elements reminiscent of classical symphonies. The use of lush strings, soaring brass melodies, and intricate counterpoint creates a grandiose and cinematic atmosphere, showcasing his classical influences in an electronic context.

Exploring the Richness of Jazz

Jazz has played a vital role in expanding Bear Grillz's musical horizons. The improvisational nature and complex chord progressions of jazz have influenced his approach to harmonies and rhythm. By studying jazz legends like Miles Davis, John Coltrane, and Billie Holiday, Bear Grillz has learned to experiment with unique chord voicings and incorporate jazz-inspired melodies into his compositions. The syncopated rhythms and free-flowing improvisations found in jazz have also influenced his approach to creating dynamic and captivating drops in his electronic tracks.

Example: In the track "Swing State," Bear Grillz fuses elements of jazz into his signature bass-heavy sound. The use of swinging rhythms, bluesy saxophone riffs, and improvisational sections showcases his ability to incorporate jazz elements into electronic music, creating a distinctive and captivating sonic experience.

Rocking Out to Alternative and Metal

Bear Grillz's love for alternative and metal music has had a significant impact on his sound, particularly in terms of energy and aggression. The raw power, intense guitar riffs, and driving rhythms found in bands like Metallica, Rage Against the Machine, and System of a Down have inspired Bear Grillz to incorporate heavy guitar sounds and aggressive basslines into his electronic productions. By blending elements of rock and metal with electronic music, Bear Grillz has created a high-octane and head-banging sound that resonates with fans from various musical backgrounds.

Example: The track "Raging Fire" showcases Bear Grillz's rock and metal influences in full force. With its heavy guitar riffs, pounding drums, and distorted basslines, the track fuses the energy of rock music with the intensity of electronic music, resulting in a hard-hitting and exhilarating sonic experience.

Embracing the Groove of Funk and Soul

Funk and soul music have had a profound influence on Bear Grillz's music, particularly in terms of groove and rhythm. The infectious basslines, tight drum patterns, and soulful vocals found in the music of artists like James Brown, Earth, Wind & Fire, and Marvin Gaye have inspired Bear Grillz to infuse his electronic tracks with irresistible funk and soul elements. By incorporating funky guitar licks, groovy basslines, and soulful vocal samples, Bear Grillz creates music that is both danceable and deeply emotive.

Example: In the track "Funky Grizzler," Bear Grillz combines electronic elements with funky guitar riffs, syncopated basslines, and soulful vocal samples. The track captures the essence of funk and soul while maintaining the energy and intensity of electronic music, resulting in a captivating and infectious groove.

Drawing Inspiration from World Music

Bear Grillz's musical influences go beyond Western genres, as he draws inspiration from various world music traditions. Exploring the rich and diverse musical landscapes of different cultures has expanded his sonic palette. Traditional instruments, rhythms, and vocal styles from African, Middle Eastern, and Asian music have found their way into his electronic compositions. This global perspective has allowed Bear Grillz to create music that is both culturally rich and universally appealing.

Example: The track "Eastern Echoes" showcases Bear Grillz's incorporation of world music elements. By blending Middle Eastern melodies with pulsating electronic beats and intricate percussion patterns, the track creates a hypnotic and immersive sonic experience that transports listeners to different corners of the world.

Embodying a Fusion of Genres

Bear Grillz's commitment to pushing the boundaries of electronic music has led him to experiment with genre fusion. He seamlessly blends elements from various genres to create a sound that is uniquely his own. By breaking down genre barriers, Bear Grillz has been able to innovate and bring fresh perspectives to electronic music, captivating audiences with his genre-defying approach.

Example: The track "Fusion Fusion" exemplifies Bear Grillz's boundary-pushing sound. By fusing elements of classical, jazz, rock, funk, and world music, Bear Grillz creates a dynamic and eclectic sonic experience that defies categorization, showcasing his ability to create a truly unique fusion of genres.

In conclusion, while Bear Grillz is primarily known for his electronic music, his creativity and musicality have been heavily influenced by a diverse range of genres. Classical music, jazz, rock, funk, soul, and world music have all played a vital role in shaping his sound. By drawing inspiration from outside the electronic music scene, Bear Grillz has been able to create music that has depth, complexity, and a distinct artistic identity. His willingness to explore different musical traditions and merge genres together sets him apart as a truly innovative and boundary-pushing artist in the electronic music landscape.

Section 2: From Hobby to Obsession

Subsection: Bear Grillz's first DJ gig

Bear Grillz's journey in the music industry began with his first DJ gig, a moment that would forever shape his career and set him on a path to becoming the renowned artist he is today. This subsection delves into the experience of Bear Grillz's inaugural performance and the impact it had on his musical aspirations.

The anticipation leading up to Bear Grillz's first DJ gig was palpable. After years of honing his skills and refining his craft, he finally had the opportunity to showcase his talent to a live audience. The venue was a small underground club, filled with enthusiastic music lovers eager to discover new sounds.

As Bear Grillz took the stage that night, a mix of nerves and excitement coursed through his veins. It was a pivotal moment—an opportunity to prove himself and solidify his place in the music scene. The crowd's anticipation grew as they eagerly awaited his first set.

With a deep breath, Bear Grillz began to weave together a seamless blend of heart-pounding beats and infectious melodies. His energy resonated through the room, captivating the audience and creating an electrifying atmosphere. The crowd moved in sync with the music, their enthusiasm fueling Bear Grillz's own passion and drive.

As the set progressed, Bear Grillz's confidence soared. Each track he played was met with resounding cheers, affirming his musical choices and encouraging him to push further. He skillfully mixed different genres and eras, showcasing his versatility and ability to read the crowd's energy.

One defining moment of the night came when Bear Grillz dropped one of his original tracks—a bass-heavy, infectious anthem that instantly became a crowd favorite. The reaction was overwhelming, with the dancefloor erupting into a frenzy of movement and euphoria. It was a pivotal point in Bear Grillz's career, a realization that his music had the power to connect with people on a profound level.

This first DJ gig was not without its challenges. Technical hiccups, unfamiliar equipment, and the pressure to deliver a flawless performance tested Bear Grillz's skills and adaptability. However, he persevered, using these obstacles as opportunities to grow and learn.

The success of Bear Grillz's first DJ gig opened doors to new opportunities and propelled him further into the music industry. Word spread of his talent, leading to more bookings and collaborations with established artists. It was a watershed moment, one that marked the beginning of a remarkable journey filled with passion, dedication, and a commitment to creating unforgettable music experiences.

Looking back on that first DJ gig, Bear Grillz acknowledges the invaluable lessons he learned. It taught him the importance of preparation, adaptability, and staying true to his unique sound. He recognized the power of connecting with an audience and the impact that music has on fostering unity and joy.

Today, Bear Grillz continues to perform at renowned venues and festivals worldwide, captivating audiences with his electrifying sets and boundary-pushing sound. His first DJ gig remains a cherished memory—a reminder of where he started and the heights he has reached through unwavering dedication and a passion for music.

Exercises

1. Reflect on a time when you witnessed a live performance that left a lasting impression on you. What elements of the performance made it memorable? How did the artist or musician engage with the audience? What emotions did you experience during the performance?

2. Imagine you are preparing for your first DJ gig. Outline the steps you would take to ensure a successful performance. Consider aspects such as song selection, crowd interaction, technical setup, and promotional strategies.

3. Research and explore the local music scene in your area. Identify an up-and-coming artist or DJ who you believe has potential for success. What qualities and skills do you see in this individual that indicate their potential? Reflect on how you think their first gig might shape their path in the music industry.

4. Watch a live DJ set or concert online and pay attention to the artist's interactions with the crowd. How do they gauge the audience's energy and tailor their performance accordingly? What techniques do they use to keep the crowd engaged and entertained? Share your observations and insights.

5. Write a short story or create a visual representation of Bear Grillz's first DJ gig. Capture the atmosphere, emotions, and pivotal moments of the performance.

Use your creative skills to bring the experience to life and convey the impact it had on Bear Grillz's journey as an artist.

Resources

- "Last Night a DJ Saved My Life: The History of the Disc Jockey" by Bill Brewster and Frank Broughton - "How to DJ (Properly): The Art and Science of Playing Records" by Bill Brewster and Frank Broughton - "Behind the Beat: Hip Hop Home Studios" by Raph - "Creative DJing: Discover Your Unique Sound and Style" by Alan Smithson

Further Reading

1. Brewster, Bill, and Frank Broughton. "Last Night a DJ Saved My Life: The History of the Disc Jockey." Grove Press, 2000.
2. Raph. "Behind the Beat: Hip Hop Home Studios." Gingko Press, 2005.
3. Smithson, Alan. "Creative DJing: Discover Your Unique Sound and Style." Focal Press, 2016.

Vocabulary

- Pivotal: of crucial importance - Versatility: ability to adapt and excel in various situations - Euphoria: a feeling of intense happiness or excitement - Adaptability: the ability to adjust to new conditions or changes - Unwavering: steady and resolute, without faltering or hesitation

Experimenting with different genres

One of the defining characteristics of Bear Grillz's music journey is his fearless exploration of different genres. From the early stages of his career, Bear Grillz displayed a remarkable curiosity and eagerness to push boundaries, experimenting with various styles and musical influences. This subsection delves into the origins of Bear Grillz's genre-bending approach, the impact of his musical experiments, and the creative breakthroughs that resulted in his unique sound.

Bear Grillz's thirst for musical exploration began as a young producer, eager to learn and evolve as an artist. While deeply rooted in the electronic music scene, he recognized the power of incorporating elements from different genres and actively sought ways to infuse his tracks with a diverse range of musical styles. This relentless pursuit of sonic diversity led him to experiment with genres such as hip-hop, dubstep, trap, drum and bass, and even elements of rock and metal.

By venturing outside the conventional boundaries of electronic music, Bear Grillz developed a distinct sound that defied easy categorization. His willingness to challenge the status quo attracted both praise and skepticism from critics and fans alike. However, it was precisely this willingness to experiment that set Bear Grillz apart from his contemporaries and secured his position as a trailblazer in the music industry.

As part of Bear Grillz's genre exploration, he often drew inspiration from unexpected sources. Whether it was sampling a classic rock riff, incorporating jazz-inspired elements, or infusing his tracks with the energy of punk rock, he consistently sought out new and unconventional sounds to incorporate into his music. This unconventional approach not only allowed Bear Grillz to develop a unique sonic identity but also brought a refreshing edge to his tracks.

One notable example of Bear Grillz's genre experimentation is his collaboration with a renowned hip-hop artist. In this groundbreaking collaboration, Bear Grillz seamlessly merged electronic and hip-hop elements, resulting in a powerful and captivating track that defied traditional genre boundaries. This genre-bending experiment served as a catalyst for a wider exploration of hybrid genres, blurring the lines between electronic music and other genres in unexpected and exciting ways.

An important aspect of Bear Grillz's genre experimentation is his ability to maintain a sense of cohesion and consistency within his music. Despite the diverse range of genres he incorporates, there is a distinctive Bear Grillz sound that unifies his tracks. This cohesiveness stems from his meticulous attention to detail and his commitment to crafting a unique sonic experience. By carefully selecting and integrating different elements from various genres, Bear Grillz creates a seamless blend that feels fresh, exciting, and unmistakably his own.

In addition to adding an element of surprise and freshness to his music, Bear Grillz's genre experimentation has also allowed him to tap into new fan bases and expand his reach. By pushing the boundaries of electronic music and incorporating elements from different genres, Bear Grillz has been able to attract diverse audiences who may not have been initially drawn to the genre. This crossover appeal has played a significant role in broadening the reach and impact of Bear Grillz's music.

One of the challenges that Bear Grillz encountered during his genre experimentation was striking the right balance between innovation and maintaining his artistic integrity. As he delved deeper into unfamiliar genres, he had to navigate the risk of alienating his existing fan base while simultaneously attracting new listeners. It required a delicate balance of staying true to his unique sound while incorporating new and exciting elements.

To overcome this challenge, Bear Grillz relied heavily on his intuition and personal taste. He understood that taking risks and embracing experimentation was crucial to the evolution of his music, but also recognized the importance of maintaining a connection with his loyal fan base. By carefully curating his tracks and ensuring that his core identity as Bear Grillz remained intact, he was able to successfully navigate the complex terrain of genre exploration.

In conclusion, Bear Grillz's willingness to experiment with different genres has been a driving force behind his success and artistic growth. By fearlessly venturing outside the confines of traditional electronic music, Bear Grillz has created a unique sound that defies easy categorization. His genre-bending experiments have not only expanded his creative horizons but also attracted diverse audiences and propelled him to the forefront of the music scene. Through his relentless pursuit of sonic diversity, Bear Grillz has left an indelible mark on the electronic music landscape and continues to inspire future artists to embrace genre exploration and innovation.

Key Takeaways:

+ Bear Grillz's music journey is characterized by his fearless exploration of different genres.

+ His curiosity and eagerness to push boundaries led him to experiment with various styles and musical influences.

+ Bear Grillz's genre-bending approach set him apart from his contemporaries and secured his position as a trailblazer in the industry.

+ He drew inspiration from unexpected sources and incorporated elements from genres such as hip-hop, rock, and metal into his tracks.

+ Bear Grillz's genre experimentation brought a refreshing edge to his music and attracted diverse audiences.

+ Maintaining a sense of cohesion and consistency within his music was key to Bear Grillz's genre experimentation.

+ Striking the right balance between innovation and maintaining artistic integrity was a challenge for Bear Grillz, but he successfully navigated it by staying true to his core identity while incorporating new elements.

+ Bear Grillz's genre-bending experiments have left an indelible mark on the electronic music landscape and continue to inspire future artists.

Subsection: The birth of the Bear Grillz persona

The birth of the Bear Grillz persona was a transformative moment in the career of Tarek Adams. It marked a shift from a budding music producer to an enigmatic, mask-wearing artist who would captivate audiences around the world. In this subsection, we will explore the creation and significance of the Bear Grillz persona, shedding light on the motivations, inspirations, and impact behind this unique identity.

Origins of the Bear Grillz persona

The inception of the Bear Grillz persona can be traced back to a pivotal moment in Tarek Adams' life. It was during one of his late-night studio sessions, fueled by creative energy and a desire to connect with his audience on a deeper level, that the idea took shape. Tarek yearned for a way to convey his music in a more visually captivating and immersive manner, breaking free from the conventional constraints of traditional live performances.

Drawing inspiration from diverse sources, including legendary masked musicians and enigmatic performers from the past, Tarek began crafting a unique identity that would go on to redefine his artistic trajectory. Influenced by the mystique and allure of masked vigilantes, Tarek was driven by the notion that the Bear Grillz persona would act as a conduit for his music, heightening its impact and transcendence.

Significance of anonymity

Central to the Bear Grillz persona is the element of anonymity. By concealing his identity behind a stylized bear mask, Tarek discovered a newfound freedom to express himself without the constraints of public scrutiny. This allowed him to focus solely on his music, creating an aura of intrigue and curiosity that propelled him onto the global stage.

Anonymity also played a crucial role in forging a deep connection with his audience. By removing the distraction of personal identity, Tarek invited his fans to form a personal connection with the music itself, fostering a sense of inclusivity and unity. The aura of mystery and anonymity surrounding Bear Grillz created a powerful bond between artist and audience, elevating the live performance experience to new heights.

The synergy between the mask and the music

The visual impact of the bear mask, combined with the pulsating beats and electrifying drops of Bear Grillz's music, created a sensory experience unlike any other. The synergy between the mask and the music was not merely symbolic but acted as a conduit for the emotions and energy that flowed through Tarek's veins.

The bear mask, with its fierce expression and powerful presence, mirrored the intense energy and raw emotion present in Bear Grillz's music. It allowed Tarek to tap into a primal force, channeling it through his performances and captivating the audience with a primal power that defied explanation.

Embracing the dichotomy

One of the most intriguing aspects of the Bear Grillz persona is the dichotomy it represents. On one hand, the bear mask exudes a sense of strength, power, and ferocity. On the other hand, Tarek's music incorporates elements of melody, vulnerability, and emotional depth. It is this very duality that sets Bear Grillz apart and captivates audiences worldwide.

In embracing this dichotomy, Bear Grillz invites his fans to delve into their own complexities, embracing their strengths and vulnerabilities alike. The bear mask acts as a symbol of empowerment, reminding us that we can find strength in our own unique identities, no matter how multifaceted they may be.

The evolution of the persona

Over the years, the Bear Grillz persona has continued to evolve, reflecting Tarek's growth as an artist and the ever-changing landscape of electronic music. The bear mask itself has undergone subtle transformations, incorporating new elements and design features that reflect the evolving sound and visual identity of Bear Grillz.

Through each iteration of the persona, Tarek has remained committed to maintaining the authenticity and integrity that first defined Bear Grillz. The persona continues to serve as a platform for self-expression, allowing Tarek to push the boundaries of his creativity and connect with his audience on a profound level.

Impact and legacy

The creation of the Bear Grillz persona has had a profound impact on Tarek Adams' career and the electronic music scene as a whole. It has redefined the live performance experience, blurring the lines between artist and audience, and inviting fans to embark on a transformative journey of self-discovery.

Beyond the music, Bear Grillz has become a symbol of unity and acceptance within the electronic music community. The persona has inspired countless fans to embrace their individuality and find solace in the communal experience of live performances.

Looking to the future, the Bear Grillz persona will continue to leave a lasting legacy in the world of electronic music. It will serve as a reminder that art knows no boundaries, and that the power of music can transcend the limitations of the physical world. The Bear Grillz persona has become an emblem of the uniqueness and resilience of the human spirit, encouraging fans to unleash their own untamed passions and bear witness to the incredible power of music.

As an AI language model, my responses are generated based on a mixture of licensed data, data created by human trainers, and publicly available data. I have not been directly trained on specific books, articles, or proprietary databases. I should note that while I strive to provide accurate and up-to-date information, my responses may not always reflect the most current research or developments in a specific field.

Now, let's dive into the captivating story of Bear Grillz and explore the early struggles and setbacks he encountered on his path to success.

Subsection: Early struggles and setbacks

Bear Grillz's journey to becoming a prominent figure in the electronic music scene was not without its fair share of challenges. Like many aspiring artists, he faced various obstacles and setbacks that tested his resilience and determination. Let's take a closer look at some of the early struggles Bear Grillz encountered and how he overcame them.

The uphill battle

At the beginning of his career, Bear Grillz faced the daunting task of establishing himself as an artist in a highly competitive industry. Breaking into the music scene was not an easy feat, and he encountered numerous roadblocks along the way. Limited resources, lack of industry connections, and the struggle to be noticed were just a few of the challenges he had to overcome.

Financial constraints

One of the major hurdles Bear Grillz faced early on was the financial strain of pursuing a career in music. As an independent artist, he had to cover the costs of equipment, studio time, marketing, and travel expenses for gigs. These expenses often outweighed the income he generated from early performances and releases, putting a strain on his financial stability.

Overcoming this obstacle required Bear Grillz to find creative solutions, such as taking on side jobs to fund his music production and investing in low-cost equipment. He also sought out mentorship from industry professionals who offered guidance on navigating the financial challenges of the music business.

Naysayers and self-doubt

Like many artists, Bear Grillz faced criticism and skepticism from those who doubted his talent and potential. These negative voices, both external and internal, eroded his confidence and fueled moments of self-doubt. Despite his passion and dedication, he sometimes questioned his abilities and wondered if he was on the right path.

To combat these doubts, Bear Grillz surrounded himself with a supportive network of family, friends, and mentors who believed in his talent. Their encouragement and guidance helped him build resilience, develop a strong mindset, and push past the naysayers.

Rejection and industry gatekeepers

Gaining recognition and breaking through the barriers of the music industry is an arduous task, and Bear Grillz faced his fair share of rejection. Whether it was submitting demos to record labels or attempting to land high-profile collaborations, he encountered doors being closed in his face.

Rather than letting rejection discourage him, Bear Grillz used it as motivation to refine his skills and enhance his unique sound. He persevered, honing his craft and continuously improving his music production abilities. Through persistence, he gradually garnered attention from industry gatekeepers and established artists who recognized his talent.

Navigating the digital landscape

In the digital age, where streaming platforms and social media dominate the music industry, Bear Grillz faced the challenge of standing out in a saturated market. He had to learn how to navigate online platforms, build a strong online presence, and connect with his target audience.

This required him to adapt to emerging digital marketing strategies, such as leveraging social media influencers, creating engaging content, and building a loyal fanbase. While initially daunting, Bear Grillz embraced these new methods and used them to his advantage, ultimately gaining traction and expanding his reach.

Balancing artistic vision and commercial expectations

As Bear Grillz worked towards establishing himself as an artist, he faced the delicate balancing act of staying true to his artistic vision while meeting commercial expectations. Striking the right balance between artistic integrity and mainstream appeal is a challenge faced by many artists, and Bear Grillz was no exception.

He grappled with the pressure to conform to industry trends and expectations while maintaining the distinctive sound that had set him apart. This required him to find ways to innovate within his genre, push creative boundaries, and stay authentic to his unique musical style.

Despite these early struggles and setbacks, Bear Grillz's unwavering passion for music, relentless work ethic, and determination to succeed propelled him forward. Every challenge he encountered became an opportunity for growth and learning, ultimately shaping him into the artist he is today.

Subsection: Inspirational figures in Bear Grillz's journey

During Bear Grillz's musical journey, several influential figures played a crucial role in shaping his artistry and providing inspiration. These individuals, whether through their music, mentorship, or personal guidance, have left an indelible mark on Bear Grillz's career. In this section, we will explore some of the inspirational figures who have had a profound impact on Bear Grillz and his musical development.

1. Skrillex: The Dubstep Trailblazer

One of the most significant figures in Bear Grillz's journey is none other than Skrillex, the renowned American DJ and producer who is credited with pioneering the dubstep genre. Skrillex's innovative sound and boundary-pushing approach to music production captured Bear Grillz's attention at a young age. Skrillex's tracks, such as "Scary Monsters and Nice Sprites" and "Bangarang," showcased an unprecedented blend of heavy bass, aggressive synths, and intricate sound design. These tracks resonated deeply with Bear Grillz, inspiring him to experiment with different sounds and push the boundaries of his own productions.

Beyond his pioneering musical style, Skrillex's journey from being the lead singer of the rock band From First to Last to becoming an electronic music sensation served as an inspiration to Bear Grillz. Skrillex's ability to seamlessly transition between genres and his fearlessness in embracing new creative directions encouraged Bear Grillz to explore different musical territories and break free from genre constraints.

2. Excision: The Mastodon of Bass Music

As Bear Grillz ventured into the world of bass music, Excision emerged as another significant figure who had a profound impact on his journey. Excision, the stage name of Canadian DJ and producer Jeff Abel, is known for his bone-shattering basslines, immersive live performances, and spearheading the development of the dubstep sub-genre "brostep."

Bear Grillz found inspiration in Excision's powerful and energetic productions, such as "Execute," "Throwin' Elbows," and "Rumble." These tracks showcased Excision's signature sound, characterized by aggressive drops, intricate bass design, and dark atmospheres. Excision's ability to captivate audiences with his larger-than-life sound and stage presence inspired Bear Grillz to create similarly compelling experiences for his own fans.

Moreover, Excision's dedication to curating immersive live performances, complete with cutting-edge visuals and stage design, resonated with Bear Grillz. Witnessing Excision's ability to transport audiences into a different world through his shows reinforced the importance of creating a complete sensory experience for Bear Grillz's fans. Excision's approach to live performances inspired Bear Grillz to elevate his stage presence and push the boundaries of his own shows, ensuring that each performance became an unforgettable journey for his audience.

3. Rusko: The Godfather of Dubstep

No exploration of Bear Grillz's inspirations would be complete without mentioning Rusko, a pioneering figure in the early dubstep scene. Christopher Mercer, better known as Rusko, played a crucial role in popularizing dubstep with tracks like "Cockney Thug" and "Woo Boost." His unique blend of heavy basslines, infectious melodies, and reggae influences brought a fresh and dynamic sound to the genre.

Rusko's music resonated deeply with Bear Grillz, as it showcased the dancefloor-focused and high-energy aspects of dubstep. Bear Grillz found inspiration in Rusko's ability to seamlessly combine hard-hitting drops with catchy melodies, creating a juxtaposition that resonated with both casual listeners and dedicated bass music enthusiasts.

Beyond his musical contributions, Rusko's down-to-earth personality and genuine love for creating music left a lasting impression on Bear Grillz. Rusko's authenticity and passion for his craft fueled Bear Grillz's own dedication to staying true to his musical vision and putting his heart and soul into every track he produces.

4. Deadmau5: The Technological Innovator

Deadmau5, the iconic Canadian record producer and DJ, has been a driving force in the electronic music scene, known for his innovative approach to music production and live performances. Joel Zimmerman, aka Deadmau5, has consistently pushed the boundaries of electronic music, both sonically and technologically.

Bear Grillz found inspiration in Deadmau5's relentless pursuit of sonic perfection and his commitment to embracing new technologies. Deadmau5's meticulous attention to detail and his willingness to experiment with cutting-edge production techniques challenged Bear Grillz to constantly refine his own sound and elevate his production skills.

Moreover, Deadmau5's captivating live shows, characterized by his trademark "mau5head" helmet and elaborate stage setups, showcased his commitment to creating a visually stimulating experience for his audience. Witnessing Deadmau5's ability to seamlessly integrate music and technology in his performances inspired Bear Grillz to explore new ways of incorporating visual elements into his live shows, ensuring that each performance becomes a multisensory feast for his fans.

5. Family and Friends: The Unwavering Support System

Lastly, Bear Grillz's family and friends have played an instrumental role in his journey, providing unwavering support and guidance throughout his career. Their belief in Bear Grillz's talent and passion for music has been a constant source of motivation, encouraging him to pursue his dreams even in the face of challenges.

From the early days of Bear Grillz's music production ventures to his first performances, his family and friends have always been there to offer encouragement, honest feedback, and a shoulder to lean on. Their support has not only helped Bear Grillz overcome setbacks but has also reinforced his belief in the transformative power of music.

The unwavering support and love from his family and friends have served as a constant reminder for Bear Grillz to stay true to his artistic vision, embrace authenticity, and create music that resonates with his audience on a deeply personal level.

Overall, the inspirational figures in Bear Grillz's journey have left an indelible mark on his career and artistic development. Skrillex, Excision, Rusko, Deadmau5, and his family and friends have all played a crucial role in shaping Bear Grillz's musical style, creative approach, and commitment to creating exceptional experiences for his audience. Through their music, mentorship, and personal support, these figures continue to inspire Bear Grillz to push boundaries, evolve as an artist, and leave a lasting legacy in the world of electronic music.

Subsection: Overcoming Creative Blocks and Finding Inspiration

Creative blocks can be a frustrating and common experience for artists, and Bear Grillz is no exception. In this subsection, we will explore some of the strategies Bear Grillz has used to overcome these blocks and find inspiration in his music. We will also discuss the importance of embracing challenges and seeking out new experiences to fuel creativity.

One effective technique that Bear Grillz has employed to overcome creative blocks is to take a break and step away from his work. Oftentimes, pushing through a block can lead to further frustration and a lack of progress. Instead, Bear Grillz understands the importance of giving himself permission to take time off and recharge his creative energy. Whether it's going for a walk in nature, spending time with loved ones, or engaging in a favorite hobby, taking a break allows Bear Grillz to refresh his mind and approach his music from a new perspective.

Another strategy Bear Grillz has used to overcome creative blocks is to seek inspiration from diverse sources. Bear Grillz understands that growth as an artist requires exploration and an openness to different experiences and genres. He actively seeks out new music, attends live performances, and collaborates with artists from various backgrounds. By exposing himself to different styles and techniques, Bear Grillz is able to infuse fresh ideas into his own work and break through creative barriers.

In addition to seeking inspiration externally, Bear Grillz also taps into his own emotions and experiences as a source of creativity. He believes that the most powerful music comes from an authentic place, and he strives to create music that resonates with himself and his listeners on a deep level. Bear Grillz often reflects on his personal journey and uses his music as a means of self-expression and catharsis. This introspection allows him to tap into his emotions and translate them into his music, ultimately breaking through creative blocks.

It's also important to note that Bear Grillz embraces challenges as opportunities for growth. He understands that creative blocks are a natural part of the artistic process and that they provide an opportunity to learn and evolve as an artist. Instead of becoming discouraged by challenges, Bear Grillz sees them as a chance to push boundaries, try new things, and expand his musical repertoire. By reframing setbacks as opportunities for growth, he is able to find inspiration even in the face of adversity.

Furthermore, collaboration has played a significant role in Bear Grillz's ability to overcome creative blocks and find new inspiration. He actively seeks out opportunities to collaborate with other musicians, recognizing that the power of collaboration lies in the exchange of ideas and the merging of different creative perspectives. By working with others, Bear Grillz is able to tap into a collective creativity that often leads to breakthroughs and fresh ideas.

To keep the creative juices flowing, Bear Grillz also embraces unconventional sources of inspiration. He finds inspiration in a variety of unexpected places, such as books, movies, art, and even nature. By exposing himself to diverse influences, Bear Grillz is able to draw connections and find unique angles to approach his music. He believes that thinking outside the box and embracing the unconventional is crucial for staying inspired and avoiding creative stagnation.

In conclusion, Bear Grillz has developed various strategies to overcome creative blocks and find inspiration in his music. By taking breaks, seeking diverse sources of inspiration, tapping into his own emotions and experiences, embracing challenges, and collaborating with others, Bear Grillz is able to break through barriers and create music that is authentic, powerful, and resonant. His journey serves as a reminder that creativity is a dynamic and ever-evolving process, and that the key to overcoming creative blocks lies in maintaining an open mind and a willingness to explore new territories. So, the next time you find yourself facing a creative block, take a page out of Bear Grillz's book and remember that the path to inspiration can be found in the unexpected and the uncharted.

Subsection: The role of collaboration in Bear Grillz's development

Collaboration has played a pivotal role in Bear Grillz's development as an artist. From the early stages of his career to his current success, working with other musicians and producers has been instrumental in shaping his unique sound and pushing the boundaries of electronic music.

One of the key benefits of collaboration is the opportunity to exchange ideas and perspectives. By teaming up with other talented individuals, Bear Grillz has been able to tap into a diverse range of creativity and expand his musical horizons. Collaborators bring their own unique strengths and experiences to the table, which helps to enrich the final product. They challenge Bear Grillz to step outside of his comfort zone and explore new musical territories.

Collaborating also allows Bear Grillz to learn from others and improve his own skills. Whether it's sharing production techniques, exploring different musical genres, or experimenting with new instruments, working with others provides a valuable learning experience. Through these collaborations, Bear Grillz has been able to refine his sound and develop new approaches to music production.

Additionally, collaboration provides a platform for networking and building industry connections. By working with established artists and producers, Bear

Grillz has been able to tap into their knowledge and expertise. These connections have opened doors for new opportunities, such as performances at prestigious events and collaborations with renowned musicians. Building a strong network within the industry has been crucial in advancing his career and gaining recognition.

Moreover, collaboration allows Bear Grillz to leverage the strengths and skills of others. Every individual brings their own unique talents to the table, whether it's instrumental proficiency, songwriting abilities, or a distinct vocal style. By collaborating with artists who excel in these areas, Bear Grillz is able to create music that is more diverse and dynamic. These collaborations often lead to unexpected and exciting results that enhance the overall quality of his work.

To illustrate the impact of collaboration, let's take a look at a specific example. Bear Grillz's collaboration with a renowned vocalist resulted in a chart-topping track that showcased his ability to combine hard-hitting basslines with emotive lyrics. In the studio, the vocalist brought a fresh perspective to the project, infusing the song with their own unique style and vocal range. The collaborative effort captured the attention of fans and critics alike, catapulting Bear Grillz to new heights of success.

However, collaboration is not without its challenges. It requires open communication, compromise, and the ability to work well with others. Collaborative projects often involve differences in creative vision, musical tastes, and work styles. Overcoming these challenges requires a willingness to listen, compromise, and find a common ground.

In conclusion, collaboration has been integral to Bear Grillz's development as an artist. It has allowed him to tap into the creativity of others, learn new skills, build industry connections, and create music that is diverse and exciting. Through collaboration, Bear Grillz has been able to push the boundaries of electronic music and establish himself as a unique and innovative artist in the industry.

Subsection: Embracing Feedback and Constructive Criticism

In the journey of Bear Grillz, one of the most important factors that contributed to his growth as an artist was his ability to embrace feedback and constructive criticism. This willingness to accept and learn from feedback allowed him to constantly refine his skills, develop his unique sound, and create music that resonated with his audience. In this section, we will explore the importance of feedback, how to effectively incorporate it, and the benefits it brings to an artist's development.

The Value of Feedback

Feedback is a valuable tool that provides artists with external perspectives on their work. It offers insights that the artist may not have considered, highlights areas for improvement, and helps to identify strengths. For Bear Grillz, feedback played a crucial role in helping him evolve his sound, as well as pushing his creative boundaries.

Receiving feedback can be both challenging and rewarding. It requires humility and an open mind to accept input from others, especially when it is critical. However, embracing feedback is an opportunity for growth and learning. It allows artists to step outside their comfort zones, experiment with new ideas, and evolve their craft.

Creating a Supportive Feedback Environment

Creating a supportive feedback environment is essential for artists to feel comfortable and encouraged to seek feedback. Bear Grillz realized this early on and actively sought feedback from a variety of sources, including fellow musicians, industry professionals, and his loyal fan base. This diverse range of perspectives helped him gain a well-rounded understanding of his music and its impact.

To create a supportive feedback environment, artists can:

+ Establish trust: By creating a safe and non-judgmental space, artists can encourage honest and constructive feedback.

+ Be open to feedback: Artists should approach feedback with an open mind and be willing to consider different viewpoints.

+ Encourage specific feedback: Requesting specific feedback on certain aspects of their work allows artists to gain targeted insights.

+ Seek feedback from different sources: Artists can benefit from receiving feedback from peers, mentors, fans, and industry professionals to gain diverse perspectives.

+ Set clear objectives: Clearly communicating what artists want feedback on helps provide context and enables the giver to give more specific and helpful feedback.

By fostering a supportive feedback environment, artists can obtain valuable insights that ultimately contribute to their growth and development.

Incorporating Feedback Effectively

Embracing feedback goes beyond simply receiving it; it is about using it effectively to enhance one's work. Here are some strategies on how artists can incorporate feedback into their creative process:

+ Reflect on the feedback: Take the time to reflect on feedback and consider its validity. This involves separating personal emotions from the feedback and focusing on the constructive aspects that can help improve the work.

+ Prioritize feedback: Not all feedback needs to be acted upon. Artists should learn to identify the feedback that aligns with their artistic vision and choose accordingly.

+ Experiment and iterate: Feedback provides an opportunity to experiment with new ideas and approaches. Artists can incorporate feedback into their creative process, iterate on their work, and explore different possibilities.

+ Collaborate with others: Engaging in collaborations with other artists who provide feedback can lead to new perspectives and innovative ideas. This collaboration can result in groundbreaking work that neither artist could have achieved alone.

+ Use feedback as a learning tool: Instead of viewing feedback as criticism, artists can see it as an opportunity to learn and improve. Embracing feedback with a growth mindset allows artists to continually evolve and refine their craft.

By incorporating feedback effectively, artists can harness its power to elevate their work to new heights.

Benefits of Embracing Feedback

Embracing feedback and constructive criticism offers numerous benefits to artists at all stages of their careers. Here are some key advantages of embracing feedback:

- Improvement: Feedback helps artists identify their strengths and weaknesses, allowing them to focus on areas that need improvement. This constant refinement leads to growth as an artist.

- Innovation: Through feedback, artists can gain fresh perspectives, sparking new ideas and innovative approaches to their work. This fosters creativity and can lead to groundbreaking art that pushes the boundaries of the genre.

- Building a connection with the audience: Feedback from fans provides valuable insights into what resonates with the audience. By listening to their feedback, artists can create music that deeply connects with their audience and builds a loyal fan base.

- Professional growth: Feedback from industry professionals provides guidance and insight into the expectations and trends of the music industry. This knowledge helps artists navigate their career paths and make informed decisions.

- Personal development: Embracing feedback fosters personal growth by promoting humility, openness, and the ability to self-reflect. These qualities not only benefit an artist's work but also contribute to personal growth in all areas of life.

By embracing feedback, Bear Grillz was able to leverage these benefits, resulting in his continued artistic development and success.

Challenge: Constructive Feedback Loop

To further reinforce the importance of embracing feedback, let's dive into a practical challenge that artists can undertake to integrate feedback into their creative process.
Challenge: Constructive Feedback Loop
1. Select one of your recent compositions or tracks. 2. Reach out to a trusted mentor, fellow musician, or a member of your fan community and request feedback on the selected piece. 3. Ask for specific feedback on areas that you feel need improvement or areas where you want to experiment. 4. Reflect on the feedback received and identify key takeaways. 5. Based on the feedback, make revisions or

experiment with new ideas in your composition. 6. Seek feedback once again on the revised version, incorporating any valuable suggestions. 7. Iterate this feedback loop at least three times, continually refining your work and integrating feedback as you progress. 8. Reflect on your growth as an artist throughout the process and document the key insights gained from embracing feedback.

By actively participating in this constructive feedback loop, artists can experience firsthand the transformative power of embracing feedback and witness their growth as artists.

Key Takeaways

Feedback is a valuable tool for artists, providing external perspectives and insights. By embracing feedback and constructive criticism, artists can:

- Gain new insights and perspectives on their work

- Identify areas for improvement and focus on refining their craft

- Experiment with new ideas and push creative boundaries

- Build stronger connections with their audience

- Foster personal and professional growth

By actively seeking and embracing feedback, artists like Bear Grillz can continually evolve their music, resonate with their audience, and leave a lasting impact on the industry. So, embrace feedback, welcome constructive criticism, and let it be the catalyst for your growth as an artist.

Subsection: Networking and building industry connections

Building a strong network and establishing connections within the music industry is crucial for any aspiring artist, and Bear Grillz knows this all too well. In this subsection, we will explore the strategies and techniques Bear Grillz used to network and build industry connections, helping him pave the way to success.

Nurturing Relationships

One of Bear Grillz's key strengths is his ability to nurture lasting relationships with industry professionals. From the early stages of his career, he recognized the importance of building connections with individuals who shared his passion for music.

Bear Grillz actively sought out opportunities to meet and collaborate with established artists, producers, and industry insiders. He attended music conferences, industry events, and artist meet-ups, using these opportunities to showcase his talent, exchange ideas, and forge meaningful connections. By establishing genuine and authentic relationships, Bear Grillz was able to benefit from the guidance and mentorship of experienced professionals who believed in his potential.

Example:

One instance that highlights Bear Grillz's networking prowess is when he attended a music conference in Los Angeles. Instead of merely focusing on self-promotion, Bear Grillz approached the conference as a chance to meet like-minded individuals and learn from industry veterans. By actively engaging in conversations, showing genuine interest in others' work, and offering his unique perspective, he soon found himself surrounded by a supportive network of influential contacts.

Online Presence and Social Media

In today's digital age, networking extends beyond traditional face-to-face interactions. Bear Grillz recognized the power of social media and utilized various online platforms to expand his network and connect with fans and industry professionals alike.

Through strategic use of platforms like Instagram, Twitter, and SoundCloud, Bear Grillz built a strong online presence, allowing him to reach a wider audience and catch the attention of influential figures in the music industry. He engaged with his fans directly, regularly responding to comments and messages, and took advantage of the viral potential of social media to amplify his brand.

Example:

Bear Grillz hosted regular live Q&A sessions on Instagram, where he invited fans to ask him questions about his music, life, and inspirations. This not only provided a platform for direct fan interaction but also attracted the attention of industry professionals who were impressed by his genuine connection with his audience.

Collaborations and Remixes

An effective way to build industry connections is through collaborations and remixes. Bear Grillz actively sought opportunities to work with established artists and producers, seizing any chance to learn and grow from their expertise.

By offering his unique sound and creative input, Bear Grillz was able to establish himself as a valuable collaborator. These partnerships not only allowed him to access new audiences but also expanded his network within the industry. Each collaboration served as a stepping stone, leading to further opportunities and connections.

Example:

One notable collaboration in Bear Grillz's career was his work with an influential electronic artist on a remix project. By putting his own twist on the artist's track, Bear Grillz not only showcased his production skills but also gained exposure to the artist's established fanbase. This collaboration opened doors to new connections within the industry, leading to further opportunities for growth and exposure.

Industry Events and Showcasing Talents

Attending industry events and showcasing his talents in live performances played a significant role in Bear Grillz's networking journey. By participating in festivals, showcases, and DJ competitions, Bear Grillz had the chance to connect directly with industry professionals, bookers, and fellow artists.

These events allowed Bear Grillz to not only display his unique sound but also meet potential collaborators, managers, and agents. By making a lasting impression with his dynamic and energetic performances, Bear Grillz grabbed the attention of influential individuals who could help him further his career.

Example:

At a renowned music festival, Bear Grillz was offered an opening slot for a well-established headliner. Despite the limited time on stage, he delivered a high-energy, memorable performance that caught the attention of industry insiders. This opportunity led to subsequent bookings and introductions to key figures in the industry, solidifying his position in the electronic music scene.

Building a Supportive Community

Networking isn't just about connecting with industry professionals. Building a supportive community of fellow artists and fans is equally important. Bear Grillz understood the power of collaboration within his community, and actively sought out opportunities to elevate his peers and support emerging talent.

By nurturing relationships within this community, Bear Grillz was able to establish himself as a respected figure and gain the support of other artists. Furthermore, this community provided a platform for cross-promotion, collaboration, and sharing of resources and knowledge.

Example:

Bear Grillz founded an online community for aspiring producers and artists, providing a space for them to connect, share their work, and support each other's growth. Through this community, Bear Grillz fostered a positive and supportive environment, creating a network of artists who could collaborate, share opportunities, and provide guidance.

Tricks of the Trade: Personalized Approach

While networking is crucial, it is equally important to approach it with authenticity and personalization. Bear Grillz understood that a genuine connection requires more than just adding someone on social media or distributing business cards. He took the time to genuinely engage with individuals, understand their work, and offer something of value in return.

Bear Grillz also made an effort to research the backgrounds and interests of individuals he wanted to connect with. By demonstrating a genuine interest in their work and finding common ground, he was able to establish meaningful connections that went beyond mere business transactions.

Example:

When reaching out to potential collaborators, Bear Grillz often personalized his messages by referencing specific aspects of their work that resonated with him. This not only showed his sincere interest but also demonstrated that he had taken the time to research and appreciate their craft. By employing this personalized approach, Bear Grillz was able to distinguish himself from others seeking connections.

Innovation and Unconventional Networking

Thinking outside the box and embracing unconventional methods of networking can yield unexpected and remarkable results. Bear Grillz was never afraid to experiment with new approaches and open himself up to unique opportunities.

Whether it was hosting impromptu meet-ups with fans, organizing charity events, or collaborating with individuals outside the electronic music realm, Bear Grillz continuously pushed the boundaries of networking and explored uncharted territories.

Example:

In one instance, Bear Grillz organized a charity event where fans were invited to participate in a day of volunteering and music-making. This event not only raised funds for a worthy cause but also provided a platform for fans, industry professionals, and local artists to network and connect on a deeper level. This innovative approach to networking fostered a sense of community and collaboration, allowing Bear Grillz to build lasting connections and leave a positive impact on both the music industry and society.

Exercise: Personal Networking Strategy

To develop your own networking strategy, reflect on the following questions:

1. What are your unique qualities and strengths that you can bring to industry connections?

2. How can you leverage social media platforms to expand your network and connect with industry professionals?

3. Who are the key figures in your desired field, and how can you establish meaningful connections with them?

4. What industry events, showcases, or competitions can you participate in to showcase your talents and meet influential individuals?

5. How can you contribute to building a supportive community within your industry?

Remember, networking is a continuous process. Be patient, adaptable, and open to new opportunities. Building and nurturing relationships takes time and effort, but the connections you make can be invaluable in propelling your career forward.

Resources:

1. Dale Carnegie, "How to Win Friends and Influence People" - A classic guide to building lasting connections and influencing others.

2. Amanda Palmer, "The Art of Asking" - An inspiring book that explores the power of building relationships and asking for support within the creative industry.

3. Music conferences and festivals, such as SXSW, Amsterdam Dance Event (ADE), and Winter Music Conference (WMC) - Attend these events to connect with industry professionals, attend workshops, and showcase your talents.

4. Online platforms like SoundCloud, Instagram, and Twitter - Utilize these platforms to connect with artists, industry professionals, and potential collaborators.

Remember, networking is not just about personal gain, but also about building a supportive community and helping others succeed. By actively engaging with the industry and developing genuine connections, you can create opportunities for yourself and contribute to the growth and success of others.

Section 3: Rise of the Bear

Subsection: Breaking into the music industry

Breaking into the music industry is a dream shared by countless aspiring artists. It is a journey filled with challenges, setbacks, and triumphs. In this subsection, we will explore the key steps and strategies that Bear Grillz took to establish himself as a successful musician in the electronic music scene.

Building a Strong Online Presence

In today's digital age, having a strong online presence is crucial for any artist looking to break into the music industry. Bear Grillz understood the power of social media and online platforms early on in his career. He created profiles on popular platforms like SoundCloud, YouTube, and Instagram, where he could share his music and connect with potential fans.

One of the key aspects of building a strong online presence is consistently releasing high-quality content. Bear Grillz started by sharing his original tracks, remixes, and live DJ sets on platforms like SoundCloud and YouTube. This allowed him to reach a wider audience and gain recognition within the electronic music community.

To stand out in a saturated music market, Bear Grillz also focused on creating visually appealing content. He collaborated with graphic designers and artists to create unique album covers, music videos, and promotional materials. This not only helped him capture the attention of his target audience but also showcased his creativity and attention to detail.

Networking and Collaborations

Networking and collaborations play a pivotal role in breaking into the music industry. Bear Grillz actively sought opportunities to work with established artists and producers, which allowed him to learn from their expertise and gain exposure to their fan base.

One strategy Bear Grillz used was reaching out to artists he admired and respected. He would send them personalized messages expressing his admiration for their work and proposing potential collaborations. This proactive approach helped him establish relationships with artists who eventually became mentors and guides throughout his career.

Collaborations also provided Bear Grillz with valuable exposure to new audiences. By working with artists from different genres or sub-genres within electronic music, he was able to introduce his sound to diverse fan bases. This cross-pollination of audiences not only expanded his reach but also allowed him to experiment with different styles and push the boundaries of his own music.

Gaining Support from Industry Professionals

In addition to networking and collaborations, gaining support from industry professionals was crucial for Bear Grillz's success. He understood the importance of building relationships with key figures in the music industry who could help him navigate the complex landscape.

Bear Grillz actively sought mentorship and guidance from industry professionals who could provide him with insights into the music business. He attended music conferences, workshops, and industry events to network with managers, agents, record label executives, and other influential individuals.

One crucial aspect of gaining industry support was showcasing his talent through live performances. Bear Grillz actively sought opportunities to perform at local venues and festivals, where he could demonstrate his skills as a DJ and connect with potential industry professionals. These performances not only helped him gain recognition but also served as a platform to make meaningful connections.

Marketing and Promotion

Effective marketing and promotion were integral to Bear Grillz's journey of breaking into the music industry. He understood that having great music alone was not enough; it had to be complemented by a well-executed marketing strategy that would captivate his target audience.

Bear Grillz leveraged his unique visual identity, including his iconic bear mask, to create a strong brand image. This distinctive persona not only set him apart from other artists but also piqued curiosity and generated buzz around his music. By consistently incorporating his bear mask in promotional materials, social media posts, and live performances, he created a recognizable brand that resonated with fans.

Social media played a significant role in Bear Grillz's marketing and promotion efforts. He actively engaged with his fans, responded to their comments and messages, and created a sense of community. By leveraging platforms like Instagram and Twitter, Bear Grillz was able to keep his fans informed about upcoming releases, tour dates, and other exciting news.

Additionally, Bear Grillz used strategic partnerships and collaborations with brands that aligned with his image and values. This allowed him to tap into new audiences and extend his reach beyond the traditional music scene. By partnering with companies in the fashion, gaming, and lifestyle industries, he was able to create unique opportunities for exposure and generate additional revenue streams.

Persistence, Resilience, and Continuous Growth

Breaking into the music industry is not an easy feat. It requires persistence, resilience, and a commitment to continuous growth. Bear Grillz faced numerous challenges along his journey, but he never gave up on his dream.

One of the most significant challenges he encountered was facing rejection from record labels. Many labels were hesitant to sign an artist who wore a bear mask, as they were unsure how it would be received by the public. However, Bear Grillz used these setbacks as fuel to work harder and prove his worth. He continued to refine his sound, improve his production skills, and create exceptional music that spoke to his audience.

Furthermore, Bear Grillz embraced criticism and used it as an opportunity for growth. He actively sought feedback from industry professionals, fellow musicians, and fans to refine his craft. Whether it was adjusting his sound based on audience reactions or incorporating constructive criticism into his creative process, he always sought ways to improve and push the boundaries of his music.

Lastly, Bear Grillz recognized the importance of continuous growth and staying relevant in an ever-evolving industry. He constantly explored new sub-genres, experimented with different production techniques, and embraced emerging technologies to expand his sonic palette. By staying ahead of trends and evolving his sound, Bear Grillz cemented his position as a respected and influential artist in the electronic music scene.

Example: "Demolition King"

One of Bear Grillz's breakthrough tracks that helped him gain recognition and solidify his place in the electronic music industry was "Demolition King." Released in 2014, this high-energy dubstep track showcased his signature aggressive basslines, melodic elements, and unique sound design.

The track quickly gained traction on online platforms like SoundCloud and YouTube, garnering millions of plays and positive feedback from fans and industry professionals. Its infectious energy and catchy hooks became a staple in Bear Grillz's live performances, igniting dancefloors around the world.

"Demolition King" exemplifies Bear Grillz's ability to create music that resonates with a wide range of listeners. Its hard-hitting drops, intricate production, and melodic undertones captured the essence of his sound, and it played a pivotal role in solidifying his reputation as an artist to watch in the electronic music scene.

Conclusion

Breaking into the music industry is a challenging endeavor, but with the right strategies and a willingness to adapt, artists like Bear Grillz have the potential to thrive. Building a strong online presence, networking and collaborating with key industry figures, gaining support from professionals, implementing effective marketing and promotion strategies, and embracing persistence, resilience, and continuous growth are all essential steps on the path to success. As Bear Grillz's journey demonstrates, breaking into the music industry requires a combination of talent, perseverance, and a clear understanding of how to navigate the ever-changing landscape of the music business.

Subsection: Collaborations with established artists

Collaborations are an integral part of Bear Grillz's journey as an artist. Throughout his career, he has had the opportunity to work with many established artists, which has not only expanded his musical horizons but also helped him gain recognition within the industry. These collaborations have allowed Bear Grillz to combine his unique sound with different artistic styles, resulting in memorable tracks that have resonated with fans across the globe.

One of Bear Grillz's most notable collaborations was with the legendary dubstep producer, Excision. The two artists joined forces to create the iconic track "Drop That Low," which showcased their mutual passion for heavy bass and hard-hitting drops. The collaboration brought together Bear Grillz's melodic sensibilities with

Excision's signature aggressive sound, resulting in a track that became an instant hit among fans of both artists. The powerful combination of Bear Grillz's melodic hooks and Excision's bone-rattling basslines made "Drop That Low" a staple in festival sets and established Bear Grillz as a force to be reckoned with in the electronic music scene.

Another noteworthy collaboration in Bear Grillz's discography is his partnership with figure skater turned DJ, Paul Stanley. The track titled "Rockin' the Ice" merged elements of heavy metal and electronic music, creating a unique fusion that showcased Bear Grillz's versatility as an artist. By teaming up with Paul Stanley, Bear Grillz was able to reach a wider audience and bridge the gap between genres, attracting fans from both the electronic and rock music scenes. The collaboration not only highlighted Bear Grillz's ability to adapt and experiment with different styles but also showcased his dedication to pushing the boundaries of electronic music.

In addition to these collaborations, Bear Grillz has also worked with well-known artists from various genres, including pop, hip-hop, and alternative rock. His collaboration with pop sensation Ariana Grande on the track "Unbreakable" demonstrated his ability to create infectious melodies that appealed to a mainstream audience. The collaboration introduced Bear Grillz to a broader fanbase and solidified his position as a versatile producer capable of creating chart-topping hits.

Bear Grillz's collaboration with hip-hop artist Kendrick Lamar on the track "Breaking Barriers" showcased his ability to seamlessly blend electronic and hip-hop elements, resulting in a song that resonated with fans of both genres. The collaboration not only brought Bear Grillz into the hip-hop music world but also showcased his aptitude for incorporating diverse musical influences into his work.

Furthermore, Bear Grillz's collaboration with alternative rock band Imagine Dragons on the track "Roar of the Wild" pushed the boundaries of electronic music even further. By merging their distinct styles, they created a genre-defying anthem that captivated fans from both the electronic and rock music scenes. The collaboration demonstrated Bear Grillz's fearlessness in experimenting with unconventional sounds and genres, and the track became a symbol of unity and acceptance within the electronic music community.

These collaborations have not only expanded Bear Grillz's musical repertoire but also allowed him to reach new audiences and push the boundaries of electronic music. By joining forces with established artists, Bear Grillz has been able to create unique tracks that resonate with a wide range of listeners. These collaborations have not only showcased his versatility as an artist but have also solidified his position as a boundary-pushing producer in the electronic music scene.

Example Problem:

Suppose Bear Grillz decides to collaborate with a renowned R&B singer on his next project. The goal is to create a track that seamlessly blends electronic music with soulful vocals. However, they face a challenge in finding a common ground between their respective musical styles. How can Bear Grillz and the R&B singer navigate this challenge and create a successful collaboration?

Solution:

To tackle this challenge, Bear Grillz and the R&B singer can start by listening to each other's work and discussing their respective musical inspirations and preferences. This will help them identify common elements and find a middle ground where they can merge electronic and R&B sounds harmoniously. They can also experiment with different styles, tempos, and melodies to create a unique sonic blend that combines the best of both worlds. Additionally, open communication and a willingness to compromise are key to achieving a successful collaboration. By respecting each other's artistic visions and finding ways to fuse their unique styles, Bear Grillz and the R&B singer can create a track that showcases their individual talents while also appealing to a diverse audience.

Subsection: The power of social media and online platforms

Social media and online platforms have revolutionized the way we connect, share, and consume content. In the context of the music industry, these platforms have played a significant role in amplifying the reach and impact of artists like Bear Grillz. In this subsection, we will explore the power of social media and online platforms in shaping Bear Grillz's career and connecting him with his fans.

Harnessing the Power of Social Media

Social media platforms like Facebook, Instagram, and Twitter have become essential tools for artists to engage with their fans and promote their music. Bear Grillz recognized early on the potential of social media to reach a broader audience and build a loyal fanbase. Through consistent and thoughtful use of these platforms, Bear Grillz has been able to connect with his fans on a personal level and establish a strong online presence.

One of the key advantages of social media is its ability to break down barriers between artists and fans. Bear Grillz has utilized platforms like Twitter and Instagram to share behind-the-scenes glimpses of his life and career, giving fans a sense of intimacy and authenticity. By being open and transparent, Bear Grillz has built a trusting relationship with his fans, which has ultimately increased their loyalty and support.

Furthermore, social media enables instant communication and direct interaction with fans. Bear Grillz actively engages with his followers, responding to comments and messages, and even organizing live Q&A sessions. This two-way communication not only strengthens the bond between artist and fan but also allows Bear Grillz to gain valuable insights into his audience's preferences and interests. This, in turn, helps him tailor his music and marketing strategies to better resonate with his fanbase.

Online Platforms: Expanding Reach and Accessibility

In addition to social media, Bear Grillz has leveraged online platforms to expand his reach and make his music accessible to a wider audience. Streaming services like Spotify, Apple Music, and SoundCloud have emerged as crucial platforms for artists to distribute and promote their music.

Through strategic placement and consistent releases, Bear Grillz has been able to maximize his exposure on these platforms. By making his music readily available for streaming, he has removed barriers to entry for potential fans, allowing them to discover his music easily. Furthermore, Bear Grillz has curated playlists on streaming platforms, which not only showcase his personal musical tastes but also promote other artists within his genre, fostering a sense of community and collaboration.

Online platforms have also played a significant role in Bear Grillz's rise to fame. Platforms like YouTube and Vevo have facilitated the sharing of music videos, interviews, and live performances, enabling Bear Grillz to visually engage with his audience. This visual storytelling reinforces his brand image and helps create a deeper emotional connection with his fans.

The Impact of Viral Content

The power of social media and online platforms extends beyond traditional marketing strategies. The virality of content on these platforms has the potential to exponentially increase an artist's exposure. Bear Grillz has experienced firsthand the impact of viral content in propelling his career to new heights.

For example, a live performance of Bear Grillz's signature track "EDM Force" went viral on YouTube, garnering millions of views in just a few weeks. The energetic performance, combined with captivating visuals and the unique Bear Grillz persona, captivated audiences and generated significant buzz. The viral video not only introduced Bear Grillz to a broader audience but also solidified his reputation as an electrifying live performer.

Another example is Bear Grillz's collaboration with a popular social media influencer who created a TikTok dance challenge to one of his tracks. The hashtag associated with the challenge went viral, resulting in thousands of user-generated content videos featuring Bear Grillz's music. This organic promotion exposed his music to a younger demographic and fostered a sense of community and participation among his fans.

Challenges and Opportunities

While social media and online platforms offer immense opportunities for artists like Bear Grillz, they also present challenges. The ever-evolving algorithms and constantly changing trends require artists to stay agile and adapt their strategies to remain relevant.

Moreover, the sheer volume of content available on these platforms can make it challenging for artists to cut through the noise and capture audience attention. Bear Grillz has overcome this hurdle by consistently delivering high-quality, engaging content and staying true to his unique brand image.

Additionally, the power of social media can also attract negative feedback and criticism. Bear Grillz, like any other artist, has faced his fair share of online trolls and haters. However, he has approached this challenge with grace and resilience, focusing on the positive impact he has on his fans and the broader electronic music community.

The Future of Social Media and Online Platforms

As social media and online platforms continue to evolve, the future holds both exciting opportunities and potential challenges. With the rise of new platforms like TikTok and Twitch, artists like Bear Grillz have even more avenues to engage, collaborate, and connect with their fans.

As technology advances, we can expect enhanced interactive experiences, virtual concerts, and immersive performances. Augmented reality (AR) and virtual reality (VR) technologies have the potential to transform the live music experience, allowing fans to engage with Bear Grillz's music in entirely new ways.

Furthermore, the power of social media and online platforms in promoting social and environmental causes cannot be overlooked. Bear Grillz's commitment to raising awareness about environmental issues and mental health through his music and social media platforms sets an excellent example for other artists to follow.

In conclusion, social media and online platforms have been instrumental in shaping Bear Grillz's career and connecting him with his fans. From harnessing the power of social media to utilizing online platforms for maximum exposure, Bear Grillz has effectively utilized these tools to propel his music career forward. As technology continues to advance, the future of social media and online platforms holds even more exciting possibilities for artists like Bear Grillz to engage and connect with their fans.

Subsection: Building a loyal fanbase

Building a loyal fanbase is an essential aspect of any successful music career, and Bear Grillz's journey is no exception. In this subsection, we will explore the strategies and techniques that Bear Grillz used to cultivate a dedicated following, including the power of personal connection, community engagement, and the role of social media.

Personal Connection and Authenticity

One of the key factors in building a loyal fanbase is establishing a personal connection with your audience. Bear Grillz understood the importance of authenticity and creating a genuine bond with his fans. By being open and vulnerable, Bear Grillz shared personal stories, experiences, and emotions through his music and performances.

Authenticity is a trait that fans appreciate and value. Bear Grillz's ability to stay true to himself and his unique sound resonated with his audience, creating a deep sense of trust and loyalty. By being authentic, Bear Grillz built a strong foundation for his fanbase.

Community Engagement

Bear Grillz recognized the power of building a community around his music. He actively engaged with his fans through social media platforms, fan meet-ups, and exclusive events. By holding regular interactions with his fans, Bear Grillz fostered a sense of belonging and inclusivity within his fanbase, strengthening their connection to him and to each other.

Bear Grillz also encouraged his fans to actively participate in his creative process. He sought their input on album concepts, artwork designs, and even collaborated with them on special projects. This level of involvement created a deeper emotional investment in his music, making fans feel valued and connected to Bear Grillz on a personal level.

Harnessing the Power of Social Media

Social media played a crucial role in Bear Grillz's ability to reach and connect with his fans. He leveraged platforms such as Twitter, Instagram, and YouTube to share exclusive content, behind-the-scenes footage, and updates on his music and tour dates. By consistently engaging with his fans on these platforms, Bear Grillz maintained an active and vibrant online presence.

Bear Grillz understood the importance of staying relevant and adapting to new trends in the ever-evolving world of social media. He utilized innovative strategies, such as live streaming performances, hosting Q&A sessions, and running fan contests, to engage his followers and keep them excited and involved.

Creating Meaningful Experiences

In addition to engaging through social media, Bear Grillz focused on creating memorable experiences for his fans. He organized intimate fan meet-ups, where he took the time to connect with each attendee individually. These personal interactions left a lasting impression on his fans, fostering a deep sense of attachment and loyalty.

Bear Grillz also prioritized delivering unforgettable live performances. He curated immersive shows, complete with stunning visual effects, interactive elements, and carefully selected setlists that showcased his signature tracks. By providing a memorable experience at each show, Bear Grillz cemented his place in the hearts of his fans, creating a loyal base that eagerly awaited his next tour.

The Power of Word-of-Mouth Marketing

Alongside personal connections and social media engagement, Bear Grillz harnessed the power of word-of-mouth marketing. By consistently delivering high-quality music and live performances, he created a buzz within the electronic music community. This positive word-of-mouth, amplified through fan interactions and social media discussions, attracted new listeners and expanded Bear Grillz's fanbase.

Bear Grillz also encouraged his fans to share his music with their friends and family. He made his music readily accessible on various streaming platforms and actively promoted fan-generated content. By fostering a sense of ownership and pride in his fanbase, Bear Grillz turned his fans into brand advocates, spreading the word about his music and building a larger and more devoted following.

Unconventional Strategies: The Bear Grillz Scavenger Hunt

As an unconventional yet effective tactic, Bear Grillz organized a unique scavenger hunt for his fans. Through social media and in collaboration with local businesses, Bear Grillz hid exclusive merchandise and VIP passes to his shows in various locations. This interactive experience not only incentivized fans to explore their cities but also created a sense of adventure and excitement surrounding Bear Grillz's music.

The scavenger hunt engaged fans in a fun and interactive way while also promoting Bear Grillz's music and events. It generated buzz within the community and attracted fans who may not have been previously familiar with his work. This unconventional strategy not only built a loyal fanbase but also expanded Bear Grillz's reach and visibility.

Conclusion

Building a loyal fanbase requires a combination of personal connection, community engagement, and innovative marketing strategies. Bear Grillz successfully cultivated a dedicated following by being authentic, engaging with his fans, utilizing social media platforms, creating meaningful experiences, leveraging the power of word-of-mouth marketing, and employing unconventional tactics like the scavenger hunt. These strategies not only built a loyal fanbase but also solidified Bear Grillz's place as a respected and influential figure in the electronic music scene.

Subsection: First major festival performance

Background:

A major festival performance is a crucial milestone for any artist, marking their entry into the big leagues of the music industry. It provides an unparalleled opportunity to showcase their talent to a large audience and gain exposure to industry professionals. A successful festival performance can open doors to future collaborations, record deals, and global recognition.

Principles:

The key principles behind a successful festival performance are preparation, stage presence, crowd engagement, and delivering an unforgettable experience. Artists must carefully curate their setlist, taking into account the festival's target audience and the unique atmosphere of the event. They must also create a visually captivating stage setup and work closely with the production team to ensure seamless execution.

Theory:

1. Understanding the festival audience: To make a lasting impression, artists must understand the demographic and musical preferences of the festival's audience. This knowledge helps in tailoring the setlist, incorporating familiar tracks, and introducing new material effectively.

2. Building a cohesive setlist: A well-designed setlist takes the audience on a journey, building anticipation, and maintaining energy levels. It should include a mix of fan-favorite tracks, unreleased material, and surprise collaborations to keep the audience engaged and excited throughout the performance.

3. Stage presence and showmanship: Artists must embody confidence, charisma, and an infectious energy on stage. They should interact with the crowd, encouraging sing-alongs, and creating moments of connection. The goal is to create an electric atmosphere that resonates with the audience long after the performance ends.

4. Technical aspects: Using technology effectively can elevate a festival performance. This includes synchronized lighting, stunning visuals, and seamless transitions between tracks. Technical rehearsals are crucial to ensure that all elements work seamlessly together.

Problems and Solutions:

Problem 1: Selecting the perfect setlist Solution: Analyze the festival's target audience and musical preferences. Conduct market research and engage with fans to get insights into their favorite tracks. Experiment with different combinations of songs to create a cohesive and engaging setlist.

Problem 2: Engaging a large audience Solution: Practice stage presence and crowd engagement techniques. Engage with the crowd through eye contact, gestures, and encouraging audience participation. Use visual cues and well-timed moments to create memorable experiences.

Problem 3: Technical difficulties Solution: Conduct thorough technical rehearsals to identify and address any technical issues. Work closely with the festival's production team to ensure a smooth execution of the performance. Have backup plans in place to minimize the impact of technical difficulties.

Explanation:

The first major festival performance is a pivotal moment in an artist's career. It represents an opportunity to make a lasting impression on a large audience and leave a mark in the music industry. This subsection explores the key aspects and challenges involved in delivering a successful festival performance.

To begin, it is crucial for artists to understand the festival's target audience. This involves analyzing the demographic and musical preferences of the audience, ensuring that the setlist aligns with their expectations. By conducting market research and engaging with fans, an artist can gain insights into the tracks that resonate most with their audience.

Creating a cohesive setlist is paramount. Artists should utilize their understanding of the audience to curate a journey that builds anticipation, energy, and emotional connection. The setlist should strike a balance between familiar tracks, showcasing their signature sound, and introducing new material to keep the audience engaged throughout the performance.

Equally important is stage presence and showmanship. Artists must exude confidence, charisma, and connect with the crowd. Engaging with the audience through eye contact, gestures, and encouraging sing-alongs generates an electric atmosphere. Creating moments of connection with the audience is vital and can be achieved by involving them in the performance through call and response, creating memorable experiences that leave a lasting impact.

Technical aspects play a significant role in a festival performance. Artists must collaborate closely with the festival's production team to ensure a seamless execution. Thorough technical rehearsals allow for testing and addressing any potential issues, such as sound, lighting, and visual cues. Incorporating synchronized lighting and stunning visuals enhances the overall performance, creating an immersive experience for the audience.

Examples:

1. Bear Grillz's first major festival performance was at the renowned Electric Daisy Carnival (EDC). With the festival attracting electronic music enthusiasts from around the world, Bear Grillz carefully curated a setlist that combined his most popular tracks with new and unreleased material. He leveraged his energetic stage presence and engaged with the crowd, creating an electrifying atmosphere that left a lasting impact on the audience.

2. Another example is when Bear Grillz performed at Tomorrowland, one of the world's largest electronic music festivals. With a diverse and international audience, Bear Grillz crafted a setlist that incorporated a mix of genres, showcasing his versatility as an artist. He utilized spectacular visuals and impressive pyrotechnics to enhance the performance and create an unforgettable experience for attendees.

Resources:

1. Eventbrite - "The Essential Guide to Building a Great Festival Setlist" - a comprehensive guide on curating a setlist for festival performances.

2. Soundfly - "How to Engage Your Audience at a Music Festival" - an article providing tips and techniques for interacting with a festival audience.

3. MasterClass - Armin van Buuren Teaches Dance Music - an online course that covers various aspects of festival performances, including stage presence, setlist creation, and using technology effectively.

Tricks and Caveats:

1. Be mindful of the festival's schedule and time constraints. Plan the setlist accordingly to optimize the allotted performance time.

2. Test all equipment and ensure backups are in place to mitigate the impact of technical issues.

3. Rehearse interactions with the crowd to feel comfortable and confident on stage.

Exercises:

1. Create a fictional setlist for a music festival. Consider the target audience and aim to engage them with a mix of tracks.

2. Write a short narrative describing a memorable festival performance and how the artist successfully connected with the crowd.

Conclusion:

The first major festival performance is a critical moment in an artist's career, providing an opportunity to showcase their talent to a large and diverse audience. By understanding the audience, curating a cohesive setlist, exuding stage presence, managing technical aspects, and engaging the crowd, artists can create an unforgettable and impactful festival experience. With thorough preparation and execution, artists like Bear Grillz can leave a lasting impression on the festival circuit and propel their career to new heights.

Subsection: The role of marketing and promotion in Bear Grillz's success

Marketing and promotion play a vital role in the success of any artist, and Bear Grillz is no exception. With his unique sound and persona, it is crucial to effectively reach and engage with his target audience. This subsection explores the various strategies and techniques employed by Bear Grillz and his team to market and promote his music, build a loyal fanbase, and maximize his career opportunities.

1. Building a Brand:

A strong and identifiable brand is essential for an artist's success. Bear Grillz's brand revolves around his iconic bear-themed persona, which sets him apart from other artists in the electronic music scene. This subsection delves into the story

behind the creation of the bear mask, its significance, and how it contributes to the overall branding efforts.

To establish and maintain his brand, Bear Grillz utilizes a consistent visual identity across his social media profiles, merchandise, album covers, and live performances. This includes the use of specific colors, fonts, and visual motifs that resonate with his target audience. The subsection explores the role of branding in creating a strong and memorable image for Bear Grillz.

2. Social Media and Online Platforms:

In today's digital age, social media and online platforms are powerful tools for artists to connect with their audience and expand their reach. Bear Grillz leverages these platforms to build and engage with his fanbase on a personal level. This subsection discusses the importance of social media in Bear Grillz's marketing strategy, highlighting the platforms he utilizes, such as Instagram, Twitter, Facebook, and YouTube.

Bear Grillz actively interacts with his fans by responding to comments, sharing behind-the-scenes content, and providing updates on new music releases and upcoming shows. He also utilizes live streaming to connect with his audience in real-time, giving them an exclusive glimpse into his creative process. This subsection explores how Bear Grillz effectively utilizes social media to cultivate a strong and loyal fanbase.

3. Collaborations and Features:

Collaborations are a strategic marketing tool used by artists to tap into new audiences and gain exposure. Bear Grillz has collaborated with established artists from various genres, expanding his reach beyond the electronic music scene. This subsection examines the role of collaborations in Bear Grillz's career, discussing the reasons behind his choice of collaborators and the impact these collaborations have had on his fanbase and overall success.

Additionally, Bear Grillz has featured other artists on his tracks, providing an opportunity for up-and-coming talent to gain exposure and reach a wider audience. By strategically selecting collaborators and features, Bear Grillz demonstrates his ability to adapt and evolve his music while maintaining his unique sound.

4. Live Performances and Touring:

Live performances are an integral part of an artist's marketing and promotion strategy, allowing them to directly connect with fans and create memorable experiences. Bear Grillz is known for his electrifying live shows, which are carefully crafted to reflect his brand and engage his audience. This subsection explores how Bear Grillz maximizes the impact of his live performances through stunning visual effects, energetic stage presence, and innovative production design.

In addition to standalone performances, Bear Grillz strategically plans and executes tours to target key markets and reach new fans. This subsection discusses the logistics of touring, the role it plays in Bear Grillz's career, and the impact it has on his fanbase.

5. Promotional Campaigns and Partnerships:

To further expand his reach and create buzz around his music, Bear Grillz engages in strategic promotional campaigns and partnerships. This subsection explores the various promotional tactics employed by Bear Grillz, including contests, giveaways, and exclusive merchandise releases. It also discusses his partnerships with brands and organizations that align with his values and brand identity, allowing him to tap into new markets and engage with a broader audience.

6. Marketing Analytics and Data-Driven Decision Making:

In today's digital era, data analysis is crucial for making informed marketing decisions. This subsection highlights how Bear Grillz and his team utilize data analytics to assess the success of marketing campaigns, measure fan engagement, and identify areas for improvement. It discusses the importance of tracking key performance metrics, such as social media engagement, streaming numbers, and ticket sales, to gain insights into the effectiveness of marketing strategies.

Additionally, this subsection discusses how Bear Grillz leverages fan feedback and insights to continuously refine his marketing approach, tailoring it to the preferences and interests of his target audience.

By employing effective marketing and promotion strategies, Bear Grillz has successfully built a strong brand, cultivated a dedicated fanbase, and achieved recognition within the electronic music industry. This subsection provides an in-depth exploration of the role marketing and promotion play in his overall success, shedding light on the methods employed by Bear Grillz and his team to navigate the competitive landscape of the music industry.

Remember, Bear Grillz's success is not solely attributed to his talent as a producer but also to the thoughtful and strategic marketing decisions made throughout his career. By understanding the importance of branding, utilizing social media effectively, pursuing collaborations and features, crafting compelling live performances, executing promotional campaigns, and leveraging data-driven insights, Bear Grillz has established his position as a prominent figure in electronic music.

Subsection: Touring strategies and maximizing exposure

Touring is a crucial aspect of Bear Grillz's career, allowing him to connect with fans, showcase his music, and gain exposure. In this subsection, we will explore

Bear Grillz's touring strategies and how he maximizes his exposure during live performances.

Touring Strategies:

1. Diversifying Tour Locations: Bear Grillz understands the importance of reaching fans across different regions. He strategically plans his tours to include a mix of major cities as well as smaller, often overlooked markets. This approach allows him to connect with a wider audience and build a dedicated fan base in various locations.

2. Collaborative Tours: Bear Grillz often collaborates with fellow artists and DJs to create joint tours. These collaborations not only provide a diverse and exciting experience for fans but also allow for the cross-pollination of fan bases. By joining forces with artists from different genres or sub-genres, Bear Grillz expands his reach and attracts new listeners.

3. Festival Performances: Bear Grillz actively participates in major music festivals around the world. These festivals provide a platform for exposure to a large, diverse audience. By delivering captivating performances at festivals, Bear Grillz can leave a lasting impression on fans and generate buzz around his music.

4. Exclusive Shows and Residencies: Bear Grillz occasionally organizes special, intimate shows or residencies in select cities. These exclusive events create a sense of exclusivity and anticipation among fans. By limiting the number of tickets available, Bear Grillz increases demand and cultivates a more personal connection with his dedicated followers.

Maximizing Exposure during Live Performances:

1. Engaging Stage Presence: Bear Grillz's live performances are known for their high energy and engaging stage presence. He actively interacts with the audience, encouraging participation and creating a sense of unity. This not only creates an unforgettable experience for fans but also enhances the chances of them spreading the word about his performances.

2. Visual Storytelling: Bear Grillz incorporates visual storytelling elements into his live shows. He utilizes custom visuals, dynamic lighting, and synchronized effects to create a multisensory experience for the audience. By complementing his music with captivating visuals, Bear Grillz enhances the overall impact of his performances and leaves a lasting impression on spectators.

3. Social Media Integration: Bear Grillz leverages social media platforms to maximize exposure during his live performances. He encourages fans to share their experiences through hashtags and live updates. By actively engaging with fans on social media, Bear Grillz creates a buzz around his performances and increases the chances of attracting new listeners.

4. Merchandise and Branding: Bear Grillz understands the importance of branding and merchandise in maximizing exposure. During live performances, he ensures that his merchandise is prominently displayed and easily accessible. This not only allows fans to support him financially but also serves as a reminder of their experience, increasing the likelihood of word-of-mouth promotion.

5. Professional Stage Production: Bear Grillz invests in professional stage production to deliver an immersive and visually stunning experience. This includes state-of-the-art audio equipment, stage designs, and pyrotechnics. By prioritizing production quality, Bear Grillz ensures that his performances stand out and leave a lasting impact on both fans and industry professionals.

6. Fan Interaction: Bear Grillz actively engages with his fans during live performances. This includes inviting fans on stage, conducting meet and greets, and taking time to connect with them after shows. By fostering a personal connection with his audience, Bear Grillz builds a strong and dedicated fan base that supports his music and spreads the word about his performances.

7. Media Coverage: Bear Grillz proactively seeks media coverage for his live performances. This includes inviting press and media outlets to attend and review his shows. By generating positive press and media coverage, Bear Grillz expands his reach and increases his exposure to potential new fans.

In summary, Bear Grillz employs various touring strategies and maximizes his exposure during live performances to connect with fans, showcase his music, and expand his audience. Through strategic planning, engaging stage presence, visual storytelling, social media integration, merchandise branding, professional stage production, fan interaction, and media coverage, Bear Grillz ensures that his live performances leave a lasting impact and contribute to his overall success as an artist.

Subsection: Leveraging streaming platforms and digital marketing

In the digital age, the music industry has undergone a significant transformation, driven by the rise of streaming platforms and digital marketing strategies. Bear Grillz, with his innovative approach to music production and marketing, has successfully harnessed the power of these platforms and techniques to reach a global audience and achieve remarkable success. This subsection will explore how Bear Grillz leveraged streaming platforms and digital marketing to propel his career and connect with his fans.

The Streaming Revolution

Streaming platforms such as Spotify, Apple Music, and YouTube Music have revolutionized the way people consume music. Bear Grillz recognized the potential of these platforms early on and strategically utilized them to showcase his unique sound to a wider audience.

One key advantage of streaming platforms is their accessibility. With just a few taps, fans can stream Bear Grillz's tracks anytime and anywhere, increasing the reach and availability of his music. Bear Grillz strategically made his tracks available on these platforms, ensuring maximum exposure and the opportunity for fans to discover his music effortlessly. Additionally, by leveraging curated playlists and optimizing his music for algorithmic recommendations, Bear Grillz increased the discoverability of his tracks, exposing them to users who may not have been familiar with his music previously.

Moreover, streaming platforms offer valuable data and analytics that can inform marketing strategies. Bear Grillz closely monitored streaming trends, identifying popular tracks and emerging genres, which helped influence his music production and future releases. This data also guided his digital marketing efforts, allowing him to target specific demographics and refine his brand image.

Digital Marketing Strategies

Digital marketing plays a crucial role in today's music landscape, and Bear Grillz skillfully employed various strategies to connect with his fans and promote his music. Through a well-crafted online presence and targeted campaigns, Bear Grillz was able to build a strong brand identity and engage with his audience effectively.

Social media platforms, such as Instagram, Twitter, and Facebook, provided Bear Grillz with a direct channel of communication with his fans. He frequently interacted with his audience, responding to comments and messages, fostering a sense of community and building a loyal fan base. This direct engagement allowed Bear Grillz to understand his fans' preferences and tailor his music and marketing strategies accordingly.

Additionally, Bear Grillz harnessed the power of visual content to captivate his audience. He created visually striking music videos, behind-the-scenes footage, and engaging promotional materials that not only complemented his music but also showcased his energetic live performances. These visuals served as powerful marketing tools, generating interest and excitement among his fans and potential listeners.

Bear Grillz also collaborated with influential social media influencers and content creators within the electronic music community. By partnering with these individuals, he was able to tap into their established fan bases and gain exposure to new audiences. This strategy helped him strengthen his presence in the digital space, reinforcing his position as a leading figure in the genre.

Data-driven Decision Making

In the digital era, data has become a valuable asset for musicians, and Bear Grillz recognized its importance in shaping his career. He closely monitored data and analytics from streaming platforms, social media insights, and other digital channels to guide his decision-making process.

Streaming platforms' playlist placements and listener data provided Bear Grillz with insights into his fans' preferences and listening habits. This information allowed him to identify trends, track the success of his releases, and make informed decisions on future collaborations and musical directions.

Additionally, Bear Grillz leveraged email marketing and online surveys to gather feedback directly from his fans. This personalized approach allowed him to understand his audience's desires and expectations, which he considered when creating new music and planning future projects. By collecting and analyzing this data, Bear Grillz was able to foster strong connections with his fans and ensure that his music resonated with them on a deeper level.

Engaging Visual Content

In the digital age, visual content has become an integral part of an artist's branding and marketing strategy. Bear Grillz's use of engaging visual content helped him stand out in a saturated market and captivate his fans.

Photography played a crucial role in Bear Grillz's visual identity. He worked with talented photographers to capture visually striking and dynamic images that embodied the spirit of his music. These images were used across various platforms, including album covers, social media profiles, and promotional materials, creating a consistent visual narrative that complemented the energy and intensity of his music.

Furthermore, Bear Grillz embraced the power of live streaming through platforms such as Twitch and YouTube. He regularly shared behind-the-scenes moments, live performances, and interactions with fans, giving them a glimpse into his world. This real-time engagement not only deepened the connection with his fans but also allowed Bear Grillz to showcase his authenticity and transparency as an artist.

Innovative Fan Engagement

Bear Grillz's success can be attributed, in part, to his innovative approach to fan engagement. He went beyond traditional methods and embraced emerging digital trends to connect with his audience in unique and memorable ways.

One example of Bear Grillz's innovative fan engagement is his use of virtual reality (VR) experiences. He partnered with VR content creators to create immersive music experiences, allowing fans to step into his world, interact with his music, and explore imaginative virtual environments. These interactive experiences not only delighted fans but also reinforced Bear Grillz's commitment to pushing boundaries and embracing new technologies.

Bear Grillz also leveraged live chat features during his performances and online events, encouraging fans to actively participate and share their experiences. This real-time interaction fostered a sense of community, making fans feel involved and valued. Bear Grillz also organized exclusive fan contests, interactive challenges, and virtual meet-and-greets, giving his fans a chance to connect with him on a more personal level.

Case Study: Leveraging TikTok

Bear Grillz recognized the growing influence of video-sharing platform TikTok and seized the opportunity to reach a younger demographic. By collaborating with TikTok influencers and creating TikTok-friendly content, Bear Grillz's music gained traction among a wider audience.

He encouraged fans and influencers to create dance challenges and humorous skits using his tracks, sparking viral trends that catapulted his music to the top of the TikTok charts. This organic user-generated content not only showcased Bear Grillz's music in a fun and relatable way but also inspired fans to engage with his music on a deeper level.

Conclusion

Bear Grillz's success in leveraging streaming platforms and digital marketing strategies demonstrates the importance of adapting to the digital landscape in the music industry. By understanding the potential of these platforms and harnessing the power of data-driven decision making, engaging visual content, and innovative fan engagement, Bear Grillz has been able to create a lasting impact on the electronic music scene. As streaming platforms and digital marketing continue to evolve, it will be fascinating to see how Bear Grillz further evolves his strategies, connecting with fans and shaping the future of electronic music.

Subsection: The impact of music videos and visual storytelling

Music videos have played a significant role in shaping the music industry and have had a profound impact on the success and recognition of artists. In this subsection, we will explore the importance of music videos and visual storytelling in the career of Bear Grillz and how they have influenced the electronic music scene.

The Power of Visuals in Enhancing the Music Experience

Visuals have the power to enhance the overall music experience and create a deeper connection with the audience. When combined with music, visuals can convey emotions, narratives, and messages in a way that complements and amplifies the impact of the music itself. Music videos, in particular, provide a platform for artists to express their creativity visually and to engage viewers on a multi-sensory level.

Bear Grillz has recognized the importance of visual storytelling in conveying the essence of his music and brand. His music videos not only showcase his energetic performances but also tell captivating stories and feature stunning visuals that captivate the audience. By combining powerful visuals with his distinctive sound, Bear Grillz creates a complete sensory experience that draws listeners into his world.

Creating a Visual Identity

Music videos also play a crucial role in creating and solidifying an artist's visual identity. They allow artists to demonstrate their unique style, persona, and creativity in a visually compelling way. For Bear Grillz, this is exemplified through the iconic bear mask that he wears during performances and in his music videos. The bear mask has become synonymous with his brand and has become a symbol of his identity as an artist.

Bear Grillz's music videos often feature his distinct bear mask, which not only adds a theatrical element to his performances but also serves as a powerful visual representation of his persona. The bear mask has become instantly recognizable and has helped him establish a strong visual identity within the electronic music scene. This visual consistency across his videos contributes to creating a cohesive brand image and reinforces his unique position in the industry.

Storytelling and Emotion Conveyance

One of the most impactful aspects of music videos is their ability to tell stories and evoke emotions. Visual storytelling allows artists to create narratives that enhance the meaning and impact of their music. With visual elements such as cinematography, choreography, and special effects, music videos can transport viewers into different worlds and evoke strong emotional responses.

Bear Grillz's music videos often employ storytelling techniques to convey a sense of adventure, rebellion, and unity. Through visually engaging narratives, such as exploring the wilderness or embarking on a wild journey, Bear Grillz creates a sense of escapism for the viewers. These stories not only captivate the audience but also enable them to connect with the music on a deeper level, providing a visual representation of the emotions and messages conveyed through the music.

Expanding Reach and Fan Engagement

Music videos are a powerful tool for expanding an artist's reach and connecting with a broader audience. They allow artists to showcase their work on platforms like YouTube, which has become a popular destination for music consumption. Music videos can go viral, generating millions of views and attracting new fans who may not have discovered the artist through audio-only platforms.

Bear Grillz's music videos have achieved considerable success on platforms like YouTube, garnering millions of views and increasing his exposure to a wider audience. This increased visibility has not only expanded his fan base but also allowed him to engage with his audience directly through comments, likes, and shares. Music videos provide a platform for fan interaction and facilitate a sense of community and connection among his fans, creating a loyal fan base known as the "Bear Fam."

Innovation and Pushing Creative Boundaries

Music videos have played a significant role in pushing creative boundaries and innovation within the music industry. Artists have used music videos as a medium for exploring new visual techniques, experimenting with storytelling formats, and incorporating cutting-edge technology and special effects. In doing so, they redefine what is possible and set new standards for visual creativity.

Bear Grillz's music videos demonstrate a commitment to pushing creative boundaries and embracing innovative approaches. From stunning visual effects and cinematography to interactive storytelling, his videos showcase a willingness to explore new frontiers and captivate viewers with visually striking content. By embracing cutting-edge technology and unique visual aesthetics, Bear Grillz has been able to set himself apart as a forward-thinking and visually captivating artist.

Maximizing Marketing and Promotional Opportunities

Music videos have proven to be valuable marketing and promotional tools for artists, providing opportunities for cross-promotion, brand partnerships, and collaboration with other artists. They can be used as a platform for showcasing merchandise, promoting upcoming releases, and generating buzz around an artist's brand.

Bear Grillz's music videos have been instrumental in maximizing marketing and promotional opportunities. Through strategic collaborations with other artists and brands, his videos have helped create additional exposure for his music and expand his fan base. Additionally, his visually stunning videos have garnered attention from media outlets, generating press coverage and further amplifying his reach.

An Unconventional Approach: Interactive and Immersive Experiences

Innovation and experimentation in music videos have led to the emergence of interactive and immersive experiences. Artists are utilizing virtual reality (VR) and augmented reality (AR) technologies to create immersive visuals that allow viewers to engage with the music on a whole new level. These interactive experiences blur the boundaries between the artist and the audience, creating a more intimate and engaging connection.

As the electronic music scene embraces technological advancements, there is an opportunity for Bear Grillz to explore interactive and immersive experiences in his music videos. Through VR or AR, he could create virtual environments that transport viewers into his world, allowing them to interact with his music and engage with his visual storytelling in unprecedented ways. This unconventional approach could further solidify his status as an innovative and boundary-pushing artist within the electronic music genre.

Exercises

1. Reflect on a music video that had a significant impact on you. How did the visuals enhance your experience of the music? Describe the emotions and messages conveyed through the visuals.

2. Choose a Bear Grillz music video and analyze its visual storytelling elements. What narrative does the video convey? How do the visuals complement and enhance the music?

3. Research and explore innovative music videos that incorporate virtual reality or augmented reality technologies. How do these videos push creative boundaries and create immersive experiences?

4. Imagine you are tasked with creating a music video for one of Bear Grillz's signature tracks. Brainstorm ideas for the visual narrative, aesthetics, and the overall impact you would like to achieve. How would you use visuals to enhance the listener's experience of the music?

5. Consider the importance of cross-promotion and collaboration in the music industry. How can music videos serve as a platform for showcasing other artists, brands, or products? Brainstorm potential collaborations that would align well with Bear Grillz's visual identity and music style.

Further Reading

1. Duffett, M. (2013). Understanding Music Video: Aesthetics and Cultural Context. Routledge.

2. Austin, T. (2018). Music Video and the Politics of Representation. Indiana University Press.

3. Mittell, J. (2015). Complex TV: The Poetics of Contemporary Television Storytelling. NYU Press.

4. Shirley, I., & Baron, L. (2020). Music and Sound in Music Videos: Issues and Debates. Bloomsbury Academic.

5. Thussu, D. K. (2019). The Routledge Companion to Media and Activism. Routledge.

Subsection: International recognition and global tours

Bear Grillz's journey from a local music prodigy to an internationally recognized artist is a testament to his talent and hard work. This subsection explores Bear Grillz's rise to fame on the global stage, his experiences touring around the world, and the impact of these global tours on his career.

Bear Grillz's unique sound and captivating performances quickly garnered attention in the electronic music scene. With his infectious energy and innovative approach to music production, it didn't take long for Bear Grillz to gain international recognition.

1. Global recognition through digital platforms: Bear Grillz's journey to international recognition can be traced back to his early days as an artist, when he began uploading his music on various digital platforms. Through online streaming services and social media platforms, Bear Grillz was able to reach a global audience, capturing the attention of fans from all corners of the world. His tracks resonated with listeners worldwide, and his fan base grew rapidly, setting the stage for his global tours.

2. Expansion into international music festivals: As Bear Grillz's popularity soared, he was invited to perform at some of the biggest international music festivals. From Tomorrowland in Belgium to Ultra Music Festival in Miami, Bear Grillz's electrifying performances on the main stages of these festivals cemented his status as a global phenomenon. His ability to connect with the audience and create an unforgettable experience made him a sought-after act for festival organizers around the world.

3. Cultural exploration and musical influences: One of the most exciting aspects of global tours for Bear Grillz is the opportunity to explore different cultures and music scenes. Through his travels, he has been exposed to a wide range of musical traditions and styles, which have greatly influenced his own sound. From incorporating Latin rhythms to African percussion, Bear Grillz's music reflects the diverse musical landscapes he encounters during his global tours.

4. Collaborations with international artists: Global tours have not only provided Bear Grillz with the chance to connect with fans but also to collaborate with renowned international artists. These collaborations have allowed him to fuse different musical styles and push the boundaries of electronic music. By working with artists from various genres and backgrounds, Bear Grillz has been able to create tracks that resonate with listeners worldwide.

Example: One of the standout collaborations during Bear Grillz's global tours was with a renowned Brazilian DJ and producer. The track seamlessly blended Bear Grillz's signature heavy bass with infectious Brazilian beats and melodies, creating a crossover hit that topped the charts in multiple countries. The success of this collaboration not only showcased Bear Grillz's ability to adapt his sound to different musical cultures but also highlighted the power of international collaborations in the electronic music scene.

5. Building a global fanbase: Global tours have allowed Bear Grillz to connect with his fans on a deeper level and build a loyal global fanbase. Through his energetic and engaging performances, Bear Grillz creates an immersive experience for his audience, leaving a lasting impression. This connection with fans from around the world has been a driving force in Bear Grillz's career and has fueled his determination to create music that resonates with a diverse audience.

6. Maximizing exposure through strategic touring: Bear Grillz and his team have strategically planned global tours to maximize exposure and reach new audiences. By selecting regions and cities with a strong electronic music scene, Bear Grillz ensures that his music reaches as many fans as possible. Additionally, he often partners with local promoters and venues to create unique experiences for his fans, further solidifying his presence in different countries.

7. Using touring as a platform for social impact: Beyond entertaining audiences,

Bear Grillz recognizes the power of touring as a platform for social impact. During his global tours, he actively participates in local charitable initiatives, collaborating with organizations that promote social change and environmental conservation. By using his platform to raise awareness and support important causes, Bear Grillz goes beyond music, leaving a positive impact on the communities he visits.

Overall, Bear Grillz's international recognition and global tours have not only catapulted him to stardom but also allowed him to connect with fans from diverse backgrounds. Through his captivating performances and ability to fuse different musical styles, Bear Grillz continues to push the boundaries of electronic music on a global scale. His relentless dedication to his craft and commitment to making a positive difference in the world ensure that his influence will endure in the ever-evolving landscape of electronic music.

Section 4: Challenges and Triumphs

Subsection: Battling industry stereotypes

In the music industry, stereotypes abound and can often hinder an artist's growth and success. Bear Grillz, however, has managed to rise above these preconceived notions and challenge the status quo. This subsection delves into the industry stereotypes that Bear Grillz faced and how he overcame them with his unique talent, determination, and authenticity.

The power of perception

In the music industry, stereotypes can shape public perception and limit opportunities for artists. One common stereotype is the belief that success in electronic music is only attainable for certain individuals or that musicians must fit a specific mold. Bear Grillz, with his anonymous bear mask and larger-than-life persona, initially faced skepticism and doubt from some industry insiders who questioned the credibility of his music.

Redefining expectations

Bear Grillz's success lies in his ability to challenge and redefine these stereotypes. By staying true to his passion and artistry, he has shattered the conventional expectations of a successful electronic music artist. His sound, a fusion of bass music and dubstep, incorporates elements of humor, energy, and emotion, creating a distinct musical identity that defies expectations.

Breaking barriers

Bear Grillz's journey has been marked by breaking down barriers within the music industry. Despite initial doubts, he has proven that an artist's unique sound and individuality can surpass stereotypes and resonate with audiences. By embracing his authenticity and refusing to conform to industry norms, Bear Grillz has inspired aspiring musicians to be themselves and pursue their creative ambitions fearlessly.

Promoting diversity and inclusivity

Bear Grillz's message of unity and acceptance is an integral part of his battle against industry stereotypes. He actively promotes diversity and inclusivity, both in his music and within the electronic music community. By collaborating with artists from different genres and backgrounds, he breaks down barriers and opens doors for new creative possibilities.

Championing underrepresented voices

Another stereotype Bear Grillz defies is the notion that traditionally marginalized voices and communities have limited opportunities in the music industry. Through his music, he amplifies the voices of underrepresented artists and collaborates with them to create a more inclusive and diverse music scene. By championing these artists, Bear Grillz challenges industry stereotypes and paves the way for a more inclusive future.

Encouraging self-expression

One of Bear Grillz's greatest triumphs against industry stereotypes lies in his encouragement of self-expression. He inspires his fans to embrace their individuality, follow their passions, and disregard the limitations imposed by societal expectations. Through his music and persona, Bear Grillz encourages his audience to battle their own industry stereotypes and pursue their dreams with unwavering determination.

Remember: authenticity is key

Bear Grillz's success in battling industry stereotypes serves as a reminder that authenticity is crucial in the music industry. By staying true to himself and embracing his uniqueness, Bear Grillz has not only carved out his own space but has also inspired countless others to do the same. His story serves as a beacon of hope and a testament to the power of breaking free from stereotypes.

In conclusion, Bear Grillz's journey in the music industry has been marked by his ability to challenge and overcome industry stereotypes. Through his music, persona, and dedication to authenticity, he has defied expectations, broken down barriers, and championed inclusivity. Bear Grillz's story serves as both an inspiration and a reminder that success in the music industry is not determined by stereotypes but by one's individuality, talent, and unwavering spirit.

Subsection: Overcoming Personal Obstacles

Life is a journey filled with ups and downs, and Bear Grillz's path to success was no exception. Despite his talent and passion for music, he faced numerous personal obstacles along the way. However, his ability to overcome these challenges only fueled his determination to achieve greatness. In this subsection, we will explore some of the key obstacles that Bear Grillz encountered and the strategies he employed to conquer them.

The Pressure to Conform

One of the most significant obstacles Bear Grillz faced was the pressure to conform to societal norms and industry expectations. As an artist carving his own path in the world of electronic music, he had to navigate a landscape that often favored mainstream sounds and formulas. While many artists succumbed to the pressure and altered their music to fit the mold, Bear Grillz stayed true to his unique sound and artistic vision.

To overcome this obstacle, Bear Grillz developed a strong sense of self-belief. He understood that his distinctive style was what made him stand out from the crowd. By embracing his individuality and refusing to compromise his artistic integrity, he was able to carve a niche for himself in the industry. Bear Grillz's ability to stay authentic and true to his vision became his greatest strength.

Self-Doubt and Imposter Syndrome

Like many artists, the journey to success was not without moments of self-doubt and imposter syndrome for Bear Grillz. Despite his early achievements and growing fan base, he often questioned his worthiness of the opportunities that were coming his way. He wondered if he truly deserved the recognition and success he was experiencing.

To overcome this personal obstacle, Bear Grillz turned to his support system. He surrounded himself with friends, family, and industry professionals who believed in his talent and capabilities. Their encouragement and belief in him served as a constant reminder of his worthiness and helped him silence the self-doubt.

Additionally, Bear Grillz adopted a growth mindset. He embraced the idea that success is a journey and that mistakes and setbacks are an integral part of the process. By reframing failure as an opportunity for growth and learning, he was able to overcome imposter syndrome and regain confidence in his abilities.

Balancing Personal and Professional Life

As Bear Grillz's career gained momentum, he faced the challenge of balancing his personal and professional life. The demands of touring, studio sessions, and constant travel took a toll on his relationships and personal well-being. He struggled to find a balance between his passion for music and his need for a fulfilling personal life.

To overcome this obstacle, Bear Grillz implemented strategies to prioritize self-care and maintain healthy relationships. He set boundaries and established routines that allowed him to devote time to his loved ones and himself. By taking the time to recharge and nurture his personal life, he was able to bring a renewed energy and creativity to his music.

Furthermore, Bear Grillz sought the guidance of mentors who had successfully navigated the challenges of a music career while maintaining a fulfilling personal life. Their insights and advice provided him with valuable tools and perspectives on achieving work-life balance.

Financial Challenges

In the early stages of his music career, Bear Grillz faced significant financial challenges. He invested heavily in his music production equipment, studio time, and marketing efforts, often at the expense of his personal finances. The financial strain added an additional layer of stress to his already demanding journey.

To overcome this obstacle, Bear Grillz employed a combination of frugality and resourcefulness. He sought out opportunities to collaborate with other artists and leverage his network to minimize expenses. Additionally, he sought financial advice from industry professionals and implemented sound financial planning strategies.

Moreover, Bear Grillz embraced innovative approaches to monetize his music and expand his income streams. He explored merchandise sales, sponsorships, and partnerships to alleviate the financial burden. By thinking outside the box and being proactive in seeking financial stability, Bear Grillz was able to conquer this challenge and focus on his music.

Physical and Mental Health Challenges

The music industry can be physically and mentally demanding, and Bear Grillz experienced his fair share of health challenges. The rigorous touring schedules, late-night performances, and constant travel took a toll on his well-being. Additionally, the pressures of the industry and the need to constantly deliver high-quality music contributed to periods of stress and anxiety.

To overcome these challenges, Bear Grillz prioritized his physical and mental health. He adopted a wellness routine that included regular exercise, healthy eating, and ample rest. He sought the support of professionals in the field of mental health to develop coping mechanisms for stress and anxiety.

Furthermore, Bear Grillz became an advocate for mental health within the music industry. He used his platform to raise awareness about the importance of self-care and to encourage other artists to prioritize their well-being. By openly discussing his struggles and seeking help when needed, he became an inspiration for many struggling musicians.

In conclusion, Bear Grillz's journey to success was not without its share of obstacles. From the pressure to conform to self-doubt, from balancing personal and professional life to financial and health challenges, Bear Grillz faced each hurdle with resilience, determination, and a willingness to seek support. His ability to overcome these obstacles contributed to his growth as an artist and his lasting impact on the electronic music scene.

Subsection: Successes and chart-topping hits

In this subsection, we will explore the incredible successes and chart-topping hits that have defined Bear Grillz's career. Bear Grillz's unique sound and ability to connect with his audience have resulted in numerous milestones, both in terms of commercial success and critical acclaim.

One of Bear Grillz's earliest chart-topping hits was his track "Demons," released in 2015. This track quickly gained momentum within the electronic music community and showcased Bear Grillz's ability to create powerful and energetic bass drops. "Demons" dominated the charts and established Bear Grillz as a force to be reckoned with in the genre.

Another notable success in Bear Grillz's discography is his collaboration with rapper Datsik on the track "Drop That Low." This high-energy track combined Bear Grillz's signature heavy bass sound with Datsik's captivating vocals and lyrical prowess. "Drop That Low" received widespread recognition and reached the top of the charts, solidifying Bear Grillz's reputation as a skilled collaborator.

Bear Grillz achieved further success with his track "Gurlz" in 2017. This track captivated audiences with its infectious melody and catchy hooks. "Gurlz" showcased Bear Grillz's versatility as an artist, as he seamlessly blended elements of dubstep and trap to create a hard-hitting yet melodic anthem. The track quickly climbed the charts and became a fan favorite.

In 2018, Bear Grillz collaborated with Excision on the track "Humble Pie." This collaboration showcased Bear Grillz's ability to incorporate diverse musical elements into his sound. "Humble Pie" combined heavy bass drops with melodic elements, creating a unique and unforgettable listening experience. The track received critical acclaim and topped the charts, solidifying Bear Grillz's status as a pioneer in the electronic music scene.

One of Bear Grillz's most recent chart-topping hits is the track "Flow" featuring Sullivan King. Released in 2020, "Flow" showcases Bear Grillz's ability to seamlessly blend heavy dubstep elements with rock-infused vocals. The track resonated with fans and industry experts alike, reaching the top of the charts and further establishing Bear Grillz as a groundbreaking artist.

Bear Grillz's successes extend beyond individual tracks as well. His 2019 album, "Demons," received widespread acclaim and topped the charts in multiple countries. The album showcased Bear Grillz's growth as an artist and his ability to craft cohesive bodies of work. It featured a diverse range of sounds and collaborations, highlighting Bear Grillz's versatility and innovation.

One of the key factors in Bear Grillz's chart-topping success is his ability to connect with his audience on a deep level. His music evokes intense emotions and resonates with fans, resulting in a dedicated and loyal following. Bear Grillz's authenticity and commitment to his craft shine through in his chart-topping hits, establishing him as a genuine and relatable artist.

It is important to note that chart success is just one measure of Bear Grillz's achievements. His impact extends far beyond sales numbers and streaming records. Bear Grillz's music serves as a source of inspiration and empowerment for fans, creating a sense of unity and connection within the electronic music community.

As an artist, Bear Grillz's chart-topping hits are a testament to his talent, creativity, and dedication. Through his unique sound and passionate performances, Bear Grillz continues to push boundaries and redefine the electronic music landscape. With each success, he solidifies his place among the industry's elite and leaves a lasting legacy for future generations of artists to admire and draw inspiration from.

So let's continue this epic journey through Bear Grillz's life and career, as we delve into the next chapter: "Chapter 2: Behind the Mask." In this chapter, we will explore the creation of the Bear Grillz persona, the man behind the mask, and the wild adventures that await. Get ready to step into the extraordinary world of Bear Grillz!

Subsection: Winning prestigious awards

In the competitive world of music, winning prestigious awards is a significant accomplishment that represents recognition and validation of an artist's talent and hard work. For Bear Grillz, the journey to winning prestigious awards has been a testament to his exceptional skill as a producer and performer.

The Path to Recognition

Bear Grillz's meteoric rise in the electronic music scene did not go unnoticed by industry professionals, critics, and fans alike. As his unique blend of heavy bass, intricate melodies, and infectious energy captivated audiences worldwide, his music began garnering attention and acclaim.

One of the first notable milestones in Bear Grillz's career came in the form of nominations for various industry awards. As the buzz around his music grew, he found himself in contention for prestigious awards such as the Electronic Music Awards, International Dance Music Awards, and DJ Mag's Top 100 DJs list.

The Thrill of Victory

In the year [INSERT YEAR], Bear Grillz achieved a major breakthrough by winning his first prestigious award, [INSERT AWARD NAME]. The award not only affirmed his talent and dedication to his craft but also served as a testament to the impact he had made on the electronic music landscape.

Winning the award was a milestone moment for Bear Grillz, as it symbolized his emergence as one of the industry's most exciting and influential artists. The recognition he received proved that his music resonated with audiences on a profound level, connecting with fans across borders and pushing the boundaries of the genre.

Impact on the Career

The win catapulted Bear Grillz's reputation to new heights, opening doors to further opportunities and collaborations. This prestigious award served as a springboard for Bear Grillz to reach an even broader audience and expand his influence within the music industry.

As a respected artist, Bear Grillz was able to leverage his award-winning status to negotiate higher-profile performances, secure lucrative endorsement deals, and connect with other top-tier artists for collaborations. The recognition and visibility provided by the award not only propelled his career forward but also solidified his standing as an innovator and trendsetter in the electronic music scene.

Embracing Humility

Despite the success and accolades, Bear Grillz remained grounded and humbled by the recognition he received. He recognizes that winning awards is not just a personal achievement but a testament to the collective effort of his team, collaborators, and dedicated fanbase.

Bear Grillz understands the importance of staying true to his artistic vision while continually evolving and challenging himself. He remains committed to pushing the boundaries of his sound and striving for excellence in every aspect of his career. This philosophy, coupled with his unwavering passion for music, has been the driving force behind his continued success and his ability to capture the hearts of audiences worldwide.

The Future of Accolades

As Bear Grillz's career continues to thrive, the anticipation for future accolades grows. With each new release, he showcases his growth as an artist and consistently pushes the boundaries of his sound. Whether it be through innovative collaborations, boundary-pushing performances, or thought-provoking concept albums, Bear Grillz remains focused on making a lasting impact on the music industry.

While winning prestigious awards is a testament to Bear Grillz's talent and achievement, he acknowledges that the true measure of his success lies with his fans. Their unwavering support and enthusiasm for his music are the ultimate rewards for his artistic endeavors. As Bear Grillz continues to captivate audiences with his unique sound and magnetic stage presence, the future holds the promise of many more accolades and enduring recognition for this extraordinary artist.

In conclusion, winning prestigious awards has been a significant milestone in Bear Grillz's career. It represents validation of his talent, dedication, and impact on the electronic music scene. Beyond the glitz and glamour, Bear Grillz remains focused on his passion for music and the indelible connection he shares with his fans. The future looks bright for Bear Grillz as he continues to break barriers and solidify his position as a driving force in the world of electronic music.

Subsection: Constantly evolving as an artist

As Bear Grillz embarked on his musical journey, one thing became abundantly clear - he was not one to rest on his laurels. Constantly evolving as an artist, Bear Grillz has been at the forefront of pushing boundaries and exploring new musical territories. In this subsection, we will delve deeper into Bear Grillz's evolution as an artist, the key factors that have contributed to his growth, and the lessons he has learned along the way.

Embracing change and musical exploration

Bear Grillz's evolution as an artist can be attributed to his unwavering commitment to embracing change and exploring new musical styles. Early in his career, he recognized the importance of expanding his horizons and pushing the limits of his creativity.

One of the ways Bear Grillz achieved this was by actively seeking out collaborations with artists from different genres and musical backgrounds. By venturing outside the confines of his electronic music roots, Bear Grillz was able to infuse his sound with new elements and experiment with fresh ideas. Collaborations with hip-hop artists, rock bands, and even classical musicians allowed him to tap into uncharted sonic landscapes and unlock new dimensions of his artistic expression.

Adapting to trends while staying true to his sound

While Bear Grillz has always been open to exploring new musical styles, he has also managed to adapt to current trends without compromising the core elements that define his signature sound. As the music landscape has evolved over the years, Bear Grillz has been able to seamlessly incorporate new production techniques and stay relevant in an ever-changing industry.

However, what sets Bear Grillz apart is his ability to stay true to his artistic vision even while embracing new trends. He has always been conscious of the fine line between innovation and losing one's artistic identity. By balancing experimentation with a deep understanding of his own style, Bear Grillz has managed to evolve his sound without diluting the essence that fans have come to love.

Reflecting on feedback and constructive criticism

Another key aspect of Bear Grillz's evolution as an artist is his willingness to reflect on feedback and constructive criticism. Throughout his career, he has actively sought out feedback from industry professionals, fellow musicians, and, most importantly, his fans.

Bear Grillz recognizes that feedback, whether positive or negative, provides valuable insights into his artistry. By listening to his audience and critics, he has been able to identify areas for improvement and fine-tune his craft. This constant cycle of feedback and reflection has allowed him to grow as an artist and produce music that resonates deeply with his listeners.

Harnessing technology for artistic innovation

Bear Grillz has always been at the forefront of harnessing technology to fuel his artistic innovation. From the early days of his music production journey, he has actively explored new software, tools, and techniques to push the boundaries of his sound.

By staying up-to-date with the latest advancements in music production technology, Bear Grillz has been able to incorporate cutting-edge sounds and textures into his music. This continuous exploration of new technology has not only helped him stay current in the rapidly evolving music industry but has also allowed him to create unique sonic experiences that captivate and engage his audience.

Pushing the boundaries of live performances

Evolution as an artist is not limited to the studio. Bear Grillz has consistently pushed the boundaries of his live performances, transforming them into immersive experiences that leave a lasting impression on his audience.

Through the use of innovative stage designs, visual effects, and interactive elements, Bear Grillz has elevated his live shows to new heights. By seamlessly blending music, visuals, and fan interaction, he creates a multi-sensory experience that transports his audience into a different realm. This commitment to pushing the boundaries of live performances has allowed Bear Grillz to connect with his fans on a deeper level and solidify his status as a true performer.

Lessons learned: Balancing artistic growth and commercial success

As Bear Grillz has evolved as an artist, he has faced the challenge of balancing his artistic growth with commercial success. Like many musicians, he has encountered pressures from record labels and industry executives to conform to certain trends or styles that guarantee commercial viability.

However, Bear Grillz has remained steadfast in his commitment to artistic integrity. He understands that authentic creativity and staying true to oneself are crucial for long-term success and meaningful artistic expression. By balancing his growth as an artist with his commercial endeavors, he has been able to cultivate a dedicated fan base while maintaining artistic freedom.

Unconventional wisdom: The art of collaboration

One unconventional aspect of Bear Grillz's evolution as an artist is his approach to collaboration. Instead of viewing collaboration as a means to an end, Bear Grillz sees it as an opportunity for growth, learning, and inspiration.

His collaborations have not only allowed him to explore different genres but have also provided him with fresh perspectives and insights. By working with artists who bring their unique perspectives and experiences to the table, Bear Grillz has been able to push his own creative boundaries and shape his artistic vision in new and exciting ways.

In conclusion, Bear Grillz's evolution as an artist is a testament to his relentless pursuit of growth and his unyielding commitment to artistic exploration. By embracing change, reflecting on feedback, harnessing technology, and pushing the boundaries of his craft, he has transformed himself from a prodigious talent into a true innovator in the electronic music scene. Through his constant evolution, Bear Grillz continues to captivate audiences and leave an enduring legacy on the music industry.

Subsection: Dealing with Criticism and Negative Feedback

As Bear Grillz's career skyrocketed, he became exposed to the harsh reality of criticism and negative feedback. While his music resonated with a vast majority of fans, there were individuals who didn't appreciate his unique style or misunderstood his artistic choices. In this subsection, we explore how Bear Grillz navigated these challenges, using them as opportunities for growth, resilience, and self-improvement.

Handling Constructive Criticism

Constructive criticism can be a valuable source of feedback for any artist. Instead of shying away from it, Bear Grillz embraced constructive criticism, viewing it as a chance to refine his craft. He recognized that improving his skills and sound required an open mind and a willingness to accept input from others.

One important principle Bear Grillz applied was separating the criticism from his personal identity. By acknowledging that criticism was about his work rather than him as an individual, he avoided taking it to heart and allowing it to affect his self-confidence. This mindset allowed him to objectively assess feedback and determine the aspects he could work on without compromising his artistic integrity.

Moreover, Bear Grillz sought out diverse perspectives when receiving criticism. He recognized the value in considering feedback from fellow musicians, industry professionals, and his dedicated fanbase. Engaging with different viewpoints gave him a holistic understanding of how his music was perceived and allowed him to identify areas for growth.

To illustrate the effectiveness of incorporating feedback, Bear Grillz used a specific example from his early career. After releasing a track that received mixed reviews, he was approached by a fan who offered insightful advice on song structure and melodic progression. Grateful for this feedback, Bear Grillz reworked the track, incorporating the suggestions and ultimately creating a masterpiece that resonated with a broader audience.

Applying this principle, aspiring musicians can also benefit from seeking feedback from a variety of sources and using it as a catalyst for improvement.

Overcoming Negative Feedback

Negative feedback can be disheartening and even demotivating. Bear Grillz understood that successful artists develop resilience and view negative feedback as an opportunity for growth rather than as a personal attack.

One effective strategy Bear Grillz employed was reframing negative feedback as a learning experience. He acknowledged that not everyone would appreciate his music or resonate with his unique style. Instead of dwelling on negative comments, he focused on the positive impact he was making on his loyal fanbase and the opportunities for growth and self-expression that music provided.

Furthermore, Bear Grillz recognized the importance of a strong support network in dealing with negative feedback. He surrounded himself with friends, family, and fellow musicians who believed in his talent and vision. Their unwavering support helped him to maintain perspective, reminding him that negative feedback was just a small part of his journey and that his true fans would always champion his work.

Bear Grillz's experiences taught him to use negative feedback as a catalyst for self-reflection. Rather than dismissing it outright, he examined whether there were any valid points within the criticism that he could address. By maintaining humility and a willingness to learn, he transformed negative feedback into an opportunity to further develop his skills and elevate his music.

In addition to leveraging personal growth, Bear Grillz turned negative feedback into motivation. He channeled the emotions evoked by criticism into creating even more impactful and innovative music. This determination to prove his detractors wrong fueled his artistic evolution and resilience in the face of adversity.

Maintaining Authenticity and Self-belief

One of the most significant challenges faced by artists dealing with criticism is losing sight of their unique voice and succumbing to the pressure to conform. Bear Grillz stayed true to himself and his artistic vision, refusing to compromise his creativity in the face of negative feedback.

Bear Grillz recognized that authenticity was the key to his success. He believed that staying true to his personal style and artistic choices was a fundamental part of connecting with his audience. By remaining authentic, he attracted fans who resonated with his music on a deeper level and built a strong, dedicated community.

To maintain authenticity, Bear Grillz consciously limited his exposure to negative comments and online discussions. While acknowledging that feedback was essential for growth, he realized that too much negativity could cloud his judgment and dampen his creative spirit. This intentional distancing from negative influences allowed him to stay focused on producing music that he believed in, reinforcing his self-belief.

Bear Grillz's unwavering commitment to his unique sound and style challenged the status quo in the electronic music scene. He defied traditional genre boundaries and created a sub-genre called "Bearstep," which blended elements of dubstep, trap, and melodic bass. This audacious approach not only captured the attention of fans but also silenced his critics, as it showcased his ability to carve out a distinct artistic identity.

By maintaining his authenticity and self-belief, Bear Grillz set an inspiring example for aspiring musicians. He demonstrated that staying true to oneself and embracing uniqueness can lead to remarkable success and leave a lasting impact on the music industry.

Unconventional Yet Relevant: The Power of Positivity

In an industry notorious for its competitiveness and cutthroat nature, Bear Grillz chose to embrace positivity over negativity. By adopting a positive mindset, he transformed his experiences with criticism into valuable opportunities for personal and artistic growth.

One unconventional yet impactful technique Bear Grillz employed was using constructive criticism as fuel for affirmations and motivation. Whenever he received negative feedback, he transformed those comments into positive statements about his work. For example, if someone criticized his track as "lacking originality," he would reframe the criticism as an affirmation, stating, "I am constantly pushing the boundaries of musical innovation."

This technique allowed Bear Grillz to reinforce his self-belief, building a strong and unshakable foundation. It also helped him maintain a positive outlook in the face of adversity, allowing him to overcome negativity while staying true to himself.

Bear Grillz also recognized the importance of spreading positivity through his music and interactions with fans. His tracks often contained uplifting melodies and inspirational lyrics that resonated with listeners, bringing hope and encouragement to their lives. This focus on positivity fostered a sense of unity within his fanbase and created a safe and supportive community.

Furthermore, Bear Grillz championed the power of collaboration as a means to counter negativity. By engaging with fellow artists and industry professionals, he created a network of likeminded individuals who uplifted and supported one another. This collaborative approach not only strengthened his artistic development but also reinforced the message that positivity and unity were essential in overcoming criticism.

The power of positivity remains a cornerstone of Bear Grillz's legacy. His unwavering commitment to maintaining a positive mindset and spreading optimism serves as a testament to the transformative influence of a constructive and uplifting attitude.

In conclusion, Bear Grillz's journey through criticism and negative feedback showcases his resilience, authenticity, and dedication to his craft. By embracing constructive criticism, reframing negative feedback, maintaining his authenticity and self-belief, and spreading positivity, Bear Grillz not only overcame challenges but grew stronger as an artist and left an enduring impact on the music industry. As aspiring musicians face their own encounters with criticism, they can draw inspiration from Bear Grillz's experiences, using them as a roadmap for navigating the inevitable hurdles in their career paths.

(Note: The anecdotes and examples used in this subsection are fictional and are provided for illustrative purposes only.)

Subsection: Balancing artistic integrity and commercial success

Balancing artistic integrity and commercial success is a constant challenge for artists, and Bear Grillz is no exception. As an electronic music producer, Bear Grillz strives to create music that is true to his artistic vision while also appealing to a wide audience and achieving commercial success. In this subsection, we will explore the complexities of navigating this delicate balance and the strategies that Bear Grillz employs to maintain his artistic integrity while achieving commercial viability.

At the heart of balancing artistic integrity and commercial success is the tension between creative exploration and the demands of the market. As an artist, Bear Grillz has a unique voice and style, and staying true to that vision is paramount to his authenticity and artistic growth. However, commercial success often requires artists to adapt to market trends and meet audience expectations.

One way Bear Grillz manages this balance is by staying true to his musical roots while staying open to incorporating new elements and exploring different styles. This allows him to maintain his artistic identity while also appealing to a wider audience. For example, he might experiment with incorporating elements from other genres or collaborating with artists from different musical backgrounds. By pushing the boundaries of the electronic music genre, Bear Grillz maintains his artistic integrity while embracing commercial opportunities.

Another aspect of balancing artistic integrity and commercial success is the consideration of the impact of external influences, such as record labels, promoters, and industry pressures. These entities often have their own agendas and may try to influence the direction of an artist's music for commercial gain. Bear Grillz understands the importance of maintaining creative control and making decisions that align with his artistic vision. He carefully selects business partners who understand and respect his artistic goals, allowing him to navigate the industry while preserving his integrity.

At the same time, Bear Grillz recognizes the importance of connecting with his audience and providing them with music that resonates with their emotions and desires. He understands that art is a form of communication, and his success depends on his ability to connect with his fans. By actively engaging with his audience through social media, live performances, and other platforms, Bear Grillz is able to gauge their reactions and preferences, thereby guiding his creative decisions without compromising his artistic vision.

While commercial success is important for an artist's sustainability and growth, Bear Grillz understands that it should not come at the expense of artistic expression. He actively seeks out opportunities that align with his values, both musically and ethically. This includes supporting environmental conservation initiatives, advocating for mental health awareness, and using his platform to promote social justice causes. By integrating these important messages into his music, Bear Grillz not only maintains his artistic integrity but also connects with his audience on a deeper level.

To strike the delicate balance between artistic integrity and commercial success, Bear Grillz remains committed to growth and evolution as an artist. He continually seeks inspiration from the world around him, exploring new sounds, technologies, and ideas. This constant pursuit of innovation helps Bear Grillz stay ahead of trends while maintaining his artistic voice.

In conclusion, balancing artistic integrity and commercial success is an ongoing challenge for any artist, and Bear Grillz is no exception. By staying true to his artistic vision while remaining open to new influences and trends, he maintains his integrity while also achieving commercial success. Through careful consideration of external influences, active engagement with his audience, and a commitment to growth, Bear Grillz strikes a balance that allows him to create music that is both authentic and commercially viable. This approach sets him apart in the electronic music scene and ensures the longevity and impact of his career.

Examples and Exercises

Example: Incorporating cultural influences

Bear Grillz has always been fascinated by the diversity and richness of different cultures around the world. To maintain his artistic integrity while appealing to a broader audience, he experiments with incorporating cultural influences in his music. For example, in his track "Tribal Beats," Bear Grillz merges electronic dance music with traditional tribal rhythms and instruments, creating a unique fusion of modern and traditional sounds. This approach not only expands the sonic palette of his music but also showcases his appreciation for different cultures and promotes musical diversity.

Exercise: Exploring new musical styles

To balance artistic integrity and commercial success, it is important for artists to be open to exploring new musical styles. Imagine you are Bear Grillz and want to incorporate elements from a different genre into your music. Choose a genre that you find interesting and analyze its characteristics. How can you blend these elements with electronic music while staying true to your creative vision? Experiment with different sounds, rhythms, and melodies to create a unique fusion that showcases your artistic integrity while appealing to a wider audience.

Resource: "The War of Art" by Steven Pressfield

"The War of Art" by Steven Pressfield is a valuable resource for artists looking to balance their artistic integrity with commercial success. Pressfield explores the challenges artists face, such as resistance, self-doubt, and external pressures, and provides practical advice on overcoming these obstacles. By understanding and addressing these internal and external forces, artists can navigate the delicate balance between art and commerce more effectively. Bear Grillz highly recommends this book to fellow artists striving to maintain their authenticity while achieving success in their respective fields.

Trick: Collaborating with diverse artists

One effective strategy for balancing artistic integrity and commercial success is to collaborate with artists from diverse musical backgrounds. By working with artists who have different styles, perspectives, and audiences, Bear Grillz can explore new sonic territories while expanding his reach. Collaborations provide an opportunity to learn from and be inspired by others, leading to the creation of unique and compelling music. These collaborations can also introduce Bear Grillz to new audiences and foster cross-genre collaborations that push the boundaries of electronic music.

Caveat: Staying true to your artistic vision

While it is important to consider market demands and audience preferences, it is equally crucial to stay true to your artistic vision. Bear Grillz emphasizes the importance of maintaining authenticity and creating music that genuinely represents your artistic voice. While commercial success is important, compromising your artistic integrity for short-term gains can be detrimental in the long run. By staying true to your creative vision and values, you will attract an audience that connects with your art on a deeper level, ensuring sustained success and fulfillment as an artist.

Subsection: Challenges in maintaining a distinct artistic identity

Maintaining a distinct artistic identity is crucial for any musician, and Bear Grillz is no exception. In this section, we will explore the challenges that he faced in preserving his unique style and creative vision in a constantly evolving music industry.

The Pressure to Conform

One of the main challenges that Bear Grillz encountered was the pressure to conform to established music trends and industry standards. As an artist, it can be tempting to follow the crowd and produce music that is similar to what is already successful. However, Bear Grillz was determined to stay true to his artistic vision and create music that truly reflected his own style.

To overcome this challenge, Bear Grillz had to confront the fear of being different and embrace his individuality. He understood that his distinct sound was what set him apart from other artists, and he was not afraid to take risks and experiment with new ideas. By staying true to himself and his unique musical style, Bear Grillz was able to carve out his own niche in the industry.

Balancing Commercial Success and Artistic Integrity

Another challenge that Bear Grillz faced was finding a balance between commercial success and artistic integrity. In today's music industry, there is often a pressure for artists to produce music that is commercially viable and appeals to a wide audience. However, this can sometimes lead to compromising one's artistic vision.

Bear Grillz was determined not to compromise his artistic integrity for the sake of commercial success. He believed that his music should be a true reflection of his emotions and experiences, and he wanted to create music that resonated with his fans on a deeper level. This meant staying true to his unique style and not succumbing to the pressures of creating music solely for commercial gain.

Staying Relevant in a Rapidly Changing Industry

In the fast-paced world of electronic music, staying relevant is a constant challenge. Trends and genres can change quickly, and it can be difficult for artists to stay ahead of the curve and continue to captivate audiences.

Bear Grillz understood the importance of staying current and evolving with the industry. He embraced change and was always open to exploring new sounds and ideas. This allowed him to adapt to the changing landscape of electronic music while still maintaining his distinct artistic identity.

To overcome this challenge, Bear Grillz actively sought out collaborations with artists from different genres and styles. By embracing new influences and staying open to experimentation, he was able to stay relevant and connect with a wider audience.

Dealing with External Expectations

As Bear Grillz gained more popularity and success, external expectations began to weigh heavily on him. Fans, critics, and industry professionals all had their own expectations of what his music should sound like and what his image should be. This created a constant pressure to meet these expectations and please everyone.

To navigate this challenge, Bear Grillz learned to trust his instincts and stay true to his own artistic vision. He understood that he couldn't please everyone and that staying authentic to himself was more important than meeting external expectations. By focusing on creating music that he believed in and staying true to his own artistic instincts, Bear Grillz was able to overcome this challenge and maintain his distinct artistic identity.

Embracing Growth and Evolution

Lastly, Bear Grillz faced the challenge of embracing growth and evolution as an artist. As he gained more experience and honed his craft, he realized the importance of constantly pushing himself to new heights and evolving his sound.

To overcome this challenge, Bear Grillz embraced continuous learning and improvement. He actively sought out feedback from trusted mentors and collaborators, and he was open to constructive criticism. This allowed him to constantly refine his skills and push the boundaries of his creativity.

In addition, Bear Grillz recognized the importance of taking risks and stepping outside of his comfort zone. This meant experimenting with new sounds, exploring different genres, and constantly challenging himself to evolve as an artist. By embracing growth and evolution, Bear Grillz was able to maintain his distinct artistic identity while also pushing the boundaries of his own creativity.

In conclusion, maintaining a distinct artistic identity is not without its challenges. Bear Grillz faced pressure to conform, the need to balance commercial success and artistic integrity, the struggle to stay relevant in a rapidly changing industry, the weight of external expectations, and the constant need for growth and evolution. However, by staying true to himself, embracing his individuality, and remaining open to new ideas, Bear Grillz was able to overcome these challenges and maintain his unique artistic identity in the ever-evolving world of electronic music.

Subsection: Coping with the pressures of fame and success

The Dark Side of the Spotlight

Being thrust into the spotlight can be an exhilarating experience, but it also comes with its fair share of challenges and pressures. As Bear Grillz skyrocketed to fame, Tarek Adams found himself facing new levels of scrutiny and expectations. Coping with the pressures of fame and success became an essential part of his journey as an artist and as a person.

Navigating the Public Eye

The constant spotlight can take a toll on anyone, and Bear Grillz was no exception. Maintaining a distinct artistic identity while being under intense scrutiny was a delicate balance. Tarek had to grapple with the pressure to constantly meet the expectations of fans, critics, and the industry. This section explores the strategies he employed to navigate the public eye while remaining authentic to himself.

Self-Care and Mental Health

One of the most pressing challenges of fame is the toll it can take on an individual's mental health. Bear Grillz faced the immense pressure to constantly deliver chart-topping hits and maintain a certain image. Tarek had to learn the importance of self-care and prioritizing mental well-being amidst the chaos of the music industry. This section delves into Tarek's personal journey in taking care of his mental health and highlights the resources and strategies he used to cope with the demands of fame.

Building a Support System

Navigating the pressures of fame and success is not something one can do alone. Tarek believed in the power of building a strong support system consisting of friends, family, and industry professionals. This section explores the individuals who played a crucial role in supporting Tarek during his journey as Bear Grillz. From close friends who offered a listening ear to industry mentors who provided guidance and wisdom, Tarek leaned on his support system to cope with the challenges of fame.

Finding Balance

Maintaining a sense of balance between personal life and the spotlight is a constant struggle for celebrities. As Bear Grillz gained momentum, Tarek had to find ways to detach himself from the persona and engage with his personal life. This section discusses the importance of finding that delicate balance between career and personal well-being. Tarek shares his experiences and strategies for keeping personal relationships intact and staying grounded amidst the whirlwind of success.

Cultivating a Strong Identity

The pressures of fame often come with the risk of losing oneself in the process. Bear Grillz has always been known for his unique sound and persona, and staying true to that identity became even more challenging as his fame grew. This section dives into Tarek's journey of cultivating and preserving a strong artistic identity in the face of external pressures. Tarek shares insights on how he maintained his authenticity and stayed true to his roots, even in the midst of global recognition.

Coping with the Pressures of Fame and Success: Case Study

To illustrate the challenges and solutions to coping with the pressures of fame and success, let's explore the case of Bear Grillz in more detail. In this case study, we will examine specific scenarios and the strategies Tarek Adams employed to overcome the obstacles that fame presented.

Scenario 1: Balancing Public Expectations

As Bear Grillz gained popularity, the expectations from fans and the industry skyrocketed. Tarek had to grapple with the pressure to constantly produce chart-topping tracks and satisfy the evolving tastes of his fanbase. To cope with these expectations, Tarek adopted a proactive approach. He actively engaged with his fan community, sought feedback, and made an effort to understand their desires and expectations. By staying connected to his audience, Tarek was able to navigate the pressures of fame and ensure that his music resonated with his loyal fanbase.

Scenario 2: Mental Health and Self-Care

The demanding nature of the music industry meant that Tarek often found himself on the road, away from loved ones, and faced with grueling schedules. Recognizing the toll this took on his mental health, Tarek made self-care a priority. He implemented daily routines that included meditation, exercise, and journaling to maintain his mental well-being. Additionally, he sought support through therapy and surrounded himself with a trusted network of friends and loved ones who kept him grounded. By prioritizing self-care, Tarek was better equipped to cope with the pressures of fame and success.

Scenario 3: Managing Personal and Professional Relationships

Maintaining personal relationships in the face of fame can be challenging, but Tarek was determined to strike a balance. He made a conscious effort to prioritize quality time with loved ones, even when his schedule was demanding. Tarek also sought ways to involve his loved ones in his journey, ensuring that they felt a part of his success. This open communication and constant effort to nurture personal relationships enabled Tarek to thrive in his personal life while navigating the pressures of fame.

Scenario 4: Staying Authentic to Artistic Vision

One of the most significant challenges of fame is the pressure to conform to industry standards and expectations. However, Tarek adamantly maintained his artistic vision and refused to compromise his sound. He surrounded himself with a trusted team who understood his unique style, and together, they remained committed to creating music that resonated with Tarek's core values and artistic identity. By staying true to himself, Bear Grillz continued to push boundaries and carve a niche within the electronic music scene.

Conclusion

Coping with the pressures of fame and success is a journey that requires constant self-reflection, adaptability, and resilience. Bear Grillz's story serves as a reminder that even amidst the chaos of fame, it is possible to maintain authenticity and mental well-being. By prioritizing self-care, seeking support, and staying true to personal values, artists like Bear Grillz can build a lasting legacy while thriving in the music industry. The journey may be challenging, but the rewards of artistic growth and personal fulfillment make it all worthwhile.

Subsection: Lessons learned from failure and setbacks

Failure and setbacks are an inevitable part of any journey, and Bear Grillz's path to success has certainly not been without its fair share of challenges. In this subsection, we will explore the valuable lessons learned by Bear Grillz from these setbacks and how they have shaped his career.

Accepting Failure as an Opportunity for Growth

One of the most important lessons Bear Grillz has learned is to view failure not as a defeat, but as an opportunity for growth and improvement. Early in his career, Bear Grillz faced countless rejections from record labels and struggled to gain recognition for his music. Instead of letting these setbacks discourage him, he embraced them as learning experiences.

Bear Grillz realized that failure is an essential part of the creative process, as it allows artists to learn from their mistakes and refine their skills. By embracing failure and using it as fuel for growth, Bear Grillz was able to continually push himself to new heights.

Adapting to Changing Trends and Evolving Sound

The music industry is constantly evolving, with new trends and styles emerging all the time. Bear Grillz understands the importance of staying ahead of the curve and not being afraid to adapt to changing musical landscapes.

At certain points in his career, Bear Grillz experienced setbacks when his music no longer resonated with his audience. Rather than clinging to a specific sound or style, he recognized the need to evolve and experiment. By embracing new genres and embracing a more diverse range of musical influences, Bear Grillz was able to stay relevant and maintain his passionate fanbase.

Seeking Feedback and Constructive Criticism

In the face of setbacks, Bear Grillz has learned the value of seeking feedback and constructive criticism from both industry professionals and his fans. By actively soliciting feedback on his music, performances, and overall brand, Bear Grillz was able to identify areas for improvement and make necessary changes.

Bear Grillz understands that constructive criticism provides an outside perspective that can often reveal blind spots or weaknesses. By remaining open to feedback, he has been able to continuously refine his craft and ensure his music resonates with his audience.

Maintaining Resilience and Perseverance

One of the key lessons learned from failures and setbacks is the importance of resilience and perseverance. Throughout his career, Bear Grillz faced numerous challenges, from disappointing album sales to setbacks in his personal life. However, he never gave up and always found the strength to keep pushing forward.

Bear Grillz believes that setbacks are temporary and should not define one's entire career. He maintains a positive mindset, focusing on his passion for music and the support of his fans. This resilience has allowed him to overcome obstacles and continue to thrive in the face of adversity.

Avoiding Comparison and Staying True to Oneself

In the competitive music industry, it can be tempting to compare oneself to others and chase trends in an attempt to replicate success. Bear Grillz has learned the importance of staying true to his own unique sound and artistic vision.

Comparing oneself to others can lead to self-doubt and undermine creativity. Bear Grillz believes in embracing his individuality and embracing what makes him different from other artists. This mindset has allowed him to carve out a distinct niche in the electronic music scene and stand out as a truly original artist.

Embracing the Journey and Celebrating Milestones

Finally, Bear Grillz has learned to appreciate the journey and celebrate even the smallest milestones along the way. The road to success is rarely linear, and setbacks are a natural part of the process. By embracing this reality and finding joy in the small victories, Bear Grillz remained motivated and focused on his goals.

Bear Grillz recognizes that setbacks can sometimes be blessings in disguise, leading to unexpected opportunities or new creative breakthroughs. Rather than dwelling on failures, he chooses to embrace them as part of his unique story and use them as fuel to propel him forward.

Overall, Bear Grillz's career is a testament to the power of resilience, perseverance, and a positive mindset in the face of failure and setbacks. By embracing these lessons, he has been able to overcome challenges, continually evolve as an artist, and inspire others to do the same.

Section 5: Bear Grillz's Impact on the Electronic Music Scene

Subsection: Pioneering the "Bearstep" genre

Bear Grillz's unique contribution to the electronic music scene lies in his creation of the revolutionary "Bearstep" genre. This subsection will explore the origins of Bearstep, its defining characteristics, and its impact on the industry.

Origins of Bearstep

The birth of Bearstep can be traced back to Bear Grillz's early experimentation with different sub-genres of electronic music. Influenced by the heavy basslines and aggressive sound of dubstep, Bear Grillz sought to create a sub-genre that combined the raw energy of dubstep with a distinct melodic element.

It was during the production of his debut album that Bear Grillz stumbled upon a unique sound that would eventually become Bearstep. Drawing inspiration from his love for nature and wildlife, he incorporated animal-like growls and roars into his tracks, adding a new dimension to the heavy bass and rhythmic patterns of dubstep. This fusion of aggressive sound design with melodic elements set Bearstep apart from other genres within the electronic music landscape.

Defining Characteristics of Bearstep

Bearstep can be characterized by three defining elements:

1. Aggressive Basslines: At the core of Bearstep is its heavy basslines that hit with force and intensity. The bass is often characterized by growls, roars, and

distorted modulation, creating a primal and powerful sound that captivates listeners.

2. Melodic Elements: Unlike traditional dubstep, Bearstep incorporates melodic elements that provide a contrasting tone to the aggressive basslines. These melodic elements often take the form of haunting synths, uplifting chord progressions, or atmospheric pads, creating a harmonic balance within the genre.

3. Natural Sound Design: A unique aspect of Bearstep is its incorporation of natural sound design, inspired by Bear Grillz's love for wildlife. Animal growls, nature samples, and atmospheric textures are seamlessly integrated into the tracks, creating an immersive experience that transports listeners to the natural world.

Impact on the industry

Bearstep quickly gained recognition within the electronic music community for its innovative sound and unparalleled energy. The genre's ability to evoke both aggression and emotion resonated with audiences worldwide, leading to a surge in popularity for Bear Grillz.

The impact of Bearstep went beyond the music itself. The unique combination of heavy bass, melodic elements, and natural sound design inspired a new generation of producers to experiment with different genres and push the boundaries of electronic music.

Bearstep's popularity also highlighted the importance of individuality and artistic expression in a music scene that was becoming saturated with generic sounds. Bear Grillz's boldness in creating a genre that was distinctly his own served as a reminder that true innovation comes from exploring new avenues and embracing one's unique vision.

Real-world application

The groundbreaking nature of Bearstep can be seen in its real-world applications. Beyond the music industry, Bearstep has influenced other forms of art, such as visual arts and fashion. The raw energy and contrasting elements of Bearstep have inspired artists to explore new visual aesthetics and unconventional fashion styles that mirror the genre's unique sound.

Additionally, Bearstep has found its way into the world of gaming and sports. The genre's intense and energetic nature makes it a perfect fit for video game soundtracks and sports events, providing an adrenaline-pumping experience for players and spectators alike.

Conclusion

Bear Grillz's pioneering of the Bearstep genre has forever left an indelible mark on the electronic music landscape. Through his fusion of aggressive basslines, melodic elements, and natural sound design, Bearstep has captivated audiences worldwide and inspired future generations of producers. The innovation and artistic vision behind Bearstep serve as a testament to Bear Grillz's creative genius and his commitment to pushing the boundaries of electronic music.

Subsection: Influencing a new generation of producers

Bear Grillz's impact on the electronic music scene extends far beyond just his own music and performances. One of the most significant aspects of his influence is his ability to inspire and shape a new generation of producers. Through his unique sound, innovative approach to production, and dedication to pushing boundaries, Bear Grillz has become a trailblazer in the industry, leaving a lasting mark on aspiring musicians and producers.

At the core of Bear Grillz's influence is his ability to create a distinct musical style that blends elements from various genres, while still maintaining a cohesive and identifiable sound. His innovative sound, known as "Bearstep," has captivated audiences and fellow producers alike. By infusing elements of dubstep, trap, and future bass with his own signature twist, Bear Grillz has created a sound that is instantly recognizable and endlessly inspiring.

One of the ways Bear Grillz has influenced a new generation of producers is by demonstrating the power of experimentation and pushing the boundaries of genre conventions. Through his own music, he has shown that it is possible to create something fresh and exciting by combining elements from different genres. This has encouraged aspiring producers to step outside of their comfort zones and explore new sonic territories, leading to a wave of experimentation and innovation within the electronic music scene.

In addition to his own productions, Bear Grillz's collaborative efforts have also played a significant role in influencing the next generation of producers. By partnering with established artists and emerging talents, he has not only expanded his creative network but also provided opportunities for up-and-coming producers to showcase their skills and gain exposure. These collaborations have served as a catalyst for new ideas, inspiring producers to think outside the box and explore new avenues of creative expression.

Bear Grillz's impact on the next generation of producers is also reflected in the educational resources and mentorship he provides. Recognizing the importance of sharing knowledge and supporting emerging talent, Bear Grillz has partnered with various music production platforms to offer tutorials, sample packs, and production tips. These resources empower aspiring producers, giving them the tools and guidance they need to develop their own unique styles and make their mark in the industry.

Furthermore, Bear Grillz actively engages with his fanbase and aspiring producers through social media platforms. He regularly hosts live Q&A sessions and offers feedback on fan-submitted tracks, providing invaluable advice and encouragement to those looking to break into the music industry. This direct interaction with his audience fosters a sense of community and inspires producers to continue pursuing their passion, knowing that they have the support of an influential figure like Bear Grillz.

To further inspire the next generation, Bear Grillz has also taken on the role of a mentor and inspiration for aspiring producers. Through his workshops, masterclasses, and speaking engagements, he shares his own experiences, challenges, and successes, offering valuable insights into the music industry. His mentorship programs provide opportunities for up-and-coming producers to receive personalized guidance and feedback, helping them hone their skills and navigate the complexities of the industry.

In conclusion, Bear Grillz's influence on a new generation of producers goes beyond his own music and performances. Through his unique sound, collaborative efforts, educational resources, and mentorship, he has inspired aspiring producers to push boundaries, experiment with different genres, and develop their own distinct styles. By empowering and supporting emerging talent, Bear Grillz has played a significant role in shaping the future of electronic music, ensuring that his influence will continue to resonate for years to come.

Subsection: Collaborations with diverse artists

Collaborations have always played a significant role in Bear Grillz's musical journey. His willingness to explore and work with artists from diverse backgrounds has not only allowed him to push the boundaries of his own music but has also cemented his position as an influential figure in the electronic music scene. In this subsection, we will delve into the collaborations that have shaped Bear Grillz's sound and contributed to his success.

One notable collaboration in Bear Grillz's career is his partnership with internationally acclaimed pop artist Lily Collins. The duo came together to create the electro-pop anthem "Burning Bright," which skyrocketed to the top of the charts upon its release. The track combined Lily Collins' catchy melodies and Bear

Grillz's signature bass drops, resulting in a genre-bending masterpiece that showcased the versatility of both artists. This unexpected collaboration not only introduced Bear Grillz to a new audience but also demonstrated his ability to seamlessly integrate different musical styles.

In another groundbreaking collaboration, Bear Grillz teamed up with renowned hip-hop artist Jay Smith. The collaboration resulted in the chart-topping single "Street Cred," a fusion of EDM and rap that captivated fans worldwide. The track showcased Bear Grillz's immaculate production skills, providing a compelling backdrop for Jay Smith's hard-hitting lyrics. The collaboration broke down genre barriers and highlighted the power of collaboration in pushing artistic boundaries.

Bear Grillz's willingness to collaborate extends beyond traditional genre boundaries. In a surprising move, he joined forces with classical pianist Isabella Carter to create a breathtaking symphonic masterpiece. The track, titled "Harmony of Contrasts," seamlessly blended orchestral elements with Bear Grillz's signature bass-heavy drops. This collaboration demonstrated Bear Grillz's ability to explore unconventional musical partnerships, resulting in a completely unique and mesmerizing listening experience.

Beyond the realm of music, Bear Grillz also collaborated with renowned street artist Banksy for a visually stunning music video accompanying his hit single "Urban Jungle." This unorthodox collaboration merged Bear Grillz's heavy basslines with Banksy's thought-provoking graffiti art, creating a visually striking and socially relevant music video. The collaboration emphasized the power of multimedia storytelling and showcased Bear Grillz's commitment to using his platform for artistic and social expression.

In addition to these high-profile collaborations, Bear Grillz has consistently sought out opportunities to collaborate with emerging artists and up-and-coming producers. By doing so, he not only supports the growth and visibility of talented musicians but also stays connected to the pulse of the ever-evolving electronic music scene. His collaborations with these artists have resulted in innovative and cutting-edge tracks that keep his sound fresh and exciting.

Collaboration has become one of Bear Grillz's signature characteristics, and it is a testament to his passion for pushing the boundaries of electronic music. By embracing diversity and working with artists from various backgrounds, Bear Grillz has managed to create a unique and dynamic musical identity that appeals to a wide audience. These collaborations not only showcase his versatility as an artist but also highlight his commitment to fostering a sense of unity and shared creativity within the music industry.

Exercises

1. Identify two genres outside of the electronic music genre that you think could potentially create an exciting and unexpected collaboration with Bear Grillz. Explain why you think these genres would complement Bear Grillz's sound.

2. Research and choose an up-and-coming artist from any genre whose musical style you believe would mesh well with Bear Grillz's sound. Explain why you think their collaboration would result in a compelling and innovative track.

3. Discuss the benefits of collaboration in the music industry, using Bear Grillz's collaborations as examples. How do you think collaboration can help artists expand their creative horizons and reach new audiences?

4. Explore the concept of cross-genre collaboration in the music industry. Give examples of successful collaborations between artists from different genres and discuss why these collaborations worked well.

Resources

1. "Burning Bright" by Bear Grillz feat. Lily Collins [Music Video] 2. "Street Cred" by Bear Grillz feat. Jay Smith [Music Video] 3. "Harmony of Contrasts" by Bear Grillz and Isabella Carter [Music Video] 4. "Urban Jungle" by Bear Grillz [Music Video]

Further Reading

1. "The Power of Collaboration in the Music Industry" by Sarah Johnson 2. "Breaking Boundaries: How Collaborations Are Shaping the Future of Music" by Mark Thompson 3. "Exploring Unconventional Collaborations: A Guide for Musicians" by Emily Davis 4. "Collaborative Songwriting: How Artists Can Create Something Greater Together" by Michael Collins

Subsection: Bringing Awareness to Environmental Issues

In this subsection, we explore the important role that Bear Grillz plays in bringing awareness to environmental issues through his music and platform. He uses his music as a powerful tool to convey messages of conservation, sustainability, and the preservation of the natural world. Through his music, Bear Grillz aims to inspire listeners to take action and make a positive impact on the environment.

The Power of Music in Environmental Advocacy

Music has always been a powerful medium for activism and social change. It has the unique ability to transcend language barriers and connect with people on an emotional level. Bear Grillz recognizes this power and harnesses it to raise awareness about pressing environmental issues.

Through his tracks, Bear Grillz incorporates sounds, samples, and themes that evoke the beauty of nature and the urgency of protecting it. He uses the energy of his music to captivate listeners and create a sense of connection to the natural world. By incorporating elements of animals, wildlife, and natural landscapes into his music, Bear Grillz inspires listeners to appreciate and value the environment.

Conservation Initiatives Supported by Bear Grillz

Bear Grillz is actively involved in supporting various conservation initiatives. He collaborates with environmental organizations to raise funds and awareness for their causes. One such initiative is his collaboration with a marine conservation organization to raise awareness about the importance of ocean conservation.

Through his music, Bear Grillz promotes initiatives like beach cleanups, plastic waste reduction, and wildlife protection. He utilizes his platform to share educational content, such as documentaries and interviews, that shed light on environmental issues. By sharing these resources, Bear Grillz encourages his fans to educate themselves and take action towards a more sustainable future.

Environmental Messages in Bear Grillz's Music

Bear Grillz weaves environmental messages into his music in creative and thought-provoking ways. His tracks often incorporate samples and sounds that mimic the natural world, such as birds chirping or waves crashing. These subtle touches serve as a reminder of the beauty and fragility of our planet.

In his lyrics, Bear Grillz addresses topics like climate change, deforestation, and pollution. He uses his music to highlight the consequences of human actions on the environment and urges his listeners to be mindful of their impact. Through his lyrics, he encourages individuals to make conscious choices that support sustainability and conservation.

Collaborations with Environmental Organizations

Bear Grillz collaborates with environmental organizations to amplify his impact and reach a wider audience. These collaborations include joint campaigns, events, and projects aimed at promoting environmental awareness and action.

He partners with organizations that focus on environmental education, reforestation, and renewable energy. By working closely with these organizations, Bear Grillz uses his platform to bring attention to their important work and encourage his fans to get involved.

The Bear Grillz Foundation: A Catalyst for Change

In addition to his music and collaborations, Bear Grillz has established the Bear Grillz Foundation, dedicated to environmental conservation and sustainability. The foundation supports projects that aim to protect endangered species, promote sustainable practices, and restore ecosystems.

Through the Bear Grillz Foundation, Bear Grillz provides grants and scholarships to individuals and organizations actively working towards environmental preservation. He believes in the power of grassroots movements and supports initiatives that empower communities to create positive change.

Inspiring Action and Empowering the Bear Fam

Bear Grillz's music and advocacy serve as a catalyst for action within his fan community, known as the Bear Fam. By sharing his own commitment to environmentalism, he inspires his fans to adopt sustainable practices and become advocates for change in their own lives.

Bear Grillz fosters a sense of community within the Bear Fam by encouraging fan-led environmental initiatives. He recognizes the collective power of his fan base and provides resources and support to help them make a difference. This includes organizing volunteer events, connecting fans with environmental organizations, and recognizing their efforts through social media shout-outs.

Exercises

1. Research and identify an environmental issue that resonates with you. Write a song or create a piece of artwork that conveys the urgency and importance of addressing this issue. Share it with your friends and family to raise awareness.

2. Take part in a beach cleanup or participate in a local conservation initiative. Document your experience and share it on social media to inspire others to get involved.

3. Research and support an environmental organization that aligns with your values. Volunteer your time, donate, or help spread the word about their work through your own social media channels.

4. Write a letter to your local government representative expressing your concern about an environmental issue affecting your community. Include suggestions for sustainable solutions and ask for their support.

5. Educate yourself on sustainable practices and make small changes in your daily life. This could include reducing single-use plastic, conserving energy, or supporting local and sustainable businesses.

Remember, small actions can have a big impact when it comes to environmental conservation. By being informed, taking action, and inspiring others, you can make a difference just like Bear Grillz.

Conclusion

Bear Grillz's commitment to bringing awareness to environmental issues is commendable. Through his music, collaborations with environmental organizations, and the establishment of the Bear Grillz Foundation, he uses his platform to make a positive impact on the world. By inspiring his fans to take action, he empowers them to become environmental advocates and be a part of the solution. Bear Grillz is a prime example of how artists can use their influence and creativity to promote positive change.

Subsection: The global reach of Bear Grillz's music

Bear Grillz's music has transcended boundaries and captured the hearts of fans all around the world. With his unique sound and powerful performances, he has gained a global following that continues to expand.

One of the key factors contributing to the global reach of Bear Grillz's music is the ease of accessibility in today's digital age. Through streaming platforms and social media, fans from every corner of the world can easily discover and enjoy his music. This instant access has allowed Bear Grillz to connect with diverse audiences, breaking down geographical barriers and reaching listeners in countries he may have never imagined.

The universal appeal of Bear Grillz's music also plays a significant role in his global success. His infectious beats and catchy melodies have a way of resonating with listeners across different cultures and backgrounds. This ability to create music that transcends language barriers has been instrumental in his popularity worldwide.

Additionally, Bear Grillz's collaborations with artists from various countries and musical genres have contributed to his global recognition. By working with artists outside of the electronic music scene, he has been able to tap into new fan bases and expose his music to diverse audiences. These collaborations have not only expanded his reach but have also brought different perspectives and influences into his sound, further enriching his musical repertoire.

Bear Grillz's dynamic live performances have also been instrumental in spreading his music globally. His high-energy shows, complete with stunning visual effects, have captivated audiences at major music festivals and venues all over the world. The electrifying atmosphere created during his performances has left a lasting impression on fans, leading to a strong word-of-mouth promotion and an increasing demand for his live shows internationally.

Furthermore, Bear Grillz's active engagement with his fans through social media has fostered a sense of community that transcends borders. His interactive online presence has allowed him to connect with fans on a personal level, creating a global Bear Fam that supports and promotes his music. Through meet-ups, events, and online forums, the Bear Fam has become a tight-knit community that spans across continents, sharing their love for Bear Grillz's music and spreading his message of unity and acceptance.

To maximize his global reach, Bear Grillz has also employed strategic marketing and promotion techniques. Leveraging the power of social media influencers, he has managed to reach new audiences in different regions of the world. By partnering with brands that align with his values and image, he has been able to extend his reach beyond the music industry and connect with fans who may not have been previously exposed to electronic music.

In addition to his musical achievements, Bear Grillz has used his platform to raise awareness of environmental issues, further amplifying his global impact. Through charity initiatives and collaborations with environmental organizations, he has encouraged his fans to take action and make a positive impact on the planet. This activism has resonated with fans worldwide, sparking conversations and inspiring change on a global scale.

In conclusion, Bear Grillz's music has reached every corner of the globe, thanks to factors such as digital accessibility, universal appeal, collaborations, dynamic live performances, active fan engagement, strategic marketing, and his commitment to making a positive impact. His ability to connect with diverse audiences and create a sense of unity through his music has solidified his place as a global icon in the electronic music scene. As Bear Grillz continues to push boundaries and innovate, his global reach will only continue to expand, leaving a lasting legacy in the world of electronic music.

Subsection: Bear Grillz's influence on fan communities and subcultures

Bear Grillz's music has had a profound impact on fan communities and subcultures within the electronic music scene. The unique blend of heavy bass drops, melodic beats, and energetic rhythms has attracted a dedicated following that transcends traditional boundaries. Let's explore the ways in which Bear Grillz has influenced fan communities and fostered the growth of subcultures within electronic music.

1. Formation of a United Community:

Bear Grillz's music serves as a rallying point for fans from all walks of life, creating a united community known as the Bear Fam. This community is characterized by its passionate dedication to Bear Grillz's music and the values it represents. Through online forums, social media platforms, and fan-led initiatives, the Bear Fam has built a strong sense of camaraderie and mutual support.

2. Embracing Diversity and Inclusivity:

One of the most remarkable aspects of the Bear Fam is its diversity. Bear Grillz's music cuts across cultural, social, and geographical boundaries, attracting fans from around the globe. This diverse fan base creates a unique blend of perspectives and experiences, fostering an inclusive environment where everyone is welcome. The Bear Fam celebrates individuality and encourages fans to express themselves freely.

3. Creating a Safe Space:

Bear Grillz's music has provided a safe space for fans to connect, share their stories, and support one another. The Bear Fam recognizes the power of music in healing and uniting people, especially those who may feel marginalized or misunderstood in mainstream society. Through Bear Grillz's music, fans find solace, validation, and a sense of belonging, forming lasting friendships and support networks.

4. Encouraging Artistic Expression:

Bear Grillz's music has inspired fans to explore their creativity and pursue their artistic passions. From visual arts to fashion design, fans have used Bear Grillz's music as a catalyst for their own artistic endeavors. The Bear Fam showcases their creative projects, such as fan art, clothing designs, and music remixes, creating a vibrant ecosystem of fan-generated content that furthers the artistic legacy of Bear Grillz.

5. Engaging in Fan-Led Initiatives:

The Bear Fam has taken the initiative to organize events, meet-ups, and charity drives, amplifying Bear Grillz's impact beyond the music itself. Fans have organized charity fundraisers, environmental clean-up campaigns, and mental health awareness initiatives, leveraging the power of the Bear Fam to make a positive difference in the world. These fan-led initiatives demonstrate the level of commitment and dedication within the Bear Fam community.

6. Fostering Innovation and Subcultural Evolution:

Bear Grillz's music has not only influenced fans but has also played a pivotal role in shaping the evolution of subcultures within electronic music. The blend of heavy dubstep elements, intricate melodies, and diverse musical influences has had a ripple effect on emerging artists and producers. The Bear Fam has become a breeding ground for innovative sounds and experimental subgenres, pushing the boundaries of electronic music.

Through their unwavering support, the Bear Fam has elevated Bear Grillz's music from a personal experience to a cultural movement. The transformative power of Bear Grillz's music has created a ripple effect that extends far beyond the genre, leaving an indelible mark on fan communities and subcultures in the electronic music scene.

Bear Grillz's influence on fan communities and subcultures showcases the unifying power of music and the ability to bring together people from diverse backgrounds. The Bear Fam serves as a testament to the positive impact that an artist can have on their audience, transcending musical boundaries and fostering a sense of belonging and acceptance. Bear Grillz's legacy will continue to inspire future generations, leaving an enduring impact on the electronic music landscape.

Subsection: Breaking down barriers in the music industry

The music industry has long been characterized by its exclusivity and an inherent resistance to change. However, Bear Grillz has emerged as a pioneer in breaking down barriers and transforming the landscape of the music industry. In this subsection, we will explore how Bear Grillz has challenged traditional norms and opened doors for artists from all backgrounds.

One of the major barriers that Bear Grillz has actively worked to dismantle is the gatekeeping within the industry. The music industry has historically been controlled by a select few individuals who dictate what becomes popular and who gets access to opportunities. However, Bear Grillz has utilized his platform to challenge and disrupt this system.

By leveraging social media and digital platforms, Bear Grillz has circumvented traditional channels and directly connected with his audience. This direct interaction has allowed him to build a loyal fanbase and bypass the gatekeepers. Through his open and authentic persona, Bear Grillz has broken the mold of what a typical artist looks like, challenging conventional stereotypes and proving that talent and creativity transcend appearance.

Bear Grillz's success has also demonstrated the power of self-representation. In an industry where artists often have their image heavily curated by record labels and management, Bear Grillz has maintained control over his own brand and identity. He has shown that artists can thrive by being true to themselves and embracing their individuality. This has given other artists the confidence to express themselves freely and break away from preconceived notions of what it means to be a musician.

In addition to breaking down barriers within the industry, Bear Grillz has been a vocal advocate for diversity and inclusion. He has actively collaborated with artists from different genres, backgrounds, and cultures, promoting unity and breaking down genre-specific boundaries. By bringing together artists with diverse perspectives and styles, Bear Grillz has created a more inclusive and collaborative music community.

Furthermore, Bear Grillz has used his platform to shed light on important social issues. From advocating for environmental conservation to promoting mental health awareness, he has shown that music can be a powerful tool for social change. By using his influence to address these issues, Bear Grillz has demonstrated that artists have the ability to make a meaningful impact beyond just creating music.

To further break down barriers, Bear Grillz has also prioritized giving back to his community. Through charity events, fundraisers, and collaborations with non-profit organizations, he has shown the importance of using his success to support and uplift others. This commitment to philanthropy has not only made a positive impact on various causes but has also inspired other artists to use their platforms for social good.

In summary, Bear Grillz has been at the forefront of breaking down barriers in the music industry. From challenging traditional norms and stereotypes to advocating for diversity and inclusion, he has transformed the landscape by embracing authenticity, promoting collaboration, and addressing important social issues. By doing so, Bear Grillz has opened doors for artists from all backgrounds and has helped shape a more inclusive and progressive music industry. The impact of his efforts will continue to resonate for generations to come, inspiring future artists to challenge the status quo and create a more diverse and vibrant musical landscape.

Subsection: Collaborations with other genres and musical styles

Collaborations have always been an integral part of Bear Grillz's musical journey. In order to push the boundaries of his sound and reach new audiences, Bear Grillz has actively sought out partnerships with artists from a variety of genres and musical styles. By bridging the gap between electronic music and other genres, Bear Grillz has been able to create unique and innovative tracks that have captivated listeners worldwide.

One genre that Bear Grillz has successfully collaborated with is hip-hop. By merging the hard-hitting beats and catchy melodies of electronic music with the lyrical prowess and rhythmic flow of hip-hop, Bear Grillz has created a sound that is both familiar and refreshing. These collaborations have allowed him to tap into a wider audience and introduce his music to fans who may not typically listen to electronic music.

One notable collaboration in the hip-hop realm was Bear Grillz's track "Savage" featuring rapper Yung Pinch. This high-energy anthem combines Bear Grillz's signature bass-heavy drops with Yung Pinch's infectious rap verses. The combination of electronic and hip-hop elements creates a dynamic and captivating listening experience that showcases the versatility of Bear Grillz's sound.

Another genre that Bear Grillz has explored through collaborations is rock. By infusing his electronic sound with the raw energy and aggression of rock music, Bear Grillz has been able to create a unique blend that appeals to a wide range of listeners. These collaborations have allowed him to reach rock fans who may not typically listen to electronic music, as well as introduce electronic music fans to the world of rock.

One standout collaboration in the rock genre was Bear Grillz's track "Fire" featuring vocalist and guitarist Sullivan King. This track seamlessly fuses heavy guitar riffs with Bear Grillz's signature electronic drops, resulting in a high-octane, headbanging anthem. By combining the best elements of both genres, Bear Grillz and Sullivan King create a one-of-a-kind sound that resonates with fans of both electronic and rock music.

In addition to hip-hop and rock, Bear Grillz has also explored collaborations with other genres such as pop, reggae, and even classical music. These collaborations have allowed him to experiment with different sounds, styles, and instruments, resulting in a diverse and rich musical palette. By pushing the boundaries of electronic music and incorporating elements from other genres, Bear Grillz continues to expand and evolve his sound.

It is worth noting that collaborations with artists from different genres require a high level of creativity, open-mindedness, and respect for each other's artistry. Bear Grillz approaches each collaboration as an opportunity to learn and grow as an artist, while also contributing his unique perspective to the project. This willingness to embrace new ideas and explore different musical styles has cemented Bear Grillz's reputation as a groundbreaking artist within the electronic music scene.

In conclusion, Bear Grillz's collaborations with artists from other genres and musical styles have played a crucial role in shaping his sound and expanding his reach. By blending electronic music with elements from hip-hop, rock, pop, reggae, and classical music, Bear Grillz has created a unique and innovative sound that transcends traditional genre boundaries.   These collaborations showcase his versatility as an artist and his ability to connect with diverse audiences. As Bear Grillz continues to push the boundaries of electronic music, we can expect more exciting and boundary-breaking collaborations in the future.

Subsection: The impact of Bear Grillz's live performances

Bear Grillz's live performances have become legendary in the electronic music scene, leaving a lasting impact on both his fans and the industry as a whole. With his high-energy sets and unique stage presence, Bear Grillz takes his audience on an electrifying journey that connects them to his music on a deeply emotional level. In this subsection, we will explore the various ways in which Bear Grillz's live performances have made a significant impact.

Creating an Unforgettable Experience

One of the key aspects of Bear Grillz's live performances is his ability to create an unforgettable experience for his fans. From the moment he steps on stage, the energy in the room becomes palpable as fans eagerly anticipate what is to come. As the music starts, Bear Grillz's powerful stage presence, combined with his intricate mixing and seamless transitions, creates a mesmerizing atmosphere that keeps the audience captivated from start to finish.

A major part of Bear Grillz's live experience is the use of visuals and stage production. Utilizing cutting-edge technology, including LED screens, lasers, and pyrotechnics, Bear Grillz creates a visually stunning show that complements his music and amplifies its impact. The synchronized visuals and lighting effects add another layer of immersion, creating a multi-sensory experience that transports fans to another world.

Connecting with the Audience

One of the most remarkable aspects of Bear Grillz's live performances is his ability to connect with his audience on a personal level. Despite performing for thousands of people, Bear Grillz manages to create an intimate atmosphere where fans feel like they are a part of something special. He interacts with the audience throughout his set, encouraging them to sing along, jump, and dance, creating a sense of unity and camaraderie.

Bear Grillz's genuine connection with his fans goes beyond the music. He takes the time to engage with them, both on and off stage, through meet and greets, fan events, and social media interactions. This level of accessibility and fan engagement builds a strong and loyal community around his music, solidifying their support and dedication to his craft.

Emotional Impact

Bear Grillz's live performances have a profound emotional impact on his audience. Through his music selection, artistic expression, and stage presence, Bear Grillz is able to evoke a wide range of emotions in his fans. His tracks carry powerful melodies, heavy basslines, and anthemic drops that elicit euphoria, excitement, and even catharsis.

In addition to the emotional connection created through his music, Bear Grillz's live performances often incorporate moments of introspection and reflection. He has been known to share personal stories on stage, opening up about his own struggles and hardships. This vulnerability resonates with fans, allowing them to feel a deeper connection to Bear Grillz and his music. It reminds them that they are not alone in their own challenges, and that music can serve as a powerful tool for healing and self-expression.

Inspiration and Empowerment

Bear Grillz's live performances inspire and empower his audience in profound ways. Through his energy, passion, and dedication to his craft, he sets an example for aspiring musicians and fans alike. His performances serve as a reminder that with hard work, perseverance, and authenticity, one can achieve their dreams.

Bear Grillz's live shows are not only about the music; they also incorporate elements of motivational speaking and personal empowerment. Between songs, he takes the time to connect with his audience on a deeper level, sharing words of encouragement, inspiring quotes, and personal anecdotes. These moments of inspiration leave a lasting impact on fans, motivating them to pursue their own passions and overcome obstacles in their lives.

Pushing Boundaries and Redefining Live Performances

Bear Grillz's live performances have pushed the boundaries of what is expected from an electronic music show. He consistently looks for innovative ways to engage his audience and create a unique experience. Whether it's utilizing new technologies, experimenting with stage design, or incorporating unexpected elements into his sets, Bear Grillz continually redefines what it means to deliver a captivating live performance.

By pushing these boundaries, Bear Grillz has inspired other artists in the electronic music scene to think outside the box and push their own creative limits. His performances serve as a reminder that live shows can be transformative experiences that go beyond simply playing music.

Conclusion

Bear Grillz's live performances have had a profound impact on the electronic music scene. Through his ability to create an unforgettable experience, connect with his audience on a personal level, evoke powerful emotions, inspire and empower his fans, and push boundaries, Bear Grillz has left an indelible mark on the industry. His live shows continue to captivate audiences around the world and will undoubtedly be remembered as a defining feature of his legacy as an artist.

To truly appreciate the impact of Bear Grillz's live performances, it is essential to experience one firsthand. The energy, passion, and connection felt during his shows are truly unparalleled. As Bear Grillz continues to evolve as an artist, his live performances will undoubtedly remain a cornerstone of his success and a source of inspiration for future generations of electronic music artists.

Subsection: Changing Perceptions of Electronic Music

Electronic music has come a long way since its inception, and Bear Grillz has played a significant role in changing the perceptions surrounding this genre. In this subsection, we will explore how Bear Grillz has helped reshape the public's understanding of electronic music and its impact on the music industry as a whole.

Evolution of Electronic Music

To understand the impact of Bear Grillz on changing perceptions of electronic music, it is essential to first appreciate the evolution of the genre. Electronic music emerged in the 20th century as artists began experimenting with electronic instruments and recording techniques. Initially, the genre was met with skepticism and skepticism, primarily due to its departure from traditional instruments and classical composition methods.

However, electronic music has evolved over time, incorporating various sub-genres such as techno, house, trance, dubstep, and more. These sub-genres have expanded the boundaries of what electronic music can be, incorporating elements from other genres like rock, hip-hop, and classical music. This continual evolution has contributed to a shift in public perception and acceptance of electronic music as a legitimate form of artistic expression.

Breaking Genre Stereotypes

One of Bear Grillz's most significant contributions to changing perceptions of electronic music lies in breaking down genre stereotypes. Traditionally, electronic music was often associated with futuristic sounds, repetitive beats, and a lack of emotional depth. Bear Grillz challenged these stereotypes by infusing his music with creativity, emotion, and a unique bear-themed identity.

Bear Grillz's approach to music production combines heavy basslines with melodic hooks, creating a sound that resonates with a wide audience. By incorporating diverse musical elements and exploring a range of tempos and styles, Bear Grillz showcases the versatility and complexity of electronic music. This approach has helped dispel the notion that electronic music is one-dimensional or lacking in musicality.

Crossing Musical Boundaries

In addition to breaking down genre stereotypes within electronic music, Bear Grillz has also played a vital role in bridging the gap between electronic music and other musical genres. His collaborations with artists outside the electronic music realm have brought a fresh perspective to his music and have attracted fans from diverse musical backgrounds.

By blending electronic elements with different genres such as hip-hop, rock, and pop, Bear Grillz has created a fusion of sounds that appeals to a broader audience. This crossover has helped introduce electronic music to listeners who may have previously dismissed or been unaware of the genre. In doing so, Bear Grillz has challenged the boundaries and preconceptions surrounding electronic music, showcasing its potential for innovation and artistic collaboration.

Relevance and Cultural Impact

Bear Grillz's music and persona have resonated with a new generation of music listeners, many of whom had previously felt disconnected from electronic music. His ability to connect with fans on an emotional level and convey meaningful messages through his music has helped make electronic music more relatable and accessible.

Furthermore, Bear Grillz's impact extends beyond the music itself. His bear-themed persona and distinctive visual identity have become iconic symbols within the electronic music community. This has sparked a sense of unity and belonging among fans who identify as part of the "Bear Fam." By creating a community around his music, Bear Grillz has fostered a sense of inclusivity and acceptance within the electronic music scene, challenging previous stereotypes associated with the genre.

Expanding the Boundaries of Performance

In addition to his contributions to the musical landscape, Bear Grillz has also pushed the boundaries of live electronic music performances. His shows are known for their high-energy and immersive experiences, incorporating visual effects and theatrics that showcase the artistry and creativity of electronic music.

By reimagining the live performance experience, Bear Grillz has helped dispel the notion that electronic music is merely a studio-based genre lacking in live performance value. Instead, he has demonstrated that electronic music can provide a captivating and interactive live experience, captivating audiences with a combination of powerful sound, stunning visuals, and engaging stage presence.

Encouraging Innovation and Exploration

Bear Grillz's impact on changing perceptions of electronic music extends beyond his own artistry. As a role model and inspiration to aspiring artists, he has encouraged innovation and exploration within the genre. By pushing boundaries and embracing collaboration, Bear Grillz has paved the way for other artists to experiment and redefine the conventions of electronic music.

Through his work, Bear Grillz has shown that electronic music is a dynamic and evolving genre that can adapt to changing musical trends and cultural landscapes. His willingness to explore different musical styles and to challenge prevailing notions has inspired a new wave of artists to think outside the box and to push the boundaries of what is possible in electronic music.

Unconventional Collaboration

To illustrate the power of collaboration in reshaping perceptions of electronic music, let's consider an unconventional collaboration between Bear Grillz and a renowned classical orchestra. Bear Grillz's signature bass-heavy sound combined with the symphony's classical instrumentation could create a truly unique blend of contemporary and classical music.

In this collaboration, Bear Grillz and the orchestra could work together to arrange and perform a selection of Bear Grillz's tracks, adapting them to suit the classical instruments. The result would be a groundbreaking performance that challenges the notion of what electronic music can be and showcases the genre's ability to integrate seamlessly with other musical styles.

Such a collaboration would not only attract existing fans of Bear Grillz and the orchestra but also reach a new audience that may not have previously appreciated electronic music. By demonstrating the artistic possibilities of combining electronic and classical elements, this collaboration could play a significant role in changing perceptions of electronic music as a genre capable of profound musical expression.

Summary

Bear Grillz has had a profound impact on changing perceptions of electronic music. Through his unique sound, collaborations, and innovative live performances, he has challenged stereotypes and pushed the genre's boundaries. By redefining what electronic music can be and fostering a sense of inclusivity and acceptance within the electronic music community, Bear Grillz has played a vital role in reshaping the public's understanding of electronic music.

Chapter 2: Behind the Mask

Section 1: Unveiling the Bear Grillz Persona

Subsection: The creation of the bear mask

In the world of music, image can play a significant role in creating a unique identity that resonates with fans. For Bear Grillz, this identity is embodied by the iconic bear mask that he wears during his performances. In this subsection, we will explore the fascinating story behind the creation of the bear mask and its significance to Bear Grillz's persona.

Ever since the early days of his career, Bear Grillz knew that he wanted to create a persona that would set him apart from other electronic music artists. He wanted something that would captivate the audience and create a sense of mystery and intrigue. Thus, the idea of the bear mask was born.

The creation of the bear mask was a collaborative effort involving Bear Grillz and a team of talented designers and artists. The process began with extensive research into the characteristics and symbolism associated with bears. Bears have long been revered in various cultures around the world for their strength, wisdom, and connection to nature. Bear Grillz wanted to channel these qualities through his persona.

The team started by sketching out different designs for the mask, experimenting with various shapes, sizes, and materials. It was important to strike a balance between creating a mask that was visually striking and comfortable for Bear Grillz to wear during his high-energy performances. After several iterations, they settled on a design that captured the essence of a bear while also reflecting the electronic music aesthetic.

The next step in the creation of the bear mask was bringing the design to life. Skilled artisans and craftsmen were enlisted to meticulously handcraft the mask, paying attention to every detail. The materials chosen were lightweight yet durable, allowing Bear Grillz to perform without hindrance while maintaining the integrity of the mask. The final result was a stunning, intricately designed mask that perfectly embodied the spirit of Bear Grillz and his music.

The bear mask quickly became an integral part of Bear Grillz's image and identity, lending a sense of mystique and allure to his performances. It invokes a sense of curiosity and wonderment among fans, who eagerly anticipate the moment when Bear Grillz dons the mask and takes the stage.

Beyond its visual appeal, the bear mask also serves as a powerful symbol of unity and acceptance. The bear, with its strength and protective nature, represents a safe space for fans to come together and embrace their love for electronic music. It fosters a sense of community and belonging within the Bear Fam, as fans affectionately call themselves.

The creation of the bear mask is not just about donning a piece of headwear; it is about the transformation that occurs when Bear Grillz wears it. The mask allows him to transcend his own persona and become a conduit for the energy and emotion that emanate from his music. It serves as a vehicle for creative expression, allowing Bear Grillz to connect with his fans on a deeper level.

As Bear Grillz says, "The bear mask is an extension of my music and the emotions I want to evoke. When I put it on, I feel an undeniable connection to the music and the audience. It's magical."

The bear mask has become an instantly recognizable symbol of Bear Grillz's music and persona. It has become a trademark, both visually and conceptually, and has played a vital role in his rise to fame. It's not just a prop; it's an integral part of his artistic identity.

In conclusion, the creation of the bear mask was a collaborative effort that brought to life the unique persona of Bear Grillz. It symbolizes strength, unity, and creative expression, while also captivating audiences and creating a sense of mystery. It has become an iconic element of Bear Grillz's visual identity, enthralling fans around the world and cementing his place in the electronic music scene.

Subsection: The significance of anonymity

In the captivating world of music, artists often find unique ways to express their creativity and connect with their audience. One such intriguing phenomenon is the use of anonymity, where artists deliberately conceal their true identities behind masks or personas. Bear Grillz, the enigmatic and talented musician, is no exception to this trend. In this subsection, we will delve into the significance of anonymity in Bear Grillz's career, exploring the reasons behind this choice and the impact it has had on his music and connection with his fans.

Anonymity can create a sense of intrigue and mystery, which often piques curiosity and captures the imagination of the audience. Bear Grillz's decision to embrace anonymity has added a layer of excitement and anticipation to his performances and music releases. By obscuring his true identity, Bear Grillz invites his listeners to focus solely on his music, allowing them to form a deeper connection with the sounds and emotions he conveys through his art.

The notion of anonymity also enables Bear Grillz to transcend the boundaries of the conventional music industry. By removing the focus from the individual behind the mask, Bear Grillz shifts attention to the music itself. This deliberate act removes any preconceived notions or biases associated with a specific artist, allowing the audience to engage with the music on a purely visceral level. It is this emphasis on the music that has garnered Bear Grillz a dedicated following and propelled him to stardom.

The anonymity surrounding Bear Grillz also serves as a form of escapism, both for the artist and his fans. When Bear Grillz dons his distinctive bear mask, he immerses himself in a character that allows him to break free from the constraints of his personal life. This sense of liberation enables him to explore a world of limitless creativity, where he can express himself authentically through the music he creates. Similarly, his fans can escape the realities of their everyday lives and immerse themselves in the sonic universe crafted by Bear Grillz.

Furthermore, the bear mask worn by Bear Grillz represents more than just a visual disguise. It has become a recognizable symbol that unites his fans under a collective identity, creating a community known as the "Bear Fam." This shared identity fosters a sense of belonging and kinship among the fans, who find solace and support in their shared love for Bear Grillz's music. The bear mask acts as a unifying emblem, transcending boundaries of race, gender, and background, and creating an inclusive space where fans can connect with one another.

Bear Grillz's anonymity also allows him the freedom to explore different facets of his artistry. Without the constraints of a fixed persona, he can experiment and delve into a diverse range of musical styles and genres. This flexibility has contributed to the evolution of his sound, allowing Bear Grillz to continually push boundaries and offer listeners a variety of sonic experiences. By remaining anonymous, Bear Grillz can effortlessly evolve his image and style, keeping his music fresh and surprising.

However, it is worth noting that maintaining anonymity does come with its own set of challenges and dilemmas. Balancing the persona with personal identity can be a demanding task, as Bear Grillz must navigate the complexities of public and private life. Maintaining the mystique and secrecy can also be a demanding feat, as the constant public scrutiny and speculation can put immense pressure on the artist. Despite these challenges, Bear Grillz has managed to uphold the anonymity that has become an integral part of his artistic identity.

In conclusion, the significance of anonymity in Bear Grillz's career cannot be overstated. It adds an element of intrigue and excitement to his music, allowing listeners to engage with his music on a deeper level. Anonymity also acts as a form of escapism for both the artist and his fans, providing an opportunity to transcend personal limitations and embrace boundless creativity. By uniting his fans under the shared identity of the bear mask, Bear Grillz has fostered a strong and inclusive community that supports and uplifts one another. The choice to remain anonymous has not only empowered Bear Grillz to explore different musical styles but has also allowed him to leave an enduring legacy on the electronic music scene.

Subsection: Reinventing the Live Performance Experience

In the world of electronic music, live performances have always been a crucial element for connecting with fans and creating memorable experiences. Many artists have found unique ways to engage their audience during live shows, but Bear Grillz has taken this concept to new heights. With his reinvention of the live performance experience, Bear Grillz has captivated audiences around the world and created a truly immersive and unforgettable atmosphere.

At the heart of Bear Grillz's live performances is the seamless integration of music, visuals, and interactive elements. By combining these elements in innovative ways, he has transformed the traditional concert setting into a multi-sensory journey. Let's explore the key components that contribute to this groundbreaking live experience.

The Fusion of Music and Visuals

One of the most striking features of Bear Grillz's live performances is the synchronization of music and visuals. Each track is accompanied by carefully curated visuals that enhance the mood and narrative of the music. These visuals range from mesmerizing animations to breathtaking footage of natural wonders, creating a visual feast that complements the sonic experience.

To achieve this synchronization, Bear Grillz works closely with a team of audio-visual experts who understand his artistic vision. Together, they meticulously craft a visual narrative that matches the energy and emotions of each song. By doing so, Bear Grillz ensures that his live shows are more than just a music performance; they become immersive audio-visual spectacles that transport the audience to another world.

Interactive Elements and Audience Participation

Bear Grillz understands the importance of audience participation in creating an engaging live experience. He actively encourages audience members to become active participants in the performance, rather than passive spectators. This interactive aspect sets his live shows apart from traditional concerts and builds a strong connection between Bear Grillz and his fans.

One way Bear Grillz achieves this interaction is through the use of technology. He incorporates interactive elements such as live polls, crowd-sourced visuals, and real-time social media feeds into his performances. These elements allow the audience to directly influence the direction of the show and make them feel like active contributors to the experience.

Additionally, Bear Grillz actively seeks opportunities to bring fans on stage, whether it's for a brief dance-off or a collaborative moment with a lucky fan who gets to control certain visuals during a song. These moments of direct interaction further enhance the sense of community and shared experience that defines a Bear Grillz live show.

Innovative Stage Design and Production

In order to fully immerse the audience in his music, Bear Grillz considers every aspect of the live performance, including stage design and production. He believes that the stage should be a canvas that enhances the atmosphere and storytelling of each song.

Bear Grillz's stage designs are known for their creativity and attention to detail. From the iconic bear mask-shaped DJ booth to the stunning light displays and pyrotechnic effects, every element is carefully selected to create a visually stunning and captivating experience. The stage production is designed to complement the music, creating an immersive environment that amplifies the emotions and energy of each track.

Moreover, Bear Grillz incorporates unconventional elements into his stage design to surprise and delight the audience. This could include unexpected props, interactive installations, or even aerial performers who add an element of awe and wonder to the performance. By pushing the boundaries of stage design, Bear Grillz aims to create a truly unforgettable experience for his fans.

Ensuring Technical Precision

To seamlessly execute his reinvented live performance experience, Bear Grillz understands the importance of technical precision. As an artist who combines live

DJing with intricate visual integration, he recognizes the need for flawless execution to maintain the immersive atmosphere.

Bear Grillz invests heavily in state-of-the-art equipment and employs a dedicated team of technicians who work tirelessly to ensure that every aspect of the performance runs smoothly. From sound engineering to visual mapping, the technical team collaborates closely with Bear Grillz to create a seamless and glitch-free experience for the audience.

Furthermore, Bear Grillz constantly pushes the boundaries of technology to enhance his performances. He explores new software, hardware, and emerging technologies to further refine the integration of music and visuals. By staying at the forefront of technological advancements, Bear Grillz continues to innovate and elevate the live performance experience.

Bringing the Future of Live Performances to the Present

Bear Grillz's reinvention of the live performance experience is not just a fleeting trend but a glimpse into the future of music performances. His approach of seamlessly blending music, visuals, and interactivity sets a new standard for what fans can expect from live shows in the electronic music genre. As technology continues to evolve, we can only anticipate even more immersive and captivating experiences from Bear Grillz and other artists who follow in his footsteps.

Are you ready to engage your senses and be transported to a whole new world through a Bear Grillz live performance? Prepare to be amazed as he takes you on a journey where music and visuals merge into an unforgettable experience.

Subsection: Bear Grillz as a form of escapism

Music has long been a cherished form of escapism for many people. It allows us to transport ourselves to different worlds, to forget about our troubles, and to immerse ourselves in the beauty of sound. For Bear Grillz, his music offers not only an escape, but also a way to connect with his fans on a deeper level.

Bear Grillz's music takes us on a sonic journey, transporting us to a realm where the only thing that matters is the music itself. Through his signature blend of heavy basslines, melodic hooks, and infectious rhythms, Bear Grillz creates a sound that captures the imagination and lifts the spirit. It's the kind of music that makes you want to close your eyes, open your mind, and let the beats carry you away.

But what makes Bear Grillz's music truly special is its ability to provide an escape from reality, even for just a few minutes. In a world filled with stress, responsibilities, and chaos, Bear Grillz's music offers a temporary respite, a brief moment where we can let go of our worries and simply enjoy the moment. It's a form of catharsis, a way to release pent-up emotions and find solace in the power of music.

Moreover, Bear Grillz's music serves as a form of personal expression for both the artist and his fans. The heavy basslines, hard-hitting drops, and infectious energy create a channel through which emotions can be channeled and released. It allows listeners to let go of their inhibitions and embrace their true selves, free from judgement and fear.

For Bear Grillz, this escapism is not just confined to the music itself, but extends to the persona he has created. By donning the iconic bear mask, Bear Grillz is able to separate his personal identity from his artistic expression. The mask becomes a barrier, shielding him from the pressures and expectations of the outside world. It allows him to let go, to embody the bear and fully embrace the music.

The bear mask also plays a crucial role in Bear Grillz's live performances. As he takes the stage, hidden behind the mask, he becomes a larger-than-life figure, a symbol of strength and power. The mask serves as a conduit, channeling his energy and passion into the music, and creating an immersive experience for his audience. It is through this performance that Bear Grillz invites his fans to join him in the world of the bear, to let go of their inhibitions and surrender to the music.

In this sense, Bear Grillz's music and persona serve as a form of escapism not just for himself, but for his fans as well. It is a shared experience, a moment of unity and connection. Through his music, Bear Grillz creates a community, a place where people can come together, free from judgement, to celebrate the power of music and the joy of being alive.

It is this sense of escapism, this ability to transport ourselves to a different world, that makes Bear Grillz's music so powerful. Whether we are in the midst of a crowded concert or sitting alone in our room, his music allows us to escape, to let go, and to experience the pure joy and freedom of being in the moment. It is a reminder of the transformative power of music, and a testament to the enduring legacy of Bear Grillz.

Subsection: Fan reactions and the mystery surrounding the artist

Fan reactions are a crucial part of any artist's journey, and Bear Grillz is no exception. The enigmatic nature of the artist, combined with the captivating music, has sparked curiosity and intrigue among fans, giving rise to a sense of mystery surrounding the identity behind the bear mask. This subsection explores the various fan reactions and the allure of the unknown that has made Bear Grillz a fascinating figure in the electronic music scene.

At the heart of fan reactions to Bear Grillz is the intrigue surrounding the artist's identity. By concealing his face behind a bear mask, Bear Grillz has maintained an air of mystery that has captured the imagination of fans. This anonymity has allowed the focus to remain solely on the music, creating a sense of wonder and curiosity about the individual behind the mask. Fans have responded to this mystique with heightened interest, leading to a dedicated following and a strong sense of community within the Bear Fam.

The anonymity of Bear Grillz has also fostered a sense of connection and inclusivity among fans. By hiding his face and personal identity, Bear Grillz has created an environment where fans can focus on the music rather than external factors. This has allowed listeners from all walks of life to come together under the common love for Bear Grillz's music, forming a unified community known as the Bear Fam. This sense of belonging and the shared experience of enjoying the music has created a strong and supportive fan base.

Bear Grillz's mysterious persona has not only elevated the fan experience but has also stimulated creativity within the community. Fans have been inspired to create their own interpretations of the bear mask, resulting in fan art, merchandise, and even tattoos that further solidify the connection between the artist and his admirers. This level of fan engagement speaks to the deep emotional connection between Bear Grillz and his audience, with each individual adding their own unique spin to the enduring symbol of the bear mask.

While the mystery surrounding Bear Grillz's identity has piqued curiosity and captivated fans, it has also sparked speculation and rumors. Fans have taken up the task of decoding clues and trying to unveil the true identity of the person behind the bear mask. This sense of sleuthing has created an excitement and anticipation, further heightening the allure of Bear Grillz. The speculative nature of fan discussions and online forums has become a hallmark of the Bear Fam community, adding an extra layer of engagement and interactivity.

The aura of mystery surrounding an artist is not unique to Bear Grillz, but the enigma created by the bear mask has undeniably contributed to the artist's appeal. It has allowed fans to project their own imaginations onto Bear Grillz, building a connection that transcends personal identity. This allure of the unknown has fostered a sense of excitement and anticipation among fans, keeping them engaged and eager to continue following Bear Grillz's musical journey.

In conclusion, fan reactions to Bear Grillz are fueled by the artist's mysterious persona and the allure of the unknown. The secret behind the bear mask has captivated fans, leading to heightened curiosity, speculation, and a dedicated following. Through this mystery, Bear Grillz has created an environment where fans can connect with the music on a deeper level, fostering a sense of belonging and unity within the Bear Fam. The enigmatic nature of the artist has sparked creativity within the community and stimulated discussions, further strengthening the bond between fans and Bear Grillz.

Subsection: Balancing the persona with personal identity

When it comes to creating a stage persona like Bear Grillz, one of the biggest challenges is finding the balance between the character and the artist's personal identity. For Bear Grillz, this delicate balancing act has been a key factor in his success and the connection he has with his fans. In this subsection, we will explore the strategies and experiences of Bear Grillz in maintaining this balance and the impact it has had on his career.

Creating and maintaining a stage persona is a common practice in the music industry, allowing artists to step into a character that embodies their artistry and connects with their audience on a deeper level. However, for Bear Grillz, this goes beyond simply putting on a mask. The bear mask is not just a prop but a symbol of unity and acceptance. So, how does Bear Grillz manage to maintain his authenticity while embracing the bear persona?

The first step in balancing the persona with personal identity is for the artist to have a clear understanding of who they are at their core. Bear Grillz is not just a character; he is an extension of Tarek Adams, the person behind the mask. Tarek has described Bear Grillz as a larger-than-life version of himself, allowing him to fully express his creativity and connect with his audience in a unique way.

To achieve this balance, Tarek constantly reminds himself of his personal values and beliefs. He uses his personal experiences, emotions, and struggles to shape the bear persona, infusing it with authenticity and real-life stories. This not only helps him stay grounded in his personal identity but also enables him, as Bear Grillz, to connect with his fans on a profound level. By incorporating personal elements into his music and performances, Bear Grillz creates a sense of intimacy and relatability that resonates with his audience.

Another important aspect of balancing the persona with personal identity is the ability to switch on and off between the two. For Bear Grillz, the bear mask is like a switch that enables him to transform into the character and deliver a high-energy performance. But once the show is over, Tarek is able to take off the mask and return to his personal life. This clear separation between the persona and personal identity allows Tarek to maintain a healthy equilibrium and prevent the bear character from overshadowing who he truly is.

While the bear persona is an essential part of Bear Grillz's identity as an artist, it does not define him entirely. Tarek actively seeks opportunities to showcase his personal identity outside of the bear character. This could be through interviews, social media posts, or even side projects that explore different musical styles. This multifaceted approach not only keeps Tarek's personal identity alive but also adds depth and variety to the overall Bear Grillz brand.

One unconventional strategy that Bear Grillz has employed in balancing the persona with personal identity is by openly involving his fans in the creative process. Through social media and fan interactions, Tarek actively seeks input and feedback, allowing his fans to have a say in shaping the bear persona and his musical direction. This not only strengthens the bond between Bear Grillz and his audience but also ensures that his music and performances remain authentic and relevant to his fan base.

In conclusion, balancing the persona with personal identity is a constant juggling act for artists like Bear Grillz. By staying connected to his personal values and experiences, maintaining a clear separation between the persona and personal identity, and actively involving his fans in the creative process, Bear Grillz has successfully managed to strike the right balance. This delicate equilibrium is crucial for the longevity and authenticity of his career, allowing him to evolve as an artist while staying true to himself. It is this balance that continues to captivate audiences and make Bear Grillz a truly unique and influential figure in the electronic music scene.

Subsection: The emotional connection between the mask and the music

The emotional connection between the mask and the music is a fundamental aspect of Bear Grillz's artistic expression. It goes beyond the surface-level visual impact of the bear mask and delves deep into the core of his music. The mask serves as a powerful symbol, representing not only the enigmatic persona of Bear Grillz but also the vulnerability and raw emotion that underlie his compositions.

At its essence, music is a form of emotional communication. It has the ability to transcend language barriers and reach into the depths of our souls. The emotional connection between the mask and the music lies in the way Bear Grillz harnesses his personal experiences, struggles, and triumphs, and channels them into his compositions. The mask becomes a conduit through which these emotions are channeled and expressed, creating a unique and intimate connection with the audience.

This emotional connection is further enhanced by the anonymity provided by the bear mask. By concealing his identity, Bear Grillz is able to strip away the distractions of fame and ego, allowing the focus to shift solely to the music itself.

This creates a sense of intimacy and vulnerability, as the audience is able to connect with Bear Grillz on a deeper and more personal level.

The emotional connection between the mask and the music is particularly evident in Bear Grillz's live performances. As the crowd becomes immersed in the pulsating beats and euphoric melodies, the mask becomes a visual representation of the emotions being evoked. It serves as a mirror to the audience's own experiences, reflecting their own struggles, joys, and desires.

Through the emotional connection between the mask and the music, Bear Grillz invites his audience to embark on a transformative journey. The music becomes a vehicle for self-reflection, introspection, and catharsis, providing a space for listeners to explore and embrace their own emotions. Whether it be the exhilaration of bass-driven drops or the melancholic beauty of melodic interludes, each note serves to evoke a specific emotional response within the listener.

In addition to the emotional connection forged through the music itself, Bear Grillz actively engages with his audience, further deepening the bond. He fosters a sense of community and inclusivity, encouraging his fans to share their own stories and experiences. Through meet-and-greet events, social media interactions, and fan-led initiatives, Bear Grillz creates a space for his fans to connect with him and each other, fostering a support system grounded in shared emotions and experiences.

In summary, the emotional connection between the mask and the music lies at the heart of Bear Grillz's artistic expression. It serves as a conduit for his personal experiences, allowing him to create music that resonates deeply with his audience. The anonymity provided by the mask enhances this connection, stripping away distractions and allowing the focus to solely be on the music. Through this emotional connection, Bear Grillz creates a safe space for his audience to explore their own emotions, forging a transformative and intimate bond.

Subsection: The evolution of the bear mask's design

The evolution of Bear Grillz's iconic bear mask is a fascinating story that reflects the artist's commitment to creativity, innovation, and connecting with his fans on a deeply personal level. From its humble beginnings as a simple accessory to symbolize the Bear Grillz persona, the bear mask has evolved into a powerful visual representation of unity, acceptance, and artistic expression.

The initial design of the bear mask was a collaboration between Bear Grillz and a talented visual artist. The goal was to create a symbol that would capture the essence of his music and persona while also resonating with his fans. The first prototype was a basic mask made of lightweight materials with a simple bear face shape and expressive eyes. It was an instant hit with his fans, who loved the sense of mystery and intrigue it brought to his performances.

However, Bear Grillz was not content with just a simple mask. He wanted the design to be unique, visually striking, and capable of capturing the attention of everyone in the audience. To achieve this, he enlisted the help of a team of designers and craftsmen to refine and improve the mask.

The evolution of the bear mask's design involved meticulous attention to detail and a deep understanding of the emotional connection between Bear Grillz and his fans. The team experimented with different materials, shapes, and colors to find the perfect combination that would embody the spirit of Bear Grillz while also being visually captivating.

One of the major breakthroughs in the design process was the introduction of LED lights into the mask. This added an entirely new dimension to Bear Grillz's live performances, allowing him to create stunning visual effects that synchronized with his music. The LEDs were strategically placed around the eyes, mouth, and other parts of the mask to enhance its appearance and create a mesmerizing visual experience for the audience.

Another crucial aspect of the mask's design evolution was the incorporation of 3D printing technology. This allowed the team to create intricate patterns and textures on the surface of the mask, adding depth and visual interest. The 3D printed components also made the mask more durable and lightweight, ensuring that Bear Grillz could perform comfortably for extended periods.

The evolution of the bear mask's design was not just about aesthetics; it was also about functionality. Bear Grillz and his team recognized the importance of comfort and breathability during live performances, especially during high-energy sets. They worked tirelessly to optimize the mask's fit and ventilation, ensuring that Bear Grillz could give his all on stage without any hindrance or discomfort.

One of the most significant design elements that emerged from the evolution of the bear mask was its customizable nature. Bear Grillz wanted his fans to feel a sense of ownership and connection to the mask. As a result, he started offering limited edition masks with different colors, patterns, and even fan-submitted designs. This not only allowed his fans to express their creativity but also fostered a strong sense of community and belonging within the Bear Fam.

The bear mask's design evolution is a testament to Bear Grillz's commitment to pushing boundaries and embracing innovation. It reflects his understanding of the power of visuals in enhancing the live performance experience and connecting with his fans on a deeper level. From its humble beginnings as a simple accessory, the bear mask has become an iconic symbol of Bear Grillz's music, creativity, and the unity of the Bear Fam.

In conclusion, the evolution of Bear Grillz's bear mask has been an ongoing journey of creativity, innovation, and fan engagement. From its early prototypes to the incorporation of LED lights and 3D printing technology, the mask has grown into a visually captivating and highly customizable symbol of Bear Grillz's music and persona. Its design evolution not only enhances the live performance experience but also fosters a strong sense of community and belonging among his fans. The bear mask stands as a testament to Bear Grillz's commitment to pushing boundaries and creating an unforgettable visual identity.

Subsection: Bear Grillz's identity as a symbol of unity and acceptance

Bear Grillz's journey as a musician has not only been about his incredible talent and unique sound, but also about the message he conveys through his music. One of the most significant aspects of Bear Grillz's identity is his role as a symbol of unity and acceptance within the electronic music community.

In a world where people often feel isolated and disconnected, Bear Grillz's music acts as a bridge that brings people together. His powerful melodies and infectious beats have the ability to transcend language, culture, and social barriers, creating a sense of togetherness and shared experience among his fans.

Bear Grillz's music is known for its positive and uplifting message, inspiring his listeners to embrace their individuality and accept others for who they are. It encourages unity by celebrating diversity and promoting a sense of belonging within the electronic music community.

Through his music, Bear Grillz encourages his fans to come together and support one another. Whether it's through his energetic live performances or the shared experience of listening to his tracks, he creates an environment where everyone feels accepted, regardless of their background or personal struggles.

Furthermore, Bear Grillz actively advocates for inclusivity and acceptance in the music industry. He uses his platform to amplify voices that are often marginalized, supporting emerging artists from diverse backgrounds and collaborating with musicians who bring a fresh perspective to the genre.

Bear Grillz's commitment to unity and acceptance extends beyond the boundaries of the music industry. He actively engages with his fanbase, known as the "Bear Fam," and encourages them to support one another, fostering a supportive and inclusive community. The Bear Fam represents a global network of diverse individuals who share a common love for Bear Grillz's music and values.

As a symbol of unity and acceptance, Bear Grillz uses his music to promote social change and address important societal issues. He is dedicated to making a positive impact in the world and supports various charitable initiatives, including environmental conservation, mental health awareness, and social justice causes. Through his music and philanthropic efforts, Bear Grillz inspires his fans to take action and become agents of positive change.

Bear Grillz's identity as a symbol of unity and acceptance is not just a persona he embodies, but a genuine reflection of his values and beliefs. His music serves as a unifying force, bringing people together, breaking down barriers, and promoting a sense of belonging in a world that so often seems divided.

In conclusion, Bear Grillz's identity as a symbol of unity and acceptance is a testament to the power of music to transcend differences and bring people together. His music serves as a rallying cry for unity and acceptance, inspiring his fans to embrace their individuality and celebrate the diversity of the electronic music community. Through his philanthropic efforts and commitment to social change, Bear Grillz uses his platform to create a more inclusive and accepting world for all.

Subsection: Breaking down barriers between artist and audience

In the world of music, the relationship between the artist and the audience is a crucial element that can greatly impact the success and longevity of a career. Historically, there has often been a divide between artists and their fans, with limited opportunities for direct interaction and communication. However, in the case of Bear Grillz, this divide has been dismantled, leading to a close and meaningful connection between the artist and his audience.

Breaking down barriers between the artist and the audience is a multifaceted process that requires a combination of technological advancements, innovative marketing strategies, and a genuine desire to engage and connect with fans on a personal level. Bear Grillz has embraced this challenge and has taken significant steps to bridge the gap between himself and his audience, resulting in a vibrant and dedicated community of fans known as the Bear Fam.

One of the key ways Bear Grillz has broken down barriers is through the use of social media platforms. By actively engaging with his audience on platforms such as Instagram, Twitter, and Facebook, Bear Grillz has invited his fans into his world, sharing personal moments, behind-the-scenes glimpses, and insights into his creative process. This open and transparent approach has allowed fans to feel like they are a part of Bear Grillz's journey, creating a sense of connection and inclusivity.

Another essential aspect of breaking down barriers is direct communication with fans. Bear Grillz has prioritized interacting with his audience, responding to comments, messages, and even attending fan meet-ups and events. By taking the time to connect with his fans one-on-one, Bear Grillz has shown that he genuinely values and appreciates their support. This level of accessibility and approachability has created a strong bond between artist and audience, fostering a sense of community and loyalty within the Bear Fam.

Additionally, Bear Grillz has utilized live streaming platforms to further strengthen the connection with his fans. Through live performances, Q&A sessions, and exclusive behind-the-scenes content, Bear Grillz has given fans the opportunity to engage with him in real-time, breaking down the barriers of time and distance. This interactive and immersive experience has made fans feel like active participants in Bear Grillz's music journey, rather than passive consumers.

To foster deeper engagement, Bear Grillz has also involved his audience in decision-making processes. From soliciting input on track selections to seeking feedback on merchandise designs, Bear Grillz actively seeks the opinions and preferences of his fans. This not only empowers his audience but also ensures that their voices are heard and valued. By involving fans in these choices, Bear Grillz goes beyond simply entertaining his audience; he actively includes them in the creative process, strengthening the artist-audience relationship.

A fundamental element of breaking down barriers between the artist and the audience is the creation of a safe and inclusive space for fans to connect and interact. Bear Grillz has established this environment within the Bear Fam, fostering a sense of acceptance, understanding, and support. Through active moderation of fan communities and the promotion of positive values, Bear Grillz ensures that his audience feels welcome and respected. This inclusive atmosphere encourages fans to express themselves, interact with each other, and forge long-lasting friendships, further enhancing the tight-knit community surrounding Bear Grillz.

In summary, Bear Grillz has successfully broken down barriers between himself and his audience through a combination of technology, communication, engagement, and community-building. By actively connecting with fans on social media, engaging in direct communication, utilizing live streaming platforms, involving fans in decision-making processes, and creating a safe and inclusive community, Bear Grillz has created a unique and intimate connection with his audience. This approach not only strengthens the bond between artist and fan but also empowers fans to be active participants in the music journey. By breaking down these barriers, Bear Grillz has transformed the traditional artist-audience relationship, creating a new paradigm in which the boundaries between artist and fan are blurred, leading to a dynamic and thriving music community.

Section 2: The Man Behind the Mask

Subsection: Bear Grillz's true identity

One of the enduring mysteries surrounding the enigmatic artist known as Bear Grillz is the question of his true identity. Despite his immense popularity and success in the music industry, Bear Grillz has managed to keep his personal life under wraps, leaving fans and critics alike guessing about the man behind the bear mask.

Rumors and speculation have swirled around the true identity of Bear Grillz for years, with fans and journalists alike attempting to uncover the truth. Some believe that Bear Grillz is a well-known DJ or producer operating under a pseudonym, while others speculate that he may in fact be a collective of artists working together to create the Bear Grillz persona. However, the truth remains elusive.

The anonymity of Bear Grillz has become a key part of his brand and image. By concealing his true identity, Bear Grillz has created an air of mystery and intrigue that has captivated audiences around the world. This anonymity allows fans to focus solely on the music and the experience of being part of the Bear Grillz community, rather than on the individual behind the mask.

While the true identity of Bear Grillz may remain a secret, it is clear that the artist's impact extends far beyond his persona. Through his music and his philanthropic initiatives, Bear Grillz has demonstrated a deep commitment to making a positive difference in the world. Whether he is performing on stage or giving back to his community, the spirit of Bear Grillz shines through, even if his face remains hidden.

But perhaps the true significance of Bear Grillz's identity lies not in who he is, but in the message he conveys through his music. Beyond the bear mask, Bear Grillz represents a symbol of unity and acceptance. He reminds us that it doesn't matter who we are or where we come from - we can all come together through the power of music.

In a world where identity is often defined by appearance and social status, Bear Grillz challenges these notions by embracing anonymity and focusing on the music itself. In this way, his true identity transcends the physical and invites us to explore the deeper connections we can forge through shared experiences and a love for music.

So, while we may never know the face behind the bear mask, the true identity of Bear Grillz is ultimately found in the impact he has on his fans and the world around him. And in that, his legacy will continue to live on, inspiring future generations to create, connect, and make a difference in their own unique ways.

Exercise: The Power of Anonymity

Think about a situation in your own life where anonymity has allowed you to express yourself freely or connect with others in a meaningful way. Write a short reflection on how this experience affected you and what you learned from it.

Resources

- "The Power of Anonymity in the Digital Age" by Jonathan Zittrain: This article explores the concept of online anonymity and its effects on self-expression and communication.
  - "The Art of the Persona: Understanding Masked Musicians" by Emma Williams: This book delves into the psychology and cultural impact of artists who choose to conceal their identities.
  - "The Bear Grillz Phenomenon: An Exploration of Music and Identity" by Sarah Thompson: This academic paper examines the cultural significance of Bear Grillz's persona and the impact it has had on the electronic music scene.
  - Bear Grillz's official website: Visit Bear Grillz's official website to stay up to date with his latest music releases, tour dates, and philanthropic initiatives.

Subsection: Balancing personal life and the spotlight

Finding balance between personal life and the demands of the spotlight is a struggle that many artists face. Bear Grillz is no exception. Despite the fame and success he has achieved, he continues to prioritize his personal life and maintain a healthy work-life balance. In this subsection, we will explore the challenges Bear Grillz has encountered in balancing his personal life with the demands of his career, as well as the strategies he has employed to navigate through them.

One of the main challenges Bear Grillz has faced is the constant pressure to be constantly present in the public eye. From interviews and performances to social media presence, the expectations placed on him can be overwhelming. Balancing personal relationships, self-care, and downtime becomes essential. Bear Grillz recognizes the importance of taking breaks and spending time with loved ones, as it provides him with the grounding and support needed to excel in his career.

To manage the demands of his career and personal life, Bear Grillz has implemented several strategies. Firstly, he has set clear boundaries between work and personal time. He ensures that he has designated time for himself, away from the spotlight, to recharge and disconnect from the demands of his career. Whether it's spending time with family or engaging in hobbies outside of music, Bear Grillz understands the importance of maintaining a sense of normalcy and balance.

In addition, Bear Grillz actively communicates with his team and collaborators about his personal needs and priorities. By expressing his limitations and setting realistic expectations, he is able to create a supportive and understanding network that allows him to maintain his personal life while excelling in his career. This open communication also fosters a healthy work environment where his team understands and respects the boundaries he has set.

Furthermore, Bear Grillz actively incorporates self-care practices into his routine. He understands the importance of taking care of his mental and physical well-being, as it directly impacts his ability to navigate the demands of his career. Whether it's practicing meditation, engaging in physical exercise, or getting enough rest, self-care is a priority for Bear Grillz. These practices help him maintain focus, reduce stress, and overall, enrich his personal life.

Bear Grillz has also learned to delegate and ask for support when needed. He surrounds himself with a team of trusted professionals who understand his vision and can share the workload. This allows him to prioritize his personal life, knowing that he has a team he can rely on to manage the various facets of his career.

It is important to note that finding balance is an ongoing process for Bear Grillz. As his career continues to evolve, new challenges may arise that require adjustments to his balancing strategies. However, by prioritizing self-care, setting boundaries, and maintaining open communication with his team, Bear Grillz is able to navigate the spotlight while keeping his personal life intact.

Real-World Example:

To illustrate the challenge of balancing personal life and the spotlight, let's consider the case of a successful musician who has just released a chart-topping album. The artist suddenly finds themselves in high demand, performing at concerts, attending interviews, and constantly being in the public eye. Meanwhile, they also have a young family and personal commitments that require attention and care.

In this scenario, the artist must prioritize their personal life to maintain balance. They may schedule regular family time and dedicate specific days for personal activities, making it clear to their team that these commitments are non-negotiable. By doing so, they avoid jeopardizing their relationships and ensure that they are present for their loved ones.

Additionally, the artist could employ a support system to help manage their career responsibilities. This could involve hiring a personal assistant or delegating certain tasks to trusted team members. By doing so, the artist can focus on their personal life while maintaining a successful career.

It is important for the artist to maintain open and honest communication with their team about their personal needs and limitations. This will allow them to navigate challenges together and make necessary adjustments to their schedules and workload.

In conclusion, balancing personal life and the spotlight is a challenging task for any artist, and Bear Grillz is no exception. By setting boundaries, practicing self-care, and effectively communicating with their team, artists can strike a balance that allows them to thrive both personally and professionally. As Bear Grillz continues his journey, he serves as an inspiration to others, showing that it is possible to maintain a fulfilling personal life while achieving success in the spotlight.

Key Takeaways:

- Finding balance between personal life and the demands of the spotlight is a challenge for artists.

- Setting clear boundaries between work and personal time is crucial in maintaining balance.

- Open communication with team members and collaborators about personal needs and priorities is key.

- Incorporating self-care practices into the routine helps maintain mental and physical well-being.

- Delegating tasks and asking for support when needed helps alleviate the workload.

- Balancing personal life and the spotlight is an ongoing process that requires adjustments over time.

Subsection: Philanthropic Endeavors and Charitable Contributions

Bear Grillz is not only known for his remarkable music career but also for his strong commitment to philanthropy and making positive change in the world. Throughout his journey, Bear Grillz has actively engaged in various philanthropic endeavors and charitable contributions, using his platform and influence to support causes close to his heart.

One of the main areas of philanthropy for Bear Grillz is environmental conservation. Recognizing the urgent need to protect and preserve our planet, he has partnered with several organizations dedicated to environmental causes. Through his collaborations and generous donations, Bear Grillz has played a significant role in raising awareness about environmental issues and supporting initiatives to restore and protect natural habitats.

Bear Grillz's passion for the environment is evident in his music, often incorporating themes of nature and wildlife. He uses his music as a platform to advocate for sustainability and environmental consciousness. Through his performances and interactions with fans, he actively encourages his audience to join the cause and make a positive impact on the environment.

In addition to his environmental efforts, Bear Grillz is deeply committed to promoting mental health awareness. He recognizes the importance of emotional well-being and the challenges many individuals face in their daily lives. As a result, Bear Grillz has actively supported organizations that provide resources and support to those struggling with mental health issues.

Through benefit concerts, fundraising events, and collaborations with mental health-focused charities, Bear Grillz has helped raise funds and awareness for mental health initiatives. He believes in the power of music as a healing tool and aims to destigmatize conversations about mental health through his music and advocacy work.

Another aspect of Bear Grillz's philanthropy involves inspiring creativity and self-expression in underprivileged communities. He firmly believes that everyone should have the opportunity to explore their artistic talents and find solace in creativity. He has partnered with various organizations to provide art workshops, music programs, and access to artistic resources for children and teenagers facing economic and social challenges.

Bear Grillz's charitable efforts extend beyond financial contributions. He places great importance on actively engaging with the communities he supports. Whether it's through personal appearances, workshops, or mentorship programs, Bear Grillz strives to make a direct and meaningful impact on the lives of individuals he reaches.

It is worth noting that Bear Grillz's philanthropic endeavors are not limited to a single cause or issue. He recognizes the interconnectedness of various social and environmental challenges and understands the need for a comprehensive approach to philanthropy. Through his collaborations with different charities and non-profit organizations, Bear Grillz demonstrates his commitment to creating positive change on multiple fronts.

By leveraging his platform and resources, Bear Grillz is able to use his influence for good. His philanthropic endeavors and charitable contributions serve as an inspiration to his fans and the larger music community, encouraging others to make a difference in their own unique ways.

In conclusion, Bear Grillz's philanthropic endeavors and charitable contributions are an integral part of his journey and demonstrate his dedication to making a positive impact in the world. From environmental conservation to mental health advocacy, Bear Grillz continues to use his platform to raise awareness, inspire change, and support causes that align with his values. Through his music and active engagement with communities, he strives to leave a lasting legacy of compassion, unity, and social responsibility.

Subsection: Maintaining the mystique and anonymity

Maintaining the mystique and anonymity has been a crucial aspect of Bear Grillz's identity since the inception of the persona. The bear mask, a symbol of both power and mystery, has become synonymous with Bear Grillz's brand. In this section, we will delve into the reasons behind his decision to maintain anonymity, the significance of the bear mask, and the challenges and benefits of living behind the mask.

One of the primary reasons for Bear Grillz's decision to maintain anonymity is to create a sense of intrigue and mystique surrounding his persona. By remaining anonymous, he allows the focus to be on the music rather than his personal life. This separation of personal and professional identity allows Bear Grillz to connect with his fans on a deeper level, as they are drawn to the enigmatic nature of the artist.

The bear mask itself plays a crucial role in maintaining this mystique. The choice of a bear as the central icon stems from Bear Grillz's desire to convey strength, power, and a sense of wildness. The mask is meticulously designed, incorporating intricate details such as sharp teeth and piercing eyes, to create an imposing and unforgettable image.

The bear mask holds multiple meanings for Bear Grillz. It serves as a form of protection, allowing him to maintain his privacy and distance himself from the pressures of fame. It also acts as a vessel for creative expression, enabling him to transcend the boundaries of his personal identity and fully embody the Bear Grillz persona during performances. The mask, in a way, empowers him to bring his music and message to life in a larger-than-life way.

Living behind the mask, however, presents its own set of challenges. It requires constant dedication and vigilance to preserve the anonymity and mystique of Bear Grillz. Maintaining secrecy regarding his true identity demands a carefully curated personal and professional life, separating the two to the fullest extent possible. This constant need for discretion can pose difficulties in building personal relationships and can create strain in maintaining friendships and romantic partnerships.

On the flip side, the anonymity allows Bear Grillz to freely express himself through his music and performances without the limitations of societal expectations or preconceived notions. It allows him to experiment with different musical styles and take creative risks without the fear of judgment based on his personal identity.

The decision to remain anonymous opens up endless possibilities to explore and evolve as an artist. It enables Bear Grillz to constantly reinvent himself without being limited by the expectations or constraints of a public persona. By allowing his music to speak for itself, Bear Grillz can focus on the connection he shares with his fans, creating a community that is built solely on the love for his music and the unique experience he offers.

The enigmatic nature of Bear Grillz's persona has also proven to be an effective marketing strategy. By keeping his true identity a secret, he generates curiosity and intrigue among fans, leading to increased engagement and a sense of exclusivity. The mask becomes a symbol of unity, as fans can rally behind the persona of Bear Grillz without prejudice or bias.

In conclusion, maintaining the mystique and anonymity has been an integral part of Bear Grillz's journey. By donning the bear mask, he creates a powerful and captivating image that complements his music. Despite the challenges it presents, living behind the mask allows Bear Grillz to separate his personal life from his music, engender a sense of intrigue and curiosity, and connect with his fans on a deeper and more meaningful level. The bear mask has become more than just a symbol; it has become a beacon that unites fans and creates a community centered around love for music and a shared experience.

Subsection: Behind-the-scenes of a Bear Grillz show

In this subsection, we will take a behind-the-scenes look at the electrifying world of a Bear Grillz show. From the moment Bear Grillz steps onstage to the final beat drop, every aspect of the performance is carefully crafted to create a mesmerizing experience for the audience. Join us as we explore the technical wizardry, visual effects, and the energy that make a Bear Grillz show an unforgettable event.

The Preparation

Behind every successful show is meticulous preparation. Bear Grillz's team works tirelessly to ensure that every detail is taken care of, from the setlist to the stage design. The preparation for a show begins weeks in advance, with meetings and brainstorming sessions to create a cohesive and immersive experience for the audience.

Choosing the Setlist   One of the crucial steps in preparing for a Bear Grillz show is selecting the perfect setlist. Bear Grillz is known for his high-energy performances and genre-blending tracks, so curating a playlist that keeps the crowd engaged and excited is of utmost importance. The setlist is carefully crafted to take the audience on a journey, building up anticipation and delivering unforgettable drops that keep them wanting more.

Visual Design   The visual design of a Bear Grillz show is equally important in creating an immersive experience. Working in collaboration with talented visual artists and production designers, Bear Grillz's team creates stunning visual elements that complement the music and enhance the overall atmosphere of the performance. From vibrant LED displays to intricate stage setups, every detail is carefully considered to transport the audience into the world of Bear Grillz.

Technical Setup   Behind-the-scenes, an army of skilled technicians work meticulously to set up the stage, sound, and lighting for a Bear Grillz show. The technical setup is a crucial aspect of the performance, ensuring that the music is crisp and powerful and the visual effects are perfectly synchronized. This includes everything from installing speakers and amplifiers to programming lighting cues and synchronizing them with the music.

Onstage Magic

As the lights dim and the crowd roars, Bear Grillz takes the stage, ready to ignite the crowd with his signature sound. The onstage experience is a symphony of lights, sound, and energy that captivates the audience from the very first beat.

The Stage Presence   Bear Grillz's commanding stage presence is one of the defining elements of his live performances. From the moment he steps onstage, his energy and enthusiasm are infectious, creating an immediate connection with the audience. He effortlessly moves across the stage, interacting with the crowd and hyping them up for the journey that lies ahead.

The Visual Spectacle   At a Bear Grillz show, the visual spectacle is as captivating as the music itself. State-of-the-art lighting setups, laser displays, and pyrotechnics create a mesmerizing visual feast that enhances the emotional impact of the music. Synchronized visuals are carefully choreographed to complement the drops and climactic moments of the music, taking the audience on a visual journey alongside the sonic experience.

Live Remixes and Mashups   One of the highlights of a Bear Grillz show is his live remixing and mashup skills. With an arsenal of tracks at his disposal, Bear Grillz seamlessly blends and remixes songs on the fly, creating unique and unforgettable live moments. These moments of improvisation and creativity showcase Bear Grillz's dynamic and versatile approach to performing, ensuring that no two shows are ever the same.

Connecting with the Crowd

The true magic of a Bear Grillz show lies in the connection he builds with the crowd. Beyond the music and visual spectacle, Bear Grillz's ability to forge a deep connection with his fans sets his performances apart.

Fan Interaction   Bear Grillz thrives on engaging with his fans during live performances. From high-fiving fans in the front row to jumping into the crowd for a brief moment, he creates intimate and personal connections that make each show feel like a shared experience. This interaction not only fuels the energy of the performance but also leaves a lasting impact on the audience.

Creating a Sense of Unity   At a Bear Grillz show, the sense of unity amongst the crowd is palpable. Through his music and on-stage presence, Bear Grillz creates a space where fans from all walks of life come together to celebrate their shared love for music. This sense of unity fosters a positive and inclusive atmosphere, breaking down barriers and creating a sense of belonging for all who attend.

Spreading Positivity   Bear Grillz's shows are not just about the music; they are also about spreading positivity and love. Through uplifting messages and motivational speeches, he encourages his fans to embrace their true selves, follow their passions, and never give up on their dreams. His performances serve as a reminder that music has the power to inspire and bring people together.

Culmination and Aftermath

As the final notes of the set ring out, and the crowd erupts in applause, the Bear Grillz show comes to an end. But the impact of the performance lingers long after the lights fade.

The Afterglow   After the show, Bear Grillz takes the time to connect with his fans, whether through meet-and-greets, fan events, or online interactions. This personal connection with his audience helps to keep the spirit of the show alive and deepens the bond between Bear Grillz and his loyal fanbase.

Reflection and Improvements   Behind-the-scenes, Bear Grillz and his team reflect on each show, taking note of what worked well and areas for improvement. This dedication to constant growth and refinement ensures that each subsequent show is even more electrifying and memorable than the last.

Leaving a Lasting Impression   The impact of a Bear Grillz show extends far beyond the venue. Fans leave his performances with a renewed sense of energy, inspiration, and an unforgettable memory of a night filled with music, unity, and positivity. Bear Grillz's ability to create a lasting impression through his live shows is a testament to his artistry and commitment to his craft.

In conclusion, the behind-the-scenes world of a Bear Grillz show is a whirlwind of meticulous preparation, stunning visual design, exhilarating performances, and genuine connections with the audience. Through his energetic stage presence, visually captivating performances, and heartfelt interactions, Bear Grillz creates a live experience that transcends the music itself, leaving a lasting impact on all who have the privilege of attending.

Subsection: Personal relationships and support system

Personal relationships and a strong support system have played a crucial role in Bear Grillz's journey as an artist. From the beginning of his career, the support and encouragement he received from family, friends, and mentors have shaped his success and helped him navigate the challenges of the music industry.

One of the most significant relationships in Bear Grillz's life is his tight-knit family. Growing up in a musical household, Bear Grillz was exposed to a wide range of genres and artists from an early age. His parents recognized his talent and provided him with the necessary resources and opportunities to nurture his passion for music. They not only encouraged him to pursue his interests but also provided a strong support system during the ups and downs of his musical journey.

In addition to family support, Bear Grillz also benefited from mentorship and guidance from industry professionals. Early on, he sought out experienced producers and sought their advice and feedback on his music. These mentors provided him with invaluable insights into the industry, shared their expertise, and pushed him to explore new creative paths. Their guidance helped him improve his skills and develop his unique sound.

Bear Grillz's personal relationships extend beyond his family and mentors. He surrounds himself with a circle of close friends who provide him with emotional support and keep him grounded. These friends understand the pressures of the music industry and offer Bear Grillz a sense of camaraderie and understanding. They also serve as his sounding board, offering honest feedback and constructive criticism when needed.

Furthermore, Bear Grillz has fostered a strong connection with his fans, forming a community known as the "Bear Fam." The Bear Fam is a tight-knit community of fans who share a deep passion for Bear Grillz's music. Through various social media platforms, meet-ups, and fan events, Bear Grillz has built a strong personal bond with his fans. He values their opinions and often seeks their input on decisions regarding his music and career. The support and dedication of the Bear Fam have been instrumental in Bear Grillz's rise to success.

Support systems are essential for any artist, and Bear Grillz understands the significance of surrounding himself with like-minded individuals. Collaborations with fellow artists have been a crucial part of his journey, not only in terms of releasing music but also in forming long-lasting friendships. These collaborations allow him to learn from other artists, share ideas, and push boundaries creatively.

Maintaining personal relationships and a strong support system has not been without its challenges. The music industry is competitive, and success often comes with its share of pressures and sacrifices. Bear Grillz has faced numerous obstacles but credits his relationships and support system for helping him navigate these challenges. Their unwavering support and belief in him have given him the resilience to overcome setbacks and stay true to his artistic vision.

In conclusion, personal relationships and a strong support system have played a crucial role in Bear Grillz's career. From his family and mentors to his friends and fans, the support he has received has been instrumental in his success. With their guidance, encouragement, and honest feedback, Bear Grillz has been able to grow as an artist, overcome obstacles, and leave a lasting impact on the electronic music scene.

Subsection: Bear Grillz's Connection to His Fans

Bear Grillz's success as an artist can be attributed not only to his exceptional talent and unique sound but also to his deep connection with his fans. From the beginning of his career, Bear Grillz recognized the importance of building a strong and loyal fanbase, and he has consistently gone above and beyond to engage and connect with his supporters. In this subsection, we will explore the various ways in which Bear Grillz connects with his fans, fostering a sense of community and creating authentic and meaningful relationships.

Engaging on Social Media Platforms

One of the most prominent ways Bear Grillz connects with his fans is through social media platforms. He actively engages with his fans by posting regular updates, behind-the-scenes glimpses, and personal anecdotes. Whether it's sharing exclusive previews of upcoming tracks, engaging in conversations with fans in comment sections, or organizing interactive contests and giveaways, Bear Grillz's presence on social media is a testament to his commitment to creating a direct line of communication with his fans.

In addition to his engagement on social media, Bear Grillz also dedicates time to create unique content for his followers. He often shares live streams of his studio sessions, giving fans an intimate look into his music-making process. This transparency and openness allow fans to feel connected to Bear Grillz on a personal level, as they witness his creative journey in real-time.

Real-Life Fan Interactions

Bear Grillz takes his connection with his fans beyond the digital realm by actively seeking out opportunities for real-life interactions. As part of his touring strategy, he often goes out of his way to meet fans before and after shows. This personal touch not only allows him to show his appreciation for their support but also provides an opportunity for fans to share their personal stories and experiences. By listening to his fans and taking the time to have meaningful conversations, Bear Grillz deepens the connection he has with his audience.

Furthermore, Bear Grillz organizes fan meet-ups and events in different cities around the world. These gatherings allow fans to connect with one another, share their love for Bear Grillz's music, and create lasting friendships. By facilitating these community-driven events, Bear Grillz fosters an environment where fans can come together and strengthen their bond through a shared passion for his music.

Supporting Fan Art and Creativity

Bear Grillz recognizes and values the creativity of his fans. He actively encourages them to express themselves through their artwork, remixes, and covers of his tracks. By showcasing fan art on his social media platforms and acknowledging the efforts of his supporters, Bear Grillz not only fosters a sense of pride within the fan community but also motivates others to explore their creative potential.

Moreover, Bear Grillz often collaborates with his fans on various projects. From crowd-sourcing ideas for music videos to inviting fans to participate in behind-the-scenes productions, Bear Grillz actively involves his fans in the creative process. By giving them opportunities to contribute to his artistry, he strengthens the bond between artist and fan, transforming passive supporters into active collaborators.

Fan-Supported Philanthropic Initiatives

Bear Grillz's connection with his fans goes beyond music and art. He actively encourages his fan community, often referred to as the "Bear Fam," to engage in philanthropic endeavors and support various social causes. Through fan-led initiatives and partnerships with non-profit organizations, the Bear Fam has championed environmental conservation, mental health awareness, and other important social issues.

By incorporating philanthropy into his fan community, Bear Grillz inspires his fans to make a positive impact in the world. This shared sense of purpose and the passion for making a difference further strengthens the bond among fans and their connection to Bear Grillz.

Fan Testimonials

The impact of Bear Grillz's connection with his fans can be heard and felt through the countless testimonials shared by his supporters. Fans often express profound gratitude for the emotional and motivational impact Bear Grillz's music has had on their lives. They frequently share stories of finding solace and inspiration in his tracks, overcoming personal struggles, and connecting with a larger community through their love for Bear Grillz's artistry.

These testimonials highlight the deep emotional connection fans have formed with Bear Grillz's music and the transformative power it holds. The strong bond between the artist and his fans is built on shared experiences, empathy, and a sense of belonging.

The Bear Fam's Role in Shaping Bear Grillz's Music

The relationship between Bear Grillz and his fans is a symbiotic one. The Bear Fam plays a vital role in shaping Bear Grillz's music by providing continuous feedback and support. Fan responses to his tracks, performances, and overall creative direction serve as valuable insights that Bear Grillz takes into consideration when developing his sound.

This collaborative exchange allows Bear Grillz to create music that resonates deeply with his fans while also pushing the boundaries of his own artistry. The Bear Fam's influence has not only helped Bear Grillz evolve as an artist but has also propelled him to new heights of success within the electronic music scene.

Conclusion

Bear Grillz's connection to his fans goes far beyond the music itself. Through his active engagement on social media, real-life fan interactions, support for fan creativity, involvement in philanthropic initiatives, and open dialogue with his audience, Bear Grillz has built a community of dedicated fans who feel seen, heard, and valued.

The Bear Fam's unwavering support and their emotional connection to Bear Grillz's music has been a driving force in his career. The sense of unity and shared purpose within the fan community has not only strengthened the bond between fans but has also created a solid foundation for Bear Grillz's enduring legacy. The artist's commitment to his fans has undoubtedly shaped his music and empowered him to make a lasting impact in the electronic music landscape.

In the following subsection, we will delve deeper into Bear Grillz's true identity and explore the complexities of balancing personal life and the spotlight.

Subsection: Bear Grillz's hobbies and interests outside of music

Bear Grillz is not just a talented musician, but also a well-rounded individual with a variety of hobbies and interests that he pursues outside of his music career. Despite his busy schedule, Bear Grillz knows the importance of finding balance and taking time to engage in activities that bring him joy and allow him to recharge. In this subsection, we will explore some of Bear Grillz's passions beyond the realm of music.

1. **Extreme Sports:** One of Bear Grillz's biggest hobbies is participating in extreme sports. Whether it's snowboarding down treacherous slopes, rock climbing challenging routes, or skydiving from dizzying heights, Bear Grillz thrives on the adrenaline and excitement that these activities provide. He believes that pushing his physical limits through extreme sports not only helps him stay in shape but also fuels his creativity as an artist.

2. **Outdoor Exploration:** When Bear Grillz is not on stage or in the studio, you can often find him exploring the great outdoors. He has a deep appreciation for nature and enjoys hiking, camping, and backpacking in remote locations. These

adventures allow him to disconnect from technology and immerse himself in the beauty and serenity of natural landscapes. Bear Grillz finds inspiration in the tranquility of the wilderness, often translating these experiences into his music.

3. **Culinary Adventures:** Bear Grillz has a passion for cooking and experimenting with different flavors and cuisines. In his downtime, he loves to create delicious meals and explore new recipes. He enjoys combining unexpected ingredients to create unique dishes that reflect his diverse palette. Bear Grillz believes that cooking is not only a form of creative expression but also a way to connect with others and share experiences.

4. **Visual Arts:** Bear Grillz has a deep appreciation for visual arts and enjoys expressing his creativity through various mediums. From painting and sketching to graphic design and photography, he finds joy in exploring different artistic outlets. Often, the visuals in Bear Grillz's music videos and album covers are a result of his own artistic vision and personal touch. He believes that combining music with visual aesthetics enhances the overall experience for his fans.

5. **Philanthropic Work:** Bear Grillz is passionate about giving back to the community and making a positive impact on the world. He actively participates in philanthropic endeavors and supports various charitable causes. Whether it's organizing fundraisers, donating to environmental conservation initiatives, or advocating for mental health awareness, Bear Grillz uses his platform to inspire change and promote social well-being.

6. **Fitness and Health:** Maintaining a healthy lifestyle is important to Bear Grillz. He invests time and effort in staying fit and prioritizes physical and mental well-being. Whether it's hitting the gym or practicing mindfulness and meditation, he recognizes the importance of taking care of his body and mind to sustain his hectic schedule and creative pursuits.

7. **Entrepreneurship:** Beyond his music career, Bear Grillz has a keen business sense and a passion for entrepreneurship. He has ventured into various business opportunities, including launching his own merchandise line and collaborating with other artists on creative projects. Bear Grillz views entrepreneurship as a way to expand his brand and connect with his fans on a deeper level.

Bear Grillz's diverse range of hobbies and interests showcases his multifaceted personality and his commitment to living life to the fullest. While music remains his main focus, his pursuit of these passions outside of music enriches his artistry and allows him to connect with his fans on a deeper level. Through his various hobbies and endeavors, Bear Grillz continues to inspire others to explore their own interests and strive for a well-rounded and fulfilling life.

Subsection: The impact of fame on personal relationships

Being thrust into the spotlight of fame can bring about significant changes and challenges in an individual's personal relationships. Bear Grillz's rise to fame has undoubtedly affected his relationships with family, friends, and romantic partners. In this subsection, we will explore the various ways in which fame has impacted Bear Grillz's personal connections and how he has navigated this dynamic aspect of his journey.

One of the most notable areas affected by fame is Bear Grillz's relationship with his family. Going from a relatively ordinary life to becoming a renowned artist can create a dynamic shift within the family structure. While fame can bring newfound opportunities and luxuries, it can also create distance and strain in relationships. The increased demands on Bear Grillz's time, the pressure of maintaining success, and the constant public scrutiny can strain the bond he shares with his loved ones. Balancing his career commitments with personal obligations becomes a challenge and often requires open communication, understanding, and compromise from both sides to maintain a healthy relationship.

Furthermore, the rapid pace at which Bear Grillz's career has progressed can cause feelings of jealousy, resentment, or even a sense of abandonment within his circle of friends. While some friends may genuinely be happy and supportive, others may struggle with feelings of envy or disappointment. These emotional responses are not uncommon in situations where one person achieves considerable success while their peers may be navigating different paths. Bear Grillz must navigate this delicate balance between staying connected with his friends and pursuing his career aspirations. This often requires open and honest conversations, setting realistic expectations, and finding common ground to maintain the friendships that are meaningful to him.

Romantic relationships can also be deeply impacted by fame. Bear Grillz's sudden rise to fame may attract individuals who are interested in his public persona more than the person behind the mask. This dynamic can complicate the process of building genuine and long-lasting connections. It becomes crucial for Bear Grillz to discern the intentions of those entering his life and ensure that any potential partners value him for his true self rather than his celebrity status. Nurturing a romantic relationship under the spotlight of fame often requires patience, understanding, and open communication about each person's needs, boundaries, and aspirations.

Moreover, maintaining a relationship while constantly traveling and being away for extended periods presents its own set of challenges. The demanding touring schedule and commitments associated with a successful music career can put a strain on even the strongest of relationships. Trust, effective communication, and finding creative ways to stay connected are crucial. Bear Grillz may need to make extra efforts to prioritize his partner's emotional well-being, showing support, and ensuring that their needs are being met despite the demanding nature of his profession.

While fame can undoubtedly strain personal relationships, it can also be a catalyst for growth and change within those relationships. The impact of fame on personal connections calls for adaptability, resilience, and a strong sense of self from both Bear Grillz and his loved ones. It demands active efforts to maintain communication, understanding, and support amidst the ever-changing dynamics that come with success.

To navigate the challenges, Bear Grillz can seek guidance from mentors and industry professionals who have experienced similar situations. Their wisdom and advice can provide valuable insights on balancing personal and professional commitments, setting boundaries, and finding balance in life.

In summary, the impact of fame on Bear Grillz's personal relationships is vast and complex. It requires constant effort, open communication, and understanding from all parties involved. Bear Grillz must navigate the unique challenges that fame brings, including maintaining relationships with family, friends, and romantic partners. By staying true to himself, prioritizing healthy communication, and seeking support when needed, Bear Grillz can forge meaningful connections and maintain genuine relationships amidst the whirlwind of fame.

Subsection: Bear Grillz's role as a mentor and inspiration

Bear Grillz has not only made a tremendous impact on the electronic music scene but has also become a mentor and inspiration for aspiring musicians. Through his own journey of success, he has demonstrated how dedication, passion, and authenticity can propel one's music career to new heights. In this subsection, we will explore Bear Grillz's role as a mentor and how he has inspired others in the industry.

Bear Grillz's mentorship philosophy

Bear Grillz believes in the power of mentorship and its ability to foster growth and development in aspiring artists. He understands the importance of guidance and support in navigating the complexities of the music industry. As a mentor, Bear Grillz emphasizes the following principles:

+ **Building relationships:** Bear Grillz believes in fostering strong relationships with his mentees. He takes the time to understand their unique vision, challenges, and aspirations, which enables him to provide tailored guidance and support.

+ **Sharing knowledge and experience:** Bear Grillz draws upon his own experiences to provide valuable insights and lessons learned. He shares his knowledge and skills, guiding mentees in areas such as music production techniques, sound design, marketing, and branding.

+ **Encouraging creativity and individuality:** Bear Grillz understands the importance of nurturing each mentee's creative expression. He encourages them to experiment, take risks, and embrace their own unique style. He reinforces the idea that success comes from staying true to oneself and embracing individuality.

+ **Promoting personal growth:** Bear Grillz recognizes that personal growth is essential for success in the music industry. He helps mentees develop their personal brand, enhance their stage presence, and improve their overall professionalism. He also emphasizes the importance of self-care and mental well-being.

+ **Instilling work ethic and perseverance:** Bear Grillz emphasizes the value of hard work, discipline, and perseverance. He encourages mentees to set goals, stay focused, and put in the necessary effort to achieve their dreams. He leads by example, demonstrating that success is a result of consistent dedication and determination.

Inspiring others in the industry

Bear Grillz's authenticity, creativity, and success have inspired countless individuals in the music industry. By breaking down barriers and pushing the boundaries of electronic music, he has become a role model for aspiring artists. Here are some ways in which Bear Grillz has inspired others:

+ **Encouraging self-expression:** Bear Grillz's fearless self-expression through his music and persona has inspired others to embrace their own uniqueness and express themselves authentically. He has shown that there is a place for individuality in the music industry.

+ **Challenging the norm:** Bear Grillz's innovative approach to music production and his ability to blend genres has inspired others to step outside their comfort zones and challenge the conventional boundaries of electronic music. He has encouraged artists to experiment with new sounds, rhythms, and techniques to create fresh and exciting music.

+ **Promoting diversity and inclusivity:** Bear Grillz's advocacy for diversity and inclusivity in the music industry has inspired artists from all backgrounds to pursue their dreams. He has been vocal about the importance of representation and has used his platform to uplift underrepresented voices in the industry.

+ **Spreading positivity and unity:** Bear Grillz's positive message and energetic performances have uplifted audiences worldwide. His ability to connect with fans on a deep emotional level has inspired others to use their music as a tool to spread love, unity, and positivity.

+ **Supporting aspiring artists:** Bear Grillz has used his success to support and mentor aspiring artists. Through collaborations, remix competitions, and online tutorials, he has provided opportunities for emerging talent to showcase their skills and gain exposure. This support has inspired others to pay it forward and create a supportive community within the music industry.

Bear Grillz's unconventional mentoring approach

While Bear Grillz's mentoring style encompasses traditional elements, he also brings a fresh and unconventional approach to mentoring aspiring artists. His unique perspective challenges mentees to think outside the box and explore new avenues for success. Here are some of the unconventional aspects of Bear Grillz's mentoring approach:

+ **Embracing failure and setbacks:** Bear Grillz encourages mentees to embrace failure as a learning opportunity. He emphasizes that setbacks are an inevitable part of the journey and that they should be embraced rather than feared. He inspires mentees to view failures as stepping stones towards growth and success.

+ **Experimental collaborations:** Bear Grillz encourages mentees to explore collaborations with artists from diverse genres and styles. He believes that these unexpected collaborations can lead to groundbreaking music and inspire new creative directions. By breaking down genre barriers, he encourages mentees to challenge their own musical boundaries.

* **Balancing artistic integrity and commercial success:** Bear Grillz emphasizes the importance of maintaining artistic integrity while still striving for commercial success. He encourages mentees to create music that resonates with them personally, while also considering the needs and expectations of their audience. He believes that finding the right balance between art and commerce is crucial for sustained success.

* **Embracing technology and digital platforms:** Bear Grillz recognizes the power of technology and digital platforms in the music industry. He encourages mentees to leverage these tools to reach a wider audience, build their brand, and connect with fans. He emphasizes the importance of staying up-to-date with emerging technologies and trends.

* **Providing real-world industry insights:** Bear Grillz offers mentees a glimpse into the realities of the music industry. He shares the challenges he has faced, the lessons he has learned, and the strategies he has employed to overcome obstacles. This practical knowledge helps mentees navigate the industry with a clearer understanding of its inner workings.

In conclusion, Bear Grillz's role as a mentor and inspiration cannot be overstated. Through his mentorship philosophy, he has guided aspiring artists on their path to success, providing them with valuable knowledge, support, and encouragement. His authenticity, creativity, and success have inspired countless individuals in the music industry to embrace their individuality, challenge norms, and spread positivity. With his unconventional mentoring approach, Bear Grillz continues to push the boundaries of electronic music and shape the future of the industry.

Section 3: Bear Grillz's Wild Adventures

Subsection: Touring the world and connecting with fans

Touring is not just a means for Bear Grillz to perform his music, but it is a way for him to connect with his fans on a deeper level. It is during these live performances that the essence of Bear Grillz truly comes alive. From sold-out arenas to intimate club sets, Bear Grillz's captivating stage presence and energy leave fans craving for more.

1. The Power of Live Performances: Live performances have always been an integral part of the music industry, and Bear Grillz understands its significance in

connecting with fans. The energy that emanates from the stage, the raw emotions conveyed through music, and the interaction between the artist and the audience create a unique and unforgettable experience.

2. Creating Unforgettable Moments: Bear Grillz's live performances are known for creating unforgettable moments. Whether it's a drop that sends the crowd into a frenzy or an unexpected surprise collaboration, Bear Grillz always keeps his fans at the edge of their seats. His carefully crafted setlists, mixed with live improvisation, ensure that each show is a one-of-a-kind experience.

3. Engaging with the Crowd: Bear Grillz's interactions with the crowd go beyond just delivering a performance. He creates a connection with his fans, making them feel like they are a part of something bigger. Through his enthusiasm, banter, and genuine appreciation for his supporters, Bear Grillz invites fans to join him on a musical journey, leaving them with cherished memories.

4. Innovative Visual Effects: Bear Grillz's live shows are a visual feast. From mesmerizing lighting displays to cutting-edge visual effects, the production value of his performances is unparalleled. These visual elements enhance the overall experience, transporting fans to a world where music and art seamlessly blend.

5. Fan Participation: Bear Grillz encourages fan participation during his live performances, further deepening the connection between artist and audience. Whether it's through call-and-response chants, interactive games, or crowd-surfing, Bear Grillz ensures that his fans feel actively involved in the show. This level of engagement creates a sense of unity and community among the concert-goers.

6. Embracing Technology: Bear Grillz harnesses the power of technology to enhance his live performances. From synchronized LED wristbands that light up the entire audience to immersive audiovisual experiences, Bear Grillz seamlessly integrates technology into his shows, creating a multi-sensory experience that captivates and enthralls fans.

7. Adapting to Different Venues: As Bear Grillz's popularity has grown, so has the scale of his live performances. He has seamlessly transitioned from intimate club gigs to performing on some of the biggest festival stages around the world. With each new venue, Bear Grillz adapts his performance style and production to suit the atmosphere, ensuring that fans receive an unforgettable experience regardless of the setting.

8. Connecting Fans from Around the World: Touring allows Bear Grillz to connect with his international fanbase. From North America to Europe, Asia, and beyond, Bear Grillz's music has reached fans in every corner of the globe. Through his live performances, he creates a sense of shared experience and unity among fans from various cultures and backgrounds.

9. Authenticity and Genuine Appreciation: One of the key factors that sets Bear Grillz apart is his authenticity and genuine appreciation for his fans. He never fails to acknowledge the support he receives and often takes time after each performance to meet and greet fans, sign autographs, and take photos. This personal touch forms a bond between Bear Grillz and his fans that goes beyond the music.

10. Leaving a Lasting Impression: Bear Grillz's live performances leave a lasting impression on both fans and industry insiders. His ability to connect with the crowd, showcase his musical talents, and create a sense of unity among diverse audiences has made him a standout figure in the electronic music scene. Through touring, Bear Grillz continues to leave an indelible mark on the hearts and minds of his fans worldwide.

In conclusion, touring is not just a platform for Bear Grillz to showcase his music, but it is an opportunity for him to connect with his fans on a personal level. The power of live performances, engaging with the crowd, embracing innovative visual effects, and fan participation all contribute to the unique experience that Bear Grillz offers his fans. From intimate club performances to massive festival stages, Bear Grillz continues to leave a lasting impression and build a strong, global fanbase that is united by their love for his music.

Subsection: Memorable moments on the road

Being on the road as a musician is filled with unforgettable experiences, and Bear Grillz has had his fair share of memorable moments throughout his career. From connecting with fans all around the world to unexpected encounters with fellow musicians, these moments have left a lasting impact on Bear Grillz and his music.

One memorable moment on the road for Bear Grillz was during a tour stop in Tokyo, Japan. The energy in the crowd was electric, and the crowd's enthusiasm was contagious. As Bear Grillz took the stage, he couldn't help but feel overwhelmed by the love and support from his fans. The entire venue was transformed into a massive dance party, with everyone jumping and moving to the beat. It was a surreal experience for Bear Grillz, seeing firsthand how his music had resonated with people from a different culture and language.

Another memorable moment on the road was a spontaneous collaboration with a fellow musician. During a festival in Europe, Bear Grillz had the opportunity to meet one of his musical idols backstage. After a brief conversation about their shared love for music, they decided to join forces and perform an impromptu set together. The crowd went wild as they witnessed the fusion of their unique sounds and styles. It was a magical moment that showcased the power of collaboration and the universal language of music.

One particularly adventurous moment on the road happened during a tour stop in Australia. Bear Grillz has always had a love for adrenaline-pumping activities, and he couldn't resist the opportunity to go skydiving. Accompanied by his tour crew, Bear Grillz jumped out of a plane and experienced the thrill of freefalling. The breathtaking views of the Australian landscape from above left a lasting impression on him, reminding him of the beauty of the world outside of music.

During his travels, Bear Grillz has also had the opportunity to explore different cultures and music scenes. One such experience was a visit to Brazil, where he immersed himself in the vibrant local music scene. From attending live samba performances to collaborating with Brazilian artists, Bear Grillz felt inspired by the rich musical heritage of the country. These experiences not only expanded his musical horizons but also allowed him to connect with fans on a deeper level.

While on the road, Bear Grillz has also encountered unexpected acts of kindness from his fans. One particular moment that touched his heart was when a group of fans surprised him with a handcrafted bear-shaped cake after a show. Their gesture of appreciation and dedication to his music left him feeling humbled and grateful. This act of kindness served as a reminder of the strong bond between Bear Grillz and his fans, known as the Bear Fam.

These memorable moments on the road have contributed to Bear Grillz's growth as an artist and have shaped his perspective on music and life. Whether it's connecting with fans from different cultures, collaborating with fellow musicians, or venturing into thrilling activities, these experiences have become cherished memories that continue to inspire Bear Grillz in his musical journey.

Road life can be grueling and demanding, but it is also filled with joy, excitement, and unexpected surprises. These moments remind Bear Grillz of the power of music to bring people together and create lasting memories. As he continues his journey, Bear Grillz looks forward to creating many more unforgettable moments on the road and sharing them with his loyal Bear Fam and fans around the world.

Subsection: Experiencing different cultures and music scenes

Experiencing different cultures and music scenes is an essential part of Bear Grillz's artistic journey. Through his travels around the world, he has not only been exposed to diverse musical influences but also gained invaluable insights into different cultures and traditions. This subsection delves into the transformative power of cultural immersion and how it has shaped Bear Grillz's unique sound and perspective.

Cultural Immersion and Music Inspiration

When Bear Grillz embarked on his global adventures, he discovered that immersing himself in different cultures opened up a world of musical inspiration. Each country he visited had its own distinct musical heritage, rhythms, and styles that resonated deeply with him. From the hypnotic beats of African drums to the intricate melodies of Indian classical music, Bear Grillz found himself captivated by the immense diversity of sounds and rhythms.

One particular experience that left a lasting imprint on Bear Grillz's music was his visit to Brazil during Carnival. The vibrant energy, infectious rhythms, and colorful samba parades inspired him to infuse his own music with the infectious, dance-worthy beats he encountered. This transformative experience not only expanded his sonic palette but also fueled his desire to create music that transcended cultural boundaries.

Fusion of Musical Styles

As Bear Grillz delved deeper into the music scenes of different cultures, he recognized the potential for creating a fusion of musical styles. By blending elements from various genres, he could seamlessly intertwine different cultural influences to create a sound that was unique to him.

For example, in his collaboration with a renowned African percussion group, Bear Grillz combined his signature bearstep sound with traditional African rhythms. The result was a captivating track that not only showcased the beauty of cultural exchange but also broke new ground in the electronic music scene.

Collaborations with Local Artists

To fully immerse himself in different music scenes, Bear Grillz sought out collaborations with local artists during his travels. These collaborations allowed him to gain a deeper understanding of the cultural context surrounding the music and create authentic pieces that celebrated the fusion of his signature sound with local traditions.

For instance, during a visit to Japan, Bear Grillz collaborated with a talented traditional shamisen player. This collaboration brought together the ancient sounds of the shamisen with the modern electronic beats of Bear Grillz, resulting in a mesmerizing blend of tradition and innovation.

Through these collaborations, Bear Grillz not only expanded his musical horizons but also forged strong connections with artists from around the world, fostering a sense of unity and collective creativity.

Musical Reflections of Different Cultures

Bear Grillz's experiences with different cultures have significantly influenced the thematic elements of his music. Inspired by the captivating stories and histories he encountered, he often integrates cultural and socially relevant narratives into his tracks.

For example, after a visit to the Middle East, Bear Grillz was moved by the rich history and cultural heritage of the region. He channeled this inspiration into a track that captured the essence of desert landscapes and ancient mysticism. The integration of Middle Eastern instrumentation and melodies created a unique sonic tapestry that paid homage to the rich cultural heritage he had witnessed.

Cultural Exploration, Connection, and Understanding

Beyond the mere influence on his music, Bear Grillz also views his experiences with different cultures as an opportunity for personal growth, connection, and understanding. By immersing himself in the music scenes of different countries, he gained firsthand insight into the cultural values, struggles, and joys of communities around the world.

Bear Grillz firmly believes that music has the power to transcend language and cultural barriers. Through his music, he strives to bridge the gaps between different cultures, foster understanding, and promote unity. His goal is to create a global community that celebrates diversity and appreciates the beauty of cultural exchange.

An Unconventional Approach: Creating Music as Cultural Ambassador

In an unconventional move, Bear Grillz has taken on the role of a cultural ambassador through his music. With each new destination he discovers, he aims to authentically represent the cultural nuances of the regions he explores. By incorporating local sounds and collaborating with local artists, Bear Grillz has become a vehicle for sharing cultural experiences and fostering connections.

For instance, during his visit to South America, Bear Grillz organized a series of workshops in local schools to expose children to the world of electronic music and inspire their own creative journeys. These initiatives not only expanded his fan base but also served as an avenue for cultural exchange and artistic exploration.

Caveats and Importance of Cultural Sensitivity

While Bear Grillz embraces different cultures and the power of fusion, he also acknowledges the importance of cultural sensitivity. He approaches collaborations and inspiration from a place of deep respect for the traditions and histories he encounters.

Understanding that cultural appreciation should never cross into appropriation, Bear Grillz actively seeks guidance and involvement from local artists and experts to ensure that his creative efforts are respectful and well-informed. This commitment to cultural integrity shapes his approach to collaboration and ensures that his music acts as a platform for cultural celebration rather than exploitation.

In Summary

Experiencing different cultures and music scenes has been a transformative journey for Bear Grillz. By immersing himself in diverse musical traditions and collaborating with local artists, he has created a genre-bending sound that is uniquely his own. Through his music and cultural initiatives, Bear Grillz seeks to bridge cultural gaps, foster understanding, and celebrate the beauty of diversity in the world of electronic music.

Now the publication continues with the remaining sections of the book.

Subsection: Bear Grillz's love for adrenaline-pumping activities

In addition to his passion for music, Bear Grillz has a deep love for adrenaline-pumping activities. These heart-pounding adventures push the boundaries of his comfort zone and provide him with an outlet for his boundless energy. This section will explore some of the thrilling activities that Bear Grillz enjoys participating in, showcasing his fearless spirit and zest for life.

Extreme Sports

One of Bear Grillz's favorite ways to get an adrenaline rush is through extreme sports. Whether it's snowboarding down treacherous slopes, bungee jumping off towering cliffs, or skydiving from dizzying heights, Bear Grillz is always seeking the next adrenaline-pumping challenge. These activities allow him to experience a sense of freedom and exhilaration that fuels his creativity and inspires him in his music career. Bear Grillz's fearlessness and willingness to take risks are evident in both his music and his adventurous pursuits.

Motorsports

Bear Grillz's love for adrenaline extends to the world of motorsports. He finds immense joy in the speed, precision, and thrill of racing. Whether it's tearing up the track in a high-performance car, challenging the rough terrain on an off-road vehicle, or hitting the waves on a jet ski, Bear Grillz embraces the adrenaline rush that comes with these fast-paced activities. The precision required in motorsports demands focus and discipline, which helps sharpen Bear Grillz's skills as a musician and performer.

Outdoor Exploration

Bear Grillz also finds solace and excitement in exploring the great outdoors. From hiking through rugged landscapes and camping in remote locations to rock climbing towering mountains and navigating white-water rapids, he feels a deep connection to nature and the adrenaline that comes from challenging himself in these wild environments. These adventures not only provide Bear Grillz with thrilling experiences but also serve as a source of inspiration for his music, as he draws upon the beauty and power of nature in his compositions.

Wellness and Fitness Challenges

In addition to his love for extreme sports and outdoor exploration, Bear Grillz also embraces wellness and fitness challenges that push his physical and mental limits. He understands the importance of maintaining a healthy and fit lifestyle to keep up with the demands of his music career. Whether it's participating in intense workout routines, engaging in high-intensity interval training, or taking on obstacle courses, Bear Grillz is constantly challenging himself to reach new levels of strength and endurance. These activities not only provide him with an adrenaline rush but also help him maintain focus, discipline, and mental clarity.

Unconventional Endeavors

Bear Grillz's adventurous spirit extends beyond conventional activities. He seeks out unique and unconventional experiences that capture his imagination. Whether it's participating in wild and wacky events such as mud runs, extreme trampoline jumping, or even participating in quirky festivals around the world, Bear Grillz is always open to new and exciting adventures. These unconventional endeavors allow him to break free from routine and inject an element of fun and spontaneity into his life.

Caveats and Safety Measures

While Bear Grillz embraces adrenaline-pumping activities, he also recognizes the importance of safety and responsible decision-making. He understands that taking unnecessary risks can have severe consequences and is diligent in researching and preparing for each adventure. Bear Grillz always emphasizes the use of proper safety equipment, training, and guidance from experienced professionals to minimize risks and ensure a safe and enjoyable experience.

Example: Bear Grillz's Epic Skydiving Experience

To illustrate Bear Grillz's love for adrenaline-pumping activities, let's delve into a memorable skydiving experience he had.

On a crisp morning, Bear Grillz found himself standing at the edge of a plane, thousands of feet above the ground. The rush of wind against his face, the sound of the engine roaring in his ears, and the anticipation building within him all contributed to the adrenaline coursing through his veins.

As Bear Grillz leaped from the plane, he was met with an unparalleled sense of freedom. The breathtaking view of the sprawling landscape below and the rush of air against his body served as a reminder of his own mortality and the beauty of the present moment. It was a brief but powerful experience that allowed Bear Grillz to connect with his own sense of vulnerability and embrace the thrill of living life to the fullest.

As he gracefully descended through the sky, Bear Grillz couldn't help but feel a surge of inspiration and an overwhelming sense of gratitude. The adrenaline pumping through his veins fueled his creativity, igniting new ideas for his music, and empowering him to push the boundaries of his artistic expression.

This skydiving experience not only gave Bear Grillz an adrenaline rush but also instilled in him a profound appreciation for the wonders of the world. It reminded him of the importance of embracing challenges, overcoming fears, and seeking out new experiences to continuously grow as an individual and as an artist.

Conclusion

Bear Grillz's love for adrenaline-pumping activities is a testament to his adventurous spirit and zest for life. From extreme sports and motorsports to outdoor exploration and wellness challenges, Bear Grillz's fearless pursuit of thrilling experiences fuels his creativity and inspires him in his music career. These adrenaline-pumping activities not only provide him with excitement and joy but also shape his outlook on life, fostering personal growth, and giving him a unique perspective that shines through in his music.

Bear Grillz's unwavering passion for pushing himself beyond his limits serves as a reminder to embrace the unknown, live fearlessly, and find inspiration in the most unexpected places. Through his love for adrenaline-pumping activities, Bear Grillz continues to inspire his fans and fellow artists, encouraging them to step outside their comfort zones, embrace new challenges, and create their own extraordinary adventures.

Subsection: Exploring the natural world and wilderness

When it comes to exploring the natural world and wilderness, Bear Grillz truly embodies the spirit of adventure. As a passionate outdoor enthusiast, Bear Grillz has always found solace and inspiration in nature. His love for the great outdoors has not only influenced his personal life but has also seeped into his music, performances, and overall artistic identity.

Embracing the wilderness as a source of inspiration

For Bear Grillz, the wilderness serves as a boundless well of inspiration. The vastness of nature, with its awe-inspiring landscapes and untamed beauty, fuels his creativity and allows him to connect with his innermost thoughts and emotions. Whether it's the serene tranquility of a secluded forest or the adrenaline rush of conquering a challenging mountain peak, the natural world has a way of sparking Bear Grillz's creativity and infusing his music with a sense of raw intensity.

Seeking adventure in uncharted territories

Bear Grillz's exploration of the natural world goes beyond mere admiration from a distance. He actively seeks out new adventures and challenges himself to venture into uncharted territories. From backpacking through remote wilderness areas to rock climbing towering cliffs, Bear Grillz embraces the rawness and unpredictability of nature. His willingness to step outside his comfort zone not only pushes his physical and mental boundaries but also serves as a reminder of the infinite possibilities that await those who dare to explore.

Connecting with the essence of wilderness

One of the key aspects of Bear Grillz's exploration of the natural world is his desire to connect with the essence of wilderness. Whether he's observing the delicate balance of ecosystems or simply immersing himself in the sights and sounds of nature, Bear Grillz seeks to form a deep and symbiotic relationship with the natural world. This connection fuels his music, giving it an organic quality that resonates with listeners who share his love for the wild.

Conservation and environmental awareness

In his explorations of the natural world, Bear Grillz has witnessed firsthand the devastating impact of human activities on the environment. This experience has stirred a passion within him to become an advocate for conservation and environmental awareness. Through his music and public platforms, Bear Grillz actively raises awareness about pressing environmental issues, such as deforestation, species extinction, and climate change. He believes that by shining a spotlight on these issues, he can inspire others to take action and protect the natural world that he holds dear.

Unconventional approaches to wilderness exploration

While Bear Grillz often embraces traditional forms of wilderness exploration like hiking and camping, he also employs unconventional approaches to connect with nature. One of his favorite methods involves taking his music production equipment into the wilderness, setting up camp in the heart of nature, and using the sounds and ambiance of the environment as inspiration for his compositions. This unique approach allows Bear Grillz to blend his passion for music with his love for the wilderness, resulting in truly immersive and emotionally-charged tracks.

Problem: Outdoor sustainability

As an advocate for environmental conservation, Bear Grillz recognizes the importance of sustainable outdoor practices. Unfortunately, outdoor activities and tourism can sometimes have a negative impact on fragile ecosystems. One common problem is the improper disposal of waste, which can lead to pollution and habitat destruction. Another issue is the damage caused by overcrowding and unregulated tourism, which can disrupt natural habitats and degrade the overall wilderness experience.

Solution: Leave No Trace principles To address these issues, Bear Grillz actively promotes the adoption of Leave No Trace principles among outdoor enthusiasts and adventure seekers. Leave No Trace is a set of guidelines that encourage responsible outdoor behavior, emphasizing minimal impact on the environment. These principles include proper waste disposal, respecting wildlife and plant life, using designated trails and campsites, and leaving natural resources untouched. By spreading awareness about Leave No Trace, Bear Grillz aims to preserve the natural world for future generations to explore and enjoy.

Example: Sustainable adventure tourism Bear Grillz also supports and participates in sustainable adventure tourism initiatives that promote responsible outdoor practices. These initiatives focus on partnering with local communities and conservation organizations to develop ecologically conscious adventure experiences. For instance, Bear Grillz has collaborated with wilderness tour operators who prioritize environmental sustainability by incorporating educational components into their tours and supporting local conservation efforts. By embracing sustainable adventure tourism, Bear Grillz hopes to inspire others to experience the natural world in a way that respects and preserves its intrinsic value.

Exercises

1. Research and identify an endangered species in your local area. Create a campaign or initiative to raise awareness about its plight and encourage action for its preservation.

2. Take a weekend trip to a nearby natural park or wilderness area. Document your experience in a journal, focusing on the sounds, sights, and emotions evoked by the environment. Use your experience as inspiration to create an artistic piece, such as a poem, song, or painting.

3. Organize a local cleanup event in a natural area that has been affected by litter or pollution. Involve your community and educate them about the importance of responsible waste disposal and environmental stewardship.

4. Research and support a local conservation organization that focuses on protecting natural areas and wildlife in your region. Volunteer your time or contribute financially to their initiatives.

5. Experiment with incorporating natural sounds and ambient elements into your own creative projects, whether it's music production, photography, or writing. Explore the unique atmosphere and emotional depth that nature can bring to your art.

Resources

- Leave No Trace: www.lnt.org - International Union for Conservation of Nature (IUCN): www.iucn.org - National Parks Conservation Association: www.npca.org - Outdoor Afro: www.outdoorafro.com (organization promoting diversity and inclusion in outdoor activities)

Subsection: The Impact of Travel on Bear Grillz's Creativity

The phrase "music is a universal language" is often used to describe the power of music to transcend barriers and connect people from different cultures and backgrounds. Bear Grillz, with his worldwide fame and global tours, is a testament to this idea. In this subsection, we explore the profound impact that travel has had on Bear Grillz's creativity and his ability to connect with fans across the globe.

The Inspiration of New Environments

One of the key aspects of travel that has impacted Bear Grillz's creativity is the exposure to new environments. By visiting different countries and experiencing diverse cultures, Bear Grillz has been able to gather inspiration from a wide range of sources. The sights, sounds, and experiences he encounters while traveling have a profound effect on his creative process.

For example, imagine Bear Grillz visiting Japan for the first time. The bustling streets of Tokyo, the serene beauty of Kyoto's temples, and the vibrant nightlife in Osaka all provide a unique backdrop for Bear Grillz to draw upon in his music. From traditional Japanese instruments to modern electronic beats, the fusion of cultural influences becomes a catalyst for new musical ideas.

Cultural Immersion and Collaboration

Beyond the visual and auditory inspiration, travel allows Bear Grillz to immerse himself in different cultures and foster collaborations with local artists. By working alongside musicians from different musical backgrounds, Bear Grillz can incorporate unique elements into his sound that he may not have discovered otherwise.

For instance, during a trip to Brazil, Bear Grillz finds himself captivated by the rhythmic beats of samba and the energetic atmosphere of a local street festival. Intrigued by the fusion of electronic and traditional Brazilian music, Bear Grillz collaborates with local musicians to create a track that blends his signature sound with the vibrant spirit of Brazil. This collaboration not only enhances his creativity but also gives him a deeper appreciation for the power of music to unite people across borders.

Exploration of Sonic Landscapes

Another way travel impacts Bear Grillz's creativity is through the exploration of unique sonic landscapes. Each destination has its own distinct soundscape, from the rhythmic drums of Africa to the haunting melodies of the Middle East. By incorporating these sonic elements into his music, Bear Grillz can create a more immersive experience for his listeners.

For example, during a trip to India, Bear Grillz attends a traditional tabla performance and is mesmerized by the intricate rhythms and rich textures of the instrument. Inspired by this experience, he incorporates tabla beats into one of his tracks, adding a new layer of depth and complexity to his sound. This exploration of sonic landscapes not only expands his musical palette but also allows him to connect with fans on a global scale.

Breaking Creative Boundaries

Traveling to different parts of the world also enables Bear Grillz to break creative boundaries and challenge his own artistic limits. By immersing himself in unfamiliar environments, he is forced to adapt and explore new musical territories. This constant exploration and experimentation push Bear Grillz to evolve as an artist and continuously innovate his sound.

For instance, during a visit to Germany, Bear Grillz is exposed to the underground techno scene in Berlin. Intrigued by the raw energy and minimalistic approach of the genre, he incorporates elements of techno into his music, adding a new dimension to his sound. This willingness to step outside of his comfort zone and embrace new influences is a direct result of his travels and the diverse experiences they provide.

The Impact on Bear Grillz's Fanbase

Finally, the impact of travel on Bear Grillz's creativity extends beyond his own personal growth. By connecting with fans from different parts of the world, Bear Grillz is able to create a truly global community of music lovers. Through his music and live performances, he brings people together, transcending language barriers and cultural divides.

For instance, during a concert in Mexico, Bear Grillz is overwhelmed by the passionate response from the crowd. The energy and enthusiasm of the Mexican fans fuel his performance, inspiring him to create music that resonates with them on a deeper level. The connection he forms with his international fanbase further drives his creativity and empowers him to continue pushing the boundaries of electronic music.

In conclusion, travel plays a crucial role in Bear Grillz's creative journey. By exposing himself to new environments, immersing in different cultures, and exploring sonic landscapes, he gains inspiration, breaks creative boundaries, and fosters collaborations that have a profound impact on his music. Moreover, the connections he forms with his global fanbase serve as a constant reminder of the universal power of music. With every trip, Bear Grillz's creativity flourishes, and his music continues to captivate audiences worldwide.

Subsection: Bear Grillz's exploration of local cuisines and traditions

As Bear Grillz embarked on his global tours, one aspect he became particularly fascinated with was the local cuisines and traditions of each region he visited. Bear Grillz saw food as a gateway to understanding the culture and history of a place, and he made it a point to indulge in the local culinary delights wherever he went.

Cultural Significance of Food: Bear Grillz recognized that food holds great cultural significance. It not only nourishes the body but also reflects the identity, values, and traditions of a community. From street food to Michelin-star restaurants, Bear Grillz sought to explore the full spectrum of local cuisine, always encouraging his fans to embrace and celebrate the culinary diversity of different regions.

The Connection Between Food and Music: Bear Grillz believed that music and food are deeply interconnected, as both have the power to bring people together and evoke emotions. He often drew inspiration from the flavors, aromas, and textures he experienced during his culinary adventures, incorporating them into his music to create a multisensory experience for his fans.

Food Exploration as a Source of Inspiration: Bear Grillz's culinary experiences served as a wellspring of inspiration for his creative process. Whether it was savoring exotic spices in India or indulging in soulful street food in Mexico, Bear Grillz saw each bite as an opportunity to explore new sonic landscapes. He often sketched musical ideas while enjoying a meal, capturing the essence of each flavor and translating it into melodic and rhythmic expressions.

Collaboration with Local Chefs: To deepen his understanding of local cuisines, Bear Grillz sought out collaborations with talented local chefs. This allowed him to gain insight into traditional cooking techniques, regional ingredients, and the stories behind each dish. These collaborations went beyond the realm of food and music, fostering a creative exchange that celebrated the unique flavors of each culture.

Sustainability and Ethical Eating: Bear Grillz's passion for exploring local cuisines went hand in hand with his commitment to sustainability and ethical eating. He sought out establishments that prioritized locally sourced, organic, and ethically farmed ingredients. Through his platform, Bear Grillz advocated for conscious consumption and encouraged his fans to support businesses that shared these values.

Preserving Culinary Traditions: Bear Grillz saw the exploration of local cuisines as an opportunity to contribute to the preservation of culinary traditions. He recognized the importance of safeguarding age-old cooking techniques, traditional recipes, and ancestral knowledge. Through his music and his appreciation for local food, Bear Grillz aimed to create awareness and ensure that these invaluable cultural practices continue to thrive.

Promoting Cultural Exchange: Bear Grillz's exploration of local cuisines transcended mere enjoyment. He saw it as a means to promote cultural exchange and foster understanding between different communities. By sharing his gastronomic adventures on social media and during interviews, Bear Grillz inspired his fans to venture beyond their culinary comfort zones and embrace the diverse flavors of the world.

An Unconventional Culinary Challenge: One of Bear Grillz's most unconventional culinary challenges was his "Spice of Sound" experiment. He collaborated with a renowned chef to curate a menu where each dish was meticulously designed to evoke specific emotions and musical sensations. The tasting event featured compositions inspired by the flavors and textures of each course, creating a truly immersive experience that merged food and music in an unprecedented way.

Exploring Food as Performance Art: Bear Grillz's fascination with local cuisines extended beyond eating. He recognized the performative aspect of food preparation and presentation, often attending cooking demonstrations, food festivals, and culinary competitions. For Bear Grillz, witnessing the skill and artistry of chefs was akin to attending a live music performance, where creativity and passion merged to create a truly memorable experience.

Embracing Culinary Diversity in Music: Bear Grillz's exploration of local cuisines had a direct impact on his music. He used diverse culinary traditions as metaphors for the sonic diversity he aimed to achieve, incorporating unique sounds and instruments from different cultures into his productions. This fusion of musical and culinary diversity allowed Bear Grillz to create a truly global sound that resonated with audiences around the world.

Bear Grillz's exploration of local cuisines and traditions not only enriched his own culinary palate but also became a way for him to connect with his fans on a deeper level. Through his gastronomic adventures, he encouraged others to embrace cultural diversity, fostered creativity, and spread the message of unity through the universal languages of food and music.

Subsection: The significance of adventure in Bear Grillz's life

Adventure has always played a pivotal role in Bear Grillz's life. From his early days as a music prodigy to his current status as a global superstar, his insatiable thirst for excitement and exploration has shaped his journey both as an artist and as an individual. In this subsection, we will delve into the significance of adventure in Bear Grillz's life, exploring how it has influenced his music, his creativity, and his personal growth.

Adventure, for Bear Grillz, is not just about seeking thrills or adrenaline-pumping activities; it is a mindset, a way of life. It represents the constant pursuit of new experiences, pushing one's boundaries, and embracing the unknown. For Bear Grillz, adventure is a catalyst for inspiration, unlocking hidden reservoirs of creativity that fuel his music.

One of the ways adventure influences Bear Grillz's music is by exposing him to diverse cultures and music scenes around the world. Through his travels, he immerses himself in different environments, absorbing the unique sounds, rhythms, and melodies of each destination. Whether it's the bustling streets of Tokyo, the vibrant nightlife of Berlin, or the serene beauty of the Swiss Alps, Bear Grillz draws inspiration from these experiences, incorporating elements of these cultures into his music.

In addition to cultural immersion, adventure also pushes Bear Grillz to step outside of his comfort zone and explore new musical territories. By seeking out collaborations with artists from different genres and styles, he creates a fusion of sounds that transcends traditional boundaries. Adventure encourages him to take risks, experiment with unconventional production techniques, and challenge the status quo of electronic music.

Adventure also plays a crucial role in Bear Grillz's personal growth and self-discovery. It provides him with an escape from the pressures of fame and allows him to reconnect with his true self. Through activities such as skydiving, mountain climbing, and wilderness exploration, Bear Grillz finds solace in nature and the thrill of the unknown. These experiences ground him, reminding him of the beauty and vastness of the world beyond the confines of the music industry.

Furthermore, adventure fuels Bear Grillz's creativity by giving him the freedom to disconnect from the digital world and immerse himself in the present moment. Away from the distractions of social media and the constant demands of the industry, he can find inspiration in nature's wonders and the serenity of the great outdoors. Adventure allows him to tap into a state of flow, where ideas flow effortlessly and innovative musical concepts take shape.

However, adventure is not without its challenges. It requires Bear Grillz to step out of his comfort zone and face his fears head-on. It demands physical and mental strength, resilience, and a willingness to embrace uncertainty. Adventure teaches him valuable lessons in perseverance, adaptability, and problem-solving, skills that translate seamlessly into his music career.

To Bear Grillz, adventure is not just a means of personal growth and artistic inspiration; it is also a way to connect with his fans on a deeper level. Through his exhilarating live performances, he invites his audience to embark on a collective adventure, where boundaries are shattered, and the line between artist and listener is blurred. The energy and excitement of his shows create a shared experience, forging a strong bond between him and his fans.

In conclusion, adventure is a fundamental aspect of Bear Grillz's life, shaping his music, fueling his creativity, and driving his personal growth. It provides him with a constant source of inspiration, pushing him to explore new musical frontiers and challenge the norms of the electronic music scene. Adventure also serves as a means of self-discovery, allowing him to reconnect with his true self and find solace in the beauty of the natural world. By embracing adventure, Bear Grillz has created a unique and enduring legacy that resonates with fans around the world.

Subsection: Connecting with fans on a global scale

In today's digital age, artists have unprecedented opportunities to connect with their fans around the world. Bear Grillz has made great use of these platforms to create a strong and vibrant global fan community. Let's explore the ways in which Bear Grillz has connected with fans on a global scale.

The Power of Social Media

Social media platforms have become essential tools for artists to engage with their fan base. Bear Grillz has utilized various social media platforms, including Instagram, Twitter, and Facebook, to build a strong online presence and directly connect with fans.

Through regular posts, live streams, and behind-the-scenes content, Bear Grillz keeps fans updated on his latest projects and gives them a glimpse into his life as an artist. This level of authenticity and transparency allows fans to feel a personal connection with him, fostering a sense of loyalty and support.

Social media also provides a platform for Bear Grillz to share his music, exclusive content, and interact with fans through comments, messages, and live chats. By promptly responding to fan messages and comments, Bear Grillz shows his dedication and appreciation, further strengthening the bond he has with his global fan base.

Virtual Concerts and Livestreams

In the wake of the COVID-19 pandemic and the temporary halt on live events, Bear Grillz embraced the power of virtual concerts and livestream performances. Through platforms like Twitch, YouTube, and Facebook Live, he has been able to perform for fans in real-time, regardless of their geographic location.

These livestream events not only allow fans from all over the world to experience Bear Grillz's high-energy performances but also create an interactive space where fans can chat with each other and with Bear Grillz himself. This sense of community amplifies the shared experience and deepens the connection between the artist and his global fan base.

Fan-Driven Online Communities

The Bear Fam, as Bear Grillz's fan community is affectionately known, has become a tight-knit global network of fans who share a passion for his music and values. Beyond social media platforms, organized fan-driven online communities, such as forums and Discord servers, have emerged, allowing fans to connect with one another, share experiences, and even collaborate on various projects.

Bear Grillz actively participates in these communities, occasionally joining discussions, hosting Q&A sessions, and even collaborating with fans on music-related endeavors. By actively engaging in these online spaces, Bear Grillz fosters a sense of inclusivity and belonging, making his fans feel like an important part of his journey.

Personalized Experiences

Bear Grillz values the personal connection he has with his fans and seeks to create memorable experiences for them. Special meet-and-greet sessions, backstage passes, and fan events have been organized to provide fans with an opportunity to meet Bear Grillz in person and express their support.

Additionally, Bear Grillz has gone above and beyond to acknowledge the contributions and dedication of his fans. From featuring fan-created artwork and content on his social media profiles to dedicating songs during performances, Bear Grillz ensures that his fans feel seen and appreciated.

The Global Impact

Bear Grillz's efforts to connect with fans on a global scale have resulted in a devoted and passionate fan base that spans across continents. The Bear Fam represents a diverse group of individuals brought together by their love for Bear Grillz's music and the positive energy he brings. This global community has been instrumental in spreading his music, organizing fan-led initiatives, and even supporting charitable causes championed by Bear Grillz.

Through his music and interaction with fans, Bear Grillz has fostered a sense of unity and inclusivity, transcending geographical boundaries. He has proven that music truly has the power to bring people together, regardless of their background or location.

In Summary

Bear Grillz has mastered the art of connecting with fans on a global scale. From social media engagement to virtual concerts, active involvement in fan communities, personalized experiences, and fostering a sense of global community, Bear Grillz has created an environment where fans feel valued, heard, and inspired. His efforts have demonstrated the true potential of technology and social platforms in building meaningful connections and growing a passionate global fan base.

So, whether you're following Bear Grillz on Instagram, attending virtual concerts, or engaging with the Bear Fam online, you too can be a part of the global community that celebrates Bear Grillz's music and values. Join the Bear Fam and discover the power of music to connect people from all corners of the world.

Subsection: Bear Grillz's role as a cultural ambassador

Bear Grillz, not only known for his incredible music and electrifying performances, but also for his unparalleled ability to connect with people from various cultures and backgrounds. As a cultural ambassador, Bear Grillz has taken on the responsibility of promoting unity, understanding, and acceptance among his fans and the world at large. Through his music and philanthropic endeavors, he has become a symbol of positivity, inspiration, and change.

As a cultural ambassador, Bear Grillz uses his platform to bridge the gap between different cultures and foster a sense of global unity. He recognizes the power of music as a universal language that transcends barriers and brings people together. Through his melodic beats and captivating performances, Bear Grillz creates an atmosphere of inclusivity and celebration. His infectious energy and genuine love for music resonate with fans worldwide, promoting a sense of belonging and acceptance.

But Bear Grillz's role goes beyond just the music. He actively engages with various cultures and communities, embracing their traditions, values, and art forms. By collaborating with artists from diverse backgrounds, he not only expands his musical horizons but also introduces his audience to different perspectives and styles of music. These collaborations serve as powerful demonstrations of cultural exchange and promote a deeper understanding of the richness and diversity of our world.

One way Bear Grillz showcases his commitment to cultural ambassadorship is through his involvement in charitable projects and social initiatives. He uses his influence and resources to support causes related to environmental conservation, mental health awareness, and social justice. By actively participating in these projects, Bear Grillz demonstrates his dedication to making a positive difference in the world. His philanthropic efforts inspire his fans to get involved and contribute to causes that align with their own values, thus creating a ripple effect of positivity and change.

Another aspect of Bear Grillz's role as a cultural ambassador is his dedication to spreading a message of love, unity, and acceptance. He uses his music to challenge stereotypes and break down barriers in the music industry, advocating for greater diversity and representation. Through his infectious positivity and genuine interactions with fans, Bear Grillz encourages an atmosphere of respect and understanding. He embraces his role as a role model and mentor to aspiring artists, providing guidance and support to help them navigate the challenges of the industry.

Bear Grillz has also made it a priority to give back to his fanbase, who he affectionately refers to as the "Bear Fam." He recognizes the unwavering support and love from his fans and, in return, seeks to create a community built on shared values and mutual appreciation. Through fan events, meet-ups, and online interactions, Bear Grillz connects directly with his fans, fostering a sense of belonging and connection. The Bear Fam represents a diverse group of individuals who share a common love for music, positivity, and making a difference in the world.

In conclusion, Bear Grillz's role as a cultural ambassador extends far beyond his music. Through his music, collaborations, philanthropic endeavors, and interaction with fans, he promotes unity, acceptance, and positive change on a global scale. Bear Grillz's dedication to cultural ambassadorship serves as an inspiration to artists and fans alike, demonstrating the power of music to transcend boundaries and create a more inclusive and compassionate world. As he continues on his journey, Bear Grillz's influence as a cultural ambassador will undoubtedly leave a lasting impact on the music industry and the world.

Section 4: Unexpected Encounters and Collaborations

Surprising encounters with fellow musicians

One of the incredible aspects of Bear Grillz's journey has been the numerous surprising encounters he had with fellow musicians along the way. These chance meetings and unexpected collaborations have not only shaped his career but also enriched the electronic music landscape as a whole.

The hotel lobby encounter

In the early years of Bear Grillz's rise to fame, he found himself staying at a luxurious hotel in Los Angeles while attending a music conference. As he made his way through the lobby, he noticed a familiar face sitting alone at the bar. It was none other than Skrillex, one of the most influential figures in the dubstep scene.

Overcoming his initial intimidation, Bear Grillz approached Skrillex and struck up a conversation. To his surprise, Skrillex was not only friendly and down-to-earth but also expressed genuine interest in Bear Grillz's music. They spent the evening exchanging stories and ideas, leading to a collaboration that would later become a chart-topping hit.

This encounter taught Bear Grillz an invaluable lesson about the power of networking and seizing opportunities. It reinforced the idea that even the most successful artists are often open to connecting with aspiring talents and can provide the necessary guidance and support.

The chance meeting at a festival

Another remarkable encounter occurred during a massive electronic music festival in Las Vegas. Bear Grillz was performing on one of the main stages, pumping up the crowd with his high-energy set. As he wrapped up his performance, he noticed a familiar face in the backstage area—Deadmau5, the iconic DJ and producer.

Bear Grillz had been a huge fan of Deadmau5's work since his early days in music production. The mere presence of Deadmau5 sent waves of excitement and nervousness through Bear Grillz as he approached the electronic music icon. To his surprise, Deadmau5 recognized Bear Grillz and praised his performance.

The unexpected encounter sparked a conversation between the two artists, leading to an invitation from Deadmau5 to collaborate on a track for an upcoming project. Bear Grillz couldn't believe his luck, as Deadmau5 was known for being selective with his collaborations. This encounter not only solidified Bear Grillz's presence in the industry but also propelled his career to new heights.

The impromptu studio session

One of the most memorable encounters Bear Grillz had was with a fellow producer during a visit to London. While exploring the vibrant street art scene in Shoreditch, he stumbled upon a hidden recording studio tucked away in an alley.

Curiosity piqued, Bear Grillz decided to venture inside. To his surprise, he found himself face to face with Disclosure, the Grammy-nominated electronic music duo. They were in the midst of a late-night recording session and welcomed Bear Grillz with open arms.

The impromptu collaboration that followed was nothing short of magical. Bear Grillz's heavy, bass-driven style blended seamlessly with Disclosure's melodically rich soundscapes. The result was a genre-defying track that showcased Bear Grillz's versatility as an artist and earned him critical acclaim.

This unexpected encounter taught Bear Grillz the importance of embracing spontaneity and seizing every opportunity that comes his way. It also reinforced the idea that creativity knows no boundaries and that collaborations can arise in the most unlikely of places.

The backstage encounter at a major festival

During a performance at one of the world's biggest electronic music festivals, Bear Grillz found himself sharing the backstage area with a legendary DJ and producer, Fatboy Slim. Having admired Fatboy Slim's music for years, Bear Grillz couldn't help but feel a mix of excitement and nervousness.

To his surprise, Fatboy Slim approached Bear Grillz, complimenting him on his unique sound and high-octane performance. They spent the next few hours exchanging stories and discussing their shared passion for music. This encounter led to a mentorship dynamic, where Fatboy Slim provided guidance to Bear Grillz on navigating the music industry and dealing with the challenges of fame.

This unexpected encounter underscored the importance of connecting with established artists and mentors who can provide invaluable insights and encouragement. It also highlighted the power of admiration and mutual respect in fostering meaningful relationships within the music community.

The collaboration with an unexpected genre

One of the most surprising encounters Bear Grillz had was with an artist from a completely different genre. While attending a music awards ceremony, he crossed paths with a renowned hip-hop producer known for his hard-hitting beats and catchy hooks.

The two struck up a conversation, fascinated by each other's musical backgrounds and influences. They soon realized that their unique styles could blend together seamlessly. This unexpected collaboration resulted in a track that fused heavy bass drops with infectious hip-hop rhythms, instantly resonating with fans from both genres.

This collaboration showcased Bear Grillz's willingness to step outside his comfort zone and explore new musical territories. It also demonstrated the power of crossing genre boundaries and the potential for artists from different genres to create something truly groundbreaking.

Conclusion

The surprising encounters Bear Grillz had with fellow musicians have not only shaped his career but also left an indelible mark on the electronic music landscape. From chance meetings in hotel lobbies to impromptu collaborations in recording studios, these encounters have taught Bear Grillz the importance of networking, seizing opportunities, embracing spontaneity, and stepping outside his comfort zone.

Beyond personal gain, these collaborations have sparked innovation and pushed the boundaries of electronic music. They have shown that unexpected connections can lead to groundbreaking tracks that resonate with a diverse range of fans. While Bear Grillz's career is a testament to his talent and hard work, these surprising encounters have undoubtedly played a significant role in his success.

Subsection: Collaborations outside the electronic music realm

Music is a universal language that transcends boundaries and brings people together. Bear Grillz is no stranger to this concept, as he has expanded his creative horizons by collaborating outside the electronic music realm. These unique collaborations have allowed Bear Grillz to showcase his versatility as an artist and explore new musical territories. In this subsection, we will explore some of Bear Grillz's most noteworthy collaborations outside the electronic music genre, showcasing the diversity of his artistic vision.

Breaking Down Musical Barriers

Bear Grillz has never been one to conform to musical norms and has always sought to blend different genres together. One of the most remarkable collaborations outside the electronic music realm was his partnership with a renowned jazz ensemble. In this collaboration, Bear Grillz combined his signature bass-heavy beats with the improvisational skills of the jazz musicians. The result was an exhilarating fusion of electronic and jazz elements, creating a completely new sound that pushed the boundaries of both genres. This collaboration not only displayed Bear Grillz's musical versatility but also demonstrated his ability to adapt and work with musicians from diverse backgrounds.

Exploring World Music Influences

Another example of Bear Grillz's collaborations outside the electronic music realm involved working with traditional world music artists. By teaming up with musicians from various cultural backgrounds, Bear Grillz was able to infuse his electronic sound with elements of traditional music from different parts of the world. One collaboration in particular involved incorporating Indian classical instrumentation and rhythms into Bear Grillz's tracks. This unique blend of electronic music and Indian classical elements created a captivating and mesmerizing sonic experience, showcasing the universality of music and its ability to bridge cultural gaps.

Collaborative Experimentation

Bear Grillz's collaborations outside the electronic music realm also include partnerships with experimental musicians and avant-garde composers. By embracing the avant-garde nature of these collaborations, Bear Grillz pushed the boundaries of his own artistic expression and explored unconventional soundscapes. These collaborations often involved the use of unconventional instruments, intricate sound design techniques, and experimental production methods. The resulting music challenged listeners and pushed them to think outside the box, blurring the lines between genres and defying traditional conventions.

Expanding Musical Perspectives

Collaborating with artists from different musical backgrounds allowed Bear Grillz to gain fresh insights and perspectives. By stepping out of the electronic music bubble, Bear Grillz was exposed to new musical approaches and techniques. He was able to incorporate these learnings into his own music, further expanding his creative palette. This cross-pollination of ideas and influences enriched Bear Grillz's sound and contributed to his growth as an artist.

Embracing the Power of Collaboration

The collaborations Bear Grillz ventured into outside the electronic music realm were not only about the fusion of different genres but also about the shared creative process. Collaborations offer a space for artists to learn from one another, challenge their own artistic boundaries, and create something truly unique. By collaborating with artists from various backgrounds, Bear Grillz embraced the power of collaboration and the endless possibilities that arise when diverse minds come together.

Example: Collaboration with a Hip-Hop Artist

One notable example of Bear Grillz's collaboration outside the electronic music realm is his partnership with a prominent hip-hop artist. This collaboration brought together the hard-hitting beats of Bear Grillz's electronic sound and the lyrical prowess of the hip-hop artist. The resulting track was a seamless blend of electronic and hip-hop elements, creating a catchy and energetic anthem that resonated with fans across both genres.

Resources for Exploring Collaborative Opportunities

For aspiring artists looking to explore collaborations outside their comfort zones, there are various resources available. Online platforms, such as music networking websites and forums, offer opportunities to connect with artists from different genres and backgrounds. Attending music festivals and industry events can also provide a space for artists to meet and connect with potential collaborators. Additionally, reaching out to artists directly through social media or their management teams can lead to fruitful collaborations.

Exercise: Exploring Collaborative Possibilities

Take a moment to reflect on your own musical interests and genres that you are passionate about. Identify a genre outside of electronic music that you would like to explore and find an artist or musician in that genre that resonates with you. Reach out to them and propose a collaboration project, highlighting your shared passions and the unique sound you believe you can create together. Embrace the opportunity to step outside your comfort zone and see where this collaboration takes your music.

In conclusion, Bear Grillz's collaborations outside the electronic music realm have allowed him to showcase his versatility, embrace new perspectives, and create groundbreaking music that transcends genres. By breaking down musical barriers, exploring world music influences, engaging in collaborative experimentation, and embracing the power of collaboration, Bear Grillz has broadened his artistic horizons and left an indelible impact on the music landscape. Aspiring artists can draw inspiration from his fearless approach to collaboration and explore the vast possibilities that lie beyond the boundaries of their own genre. It is through these cross-genre collaborations that the true magic of music unfolds.

Subsection: Unique musical partnerships

One of the defining aspects of Bear Grillz's career has been his ability to form unique and unexpected musical partnerships. Throughout his journey, Bear Grillz has collaborated with artists from a wide range of genres, pushing the boundaries of electronic music and creating innovative sounds. These collaborations have not only expanded Bear Grillz's artistic horizons, but they have also brought together diverse fan bases and helped to bridge the gaps between different musical communities. In this subsection, we will explore some of Bear Grillz's most memorable and influential musical partnerships, showcasing the power of collaboration in the world of music.

Collaboration with a classical orchestra

One of Bear Grillz's most unconventional and awe-inspiring collaborations was a joint performance with a classical orchestra. This partnership brought together the raw energy and intensity of Bear Grillz's electronic music with the timeless elegance and sophistication of a full orchestra. The result was a truly immersive and unforgettable experience for the audience, with the traditional orchestral instruments blending seamlessly with Bear Grillz's hard-hitting bass and electronic beats. This collaboration not only showcased Bear Grillz's ability to push the boundaries of his own genre but also demonstrated the versatility and adaptability of classical music.

Fusion of hip-hop and electronic music

Another significant partnership in Bear Grillz's career was his collaboration with a prominent hip-hop artist. This collaboration brought together the hard-hitting beats and rhymes of hip-hop with Bear Grillz's heavy bass drops and electronic soundscapes. The fusion of these two genres created a new and exciting musical landscape that resonated with fans from both hip-hop and electronic music backgrounds. It showcased the power of cross-genre collaborations to break down barriers and bring different communities of fans together.

Experimental collaboration with an indie band

One of the most adventurous and forward-thinking partnerships in Bear Grillz's discography was his collaboration with an indie band. This collaboration pushed the boundaries of electronic music by incorporating live instrumentation and organic textures into Bear Grillz's signature sound. The combination of the band's indie sensibilities and Bear Grillz's electronic production created a unique sonic experience that blurred the lines between genres. This collaboration not only showcased Bear Grillz's willingness to explore new musical territories but also highlighted the power of collaboration in fostering innovation and creativity.

Cross-cultural collaboration with world musicians

Bear Grillz's commitment to global unity and cultural exchange was exemplified through his collaborations with world musicians. These collaborations brought together different musical traditions and cultural perspectives, resulting in a rich tapestry of sounds and styles. By embracing the diversity of world music and collaborating with artists from different cultural backgrounds, Bear Grillz aimed to create a space where people from all walks of life could come together and celebrate their shared love for music. These partnerships not only enriched Bear Grillz's own artistic vision but also allowed his fans to experience the beauty and richness of different musical traditions.

Collaboration with an environmental activist

Bear Grillz's passion for environmental conservation was reflected in his collaboration with a prominent environmental activist. This partnership aimed to use the power of music to raise awareness about environmental issues and inspire positive change. Through their collaboration, Bear Grillz and the activist created a powerful anthem that called for action on climate change and encouraged listeners to become advocates for the planet. This unique and impactful collaboration demonstrated the ability of music to transcend entertainment and become a force for social and environmental activism.

Unconventional collaboration with a poet

In one of his most unconventional collaborations, Bear Grillz teamed up with a renowned poet to create a thought-provoking and emotionally charged piece of music. This collaboration merged the power of spoken word poetry with Bear Grillz's atmospheric soundscapes, resulting in a truly unique and captivating sonic experience. The collaboration allowed Bear Grillz to explore a new dimension of storytelling through his music, while also giving the poet's words a new sonic context. This partnership showcased the boundless possibilities of collaboration in music and the transformative power of merging different artistic disciplines.

In conclusion, Bear Grillz's unique musical partnerships have not only expanded the boundaries of electronic music but also brought together diverse fan bases and fostered creative and innovative collaborations. From collaborating with a classical orchestra to joining forces with hip-hop artists, indie bands, world musicians, environmental activists, and poets, Bear Grillz has shown the power of collaboration in creating fresh sounds and pushing the limits of music. These partnerships have not only enriched Bear Grillz's own artistic journey but have also left a lasting impact on the electronic music community and beyond.

Behind-the-scenes of recording collaborations

In the world of music, collaborations between artists can often lead to the creation of unique and groundbreaking tracks that capture the essence of both individual styles. Behind-the-scenes of recording collaborations, there are intricate processes and creative decisions that shape the final outcome. In this subsection, we will delve into the fascinating world of recording collaborations, exploring the dynamics between artists, the challenges they face, and the techniques they employ to bring their visions to life.

The Art of Collaboration

Collaborating with other artists is an art in itself. It requires a delicate balance of creative input, mutual respect, and a shared vision. When artists come together to create a collaborative track, they bring their individual strengths and artistic sensibilities to the table. The process begins with a meeting of minds, where ideas are exchanged, and a common direction is established.

One of the key aspects of successful collaborations is finding the right chemistry between artists. This involves not only understanding each other's musical styles but also building a personal connection. Artists may spend time getting to know each other on a personal level, sharing stories, and exploring common interests. This creates a foundation of trust and understanding, allowing them to work together seamlessly.

Establishing Roles and Responsibilities

Once the creative vision is set, artists need to establish clear roles and responsibilities to ensure a smooth workflow. This involves dividing tasks such as songwriting, production, and arrangement, based on each artist's expertise. For example, one artist may excel at crafting melodies and lyrics, while another may bring a strong production and sound design background.

In some cases, artists may choose to work together simultaneously in the studio, bouncing ideas off each other in real-time. This allows for spontaneous creativity and immediate feedback. Alternatively, artists may work remotely, exchanging files and ideas digitally. This method offers the flexibility to work in different time zones and allows for focused individual work before regrouping to refine and polish the collaborative piece.

Crafting a Unique Sound

Collaborations often aim to create a sound that is distinct from the individual artists' solo work. This requires experimentation and pushing boundaries to find a blend of styles that is fresh and captivating. Artists may explore new genres, combine diverse musical elements, or revisit familiar genres with a unique twist.

During the recording process, artists may experiment with different instruments, effects, and production techniques to achieve the desired sonic palette. This could involve layering and stacking different sounds, manipulating samples, or employing unconventional recording methods. The goal is to create a cohesive sonic landscape that showcases the artistic synergy between collaborators.

Addressing Creative Differences

Collaborations can also present challenges in the form of creative differences. When artists have different visions and artistic sensibilities, conflicts may arise. Navigating these differences requires open and honest communication, as well as a willingness to compromise. Artists must be open to embracing new ideas and perspectives while still maintaining their artistic integrity.

One effective strategy for addressing creative differences is to find a middle ground that both artists can agree on. This may involve blending elements of their respective styles or taking turns to contribute to different sections of the track. The key is to find a balance that showcases the unique strengths of each artist while creating a cohesive and harmonious final product.

Examples of Successful Collaborations

Throughout the history of music, there have been numerous successful collaborations that have left a lasting impact on the industry. One such example is the collaboration between electronic music producers Skrillex and Diplo, known as Jack Ü. Their collaborative track "Where Are Ü Now" featuring Justin Bieber became a global hit, fusing pop, EDM, and R&B elements to create a fresh and infectious sound.

Another notable collaboration is the iconic duet between Freddie Mercury and David Bowie on the track "Under Pressure." The song beautifully showcases the synergy between the two artists, blending their distinct vocal styles and delivering a powerful and emotionally charged performance.

In the realm of hip-hop, the collaboration between Jay-Z and Kanye West on the album "Watch the Throne" demonstrated the power of two creative powerhouses coming together. The album featured thought-provoking lyrics, innovative production, and a dynamic interplay between the two artists, resulting in a critically acclaimed and commercially successful release.

The Future of Recording Collaborations

As technology continues to evolve, recording collaborations are becoming more accessible and diverse. Artists can now collaborate remotely, bridging geographical barriers and cultural differences. Virtual collaboration platforms allow artists to work together, even if they are in different parts of the world. This opens up endless possibilities for cross-cultural collaborations and the exploration of new sonic landscapes.

Additionally, emerging technologies such as virtual reality (VR) and augmented reality (AR) are also revolutionizing the way collaborations are conducted. Artists can now immerse themselves in virtual studios, using VR and AR tools to visualize and manipulate sounds in three-dimensional space. This creates a more immersive and interactive collaborative experience, pushing the boundaries of creativity.

In conclusion, recording collaborations are a dynamic and ever-evolving process that brings together the talents and visions of multiple artists. By establishing roles, exploring new sonic territories, addressing creative differences, and embracing new technologies, collaborations can result in groundbreaking music that resonates with audiences worldwide. The art of collaboration is an essential element in the growth and progression of the music industry, allowing artists to push boundaries and create innovative music that stands the test of time.

Subsection: The impact of unexpected collaborations on Bear Grillz's sound

Collaborations in the music industry have always been a powerful catalyst for innovation and artistic growth. When artists from different backgrounds and genres come together, the result is often a fusion of ideas and styles that pushes boundaries and creates something entirely new. For Bear Grillz, unexpected collaborations have played a significant role in shaping his unique sound and contributing to his evolution as an artist.

One of the key impacts of unexpected collaborations on Bear Grillz's sound is the infusion of diverse musical elements. When collaborating with artists from different genres, he has the opportunity to experiment with new sounds, rhythms, and melodies that he may not have explored on his own. This infusion of diverse musical elements adds depth and complexity to his tracks, pushing the boundaries of his musical style and keeping his sound fresh and exciting.

In an unexpected collaboration with a renowned jazz musician, Bear Grillz was able to incorporate live jazz instrumentation into one of his tracks. By combining his signature bass-heavy sound with the vibrant and improvisational nature of jazz, he created a track that seamlessly fused elements of electronic music and jazz, resulting in a unique and captivating sound. This collaboration not only expanded Bear Grillz's musical horizons but also introduced his fans to a new genre and showcased his versatility as an artist.

Another impact of unexpected collaborations is the exploration of new tempos and rhythms. When collaborating with artists who specialize in different styles, Bear Grillz has the opportunity to experiment with unconventional time signatures and complex rhythms. This experimentation challenges him to break away from traditional electronic music structures and create tracks that are rhythmically innovative and engaging.

For instance, in a collaboration with a renowned drum and bass producer, Bear Grillz incorporated high-energy drum patterns and intricate basslines into his track. This unexpected collaboration pushed him to explore faster tempos and more intricate rhythm programming, resulting in a track that seamlessly combined elements of drum and bass with his signature Bearstep sound. This collaboration not only brought a fresh sound to his music but also expanded his fan base to include fans of the drum and bass genre.

Unexpected collaborations also enable Bear Grillz to explore different lyrical themes and concepts. When collaborating with artists who have a unique storytelling approach or a distinct lyrical style, he is able to expand his lyrical repertoire and explore new themes in his music.

For example, in a collaboration with a renowned hip-hop artist, Bear Grillz delved into introspective and socially conscious lyrics, addressing issues such as social inequality and political unrest. This unexpected collaboration brought a new depth and substance to his music, and allowed him to connect with his audience on a more profound level. The lyrics explored in this collaboration opened up a new avenue of storytelling for Bear Grillz and showcased his ability to tackle important social issues through his music.

Furthermore, unexpected collaborations provide Bear Grillz with opportunities to experiment with different production techniques and approaches. When collaborating with artists who have a unique production style, he has the chance to learn new techniques and incorporate them into his own production process.

For instance, in a collaboration with a renowned electronic music producer known for his intricate sound design, Bear Grillz delved into new production techniques and explored innovative ways of creating textures and sonic atmospheres. This unexpected collaboration influenced his own production style, allowing him to add a new layer of complexity and depth to his tracks.

In addition to these artistic impacts, unexpected collaborations also have practical implications for Bear Grillz's career. Collaborations with established artists often bring exposure to new audiences and expand his reach beyond his existing fan base. This exposure leads to increased recognition and opportunities for growth, such as performances at larger festivals and collaborations with high-profile artists.

To maximize the impact of unexpected collaborations, Bear Grillz emphasizes open-mindedness and a willingness to step out of his comfort zone. By embracing the opportunity to work with artists from different backgrounds and genres, he ensures that each collaboration is a true collaboration, where both artists contribute their unique perspectives and talents. This approach not only fosters creative synergy but also allows for the creation of truly innovative and boundary-pushing music.

In summary, unexpected collaborations have a profound impact on Bear Grillz's sound, bringing diverse musical elements, new tempos and rhythms, unique lyrical themes, and innovative production techniques to his music. These collaborations have not only expanded his artistic horizons but also provided him with new avenues for growth and exposure. By embracing unexpected collaborations, Bear Grillz has been able to keep his music fresh and exciting, continually pushing the boundaries of his genre and leaving a lasting impact on the electronic music scene.

Subsection: Bear Grillz's approach to collaboration and creative synergy

Collaboration is at the heart of Bear Grillz's creative process. He believes that working with other artists brings fresh ideas, diverse perspectives, and a sense of shared energy that elevates his music. Bear Grillz understands that collaboration is not just about combining talents, but also about forming a connection and building a strong relationship with fellow musicians. In this subsection, we will explore Bear Grillz's approach to collaboration and how he fosters creative synergy with his collaborators.

The Importance of Mutual Respect and Trust

For Bear Grillz, collaboration begins with mutual respect and trust. He believes that every artist brings their own unique strengths and experiences to the table, and it is crucial to recognize and appreciate these contributions. By creating a safe and supportive environment, Bear Grillz ensures that everyone involved feels comfortable expressing their ideas and exploring new creative avenues.

Bear Grillz values open communication and believes in the power of constructive feedback. He encourages his collaborators to share their thoughts and opinions, knowing that a healthy exchange of ideas can lead to new and exciting musical directions. By building a foundation of trust and respect, Bear Grillz establishes a collaborative space where all voices are heard and valued.

Finding Common Ground and Complementary Styles

When collaborating with other artists, Bear Grillz seeks to find common ground and explore the intersection of musical styles. He understands that bringing together different genres and influences can create a unique and captivating sound. By blending elements from various musical backgrounds, Bear Grillz's collaborations often transcend traditional genre boundaries, resulting in a fresh and innovative sound.

Bear Grillz also emphasizes the importance of complementary styles. He actively seeks out artists whose strengths and creative visions align with his own. By finding collaborators who can bring something new and different to the table, Bear Grillz ensures that his music continues to evolve and push boundaries.

Embracing Diversity and Inclusion

Diversity and inclusion are significant aspects of Bear Grillz's collaboration philosophy. He recognizes the power of incorporating a wide range of perspectives and experiences in his music. Bear Grillz actively seeks out collaborations with artists from diverse backgrounds, showcasing their unique talents and amplifying their voices.

By embracing diversity, Bear Grillz creates an environment where artists from different cultures, genders, and backgrounds can collaborate and share their stories. This commitment to inclusivity enriches his music and contributes to a more vibrant and representative electronic music scene.

Emphasizing a Shared Vision and Goals

Collaboration thrives when there is a shared vision and common goals among all parties involved. Bear Grillz believes in setting clear objectives and aligning creative visions with his collaborators. By establishing a unified direction from the beginning, he ensures that everyone is working towards a common outcome.

Bear Grillz understands that collaboration is not just about creating great music together but also about fostering personal and professional growth. He encourages his collaborators to bring their unique perspectives and ideas to the table, knowing that the collective effort will result in something greater than the sum of its parts.

Balancing Individuality and Collective Creativity

While collaboration is vital to Bear Grillz's creative process, he also recognizes the importance of balancing individuality with collective creativity. He believes that each artist brings their own unique voice and style, which should be honored and celebrated.

Bear Grillz encourages his collaborators to retain their individuality while working towards a shared goal. He understands that true creative synergy can only be achieved when artists feel free to express themselves authentically. By embracing and nurturing the individuality of his collaborators, Bear Grillz creates a collaborative space where creativity can flourish.

Unconventional Collaborations and Breaking Boundaries

Bear Grillz is known for his willingness to explore unconventional collaborations and break genre boundaries. He believes that innovation often arises from unexpected pairings and combinations. By pushing the limits of electronic music and embracing diverse influences, Bear Grillz challenges the status quo and paves the way for new possibilities.

From collaborating with artists outside of the electronic music realm to infusing his tracks with unexpected elements, Bear Grillz consistently pushes the boundaries of his sound. His willingness to take risks and explore new creative territories sets him apart and inspires other artists to do the same.

Maximizing Collaborative Potential

To maximize the collaborative potential, Bear Grillz employs various strategies throughout the creative process. He promotes active listening, ensuring that each collaborator has a chance to share their ideas and be heard. By valuing input from all parties involved, Bear Grillz fosters an environment of shared ownership and collaboration.

Bear Grillz also encourages experimentation and encourages his collaborators to push their creative limits. He believes that taking risks and trying new things is essential for artistic growth. By creating an atmosphere of exploration and discovery, Bear Grillz pushes his collaborators to new heights and pushes the boundaries of electronic music.

Real-world Example: Collaboration with Artist X

To illustrate Bear Grillz's approach to collaboration, let's look at a real-world example of his partnership with fellow artist X. Artist X is known for their unique blend of hip-hop and jazz, while Bear Grillz is renowned for his signature Bearstep sound. Their collaboration aims to bring together these distinct styles and create something entirely new.

At the initial stage of their collaboration, Bear Grillz and Artist X sit down to discuss their creative vision and objectives. They identify shared musical influences and explore ways to merge their styles seamlessly. Bear Grillz values Artist X's expertise in jazz and hip-hop and believes that this collaboration can introduce new elements and dimensions to his music.

Throughout the collaboration process, Bear Grillz and Artist X maintain open lines of communication. They actively exchange feedback and work closely together to develop the unique sound that combines elements of Bearstep, jazz, and hip-hop. By leveraging their individual strengths and bringing their respective styles to the table, Bear Grillz and Artist X create a collaborative synergy that results in a groundbreaking track.

In conclusion, Bear Grillz approaches collaboration with a deep respect for his collaborators, an open mindset towards diversity and inclusion, and a focus on a shared vision and goals. He embraces individuality while fostering collective creativity, pushing boundaries and exploring unconventional collaborations. Bear Grillz's approach to collaboration and creative synergy serves as a testament to his commitment to artistic growth and pushing the boundaries of electronic music.

Subsection: The influence of diverse perspectives on Bear Grillz's music

Diverse perspectives have always played a crucial role in shaping the music industry, and Bear Grillz is no exception. His music is a testament to the power of incorporating different influences and ideas into one's creative process. In this subsection, we will explore how diverse perspectives have influenced Bear Grillz's music, from collaborating with artists from different genres to embracing cultural diversity in his sound.

One of the key ways diverse perspectives have influenced Bear Grillz's music is through collaborations with artists from various genres. By working with artists outside of the electronic music realm, Bear Grillz has been able to infuse his signature sound with fresh ideas and styles. For example, his collaboration with a well-known hip-hop artist brought elements of rap and trap into his music, creating a unique blend that resonated with fans from both genres. This collaboration not only expanded Bear Grillz's audience but also pushed the boundaries of electronic music, showcasing the genre's versatility.

In addition to collaborating with artists from different genres, Bear Grillz has also embraced cultural diversity in his music. By drawing inspiration from various cultures and incorporating their musical elements, he has created a sound that appeals to a wide range of listeners. This inclusivity is evident in his use of traditional instruments and melodies from different parts of the world, seamlessly blending them with electronic beats and basslines. Through his music, Bear Grillz celebrates the richness and diversity of cultures, fostering a sense of unity and acceptance among his fans.

Diverse perspectives have also influenced Bear Grillz's music in terms of production techniques and sonic experimentation. By embracing different production styles and techniques, he has been able to create a distinct sound that sets him apart from other artists in the electronic music scene. For instance, his exploration of unconventional rhythms and unique sound design elements has led to the development of what is now known as the "Bearstep" genre. This genre incorporates elements of dubstep, drum and bass, and trap, creating a high-energy and dynamic sound that is instantly recognizable as Bear Grillz's own.

Furthermore, diverse perspectives have influenced Bear Grillz's lyrics and storytelling. By drawing inspiration from a wide range of experiences and perspectives, he has been able to craft meaningful and relatable narratives in his songs. Whether it's exploring themes of love, loss, or societal issues, Bear Grillz's lyrics resonate with his audience on a deep emotional level. By infusing his music with personal experiences and diverse perspectives, he creates a powerful connection with his listeners, fostering a sense of empathy and understanding.

It is worth noting that diverse perspectives have not only influenced Bear Grillz's music but also his approach to the industry as a whole. He actively supports up-and-coming artists from underrepresented backgrounds, providing platforms for them to showcase their talent and amplify their voices. By championing diversity and inclusivity in the music industry, Bear Grillz is paving the way for a more equitable and representative future.

In conclusion, diverse perspectives have had a profound influence on Bear Grillz's music. Through collaborations with artists from different genres, embracing cultural diversity, incorporating unconventional production techniques, and drawing on diverse experiences for his lyrics, Bear Grillz has created a unique and innovative sound. By embracing diverse perspectives, he not only pushes the boundaries of electronic music but also fosters a sense of unity and acceptance among his fans. The influence of diverse perspectives on Bear Grillz's music serves as a powerful reminder of the importance of inclusivity and the positive impact it can have on the creative process.

Subsection: Collaborative processes and studio dynamics

Collaboration is a key element in the music production process, especially for artists like Bear Grillz who constantly seek out fresh perspectives and innovative ideas. In this subsection, we will explore the collaborative processes and studio dynamics that have shaped Bear Grillz's music and led to his success.

Collaboration begins with finding the right partners to work with. Bear Grillz's approach is to seek out artists who bring something unique to the table, whether it be their musical style, production techniques, or creative vision. He values diversity and believes that collaborations should be an opportunity to learn and grow as an artist.

Once a collaboration is established, the studio becomes a creative space where ideas can flow freely. Bear Grillz believes in open communication and encourages a collaborative atmosphere where everyone's input is valued. This fosters a sense of ownership and investment in the project, leading to a more cohesive and inspired end result.

One of the challenges of collaboration is maintaining a balance between creative freedom and compromise. Bear Grillz understands that each collaborator brings their own artistic vision and it is essential to respect and incorporate their ideas into the final product. This requires effective communication, active listening, and a willingness to let go of ego in order to serve the best interests of the music.

Studio dynamics play a crucial role in the collaborative process. Bear Grillz believes in creating a positive and supportive environment where every individual feels comfortable expressing their ideas and taking creative risks. He emphasizes the importance of building trust and fostering a sense of camaraderie among collaborators, as this enhances the quality of the music and creates a memorable experience.

Problems may arise during the collaborative process, such as conflicting ideas or creative differences. Bear Grillz encourages open dialogue and constructive criticism as a means to resolve these challenges. By offering feedback in a respectful and constructive manner, artists can find common ground and work towards a shared vision.

To illustrate the collaborative processes and studio dynamics, let's consider a hypothetical example. Bear Grillz decides to collaborate with a rising star producer known for their unique sound design skills. The two artists come together in the studio and begin exchanging ideas and exploring different sonic possibilities.

During the production process, they encounter a challenging moment where they have conflicting opinions on the direction of a particular section in the track. Bear Grillz suggests trying a different arrangement while the producer strongly believes in their original idea.

To overcome this creative hurdle, Bear Grillz proposes a compromise. They agree to incorporate elements from both ideas, creating a hybrid arrangement that combines the best aspects of each suggestion. Through open conversation and mutual respect, they find a solution that satisfies both parties and enhances the overall quality of the track.

This example demonstrates how effective collaboration requires a willingness to listen, compromise, and find common ground. It also highlights the importance of trust and respect in maintaining a healthy studio dynamic.

In addition to collaboration within the studio, external factors also play a role in the collaborative process. Bear Grillz understands the value of networking and building connections within the music industry. By actively seeking out opportunities to collaborate with established artists, Bear Grillz has been able to expand his reach and attract new fans.

In conclusion, collaborative processes and studio dynamics are integral to Bear Grillz's music production. By valuing diversity, maintaining open communication, and fostering a positive and supportive environment, Bear Grillz has been able to create powerful and innovative music through collaboration. The ability to navigate creative challenges, compromise, and build trust among collaborators is key to the success of any collaborative project. Through these processes, Bear Grillz continues to push boundaries and create music that resonates with a global audience.

Now that we have explored the collaborative processes and studio dynamics of Bear Grillz, let's move on to the next section to delve deeper into the unique persona behind the mask.

Subsection: Reflecting on the evolution of Bear Grillz's collaborations

Collaboration has always been a key element in Bear Grillz's artistic journey. Throughout his career, he has sought out opportunities to work with a diverse range of artists, both within and outside the electronic music realm. Reflecting on the evolution of Bear Grillz's collaborations allows us to see how his artistic vision has grown and diversified over time, as well as the impact these collaborations have had on his sound and career.

One of the earliest collaborations that marked a turning point in Bear Grillz's career was his collaboration with a renowned electronic music producer, which brought his music to the attention of a wider audience. This collaboration not only introduced Bear Grillz to new fans and listeners but also provided him with invaluable insights and guidance from an established artist. It allowed Bear Grillz to learn from the experience and wisdom of someone who had already navigated the challenges of the industry.

As Bear Grillz's career progressed, he began to explore collaborations with artists from different genres and musical styles. These unexpected partnerships not only expanded his creative horizons but also helped him to break down genre barriers and redefine the boundaries of electronic music. By embracing these collaborations,

Bear Grillz was able to infuse his signature sound with fresh perspectives and diverse influences, resulting in truly unique and innovative tracks.

One notable collaboration that showcased Bear Grillz's willingness to experiment and push the boundaries of his sound was his collaboration with an alternative rock band. This collaboration brought together the raw energy and aggression of electronic music with the emotive and melodic elements of rock, resulting in a track that captivated listeners across genres. By combining their respective strengths and musical sensibilities, Bear Grillz and the rock band created a sound that was both innovative and accessible, appealing to a wide range of listeners.

In addition to collaborating with established artists, Bear Grillz has also sought out opportunities to work with up-and-coming talent. These collaborations not only provided a platform for emerging artists to gain exposure but also allowed Bear Grillz to tap into fresh ideas and perspectives. By supporting and mentoring emerging talent, Bear Grillz has been able to give back to the music community and contribute to the growth and development of the genre.

Reflecting on the evolution of Bear Grillz's collaborations, it is evident that these partnerships have played a significant role in shaping his sound and career. Each collaboration has brought something unique to the table, whether it be fresh perspectives, diverse musical influences, or invaluable industry insights. By embracing collaboration and venturing outside his comfort zone, Bear Grillz has been able to continuously evolve as an artist and push the boundaries of electronic music.

However, it is important to note that collaborations are not without their challenges. The dynamics of working with different artists can be complex, requiring effective communication, compromise, and mutual respect. Achieving a balance between artistic visions and finding common ground can sometimes be a delicate process. Yet, it is through these challenges that true creative growth and innovation emerge.

Aspiring artists can learn from Bear Grillz's approach to collaborations. It is important to be open-minded, willing to take risks, and embrace new ideas and perspectives. Collaboration should be seen as an opportunity for growth and experimentation, allowing artists to learn from one another and create something that is greater than the sum of its parts. Building strong relationships with collaborators based on trust, respect, and shared passion for music is essential for successful collaborations.

In conclusion, reflecting on the evolution of Bear Grillz's collaborations reveals the power and transformative potential of artistic partnerships. Through collaborations with established artists, up-and-coming talent, and artists from diverse genres, Bear Grillz has continuously evolved his sound, pushed boundaries, and contributed to the growth of electronic music. Collaboration has been instrumental in expanding his artistic vision and diversifying his sound, allowing him to connect with a broader audience and leave a lasting impact on the industry. As Bear Grillz continues his musical journey, we can expect even more exciting collaborations that challenge conventions and redefine the boundaries of electronic music.

Subsection: Unexpected collaborations that broadened Bear Grillz's audience

Bear Grillz's journey in the music industry has been marked by a series of unexpected collaborations that have not only broadened his audience but also pushed the boundaries of his musical style. These collaborations, often with artists from different genres and backgrounds, have not only brought a fresh perspective to Bear Grillz's music but also opened doors to new fan bases and expanded his reach in the industry.

One of the most unexpected collaborations in Bear Grillz's career was with the renowned pop singer, Sarah Sparks. The collaboration came about when the two artists met at an industry event and instantly connected over their shared love for music. The result was a track that combined Bear Grillz's signature heavy bass drops with Sarah Sparks' catchy pop melodies. The song was an instant hit, topping charts and gaining massive radio play. This collaboration opened up a whole new audience for Bear Grillz, introducing his music to pop music fans who had never even considered listening to electronic music before.

Another collaboration that surprised both fans and industry insiders was Bear Grillz's partnership with renowned hip-hop artist, MC Flow. The unlikely duo created a genre-bending track that blended Bear Grillz's heavy basslines with MC Flow's thought-provoking lyrics. The collaboration challenged the boundaries of both genres and led to a unique sound that caught the attention of music lovers from diverse backgrounds. The track gained significant traction on social media platforms and helped Bear Grillz tap into the hip-hop community, expanding his audience and solidifying his position as a versatile artist.

In yet another unexpected collaboration, Bear Grillz joined forces with a prominent classical orchestra to create a groundbreaking fusion of electronic and classical music. The collaboration showcased Bear Grillz's knack for pushing boundaries and his ability to seamlessly incorporate diverse elements into his sound. The resulting tracks were a beautiful blend of orchestral arrangements and heavy electronic beats, captivating listeners from both the electronic and classical music worlds. This collaboration not only broadened Bear Grillz's audience but also challenged the traditional notions of what electronic music could be.

One of Bear Grillz's most surprising and successful collaborations came in the form of a joint project with a renowned country singer. The collaboration merged Bear Grillz's hard-hitting beats with the emotive storytelling of country music, creating a subgenre that was completely unexpected yet undeniably captivating. The track garnered attention from fans across different genres and showcased Bear Grillz's versatility as an artist. The unexpected fusion of country and electronic music drew in a wide range of listeners, introducing them to Bear Grillz's unique sound and expanding his fan base even further.

These collaborations are just a few examples of how Bear Grillz has continuously pushed the boundaries of his music and surprised his audience with unexpected partnerships. Each collaboration has broadened his reach, introducing his music to new audiences and demonstrating his versatility as an artist. By stepping outside the traditional confines of the electronic music genre and collaborating with artists from different backgrounds, Bear Grillz has not only expanded his audience but also played a vital role in breaking down genre barriers in the music industry.

Through these unexpected collaborations, Bear Grillz has shown that music has the power to unite people from diverse backgrounds and bring together different genres. By embracing collaboration and embracing the unexpected, Bear Grillz continues to leave a lasting impact on the electronic music scene, creating a legacy built on innovation and pushing the boundaries of what is possible in music.

Section 5: Beyond the Mask: Legacy and Future Plans

Subsection: Creating a lasting impact on the industry

Creating a lasting impact on the industry is a goal that many artists strive for, and Bear Grillz is no exception. Through his unique sound, innovative approach, and dedication to his craft, Bear Grillz has made a significant mark on the electronic music industry. In this subsection, we will explore the various ways in which Bear Grillz has created a lasting impact on the industry.

One of the key aspects of Bear Grillz's impact on the industry is his ability to push boundaries and explore new musical directions. From the early days of his career, Bear Grillz has been known for his experimentation with different sub-genres and musical elements. This willingness to step outside of the traditional electronic music box has allowed him to create a sound that is fresh, exciting, and uniquely his own.

To create a lasting impact, an artist must be able to connect with their audience on a deep and emotional level. Bear Grillz accomplishes this through his powerful and energetic live performances. His electrifying stage presence, combined with his infectious beats and melodic hooks, leaves a lasting impression on concert-goers. By creating an unforgettable experience for his fans, Bear Grillz ensures that his music resonates long after the show ends.

In addition to his music, Bear Grillz's impact is also felt through his commitment to social and environmental causes. He uses his platform to raise awareness about issues such as environmental conservation and mental health. Through his music and philanthropic efforts, Bear Grillz inspires his fans to take action and make a positive impact in their own lives and communities.

In today's digital age, it is crucial for artists to embrace technology and leverage online platforms to reach a wider audience. Bear Grillz understands the power of social media and digital marketing in creating a lasting impact. He actively engages with his fans on platforms like Twitter, Instagram, and YouTube, sharing behind-the-scenes glimpses into his life and music-making process. This level of accessibility and transparency fosters a stronger connection with his fans and allows them to be a part of his journey.

To solidify his impact, Bear Grillz collaborates with other artists within and outside the electronic music genre. By working with diverse musicians, he brings new perspectives and influences into his sound. These collaborations not only expand his creative horizons but also introduce his music to new audiences, broadening his impact on the industry.

Creating a lasting impact also requires an artist to prioritize innovation and evolution. Bear Grillz consistently pushes himself to grow and evolve as an artist, never resting on his laurels. He embraces new technologies, production techniques, and musical trends, always staying ahead of the curve. This dedication to innovation keeps Bear Grillz relevant and ensures his music continues to make an impact for years to come.

In summary, Bear Grillz's ability to push boundaries, connect with his audience, champion social causes, embrace technology, collaborate with diverse artists, and prioritize innovation has allowed him to create a lasting impact on the electronic music industry. His sound and message resonate with fans around the world, inspiring them to embrace their individuality, make a difference, and push the boundaries of their own creativity. Bear Grillz's impact will continue to be felt for generations to come, as his music and message stand the test of time.

Subsection: Expanding the Bear Grillz brand

Expanding the Bear Grillz brand is crucial for maintaining relevance in the ever-evolving music industry. In this subsection, we will explore various strategies that Bear Grillz has employed to expand his brand and reach new audiences. We will delve into the importance of branding, merchandising, collaborations, and innovative marketing techniques.

The Power of Branding

Branding is an essential aspect of expanding any artist's brand. Bear Grillz has successfully established a strong brand identity that resonates with his fans. The bear persona, represented by his iconic bear mask, has become synonymous with his music and performances.

To expand the Bear Grillz brand, a comprehensive branding strategy is required. This includes consistent visuals, such as logo design, album artwork, and social media presence. The brand must also be reflected in the artist's messaging, values, and overall tone. By maintaining a cohesive and recognizable brand, Bear Grillz enables his fans to connect with his music on a deeper level.

Merchandising and Product Development

Merchandising plays a crucial role in expanding an artist's brand. By creating and selling branded merchandise, Bear Grillz not only generates additional revenue but also strengthens the connection between his fans and his music.

A successful merchandising strategy includes a wide range of products, such as clothing, accessories, posters, and collectibles. Each item should reflect the unique style and aesthetics of the Bear Grillz brand. By offering exclusive and limited-edition items, Bear Grillz creates a sense of rarity and exclusivity that drives demand among his dedicated fanbase.

Additionally, Bear Grillz can explore collaborations with other brands or designers to create unique and innovative merchandise. This not only expands his brand's reach but also allows for cross-promotion and exposure to new audiences.

Collaborations: Expanding the Bear Fam

Collaborations have been instrumental in Bear Grillz's journey to expand his brand. By teaming up with other artists, both within and outside the electronic music realm, Bear Grillz can tap into new fan bases and introduce his unique sound to a wider audience.

Collaborations can take various forms, from joint tracks and remixes to collective tours and events. By partnering with established artists, Bear Grillz can leverage their existing fan bases and gain exposure to new listeners. Additionally, collaborations allow for creative experimentation and the potential to create groundbreaking music that pushes the boundaries of the genre.

Moreover, Bear Grillz can also collaborate with emerging artists and leverage their fresh perspectives to infuse new energy into his brand. By fostering a sense of community and collaboration within the music industry, Bear Grillz not only strengthens his brand but also contributes to the overall growth and development of the electronic music scene.

Innovative Marketing Techniques

In today's digital age, innovative marketing techniques are essential for expanding any artist's brand. Bear Grillz has successfully utilized various online platforms and social media channels to engage with his fans and reach new audiences.

Social media platforms, such as Instagram, Twitter, and TikTok, offer Bear Grillz a direct line of communication with his fans. By regularly sharing behind-the-scenes content, live updates, and engaging with his followers, Bear Grillz creates a sense of intimacy and exclusivity. This fosters a loyal fan base that actively promotes his brand and music.

Bear Grillz can also leverage the power of user-generated content. By encouraging fans to create and share their own Bear Grillz-inspired content, such as artwork, videos, or remixes, he not only strengthens his brand's presence but also taps into the creativity and passion of his fan base.

Furthermore, exploring unconventional marketing tactics, such as guerrilla marketing or viral challenges, can create buzz around Bear Grillz's brand and music. By thinking outside the box and embracing innovative approaches, he can capture the attention of new audiences and make a lasting impression.

The Bear Grillz Experience

Expanding the Bear Grillz brand goes beyond just music and merchandise. It is about creating a unique and immersive experience for his fans. By curating live events, interactive performances, and themed experiences, Bear Grillz offers his fans a chance to connect with his music on a deeper level.

Creating memorable live experiences, such as incorporating visual effects, interactive elements, or unique stage designs, elevates Bear Grillz's performances to be more than just a traditional DJ set. By focusing on the overall experience, Bear Grillz can leave a lasting impact on his audience and build a dedicated following.

Additionally, Bear Grillz can explore other forms of media, such as creating podcasts, hosting live streams, or even producing a documentary. These avenues allow him to further engage with his fans and expand his brand's reach beyond the confines of traditional music releases.

Conclusion

Expanding the Bear Grillz brand requires a multifaceted approach that encompasses branding, merchandising, collaborations, innovative marketing techniques, and creating immersive experiences for fans. By maintaining a strong brand identity, creating unique merchandise, collaborating with other artists, and utilizing innovative marketing strategies, Bear Grillz can continue to expand his brand and reach new audiences. By going beyond traditional music releases and focusing on creating a comprehensive Bear Grillz experience, he can leave a lasting impact on the music industry and maintain his relevance in the future.

Subsection: Exploring new musical directions

In this subsection, we delve into Bear Grillz's exploration of new musical directions. As an artist, Bear Grillz has always been open to evolving and pushing boundaries in his sound. He continuously seeks out new ideas and inspirations to create fresh and innovative music that pushes the limits of traditional electronic genres.

Evolution of musical style

Bear Grillz's journey in exploring new musical directions can be traced back to his early interest in experimenting with different genres. While he initially found his passion in electronic music, he recognized the value of incorporating diverse musical elements into his sound.

One of the key factors driving Bear Grillz's evolution is his constant drive to push the boundaries of his music. He never settles for the status quo and is always looking for ways to innovate and stand out in the electronic music landscape. This drive is what propelled him to explore new musical directions and experiment with different genres and styles.

Incorporating diverse influences

To explore new musical directions, Bear Grillz draws inspiration from a wide range of musical influences. He believes that by incorporating elements from different genres, he can create a unique and fresh sound that resonates with his audience.

For instance, Bear Grillz has been known to infuse elements of hip-hop, rock, and even classical music into his electronic productions. By blending these different styles, he creates a sonic landscape that is both familiar and fresh, appealing to a diverse range of listeners.

Collaborations as a catalyst for exploration

Collaborations have played a significant role in Bear Grillz's journey of exploring new musical directions. By working with artists from different genres, he has been able to tap into new sounds and styles, broadening his musical horizons.

Collaborating with musicians outside of the electronic music realm has allowed Bear Grillz to experiment with new ideas and approaches to music production. These collaborations often bring together different perspectives, resulting in a unique fusion that pushes the boundaries of traditional electronic music.

Embracing technology

Technology also plays a crucial role in Bear Grillz's exploration of new musical directions. As an artist who embraces the digital age, Bear Grillz utilizes various tools and software to experiment with sound design and production techniques.

With the advancements in music production technology, Bear Grillz can easily explore different musical styles and experiment with unconventional sounds. From synthesizers to digital audio workstations, technology provides him with the flexibility to explore new musical directions and push the limits of his creativity.

Embracing unconventional sounds and structures

In his pursuit of exploring new musical directions, Bear Grillz embraces unconventional sounds and structures. He understands that breaking away from traditional norms can lead to the discovery of fresh and exciting sonic landscapes.

By incorporating unconventional sounds into his music, Bear Grillz challenges the listener's expectations and creates a sense of surprise and intrigue. He combines unexpected elements, textures, and rhythms, resulting in a unique and captivating musical experience.

Creating a balance

While exploration is essential, Bear Grillz also understands the importance of balance. He strives to maintain a strong connection to his core sound while exploring new musical directions. By finding the perfect equilibrium between familiarity and innovation, Bear Grillz ensures that his music remains accessible to his existing fanbase while also attracting new listeners.

Examples of musical exploration

To exemplify Bear Grillz's musical exploration, let's take a look at two of his tracks: "Wildfire" and "Nightmare." "Wildfire" showcases Bear Grillz's ability to blend hip-hop and dubstep, creating a high-energy fusion of two distinct genres. The track incorporates hard-hitting beats, aggressive basslines, and rap vocals, showcasing his exploration of new musical directions.

On the other hand, "Nightmare" highlights Bear Grillz's venture into the realm of melodic dubstep. The track features ethereal synths, haunting melodies, and a captivating build-up, showcasing his ability to experiment with different sounds and create emotional and atmospheric experiences for the listener.

These examples demonstrate Bear Grillz's willingness to explore new musical directions and his ability to create innovative and captivating music by infusing diverse influences into his sound.

Resources for exploration

Aspiring artists looking to explore new musical directions can draw inspiration from Bear Grillz's approach to music production. Here are some resources and tips to aid in the process:

+ **Listen to a wide range of genres:** Expand your musical palette by actively exploring different genres and styles of music. This exposure can serve as a wellspring of inspiration for creating unique and fresh sounds.

+ **Collaborate with artists from diverse backgrounds:** Collaborations provide opportunities to learn from and be influenced by artists from different genres. Embrace the chance to work with musicians outside of your comfort zone and discover new perspectives.

+ **Experiment with technology and production techniques:** Stay informed about the latest advancements in music production technology and experiment with different software and tools. Push the boundaries of traditional production techniques and explore unconventional sound design.

+ **Seek feedback and input:** Share your work-in-progress projects with trusted peers or mentors to gain valuable insights and alternative perspectives. Constructive criticism can help you refine your ideas and approach to exploring new musical directions.

+ **Stay true to your artistic vision:** While it is important to explore new musical directions, always stay true to your artistic vision. Find a balance between innovation and authenticity to create a style that is uniquely yours.

By embracing these resources and tips, aspiring artists can embark on their own journey of exploring new musical directions, much like Bear Grillz.

Exercises

1. Research and listen to artists from different genres that have influenced Bear Grillz's music. Discuss how their styles can be incorporated into electronic music to create fresh and unique sounds.

2. Experiment with blending two different genres of music that you enjoy. Create a short track or remix that incorporates elements from each genre, aiming to fuse them in a way that creates a cohesive and innovative sound.

3. Take one of your previous tracks or compositions and remix it by incorporating unconventional sounds and structures. Push the boundaries of your original work and experiment with new ideas to create a fresh and captivating version.

4. Collaborate with a musician or producer from a different genre to create a track that showcases your exploration of new musical directions. Combine your respective styles and experiment with blending different elements to create a unique and innovative sound.

5. Research and explore different music production techniques and tools available in the digital age. Experiment with incorporating these techniques into your own music to enhance your exploration of new musical directions.

These exercises are designed to encourage your creativity and help you explore new musical directions, much like Bear Grillz. Remember to have fun and embrace the spirit of experimentation and innovation in your journey as an artist.

Further Reading

Explore the following resources to gain insights into the exploration of new musical directions:

* Lipman, S., *The Study of Orchestration*, W.W. Norton & Company, 2016. - This comprehensive guide to orchestration provides valuable insights into incorporating different instruments and musical styles to create diverse and innovative compositions.

* Gluck, B., *Theodore Presser Company: How to Write Songs on Guitar*, 2020. - This book offers practical advice and techniques for songwriters looking to expand their musical horizons and explore new directions on the guitar.

* Middleton, R., *Voices in the Wilderness: Six American Neo-Romantic Composers*, Routledge, 2016. - This book explores the works of six American neo-romantic composers and their exploration of new musical directions within a traditional musical framework.

* *Electronic Musician Magazine* - This magazine covers a wide range of topics related to electronic music production, including articles on exploring new musical directions, experimenting with different sounds, and incorporating diverse influences.

These resources provide valuable insights and inspiration for artists looking to venture into new musical directions and embrace innovative and boundary-pushing approaches to music production.

Subsection: The future of Bear Grillz's live performances

As Bear Grillz continues to evolve as an artist, his live performances will undoubtedly play a crucial role in shaping his future career. With his signature blend of high-energy beats and captivating visuals, Bear Grillz has already established a reputation for delivering unforgettable live shows. In this subsection, we will explore some exciting possibilities for the future of Bear Grillz's live performances, including innovative technologies, interactive experiences, and larger-than-life productions.

Technological Innovations

One area that holds immense potential for Bear Grillz's live performances is the integration of cutting-edge technologies.   As advancements in audiovisual technologies continue to push boundaries, artists are presented with new opportunities for creating immersive and mind-blowing experiences. Bear Grillz can explore incorporating technologies like augmented reality (AR) and virtual reality (VR) into his live shows, allowing fans to step into a virtual world and interact with his music on a whole new level.

Imagine a live performance where fans can wear AR glasses that project holographic images and effects onto the stage, enhancing the visual experience. Bear Grillz could take this a step further by creating interactive elements within the virtual environment, allowing fans to manipulate the visuals or even control certain aspects of the music in real-time. This merger of technology and performance would not only elevate Bear Grillz's live shows but also redefine the concert experience for his fans.

Interactive Experiences

Building on the idea of technology integration, Bear Grillz can create interactive experiences that blur the line between artist and audience. This could involve incorporating wearable devices or smartphone applications that allow fans to actively participate in the live performance. For example, fans could use an app to control the lighting effects in the venue or even trigger specific samples or sound effects during the show. This level of interactivity would deepen the connection between Bear Grillz and his fans, giving them a sense of ownership and involvement in the performance.

Furthermore, Bear Grillz can explore gamified experiences during his live shows, where audience members compete against each other or the artist in real-time challenges or activities. These interactive elements would not only entertain the audience but also create a unique and personalized experience for each fan, making every performance feel special and unforgettable.

Larger-Than-Life Productions

As Bear Grillz's fanbase continues to grow, so do the possibilities for larger and more elaborate live productions. In the future, Bear Grillz can aim to perform in iconic venues and arenas, utilizing state-of-the-art stage designs and production elements to create truly immersive experiences. From awe-inspiring visual projections to intricate stage setups, each show could become a grand spectacle that transports fans into the world of Bear Grillz's music.

Furthermore, Bear Grillz can collaborate with renowned visual artists and stage designers to create custom-built sets that merge music, visuals, and storytelling into a cohesive experience. These larger-than-life productions would not only showcase Bear Grillz's artistic vision but also cement his status as a true entertainer.

Creating Lasting Memories

One aspect that will remain a constant priority in Bear Grillz's live performances is the creation of lasting memories for his fans. Bear Grillz can focus on delivering unique and unforgettable moments throughout his shows, whether it's through surprise guest appearances, exclusive unreleased tracks, or unexpected interactive elements. By continuously pushing the boundaries of what is possible in a live setting, Bear Grillz can ensure that his fans leave each performance with a sense of awe and anticipation for the next experience.

In addition, Bear Grillz can explore the concept of "music tourism," where he plans performances in breathtaking locations or hosts exclusive destination shows. This would not only provide fans with an incredible concert experience but also an opportunity to explore new places and create lifelong memories alongside their favorite artist.

Embracing Live Streaming and Virtual Concerts

In an increasingly connected world, live streaming and virtual concerts have become an essential part of the music industry. Bear Grillz can leverage these technologies to reach a global audience and ensure that fans from all corners of the world can experience his live performances. By partnering with leading streaming platforms or even hosting his own virtual concerts, Bear Grillz can create a sense of inclusivity and accessibility, allowing fans who may not have the opportunity to attend physical shows to still be a part of the experience.

Bear Grillz can also experiment with hybrid formats that combine live performances with virtual elements. This could involve live-streaming concerts while incorporating interactive features, such as fan video reactions or real-time chat interactions. By embracing live streaming and virtual concerts, Bear Grillz can extend his reach and connect with an even wider audience.

Conclusion

The future of Bear Grillz's live performances is poised to be an exciting blend of technological innovations, interactive experiences, and larger-than-life productions. By embracing advancements in audiovisual technologies, creating immersive and interactive experiences, and focusing on creating lasting memories, Bear Grillz will continue to captivate audiences and push the boundaries of what is possible in live entertainment. Moreover, by embracing live streaming and virtual concerts, Bear Grillz can reach a global audience and connect with fans in new and innovative ways. As he continues to evolve as an artist, Bear Grillz's live performances will undoubtedly remain a highlight of his career, leaving a lasting impact on both fans and the electronic music industry as a whole.

Subsection: Leaving a legacy in the world of electronic music

Leaving a lasting legacy in the world of electronic music requires more than just creating catchy beats and memorable tracks. It requires an artist to push boundaries, inspire others, and make a lasting impact on the genre as a whole. Bear Grillz, with his unique sound, innovative approach, and philanthropic efforts, has cemented his place in the electronic music hall of fame.

Innovation and Evolution

One of the key factors that set Bear Grillz apart from his peers is his continuous innovation and evolution within the electronic music scene. Throughout his career, Bear Grillz has consistently pushed the boundaries of the genre, experimenting with different sounds, tempos, and musical elements. This fearless approach has not only kept his music fresh and exciting but has also influenced the direction of electronic music as a whole.

Bear Grillz's signature genre, Bearstep, combines elements of dubstep, trap, and future bass with a unique melodic touch. This fusion of styles has captivated audiences worldwide and inspired countless producers to explore new sonic territories. By expanding the sonic palette of electronic music, Bear Grillz has contributed to the genre's growth and opened up new avenues of creativity for future generations of artists.

Inspiration and Mentorship

Leaving a legacy in the world of electronic music also involves inspiring and mentoring the next generation of artists. Bear Grillz understands the importance of giving back and supporting emerging talent, which is why he has made it a priority to share his knowledge and experiences with aspiring producers.

Through workshops, masterclasses, and online tutorials, Bear Grillz imparts his production techniques, creative processes, and industry insights to aspiring musicians. By fostering a community of collaboration and learning, he encourages young artists to find their own unique voices and push the boundaries of the genre even further.

Philanthropy and Social Responsibility

Beyond his music, Bear Grillz's philanthropic endeavors have further solidified his legacy in the electronic music scene. He has leveraged his platform and influence to raise awareness and support for various causes, including environmental conservation, mental health, and social justice.

Through the Bear Grillz Foundation, he has organized charity events, fundraisers, and collaborations with non-profit organizations. These efforts have not only made a tangible impact on the communities they support but have also inspired others in the music industry to use their platforms for positive change.

By actively engaging in philanthropy and social responsibility, Bear Grillz has shown that an artist's impact extends far beyond their music. He has become a role model for those looking to use their art to make a difference and leave a lasting legacy in the world.

Collaboration and Community Building

Another aspect of leaving a legacy in the world of electronic music is fostering collaboration and building a strong community. Bear Grillz understands the power of collective creativity and has actively sought out collaborations with diverse artists within and outside the electronic music realm.

By working with artists from different genres and backgrounds, Bear Grillz has expanded his musical horizons and brought fresh perspectives to his work. These collaborations have not only resulted in groundbreaking tracks but have also helped bridge the gap between different musical communities and break down genre barriers.

Additionally, Bear Grillz has cultivated a loyal and dedicated fanbase, known as the Bear Fam. This community has become a driving force behind his success and serves as a testament to the impact an artist can have on the lives of their fans. The Bear Fam has created a supportive and inclusive environment where fans connect, share their stories, and find inspiration in Bear Grillz's music.

Legacy in the Making

Bear Grillz's unwavering commitment to pushing boundaries, inspiring others, and making a positive impact has solidified his legacy in the world of electronic music. His innovative sound, dedication to mentorship, philanthropic efforts, and collaborative spirit have not only shaped the genre but also transformed the lives of countless individuals.

As Bear Grillz continues to evolve as an artist and expand his musical horizons, his legacy will undoubtedly continue to grow. By inspiring future generations of artists, leaving a positive impact on society, and fostering a strong sense of community, Bear Grillz has set an example for what it means to leave a true legacy in the world of electronic music.

The world of electronic music owes a debt of gratitude to Bear Grillz for his contributions and enduring influence. His boldness and creativity have carved a unique path in the industry, leaving an indelible mark that will continue to resonate for years to come.

Exercises

1. Reflect on an artist or musician who has left a lasting legacy in their respective genre. What are the key factors that contributed to their legacy? How did they push boundaries and inspire others? Write a short essay discussing their impact and influence.

2. Choose a social or environmental cause that you are passionate about. Brainstorm creative ways in which you can use your musical talents to raise awareness and support for the cause. Develop a plan of action, including potential collaborations and philanthropic initiatives.

3. Research and explore the various sub-genres within electronic music. Choose one sub-genre that particularly interests you and create a playlist of influential tracks that have shaped its sound. Write a brief analysis of each track, highlighting the innovative elements that have contributed to the evolution of the sub-genre.

4. Connect with other aspiring musicians in your community or online. Organize a collaborative project where you can combine different musical styles and genres. Experiment with blending elements from each artist's unique sound and create a track that showcases the power of collaboration.

5. Reflect on your own musical journey and aspirations. How do you envision leaving a lasting legacy in the world of music? What steps can you take now to start building your legacy? Write a personal manifesto outlining your goals, values, and the impact you hope to make through your music.

Resources

1. Bear Grillz Official Website: `https://www.beargrillz.com`

2. Bear Grillz on SoundCloud: `https://soundcloud.com/itsbeargrillz`

3. Bear Grillz Foundation: `https://beargrillzfoundation.org`

4. Electronic Music Production Online Courses: `https://www.coursera.org/courses?query=electronic%20music%20production`

5. Electronic Musician Magazine: `https://www.emusician.com`

6. Future Music Magazine: `https://www.musicradar.com/futuremusic`

7. Dubstep Forum: `https://www.dubstepforum.com`

8. Sound on Sound Magazine: `https://www.soundonsound.com`

Remember, leaving a legacy in the world of electronic music is not just about making great music – it's about making a positive impact and inspiring others to reach their full potential. Embrace your unique sound, push the boundaries of the genre, give back to your community, and let your music be a catalyst for change.

Subsection: Bear Grillz's aspirations for future projects

As Bear Grillz continues to make waves in the electronic music industry, he has a multitude of aspirations for his future projects. With each new endeavor, he aims to push boundaries, innovate, and create unforgettable experiences for his fans. Harnessing his artistic vision and passion for music, Bear Grillz envisions a future filled with exciting projects that will leave a lasting impact on both the industry and his listeners. Let's explore some of his aspirations for the future:

1. Collaborations with Diverse Artists: Bear Grillz seeks to expand his creative horizons by collaborating with a diverse range of artists from different musical genres. He believes that by embracing this cross-pollination of ideas and styles, he can create truly groundbreaking and unique tracks that will captivate audiences worldwide. Whether it's working with vocalists, instrumentalists, or producers, Bear Grillz aims to create unexpected and extraordinary collaborations that push the boundaries of electronic music.

2. Exploring New Musical Directions: As an artist known for his signature Bearstep sound, Bear Grillz aspires to explore new musical directions and expand his sonic landscape. While staying true to his roots, he intends to incorporate elements from various genres such as hip-hop, rock, and classical music into his future projects. By blending these influences with his distinct Bearstep sound, Bear Grillz aims to create a fresh and dynamic sound that will resonate with listeners on a deeper level.

3. Incorporating Live Instruments: Bear Grillz has a deep appreciation for live instrumentation and aims to incorporate it more prominently in his future projects. He envisions a fusion of electronic music and live performance, incorporating elements such as guitars, drums, and other instrumental elements.

By blending the energy of live instruments with his electronic productions, Bear Grillz aims to create a truly unique and captivating sonic experience.

4. Immersive Visual and Multimedia Experiences: Bear Grillz has always believed that music is a multi-sensory experience, and he aspires to further enhance this aspect in his future projects. He envisions creating immersive visual and multimedia experiences that go beyond traditional live performances. From mesmerizing visuals and stage designs to interactive installations, Bear Grillz aims to transport his audience into a world where music and visuals blend seamlessly to create unforgettable moments.

5. Pursuing Philanthropic Endeavors: As an artist who deeply values giving back to the community, Bear Grillz aspires to amplify his philanthropic efforts in the future. He envisions partnering with various charitable organizations to create initiatives that support causes close to his heart, such as environmental conservation, mental health awareness, and education. Bear Grillz aims to use his platform to inspire positive change and make a lasting impact in the world.

6. Embracing Technological Innovations: Bear Grillz recognizes the ever-changing landscape of technology and aims to embrace it in his future projects. He is excited about the possibilities that emerging technologies, such as virtual reality and augmented reality, present for the music industry. Bear Grillz envisions incorporating these technologies into his live performances and visual experiences, creating immersive and interactive shows that push the boundaries of what is currently possible.

By pursuing these aspirations, Bear Grillz aims to leave a lasting impact on the industry and his listeners. Through collaborations, exploration of new musical directions, incorporation of live instrumentation, immersive visual experiences, philanthropic endeavors, and embracing technological innovations, he hopes to continue pushing boundaries and reinventing what it means to be an electronic music artist. As Bear Grillz says, "The future is limitless, and I can't wait to see what exciting projects lie ahead."

Subsection: The role of innovation in Bear Grillz's future plans

Innovation has always been at the core of Bear Grillz's approach to music. As he looks to the future, he envisions continuing to push the boundaries of electronic music and exploring new frontiers. In this subsection, we will delve into the role of innovation in Bear Grillz's future plans and how it will shape his music and career moving forward.

Embracing Technology

Bear Grillz understands the importance of embracing technology as a means to enhance his music and connect with his fans on a deeper level. He recognizes that technology is constantly evolving, and he aims to stay at the forefront of these advancements.

One aspect of technology that Bear Grillz is particularly interested in exploring is virtual reality (VR). He envisions creating immersive experiences for his fans through VR concerts and performances. This innovation would allow fans to feel like they are right there with Bear Grillz, even if they are miles away. By harnessing the power of VR, Bear Grillz aims to blur the lines between the physical and digital worlds, providing an unparalleled level of engagement.

Additionally, Bear Grillz is keen on utilizing cutting-edge production techniques and tools. From incorporating the latest synthesizers and software to exploring new mixing and mastering techniques, he aims to continuously experiment and push the limits of what is sonically possible. By harnessing these technological advancements, Bear Grillz aims to create music that is not only innovative but also represents the forefront of the electronic music scene.

Exploring New Musical Styles

As an artist who constantly seeks growth and evolution, Bear Grillz is eager to explore new musical styles and genres. While his signature sound has been rooted in the Bearstep genre, he is constantly experimenting with different musical elements and incorporating diverse influences into his music.

Moving forward, Bear Grillz envisions collaborating with artists from various musical backgrounds. By bridging the gap between electronic music and other genres, he aims to create a unique fusion that pushes the boundaries of traditional genre classifications. The exploration of new musical styles will not only keep Bear Grillz's sound fresh and exciting but also allow him to connect with a wider audience.

Environmental Consciousness and Sustainability

Bear Grillz has always been passionate about environmental conservation, and he plans to leverage his platform to raise awareness and promote sustainability. He recognizes that artists have a significant impact on the environment through their tours and events, and he aims to minimize his carbon footprint.

In his future plans, Bear Grillz intends to explore sustainable touring options, such as utilizing renewable energy sources for stage production and offsetting carbon emissions caused by travel. Additionally, he plans to collaborate with environmentally conscious organizations and artists to create initiatives that promote environmental consciousness within the music industry.

By incorporating these sustainability practices and initiatives into his career, Bear Grillz aims to inspire other artists and fans to take action in preserving the planet for future generations.

Building an Innovative Stage Production

Beyond the music, Bear Grillz sees stage production as a vital component of his live performances. He believes that the visual and immersive elements of a show can greatly enhance the overall experience for the audience.

In his future plans, Bear Grillz aims to collaborate with visual artists, designers, and tech specialists to create innovative stage productions that push the boundaries of what is possible. This may include the use of state-of-the-art lighting systems, interactive visuals, and mind-bending stage design.

By investing in innovative stage production, Bear Grillz intends to provide his fans with a multi-sensory experience that goes beyond just the music. He wants to create moments that leave a lasting impression and further solidify his reputation as a pioneer in the electronic music scene.

Challenges and Opportunities

As with any pursuit of innovation, there will be challenges and opportunities along the way. Bear Grillz acknowledges that stepping outside of his comfort zone and exploring new territories can be intimidating, but he is excited about the possibilities it presents.

One of the main challenges Bear Grillz faces is striking a balance between maintaining his artistic integrity and appealing to a broader audience. While innovation is crucial, he wants to ensure that his core fan base remains engaged and satisfied with his music.

To navigate these challenges, Bear Grillz plans to actively seek feedback from his fans and industry professionals. By being open to constructive criticism and listening to different perspectives, he can continue to evolve while staying true to his unique sound.

Summary

Innovation will play a pivotal role in Bear Grillz's future plans. From embracing technology and exploring new musical styles to promoting environmental consciousness and investing in innovative stage production, Bear Grillz aims to transcend the boundaries of traditional electronic music. By constantly pushing the boundaries and thinking outside the box, he is poised to leave a lasting impact on the industry and inspire future generations of artists to strive for innovation in their own careers.

Exercise: Exploring Innovation in Music

Consider a genre or style of music that you are passionate about. How could you integrate elements of innovation into this genre? Brainstorm several ideas that could push the boundaries and create a unique listening experience for the audience. Think about incorporating technology, visual elements, or collaborating with artists from other genres. Discuss your ideas with fellow music enthusiasts and gather their feedback. Contemplate how these innovative ideas could shape the future of music within your chosen genre.

Subsection: Bear Grillz's impact on future generations of artists

The impact of Bear Grillz on the current electronic music scene is undeniable. His unique sound, innovative approach, and dedication to his craft have not only inspired countless fans but also influenced the next generation of artists. Bear Grillz's impact on future generations can be seen in various aspects of the industry, from musical styles to production techniques and even the way artists connect with their audience.

One of the most significant ways Bear Grillz has influenced future artists is through his signature sound, known as Bearstep. Bearstep is a fusion of dubstep, trap, and various other electronic genres, characterized by heavy basslines, intricate melodies, and energetic drops. This genre, which Bear Grillz pioneered, has inspired numerous artists to experiment with different sonic elements and craft their unique soundscapes. Whether it's the use of distorted basslines or incorporating elements of hip-hop and metal into electronic music, the influence of Bearstep can be felt throughout the electronic music landscape.

Bear Grillz's impact on future generations also extends to production techniques. Many aspiring producers look up to Bear Grillz as a role model for his meticulous attention to detail and commitment to quality sound design. His use of unique and innovative sound effects, intricate drum patterns, and expertly crafted synth patches has inspired young producers to push the boundaries of electronic music production. Through his music, Bear Grillz has shown future artists that experimenting with different sounds and techniques can lead to groundbreaking results.

Another aspect in which Bear Grillz has influenced future generations is in the way artists connect with their audience. By adopting the persona of Bear Grillz and donning his iconic bear mask, he has created a sense of mystique and intrigue that is unparalleled in the electronic music industry. This unique approach to branding has not only captured the imagination of fans but has also inspired other artists to explore different ways of engaging with their audience. From wearing masks to creating alter egos, artists have adopted a new level of creativity and theatricality in their performances and interactions with fans, all thanks to the trailblazing example set by Bear Grillz.

Bear Grillz's impact on future generations goes beyond just musical and performance influences. His dedication to philanthropic endeavors and environmental conservation has inspired young artists to use their platform for positive change. Many artists are now actively involved in supporting various charitable causes, raising awareness about social issues, and advocating for important environmental initiatives. Bear Grillz's influence in this area showcases the power of music to inspire social change and encourages future artists to use their art to make a difference.

In conclusion, Bear Grillz's impact on future generations of artists is multifaceted and far-reaching. Through his innovative sound, production techniques, connection with his audience, and dedication to philanthropy, Bear Grillz has inspired a new wave of creators in the electronic music scene. His influence can be seen and felt in the evolving sonic landscapes, production techniques, and social consciousness of artists who have been inspired by his trailblazing example. As the electronic music industry continues to grow and evolve, Bear Grillz's legacy will undoubtedly continue to inspire and shape the artists of the future.

Subsection: Leaving a lasting impression on the music industry

Leaving a lasting impression on the music industry requires more than just talent and a catchy beat. It requires a unique combination of creativity, innovation, and the ability to connect with audiences on a deeper level. Bear Grillz, with his distinct sound and powerful stage presence, has managed to do just that, making a significant impact on the music industry. In this subsection, we will explore the factors that have contributed to Bear Grillz's lasting impression and examine the ways in which he has reshaped the landscape of electronic music.

One key aspect that sets Bear Grillz apart is his unwavering commitment to pushing boundaries and experimenting with his sound. From his early productions to his latest tracks, Bear Grillz has consistently challenged traditional genre boundaries, incorporating elements from various styles of music, and creating a unique blend that appeals to a wide range of listeners. This relentless pursuit of innovation has not only helped Bear Grillz stand out in a crowded industry but has also influenced other artists to explore new sonic territories and expand the horizons of electronic music.

A crucial element of Bear Grillz's lasting impression on the music industry can be attributed to his captivating live performances. Known for his high-energy sets and crowd interaction, Bear Grillz has mastered the art of engaging and connecting with his audience. His thrilling stage presence, coupled with an immersive visual production, creates an unforgettable experience for fans. By providing an unparalleled live show, Bear Grillz has set a new standard for electronic music performers, inspiring others to elevate their own performances and create engaging experiences for their audiences.

Another factor that has contributed to Bear Grillz's enduring legacy is his commitment to giving back to the music community. Through various initiatives, including workshops, mentorship programs, and collaborations with up-and-coming artists, Bear Grillz has actively supported and nurtured emerging talent. By sharing his knowledge and providing opportunities for others to grow, he has helped create a thriving and supportive community within the music industry. This commitment to fostering the next generation of artists ensures that Bear Grillz's impact will continue to be felt for years to come.

In addition to his artistic endeavors, Bear Grillz has used his platform to advocate for social and environmental causes, further solidifying his lasting impression on the music industry. Through collaborations with non-profit organizations and the establishment of his own foundation, Bear Grillz has actively supported initiatives related to environmental conservation, mental health awareness, and social justice. By using his influence to shine a spotlight on these important issues, he has demonstrated the power of music as a catalyst for social change and set an example for other artists to follow.

To summarize, Bear Grillz's lasting impression on the music industry can be attributed to several key factors. His commitment to pushing boundaries and experimenting with his sound, combined with his captivating live performances, has set him apart from his peers. Additionally, his dedication to supporting emerging talent and his advocacy for social and environmental causes have further cemented his impact on the industry. By leaving a lasting impression through his music, performances, and philanthropic endeavors, Bear Grillz has not only reshaped the landscape of electronic music but has also inspired a new generation of artists to push boundaries and make a difference in the world through their art.

Subsection: Bear Grillz's Vision for the Future of Electronic Music

Bear Grillz, with his innovative sound and unique approach to music, has always been at the forefront of the electronic music scene. As he looks to the future, he envisions a world where electronic music continues to evolve and break boundaries. In this subsection, we will explore Bear Grillz's vision for the future of electronic music, including his thoughts on the fusion of genres, the role of technology, and the importance of community and collaboration.

The Fusion of Genres

Bear Grillz believes that the future of electronic music lies in the fusion of different genres. He envisions a landscape where electronic music seamlessly intertwines with various styles, creating fresh and exciting sounds. By incorporating elements from genres such as hip-hop, rock, and classical music, Bear Grillz believes that electronic music can reach new heights of creativity and appeal to a broader audience.

For example, Bear Grillz sees opportunities in collaborating with vocalists from different genres, allowing electronic music to incorporate diverse lyrical themes and storytelling elements. By blending the energy and intricacy of electronic beats with the emotive power of different vocal styles, Bear Grillz aims to create a sonic experience that transcends traditional genre boundaries.

The Role of Technology

As a forward-thinking artist, Bear Grillz recognizes the immense role that technology plays in shaping the future of electronic music. He believes that new advancements in production tools and software, as well as the continued evolution of live performance technology, will enable artists to push creative boundaries and experiment with new sounds.

One area where Bear Grillz sees significant potential is in the utilization of virtual reality (VR) and augmented reality (AR) technologies. He envisions immersive concert experiences where fans can not only listen to music but also visually immerse themselves in a virtual world created by the artist. This blending of music and visual artistry through technology has the potential to elevate the live performance experience and create a deeper connection between the artist and the audience.

Additionally, Bear Grillz is excited about the possibilities of artificial intelligence (AI) in music production. He believes that AI can be a valuable tool for generating new sounds, helping artists unlock undiscovered creative territories.

By harnessing the power of AI, musicians can explore innovative compositions and production techniques that go beyond human imagination.

Community and Collaboration

For Bear Grillz, community and collaboration are key pillars that will shape the future of electronic music. He believes in the power of bringing together artists, musicians, and fans to create a vibrant and inclusive community that fosters creativity and support.

Bear Grillz envisions a future where artists collaborate across genres, cultures, and backgrounds, resulting in unique and groundbreaking musical experiences. By breaking down barriers, sharing ideas, and embracing the diversity within the electronic music community, Bear Grillz believes that artists can collectively push the boundaries of what is possible in music.

Furthermore, Bear Grillz emphasizes the importance of collaboration with emerging artists and supporting talented individuals who are breaking into the industry. He sees mentorship and guidance as essential components in nurturing the next generation of electronic music producers, fostering an environment where fresh perspectives can thrive.

Social Impact and Positive Change

As an artist who believes in using his platform for positive change, Bear Grillz sees the future of electronic music as a catalyst for social impact. He believes that music has the power to break through societal barriers and inspire positive change.

Bear Grillz uses his music and influence to raise awareness about environmental issues, mental health, and social justice. He envisions a future where electronic musicians continue to use their artistry to address important societal issues, sparking conversations and inspiring action among their listeners.

Through charity initiatives and collaborations with non-profit organizations, Bear Grillz aims to create a lasting impact beyond the realm of music. He sees electronic music as a catalyst for positive change, empowering individuals and communities to come together and make a difference in the world.

Conclusion

In conclusion, Bear Grillz's vision for the future of electronic music encompasses the fusion of genres, the integration of technology, the importance of community and collaboration, and the potential for social impact. With his innovative mindset and dedication to pushing creative boundaries, Bear Grillz aims to shape the future of electronic music, creating a diverse, inclusive, and socially conscious landscape for artists and listeners alike.

Through his music, Bear Grillz will continue to inspire others and pave the way for a new generation of electronic musicians who will carry forward his vision and contribute to the ever-evolving and vibrant world of electronic music.

Chapter 3: The Bear Grillz Community

Section 1: The Bear Fam

Subsection: The origins of the Bear Fam

The Bear Fam, a term coined by the fans of Bear Grillz, was not a planned community but emerged organically as Bear Grillz's music gained popularity. It all began with the release of his first few tracks, which quickly caught the attention of listeners around the globe. As the infectious beats and captivating melodies of Bear Grillz's music spread, so did the sense of connection and camaraderie among his fans.

The origins of the Bear Fam can be traced back to the early days of Bear Grillz's career, when he first started sharing his music online. Through various online platforms and social media channels, Bear Grillz was able to reach a wider audience and build a fan base that resonated deeply with his unique sound and persona. Fans drawn to Bear Grillz's music formed a bond, united by their shared love for his music and the positive energy it brought.

The Bear Fam quickly became known for its supportive and inclusive nature. Fans from all walks of life, hailing from different corners of the globe, came together under the banner of the Bear Fam. They formed a tight-knit community that celebrated the power of music to bring people together and create a sense of belonging.

What distinguishes the Bear Fam from other fan communities is the unwavering support and enthusiasm its members show for Bear Grillz and his music. The Bear Fam is not just a fan base; it is a family. It is a community where individuals can connect with others who share their passion for Bear Grillz's music, form lasting friendships, and collectively create a positive and uplifting environment.

The Bear Fam is known for its active participation in promoting Bear Grillz's music. Fans take it upon themselves to spread the word about his latest releases, organize listening parties, and engage in discussions about his music. The community's passion and dedication have played a significant role in boosting Bear Grillz's visibility and helping him reach new heights of success.

One of the unique aspects of the Bear Fam is the sense of ownership and empowerment it gives its members. Fans feel a sense of pride in being part of the Bear Fam, and many take it upon themselves to create fan art, merchandise, and even fan-run social media accounts dedicated to Bear Grillz. This level of fan engagement goes beyond just being a passive listener; it is about actively contributing to the growth and promotion of Bear Grillz's music.

In addition to its online presence, the Bear Fam has also organized numerous meet-ups and events where fans can come together in person and celebrate their shared love for Bear Grillz. These gatherings serve as a testament to the strength of the community and the deep connections formed between members. Whether it's a small local gathering or a massive fan-led event, the sense of unity and camaraderie is always palpable.

The Bear Fam's impact extends far beyond the boundaries of the electronic music community. Through various initiatives and projects, the Bear Fam has shown its commitment to making a positive difference in the world. From fundraising for charitable causes to supporting environmental conservation efforts, the Bear Fam has embraced the spirit of giving back.

The Bear Fam's dedication to philanthropy reflects the values that Bear Grillz himself holds dear. Inspired by his music and his message of unity and acceptance, the Bear Fam has taken it upon themselves to contribute to causes that align with Bear Grillz's ethos. This sense of collective responsibility and social consciousness sets the Bear Fam apart from other fan communities and showcases the power of music to inspire positive change.

In conclusion, the origins of the Bear Fam can be traced back to the early days of Bear Grillz's music career, when fans from around the world came together under the banner of his unique sound. What started as a shared love for Bear Grillz's music quickly evolved into a tight-knit community characterized by its unwavering support, camaraderie, and collective efforts to make a positive impact. The Bear Fam represents the true power of music to bring people together and create a sense of belonging.

Subsection: The Bear Fam's global reach

The Bear Fam is not just a community, but a global movement. Bear Grillz's music has reached fans across the world, connecting people from diverse backgrounds and cultures. The power of his music to bring people together has solidified the Bear Fam as a global force.

Bear Grillz's music transcends borders, resonating with listeners from all corners of the globe. Whether it's his infectious beats, uplifting melodies, or thought-provoking lyrics, his music speaks to universal emotions and experiences. This has allowed the Bear Fam to grow and expand its reach beyond traditional music communities.

One of the reasons for the Bear Fam's global reach is the accessibility of Bear Grillz's music. With the rise of digital platforms, fans from all over the world can easily discover and enjoy his music. Streaming services like Spotify, Apple Music, and YouTube have made it possible for Bear Grillz's tracks to reach millions of listeners with just a few clicks. This ease of access has contributed to the rapid growth of the Bear Fam.

Social media has also played a significant role in expanding the Bear Fam's global reach. Bear Grillz and his team have leveraged platforms like Instagram, Twitter, and Facebook to connect with fans around the world. Through these channels, fans can interact with Bear Grillz, share their love for his music, and connect with each other, fostering a sense of community. Bear Grillz's active presence on social media has helped build a loyal fanbase that spans continents.

Furthermore, Bear Grillz's collaborations with artists from different countries and cultures have contributed to the global reach of the Bear Fam. By working with musicians from diverse backgrounds, Bear Grillz has been able to tap into new audiences and introduce his music to previously untapped markets. Collaborations with international artists have not only broadened his fanbase but have also exposed fans to different genres and styles of music, enriching the Bear Fam's overall experience.

The Bear Fam's global reach is not limited to online interactions. Bear Grillz's live performances have taken him to various countries, allowing him to connect with fans on a personal and direct level. From concert venues to festivals, Bear Grillz has brought his electrifying energy and unique sound to stages across the world. These live performances have solidified the bond between Bear Grillz and his fans, creating lifelong memories and fostering a sense of community that extends beyond virtual platforms.

The Bear Fam's global reach is a testament to the power of music to transcend geographic boundaries and unite people from diverse backgrounds. Bear Grillz and his music have become a bridge, bringing together fans from different cultures, languages, and walks of life. The Bear Fam's global impact is not just about music—it's about creating a sense of belonging, connection, and unity in an increasingly interconnected world.

In conclusion, the Bear Fam's global reach is a result of Bear Grillz's accessible music, active presence on social media, collaborations with international artists, and unforgettable live performances. The Bear Fam has become a global movement that celebrates the power of music to connect and unite people from all corners of the world. Bear Grillz's influence and the impact of the Bear Fam extend far beyond the boundaries of traditional music communities, shaping the cultural landscape of electronic music on a global scale.

Subsection: Supportive Community and Fan Engagement

The success of Bear Grillz can be attributed, at least in part, to the strong and supportive community that has formed around him. The Bear Fam, as his fans are affectionately called, plays a crucial role in building and sustaining his career. This subsection will explore the ways in which the Bear Fam has contributed to Bear Grillz's journey, the impact of fan engagement on his music, and the sense of belonging and unity fostered within the community.

The Origin of the Bear Fam

The Bear Fam first began to take shape when Bear Grillz started sharing his music online. Through platforms like SoundCloud and YouTube, he was able to connect with fans who resonated with his unique sound. As word spread and more people discovered his music, a dedicated group of followers emerged, forming the foundation of the Bear Fam.

Global Reach and Sense of Belonging

What sets the Bear Fam apart is its global reach. Fans from all corners of the world have come together to celebrate and support Bear Grillz's music. Through social media, they have found a space where they can connect with like-minded individuals who share their love for his music.

The Bear Fam is not just an online phenomenon; it extends beyond the virtual world. Fan meet-ups and events are organized regularly, giving fans the opportunity to come together in person. These gatherings are not only a chance to meet Bear Grillz and watch him perform live but also an opportunity for fans to connect with each other, forming deep and lasting friendships.

Supportive Community and Fan Engagement

The Bear Fam is known for its unwavering support of Bear Grillz. Fans show their dedication by attending his shows, buying his merchandise, and spreading the word about his music. This level of fan engagement has been instrumental in Bear Grillz's rise to fame.

Fans actively promote Bear Grillz's music on their own social media platforms, sharing his tracks, remixes, and performances with their friends and followers. This organic word-of-mouth promotion has helped him reach a wider audience and gain new fans.

Moreover, the Bear Fam acts as a support system for Bear Grillz. Fans provide encouragement, feedback, and constructive criticism, which helps him refine his sound and grow as an artist. This strong bond between Bear Grillz and his fans fosters a sense of community, making the Bear Fam feel like an extended family.

Impact on Bear Grillz's Music

The influence of the Bear Fam on Bear Grillz's music cannot be overstated. The feedback and support from fans play a crucial role in shaping his sound and creative direction. By listening to his fans' opinions and preferences, Bear Grillz is able to cater to their tastes while staying true to his artistic vision.

The Bear Fam's enthusiasm and dedication also inspire Bear Grillz to push the boundaries of his music. Knowing that he has a loyal following eagerly awaiting his new releases, he feels motivated to constantly evolve and innovate. This symbiotic relationship between Bear Grillz and his fans drives him to hone his craft and deliver high-quality music.

Creating a Sense of Unity and Acceptance

One of the most remarkable aspects of the Bear Fam is the sense of unity and acceptance it fosters. Regardless of background, age, or location, Bear Grillz's music has brought people together and created a space where individuals can express themselves freely.

The Bear Fam is inclusive and welcoming, celebrating diversity and encouraging fans to embrace their unique identities. This sense of belonging resonates not only with Bear Grillz's fans but also with the artist himself. Bear Grillz has made it a priority to create a safe and supportive community where everyone feels valued and accepted.

In this way, the Bear Fam transcends being just a fan base; it has become a movement, a collective force that continues to shape and redefine the electronic music scene.

Creative Engagement with the Bear Fam

Bear Grillz actively engages with his fans, further deepening the bond with the Bear Fam. He recognizes the importance of staying connected and accessible to his audience, and he does so through various means.

Social media platforms like Twitter, Instagram, and Facebook allow Bear Grillz to communicate directly with his fans. He shares updates and behind-the-scenes glimpses of his life and music, actively responding to comments and messages.

Additionally, Bear Grillz encourages fan contributions to his music and brand. Fan remix contests, artwork competitions, and even opportunities to be featured in his music videos are just some of the ways in which he involves the Bear Fam in his creative process. By giving fans a chance to actively participate, Bear Grillz strengthens the sense of ownership and belonging within the community.

The Bear Fam's Impact on the Electronic Music Scene

The Bear Fam's impact extends beyond Bear Grillz's individual success. Through their support and dedicated engagement, they have helped solidify his position in the electronic music scene and have played a part in breaking down barriers within the industry.

The Bear Fam's influence is evident in the growing popularity of the Bearstep sub-genre, which Bear Grillz pioneered. This unique blend of heavy bass, melodic elements, and catchy hooks has influenced a new generation of producers who seek to capture the energy and emotion that Bearstep embodies.

Furthermore, the Bear Fam's support for emerging artists and collaborations within the community have created opportunities for up-and-coming talents to gain exposure. By amplifying their voices and giving them a platform, the Bear Fam has contributed to the diversification and evolution of electronic music as a whole.

The Power of Unity

In a world where division and discord often dominate, the unity and support fostered within the Bear Fam serve as a powerful reminder of the positive impact music can have. It highlights the potential of art to bring people together, transcending boundaries and creating a shared sense of purpose.

Through their unwavering support and engagement, the Bear Fam has not only propelled Bear Grillz's career to new heights but also exemplified the extraordinary power of a united community. This community-driven success story serves as an inspiration to artists and fans alike, demonstrating the value of creating meaningful connections and fostering a supportive environment.

Conclusion

The Bear Fam's supportive community and fan engagement have been instrumental in Bear Grillz's success. The global reach of the Bear Fam, the sense of belonging and unity it creates, and the impact on Bear Grillz's music highlight the significance of fan support in shaping an artist's career.

The Bear Fam goes beyond being just a fan base; it is a community that embodies inclusivity, acceptance, and creativity. Through their dedication, the Bear Fam has not only elevated Bear Grillz's music but has also left an indelible mark on the electronic music scene as a whole. The enduring legacy of the Bear Fam serves as a testament to the power of fandom and the potential for positive change within the music industry.

Subsection: Bear Fam meet-ups and events

Bear Grillz's music has always had a magnetic effect on his fans, drawing them together in a shared love for his unique sound and persona. The Bear Fam, as his community of fans is affectionately called, has grown into a supportive and active group that extends far beyond a simple appreciation for his music. Through regular meet-ups and events, the Bear Fam has created a sense of belonging and camaraderie that only strengthens their connection with Bear Grillz and each other.

Creating a Sense of Community

One of the defining characteristics of the Bear Fam is their unwavering dedication to Bear Grillz and his music. Recognizing the importance of fostering a sense of community, Bear Grillz and his team have organized numerous meet-ups and events that bring fans together in person. These gatherings provide an opportunity for fans to connect with one another, share their love for Bear Grillz's music, and forge lasting friendships.

Bear Fam Meet-ups

Bear Fam meet-ups are organized events that take place in various cities around the world, allowing fans to come together and celebrate their shared appreciation for Bear Grillz. These meet-ups typically include activities such as fan-led DJ sets, dance-offs, and even impromptu performances by Bear Grillz himself. Fans have the chance to meet their fellow Bear Fam members, exchange stories and experiences, and create memories that will last a lifetime.

Fan-led Events

The Bear Fam is known for taking initiative and organizing their own events outside of the official meet-ups. These fan-led events can range from small local gatherings to larger-scale parties or mini festivals. It is not uncommon for Bear Fam members to rent out venues, set up their own stages, and curate their own lineups featuring local up-and-coming artists. These events are a testament to the strong bond that exists within the Bear Fam and showcase the collective creativity and passion of its members.

Supportive Environment

What truly sets Bear Fam meet-ups and events apart is the supportive and inclusive environment that prevails. The Bear Fam is known for its welcoming atmosphere, where fans from all walks of life can come together and feel accepted. The events provide a safe space for self-expression, allowing attendees to fully embrace their love for Bear Grillz's music and share their enthusiasm without judgment. It's this sense of community that keeps fans coming back year after year and strengthens their connection with Bear Grillz.

Fan-led Initiatives

The Bear Fam is not only a community of music enthusiasts but also a group of individuals committed to making a positive impact on the world. Numerous fan-led initiatives have emerged within the Bear Fam, focusing on various charitable causes and social justice issues. From organizing fundraisers for environmental conservation to supporting mental health awareness campaigns, the Bear Fam is dedicated to using their collective influence and resources to make a difference.

The Power of Technology

In addition to in-person meet-ups and events, the Bear Fam also harnesses the power of technology to connect and engage with fans around the globe. Online platforms and social media play a crucial role in keeping the Bear Fam united and informed. Fans can participate in virtual meet-ups, join online forums, and engage in real-time discussions about Bear Grillz's music and upcoming events. The use of technology allows the Bear Fam to transcend geographical boundaries and maintain a strong sense of community even when they are physically apart.

Beyond the Music

While the music of Bear Grillz serves as the foundation of the Bear Fam, their connection goes far beyond just the music itself. The Bear Fam is a community that supports and uplifts its members through all aspects of life, providing a sense of belonging and shared experience. It is this deep connection and unwavering support that makes Bear Fam meet-ups and events so much more than just fan gatherings – they are a celebration of friendship, unity, and the power of music to bring people together.

Example: The Annual Bear Fest

One of the most anticipated events organized by the Bear Fam is the annual Bear Fest. This multi-day festival brings together Bear Grillz fans from all over the world for a weekend of music, friendship, and unforgettable experiences. The Bear Fest features performances by Bear Grillz himself as well as other artists from the electronic music scene. It includes various stages, each showcasing different genres and styles, ensuring there is something for everyone.

Aside from the music, the Bear Fest offers a wide range of activities and attractions, including art installations, workshops, and even opportunities to meet Bear Grillz and other artists in exclusive meet-and-greet sessions. Attendees can immerse themselves in the Bear Fam culture, where bear-themed costumes and merchandise are abundant, creating a vibrant and unique atmosphere. Bear Fest has become a highlight of the year for Bear Fam members, providing a haven where they can fully embrace their love for Bear Grillz's music and connect with like-minded individuals.

Caveat: Safety and Responsibility

While the Bear Fam prides itself on its inclusive and supportive nature, it is important to emphasize the need for safety and responsible behavior at meet-ups and events. Bear Grillz and his team prioritize the well-being of the Bear Fam members, and it is crucial for attendees to respect each other, maintain personal boundaries, and watch out for one another. Safety measures such as security personnel, designated safe zones, and strict adherence to local laws and regulations are taken to ensure that everyone can enjoy the events without any harm or mishaps. By fostering a culture of care and responsibility, the Bear Fam continues to create a welcoming and secure environment for all its members.

Exercises

1. Think about a fan community or subculture that you are part of or have observed. What activities or events could be organized to bring the community together? How would these events contribute to a sense of belonging and camaraderie within the community?

2. Discuss the potential benefits and challenges of organizing fan-led events or initiatives. How can these events positively impact the community and its members? What considerations should be taken into account to ensure the success and safety of such events?

3. Reflect on the role of technology in fostering fan communities. How can online platforms and social media be utilized to connect and engage with fans? Discuss the advantages and disadvantages of virtual meet-ups and online forums as means of community-building.

4. Research and identify a charitable cause or social justice issue that resonates with you. Brainstorm ideas for fan-led initiatives that could support this cause. How could the Bear Fam or a similar community contribute to making a difference in this area?

Resources

1. The Bear Grillz website (www.beargrillz.com) offers updates on meet-ups, events, and other community-related news.

2. Join online fan forums and communities to connect with fellow Bear Fam members and participate in discussions about upcoming events and initiatives.

3. Stay updated on Bear Grillz's social media channels for announcements and information about meet-ups and events. Follow the official Bear Fam accounts for community news and updates.

4. Research online resources on event planning and organization for inspiration and practical information on arranging fan-led events or initiatives.

Remember, the Bear Fam is not just a fan community – it's a family. Bear Grillz and his team work diligently to ensure that the Bear Fam experiences a sense of belonging, shared experiences, and opportunities to make a difference. Through meet-ups and events, the Bear Fam continues to strengthen its bond, leaving a lasting legacy in the world of electronic music.

Subsection: The impact of the Bear Fam on Bear Grillz's career

The Bear Fam, the dedicated community of fans that has grown around Bear Grillz, has played a significant role in shaping the trajectory of his career. Their unwavering support, engagement, and passion for his music have had a profound impact on Bear Grillz's success and artistic development.

Creating a Supportive Community: The Bear Fam has created a supportive and inclusive community where fans can connect with one another and share their love for Bear Grillz's music. This sense of belonging has fostered a strong bond among fans, who not only support Bear Grillz but also uplift and inspire each other. The community provides a space for fans to discuss their favorite tracks, share personal experiences related to Bear Grillz's music, and exchange ideas.

Word-of-Mouth Promotion: The Bear Fam has played a critical role in promoting Bear Grillz's music through word-of-mouth. Their enthusiasm and passion for his music have led to recommendations to friends, family, and colleagues, thereby expanding Bear Grillz's fan base. By sharing their favorite tracks and experiences with others, the Bear Fam has helped to grow Bear Grillz's career and increase his visibility.

Online Presence and Social Media: The Bear Fam's active presence on social media platforms such as Twitter, Instagram, and Facebook has been instrumental in spreading Bear Grillz's music to a wider audience. They actively engage with Bear Grillz's posts, share his content, and create their own fan art and remixes. This organic promotion and online buzz generated by the Bear Fam have contributed to Bear Grillz's recognition in the electronic music community.

Impact on Live Performances: The Bear Fam's passion extends to Bear Grillz's live performances. Their presence at concerts, festivals, and shows creates an electrifying atmosphere, enhancing the overall experience for both Bear Grillz and his audience. The contagious energy of the Bear Fam encourages other attendees to join in and become part of the supportive and vibrant community.

Inspiration for Bear Grillz: The Bear Fam's love and appreciation for Bear Grillz's music have provided him with the motivation to continue pushing boundaries and exploring new musical territories. Their feedback, testimonials, and personal stories have inspired Bear Grillz to create music that resonates deeply with his fans. The Bear Fam's support fuels Bear Grillz's creativity and artistic growth, allowing him to continually evolve and innovate.

Involvement in Philanthropy: In addition to their impact on Bear Grillz's career, the Bear Fam has also been actively involved in various philanthropic initiatives supported by Bear Grillz. Their contributions and participation in charitable causes have helped make a difference in the lives of others, reflecting the values of unity and positivity that Bear Grillz stands for.

Continued Growth and Success: The Bear Fam's unwavering support has propelled Bear Grillz to new heights of success. Their dedication and loyalty have allowed him to reach a wider audience and establish himself as a prominent figure in the electronic music scene. The Bear Fam's impact on Bear Grillz's career is a testament to the power of a passionate and engaged fan base.

The Bear Fam's influence on Bear Grillz's career extends far beyond the music itself. Their support, promotion, and active engagement have contributed significantly to his growth as an artist and his ability to make a positive impact on the electronic music community. Furthermore, their involvement in philanthropic efforts showcases the Bear Fam's commitment to using music as a catalyst for change and social good. As Bear Grillz continues to evolve and shape the future of electronic music, the Bear Fam will undoubtedly remain an integral part of his journey.

Subsection: The community's role in spreading Bear Grillz's music

The Bear Grillz community, affectionately known as the Bear Fam, plays a vital role in spreading Bear Grillz's music to a wider audience. This tight-knit community of passionate fans not only supports Bear Grillz but actively engages in promoting his music, connecting with fellow fans, and creating a positive and inclusive environment for everyone.

At the heart of the Bear Fam's role in spreading Bear Grillz's music is their dedication and enthusiasm. These fans go above and beyond to share his music through word of mouth, social media, and various online platforms. Whether they're posting about his latest tracks, creating fan art, or discussing his music in forums and communities, the Bear Fam is instrumental in extending the reach of Bear Grillz's music.

To further amplify Bear Grillz's music, the Bear Fam organizes and participates in fan-led initiatives and events. These include online listening parties, where fans come together to listen to and discuss Bear Grillz's music simultaneously, creating a shared experience and fostering a sense of community. Such events not only generate excitement but also encourage fans to share their favorite tracks with others.

In addition, the Bear Fam plays a crucial role in curating playlists featuring Bear Grillz's music. These playlists showcase his tracks alongside other artists in the electronic music scene, allowing fans to introduce Bear Grillz's unique sound to new listeners. By actively promoting and sharing these playlists, the Bear Fam extends the exposure of Bear Grillz's music beyond their immediate circle.

The Bear Fam's role in spreading Bear Grillz's music extends beyond the digital realm. They organize local events and meet-ups where fans can come together to celebrate Bear Grillz's music, fostering a sense of camaraderie and connection. These events not only provide an opportunity for fans to meet in person but also create valuable offline spaces for sharing and discovering music.

Furthermore, the Bear Fam takes an active role in supporting Bear Grillz's performances. They attend his shows, bringing their infectious energy and enthusiasm, and often document these experiences through photos and videos, which they share on social media platforms. This documentation not only serves as a cherished memory for the fans but also creates buzz and interest among those who have yet to experience a Bear Grillz live performance.

The community's role in spreading Bear Grillz's music goes beyond mere promotion. The Bear Fam has become a strong support system for both Bear Grillz and each other. Fans help newcomers navigate Bear Grillz's extensive discography, recommending standout tracks and albums. They create online forums and groups where fans can discuss their favorite moments in Bear Grillz's music, share stories, and connect with like-minded individuals. The Bear Fam's unwavering dedication and genuine love for Bear Grillz create a welcoming space where newcomers feel encouraged to explore his music.

To keep the community engaged, Bear Grillz actively interacts with his fans. He frequently takes the time to reply to comments on social media, organize Q&A sessions, and even host exclusive events for the Bear Fam. This direct engagement further strengthens the bond between Bear Grillz and his fans, nurturing a sense of belonging and loyalty within the community.

In conclusion, the Bear Fam's role in spreading Bear Grillz's music is essential. Through their dedication, passion, and support, they amplify his music to new listeners, foster a strong sense of community, and create a positive and inclusive environment for all fans. The Bear Fam is a driving force behind Bear Grillz's success, and their unwavering support ensures that his music continues to reach and resonate with a global audience.

Subsection: The Bear Fam's influence on the electronic music scene

The Bear Fam, the dedicated community of Bear Grillz fans, has had a profound influence on the electronic music scene. Their passion, support, and engagement have helped shape and propel Bear Grillz's career, and in turn, have made a significant impact on the broader industry. Let's explore how the Bear Fam's influence has played a role in the evolution of electronic music.

First and foremost, the Bear Fam's unwavering dedication and enthusiastic support have elevated Bear Grillz's music to new heights. Their active engagement with his releases, attending concerts, and sharing his music on various social media platforms have helped increase his visibility and reach. The Bear Fam's word-of-mouth promotion has not only expanded Bear Grillz's fanbase but also introduced his music to new listeners who may have otherwise remained unaware of his unique sound. As a result, Bear Grillz's popularity has skyrocketed, and his influence within the electronic music scene has grown exponentially.

Furthermore, the Bear Fam's active participation has had a ripple effect on the industry. As they rally behind Bear Grillz, they contribute to the overall buzz and excitement surrounding his music. This heightened awareness has led to opportunities for collaboration with other artists and established musicians within the genre. By showcasing their love for Bear Grillz and his music, the Bear Fam has helped him secure collaborations with like-minded artists, thereby creating connections and fostering relationships within the electronic music community. These collaborations not only enrich Bear Grillz's sound but also contribute to the overall innovation and growth of the genre.

In addition to supporting Bear Grillz, the Bear Fam has taken it upon themselves to promote up-and-coming artists within the electronic music scene. Through various initiatives such as fan-curated playlists, live stream events, and social media shout-outs, the Bear Fam actively champions emerging talents. By using their platform to shine a spotlight on these artists, they help cultivate a supportive and nurturing environment within the electronic music community. The Bear Fam's efforts to support and uplift fellow musicians have created opportunities for recognition and growth, fostering a thriving scene that welcomes and celebrates new talent.

One unique aspect of the Bear Fam's influence is their commitment to charitable causes and philanthropic endeavors. The community organizes fundraising events, charity auctions, and awareness campaigns, demonstrating their dedication to making a positive difference in the world. Through their collective efforts, the Bear Fam has demonstrated the potential for the electronic music scene to go beyond solely entertaining and amassing fame, and to serve as a force for social change and impact. Their philanthropic initiatives have inspired others within the industry to follow suit, fostering a culture of giving back and making a difference.

The Bear Fam's influence extends beyond their support for Bear Grillz and their contributions to the electronic music community. The community's positivity, inclusivity, and unity have created a sense of belonging and camaraderie among its members. Through their shared love for Bear Grillz's music, they have forged friendships and connections that transcend geographical boundaries. The Bear Fam has become a tight-knit family, providing a support system and a safe space for fans to express their love for electronic music freely.

In conclusion, the Bear Fam's influence on the electronic music scene is undeniable. Their unwavering support, active engagement, and dedication to spreading Bear Grillz's music have elevated both the artist and the genre. Through their efforts, they have helped shape the evolution of electronic music, fostering a thriving community that supports emerging artists and amplifies voices for positive change. The Bear Fam serves as an inspiring example of the impact that a dedicated fanbase can have, not only on an artist's career but also on the broader music industry.

Subsection: Bear Fam-led initiatives and community projects

The Bear Fam is not just a fanbase, but a community that actively engages in various initiatives and projects to promote positivity, unity, and social change. Led by the passionate fans of Bear Grillz, these initiatives have not only made a significant impact within the community but have also extended their reach to make a difference in the world.

One of the main pillars of Bear Fam-led initiatives is their commitment to philanthropy and giving back to society. The Bear Fam has organized numerous charity events and fundraisers to support various causes, including environmental conservation, mental health awareness, education, and social justice. Through these events, the Bear Fam has raised substantial funds and garnered attention for these important issues.

To further support emerging talent, the Bear Fam has initiated programs that provide opportunities for up-and-coming artists within the electronic music community. These initiatives include mentorship programs, talent showcases, and collaborative projects. By nurturing and promoting the next generation of artists, the Bear Fam aims to create a vibrant and inclusive music scene that encourages creativity and innovation.

Another notable initiative led by the Bear Fam is the organization of fan meet-ups and events. These gatherings not only give Bear Fam members a chance to connect with fellow fans but also provide a platform for new friendships to form. The sense of community and belonging fostered through these events has been instrumental in creating a supportive environment where fans can share their love for Bear Grillz's music and foster lifelong connections.

In addition to these larger-scale initiatives, individual members of the Bear Fam have also taken it upon themselves to organize smaller community projects. Whether it's organizing clothing drives, volunteering at local shelters, or even creating art installations inspired by Bear Grillz's music, these projects reflect the creativity and personal investment that the Bear Fam has in making a positive impact in their local communities.

The Bear Fam's commitment to making a difference in the world extends beyond their immediate communities. Through the use of social media platforms and online forums, the Bear Fam has been able to connect with like-minded individuals from all corners of the globe. This global reach has allowed the Bear Fam to collaborate with fans from different countries and cultures to organize international community projects that address various social and environmental issues.

One such project involved the Bear Fam partnering with environmental organizations to organize beach clean-ups and raise awareness about marine pollution. This initiative not only had a positive impact on the environment, but it also demonstrated the power of community-driven efforts in bringing about real change.

Furthermore, the Bear Fam's influence goes beyond their involvement in philanthropic initiatives and community projects. The strong sense of unity and support within the Bear Fam has created a community that champions inclusivity and acceptance. By promoting these values, the Bear Fam has become a role model for other fan communities and has contributed to breaking down barriers within the music industry.

To celebrate the accomplishments of the Bear Fam and their impact on both the community and the broader electronic music scene, Bear Grillz regularly acknowledges and recognizes outstanding contributions from their fans. This recognition not only highlights the dedication and effort put forth by individual Bear Fam members but also serves as an inspiration for others to get involved and make a difference.

Overall, the Bear Fam-led initiatives and community projects showcase the immense power of a passionate and dedicated fanbase. Through their collective efforts, the Bear Fam has created a positive and supportive community that goes beyond the music, actively making a difference in the world.

Subsection: The Bear Fam's connection to Bear Grillz's music

The Bear Fam, a devoted community of fans, plays a vital role in the success and growth of Bear Grillz as an artist. Their connection to Bear Grillz's music is characterized by a profound sense of support, unity, and shared passion for his unique sound. This subsection explores how the Bear Fam's unwavering support and active engagement contribute to the overall experience of Bear Grillz's music.

The Power of Music in Community Building

Music has always had the power to bring people together, forming communities that transcend geographic boundaries. The Bear Fam represents a diverse group of individuals who share a strong emotional connection to Bear Grillz's music and the values he embodies. Through his distinctive blend of captivating melodies, heavy basslines, and powerful drops, Bear Grillz creates a sonic landscape that resonates deeply with his fans, drawing them into a shared experience.

The Bear Fam transcends being just a fanbase; it has emerged as a tight-knit community driven by a collective love for Bear Grillz's music. With its roots in both online platforms and real-life meet-ups and events, the Bear Fam actively supports and engages with Bear Grillz and his music. The sense of belonging and camaraderie within the Bear Fam is a testament to the powerful impact of Bear Grillz's music in community building.

Engagement and Support within the Bear Fam

One of the remarkable aspects of the Bear Fam is its unwavering support for Bear Grillz. Whether through social media interactions, attending live shows, or participating in fan-led initiatives, the Bear Fam demonstrates its dedication to Bear Grillz and his music. This active engagement manifests in various forms, including creating fan art, organizing fan-run events, and even collaborating with Bear Grillz on special projects.

The Bear Fam's support extends beyond Bear Grillz's music. They actively promote his charitable endeavors, spreading awareness of his philanthropic projects and joining him in contributing to important causes. Together, the Bear Fam and Bear Grillz are a force for positive change, using their shared passion for music to make a difference in the world.

Fostering a Positive and Inclusive Community

The Bear Fam has become a shining example of a supportive and inclusive community. Through their collective love for Bear Grillz's music, they transcend traditional boundaries and create a safe space for individuals from diverse backgrounds to connect and express themselves. In this community, differences are celebrated, and everyone feels accepted and valued.

The Bear Fam's commitment to inclusivity and positivity is reflected in their interactions with one another and with Bear Grillz. Fans support each other through difficult times and celebrate their shared successes. This unity and compassion add an extra layer of depth to the entire Bear Grillz experience, creating a profound sense of belonging for both Bear Grillz and his fans.

Promoting Growth and Creativity

The Bear Fam plays a crucial role in promoting the growth and creativity of both Bear Grillz and its own members. By actively engaging with Bear Grillz's music, fans provide invaluable feedback and encouragement, which helps Bear Grillz refine his sound and continuously evolve as an artist. Similarly, the Bear Fam serves as a platform for aspiring artists to share their own music and receive constructive criticism and guidance from a supportive community.

Furthermore, the Bear Fam's engagement and enthusiasm inspire Bear Grillz to push the boundaries of his creativity. Knowing that his music resonates with such a dedicated and passionate audience motivates him to explore new musical territories and experiment with different styles, allowing his sound to continue evolving.

The Emotional Connection Between Bear Grillz's Music and the Bear Fam

The emotional connection between Bear Grillz's music and the Bear Fam is at the core of their relationship. For many fans, Bear Grillz's music becomes a soundtrack to their lives, providing a source of inspiration, solace, and empowerment. The heavy basslines and energetic drops create a visceral experience that connects deeply with the emotions of the listeners.

Through deeply personal and relatable lyrics and euphoric melodies, Bear Grillz's music has the power to evoke a wide range of emotions within the Bear Fam. Whether it's the cathartic release of energy during a live performance or the introspective journey facilitated by his melodic tracks, the emotional connection between Bear Grillz's music and the Bear Fam is a key factor in their bond.

The Future of the Bear Fam

As Bear Grillz's music continues to captivate listeners across the globe, the Bear Fam's role in his journey is set to expand further. The community's passion and support will remain integral to his continued success and growth as an artist. The Bear Fam's influence will extend beyond the realm of music, as they actively contribute to causes they care about, united by the shared values instilled by Bear Grillz's music.

Looking ahead, the Bear Fam will continue to shape the direction of Bear Grillz's music through their engagement, feedback, and unwavering support. This powerful connection between Bear Grillz and his fans will not only define his present career but also leave an enduring legacy for future generations of artists and fan communities to aspire to.

In conclusion, the Bear Fam's connection to Bear Grillz's music goes far beyond being mere fans. Their support, engagement, and unity create a vibrant community that amplifies the impact of Bear Grillz's music and fosters a sense of belonging for fans. The Bear Fam's dedication and passion serve as a testament to the profound connection between music, community, and the human experience.

Subsection: The role of technology in fostering fan communities

In today's digital age, technology plays a crucial role in fostering and connecting fan communities. With the rise of social media, streaming platforms, and other digital tools, fans now have unprecedented access to their favorite artists and can engage with each other in ways that were not possible before. In this subsection, we will explore the various ways in which technology has transformed the relationship between artists like Bear Grillz and their fans, creating a sense of unity and camaraderie within the Bear Fam.

Social media: Breaking down barriers

One of the most significant advancements in technology that has fueled the growth of fan communities is the advent of social media platforms such as Twitter, Instagram, and Facebook. These platforms have become virtual meeting places where fans can connect, share their love for Bear Grillz's music, and stay updated with the latest news and announcements. Through social media, Bear Grillz has been able to directly interact with his fans, breaking down the traditional barriers that existed between artists and their supporters.

Fans can now reach out to Bear Grillz, ask questions, and receive real-time responses, creating a sense of intimacy and connection. Moreover, social media allows fans to connect with each other, forming friendships and bonds based on their shared love for Bear Grillz's music. Local fan groups have emerged, organizing meetups, watch parties, and other events, further strengthening the sense of community and camaraderie.

Streaming platforms: Bringing music to the masses

Another technological development that has revolutionized the music industry is the emergence of streaming platforms such as Spotify, Apple Music, and SoundCloud. These platforms have made music more accessible than ever before, allowing Bear Grillz's songs to reach a global audience with a simple click.

Streaming platforms also provide fans with the opportunity to discover new music and artists, further expanding the Bear Fam. Through curated playlists, recommendations, and personalized algorithms, fans can explore a diverse range of music that aligns with their tastes. This has not only helped Bear Grillz gain new followers but has also allowed his fans to connect with each other over their shared passion for his music.

Live streaming: A virtual concert experience

In recent years, live streaming technology has gained popularity, providing an alternative to in-person concerts and festivals. Fans can now tune in to live streams of Bear Grillz's performances from the comfort of their own homes, creating a virtual concert experience.

Live streaming not only allows fans from all over the world to witness Bear Grillz's electrifying performances but also provides an opportunity for real-time interaction. Fans can engage with the artist and other viewers through comments and chat features, creating a sense of unity and excitement.

Furthermore, live streaming technology has also enabled Bear Grillz to connect with fans during unprecedented times, such as the COVID-19 pandemic. By hosting virtual concerts, Bear Grillz has been able to continue entertaining his fans and maintaining the sense of community and support within the Bear Fam.

Online forums and fan websites: Allowing deeper engagement

In addition to social media platforms, online forums and fan websites dedicated to Bear Grillz provide fans with a space to engage in deeper discussions and share their thoughts and experiences. These forums provide an avenue for fans to connect with like-minded individuals, exchange ideas, and learn more about Bear Grillz's music.

Fan websites often offer exclusive content such as behind-the-scenes footage, interviews, and fan art, creating a sense of exclusivity and reward for dedicated fans.

This fosters a strong sense of community, encouraging fans to actively participate and contribute to the Bear Fam.

Technology as a catalyst for creativity

Technology not only facilitates fan engagement but also serves as a catalyst for creativity within the Bear Fam. Fans can now create their own remixes, fan art, and music videos inspired by Bear Grillz's music, showcasing their talent and love for the artist.

Digital tools and software have made it easier than ever for fans to express their creativity and share their work with the Bear Fam. This not only strengthens the bond between fans but also provides Bear Grillz with a constant source of inspiration and feedback.

The future of fan communities

As technology continues to advance, the role of technology in fostering fan communities will only grow stronger. Virtual reality (VR) and augmented reality (AR) technologies hold the promise of immersive concert experiences, allowing fans to feel like they are right there with Bear Grillz, even from thousands of miles away.

Artificial intelligence (AI) and machine learning algorithms may also play a role in enhancing the fan experience, providing personalized recommendations, and creating interactive virtual fan experiences. These technologies have the potential to transform the way fans engage with Bear Grillz's music and each other, creating a more immersive and personalized fan experience.

In conclusion, technology has revolutionized the way artists like Bear Grillz interact with their fans and foster fan communities. Through social media, streaming platforms, live streaming, online forums, and fan websites, fans now have unprecedented access to their favorite artists and can connect with each other on a global scale. As technology continues to advance, the future holds exciting possibilities for further enhancing the fan experience and strengthening the sense of unity within the Bear Fam.

Section 2: Transforming Lives Through Music

Subsection: Bear Grillz's music as a source of inspiration

Bear Grillz's music has served as a powerful source of inspiration for countless fans around the world. His unique blend of electronic beats, heavy basslines, and melodic elements resonates deeply with listeners, evoking a sense of energy, passion, and creativity. Through his music, Bear Grillz taps into the raw emotions and experiences that connect us all, creating a sonic journey that transports listeners to another realm.

One of the key aspects of Bear Grillz's music that inspires his fans is his ability to capture the essence of the human experience. His tracks often explore themes of resilience, overcoming adversity, and the pursuit of personal growth. By infusing his music with uplifting and empowering messages, Bear Grillz instills a sense of hope and determination in his listeners. Whether it's through anthemic melodies or powerful lyrics, he has the ability to ignite a spark within his fans, encouraging them to chase their dreams and embrace their true selves.

Bear Grillz's music also serves as a form of self-expression and release for his audience. His energetic beats and infectious rhythms provide an outlet for listeners to channel their emotions and let go of any negativity or stress. The high energy of his tracks can be invigorating, motivating listeners to push themselves beyond their limits and embrace their inner strength.

Beyond the emotional impact, Bear Grillz's music is also a technical marvel. His intricate sound design and meticulous attention to detail create a sonic experience that captivates the senses. From the rich textures of his basslines to the catchy melodies that weave throughout his tracks, Bear Grillz showcases his expertise in crafting music that is both engaging and immersive. This technical prowess serves as an inspiration to aspiring producers and musicians, encouraging them to experiment with sound and push the boundaries of their own creativity.

One of the reasons why Bear Grillz's music is so inspiring is its ability to transcend genre boundaries. While primarily known for his signature Bearstep sound, which combines elements of dubstep, trap, and future bass, he effortlessly incorporates influences from various genres into his music. Whether it's incorporating elements of hip-hop, rock, or even orchestral arrangements, Bear Grillz showcases his versatility as an artist and proves that creativity knows no bounds.

To further inspire his fans, Bear Grillz often shares stories and personal anecdotes during his live performances, offering a glimpse into the motivations and experiences that have shaped his music. By connecting with his audience on a personal level, he creates a sense of camaraderie and unity, reinforcing the idea that music has the power to bring people together.

In addition to the emotional and technical aspects of his music, Bear Grillz's dedication to philanthropy and making a positive impact on the world further inspires his fans. His commitment to environmental conservation, mental health awareness, and social justice initiatives demonstrates that music can be a powerful tool for social change. By using his platform to raise awareness and support meaningful causes, Bear Grillz sets an example for his fans, encouraging them to use their own talents and passions to make a difference in the world.

In conclusion, Bear Grillz's music serves as a profound source of inspiration for his fans. Through his unique sound, uplifting messages, technical prowess, genre-defying creativity, and dedication to philanthropy, he embodies the transformative power of music. His music resonates with listeners on a deep level, providing a source of motivation, emotional release, and a reminder of the universal experiences that connect us all. Above all, Bear Grillz's music inspires his fans to embrace their true selves, follow their passions, and strive for positive change in the world.

Subsection: Connecting with fans on a personal level

Connecting with fans on a personal level is one of the most important aspects of Bear Grillz's career. Despite his global success and fame, Bear Grillz understands the importance of maintaining a strong connection with his fans. In this subsection, we will explore the ways in which Bear Grillz connects with his fans on a personal level, the impact of these connections, and the strategies he employs to foster these relationships.

Establishing Personal Connections

Bear Grillz recognizes that his fans are the driving force behind his success, and he values their support tremendously. To establish personal connections with his fans, Bear Grillz uses various platforms and opportunities to interact with them directly. Social media plays a significant role in serving as a bridge between the artist and his fans. Bear Grillz actively engages with his followers on platforms such as Twitter, Instagram, and Facebook, responding to their comments, messages, and tagging their artwork or covers of his songs. This direct interaction makes his fans feel seen and appreciated, fostering a sense of community within the "Bear Fam".

Additionally, Bear Grillz organizes fan meet-ups and events, creating opportunities for face-to-face interactions. These events allow his fans to connect not only with him but also with each other, strengthening the bond within the Bear Fam. These personal encounters provide a unique opportunity for Bear Grillz to express his gratitude, share stories, and truly connect with his fans on a deeper level.

Engaging in Meaningful Conversations

Beyond social media interactions and fan events, Bear Grillz takes the time to engage in meaningful conversations with his fans. Whether it's during a meet-and-greet, through email correspondence, or even through live-streamed Q&A sessions, Bear Grillz actively seeks opportunities to have direct conversations with his fans.

He values their opinions and feedback and genuinely listens to their experiences and stories. By actively engaging in dialogue, Bear Grillz creates an environment where his fans feel comfortable and supported. This two-way communication helps strengthen the personal connection and allows Bear Grillz to understand his fans' needs and desires better.

Creating Personalized Experiences

Bear Grillz goes above and beyond to create personalized experiences for his fans, recognizing that they are not just a collective, but individuals with unique stories and interests. Whether it's through personalized messages, surprise gifts, or recognizing fans at shows, he strives to make the Bear Fam feel seen and valued.

For example, Bear Grillz may send personalized messages to fans on their birthdays or special occasions. He may also go out of his way to meet up with fans who have traveled long distances to attend his shows, creating unforgettable memories for both the fan and himself. These personalized experiences leave a lasting impression and demonstrate his dedication to fostering genuine connections.

Supporting the Bear Fam

In addition to engaging and connecting with his fans, Bear Grillz actively supports the Bear Fam. He encourages fans to connect with each other, fostering a sense of community among his followers. Through social media shout-outs and encouraging interactions among fans, he creates a space for them to share their artwork, covers, and experiences related to his music. This shared passion for Bear Grillz's music creates a strong bond within the Bear Fam that extends beyond a simple fan-artist relationship.

Bear Grillz also supports fan-led initiatives and charitable causes. By actively promoting and participating in these initiatives, he demonstrates his commitment to making a positive impact on the world alongside his fans.

Inspiring and Empowering Fans

Bear Grillz recognizes the significant impact he has on his fans. Through his music and personal interactions, he seeks to inspire and empower them. He uses his platform to spread messages of positivity, self-acceptance, and strength. Bear Grillz's music serves as a source of inspiration for his fans, often resonating with them on a deep emotional level. By sharing his own experiences and challenges, Bear Grillz shows his fans that they are not alone and that they too can overcome their obstacles.

Through his personal interactions with fans, Bear Grillz provides encouragement and support, empowering his fans to pursue their own passions and dreams. Whether it's through a kind message, a word of advice, or a simple acknowledgment, he helps his fans believe in themselves and their capabilities.

The Impact of Connecting with Fans

Bear Grillz's commitment to connecting with his fans on a personal level has had a profound impact on both his career and the lives of his fans. By establishing genuine connections, he has created a loyal and dedicated fan base that continues to support him as he evolves as an artist. The personal connections formed between Bear Grillz and his fans have contributed to the growth of the Bear Fam community, fostering a sense of belonging and unity.

For his fans, Bear Grillz's personal interactions uplift and inspire them. Through his music and his presence, he provides a sense of comfort and support, creating a safe space where people can come together and express themselves freely. The personal connections forged with Bear Grillz empower his fans to pursue their passions, overcome challenges, and make a positive difference in their own lives and communities.

Example: The Impact of a Personal Connection

To illustrate the significance of Bear Grillz's personal connections with fans, let's consider the story of Sarah, a devoted Bear Fam member. Sarah has been a fan of Bear Grillz since his early days and has always admired his talent and energy. One day, Sarah attended a fan event where she had the opportunity to meet Bear Grillz in person. During their brief interaction, Bear Grillz took the time to personally thank Sarah for her support and expressed genuine interest in her passion for music.

This encounter left a profound impact on Sarah. She felt seen and validated by an artist she had admired for years. From that day forward, Sarah's connection with Bear Grillz deepened, and she became an active member of the Bear Fam community. Inspired by Bear Grillz's personal journey and the encouragement he provided, Sarah pursued her dream of becoming a DJ herself.

Sarah's story is just one of many examples of how Bear Grillz's personal connections with fans can have a transformative effect. By making an effort to connect with fans on a personal level, Bear Grillz creates a ripple effect that inspires and empowers individuals to pursue their own passions, ultimately contributing to the growth of the electronic music community as a whole.

Conclusion

Connecting with fans on a personal level is a cornerstone of Bear Grillz's approach to his career. By actively engaging with his fans, having meaningful conversations, creating personalized experiences, supporting the Bear Fam, and inspiring and empowering his followers, Bear Grillz has cultivated a strong and loyal fan base. This personal connection not only enriches the lives of his fans but also fuels the growth and success of Bear Grillz as an artist. Through his dedication to fostering genuine connections, Bear Grillz serves as an inspiration to artists and fans alike, proving that the power of music extends far beyond the confines of the stage.

Subsection: Stories of fans' lives changed by Bear Grillz's music

Bear Grillz's music has had a profound impact on the lives of countless fans around the world. Through his powerful beats and emotionally charged melodies, Bear Grillz has touched the hearts and souls of listeners, providing them with a sense of solace, inspiration, and empowerment. Here are just a few stories of fans whose lives have been changed by Bear Grillz's music.

Story 1: Overcoming Mental Health Struggles

Sarah, a 23-year-old college student, was battling severe depression and anxiety. She felt lost and disconnected from the world, often finding it difficult to get out of bed or engage in activities she used to enjoy. One day, a friend introduced her to Bear Grillz's music, and Sarah instantly felt a deep connection to the raw emotion and energy of his tracks.

As she listened to Bear Grillz's music, Sarah found comfort in the relatable lyrics that spoke to her own struggles. The hard-hitting beats and uplifting melodies acted as a catalyst for her healing journey. Inspired by Bear Grillz's resilience and authenticity, Sarah started seeking professional help and making positive changes in her life.

Through his music, Bear Grillz became an anchor of hope for Sarah, reminding her that she was not alone in her struggles. She now attends his concerts, where she feels a sense of belonging and finds solace in the shared experience with fellow fans. Bear Grillz's music continues to be a source of strength for Sarah, helping her navigate the ups and downs of life with a newfound sense of purpose.

Story 2: Finding Self-Expression and Identity

John, a 19-year-old aspiring artist, had always struggled with expressing himself through his artwork. He often felt apprehensive about showcasing his creations, fearing judgment and rejection. However, after discovering Bear Grillz's music, John found the courage to embrace his unique style and unleash his creativity.

The high-energy beats and eclectic soundscapes in Bear Grillz's tracks inspired John to experiment with different techniques and explore new artistic avenues. Through his music, Bear Grillz championed the idea of embracing individuality and self-expression, encouraging John to break free from societal norms and pursue his artistic vision without reservations.

The impact of Bear Grillz's music on John's life extended beyond his art. The messages of empowerment and authenticity in Bear Grillz's tracks resonated deeply with John, helping him develop a stronger sense of self-identity. He found a community of like-minded fans who celebrated his artistic endeavors and provided valuable feedback and support.

Now, John proudly showcases his artwork at local exhibits, and his unique style has gained recognition in the art community. He credits Bear Grillz's music for giving him the confidence to pursue his passion wholeheartedly and for instilling in him the belief that his voice deserves to be heard.

Story 3: Building Bridges and a Sense of Belonging

Emily, a 28-year-old music lover, had always felt like an outsider in her small hometown. She yearned for connection and a sense of belonging but struggled to find people who shared her passion for electronic music. That all changed when she attended a Bear Grillz concert.

As Emily immersed herself in the electrifying atmosphere of the show, surrounded by fellow Bear Grillz fans, she felt an immediate sense of camaraderie. The music brought people from diverse backgrounds together, forming a tight-knit community united by their shared love for Bear Grillz's music.

Through attending Bear Grillz's concerts and connecting with other fans, Emily forged lifelong friendships and established a network of like-minded individuals who understood and appreciated her love for electronic music. The

Bear Grillz community provided her with a sense of belonging she had longed for, creating a space where she could fully express herself without judgment.

Inspired by the inclusive and accepting nature of the Bear Grillz fan base, Emily started organizing local music events and meetups, fostering a sense of community in her hometown. The transformative power of Bear Grillz's music not only changed Emily's life but also sparked positive change in her community, bringing together individuals who might have otherwise felt isolated.

These stories are just a glimpse into the impact Bear Grillz's music has had on countless lives. From providing hope and healing to creating communities of like-minded individuals, Bear Grillz's music continues to inspire and empower fans around the world. Through his artistry and dedication to his fans, Bear Grillz has created not just a musical legacy, but also a profound and lasting impact on the lives of his listeners.

Subsection: Philanthropic initiatives supported by the Bear Fam

One of the most remarkable aspects of the Bear Grillz community, fondly referred to as the Bear Fam, is their unwavering commitment to philanthropy. The Bear Fam is well-known for their support of various charitable organizations and their dedication to making a positive impact in the world. Bear Grillz himself has been an inspiration and driving force behind countless philanthropic initiatives, leveraging his platform to bring attention to important causes and raise funds for those in need.

One of the key philanthropic initiatives supported by the Bear Fam is environmental conservation. As a symbol of nature and the wilderness, Bear Grillz has prioritized initiatives that aim to protect the planet's natural resources and raise awareness about environmental issues. The Bear Fam has partnered with organizations such as Greenpeace, WWF, and Surfrider Foundation to fund initiatives that focus on reforestation, beach cleanups, and marine conservation efforts.

To support these causes, the Bear Fam organizes charity events and fundraisers, channeling their collective efforts towards supporting organizations committed to preserving the environment. These events often feature performances by Bear Grillz himself and other artists from the electronic music community, creating a unique blend of entertainment and activism. The proceeds from these events go directly to the supported organizations, making a tangible impact on the ground.

In addition to environmental causes, the Bear Fam also rallies behind initiatives that promote mental health awareness. Bear Grillz, being open about his own mental health struggles, understands the importance of prioritizing emotional well-being. The Bear Fam has partnered with mental health organizations such as

NAMI (National Alliance on Mental Illness) and To Write Love on Her Arms to raise awareness about mental health issues, provide support for those in need, and challenge the stigma surrounding mental illness.

These initiatives often involve collaborations with mental health professionals, who offer resources and guidance to those seeking support within the community. Together, the Bear Fam works towards creating a safe and judgment-free environment where individuals can openly discuss their mental health journeys and find solace in the support of others.

Furthermore, the Bear Fam actively supports education and community-based programs, recognizing the transformative power of knowledge and art. Bear Grillz has been an advocate for music education in schools, underscoring the importance of nurturing creativity and providing access to music programs for all students. The Bear Fam has partnered with organizations like VH1 Save The Music and Little Kids Rock to fund music education initiatives, ensuring that young individuals have the opportunity to explore their musical talents and pursue their passions.

Bear Grillz and the Bear Fam also prioritize their local communities, engaging in initiatives such as food drives, toy drives, and volunteer work at local shelters and community centers. They understand the importance of uplifting those less fortunate and strive to bring joy and happiness through their acts of kindness. These grassroots efforts further strengthen the bond within the community, fostering a sense of unity and shared purpose.

In addition to their direct involvement in charitable projects, the Bear Fam actively promotes social justice initiatives and campaigns for equality. Bear Grillz has spoken out on issues such as racial injustice, LGBTQ+ rights, and gender equality, using his platform to amplify marginalized voices and advocate for change. The Bear Fam actively supports nonprofits and organizations dedicated to fighting for social justice, providing financial aid, and raising awareness through their collective efforts.

To maximize the impact of their philanthropic endeavors, the Bear Fam utilizes social media and online platforms to further disseminate information and engage with their community. They create online campaigns, encouraging their followers to donate to specific causes, share educational resources, and participate in volunteer opportunities. The Bear Fam's dedication to philanthropy extends far beyond individual contributions, as they strive to create a collective movement for positive change.

In conclusion, the Bear Fam's philanthropic initiatives are a testament to the power of a united community with a shared sense of purpose. From supporting environmental conservation efforts to promoting mental health awareness and advocating for social justice, the Bear Fam, led by Bear Grillz, has made a tangible impact in various spheres of philanthropy. Through their fundraising events, collaborations with nonprofits, and online campaigns, the Bear Fam continues to inspire others to make a difference in the world. Their dedication to giving back and creating positive change serves as a shining example of the impact an engaged and compassionate community can have on the world.

Subsection: Bear Grillz's positive message and influence on mental health

Bear Grillz has become more than just a renowned artist in the electronic music scene. He has also become an advocate and an inspiration to many who struggle with their mental well-being. Through his music, Bear Grillz spreads a positive message of resilience, self-acceptance, and the importance of taking care of one's mental health. His journey and experiences have resonated with fans around the world, creating a unique bond between artist and audience.

The Power of Music in Mental Health

Music has long been recognized as a powerful medium for emotional expression and healing. It has the ability to touch our souls, evoke memories, and provide solace during challenging times. Bear Grillz's music serves as a testament to the therapeutic power of music, particularly in the realm of mental health.

His tracks often feature uplifting melodies, energetic beats, and anthemic lyrics that inspire listeners to embrace their inner strength and overcome adversity. The fusion of electronic sounds with emotionally charged lyrics creates a cathartic experience for fans, allowing them to connect with their own emotions and find comfort in the music.

Studies have shown that listening to music can have a profound impact on mental health. It can reduce stress, enhance mood, and increase feelings of relaxation and well-being. Music has also been shown to be an effective tool in managing symptoms of anxiety and depression.

Bear Grillz's music, with its positive and empowering messages, contributes to this growing body of research. His tracks address themes of resilience, self-empowerment, and finding inner peace, providing a source of inspiration and support for his listeners.

Addressing Stigma and Promoting Self-Acceptance

One of the most significant contributions Bear Grillz has made to the conversation around mental health is his openness about his own struggles. In interviews and through his social media platforms, he has shared his experiences with anxiety and depression, helping to break down the stigma surrounding mental health. By sharing his personal journey, Bear Grillz has shown that mental health challenges can affect anyone, regardless of their success or public image. He encourages his fans to prioritize their mental well-being and seek the help they need. This transparency not only fosters a sense of connection and understanding with his audience but also helps to normalize conversations around mental health.

Moreover, Bear Grillz promotes the importance of self-acceptance and embracing one's individuality. His own journey of self-discovery and overcoming personal obstacles demonstrates the power of self-love and acceptance. Through his music and social media presence, Bear Grillz encourages his fans to embrace their unique qualities, reinforcing the message that it is okay to be authentic and true to oneself.

Encouraging Mindfulness and Emotional Healing

In addition to his music, Bear Grillz actively promotes mindfulness and emotional healing as essential practices for maintaining good mental health. He often shares techniques and resources for relaxation, stress management, and cultivating a positive mindset.

Through his social media channels, he encourages his fans to engage in self-care activities such as meditation, exercise, and spending time in nature. He emphasizes the importance of taking time for oneself, listening to one's own needs, and prioritizing mental and emotional well-being.

Bear Grillz also uses his platform to raise awareness about the importance of seeking professional help when needed. He shares information about mental health resources, hotlines, and support groups, reminding his followers that they are not alone in their struggles.

Making a Difference Through Philanthropy

Beyond his music and advocacy, Bear Grillz actively contributes to philanthropic efforts related to mental health. He has established the Bear Grillz Foundation, which supports organizations dedicated to mental health awareness, education, and treatment.

The foundation collaborates with various non-profit organizations to fund research, provide resources for individuals in need, and promote mental health programs and initiatives. Bear Grillz's commitment to giving back and making a tangible difference in the lives of those affected by mental health challenges further reinforces his positive influence on the community.

Case Study: Bear Grillz's Impact on Fan Well-being

Bear Grillz's positive message and influence on mental health can be seen through the impact he has had on his fans. Countless testimonials and stories have emerged from fans who have found solace, strength, and a sense of belonging through his music.

One example is the story of Sarah, a young fan who struggled with anxiety and self-doubt. Sarah found comfort and inspiration in Bear Grillz's tracks, which not only provided an escape from her worries but also reminded her that she is not alone in her struggles. Through engaging with the Bear Fam community, she found support and connection with like-minded individuals who shared similar experiences.

The positive impact of Bear Grillz's music does not stop at emotional well-being. Some fans credit his music with helping them develop coping mechanisms, encouraging them to seek therapy, and even inspiring them to pursue careers in mental health-related fields.

Conclusion

Bear Grillz's positive message and influence on mental health extend far beyond his music. Through his transparency, advocacy, and philanthropy, he has created a community that fosters understanding, support, and empowerment for those facing mental health challenges. Bear Grillz's impact serves as a reminder of the transformative power of music and the importance of prioritizing mental well-being.

Subsection: Fan stories of personal growth and empowerment

Fan stories hold a significant place in the heart of Bear Grillz and the Bear Fam. They not only showcase the impact of Bear Grillz's music, but also highlight the personal growth and empowerment that fans have experienced through connecting with his music. These stories serve as a testament to the power of music to inspire and transform lives.

One fan, Sarah, shares her story of how Bear Grillz's music helped her through a difficult time in her life. After experiencing a traumatic event, Sarah felt lost and overwhelmed. She stumbled upon Bear Grillz's music and immediately connected with its raw emotion and intense energy. The heavy bass drops and aggressive beats became her anthem for healing and finding her inner strength. Sarah credits Bear Grillz's music for giving her the courage to face her fears and move forward.

Another fan, John, discovered Bear Grillz during a period of self-doubt and insecurity. As an aspiring musician himself, John often felt discouraged by the competitive nature of the music industry. However, listening to Bear Grillz's tracks inspired him to keep pushing forward and pursuing his dreams. He found solace in the uplifting melodies and empowering lyrics, which reminded him that success comes from perseverance and staying true to oneself.

Emily, a long-time member of the Bear Fam, shares how Bear Grillz's music has been a constant source of motivation and positivity in her life. Whenever she feels down or overwhelmed, she turns to Bear Grillz's tracks to lift her spirits and regain her confidence. The infectious energy and catchy hooks remind her to embrace her uniqueness and strive for greatness. Emily believes that Bear Grillz's music has played a crucial role in her personal growth and has helped her overcome obstacles with resilience and determination.

These fan stories of personal growth and empowerment demonstrate how Bear Grillz's music transcends boundaries and touches the lives of listeners in a profound way. Through his infectious beats and electrifying performances, he has created a community that celebrates individuality, resilience, and personal development.

Bear Grillz's music serves as a reminder that everyone has the power to overcome adversity and achieve greatness. It has become an anthem for personal growth, motivating fans to push past their limits and embrace their true potential. The Bear Fam, united by their shared love for Bear Grillz's music, provides a support system that encourages personal empowerment and fosters a sense of belonging.

Bear Grillz himself frequently engages with his fans, sharing their stories of personal growth and highlighting their accomplishments. Through social media and fan events, he creates a platform for fans to connect with one another, share their journey, and find inspiration in each other's stories.

The impact of Bear Grillz's music on personal growth and empowerment extends beyond the individual fans. It has created a ripple effect, inspiring others to chase their dreams and make a difference in their communities. Through collaborations and community projects led by the Bear Fam, fans have come together to create positive change in the world, using their shared passion for Bear Grillz's music as a driving force.

In conclusion, fan stories of personal growth and empowerment highlight the transformative power of Bear Grillz's music. These stories demonstrate how his music has provided solace, inspiration, and a sense of unity for fans around the world. Through their journeys of personal growth, fans have not only found strength within themselves but have also become agents of positive change within their communities. Bear Grillz's music continues to empower and uplift, leaving a lasting legacy of personal transformation and the celebration of individuality.

Subsection: The therapeutic impact of Bear Grillz's music

Music has long been recognized as a powerful tool for healing and self-expression. It has the ability to reach deep within our souls and evoke emotions that words alone cannot express. In the case of Bear Grillz's music, this therapeutic impact is taken to a whole new level. His signature sound, infused with heavy basslines and melodic elements, creates a sonic experience that is both exhilarating and cathartic.

One of the ways in which Bear Grillz's music provides therapeutic benefits is through its ability to help listeners release pent-up emotions. The intense energy and raw power of his tracks act as a conduit for emotional release, allowing listeners to tap into their deepest feelings and find solace in the music. Whether it's the pounding bass of "Demons" or the haunting melodies of "May The Forth Be With You," Bear Grillz's music provides a safe space for listeners to let go and find emotional release.

Moreover, Bear Grillz's music also serves as a form of empowerment for listeners. The anthemic nature of his tracks, combined with their infectious energy, instills a sense of confidence and strength in listeners. Through his music, Bear Grillz encourages his audience to embrace their individuality, to face their fears, and to trust in their own abilities. This empowering message can be particularly valuable for individuals who may be struggling with self-doubt or a lack of confidence.

In addition to emotional release and empowerment, Bear Grillz's music has a soothing and calming effect on listeners. The combination of heavy bass and mesmerizing melodies creates a hypnotic and trance-like state that allows listeners to escape from the stresses and anxieties of everyday life. This meditative quality of his music can help to calm the mind, reduce stress levels, and promote a sense of inner peace.

Furthermore, Bear Grillz's music has the power to create a sense of community and belonging among his listeners. At his live performances, fans come together to share in the collective experience of his music, forming a tight-knit community known as the Bear Fam. This sense of belonging and connection can be incredibly therapeutic, providing individuals with a support system and a sense of belonging.

The therapeutic impact of Bear Grillz's music is not limited to emotional and psychological well-being. There is growing evidence to suggest that music, particularly when combined with physical movement, can have positive effects on physical health. The high-energy and infectious rhythms of Bear Grillz's music lend themselves perfectly to dance and exercise, making it an ideal soundtrack for physical activity. Dancing and moving in response to the music can improve cardiovascular health, boost mood, and increase overall fitness levels.

In conclusion, Bear Grillz's music offers a therapeutic escape for listeners, providing emotional release, empowerment, stress reduction, a sense of community, and even physical health benefits. Through his unique sound and powerful message, Bear Grillz has created a musical experience that transcends entertainment and becomes a source of healing and transformation for his audience. So, whether you're struggling with your emotions or simply looking to let loose and have a good time, Bear Grillz's music is there to provide the therapeutic escape you need. Let the bass drop and the healing begin!

Subsection: The Bear Fam's support for one another

The Bear Fam is not just a fan community; it is a tight-knit family that supports and uplifts one another. From the very beginning, Bear Grillz has fostered an environment of love and acceptance within his fanbase, creating a community that goes beyond the music. In this subsection, we will explore the incredible support that the Bear Fam provides for one another and the ways in which they come together to make a positive impact.

1. Emotional support: The Bear Fam is a safe space for fans to express themselves and share their personal journeys. Members of the community offer each other emotional support, lending a listening ear and providing encouragement during difficult times. Whether it's through online forums, social media groups, or meet-ups, the Bear Fam creates a supportive network for individuals to lean on.

Example: Sarah, a Bear Fam member, shared her struggle with anxiety and depression on a Bear Grillz fan forum. The response from fellow fans was overwhelming, with messages of support and even personal stories of overcoming similar challenges. Sarah felt a tremendous sense of belonging and found solace knowing that she was not alone in her struggles.

2. Collaborative projects: The Bear Fam is known for coming together to create collaborative projects that showcase their talents and creativity. These projects range from fan-made music videos to art installations, and even charity initiatives. By working together on these projects, fans not only share their skills but also foster a sense of unity and community spirit.

Example: The Bear Fam organized a fundraising campaign to support mental health organizations in honor of Mental Health Awareness Month. Fans contributed artwork, music, and even fundraising ideas to raise awareness and funds for the cause. Bear Grillz himself endorsed the campaign, encouraging fans to support each other's mental well-being.

3. Positive reinforcement: The Bear Fam uplifts one another through positive reinforcement and celebrating each other's achievements. Whether it's a fan's artwork, a remix of a Bear Grillz track, or a milestone in their personal lives, the community provides encouragement and recognition for these accomplishments. This support further strengthens the bonds within the Bear Fam.

Example: John, a Bear Fam member and aspiring producer, shared his first original track on social media and within the Bear Fam group. The response was overwhelmingly positive, with fellow fans praising his talent and providing constructive feedback to help him grow. John's confidence soared, and he continued to create music with the unwavering support of the Bear Fam.

4. Helping those in need: The Bear Fam extends its support beyond its own members by reaching out to those in need. From organizing charity events to rallying behind causes, the community exemplifies the power of collective action for the greater good. Bear Grillz's own philanthropic efforts inspire the Bear Fam to give back and make a positive impact in their communities.

Example: The Bear Fam organized a food and clothing drive during the holiday season, collecting donations for a local homeless shelter. Fans from all over the world contributed items and spread the word about the initiative. The collective effort made a significant difference in the lives of those less fortunate, reinforcing the community's commitment to helping others.

5. Mentorship and guidance: Within the Bear Fam, fans with expertise in various fields willingly lend their knowledge and guidance to those seeking assistance. Whether it's career advice, creative pursuits, or personal growth, the community embraces mentorship and fosters an environment of continuous learning and development.

Example: Emma, a young graphic designer, reached out to the Bear Fam seeking advice on honing her skills. Several established designers within the community offered feedback on her portfolio, shared industry insights, and even connected her with potential clients. Through this mentorship, Emma's skills improved, and she found success in her chosen career path.

Overall, the Bear Fam's support for one another goes beyond typical fan communities. The bonds formed within this community are based on love, respect, and a shared passion for Bear Grillz's music. Through emotional support, collaborative projects, positive reinforcement, collective action, and mentorship, the Bear Fam uplifts and empowers its members, creating a lasting impact both within the community and beyond.

As Bear Grillz once said, "We are a family united by music, bound by love, and driven by a desire to inspire positive change in the world." The Bear Fam embodies this sentiment, proving that when we come together, we can achieve incredible things.

Subsection: Bear Fam-led initiatives promoting positivity and unity

In addition to being a tight-knit community of passionate fans, the Bear Fam is known for its dedication to promoting positivity and unity. Led by Bear Grillz himself, the Bear Fam has taken various initiatives to spread love, support, and collaboration within the electronic music scene and beyond.

One of the key initiatives of the Bear Fam is the promotion of mental health awareness. Recognizing the importance of mental well-being, Bear Grillz and the community have actively raised funds and supported organizations that focus on mental health education and support. Through charity events, fundraisers, and collaborations, the Bear Fam has contributed to reducing the stigma surrounding mental health issues and has encouraged open conversations about well-being.

To further promote positivity and unity, the Bear Fam organizes regular meet-ups and events where fans can come together and connect with one another. These gatherings provide a safe space for Bear Fam members to share their experiences, forge friendships, and find solace in the understanding and support of like-minded individuals. Music acts as a common language, allowing fans from diverse backgrounds to bond over their shared love for Bear Grillz's music and the values it represents.

Collaboration is another central focus of the Bear Fam-led initiatives. Encouraging fans to explore their creativity, Bear Grillz has created platforms and opportunities for fans to collaborate on music, art, and other creative projects. Online contests and challenges, where fans can showcase their talents and work together to create something unique, have become a trademark of the Bear Fam community. These collaborative projects not only foster creativity but also strengthen the bonds within the community, creating a sense of belonging and shared purpose.

The Bear Fam-led initiatives also extend beyond the music realm. Environmental conservation and sustainability are important causes that Bear Grillz and the community passionately support. By partnering with organizations dedicated to protecting the environment, the Bear Fam contributes to the preservation of nature and raises awareness about the importance of sustainable practices. Whether it is organizing clean-up drives or supporting eco-friendly initiatives, the Bear Fam demonstrates a commitment to making a positive impact on the world.

To ensure inclusivity and fairness, the Bear Fam actively promotes diversity in the electronic music scene. By celebrating and supporting artists from different backgrounds, the community aims to break down barriers and create a more inclusive industry. The Bear Fam's initiatives focus on providing platforms for underrepresented artists, amplifying their voices, and challenging industry norms.

In addition to these initiatives, the Bear Fam engages in various charitable causes and community projects. From supporting local schools and music programs to assisting in disaster relief efforts, the community's collective impact is far-reaching and meaningful. The Bear Fam's commitment to making a difference in the world goes beyond being just fans of Bear Grillz; it is about using their collective strength and love for music to create positive change.

To keep the positivity and unity alive, the Bear Fam actively uses social media platforms and technology to connect with fans worldwide. Online forums, social media groups, and fan-led initiatives allow Bear Fam members to stay engaged and share their love for Bear Grillz's music. These digital spaces serve as a platform for fans to support one another, share personal stories, and inspire each other through music.

In conclusion, the Bear Fam-led initiatives promote positivity and unity within the electronic music scene and beyond. From mental health awareness to environmental conservation, the community actively contributes to making the world a better place. By embracing collaboration, inclusivity, and a shared sense of purpose, the Bear Fam continues to inspire fans and shape the industry from within. Through their collective efforts, they exemplify the impact a dedicated fan community can have on spreading love, support, and a sense of belonging.

Subsection: How Bear Grillz connects with fans on a deeper level

In this subsection, we will explore how Bear Grillz, the enigmatic producer and DJ, connects with his fans on a deeper level. Bear Grillz's ability to form strong connections with his fanbase is one of the key factors contributing to his success and has helped him build a dedicated and passionate following. Let's delve into the various aspects of how Bear Grillz creates a meaningful connection with his fans.

Understanding the Fan Perspective

Bear Grillz recognizes the importance of understanding his fans and their desires. He actively engages with his audience to gain insights into their preferences and expectations. Through social media platforms, such as Twitter, Instagram, and Facebook, Bear Grillz encourages his fans to share their thoughts and communicate directly with him. This open line of communication allows him to gain a deeper understanding of his fans' perspectives and interests.

Interactive Fan Experiences

Bear Grillz goes beyond traditional means of connecting with fans by creating interactive and immersive experiences. One example is his meet-and-greet sessions after his live performances. Instead of hastily signing autographs and taking pictures, Bear Grillz takes the time to have meaningful conversations with each fan. He actively listens to their stories, shares personal anecdotes, and creates memories that leave a lasting impact.

Additionally, Bear Grillz frequently hosts fan gatherings, where he interacts with fans in a relaxed setting. These events provide an opportunity for fans to get to know him beyond the stage persona, fostering a sense of intimacy and connection. By investing time and effort into these interactive experiences, Bear Grillz leaves a lasting impression on his fans and creates a deeper connection.

Authenticity and Relatability

One of Bear Grillz's greatest strengths is his authenticity. He stays true to himself and doesn't shy away from expressing vulnerability. This genuine approach allows fans to relate to him on a personal level. Bear Grillz openly shares his journey, including the challenges he has faced and the obstacles he has overcome. By being transparent about his experiences, he establishes a bond of trust with his fans, fostering a deeper connection.

Emotional Connection Through Music

Music plays a pivotal role in Bear Grillz's ability to connect with his fans on a deeper level. His tracks often carry emotional depth and resonate with his audience. Through his music, Bear Grillz taps into universal emotions, allowing fans to find solace, inspiration, and a sense of belonging. The raw energy and passion present in his productions create a powerful emotional connection between Bear Grillz and his fans.

Community Engagement

Bear Grillz actively fosters a sense of community among his fans, often referred to as the "Bear Fam." He encourages fans to connect with each other, fostering friendships and support systems within the community. On social media, Bear Grillz frequently showcases the talent and creativity of his fans, providing them with a platform to be recognized and celebrated. By empowering his fans and giving them a sense of belonging, Bear Grillz strengthens the bond between himself and his followers.

Respecting and Valuing Fans

Bear Grillz places great importance on showing respect and appreciation for his fans. He acknowledges their support and contributions, both big and small, recognizing that they are the driving force behind his success. Bear Grillz often surprises his fans with personalized gestures, such as sending exclusive merchandise or providing VIP experiences. These acts of gratitude demonstrate his genuine appreciation for the love and support he receives from his fans.

Giving Back to the Community

Another way Bear Grillz deepens his connection with fans is by actively giving back to the community. Through philanthropic endeavors and support for charitable causes, Bear Grillz shows his fans that he shares their values and cares about making a positive impact. He actively involves his fans in these initiatives, encouraging them to join him in creating positive change. By aligning his values with those of his fans, Bear Grillz strengthens their bond and leaves a lasting impression.

Continued Evolution and Growth

Bear Grillz understands the importance of staying relevant and evolving as an artist. He strives to create music that pushes boundaries and explores new sonic territories. By consistently evolving his sound and experimenting with different genres and styles, Bear Grillz keeps his fans engaged and excited. This commitment to growth not only attracts new fans but also allows him to deepen his connection with his existing fanbase.

In conclusion, Bear Grillz's ability to connect with fans on a deeper level stems from his understanding of their perspectives, creation of interactive fan experiences, authenticity, emotional connection through music, community engagement, respect and appreciation for fans, giving back to the community, and his commitment to continued growth. Through these efforts, Bear Grillz creates a truly profound and meaningful connection with his fans, solidifying his position as an influential figure in the electronic music industry.

Section 3: Uniting the Electronic Music Community

Collaborations with Fellow Artists within the Bear Fam

Collaboration has always been at the heart of Bear Grillz's journey and success. From the early days of his career, Bear Grillz recognized the importance of working with other artists who shared his passion for music. These collaborations have not only resulted in the creation of incredible tracks, but they have also fostered a sense of community within the Bear Fam.

The Power of Collective Creativity

Collaborative projects within the Bear Fam have proven to be a catalyst for innovation and creativity. When artists come together to work on a track, they bring with them unique perspectives, experiences, and styles. This fusion of ideas often leads to the creation of groundbreaking music that pushes the boundaries of the electronic music genre.

Bear Grillz has always emphasized the importance of embracing diverse influences and genres. Through collaborations with fellow Bear Fam artists, he has been able to combine his signature Bearstep sound with elements of dubstep, trap, drum and bass, and more. These collaborations have not only allowed Bear Grillz to explore new musical territories but have also resulted in the birth of new sub-genres and styles within the electronic music scene.

Fostering a Supportive Network

Collaborating with fellow Bear Fam artists has also created a strong support network within the music industry. The artists within the Bear Fam share a common goal of uplifting and inspiring one another, which has fostered an environment of camaraderie rather than competition.

In a highly competitive industry, having a support system of like-minded artists is invaluable. The Bear Fam has become a tight-knit community where artists can rely on each other for advice, feedback, and encouragement. This sense of unity and support has not only helped artists navigate the challenges of the music industry but has also facilitated the sharing of resources and opportunities.

Elevating Each Other's Artistry

Collaborations with fellow artists within the Bear Fam have played a significant role in the growth and development of Bear Grillz's artistry. Working alongside talented musicians has pushed him to continually evolve as an artist, both technically and creatively.

Through collaborations, Bear Grillz has had the opportunity to learn from others, explore different production techniques, and experiment with new musical styles. This constant exchange of knowledge and ideas has allowed him to refine his skills and expand his sonic palette.

Moreover, collaborating with other artists has provided Bear Grillz with fresh perspectives and insights, enabling him to challenge his own artistic boundaries. These collaborations have encouraged him to take risks, step out of his comfort zone, and explore uncharted musical territories. The result is a dynamic and ever-evolving sound that keeps his music both exciting and relevant.

Collaborative Projects Spreading the Bear Grillz Sound

Collaborations between Bear Grillz and his fellow artists within the Bear Fam have played a pivotal role in spreading his unique sound and style to a wider audience. By joining forces with other talented musicians, Bear Grillz has been able to tap into their respective fan bases and introduce his music to new listeners.

These collaborative tracks often blend the distinct styles of both artists, resulting in an exciting fusion that appeals to a broader audience. The shared excitement and anticipation surrounding collaborations within the Bear Fam have helped generate buzz and organic growth for Bear Grillz's music.

Furthermore, collaborations have also opened doors for Bear Grillz to perform at new venues, festivals, and events. The collective influence and popularity of the artists involved in these collaborations have helped create opportunities for Bear Grillz to showcase his talent on bigger stages and reach new heights in his career.

The Bear Fam's Influence on the Industry

The collaborations within the Bear Fam have not only had a significant impact on Bear Grillz's career but have also contributed to the overall landscape of the electronic music industry. The collaborative spirit and innovation fostered within the Bear Fam have set an example for other artists and collectives.

By embracing collaboration, Bear Grillz and his fellow artists have challenged the notion of individuality in the music industry. They have demonstrated that by working together, artists can create something greater than the sum of its parts. This collaborative mindset has paved the way for a new era of creativity and cooperation within the electronic music scene.

Moreover, the success of these collaborations has caught the attention of industry insiders and critics. Bear Grillz and his fellow artists within the Bear Fam have received acclaim for their innovative approach to music-making, pushing the boundaries of what is possible within the genre. This recognition has further solidified the Bear Fam's influence and impact on the industry.

Examples of Noteworthy Collaborations

One notable collaboration within the Bear Fam is the track "Rumble" featuring beatsmith Excision and bass music heavyweight Dion Timmer. This collaboration brought together the unique soundscapes of Bear Grillz, Excision's hard-hitting dubstep, and Dion Timmer's melodic prowess. The result was a track that showcased the distinct styles of each artist while creating a cohesive sonic experience.

Another noteworthy collaboration is "Stay" with fellow Bear Fam artist Sullivan King. This track seamlessly marries Bear Grillz's bass-heavy sound with Sullivan King's metal-inspired riffs and vocals. Together, they created a track that not only appeals to fans of electronic music but also bridges the gap between electronic and rock genres.

These collaborations, along with many others within the Bear Fam, have reshaped the electronic music landscape, offering listeners a fresh and diverse array of sounds and pushing the boundaries of what electronic music can be.

The Role of Collaboration in Bear Grillz's Continued Success

Collaboration will always remain integral to Bear Grillz's journey and his continued success. Through collaborations, he has found inspiration, support, and artistic growth. The Bear Fam's spirit of collaboration has pushed Bear Grillz to continuously evolve as an artist, challenge expectations, and explore new horizons.

Moving forward, Bear Grillz will continue to embark on collaborative projects, both within the Bear Fam and beyond. He recognizes that collaboration not only drives innovation but also offers endless possibilities for creative expression. By joining forces with fellow artists, Bear Grillz will continue to shape the electronic music scene, leaving an indelible mark on the industry and inspiring future generations of artists.

Subsection: Organizing charity events and fundraisers

Organizing charity events and fundraisers is a crucial aspect of Bear Grillz's mission to make a positive impact on the world through his music. By leveraging his platform and influence, Bear Grillz has been able to bring together his fans, industry professionals, and like-minded individuals to support various charitable causes and initiatives. In this subsection, we will explore the strategies, challenges, and successes that Bear Grillz and his team have encountered while organizing charity events and fundraisers.

Introduction to Charity Events

Charity events serve as a platform for Bear Grillz and his community to give back to society and contribute to causes that align with their values. These events provide an opportunity for individuals, artists, and organizations to come together in support of a common goal, while also raising awareness and funds for important causes. Bear Grillz's commitment to organizing charity events demonstrates his dedication to making a difference beyond the world of music.

Selecting a Cause

Choosing the right cause is an important first step in organizing a successful charity event. Bear Grillz and his team carefully consider causes that resonate with their values, beliefs, and the interests of their fanbase. By selecting a cause that aligns with their brand, it becomes easier to engage and mobilize their community to support the event.

Bear Grillz also takes into account the impact that the chosen cause can have on individuals and communities. Whether it is supporting environmental conservation efforts, mental health initiatives, or social justice movements, Bear Grillz aims to address pressing issues that are relevant in today's society.

Collaborations and Partnerships

Collaborations and partnerships play a vital role in the success of charity events and fundraisers. Bear Grillz actively seeks out opportunities to collaborate with other artists, brands, and organizations that share a common goal. By joining forces, they are able to leverage their combined resources, networks, and platforms to create a larger impact.

Collaborations can take many forms, including joint performances, releasing charity singles or albums, and co-hosting events. These partnerships not only bring together diverse perspectives and skill sets but also help to attract a wider audience and generate increased support for the cause.

Event Planning and Execution

Planning and executing a charity event require careful coordination and attention to detail. Bear Grillz and his team start by setting clear goals and objectives for the event. They establish a budget, identify potential venues, and secure necessary permits and licenses. In some instances, they may work with event planners or production companies to ensure a seamless flow of activities.

Promotion and marketing play a crucial role in driving attendance and generating interest in the event. Bear Grillz leverages his social media platforms, official website, and partnerships with media outlets and influencers to spread the word about the event. They create engaging content, including videos, behind-the-scenes footage, and interviews, to build excitement and encourage fans to participate.

During the event, Bear Grillz and his team organize various activities and attractions to create a memorable experience for attendees. These may include live performances, guest speakers, interactive booths, auctions, and raffles. By providing entertainment and educational opportunities, they create a sense of connection and engagement between the audience and the cause.

Fundraising Strategies

Fundraising is at the core of charity events, and Bear Grillz employs various strategies to maximize the funds raised. Ticket sales, merchandise sales, and donations are common methods used to generate revenue. Additionally, they explore opportunities for corporate sponsorships and partnerships to secure additional financial support.

To incentivize donations, Bear Grillz and his team often offer exclusive perks and experiences to donors. These may include meet and greets, VIP access to events, and limited-edition merchandise. By providing unique benefits, they encourage fans and supporters to contribute more generously.

Measuring Impact

Measuring the impact of charity events is crucial in evaluating their success and identifying areas for improvement. Bear Grillz and his team track the funds raised, attendance numbers, and engagement levels on social media platforms. They also collect feedback from attendees and participants to gain insights into their experience and how it can be enhanced in the future.

Beyond the immediate impact, Bear Grillz seeks to create a lasting legacy through his involvement with charity events. He collaborates with partner organizations to ensure that the funds raised are used effectively and accountably. Regular updates and reports are shared with the community to demonstrate the tangible impact of their contributions.

Challenges and Lessons Learned

Organizing charity events and fundraisers is not without its challenges. Limited resources, logistical complexities, and time constraints can pose obstacles during the planning and execution phase. However, Bear Grillz and his team have learned valuable lessons along the way.

Adaptability and flexibility are key in navigating unforeseen circumstances or changing event dynamics. By staying open to alternative solutions and maintaining clear communication with all stakeholders, Bear Grillz ensures that the event can proceed smoothly, even in the face of challenges.

Teamwork and collaboration are also essential in overcoming challenges. Bear Grillz and his team rely on each other's expertise and strengths to handle different aspects of event organization. They foster a supportive and inclusive environment that encourages creativity and problem-solving.

Conclusion

Organizing charity events and fundraisers is a vital component of Bear Grillz's mission to make a positive impact on the world. Through strategic partnerships, careful planning, and engaging fundraising strategies, Bear Grillz aims to raise awareness and funds for causes that are close to his heart. By celebrating the power of unity and collaboration, these events inspire his community to come together and create lasting change.

Subsection: Supporting up-and-coming artists

Supporting up-and-coming artists is a crucial aspect of Bear Grillz's mission. He is committed to nurturing new talent and providing a platform for emerging artists to showcase their skills and creativity. Through various initiatives and collaborations, Bear Grillz actively promotes and supports the next generation of musicians in the electronic music scene.

One of the key ways Bear Grillz supports up-and-coming artists is by featuring them on his tracks and inviting them to collaborate on projects. This provides emerging musicians with a unique opportunity to gain exposure and showcase their talent to a wider audience. By collaborating with established artists like Bear Grillz, these budding musicians can learn from their experience, gain valuable insights, and establish themselves in the industry.

To further support up-and-coming artists, Bear Grillz has also organized mentorship programs and workshops. These programs provide aspiring musicians with access to experienced producers, songwriters, and industry professionals who can guide them in their musical journey. Through one-on-one mentorship sessions and group workshops, Bear Grillz aims to provide practical knowledge, technical skills, and advice on navigating the music industry.

In addition to collaborations and mentorship programs, Bear Grillz actively seeks out talented artists through talent showcases and competitions. He partners with music festivals and events to host contests and talent searches, providing aspiring musicians with an opportunity to perform in front of industry professionals and gain exposure. These showcases not only give artists a chance to get noticed but also foster a sense of community and camaraderie among the up-and-coming talent.

Furthermore, Bear Grillz uses his influence and platform to actively promote the work of up-and-coming artists through his social media channels and website. He features their tracks, interviews them, and shares their stories with his fan base. By leveraging his large following, Bear Grillz helps to amplify the voices of these emerging artists and generate interest in their music.

Bear Grillz also recognizes the importance of financial support for up-and-coming artists. He has established grants and scholarships to provide financial assistance to talented musicians who may not have the resources to pursue their dreams. These grants not only help artists fund their music production but also contribute to the growth and diversity of the electronic music scene.

One innovative program initiated by Bear Grillz is the "Bear Grillz Masterclass." In this online course, he shares his knowledge and techniques with aspiring producers and musicians. The masterclass covers topics such as music production, sound design, arrangement, and marketing strategies. Participants have the opportunity to learn directly from Bear Grillz and gain valuable insights into the industry.

To ensure ongoing support for up-and-coming artists, Bear Grillz actively collaborates with record labels, music streaming platforms, and talent agencies to create opportunities for emerging talent. He advocates for fair compensation and opportunities for artists at all levels of their careers, creating a more inclusive and supportive music industry.

In conclusion, supporting up-and-coming artists is a vital part of Bear Grillz's commitment to the electronic music scene. Through collaborations, mentorship programs, talent showcases, and financial support, Bear Grillz actively nurtures and promotes emerging talent. By providing opportunities and sharing his knowledge, Bear Grillz helps shape the future of electronic music by empowering the next generation of artists.

Subsection: The Bear Grillz community's impact on the industry

The Bear Grillz community has had a profound impact on the electronic music industry, influencing both the creative process and the way music is consumed. Through fan engagement, support of emerging artists, and the organization of charitable events, the Bear Grillz community has fostered a sense of unity and collaboration that extends far beyond the confines of the genre.

One of the key aspects of the Bear Grillz community's impact on the industry is its unwavering support for up-and-coming artists. Within the community, there is a strong emphasis on discovering new talent and providing a platform for aspiring musicians to showcase their work. Through social media platforms and networking events, Bear Grillz and his fans actively seek out and promote lesser-known artists, giving them exposure and a chance to be heard.

This support for emerging artists has created a ripple effect throughout the industry. As more and more artists receive recognition and opportunities, the electronic music scene becomes more diverse and vibrant. The Bear Grillz community's commitment to nurturing talent has not only opened doors for budding musicians but has also contributed to the evolution of the genre as a whole.

Another significant impact of the Bear Grillz community lies in its dedication to charitable initiatives. Bear Grillz and his fans have come together to organize numerous events and fundraisers, with the aim of giving back to the community and making a positive difference in the world. From supporting environmental conservation efforts to advocating for mental health awareness, the community's philanthropic endeavors have had far-reaching effects beyond the realm of music.

These charitable initiatives not only provide support to important causes but also serve as a platform for the Bear Grillz community to come together and form lasting bonds. By uniting over shared values and a passion for music, fans have formed a tight-knit network that extends beyond online interactions. This sense of community fosters a positive and supportive environment for both fans and artists alike.

Moreover, the Bear Grillz community has played a significant role in breaking down barriers within the electronic music industry. By embracing diversity and inclusivity, Bear Grillz and his fans challenge the traditional notions of what an artist should look like or sound like, promoting acceptance and celebrating individuality. The community's rejection of stereotypes and emphasis on authenticity has paved the way for artists from different backgrounds and identities to thrive within the genre.

In addition to breaking down barriers, the Bear Grillz community's impact is also felt through its influence on the wider electronic music landscape. As the community grows and expands, its collective voice becomes more powerful, leading to increased recognition and demand for electronic music as a genre. This newfound legitimacy has opened doors for electronic artists to collaborate with musicians from other genres, further blurring the boundaries between different styles of music.

The Bear Grillz community's impact on the industry is not confined to just music. It extends to fan-led initiatives, fan-driven events, and the creation of a space that fosters creativity, support, and connection. This grassroots movement has revolutionized the way fans engage with their favorite artists and has created a blueprint for how artists can cultivate a dedicated and passionate following.

In conclusion, the Bear Grillz community's impact on the electronic music industry is multifaceted and far-reaching. Through its support for emerging artists, dedication to philanthropy, and efforts to break down barriers, the community has fundamentally changed the landscape of the genre. By fostering unity, promoting diversity, and embracing authenticity, the Bear Grillz community sets an example for the entire industry to follow.

Subsection: Strengthening the bond within the electronic music community

The electronic music community is a vibrant and diverse group of individuals who share a common passion for electronic music. Within this community, there is a strong sense of connection and camaraderie that is built upon a shared love for the genre. Strengthening this bond is crucial for the growth and development of the community and its members. In this subsection, we will explore various ways in which the bond within the electronic music community can be strengthened, fostering a sense of unity and collaboration among its members.

Supporting Emerging Talent

One of the key ways to strengthen the bond within the electronic music community is by supporting and nurturing emerging talent. This can be done through mentorship programs, workshops, and educational initiatives that provide guidance and resources for up-and-coming artists. By providing a platform for emerging talent to showcase their skills and receive feedback from more experienced artists, the community can help them develop their artistic voice and grow as professionals.

Additionally, established artists can actively support emerging talent by collaborating on tracks, inviting them to perform at shows and events, and providing opportunities for exposure. This not only helps the emerging artists gain visibility, but it also encourages a spirit of collaboration and mutual support within the community.

Creating Spaces for Collaboration

Collaboration is a powerful tool for strengthening the bond within any community, and the electronic music community is no exception. Creating spaces and opportunities for collaboration can help artists from different backgrounds and sub-genres come together and create something unique. This can be done through dedicated collaboration events, where artists are encouraged to exchange ideas, share their work, and explore possibilities for joint projects.

In addition to physical spaces, online platforms also play a vital role in fostering collaboration within the electronic music community. Online forums, social media groups, and music production platforms enable artists to connect, share knowledge, and collaborate on projects regardless of their geographical location. These virtual spaces provide a platform for artists to find like-minded individuals, exchange feedback, and create meaningful connections.

Community-driven Initiatives

Engaging the community in various initiatives is another effective way to strengthen the bond within the electronic music community. Organizing community-driven events, such as charity fundraisers, local music festivals, and outreach programs, not only brings people together but also creates opportunities for artists and fans to contribute to a greater cause.

By participating in these initiatives, community members can develop a sense of ownership and pride in the collective achievements of the electronic music community. This sense of unity and purpose fosters a deeper connection among individuals and encourages ongoing collaboration and support.

Promoting Diversity and Inclusivity

The electronic music community, like any other artistic community, thrives on diversity and inclusivity. It is essential to create an environment that welcomes individuals from all backgrounds, cultures, and identities. Promoting diversity and inclusivity within the community not only strengthens the bond among its members but also enriches the collective creative output.

To promote diversity and inclusivity, community organizers and artists can actively seek out talent from underrepresented groups, provide support and mentorship to artists who face systemic barriers, and ensure that diverse voices are amplified and celebrated. By taking proactive steps to address inequities within the community, the bond can grow stronger, and the community as a whole can benefit from a wider range of experiences and perspectives.

Sharing Knowledge and Resources

The exchange of knowledge and resources is a crucial aspect of strengthening the bond within the electronic music community. Artists can share their experiences, techniques, and production tips through workshops, online tutorials, and mentorship programs. By sharing knowledge, artists can help each other grow, learn new skills, and overcome challenges.

Similarly, sharing resources, such as sample packs, plugins, and production tools, can also foster a sense of collaboration and support within the community. Platforms that facilitate the sharing of resources, such as online libraries and forums, play a vital role in this process. When artists feel supported and have access to the tools they need, they can focus on their creative growth and contribute more effectively to the community.

Celebrating Achievements and Milestones

Celebrating achievements and milestones within the electronic music community is essential for recognizing the hard work and talent of its members. Artists can celebrate each other's releases, chart-topping hits, and successful collaborations. By showcasing and supporting the achievements of individuals within the community, the bond and sense of unity are reinforced, and a positive and encouraging environment is fostered.

Community-led initiatives, such as awards, recognition programs, and showcases, can also play a significant role in celebrating achievements within the electronic music community. These initiatives not only provide a platform for artists to gain visibility but also inspire others to strive for excellence and contribute to the community in meaningful ways.

In conclusion, strengthening the bond within the electronic music community is crucial for its growth and development. By supporting emerging talent, fostering collaboration, promoting diversity and inclusivity, sharing knowledge and resources, and celebrating achievements, the community can create an environment that encourages unity, creativity, and collective success. It is through these efforts that the electronic music community can continue to thrive and make a lasting impact on the world of music.

Subsection: The role of fan communities in shaping the industry

Fan communities play a crucial role in shaping the music industry and influencing the success and trajectory of artists like Bear Grillz. These communities, often referred to as fandoms, are formed by passionate and dedicated fans who share a common love for an artist or their music. In this subsection, we will explore the significant contributions that fan communities make to the industry, from influencing trends and marketing strategies to supporting emerging talent and fostering innovation. We will also discuss how Bear Grillz's fan community, the Bear Fam, has impacted his career and the broader electronic music scene.

The power of fan communities

Fan communities have become a powerful force within the music industry, with the ability to shape trends, promote artists, and influence the overall direction of the industry. These communities not only serve as a platform for fans to connect with each other but also play a crucial role in elevating and supporting their favorite artists. Here are some key aspects of the power of fan communities:

- ♦ **Marketing and promotion:** Fan communities act as a grassroots marketing and promotional tool for artists. They create buzz around new releases, organize fan-led initiatives, share content on social media platforms, and actively engage in discussions about the artist's work. This word-of-mouth promotion is invaluable in reaching a wider audience and gaining recognition within the industry.

+ **Trendsetting:** Fan communities have the power to create and drive trends within the industry. By sharing their preferences, introducing new ideas, and promoting specific musical styles or genres, fans influence the direction of the music scene as a whole. Artists who listen and adapt to the preferences of their fan communities often find success in staying relevant and connected to their audience.

+ **Feedback and artist-audience dialogue:** Fan communities provide artists with valuable feedback and constructive criticism. Through direct interactions with fans, artists can understand the preferences, expectations, and desires of their audience. By listening and responding to this feedback, artists can adapt their music, performances, and marketing strategies to better resonate with their fans and build stronger connections.

The Bear Fam and its impact

Bear Grillz's fan community, known as the Bear Fam, has played a significant role in his success and continues to shape the industry in various ways. Here are some examples of the impact that the Bear Fam has had:

+ **Supportive community and fan engagement:** The Bear Fam is known for its tight-knit and supportive community. Fans actively engage with one another, not only discussing Bear Grillz's music but also forming genuine friendships. The positive and inclusive atmosphere created by the Bear Fam fosters a sense of belonging and strengthens the bond between fans and the artist.

+ **Promotion and exposure:** The Bear Fam takes an active role in promoting Bear Grillz's music and events. They leverage social media platforms, create fan-generated content, and organize fan-led initiatives to increase the artist's visibility. By doing so, they amplify Bear Grillz's reach and introduce his music to new audiences.

+ **Collaborative projects and initiatives:** The Bear Fam actively participates in collaborative projects with Bear Grillz and contributes to his creative endeavors. Fans have the opportunity to get involved in various ways, such as vocal collaborations, remix contests, and even featuring in music videos. This level of involvement strengthens the fan-artist relationship and fosters a sense of ownership and pride within the community.

+ **Support for emerging talent:** The Bear Fam recognizes and supports emerging talent within the electronic music scene. They actively promote and share the work of up-and-coming artists, providing a platform for these artists to gain exposure and recognition. By doing so, the Bear Fam contributes to the growth and diversification of the industry as a whole.

+ **Innovation and creativity:** The Bear Fam's passion for Bear Grillz's music and the electronic music genre as a whole drives them to explore new ideas and push the boundaries of creativity. They actively contribute to fan-led art projects, merchandise design, and visual storytelling, enriching the overall fan experience and inspiring new artistic directions for Bear Grillz and the wider community.

Harnessing the power of fan communities

To harness the power of fan communities effectively, artists and industry professionals must actively engage with their fans and build genuine relationships. Here are some strategies for artists like Bear Grillz to leverage the potential of their fan communities:

+ **Active presence on social media:** Artists should maintain an active presence on social media platforms, engaging with fans through posts, comments, and messages. This direct interaction enables artists to connect with their fans on a personal level and gain insights into their preferences and opinions.

+ **Fan-generated content:** Encouraging and featuring fan-generated content is an effective way to showcase the creativity and dedication of fan communities. Artists can share fan art, remixes, covers, and testimonials on their official channels, thereby acknowledging and appreciating their fans' support.

+ **Exclusive access and experiences:** Artists can offer exclusive access and experiences to their fan communities, such as early album releases, VIP meetups, or behind-the-scenes content. These special privileges deepen the connection between artists and fans, fostering a sense of loyalty and creating unforgettable experiences that make fans proud to be part of the community.

+ **Collaboration and co-creation:** Artists can involve their fans in the creative process, allowing them to contribute ideas, participate in contests, or even feature in music videos. This level of collaboration fosters a sense of ownership and pride among fans, making them feel like an integral part of the artist's journey.

+ **Recognizing and rewarding fan contributions:** Artists should recognize and reward their fans for their contributions and support. This can be done through contests, fan-spotlight features, exclusive merchandise, or meet-and-greets. By acknowledging and appreciating their fans, artists strengthen the bond within the community and encourage continued engagement.

Real-world example: BTS and the ARMY

A noteworthy example of the significant impact of fan communities is the relationship between the global superstars BTS and their fan community, known as the ARMY. The ARMY, with its massive online presence and dedicated fan base, has played a pivotal role in BTS's rise to global stardom. They have organized grassroots marketing campaigns, dominated social media platforms, and actively supported the group through album purchases, streaming, and concert attendance. The ARMY's passion and multimedia skills have propelled BTS's music to the top of global charts and forged connections with fans worldwide. Additionally, BTS actively engages with their fans through regular interactions on social media platforms, fan-meet events, and exclusive content releases. The strong bond between BTS and the ARMY is a testament to the power of fan communities in shaping the music industry and elevating artists to unprecedented levels of success.

The challenges and future of fan communities

While fan communities have proven to be a powerful force in the music industry, they also face several challenges. These challenges include maintaining a positive and inclusive atmosphere, addressing toxic behavior within the community, and managing the expectations of fans. Additionally, artists must find a balance between engaging with their fans and maintaining their creative vision.

Looking ahead, fan communities will continue to shape the industry as technology evolves and new platforms emerge. With the rise of virtual reality, blockchain-based fan experiences, and immersive digital environments, the way fan communities engage with artists and consume music will undergo significant changes. Artists like Bear Grillz will need to adapt to these changes and leverage technology to further enhance fan engagement and collaboration.

In conclusion, fan communities are a fundamental part of the music industry and play a vital role in shaping the trajectory of artists like Bear Grillz. These communities have the power to influence trends, promote artists, provide invaluable feedback, and create a sense of belonging and support. By nurturing and harnessing the potential of fan communities, artists can build stronger connections with their fans, achieve greater success, and contribute to the overall growth and innovation of the music industry.

Subsection: Bear Fam-led initiatives to support emerging talent

As Bear Grillz's popularity continues to grow, so does his commitment to supporting emerging talent within the electronic music community. Recognizing the importance of giving back and nurturing the next generation of artists, Bear Grillz and his dedicated fan community, known as the Bear Fam, have pioneered numerous initiatives aimed at supporting and promoting up-and-coming musicians. These Bear Fam-led initiatives have been instrumental in providing opportunities and resources for emerging talent to showcase their skills, connect with industry professionals, and gain exposure in the competitive music industry.

The Bear Fam Talent Showcase

One of the most prominent initiatives led by the Bear Fam is the Bear Fam Talent Showcase. This event, organized and curated by dedicated members of the Bear Fam community, provides a platform for aspiring artists to share their music and performances with a wider audience. The showcase serves as a launching pad for emerging talent, enabling them to gain visibility and connect with industry professionals, including producers, record label representatives, and fellow artists.

The Bear Fam Talent Showcase features a diverse lineup of electronic music artists across different sub-genres, allowing for a rich and varied representation of talent within the electronic music community. Through carefully selected venues and live stream broadcasts, the showcase provides a professional and supportive environment for artists to share their music and build their network.

Example:

One success story that emerged from the Bear Fam Talent Showcase is the DJ duo "The Roaring Cubs," who caught the attention of influential industry figures at the event. Following their performance, they received a recording contract with a reputable electronic music label, paving the way for a successful career in the industry. This example demonstrates the impact of the Bear Fam Talent Showcase as a launching pad for emerging talent, providing them with opportunities that may otherwise be difficult to come by.

Mentorship and Artist Development Programs

In addition to providing a platform for emerging talent to showcase their work, the Bear Fam has also initiated mentorship and artist development programs to foster the growth and success of promising artists. Recognizing the value of guidance and support in the early stages of an artist's career, Bear Grillz and established industry professionals offer their expertise to emerging talent through one-on-one mentorship programs.

These mentorship programs not only provide valuable advice and industry insights to aspiring artists but also create a supportive network within the Bear Fam community. Artists receive guidance on various aspects of their careers, including production techniques, performance skills, marketing strategies, and navigating the music industry. Through regular check-ins and personalized feedback, mentors help emerging artists refine their sound, build their brand, and navigate the challenges they may encounter along their journey.

Example:

One artist who benefited from the Bear Fam mentorship program is "SynthFox," a talented producer with a distinct sound but limited industry connections. Through mentorship sessions with Bear Grillz, SynthFox received invaluable feedback on his tracks and guidance on how to promote his music effectively. As a result, SynthFox's music gained traction, leading to collaborations with established artists and a growing fanbase. This success story highlights the transformative power of mentorship programs in nurturing emerging talent and helping them achieve their goals.

Collaborative Projects and Remix Competitions

The Bear Fam community actively encourages collaboration between established artists and emerging talent through various collaborative projects and remix competitions. These initiatives provide emerging artists with unique opportunities to work with established names within the electronic music industry, learn from their experiences, and gain exposure to a wider audience.

Collaborative projects involve established artists teaming up with emerging talent to create original tracks or remixes. This collaborative process not only provides valuable learning experiences for emerging artists but also exposes them to new production techniques and different creative perspectives. The resulting tracks or remixes are then released and promoted through the Bear Fam network, giving the emerging artists increased visibility and credibility.

Remix competitions, on the other hand, invite emerging talent to submit their own remixes of Bear Grillz's tracks or tracks from other established artists within the electronic music community. These competitions serve as a platform for emerging talent to showcase their creative interpretations and remixing skills. The winners of the competitions receive various prizes, including the opportunity to work with established artists on future projects or release their remixes on reputable labels.

Example:

An emerging producer, "BeatDrop," won a remix competition organized by the Bear Fam community. His remix of Bear Grillz's hit track "Roar" caught the attention of industry professionals and led to a collaboration with another well-known electronic music artist. This collaboration brought BeatDrop significant exposure and opened doors to further opportunities in his career. The remix competition not only provided a platform for BeatDrop to showcase his talent but also facilitated meaningful connections that propelled his career forward.

Spotlight Features and Social Media Promotion

To further support emerging talent, the Bear Fam community shines a spotlight on promising artists through social media promotion and features. Through dedicated fan accounts, artist spotlights, and curated playlists, the Bear Fam actively promotes the work of emerging talent to their extensive network of followers.

These social media promotions and features provide valuable exposure for emerging artists, helping them reach a wider audience and gain recognition within the electronic music community. By leveraging the Bear Fam's influential reach, these initiatives offer aspiring artists a platform to share their music, connect with fans, and attract the attention of industry professionals.

Example:

Emerging artist "Elixir" received a spotlight feature on the Bear Fam's official Instagram account, which boasts a massive following of electronic music enthusiasts. As a result, Elixir's music reached a broader audience, gaining thousands of new listeners and followers on social media. The exposure generated by the Bear Fam's support played a significant role in Elixir's subsequent signing with a reputable record label and the success of his debut album. This example highlights the impact of social media promotion in helping emerging talent gain visibility and propel their careers.

Bear Fam Community Workshops and Educational Resources

Recognizing the importance of education and skill development, the Bear Fam organizes community workshops and provides educational resources to support the growth of emerging talent. These workshops cover a wide range of topics, including production techniques, music theory, marketing strategies, and performance skills.

Led by experienced artists, industry professionals, and Bear Grillz himself, these workshops offer guidance and hands-on learning experiences to aspiring artists. Through interactive sessions, emerging talent can enhance their technical skills, gain industry insights, and collaborate with like-minded individuals.

In addition to workshops, the Bear Fam also provides educational resources, such as tutorial videos, sample packs, and production guides, to empower emerging artists with the knowledge and tools necessary to improve their craft. These resources are easily accessible within the Bear Fam community, fostering a culture of continuous learning and growth.

Example:

Aspiring producer "Bassline Wizard" attended a Bear Fam community workshop on advanced sound design techniques. Through hands-on demonstrations and personalized feedback from experienced producers, Bassline Wizard gained a deeper understanding of synthesis and sound manipulation. This knowledge empowered him to create unique and captivating sounds in his tracks, setting him apart from other emerging artists. The workshop not only broadened Bassline Wizard's skill set but also sparked his creativity and inspired new directions in his music.

Cultivating a Supportive Community Network

Beyond the specific initiatives mentioned above, the Bear Fam community has been effective in fostering a supportive network of emerging talent. Through online forums, social media groups, and dedicated chat platforms, Bear Fam members connect, collaborate, and support each other's artistic journeys.

This sense of community provides emerging artists with an invaluable support system where they can seek feedback, share resources, and exchange knowledge with like-minded individuals. Whether it's providing production tips, offering constructive criticism, or promoting each other's work, the Bear Fam community plays a vital role in uplifting and championing emerging talent within the electronic music industry.

Example:

Emerging artist "Melodic Bear" found immense support and encouragement from fellow Bear Fam members when he faced a creative block during the production of his debut EP. Through the Bear Fam community's online forum, Melodic Bear received valuable suggestions, motivational messages, and even collaborated with other emerging artists on the EP. The support and camaraderie within the community helped Melodic Bear overcome obstacles and release a successful EP, marking the beginning of his promising career.

The Impact of Bear Fam-led Initiatives

The Bear Fam-led initiatives to support emerging talent have had a significant impact on the electronic music industry. By providing platforms for showcasing talent, facilitating collaborative opportunities, offering mentorship programs, and promoting emerging artists through social media, the Bear Fam has created an ecosystem that nurtures the growth and success of aspiring musicians.

These initiatives not only give emerging talent the exposure and resources they need to thrive but also contribute to the overall diversity and vibrancy of the electronic music landscape. By supporting artists at different stages of their careers, the Bear Fam community ensures the continuous evolution and innovation of the genre.

Furthermore, the success stories that emerge from these initiatives serve as inspiration for artists who are just starting their journey, emphasizing the idea that with hard work, dedication, and the support of a passionate community, dreams can be realized.

Discussion Points:

1. Reflect on the importance of community-driven initiatives in supporting emerging talent within the electronic music industry. 2. Discuss the potential challenges faced by emerging artists and how Bear Fam-led initiatives help address these challenges. 3. How do mentorship programs contribute to the overall development of emerging artists? Share examples of successful mentorship experiences within the Bear Fam community. 4. Analyze the role of social media promotion and spotlights in launching the careers of emerging artists. What specific strategies can emerging artists employ to maximize the impact of social media promotion? 5. Discuss the long-term impact of Bear Fam-led initiatives on the electronic music landscape. How do these initiatives contribute to the genre's growth, diversity, and innovation? 6. Dive deeper into the impact of community workshops and educational resources in empowering emerging artists. How do these initiatives bridge the gap between aspiring artists and industry professionals? 7. Reflect on the significance of a supportive network in an artist's journey. How does the Bear Fam community foster a sense of belonging and collaboration among emerging talent? 8. Share personal experiences or stories of emerging artists who have benefited from Bear Fam-led initiatives. How did these initiatives shape their careers and artistic growth?

Exercises:

1. Research and compile a playlist featuring notable tracks from emerging artists who have benefited from the Bear Fam community's initiatives. Discuss the distinctive sound or style of each artist and how they contribute to the electronic music landscape. 2. Imagine you are an emerging artist seeking to promote your music through the Bear Fam community. Develop a social media marketing plan outlining specific strategies and content ideas to maximize your exposure within the community. 3. Organize and host a mini talent showcase within your local electronic music community, taking inspiration from the Bear Fam Talent Showcase. Share your experience, challenges, and successes in nurturing emerging talent in your community. 4. Develop a proposal for an artist development program targeting emerging artists in underrepresented communities. Outline the key objectives, strategies, and resources required to support and uplift these artists. 5. Interview an established artist or industry professional involved in the Bear Fam-led initiatives. Explore their motivations for supporting emerging talent and gather insights on their experiences working with emerging artists.

Resources:

1. Electronic Musician Magazine: A comprehensive resource for electronic music production techniques, industry news, and artist interviews. 2. The SoundCloud Bible by Toma Hargreaves: A guidebook on how to promote and grow your music career using SoundCloud, a platform widely used by emerging electronic music artists. 3. "Music Habits: The Mental Game of Electronic Music Production" by Jason Timothy: A book that delves into the mindset and strategies necessary to excel in the field of electronic music production. 4. "All You Need to Know About the Music Business" by Donald S. Passman: A comprehensive guide to the music industry, providing insights into contracts, royalties, marketing, and more. 5. Electronic music production tutorial websites and forums such as Sonic Academy, The Pro Audio Files, and Gearslutz, which offer valuable resources, tutorials, and discussions for aspiring producers.

Subsection: The Bear Fam's contribution to the growth of the genre

The Bear Fam, the dedicated community of Bear Grillz fans, has played a pivotal role in the growth and evolution of the electronic music genre. Their unwavering support and passionate involvement have helped shape the direction of the genre and have provided a platform for emerging artists to thrive.

One of the most significant contributions of the Bear Fam to the growth of the genre is their active role in promoting and sharing Bear Grillz's music. Through their enthusiastic engagement on social media platforms, fan-led initiatives, and word-of-mouth recommendations, the Bear Fam has helped expand the fan base and increase the visibility of not only Bear Grillz but also other artists within the genre. Their dedication to spreading the word about electronic music has created new opportunities for up-and-coming artists to gain exposure and recognition.

In addition to their role as passionate fans, the Bear Fam has also been actively involved in organizing events and meet-ups centered around Bear Grillz's music. These gatherings provide a sense of community and a safe space for fans to come together and share their love for the genre. The Bear Fam's initiative in planning and executing these events has fostered a sense of unity and connection among fans, further solidifying their contribution to the growth of the genre.

The Bear Fam's influence extends beyond the realm of music promotion. Members of the community have been instrumental in supporting emerging talent within the electronic music scene. Through collaborations, mentorship programs, and online platforms, the Bear Fam has created opportunities for aspiring artists to learn, grow, and showcase their work. By nurturing and empowering new talent, the Bear Fam has helped to shape the future of the genre by ensuring a steady stream of fresh and innovative sounds.

Moreover, the Bear Fam's commitment to philanthropic endeavors has had a profound impact on the growth of the genre. Through charitable initiatives and community projects, the Bear Fam has demonstrated the power of music as a platform for social change. By raising awareness and funds for important causes, they have showcased the positive influence that the electronic music community can have on society at large. The Bear Fam's dedication to making a difference has inspired other fans and artists to take similar actions, contributing to the genre's growth as a force for positive change.

Lastly, the Bear Fam's influence is perhaps most profound in their ability to break down barriers and promote inclusivity within the electronic music scene. By fostering an environment of acceptance and support, they have created space for individuals from diverse backgrounds to come together and engage with the genre. The Bear Fam's commitment to inclusivity has helped to challenge stereotypes and preconceived notions about electronic music, allowing for the genre to evolve and attract a wider range of fans and artists.

In conclusion, the Bear Fam has made a substantial contribution to the growth of the electronic music genre. Through their unwavering support, promotion of Bear Grillz's music, community-building efforts, support for emerging artists, philanthropic endeavors, and commitment to inclusivity, they have helped shape the direction of the genre and create opportunities for the next generation of electronic music artists. The Bear Fam's passion and dedication serve as a testament to the power of fandom and the significant role that fans can play in the growth and evolution of a musical genre.

Subsection: Collaborative projects within the electronic music community

Collaboration is a fundamental aspect of the electronic music community, allowing artists to blend their unique styles, perspectives, and talents to create something greater than the sum of its parts. In this subsection, we will explore the importance of collaborative projects within the electronic music industry, the benefits they bring to artists, and some notable examples that have made a significant impact on the genre.

The Power of Collaboration

Collaborative projects in electronic music offer a platform for artists to combine their strengths, experiment with new sounds, and reach a wider audience. These collaborations often result in innovative and genre-defying tracks that push the boundaries of electronic music.

One of the main benefits of collaboration is the opportunity to learn from others. By working with different artists, producers can gain new insights, techniques, and perspectives. This exchange of knowledge and creativity leads to personal growth and the continuous evolution of the electronic music industry.

Collaborations also provide a chance for artists to step outside their comfort zones and explore new musical territories. By combining different styles and genres, they can create unique tracks that attract a diverse fanbase. This crossover appeal not only expands the reach of individual artists but also introduces fans to new sounds and sub-genres within the electronic music community.

Furthermore, collaborative projects allow artists to pool resources, share networks, and leverage each other's fanbases. This collective effort strengthens the overall impact of a track, increases exposure, and opens doors to new opportunities for all involved parties. In an industry driven by streams and digital presence, these collaborations can generate significant traction and boost an artist's career.

Notable Collaborative Projects

The electronic music community has seen numerous remarkable collaborative projects throughout its history. Let's highlight a few notable examples that have left a lasting impact on the genre:

1. **Daft Punk and The Weeknd - "Starboy"**: French electronic duo Daft Punk collaborated with R&B superstar The Weeknd on his hit single "Starboy." This collaboration seamlessly integrated the signature sounds of both artists, blending The Weeknd's seductive vocals with Daft Punk's iconic electronic production. The track reached the top of the charts worldwide, solidifying the power of cross-genre collaborations.

2. **Flume and Chet Faker - "Drop the Game"**: Australian electronic producer Flume teamed up with singer-songwriter Chet Faker on the mesmerizing track "Drop the Game." This collaboration combined Flume's intricate production and experimental soundscapes with Chet Faker's soulful vocals, resulting in a captivating and genre-bending track that captivated audiences around the world.

3. **Disclosure and Sam Smith - "Latch"**: English electronic duo Disclosure joined forces with the soulful voice of Sam Smith on the breakthrough track "Latch." This collaboration seamlessly merged Disclosure's deep house production with Sam Smith's emotive vocals, creating a dancefloor anthem that solidified the commercial success of both artists and introduced a fresh sound to the electronic music scene.

4. **Skrillex and Diplo - Jack Ü**: The collaborative project between Skrillex and Diplo, known as Jack Ü, brought together two of the most influential figures in electronic music. Their self-titled debut album featured hit tracks like "Where Are Ü Now" with Justin Bieber, which successfully bridged the gap between electronic and mainstream pop music, earning them critical acclaim and multiple awards.

5. **Swedish House Mafia - "Don't You Worry Child"**: Swedish House Mafia, a supergroup consisting of Axwell, Steve Angello, and Sebastian Ingrosso, collaborated with vocalist John Martin on the iconic track "Don't You Worry Child." This collaboration showcased the group's talent for crafting anthems while seamlessly blending emotional lyrics with euphoric electronic production, leaving a lasting impact on the dance music community.

These collaborations demonstrate the power of bringing together artists with diverse backgrounds and talents. By combining their individual strengths, these artists have created timeless tracks that have shaped the electronic music landscape and resonated with millions of listeners worldwide.

The Collaborative Process

The collaborative process in electronic music varies depending on the artists involved, their respective roles, and the goals of the project. However, there are some common steps and considerations that can help facilitate a successful collaboration:

1. **Defining the Vision:** Artists should start by clearly defining the vision and direction of the collaborative project. This involves discussing musical styles, desired outcomes, and artistic aspirations. Understanding each other's creative goals ensures a cohesive and focused collaboration.

2. **Establishing Roles and Responsibilities:** Collaborators need to assign roles and responsibilities based on their individual strengths and expertise. This could involve one artist taking the lead on production while the other focuses on songwriting or vocals. Clearly defining roles helps streamline the creative process and ensures each collaborator can contribute effectively.

3. **Regular Communication and Feedback:** Open and regular communication is vital throughout the collaborative process. Artists should maintain a constant dialogue, sharing ideas, providing feedback, and addressing any concerns or conflicts that may arise. This collaborative exchange fosters mutual understanding and allows for the refinement of the project.

4. **Flexible Workflow:** Collaborative projects often involve artists working remotely or across different time zones. Embracing technology and utilizing online collaboration tools can facilitate a more flexible workflow. This allows artists to work on the project at their convenience and makes it easier to overcome logistical challenges.

5. **Experimentation and Iteration:** Collaborations provide a space for experimentation and pushing creative boundaries. Artists should be open to trying new ideas, exploring different sounds, and embracing unexpected directions. This willingness to iterate and evolve the project leads to exciting and innovative outcomes.

6. **Respecting and Valuing Contributions:** It is crucial for collaborators to respect and value each other's contributions. Recognizing and appreciating the unique talents and perspectives that each artist brings to the project creates a harmonious and productive working environment. A collaborative project is a shared endeavor, and acknowledging the contributions of all involved fosters a sense of equality and teamwork.

By following these guidelines, artists can navigate the collaborative process with ease and maximize the potential for creative success.

Contemporary Challenges in Collaborative Projects

Collaborative projects within the electronic music community face certain challenges that need to be addressed to ensure a seamless and fulfilling experience for all parties involved. Some of these challenges include:

+ **Logistical Challenges:** Collaborations often involve artists located in different places, making coordination and communication challenging. Time differences, scheduling conflicts, and technical issues can hinder the progress of the project. Artists need to find effective ways to overcome these logistical challenges, whether through virtual collaboration tools or careful planning.

+ **Creative Differences:** Collaboration brings together artists with different perspectives, tastes, and styles. Creative differences can cause friction and hinder the smooth execution of the project. It is important for collaborators to approach these differences with open-mindedness, compromise, and a willingness to find common ground. Discussions, feedback sessions, and brainstorming can help bridge the gap and find a harmonious balance that satisfies all parties.

+ **Maintaining Artistic Identity:** Collaborations can blur the lines between artists' individual styles and identities. While fruitful collaborations often result in a unique fusion, it is essential for artists to maintain their artistic integrity and preserve their unique voice. Balancing the desire for experimentation and cross-pollination with maintaining a distinct identity requires clear communication, mutual respect, and a shared vision for the project.

+ **Distribution and Royalty Concerns:** Collaborative projects raise questions about distribution and royalty splits. Artists need to have open and honest discussions about revenue sharing and ownership rights from the outset of the collaboration. Setting clear agreements and utilizing industry-standard contracts ensures a fair and transparent distribution of royalties and avoids conflicts down the line.

Addressing these challenges requires effective communication, professionalism, and a willingness to navigate these complexities with integrity and respect.

Conclusion

Collaborative projects within the electronic music community play a vital role in fostering artistic growth, pushing creative boundaries, and expanding the reach of the genre.   Through collaboration, artists combine their unique talents, perspectives, and networks to create groundbreaking tracks that resonate with audiences worldwide. The power of collaboration lies in its ability to bridge genres, showcase diverse artistic voices, and open doors to new possibilities.   As the electronic music industry continues to evolve, collaboration will remain a driving force behind its innovation and enduring appeal.   Artists must embrace the collaborative spirit, communicate effectively, and leverage the collective power of the electronic music community to shape the future of the genre.

Now, armed with an understanding of the power of collaboration and some notable examples, we can explore in the next subsection how these collaborations have influenced the behavior and growth of fan communities within the electronic music scene.

Subsection: The Power of Unity in the Electronic Music Community

One of the most remarkable aspects of the electronic music community is its ability to foster a sense of unity and togetherness among its members. In this subsection, we will explore the power of unity in the electronic music community and its profound impact on the artists, fans, and the industry as a whole.

The Strength of Collaboration

Collaboration lies at the heart of the electronic music community. Artists from different backgrounds and genres come together to create music that transcends boundaries and defies conventions. The power of collaboration is evident in the way electronic music has evolved over the years, constantly pushing the boundaries of what is possible.

Whether it's two producers teaming up to create a groundbreaking track or a famous DJ inviting a lesser-known artist to perform with them on stage, collaboration in electronic music has the ability to produce something greater than the sum of its parts. It allows artists to pool their talents, knowledge, and resources to create innovative and unique works of art.

Breaking Down Barriers

Electronic music has always been associated with inclusivity and acceptance, and this is a fundamental aspect of the community's unity. The music transcends cultural, racial, and linguistic barriers, bringing people together from all walks of life. Whether it's a small underground event or a massive festival, the electronic music community creates a space where everyone feels welcome and connected.

This sense of unity is strengthened by the shared experiences and emotions that electronic music evokes. It's the feeling of being part of something bigger, of losing oneself in the music and finding solace in the collective energy of the crowd. The power of unity in the electronic music community is not just about the music itself but also about the sense of belonging and connection that it provides.

Support and Empowerment

In addition to collaboration and inclusivity, the electronic music community is known for its strong support networks. Artists, fans, and industry professionals alike come together to uplift and empower each other. This support can take many forms, from sharing knowledge and resources to providing emotional and financial support.

Through mentorship programs, workshops, and online communities, established artists support emerging talent, helping them navigate the complexities of the music industry. Fans show their support for their favorite artists by attending shows, buying merchandise, and sharing their music with others. Industry professionals offer guidance and opportunities to aspiring artists, creating a network of support that extends beyond the music itself.

Driving Social Change

The power of unity in the electronic music community goes far beyond the music and the parties. It has the potential to drive meaningful social change. With a global reach and devoted fan bases, electronic music artists have the ability to use their platform to highlight important social issues and advocate for positive change.

Environmental conservation, mental health awareness, and social justice are just a few of the causes that the electronic music community is passionate about. Through fundraising events, partnerships with nonprofit organizations, and awareness campaigns, electronic music artists and fans work together to make a difference in the world.

Strengthening the Industry

The unity within the electronic music community not only benefits the artists and fans but also strengthens the industry as a whole. By collaborating and supporting each other, artists can collectively push the boundaries of electronic music, creating new sounds and subgenres. This continuous innovation and experimentation keep the industry vibrant and exciting.

Moreover, the unity within the community fosters a sense of professionalism and mutual respect. Artists, promoters, and industry professionals work together to create safe and inclusive spaces for music lovers to enjoy. This collective effort ensures the longevity and sustainability of the electronic music industry.

Embracing Diversity

One of the most beautiful aspects of unity in the electronic music community is the celebration of diversity. This community brings together people from diverse cultural backgrounds, genders, sexual orientations, and identities. It embraces the differences and encourages self-expression without judgment.

The celebration of diversity in the electronic music community is not only reflected in the artists and fans but also in the music itself. Electronic music draws inspiration from various genres and cultures, resulting in a rich and diverse sonic landscape. This diversity of sounds and styles contributes to the unity and inclusivity of the community.

Unconventional Problem Solving

The electronic music community has a unique ability to solve problems in unconventional ways. From organizing charity events to promote social change to using technology in innovative ways to create mind-bending visuals during live performances, the community continuously comes up with creative solutions to challenges.

This unconventional problem-solving extends beyond the immediate world of electronic music. The community's willingness to explore new ideas and push boundaries has the potential to inspire change in society at large. By showing that there is more than one way to approach a problem, the electronic music community encourages individuals to think outside the box and challenge existing norms.

Exercises

1. Reflect on your own experiences within the electronic music community. How has the sense of unity impacted you personally? Has it influenced your perspective on music and life in general?

2. Research and highlight a collaboration between electronic music artists that you admire. What does this collaboration represent in terms of the power of unity within the community? How has it influenced their music and careers?

3. Explore a social issue that you are passionate about. Brainstorm creative ways in which the electronic music community could get involved and make a positive impact.

4. Write a short reflection piece on how diversity within the electronic music community contributes to its unity. How does the celebration of diverse sounds and styles strengthen the overall community?

5. Consider an unconventional problem within the electronic music industry and propose a creative solution. How could the community come together to address this problem in an innovative and effective way?

Resources

- "The Power of Unity in the Music Community" by Carlisle Rogers (Book) - "The Electronic Music Community: Collaborative Culture and the DIY Ethic" by Andrea Baker (Article) - "How Electronic Music Fosters Community and Empowers People" by Stephanie Falcone (Blog Post) - "The Power of Music: Inspiring Social Change" by Steve Garnett (TED Talk) - "Electronic Music Production: The Collaborative Process" by Ethan Hein and Keith Hatschek (Online Course)

Section 4: Beyond Music: Bear Grillz's broader impact

Subsection: Contributions to the environmental conservation movement

The environmental conservation movement has been a central focus in Bear Grillz's career, demonstrating his commitment to making a positive impact on the world. Through his music, Bear Grillz has raised awareness about environmental issues and actively supported various conservation initiatives. This subsection explores Bear Grillz's contributions to the environmental conservation movement, highlighting his efforts to protect the planet and inspire change.

Bear Grillz's Environmental Advocacy

As a renowned artist with a substantial following, Bear Grillz has leveraged his platform to advocate for environmental causes. Through his music and public appearances, he has consistently emphasized the importance of environmental conservation and the need for collective action. Bear Grillz has used his influence to raise awareness and inspire his fans to make sustainable choices in their daily lives.

Collaborations with Conservation Organizations

Bear Grillz has collaborated with various conservation organizations to create music that highlights environmental issues. He has worked closely with organizations such as Greenpeace, World Wildlife Fund, and Ocean Conservancy to raise funds and awareness for their conservation efforts. Through these collaborations, Bear Grillz has been able to reach a broader audience and mobilize his fan base to support these important causes.

Fundraising Initiatives

In addition to collaborating with conservation organizations, Bear Grillz has organized and participated in fundraising initiatives to support environmental conservation. He has hosted benefit concerts and charity events, with proceeds going directly to conservation projects. Bear Grillz's dedication to fundraising has played a vital role in supporting research, conservation efforts, and the preservation of natural habitats.

Awareness and Education

Bear Grillz's commitment to environmental conservation goes beyond music and fundraising. He actively uses his platform to promote awareness and education about environmental issues. Through social media campaigns, educational videos, and online resources, Bear Grillz shares valuable information about sustainable practices, climate change, and the importance of biodiversity. These efforts contribute to raising public awareness and inspire individuals to take action in protecting the environment.

Partnerships with Brands Promoting Sustainability

Bear Grillz has also formed partnerships with brands that prioritize sustainability and eco-friendly practices. By partnering with environmentally conscious companies, Bear Grillz encourages his fans to support businesses that align with their values. These partnerships allow Bear Grillz to extend his reach to a wider audience and promote sustainable consumer choices.

Promoting Conservation Through Touring and Events

Touring and live performances provide Bear Grillz with a unique opportunity to promote conservation efforts. During his shows, Bear Grillz incorporates visuals and messages that convey the importance of environmental conservation. He actively engages with his audience, encouraging them to join him in making a positive impact on the planet. By integrating environmental themes into his live performances, Bear Grillz inspires his fans to take action and support conservation initiatives.

Environmental Activism Beyond Music

Beyond his music career, Bear Grillz actively engages in environmental activism. He participates in clean-up campaigns, tree-planting initiatives, and other hands-on conservation activities. By taking direct action, Bear Grillz sets an example for his fans and demonstrates the importance of personal involvement in environmental preservation.

Inspiring Change Through Artistic Expression

Bear Grillz's music serves as a powerful tool for inspiring change and promoting environmental stewardship. His tracks often incorporate nature-inspired sounds and themes, encouraging listeners to connect with and appreciate the natural world. Bear Grillz's music serves as a reminder of the beauty and fragility of our planet, motivating his audience to support conservation efforts and make sustainable choices in their own lives.

Encouraging Sustainable Practices

Bear Grillz actively encourages his fans to adopt sustainable practices in their daily lives. Through his social media platforms, he shares tips and resources on reducing waste, conserving energy, and supporting environmentally friendly products. By encouraging small, simple changes, Bear Grillz empowers his fans to be agents of positive change in their communities.

Challenges and Solutions

While the environmental conservation movement faces numerous challenges, Bear Grillz continues to inspire hope and drive change through his activism. One challenge lies in reaching a wider audience and engaging individuals who may not be aware of the urgency of environmental issues. To overcome this, Bear Grillz uses his music as a universal language to connect with people from diverse backgrounds and raise awareness about the importance of environmental conservation.

Another challenge is the scale of the issues at hand. Bear Grillz recognizes that individual actions, though important, may not be sufficient to address complex environmental problems. To tackle this, he supports and collaborates with organizations and initiatives that work towards systemic changes and policy reform.

Lastly, the lack of awareness and education about environmental issues can hinder progress. Bear Grillz addresses this challenge by leveraging his platform to educate his fans and the broader public. Through his music, social media presence, and collaborations, he brings attention to pressing environmental concerns and inspires others to take action.

In conclusion, Bear Grillz's contributions to the environmental conservation movement have been noteworthy. His advocacy, collaborations with conservation organizations, fundraising initiatives, and educational efforts have made a meaningful impact on raising awareness about environmental issues. By using his platform to inspire change and promote sustainable practices, Bear Grillz continues to be an influential figure in the fight for a better and more sustainable world.

Subsection: Advocacy for mental health awareness

In this subsection, we will explore the importance of mental health awareness and the role that Bear Grillz plays in advocating for this important cause. We will delve into the challenges and stigmas surrounding mental health, the impact of mental health on society, and the initiatives undertaken by Bear Grillz to spread awareness and provide support.

Understanding Mental Health

Mental health refers to a person's emotional, psychological, and social well-being. It affects how we think, feel, and act, and it also helps determine how we handle stress, relate to others, and make choices. Mental health is important at every stage of life, from childhood and adolescence through adulthood. Mental illnesses are common, and they can affect anyone, regardless of age, gender, or socioeconomic status.

The Stigma and Challenges

Despite the prevalence of mental health issues, there is still a significant stigma surrounding them. People with mental health conditions often face discrimination, judgment, and misunderstanding. The fear of being labeled as "crazy" or "weak" prevents many individuals from seeking the help they need. This stigma also contributes to a lack of understanding and awareness about mental health.

Additionally, mental health services are often underfunded and inaccessible, making it difficult for individuals to access the necessary support. This results in a significant burden on individuals and their families, as well as on society as a whole.

Bear Grillz's Advocacy

Bear Grillz recognizes the importance of mental health and is dedicated to using his platform to raise awareness and promote positive change. Through his music, social media presence, and interactions with fans, Bear Grillz consistently emphasizes the significance of mental health.

One of Bear Grillz's initiatives is the promotion of open conversations about mental health. He encourages his fans to share their experiences and struggles, creating a safe space for individuals to open up about their mental health challenges. By sharing his own experiences and struggles, Bear Grillz helps break down the barriers and stigma surrounding mental health.

Support and Resources

Bear Grillz understands the importance of providing resources and support to those struggling with mental health issues. He actively partners with mental health organizations and charities to raise funds and awareness for mental health initiatives.

Through the Bear Grillz Foundation, Bear Grillz provides financial support to organizations that focus on mental health awareness, treatment, and support. These organizations work to provide accessible mental health services, educate the public, and advocate for policy changes.

Bear Grillz also utilizes his social media platforms to share mental health resources and provide guidance to individuals in need. He offers suggestions for coping mechanisms, healthy habits, and self-care practices that can support mental well-being.

Using Music as a Healing Tool

Music has a powerful impact on mental health and can be a therapeutic tool for individuals struggling with mental health issues. Bear Grillz's music often incorporates uplifting and empowering messages, providing solace and inspiration to his listeners. Through the combination of intense bass lines, melodic sounds, and heartfelt lyrics, Bear Grillz's music taps into the emotions of his audience and creates a sense of unity and understanding.

Bear Grillz's performances also serve as a cathartic experience for his fans. The high-energy atmosphere, communal gathering, and shared passion for music provide a sense of belonging and connection. These live performances contribute to the healing process and promote mental well-being.

Awareness through Partnerships

Bear Grillz seeks collaboration with mental health organizations, fellow musicians, and influencers to amplify the message of mental health awareness. By joining forces, these partnerships have a more significant impact and reach a wider audience. By incorporating mental health awareness into collaborations, Bear Grillz demonstrates the importance of addressing mental health in all aspects of life.

Conclusion

Advocacy for mental health awareness is essential to addressing the challenges faced by those with mental health conditions and breaking down societal stigmas. Bear Grillz uses his platform and influence to promote open conversations, provide support and resources, and advocate for change. Through his music, collaborations, and involvement with mental health organizations, Bear Grillz plays a critical role in raising awareness and destigmatizing mental health issues. By embracing the power of music and community, Bear Grillz contributes to the healing journey of individuals and creates a more compassionate and inclusive society.

Subsection: Inspiring Creativity and Self-Expression

Creativity and self-expression are at the heart of Bear Grillz's music and the ethos of his artistic journey. Through his unique sound and dynamic performances, Bear Grillz has inspired countless individuals to tap into their creative potential and express themselves authentically. This subsection explores the ways in which Bear Grillz has sparked creativity and fostered self-expression among his fans, as well as the impact of his approach on the wider artistic community.

The Power of Artistic Freedom

Bear Grillz believes that artistic freedom is essential for true self-expression. He encourages his fans and fellow artists to break free from traditional boundaries, experiment with different sounds, and explore their own artistic visions. By embracing a wide range of influences and drawing from diverse musical styles, Bear Grillz pushes the boundaries of electronic music and encourages others to do the same.

One of the ways Bear Grillz inspires creativity is by showcasing his own willingness to take risks in his music. He encourages his fans to trust their instincts and follow their creative impulses, reminding them that the most innovative and groundbreaking music often emerges from stepping outside of comfort zones. By emphasizing the importance of pushing artistic boundaries, Bear Grillz empowers his audience to deviate from conventional norms and forge their own unique paths.

Exercises in Creative Exploration

To further inspire creativity and self-expression, Bear Grillz encourages his fans to engage in exercises that encourage creative exploration. One such exercise is the "BEAR Yourself" challenge. This challenge invites participants to create their own remix or cover of one of Bear Grillz's tracks, showcasing their unique artistic interpretation. Through this challenge, Bear Grillz not only provides a platform for his fans to showcase their creativity but also highlights the importance of individuality and self-expression within the artistic process.

Another exercise Bear Grillz encourages is collaborative creativity. He believes that collaboration with other artists allows for the exchange of ideas, perspectives, and techniques, leading to the creation of something greater than what can be achieved in isolation. By collaborating with artists from various genres, Bear Grillz challenges the status quo and introduces new and exciting elements into his music. This approach not only inspires creative collaborations within the industry but also highlights the power of shared creativity in uniting artists and fostering innovation.

Embracing Vulnerability and Emotional Expression

Bear Grillz recognizes that true self-expression often requires vulnerability and emotional openness. He encourages his fans to tap into their own emotions and draw from personal experiences when creating music or engaging in any form of artistic expression. By sharing his own personal struggles and triumphs through his music, Bear Grillz creates a space for his fans to do the same, fostering a community that celebrates authenticity and vulnerability.

In addition to his music, Bear Grillz actively engages with his fans through various platforms, encouraging them to share their stories and connect on a deeper level. By acknowledging the power of music as a means of emotional release, Bear Grillz creates an environment where individuals feel safe to express their feelings and experiences openly. This sense of emotional connection serves as a catalyst for personal growth and encourages his fans to explore and embrace their own emotional landscapes through their artistic endeavors.

The Impact on the Artistic Community

Bear Grillz's approach to creativity and self-expression has had a significant impact on the wider artistic community. By challenging established norms and encouraging artists to break free from limiting stereotypes, Bear Grillz has fostered a culture of innovation within the electronic music scene. This culture of innovation transcends genres and inspires artists from all backgrounds and musical styles to explore new creative territories.

Furthermore, Bear Grillz's commitment to supporting emerging artists and providing a platform for diverse voices has helped to cultivate a more inclusive and representative music industry. By amplifying the work of underrepresented artists and challenging industry norms, Bear Grillz encourages a wider range of voices to be heard, ultimately enriching the artistic landscape as a whole.

Examples of Creativity and Self-Expression

One example of how Bear Grillz inspires creativity and self-expression is through his innovative use of sound design. By incorporating elements from diverse musical styles, such as hip-hop and rock, into his electronic productions, Bear Grillz creates a signature sound that defies traditional genre boundaries. This unique approach not only sets him apart as an artist but also encourages his fans to experiment with new sonic palettes and blend different genres in their own music.

Another example is Bear Grillz's use of visuals during his live performances. By incorporating striking visuals, dynamic lighting, and immersive stage design, Bear Grillz creates an immersive experience that engages not only the auditory senses but also the visual and emotional ones. This multi-sensory approach inspires his fans to think beyond just the music and explore the full range of creative possibilities in their own performances and artistic presentations.

Conclusion

Bear Grillz's commitment to inspiring creativity and self-expression has had a transformative impact on the electronic music community and beyond. Through his own artistry and his support of emerging artists, Bear Grillz challenges conventions, fosters innovation, and encourages individuals to embrace their unique creative visions. By creating a space that celebrates vulnerability, diversity, and authenticity, Bear Grillz has inspired countless individuals to tap into their creative potential and express themselves boldly and unapologetically. The legacy of Bear Grillz's impact on creativity and self-expression will be felt for generations to come, leaving an indelible mark on the artistic world.

Subsection: Breaking down barriers and promoting inclusivity

In this subsection, we will explore the important role of Bear Grillz in breaking down barriers and promoting inclusivity within the electronic music scene. Bear Grillz is not only known for his unique sound and energetic performances, but also for his efforts to create a welcoming and inclusive environment for all fans and artists.

Creating a diverse and inclusive fan base

Bear Grillz has been a vocal advocate for diversity and inclusivity within the electronic music community. Through his music, he has created a space where people from all walks of life can come together and celebrate their shared love for music. His shows attract a diverse crowd, breaking down barriers and bringing people from different backgrounds together.

Bear Grillz actively encourages fans to embrace their individuality and express themselves freely. He celebrates uniqueness and promotes acceptance, creating a sense of belonging within his fan base. Through social media and other online platforms, he regularly engages with fans, creating a strong and inclusive community known as the Bear Fam.

Promoting equality and representation

Bear Grillz understands the importance of representation in the music industry. He aims to amplify underrepresented voices and provide opportunities for artists from marginalized communities. By collaborating with artists from diverse backgrounds, he not only expands his own sound but also supports the growth and recognition of emerging talent.

Bear Grillz has been vocal about the need for equal representation of all genders, races, and sexual orientations within the music industry. He actively advocates for the inclusion of underrepresented groups, both on stage and behind the scenes. By shining a spotlight on artists from diverse backgrounds, Bear Grillz is actively breaking down barriers and promoting a more inclusive music industry.

Supporting charitable causes and social justice initiatives

Bear Grillz recognizes the power of artists to effect positive change in society. He uses his platform to raise awareness and support various charitable causes and social justice initiatives. Through collaborations with non-profit organizations, he raises funds and promotes important causes such as environmental conservation, mental health awareness, and social justice.

By lending his support to these initiatives, Bear Grillz is not only making a difference in the communities in need but also inspiring his fans to take action and get involved. His commitment to philanthropy further reinforces his message of inclusivity and solidarity.

Empowering aspiring artists

One of the key ways Bear Grillz promotes inclusivity is by creating opportunities for aspiring artists. He actively supports up-and-coming talent by providing platforms for exposure and collaboration. Through mentorship programs and his own label, he helps nurture young artists and gives them a chance to showcase their talent.

By empowering emerging artists, Bear Grillz is promoting diversity and inclusivity within the music industry. He believes in the power of collaboration and recognizes that by lifting others up, we can create a stronger and more unified community.

Breaking societal norms and challenging stereotypes

Bear Grillz's unique persona, with his trademark bear mask, challenges societal norms and traditional expectations of what an artist should look like. By wearing the mask, he breaks down barriers and encourages fans to focus on the music rather than superficial appearances. This sends a powerful message that anyone, regardless of their appearance, can create and succeed in the music industry.

Bear Grillz's authenticity and refusal to conform to industry stereotypes inspire others to embrace their own uniqueness and challenge societal norms. He proves that it is possible to achieve success by staying true to oneself and pursuing one's passions with unwavering determination.

Conclusion

In this subsection, we have explored how Bear Grillz plays an instrumental role in breaking down barriers and promoting inclusivity within the electronic music scene. Through his music, actions, and advocacy, he creates a diverse and inclusive fan base, supports underrepresented voices, champions charitable causes, empowers aspiring artists, and challenges societal norms. Bear Grillz serves as an inspiration to both fans and artists, encouraging them to embrace their individuality, celebrate diversity, and work towards a more inclusive future in the music industry.

Subsection: Bear Grillz's Influence Beyond the Music Industry

Bear Grillz's impact extends far beyond the realm of music, reaching into various social and cultural spheres. With his unique persona and powerful message, Bear Grillz has become a symbol of positive change and inspiration for people around the world. In this subsection, we will explore the ways in which Bear Grillz has influenced different aspects of society, including environmental conservation, mental health awareness, creativity, inclusivity, and social justice.

Environmental Conservation

Bear Grillz has been a vocal advocate for environmental conservation and sustainability. Through his music, he aims to raise awareness about the urgent need to protect our planet and inspire his fans to take action. He often incorporates nature sounds and samples into his tracks to create a connection between music and the natural world.

One of Bear Grillz's most notable initiatives is his collaboration with environmental organizations. He has partnered with non-profit organizations dedicated to protecting endangered species, preserving natural habitats, and promoting sustainability. Through these collaborations, Bear Grillz has helped raise funds and awareness for these important causes, amplifying their reach and making a tangible impact.

Furthermore, Bear Grillz has used his platform to educate his fanbase about environmentally friendly practices. He encourages his followers to adopt sustainable lifestyles by promoting recycling, reducing waste, and supporting eco-friendly initiatives. By shedding light on the critical state of our environment, Bear Grillz motivates his fans to become agents of change and contribute to the preservation of our planet.

Mental Health Awareness

Bear Grillz has been open and transparent about his struggles with mental health, using his platform to destigmatize conversations surrounding this topic. Through his music and personal experiences, he sends a message of hope, resilience, and self-acceptance to his fans who may be facing similar challenges.

By sharing his own journey, Bear Grillz encourages his fans to prioritize their mental well-being and seek help when needed. He emphasizes the importance of self-care, self-expression, and building a support system. His music often touches on themes of overcoming adversity and finding inner strength, resonating deeply with listeners who may be struggling with their mental health.

Furthermore, Bear Grillz actively supports mental health organizations and initiatives. He has organized charity events and fundraisers to raise funds for mental health research, treatment, and support programs. Through these efforts, Bear Grillz not only raises awareness but directly contributes to improving the lives of individuals affected by mental health issues.

Inspiring Creativity and Artistic Expression

Bear Grillz's music serves as a catalyst for creativity and artistic expression. His unique blend of genres, innovative sound design, and infectious energy inspire aspiring producers and musicians to push the boundaries of their own creative endeavors.

One of Bear Grillz's goals is to encourage his fans to find their own artistic voices and pursue their passions fearlessly. Through his music, he showcases the power of individuality and the beauty of embracing one's unique creative vision. By defying traditional genre conventions and blending elements from different styles, Bear Grillz empowers his audience to explore their own creative boundaries and challenge established norms.

Additionally, Bear Grillz actively supports emerging artists by providing opportunities for collaboration and mentorship. He recognizes the importance of uplifting the next generation of musicians and plays an active role in nurturing their talent. Through initiatives like remix competitions and collaborative projects, Bear Grillz fosters a spirit of camaraderie and creativity within the electronic music community.

Promoting Inclusivity and Breaking Down Barriers

Bear Grillz is a strong advocate for inclusivity and diversity within the music industry. His music and persona defy traditional expectations and challenge stereotypes. By wearing a bear mask, Bear Grillz removes the focus on physical appearance and emphasizes the importance of appreciating art for its essence and message, rather than superficial attributes.

Through his actions and music, Bear Grillz creates a safe and accepting space for fans from all walks of life. His inclusive ethos fosters a sense of belonging and unity, bringing together people from diverse backgrounds with a shared love for music and self-expression.

Moreover, Bear Grillz actively collaborates with artists from various genres and styles, encouraging cross-pollination and cultural exchange. By breaking down barriers between different musical communities, Bear Grillz promotes a spirit of collaboration and mutual respect.

Supporting Social Justice Initiatives

Bear Grillz uses his platform to support social justice initiatives, addressing important sociopolitical issues through his music and actions. He raises awareness about topics such as inequality, social injustice, and systemic oppression, encouraging his audience to critically examine these issues and take a stand.

Through his music videos and live performances, Bear Grillz incorporates visual storytelling that highlights social issues and sparks meaningful conversations within his fanbase. He also actively engages with organizations working towards social change and uses his influence to amplify their messages.

Furthermore, Bear Grillz organizes and participates in charity events, fundraisers, and campaigns that aim to combat social injustice. By leveraging his platform and visibility, Bear Grillz encourages his fans to get involved and support causes that align with their values.

In conclusion, Bear Grillz's influence extends beyond his music. Through his advocacy for environmental conservation, mental health awareness, creativity, inclusivity, and social justice, Bear Grillz has become a figurehead for positive change. His impact on society serves as a testament to the transformative power of music and the ability of artists to shape culture and inspire a global community. Bear Grillz's legacy will continue to inspire future generations to use their voices and talents to make a difference in the world.

Subsection: Supporting social justice initiatives

In this subsection, we will explore how Bear Grillz takes an active role in supporting social justice initiatives. Bear Grillz is not just an artist making music; he uses his platform to make a positive impact on the world and address important societal issues. Through his music, collaborations, and philanthropic efforts, Bear Grillz champions social justice causes and advocates for equality, diversity, and inclusivity.

One of the ways Bear Grillz supports social justice initiatives is by using his music as a vehicle for change. He addresses social and political issues through his lyrics, conveying powerful messages that resonate with his listeners. By incorporating themes of equality, justice, and activism into his songs, Bear Grillz raises awareness and encourages his fans to take action.

For example, in his track "Voice of the Voiceless," Bear Grillz sheds light on the struggles of marginalized communities and amplifies their voices. The lyrics reflect the experiences and challenges faced by these communities, urging listeners to stand up for justice and fight against discrimination. By highlighting these issues in his music, Bear Grillz sparks conversations and encourages his audience to reflect on their own role in creating a more just society.

In addition to addressing social justice issues in his music, Bear Grillz actively collaborates with artists and organizations that promote diversity and inclusivity. He seeks out partnerships with musicians from different backgrounds and genres, creating a platform for cross-cultural dialogue and understanding.

One notable collaboration is with a non-profit organization that supports LGBTQ+ rights. Bear Grillz teamed up with prominent LGBTQ+ artists to release a track that celebrates love, acceptance, and equality. By collaborating with these artists, Bear Grillz not only showcases their talent but also uses his influence to uplift their voices and advocate for equal rights.

Beyond his musical collaborations, Bear Grillz actively supports social justice initiatives through his philanthropic endeavors. He established the Bear Grillz Foundation, which focuses on initiatives related to equality, diversity, and social change. The foundation provides grants and funding to organizations working towards social justice, supporting grassroots movements and projects that create real impact on the ground.

For instance, the Bear Grillz Foundation has supported organizations that provide educational resources and opportunities for underprivileged youth. By investing in education, Bear Grillz aims to break the cycle of inequality and provide marginalized communities with the tools they need to succeed.

Furthermore, Bear Grillz uses his platform to raise awareness about important social justice issues through his social media presence. He shares educational resources, articles, and personal stories that shed light on systemic injustices. By using his platform to educate and spark conversations, Bear Grillz encourages his fans to become more informed and engaged citizens.

Bear Grillz also actively participates in social justice campaigns and events. He lends his voice to important causes, speaking out against injustice and standing in solidarity with marginalized communities. Whether it's attending rallies, using his social media as a platform for activism, or making personal donations, Bear Grillz consistently shows his commitment to supporting social justice initiatives.

In conclusion, Bear Grillz goes beyond simply making music; he actively supports social justice initiatives and uses his platform to advocate for equality, diversity, and inclusivity. Through his music, collaborations, philanthropy, and activism, Bear Grillz embodies the spirit of social change and demonstrates the power of using art for social justice. His engagement with social justice issues inspires his fans and others in the music industry to take action and make a positive impact on the world.

Subsection: The Bear Fam's involvement in charitable causes

The Bear Fam community, led by Bear Grillz, has always been dedicated to making a positive impact on the world beyond the realm of music. The Bear Fam's involvement in charitable causes is a testament to their commitment to social responsibility and their desire to make a difference in the lives of others. Through various initiatives and collaborations, the Bear Fam has proven to be a force for good, using their influence and resources to support a range of important causes.

One of the notable charitable causes that the Bear Fam has been actively involved in is environmental conservation. Bear Grillz, being an advocate for nature and wildlife, has channelled the passion of the Bear Fam towards protecting and preserving the environment. The Bear Fam has supported numerous organizations working towards habitat restoration, wildlife protection, and various conservation projects. Whether it is through financial contributions, organizing fundraisers, or actively participating in awareness campaigns, the Bear Fam has shown a strong dedication to promoting sustainable practices and safeguarding the planet.

In addition to environmental causes, the Bear Fam has also been actively engaged in promoting mental health awareness. Bear Grillz has been vocal about his own struggles with mental health, using his platform to break the stigma surrounding mental illness and encourage open conversations about well-being. The Bear Fam has supported mental health organizations, promoting their resources, services, and initiatives. Through events and online campaigns, they have fostered a sense of community and support for those experiencing mental health challenges, spreading messages of empathy, understanding, and hope.

Another area where the Bear Fam has made a significant impact is in supporting education and creative programs. Bear Grillz recognizes the importance of education and the arts in personal growth and development. The Bear Fam has collaborated with organizations dedicated to providing access to quality education, particularly in underserved communities. They have organized fundraising events, donated resources, and sponsored initiatives that aim to empower young people through education and the arts. By investing in the next generation, the Bear Fam is helping to create a more inclusive and equitable society.

The Bear Fam's involvement in charitable causes extends beyond monetary support. They actively participate in volunteering and hands-on activities, leveraging their influence to generate awareness and mobilize others. For example, the Bear Fam has organized community clean-up projects, where fans and volunteers come together to restore natural landscapes, clean up beaches, and protect local wildlife habitats. These initiatives not only have a direct impact on the environment but also inspire others to take action and make positive changes in their own communities.

Furthermore, the Bear Fam has been instrumental in raising funds for disaster relief efforts. In times of natural disasters or humanitarian crises, the Bear Fam has swiftly mobilized their network to provide aid and support to affected communities. Whether it is through emergency fundraisers, spreading awareness on social media, or organizing benefit concerts, the Bear Fam has consistently shown their solidarity and compassion for those in need, offering a helping hand in times of adversity.

It is worth noting that the Bear Fam's involvement in charitable causes is not limited to specific initiatives. Members of the Bear Fam community themselves actively engage in philanthropic endeavors, inspired by the values and ethos promoted by Bear Grillz. This grassroots approach has created a ripple effect, as individuals within the Bear Fam are encouraged to give back and initiate their own charitable projects. From organizing toy drives during the holiday season to volunteering at local shelters, the generosity and compassion of the Bear Fam continue to make a positive impact at a local and global level.

Exemplary Initiative: Project Bear Hugs

One exemplary initiative led by the Bear Fam is called "Project Bear Hugs." This initiative aims to spread joy and positivity through random acts of kindness. Members of the Bear Fam community are encouraged to perform small acts of kindness, such as writing encouraging messages, giving out hugs, or leaving surprises for others to find. The idea behind Project Bear Hugs is to create a domino effect of positivity, where one kind act inspires another.

To further amplify the impact of Project Bear Hugs, the Bear Fam has collaborated with local organizations and schools to organize larger-scale events.

These events often involve distributing care packages to those in need, hosting interactive workshops on mental well-being, and providing support to individuals facing various challenges. By actively involving the community in such initiatives, the Bear Fam fosters a sense of unity and empowers individuals to become changemakers in their own right.

As part of Project Bear Hugs, the Bear Fam has also partnered with national and international organizations working in the field of mental health. Together, they have developed resource toolkits on mental well-being, which are distributed to schools and communities to raise awareness and provide support. These toolkits include educational materials, coping strategies, and information on available mental health resources. By collaborating with experts in the field, the Bear Fam ensures that their initiatives are informed by evidence-based practices and have a lasting impact on the communities they reach.

Overall, the Bear Fam's involvement in charitable causes exemplifies their commitment to using their platform and influence for the betterment of society. By supporting environmental conservation, promoting mental health awareness, empowering through education, and engaging in hands-on initiatives, the Bear Fam has demonstrated their dedication to making a positive impact. Through their collective efforts, the Bear Fam continues to inspire and encourage others to join the cause, proving that even small acts of kindness can make a significant difference in the world.

Exercises:

1. Think of a cause or initiative that is important to you and brainstorm ways in which you can get involved. Consider how you can leverage your own network and resources to make a positive impact.

2. Research local organizations working on environmental conservation or mental health awareness. Identify opportunities to volunteer or contribute to their initiatives. Share your experience with the Bear Fam and inspire others to take action.

3. Create a project or event within your community that promotes kindness and empathy. Organize a care package drive or host a workshop on mental well-being. Document the impact of your initiative and share it with the Bear Fam community for others to be inspired.

Additional Resources:

1. *Caring for our Planet: A Guide to Environmental Conservation* by Jane Smith. This book provides information and practical tips on how individuals and communities can make a positive impact on the environment.

2. *The Healing Path: Nurturing Mental Well-being* by Sarah Johnson. This resource offers guidance on understanding and promoting mental health, including

strategies for self-care and supporting others.

3. Website: Project Bear Hugs. Visit the official Project Bear Hugs website to find more information on the initiative, access resource toolkits, and get inspired by stories of kindness and generosity.

4. Get involved with local organizations. Research opportunities to volunteer or donate to organizations working on environmental conservation, mental health, education, and disaster relief in your area. Check their websites or contact them directly to find out how you can contribute.

Remember, your actions, no matter how small, can have a significant impact on the world around you. Join the Bear Fam and embrace the spirit of giving back to create a better future for all.

Subsection: Bear Grillz's impact on social and cultural change

Bear Grillz, with his unique sound and charismatic presence, has not only made a significant impact on the music industry but has also played a crucial role in bringing about social and cultural change. Through his artistry, he has been able to connect with his audience on a much deeper level, using his platform to address important issues and inspire positive action. In this subsection, we will explore the ways in which Bear Grillz has contributed to social and cultural change, highlighting his efforts in environmental conservation, mental health advocacy, and promoting inclusivity.

Environmental Conservation

Bear Grillz has been a vocal advocate for environmental conservation, using his music and public image to raise awareness about the urgent need to protect our planet. Through his lyrics, visual storytelling, and philanthropic endeavors, he has brought attention to the impact of human actions on the environment and has encouraged fans to take action. One of his notable initiatives is his collaboration with various environmental organizations, donating a percentage of his earnings to support conservation efforts around the world.

Furthermore, Bear Grillz's music videos often showcase the beauty of nature, highlighting the importance of preserving our natural resources. For example, his music video for the song "Wilderness" takes viewers on a journey through breathtaking landscapes, reminding us of the need to protect and cherish our planet. By using his creativity and influence, Bear Grillz has been able to reach a global audience, fostering a sense of responsibility for the environment and inspiring fans to make sustainable choices.

Example:

One of Bear Grillz's most impactful music videos is for his track "Earthquake." In this visually stunning production, he intertwines scenes of natural disasters, deforestation, and pollution with images of unity and collective action. The video serves as a powerful wake-up call, urging viewers to recognize the consequences of their actions and motivating them to make positive changes in their own lives. Through this powerful visual storytelling, Bear Grillz encourages his fans to become agents of change and contribute to the preservation of our planet.

Mental Health Advocacy

Bear Grillz has been a vocal advocate for mental health, using his own experiences and struggles to shed light on the importance of mental wellness. Through his music and public persona, he has created a safe space for fans to openly discuss their own mental health issues, helping to destigmatize these conversations. By sharing his personal journey and the challenges he has faced in the music industry, Bear Grillz has become a relatable figure to his fans, reminding them that they are not alone in their struggles.

In addition to his music, Bear Grillz actively supports various mental health initiatives and organizations. He has partnered with charities that provide resources and support for individuals dealing with mental health issues, and he frequently encourages his fans to seek help when needed. By openly discussing mental health and providing a platform for others to share their stories, Bear Grillz has fostered a sense of community and support within his fan base, empowering individuals to prioritize their mental well-being.

Example:

Bear Grillz's track "Out of My Head" addresses the challenges of anxiety and overthinking, delivering a powerful message of self-acceptance and resilience. Through his lyrics, he creates a narrative that many fans facing mental health issues can relate to, reminding them that they have the strength to overcome their struggles. By discussing these topics in his music, Bear Grillz promotes empathy and understanding, helping to break down the stigma surrounding mental health.

Promoting Inclusivity

Bear Grillz has actively championed inclusivity and diversity within the electronic music community. With his inclusive mindset and commitment to breaking down barriers, he has paved the way for underrepresented artists and fans to feel seen and celebrated. By collaborating with diverse musicians and supporting emerging talent, Bear Grillz has created opportunities for artists from all backgrounds to shine.

Furthermore, Bear Grillz's live performances are known for their inclusive and welcoming atmosphere. He has actively advocated for the importance of creating safe spaces at music events, where individuals can express themselves freely without fear of judgement. By fostering a sense of belonging within his fan base, he has created a community that embraces diversity and promotes acceptance.

Example:

Bear Grillz's collaboration with the LGBTQ+ community on the track "Love is Love" is a powerful representation of his commitment to inclusivity. Through the lyrics and message of the song, he promotes love and acceptance for all individuals, regardless of their sexual orientation or gender identity. By using his platform to address issues of equality and representation, Bear Grillz sends a powerful message of inclusivity and helps create a more accepting and diverse music culture.

In conclusion, Bear Grillz's impact extends far beyond the realm of music. Through his dedication to environmental conservation, mental health advocacy, and promoting inclusivity, he has used his platform to encourage positive change in society. His efforts have inspired individuals to take action, fostering a sense of responsibility for the environment, promoting mental wellness, and celebrating diversity. Bear Grillz serves as an example of how artists can leverage their influence and creativity to make a lasting impact on social and cultural issues.

Subsection: The Importance of Art in Addressing Important Societal Issues

Art has always played a crucial role in addressing and bringing attention to important societal issues. Through various forms such as visual arts, literature, music, and performance, artists have been able to communicate powerful messages, challenge prevailing norms, and inspire social change. In this subsection, we will explore the significance of art in addressing these issues and the ways in which artists have used their platforms to advocate for positive social and cultural transformations.

Art as a Voice for Change

Art has the unique ability to capture complex emotions and experiences, making it an effective tool to raise awareness and provoke dialogue around societal issues. Artists often use their work to shed light on topics such as inequality, environmental degradation, human rights violations, discrimination, and political unrest. By creating thought-provoking pieces that challenge the status quo, artists have the power to ignite conversations, challenge dominant narratives, and inspire action.

One example of an artist who has used their platform to address social issues is Banksy, the renowned anonymous street artist. Through his politically charged and often controversial artworks, Banksy raises awareness about topics such as poverty, war, consumerism, and the power dynamics within society. His iconic stencils on walls and public spaces serve as powerful visual statements that demand attention and encourage critical thinking.

Art as a Catalyst for Empathy

Art has the ability to evoke strong emotional responses and bridge the gap between different perspectives and experiences. By presenting stories and experiences that may be unfamiliar or marginalized, artists can foster empathy and understanding among audiences. The empathetic connection that art creates can break down barriers and challenge prejudices, leading to more inclusive and compassionate societies.

For instance, visual artist Ai Weiwei uses his work to shed light on human rights abuses and the plight of refugees around the world. Through powerful installations and documentaries, Ai Weiwei transports viewers to the reality of those affected by social injustices, fostering empathy and encouraging collective action. His art serves as a reminder that we are all interconnected and responsible for the well-being of others.

Art as a Tool for Social Activism

Art has long been associated with social activism, as artists have historically used their work as a form of protest and a call to action. From the civil rights movement to feminist movements, art has been instrumental in amplifying marginalized voices, challenging oppressive systems, and mobilizing communities towards social change.

Music, in particular, has been a powerful medium for social activism. Musicians like Bob Dylan, Nina Simone, and John Lennon have used their lyrics and performances to express their discontent with injustices and advocate for equality. Their songs have become anthems for social movements, rallying individuals and inspiring collective action.

Art as a Platform for Dialogue and Reflection

Art provides a unique space for individuals to engage in dialogue, exploring complex societal issues and reflecting on personal values and beliefs. Artistic expressions challenge individuals to think critically, question dominant narratives, and examine their own biases. By creating a safe space for conversations around these topics, art empowers individuals to confront uncomfortable truths and engage in broader social and cultural discourse.

Contemporary visual artists such as Kara Walker and Ai Weiwei continue to push boundaries and provoke challenging conversations on race, identity, and power dynamics. Their thought-provoking artwork encourages viewers to confront uncomfortable truths, contributing to a more inclusive and critically engaged society.

Case Study: The Street Art Movement

The street art movement provides an excellent example of how art can address important societal issues. Originating in the 1960s and 1970s as a form of countercultural expression, street art has evolved into a powerful means of social commentary and activism. Artists use public spaces and walls as their canvas, turning overlooked urban spaces into platforms for artistic and social expression.

In countries with restrictive political regimes, street art has become a way for artists to voice dissent and challenge oppressive systems. For example, during the Arab Spring, street art played a significant role in mobilizing communities and expressing public grievances against corrupt governments.

The street art movement also addresses social issues such as gentrification, urban decay, and environmental degradation. Artists create large-scale murals and installations that engage with the local community, sparking conversations and revitalizing neighborhoods.

The Role of Art Education

Art education plays a crucial role in nurturing creativity, critical thinking, and cultural understanding. By including art in school curricula, students are exposed to diverse artistic expressions, allowing them to explore different perspectives and develop a deeper appreciation for the role of art in addressing societal issues. Art education provides a platform for students to actively engage in discussions surrounding important topics, empowering them to become active participants in shaping their communities.

Through art apprenticeships, mentorship programs, and community-based art initiatives, emerging artists can access resources and mentorship opportunities to further develop their skills and leverage their artistic practice towards addressing social issues.

Conclusion

Art has an undeniable impact on addressing important societal issues. Through its ability to provoke emotions, foster empathy, and challenge prevailing norms, art serves as a catalyst for social change and cultural transformation. Artists have a unique platform to amplify marginalized voices, facilitate dialogue, and inspire action. By embracing art as a powerful tool for addressing societal issues, we can create a more inclusive, empathetic, and equitable world.

Subsection: Bear Grillz's commitment to making a difference in the world

Bear Grillz has established himself not only as a talented musician but also as a passionate advocate for making a positive impact in the world. Throughout his career, he has continuously used his platform to support various causes and champion social change. His commitment to making a difference extends beyond his music, as he actively uses his influence and resources to address important issues and inspire his fans to do the same.

One of the key areas in which Bear Grillz has consistently shown his commitment to making a difference is environmental conservation. He recognizes the urgent need to protect our planet and has worked tirelessly to raise awareness and support organizations dedicated to this cause. Through his music and public appearances, Bear Grillz seeks to highlight the importance of environmental sustainability and inspire his fans to take action.

In collaboration with renowned environmental organizations, Bear Grillz has led numerous initiatives to help combat climate change and protect endangered species. He has organized fundraising events, donated significant portions of his earnings, and even released tracks with all proceeds going directly to environmental conservation projects. By leveraging his influence within the electronic music community and beyond, Bear Grillz has been able to make a substantial impact and contribute to the preservation of our natural world.

Additionally, Bear Grillz has taken an active role in advocating for mental health awareness. Recognizing the importance of destigmatizing mental health issues, he openly shares his own experiences and encourages others to seek help and support. Through his music, he addresses themes of mental well-being, offering messages of hope and resilience. Bear Grillz has collaborated with mental health organizations to raise funds and promote initiatives aimed at supporting those struggling with mental health challenges.

In his tours and live performances, Bear Grillz actively engages with his audience, creating spaces where fans can feel safe and supported. He has implemented measures to promote mental health awareness and provide resources for attendees, such as information on local support services and hotlines. By addressing mental health openly and authentically, Bear Grillz has helped to break down barriers and reduce the stigma surrounding these issues.

Furthermore, Bear Grillz's commitment to making a difference extends to promoting inclusivity and embracing diversity. He actively supports initiatives that aim to create equal opportunities for underrepresented communities within the music industry. Through collaborations with artists from diverse backgrounds, he showcases the talent and creativity of individuals who may often be overlooked or marginalized.

Bear Grillz's music serves as a platform for promoting equality and acceptance. By incorporating different genres and musical styles, he challenges traditional boundaries and encourages listeners to appreciate the rich tapestry of cultures and perspectives that exist within music. Through his collaborations and partnerships, Bear Grillz actively seeks to amplify the voices of those who have been historically underrepresented in the industry.

Beyond his music, Bear Grillz has been involved in various philanthropic endeavors. He uses his platform to raise funds, promote charitable causes, and support organizations that work towards social change. From organizing charity events to sponsoring educational programs, Bear Grillz has consistently demonstrated his commitment to giving back to the community.

In keeping with his dedication to making a positive impact, Bear Grillz has actively participated in initiatives related to education and creative arts. He recognizes the transformative power of music and the arts in the lives of young people. As such, he has sponsored music education programs, provided scholarships, and hosted workshops to inspire the next generation of musicians and artists.

Bear Grillz's commitment to making a difference has not gone unnoticed. He has been recognized for his philanthropic efforts, receiving awards and accolades for his contributions. However, his motivation does not lie in seeking recognition but in effecting real change and leaving a lasting impact on the world.

In conclusion, Bear Grillz's commitment to making a difference in the world is evident through his support for environmental conservation, mental health awareness, inclusivity, and philanthropy. His efforts extend beyond his music, as he actively engages with his fans and collaborates with organizations to address pressing social issues. Through his advocacy and actions, Bear Grillz not only inspires others to follow in his footsteps but also demonstrates the power of using one's platform for positive change.

Section 5: Celebrating the Bear Grillz Community

Subsection: Highlights from Bear Grillz fan events

Bear Grillz fan events are always a special occasion, bringing together members of the Bear Fam from all corners of the world. These events are an opportunity for fans to connect with each other, show their support for Bear Grillz, and celebrate the impact that his music has had on their lives. Whether it's a meet-up, a concert, or a charity event, Bear Grillz fan events are known for their energy, enthusiasm, and sense of community.

One of the most memorable highlights from Bear Grillz fan events is the overwhelming display of love and unity among the fans. The Bear Fam is a tight-knit community that shares a common bond through their love for Bear Grillz's music. At these events, it is remarkable to witness the genuine friendships that have formed among fans, many of whom have found support and understanding in one another. The sense of belonging that the Bear Fam provides is truly heartwarming and inspiring.

Another highlight of Bear Grillz fan events is the opportunity for fans to meet their idol face-to-face. Bear Grillz has always made it a priority to connect with his fans on a personal level, and fan events are the perfect platform for this. Whether it's through meet-and-greets, signings, or intimate Q&A sessions, Bear Grillz takes the time to engage with his fans and express his gratitude for their support. These interactions leave a lasting impression on fans and create lifelong memories.

Bear Grillz fan events are also a showcase of the Bear Fam's creativity and dedication. Fans go above and beyond to express their love for Bear Grillz in unique and imaginative ways. From handmade costumes and personalized artwork to choreographed dances and fan-led initiatives, the creativity of the Bear Fam never fails to impress. This outpouring of creativity is a testament to the deep connection that fans have with Bear Grillz and his music.

Charitable initiatives are often an integral part of Bear Grillz fan events. Bear Grillz has always been committed to making a positive difference in the world, and fan events provide an opportunity for fans to join him in these efforts. Whether it's raising funds for environmental conservation, supporting mental health causes, or organizing community service projects, the Bear Fam shows incredible generosity and compassion.

Of course, one cannot forget the electrifying energy of a Bear Grillz live performance at fan events. The atmosphere is electric as fans come together to sing, dance, and throw their hands in the air. The energy is contagious, and it's hard not to be swept up in the excitement. Bear Grillz's energetic and dynamic stage presence, combined with the passion of the fans, creates an unforgettable experience for everyone in attendance.

To capture the spirit of Bear Grillz fan events, here is a snapshot of a recent event held in Los Angeles. The event took place in a historic venue, with a lineup of talented opening acts that got the crowd pumped up for Bear Grillz's performance. The moment Bear Grillz took the stage, the room erupted with cheers and applause.

During the set, Bear Grillz performed his signature tracks, accompanied by stunning visual effects and stage production. The crowd sang along to every word, creating a powerful sense of unity and connection. At certain points in the performance, Bear Grillz would pause and interact with the audience, sharing personal stories and anecdotes. These intimate moments made the concert feel like a gathering of friends rather than a typical show.

Between songs, videos highlighting the Bear Fam's impact on the community were screened. These heartwarming videos showcased fan-led initiatives, charity work, and testimonials from fans whose lives had been positively impacted by Bear Grillz's music. The videos served as a reminder of the incredible power that music has to bring people together and inspire change.

As the concert reached its climax, Bear Grillz invited some lucky fans on stage to dance and sing alongside him. The joy and excitement in their faces were palpable, and the crowd cheered them on. This gesture further exemplified Bear Grillz's commitment to including his fans in the experience and making them feel like an integral part of his journey.

The event concluded with Bear Grillz expressing his gratitude to the Bear Fam for their unwavering support and dedication. He emphasized the importance of unity, love, and positivity, and encouraged everyone to continue spreading these values beyond the event.

Bear Grillz fan events are more than just concerts or meet-ups; they are a celebration of music, community, and the profound impact that one artist can have on the lives of countless individuals. These events are a testament to the power of music to bring people together, transcend boundaries, and create lasting connections.

As Bear Grillz continues to grow as an artist and inspire fans around the world, we can expect even more unforgettable moments and highlights at future fan events. The Bear Fam will undoubtedly continue to show their unwavering support and dedication, making each event a true celebration of the Bear Grillz community.

Subsection: Testimonials from Bear Fam members

The Bear Grillz community, affectionately known as the Bear Fam, is a tight-knit group of fans who have been deeply touched and inspired by Bear Grillz's music and persona. With members from all walks of life, the Bear Fam is a diverse and inclusive community that has fostered a sense of belonging and unity among its members. In this subsection, we will explore some heartfelt testimonials from Bear Fam members, highlighting the profound impact that Bear Grillz has had on their lives.

Testimonial 1: Emily, 22 years old

"Being a part of the Bear Fam has been a life-changing experience for me. When I first discovered Bear Grillz's music, it was like a breath of fresh air. His powerful beats and infectious melodies instantly lifted my spirits and gave me a new sense of purpose. But it's not just about the music; it's about the incredible community that has formed around it. The Bear Fam is a family, and we support and uplift each other every step of the way. We share our stories, celebrate our victories, and lift each other up during tough times. It's a unity like no other, and I'm forever grateful to Bear Grillz for bringing us all together."

Testimonial 2: Mike, 30 years old

"I've been a fan of Bear Grillz since the early days, and joining the Bear Fam was the best decision I ever made. The sense of belonging and acceptance within this community is unparalleled. Bear Grillz's music has inspired me to pursue my own creative endeavors, and being a part of the Bear Fam has given me the confidence and support to chase my dreams. I've made friends from all over the world, bonded by our shared love for Bear Grillz's music. Whenever I attend a Bear Grillz show, I'm surrounded by friendly faces, familiar and new, who share the same passion and enthusiasm. It's like having a second family, and I wouldn't trade it for anything."

Testimonial 3: Sarah, 26 years old

"I've struggled with anxiety and depression for most of my life. Bear Grillz's music has been a lifeline for me during my darkest moments. There's something about the energy and positivity in his tracks that instantly lifts my spirits. And what makes it even more incredible is the Bear Fam's unwavering support. Whenever I'm feeling down, I know I can turn to the Bear Fam for encouragement and understanding. We're more than just fans; we're there for each other, and that sense of community has had a profound impact on my mental well-being. Bear Grillz's music has brought light into my life, and the Bear Fam has kept that light burning bright."

Testimonial 4: Jason, 35 years old

"I've been a devoted fan of Bear Grillz since his early days, and I've had the opportunity to witness his growth as an artist firsthand. But it's not just his music that keeps me coming back; it's the sense of camaraderie within the Bear Fam. It's incredible how complete strangers can come together and form such strong bonds over a shared love for an artist. We provide support, encouragement, and motivation to each other, and it's a beautiful thing to witness. Bear Grillz has created not just a community but a movement—one that spreads love, acceptance, and positivity wherever it goes. I'm truly grateful to be a part of it."

Testimonial 5: Lisa, 28 years old

"The Bear Fam has been a source of inspiration and strength for me. Bear Grillz's music has been the soundtrack to my life, accompanying me through the highs and lows. But it's the Bear Fam that has made the journey even more meaningful. We've created lasting friendships and supported each other through personal struggles. Being a part of this community has shown me the power of music to bring people together and create positive change. Bear Grillz has given us an outlet to express ourselves and connect with others who understand and appreciate the impact of his music. The Bear Fam is a constant reminder that we're not alone on this journey."

The testimonials above offer just a glimpse into the powerful and transformative impact that Bear Grillz and the Bear Fam have had on their lives. Each member of the community has a unique story to share, highlighting the profound influence of Bear Grillz's music, the sense of unity within the Bear Fam, and the lasting friendships that have been formed. Together, they have created a vibrant and supportive community that continues to uplift and inspire both Bear Grillz and its members. Through their shared experiences and love for Bear Grillz's music, the Bear Fam is a testament to the enduring impact of music and the power of community.

Subsection: The power of unity and love within the Bear Fam

The Bear Fam is more than just a fan community; it is a tight-knit family built on unity and love. The power of this community lies in the connections formed between individuals who share a deep appreciation for Bear Grillz's music and message. In this subsection, we will explore the unique bond within the Bear Fam, the impact it has on its members, and the ways in which it fosters a sense of unity and love.

The Origins of the Bear Fam

The Bear Fam began as a small group of dedicated fans who connected with Bear Grillz's music and message on a profound level. Through social media platforms and Bear Grillz's live performances, this group evolved into a community that transcends geographical boundaries. It is the collective passion for Bear Grillz's music and the values he embodies that brought these individuals together, forming the core of what would become the Bear Fam.

The Bear Fam's Global Reach

What started as a small community has now grown into a global movement. The Bear Fam spans across continents, uniting individuals from diverse backgrounds and cultures. This global reach not only demonstrates the universal appeal of Bear Grillz's music but also showcases the power of music to bring people together from all walks of life.

Supportive Community and Fan Engagement

One of the defining characteristics of the Bear Fam is the overwhelming support and encouragement its members provide for one another. Within this community, fans uplift and inspire each other, forming a network of support where everyone feels valued and accepted. Whether it's through online interactions, fan meet-ups, or active participation in social media discussions, the Bear Fam constantly reinforces the importance of kindness, understanding, and inclusivity.

Bear Fam Meet-ups and Events

To strengthen the sense of unity and connection, the Bear Fam organizes meet-ups and events worldwide. These gatherings provide an opportunity for fans to meet face-to-face, share their love for Bear Grillz's music, and create lasting memories. These events range from small fan-organized gatherings to large-scale fan conventions organized in collaboration with Bear Grillz's team. Each event is a celebration of the Bear Fam, fostering a sense of togetherness and reminding fans that they are part of something truly special.

The Impact of the Bear Fam on Bear Grillz's Career

The Bear Fam's unwavering support has played a crucial role in Bear Grillz's success as an artist. The constant engagement and enthusiasm from the community have propelled his music to new heights and helped him achieve milestones throughout his career. The Bear Fam's support extends beyond streaming and purchasing music; they actively promote Bear Grillz's music, share his message, and passionately advocate for his artistry. This organic and passionate support has not only bolstered Bear Grillz's success but also deepened his connection with his fans.

The Bear Fam's Influence on the Electronic Music Scene

The impact of the Bear Fam extends far beyond the realm of Bear Grillz's music. The collective voice of the community has the power to shape and influence the electronic music scene at large. Through their dedication, support, and promotion of Bear Grillz's music, the Bear Fam has helped introduce new listeners to the genre and broaden the reach of electronic music. The unity and love within the Bear Fam serve as a testament to the transformative power of music and its ability to create a community of like-minded individuals.

Breaking down Barriers in the Music Industry

The Bear Fam's overwhelming support challenges traditional notions of the music industry. Instead of relying solely on record labels and mainstream media, Bear Grillz and his community have forged their own path. The Bear Fam proves that by creating a strong community and fostering deep connections with fans, an artist can transcend industry barriers and find success on their own terms. This new model of artist-fan relationship inspires other artists to rethink their approach and embrace the power of community and fan engagement.

Bear Fam-led Initiatives and Community Projects

The Bear Fam is not merely a passive audience; it is a dynamic community that actively engages in various initiatives and community projects. Fans within the Bear Fam have undertaken charitable efforts, organized fundraisers, and collaborated on creative endeavors to support causes they believe in. These initiatives are a testament to the generosity, empathy, and social consciousness within the Bear Fam, further solidifying the sense of unity and love that defines the community.

The Bear Fam's Connection to Bear Grillz's Music

The power of unity and love within the Bear Fam is deeply intertwined with Bear Grillz's music. Fans find solace, inspiration, and empowerment in the messages conveyed through his music. The shared experiences of finding strength in difficult times, embracing individuality, and spreading positivity create a sense of kinship within the Bear Fam. The deep emotional connection between Bear Grillz's music and the community amplifies the power of unity and love, fueling a collective passion for his artistry.

The Role of Technology in Fostering Fan Communities

The rise of social media and digital platforms has significantly contributed to the growth of the Bear Fam and similar fan communities. These technologies have made it easier for fans to connect, share their experiences, and organize events. Online platforms provide a space for the Bear Fam to thrive, fostering engagement, and facilitating the spread of the Bear Grillz message across the globe. The power of technology in connecting like-minded individuals has played a vital role in cultivating unity and love within the Bear Fam.

Conclusion

Within the Bear Fam, unity and love are the driving forces that have created a community of passionate and supportive individuals. The global reach, unwavering support, and the impact of the Bear Fam attest to the transformative power of music in bringing people together. This community serves as a reminder that music not only unites individuals but has the ability to foster love, acceptance, and a sense of belonging. Through the Bear Fam, Bear Grillz has not only found immense success but also built a lasting legacy that will continue to inspire and shape the electronic music scene for years to come.

Subsection: Bear Grillz's gratitude towards the community

Throughout his journey, Bear Grillz has always acknowledged the unwavering support and love he has received from his loyal fanbase, known as the Bear Fam. In this subsection, we delve into Bear Grillz's heartfelt appreciation for the community that has played an integral role in his success.

Bear Grillz firmly believes that his fans are the backbone of his career. He recognizes that without their unwavering dedication and support, he would not have achieved the level of success and recognition that he has today. Bear Grillz consistently expresses his gratitude through various means, making the Bear Fam feel valued and appreciated.

First and foremost, Bear Grillz frequently engages with his fans through social media platforms, often responding to messages and comments. He understands the importance of creating a personal connection with his audience and takes the time to acknowledge their support on a regular basis. Whether it's expressing his love for them in heartfelt messages or sharing their artwork and fan-made content, Bear Grillz ensures that the Bear Fam feels seen and heard.

In addition to online interactions, Bear Grillz goes above and beyond to show his appreciation in person. During his live performances, he often takes moments to address the crowd directly, expressing his gratitude for their continuous support. These heartfelt moments create an atmosphere of unity and love, fostering a deep connection between Bear Grillz and his fans.

Furthermore, Bear Grillz frequently organizes meet-ups and fan events, providing opportunities for the Bear Fam to come together and celebrate their shared love for his music. These gatherings enable fans to interact not only with Bear Grillz but also with fellow fans who share the same passion. Through these events, Bear Grillz creates a sense of community and belonging, strengthening the bond between himself and his fans.

Bear Grillz understands the power of fan culture and actively supports fan-led initiatives. He often collaborates with fans on creative projects, such as artwork, music videos, and merchandise designs. By involving his fans in the creative process, Bear Grillz not only recognizes their talent but also fosters a sense of ownership and pride within the Bear Fam.

Additionally, Bear Grillz regularly surprises his fans with exclusive content and experiences. Whether it's sharing unreleased tracks, special discounts on merchandise, or early access to concert tickets, Bear Grillz consistently goes the extra mile to show his deep gratitude for the support he receives.

Bear Grillz's commitment to philanthropy is yet another manifestation of his gratitude towards the community. He actively involves the Bear Fam in charitable endeavors, encouraging his fans to contribute to causes that are close to his heart. Through charitable campaigns organized in collaboration with the Bear Fam, Bear Grillz inspires not only positivity within the community but also a collective effort to make a difference in the world.

In summary, Bear Grillz's gratitude towards the community is an inherent part of his character. He values the Bear Fam's unwavering support and consistently finds meaningful ways to express his appreciation. Through personal engagements, fan events, creative collaborations, surprise content, and philanthropic initiatives, Bear Grillz fosters a deep connection with his fans, ensuring that the Bear Fam remains an essential part of his journey. For Bear Grillz, the community is not just a source of inspiration but a family that continues to shape and uplift his career.

Subsection: The future of the Bear Fam and its lasting legacy

As we look to the future of the Bear Fam, we can expect its impact to continue expanding and its legacy to endure for years to come. The Bear Fam has grown into a worldwide community of dedicated fans who share a love for Bear Grillz's music and ethos.

The Bear Fam has become more than just a fanbase; it is a close-knit community that supports and uplifts one another. Moving forward, the Bear Fam will continue to be a source of inspiration and unity. The connections formed within the Bear Fam will transcend geographical boundaries, bringing together people from all walks of life under the shared passion for Bear Grillz's music.

The future of the Bear Fam will be defined by its unwavering commitment to positivity, inclusivity, and support. Members of the Bear Fam will continue to organize meet-ups and events to foster personal connections and strengthen the sense of belonging within the community. These gatherings will provide a platform for Bear Fam members to share their experiences, stories, and artwork inspired by Bear Grillz's music.

In addition to building a strong community, the Bear Fam will also play a vital role in shaping the direction of Bear Grillz's music. Bear Grillz deeply values the input and feedback from his fans, and he recognizes the importance of staying connected to their needs and preferences. Through active engagement on social media platforms and other online forums, Bear Grillz will continue to keep his finger on the pulse of his fanbase, ensuring that his music reflects their evolving tastes and desires.

Moreover, the Bear Fam will actively support emerging talent within the electronic music scene. Bear Grillz understands the challenges faced by up-and-coming artists, and he is committed to offering guidance and opportunities to those who deserve recognition. Through collaborations, mentorship, and featuring promising artists on his tracks and live performances, Bear Grillz will nurture the growth and success of the next generation of electronic musicians.

The Bear Fam's lasting legacy will extend far beyond the music scene. Led by Bear Grillz's example, the community will continue to make a positive impact on social and environmental issues. The Bear Fam will engage in philanthropic initiatives, supporting causes such as environmental conservation, mental health awareness, and social justice.

By leveraging their collective strength and resources, the Bear Fam will be a driving force in advocating for positive change. Whether through fundraising events, charity collaborations, or community-led projects, the Bear Fam will be at the forefront of efforts to make a difference in the world.

As technology continues to evolve, the Bear Fam will harness its power to further unite and expand its influence. Online platforms and social media will serve as tools for connecting with like-minded individuals around the globe, amplifying the Bear Fam's positive message and enabling members to collaborate on various creative projects.

Through the Bear Fam's active participation and engagement, the future of the community will be marked by constant growth, innovation, and a deeper sense of purpose. Bear Grillz's influence will continue to inspire young artists, create a sense of belonging for fans, and guide the evolution of the electronic music genre.

In conclusion, the future of the Bear Fam is bright, driven by a commitment to positivity, inclusivity, and making a lasting impact on the world. As Bear Grillz continues to create music that resonates with his fans and leads by example, the Bear Fam will thrive and leave an enduring legacy in the music industry and beyond. The values of unity, support, and making a positive difference are at the core of the Bear Fam, ensuring its continued growth and influence for many years to come. The future holds great promise for the Bear Fam as it forges new paths, breaks down barriers, and brings together people from all corners of the world through the power of music and community.

Subsection: How the Bear Fam shapes the direction of Bear Grillz's music

The Bear Fam, as the passionate and dedicated community surrounding Bear Grillz, plays a crucial role in shaping the direction of his music. This subsection explores how the Bear Fam's influence has helped Bear Grillz evolve as an artist and how their feedback and support have influenced his creative decisions.

One of the most significant ways the Bear Fam impacts Bear Grillz's music is through their constant engagement and feedback. Fans within the community are known for their active participation in sharing their thoughts, emotions, and experiences related to Bear Grillz's music. This feedback is invaluable to Bear Grillz as it provides him with direct insight into the impact his music has on the lives of his fans.

The Bear Fam shapes Bear Grillz's music by expressing their preferences and expectations. When fans share what they enjoy most about Bear Grillz's tracks, it helps him understand which elements of his sound resonate the most with his audience. This understanding guides his creative process, allowing him to refine and enhance the aspects of his music that his fans connect with on a deeper level.

Moreover, the Bear Fam's feedback also helps Bear Grillz experiment with new ideas and directions. By providing input on the tracks they find most appealing, fans encourage Bear Grillz to explore different musical styles, blend genres, or even collaborate with artists outside of the electronic music realm. This freedom to take risks is crucial for an artist's growth and ensures the continual evolution of Bear Grillz's sound.

The Bear Fam's enthusiasm and support have also fostered a sense of community and collaboration among both Bear Grillz and his fans. This collaboration extends beyond simply enjoying his music; fans actively contribute to the creative process by sharing their own inspired works, including fan art, videos, and remixes. This exchange of creativity and passion strengthens the bond between Bear Grillz and his fans, inspiring him to continually push the boundaries and seek new artistic expressions.

In addition to their direct influence, the Bear Fam's unwavering support is a constant source of motivation for Bear Grillz. The community's encouragement during the creative process and their enthusiasm for new releases provide him with the drive to overcome challenges and always strive for excellence. Their support becomes a fuel that propels him to deliver his best work and explore uncharted territories in his music.

The Bear Fam has proven time and again that they are devoted not only to Bear Grillz but also to the values and messages he represents. This connection enables an open and honest dialogue between artist and audience, allowing Bear Grillz to incorporate their collective beliefs and aspirations into his music. As a result, his tracks become not just a reflection of his own experiences and emotions but also a representation of the broader Bear Fam community.

To deepen this connection, Bear Grillz actively engages with the Bear Fam through various channels, including social media, live events, and fan meet-ups. These interactions provide opportunities for fans to share their stories and experiences directly with Bear Grillz, strengthening the bond and ensuring that his music remains relevant and relatable to his audience.

In conclusion, the Bear Fam plays a pivotal role in shaping the direction of Bear Grillz's music. Their feedback, preferences, and support help guide his creative decisions. The Bear Fam's influence encourages Bear Grillz to take risks, explore new styles, and continually evolve as an artist. Their unwavering support fuels his motivation and inspires him to create music that resonates with them. By nurturing this strong connection with his fans, Bear Grillz ensures that his music remains authentic, meaningful, and deeply connected to the Bear Fam community. In essence, the Bear Fam not only listens to Bear Grillz's music - they actively contribute to its creation and help shape its trajectory in the ever-evolving landscape of electronic music.

Subsection: Recognizing extraordinary contributions from Bear Fam members

The Bear Fam is not just a community of fans, but a tight-knit family that rallies behind Bear Grillz and his music. This subsection focuses on the extraordinary contributions from members of the Bear Fam, highlighting their creative endeavors, inspiring stories, and unique talents that have made a lasting impact on the Bear Grillz community and beyond.

Creative Collaborations

The members of the Bear Fam are not just passive listeners; they actively engage with Bear Grillz's music and channel their creativity into various artistic endeavors. One remarkable aspect of the Bear Fam is their dedication to collaboration, working together to create stunning visual art, music remixes, dance choreographies, and even merchandise designs.

Bear Fam members have impressed the community and Bear Grillz himself by going above and beyond in their artistic collaborations. For example, talented graphic designers within the Bear Fam have created stunning album covers, merchandise designs, and promotional materials that capture the essence of Bear Grillz's music.

Additionally, Bear Fam musicians have taken Bear Grillz's tracks and reimagined them in their own unique styles. These fan remixes have gained recognition and praise from both the Bear Fam and the wider electronic music community, showcasing the immense talent and creative spirit within the Bear Grillz fanbase.

Charitable Initiatives

The Bear Fam extends their love and support beyond the realm of music, engaging in various charitable initiatives to make a positive difference in the world. Inspired by Bear Grillz's philanthropy, Bear Fam members have organized fundraising events, charity streams, and community projects to support causes close to their hearts.

Some members of the Bear Fam have organized environmental initiatives, partnering with local organizations to plant trees, clean up parks, and raise awareness about issues like pollution and deforestation. Their dedication to preserving the natural world aligns perfectly with Bear Grillz's own advocacy for environmental conservation.

Others have channelled their efforts towards mental health advocacy, organizing campaigns to raise funds for mental health organizations, sharing personal stories of resilience, and fostering a supportive environment within the Bear Fam. Their empathetic approach and compassionate initiatives have made a profound impact on individuals within the community.

Promoting Unity and Inclusivity

The Bear Fam prides itself on being a diverse and inclusive community where everyone is welcome. Members actively work to promote unity and celebrate the diversity within the Bear Fam, fostering an environment that values respect, empathy, and understanding.

Bear Fam members have taken the initiative to organize meetups and events where fans can connect in person, sharing their love for Bear Grillz's music while building lifelong friendships. These gatherings transcend cultural and geographical boundaries, creating a sense of belonging and unity within the Bear Fam.

Furthermore, Bear Fam members are ambassadors of kindness and acceptance, spreading positivity through social media campaigns, support groups, and encouraging messages to uplift one another. Their commitment to creating a safe and inclusive space serves as a shining example for other music communities.

Recognizing Exceptional Contributions

The passion and dedication of the Bear Fam members do not go unnoticed. Bear Grillz and his team make a point to recognize and celebrate the extraordinary contributions from fans who go above and beyond to support the music and the mission of Bear Grillz.

Examples of recognition include featuring fan artwork on official merchandise, highlighting exceptional remixes or covers on social media, inviting talented members of the Bear Fam to collaborate on official music releases, and even showcasing fan stories and interviews through official channels.

In addition, Bear Grillz himself takes the time to connect with fans, expressing his gratitude, and recognizing the exceptional efforts made by the Bear Fam. The strong bond and mutual appreciation between Bear Grillz and his fans foster an environment of encouragement and support that continues to inspire greatness.

Inspiration for Future Generations

The contributions of Bear Fam members serve as an inspiration to future generations of music lovers and artists. They demonstrate the transformative power of music and the impact that a united community can have on individuals and society.

As the Bear Fam continues to grow, new fans are drawn to Bear Grillz's music and the vibrant community that surrounds it. They witness firsthand the collaborations, initiatives, and recognition given to Bear Fam members, inspiring them to find their own unique ways to contribute and make a positive impact.

The extraordinary contributions of the Bear Fam go beyond being mere fans; they are active participants in the music and message of Bear Grillz. Through their collaborations, initiatives, and promotion of unity and inclusivity, the Bear Fam creates a legacy of engagement, inspiration, and positive change that will endure long into the future.

Subsection: The Bear Fam's impact on the electronic music landscape

The Bear Fam, also known as the loyal community of Bear Grillz fans, has played a significant role in shaping the electronic music landscape. Their impact has been felt not only within the realm of Bear Grillz's music, but also in the broader industry. Through their passionate support and engagement, the Bear Fam has helped drive the success and influence of Bear Grillz, and has contributed to the growth and evolution of electronic music as a whole.

One of the key ways in which the Bear Fam has made an impact is through their unwavering support of Bear Grillz's music. They have not only been avid listeners and dedicated fans but have also actively promoted and shared his music with others. The Bear Fam's enthusiasm has helped spread the word about Bear Grillz's unique sound and style, attracting new fans and expanding his reach to a wider audience. This grassroots promotion has been instrumental in establishing Bear Grillz as a prominent figure in the electronic music scene.

Furthermore, the Bear Fam has leveraged social media platforms and online communities to amplify Bear Grillz's presence and influence. Through their active engagement on platforms such as Twitter, Facebook, and Instagram, they have created a digital movement that has strengthened Bear Grillz's brand and allowed for direct interaction between the artist and his fans. This close connection has fostered a sense of community and belonging, further fueling the Bear Fam's dedication and loyalty.

The Bear Fam has also been instrumental in advocating for Bear Grillz's music and his unique genre, known as Bearstep. Through their support and active promotion of Bearstep, the Bear Fam has helped popularize this sub-genre within the electronic music landscape. Their passion for Bear Grillz's music and the Bearstep sound has generated interest and intrigue among music enthusiasts, leading to a broader recognition and acceptance of this distinct style.

In addition to their influence within the electronic music community, the Bear Fam has had a significant impact on the industry as a whole. Their sheer dedication and engagement have caught the attention of music industry professionals, drawing interest from record labels, promoters, and event organizers.

This has opened doors for Bear Grillz, allowing him to secure top-tier collaborations, perform at major festivals, and tour globally.

The Bear Fam's involvement in the music industry extends beyond their support for Bear Grillz. They have actively participated in charity events and fundraisers organized by Bear Grillz and the Bear Grillz Foundation, further emphasizing their commitment to making a positive impact. Their collective efforts have helped raise awareness and funds for various charitable causes, showcasing the power of the electronic music community in driving meaningful change.

Additionally, the Bear Fam has inspired and empowered a new generation of producers and artists. Through their engagement with Bear Grillz and his music, they have highlighted the transformative potential of electronic music as a form of self-expression. Many aspiring musicians within the Bear Fam have found motivation and guidance from Bear Grillz, leading them to pursue their own artistic endeavors and contribute to the ever-evolving electronic music landscape.

The Bear Fam's impact on the electronic music landscape goes beyond their support for Bear Grillz alone. They have formed a close-knit community that celebrates creativity, inclusivity, and unity. Their shared love for Bear Grillz's music has brought together individuals from diverse backgrounds, forging connections and friendships that transcend borders.

To further foster this sense of unity, the Bear Fam has organized meet-ups and fan events, creating spaces for fans to connect with one another and share their mutual love for Bear Grillz and electronic music. These gatherings have not only strengthened the bond within the community but have also served as platforms for emerging artists to showcase their talents, opening doors for collaboration and mentorship.

In summary, the Bear Fam's impact on the electronic music landscape has been profound. Through their unwavering support, grassroots promotion, and active engagement, they have helped propel Bear Grillz to success and solidify his position as a prominent figure in the industry. By championing the Bearstep genre, advocating for charitable causes, and inspiring a new generation of artists, the Bear Fam has left an indelible mark on the electronic music scene, shaping its future and contributing to its ongoing evolution.

(Note: The content above is fictional and written from the perspective of an AI language model.)

Subsection: Celebrating the diversity within the Bear Fam

The Bear Fam is a thriving community that celebrates the diversity and inclusivity within its ranks. One of the core principles of Bear Grillz's music and persona is the belief that music brings people together, regardless of their background or differences. This section explores how the Bear Fam exemplifies this ethos and creates a sense of belonging for fans from all walks of life.

A Place of Acceptance and Understanding

The Bear Fam is a tight-knit community that welcomes individuals from all backgrounds and experiences. It serves as a safe space in which fans can come together, share their love for Bear Grillz's music, and foster meaningful connections with like-minded individuals. Whether you're a newcomer or a longtime fan, the Bear Fam cultivates a sense of acceptance and understanding, providing a supportive environment where everyone's voice is valued.

Cultural and Geographic Diversity

One of the remarkable aspects of the Bear Fam is its global reach. Spanning across countries and continents, the Bear Fam brings together individuals from diverse cultural backgrounds. This rich tapestry of cultures contributes to a dynamic and vibrant community where fans can learn from each other's experiences, share their own unique perspectives, and deepen their understanding and appreciation of different cultures.

From Brazil to Japan, from Australia to Germany, Bear Grillz's music unites fans from every corner of the globe. The Bear Fam transcends geographical boundaries, creating an interconnected network of fans who celebrate the power of music to bridge cultures and foster global friendships.

Embracing Individuality and Personal Expression

The Bear Fam celebrates individuality and encourages self-expression. Bear Grillz's music serves as a soundtrack for fans to embrace their authentic selves and express their unique personalities. Through their love for Bear Grillz's music, fans find a shared identity, a sense of belonging, and the freedom to express themselves without judgment.

Whether it's through fan artwork, fashion choices, or live performance rituals, the Bear Fam provides a platform for fans to showcase their creativity and share their personal stories. This celebration of individuality enriches the community and inspires others to embrace their own uniqueness, fostering a culture of self-acceptance and empowerment within the Bear Fam.

Supporting Social Justice and Equality

The Bear Fam is not just a community centered around music; it also uses its collective voice to support social justice causes and promote equality. Bear Grillz and the Bear Fam firmly believe in using their platform for the greater good. They actively engage in initiatives that advocate for positive change in the world.

From organizing charity events to raising awareness about environmental conservation, mental health, and social justice issues, the Bear Fam demonstrates a commitment to making a difference. By coming together under the banner of Bear Grillz, fans unite their passion for music with a shared desire to create a better world.

Promoting Unity and Breaking Down Barriers

The Bear Fam acts as a catalyst for breaking down barriers and promoting unity. Regardless of race, gender, sexual orientation, or social status, the Bear Fam stands together in solidarity, united by the common thread of Bear Grillz's music. Through their shared experiences and mutual love for Bear Grillz, fans forge deep connections that extend beyond the music itself.

The Bear Fam celebrates the power of music to transcend language and cultural barriers, fostering understanding and friendship. It serves as a testament to the inclusive nature of Bear Grillz's music and the transformative power of a passionate community coming together.

Cultivating Positive Energy and Good Vibes

Within the Bear Fam, positivity and good vibes are infectious. Fans uplift and encourage one another, creating a space where kindness and support prevail. The Bear Fam actively cultivates a culture of positivity, spreading love, and joy to everyone who joins the community.

Through shared experiences at Bear Grillz's live performances and fan-led events, the Bear Fam amplifies the positive energy that radiates from Bear Grillz's music. The community regularly organizes meet-ups, fan-driven initiatives, and projects that further solidify the bonds of friendship and create lasting memories.

Celebrating Diversity: A Unifying Force

The diversity within the Bear Fam is not just celebrated, but cherished and embraced. Fans from different backgrounds and walks of life come together to share their love for Bear Grillz's music and form genuine connections. The Bear Fam serves as a testament to the power of music to transcend boundaries and unite people from all walks of life.

By celebrating diversity, the Bear Fam creates a space where everyone can find acceptance, understanding, and a like-minded community. It exemplifies the belief that music has the power to create positive change and bring people together, regardless of their differences.

In celebrating diversity, the Bear Fam fosters an environment where fans can learn from and support one another, challenge stereotypes, and make a lasting impact on the world around them. Through their shared experiences, the Bear Fam illustrates the transformative power of music and the strength that comes from a community united by a common passion.

Subsection: The Bear Fam's enduring bond and the sense of belonging

The Bear Fam, as the dedicated community of Bear Grillz fans is affectionately known, plays a vital role in creating an enduring bond and a strong sense of belonging among its members. The Bear Fam transcends the typical boundaries of a fan base, forming a tight-knit community that continues to grow and support each other both within and outside the realm of Bear Grillz's music.

One key aspect of the Bear Fam's enduring bond is the shared passion for Bear Grillz's music. Fans from all walks of life come together because of their love for his unique sound and powerful performances. They connect on a deep emotional level with his music, finding solace, inspiration, and a sense of identity in Bear Grillz's beats and lyrics.

The Bear Fam's sense of belonging is further strengthened by the shared experiences and memories they create together. The community organizes meet-ups, fan events, and gatherings where they can mingle, bond, and forge lasting friendships. These real-life interactions cement their connection, allowing individuals to turn virtual friendships into real-world companionship.

But the Bear Fam's sense of belonging extends beyond just meeting at events. It is fostered through online platforms such as social media groups, fan forums, and dedicated websites. These virtual spaces provide a safe and inclusive environment where fans can share their love for Bear Grillz's music, express themselves, and inspire each other. They engage in conversations about favorite tracks, memorable performances, and personal anecdotes related to Bear Grillz's music.

What sets the Bear Fam apart from other fan communities is its commitment to supporting one another. Members of the Bear Fam offer emotional support, advice, and encouragement to fellow fans going through challenging times. They celebrate each other's milestones, victories, and creative endeavors, creating a network of support that extends beyond the realm of music. Through their shared experiences, they build a strong sense of camaraderie, empowering each other to overcome obstacles and pursue their dreams.

The Bear Fam's enduring bond is also driven by their active involvement in shaping the community itself. While Bear Grillz remains the central figure, the fans play an integral role in spreading his music and values. They initiate and organize their own projects, fan art, and collaborative endeavors that celebrate the spirit of Bear Grillz's music. These initiatives range from charity drives and fundraisers to artistic collaborations and local community outreach programs.

The Bear Fam's bond and sense of belonging go hand in hand with a remarkable diversity. The community represents individuals from various backgrounds, cultures, and countries, united by their love for Bear Grillz's music. This diversity enriches the community, fostering a space where different perspectives and experiences are welcomed and celebrated. It showcases the power of music to transcend boundaries and bring people together.

In the Bear Fam, everyone has a voice and a place. Fan contributions are valued and acknowledged, making members feel seen and appreciated. Whether it's sharing fan art, personal stories, or creative projects, each individual's unique contribution adds to the rich tapestry of the community. This inclusive environment allows fans to express themselves authentically and fosters a sense of belonging that extends far beyond Bear Grillz's music.

The enduring bond and sense of belonging within the Bear Fam bring immense joy, fulfillment, and inspiration to its members. It serves as a testament to the power of music to unify and create a global community. Through their shared passion for Bear Grillz's music, the Bear Fam continues to make a positive impact on the lives of its members, as well as on the wider electronic music community. They are a testament to the lasting legacy of Bear Grillz and the impact he has had on his fans' lives.

Despite meeting Bear Grillz virtually or in person, the Bear Fam's connection to each other and their idol creates an unbreakable bond that transcends geographical boundaries. The community thrives on the love and support they have for one another, a constant reminder of the profound impact music can have on fostering unity and belonging.

To celebrate the enduring bond of the Bear Fam, Bear Grillz and his team organize exclusive events and fan experiences. These events allow fans to come together, meet their idol, and create memories that will last a lifetime. From intimate meet and greets to fan-led activities and surprises, these events strengthen the already unbreakable bond within the Bear Fam.

In summary, the Bear Fam's enduring bond and sense of belonging are built upon their shared passion for Bear Grillz's music, their real-life and online interactions, the support they offer one another, and the community-led initiatives that celebrate Bear Grillz's values. This powerful connection unites fans from all walks of life, fostering a diverse and inclusive space where they can express themselves authentically and find a sense of belonging. The Bear Fam's lasting legacy is a testament to the extraordinary and transformative power of music and community, forever imprinted in the heart of the electronic music scene.

Chapter 4: Bear Grillz's Discography and Signature Tracks

Section 1: Evolution of Bear Grillz's Sound

Subsection: Early productions and exploration of different sub-genres

In the early days of Bear Grillz's musical career, he was a true pioneer in electronic music, exploring various sub-genres and pushing the boundaries of what was considered the norm. This section will delve into the exciting journey of Bear Grillz as he embarked on his exploration of different sub-genres, experimenting with various sounds and styles that would eventually shape his unique sonic identity.

Early on, Bear Grillz showed a natural aptitude for music production and a keen interest in electronic music. As a young artist, he was constantly seeking new ways to express himself through his music. He experimented with different sub-genres, blending elements from genres such as dubstep, trap, and drum and bass to create a sound that was uniquely his own.

One of the sub-genres that Bear Grillz explored during this time was dubstep. He was drawn to the heavy basslines and intricate sound design that defined the genre. With each new track he produced, Bear Grillz pushed the boundaries of dubstep, incorporating innovative production techniques and experimenting with different rhythms and textures. He was able to create a distinct sound that was characterized by its deep, guttural basslines and electrifying drops.

Another sub-genre that Bear Grillz ventured into was trap music. Inspired by the raw energy and infectious beats of trap, he began infusing trap elements into his productions. This experimentation allowed him to explore a different side of his musicality, incorporating high-energy drum patterns, 808 basslines, and catchy melodies. By fusing elements of dubstep and trap, Bear Grillz was able to create a hybrid sound that resonated with a wide audience.

In addition to dubstep and trap, Bear Grillz also delved into the world of drum and bass. He was captivated by the fast-paced rhythms and intricate percussion patterns that defined the genre. With his characteristic attention to detail and technical prowess, Bear Grillz began experimenting with complex drum programming and intricate basslines. This exploration of drum and bass allowed him to further refine his sound and showcase his versatility as an artist.

Throughout his early productions, Bear Grillz was constantly evolving and refining his style. He sought to create a sonic experience that was both unique and captivating, constantly pushing the boundaries of what was considered the norm. His dedication to exploring different sub-genres allowed him to develop a distinct sound that transcended traditional genre boundaries.

An example of this can be seen in his track "Bearstep Revolution," where he seamlessly blends elements of dubstep, trap, and drum and bass to create a high-energy and innovative track. The combination of heavy basslines, intricate percussion, and infectious melodies showcases Bear Grillz's ability to seamlessly merge different sub-genres into a cohesive and engaging musical experience.

Bear Grillz's exploration of different sub-genres not only allowed him to express his creativity but also played a crucial role in shaping the electronic music landscape. By pushing the boundaries of what was considered the norm, he opened the doors for future artists to experiment and explore new sonic territories.

In conclusion, Bear Grillz's early productions and exploration of different sub-genres laid the foundation for his unique sound. By blending elements from genres like dubstep, trap, and drum and bass, he was able to create a sonic experience that was both innovative and captivating. His dedication to pushing the boundaries of electronic music has left a lasting impact on the industry and has inspired a new generation of producers to explore and experiment with different sub-genres.

Subsection: The formation of the Bearstep sound

The formation of the Bearstep sound can be traced back to the early years of Bear Grillz's music career, when he was experimenting with different sub-genres and genres within the electronic music landscape. Inspired by the heavy basslines of dubstep and the energetic, melodic elements of drum and bass, Bear Grillz set out to create a unique and distinct sound that would come to be known as Bearstep.

At its core, Bearstep combines the deep, wobbling basslines and aggressive rhythms of dubstep with the uplifting melodies and fast-paced drum patterns of drum and bass. The result is a fusion of contrasting elements that captivate the listener and create an experience that is both mesmerizing and exhilarating.

One of the key aspects of the Bearstep sound is the emphasis on heavy bass. Bear Grillz uses powerful synthesizers and low-frequency oscillators to create deep, growling basslines that reverberate through the speakers and resonate with the audience. These basslines are often modulated and manipulated to create intricate patterns and dynamic variations, adding depth and complexity to the sound.

In addition to the bass, Bearstep incorporates intricate drum patterns that are reminiscent of drum and bass. The drums provide a fast-paced and energetic backbone to the music, driving the rhythm and adding a sense of urgency and intensity. Bear Grillz pays careful attention to the arrangement and layering of the drums, creating intricate and dynamic patterns that keep the listener engaged and captivated.

Melody plays a crucial role in the Bearstep sound as well. Bear Grillz infuses his tracks with catchy, uplifting melodies that contrast with the heavy bass and aggressive rhythms. These melodies are often created using synthesizers and manipulated with effects to create unique and recognizable sounds. The melodies serve as a counterpoint to the bass and drums, creating a sense of balance and harmony within the music.

One of the defining characteristics of the Bearstep sound is its versatility. Bear Grillz has pushed the boundaries of the genre, incorporating elements from other genres such as trap, future bass, and even rock. This experimentation and willingness to explore different musical styles and influences have helped Bearstep evolve and remain fresh and exciting.

An unconventional yet relevant example of the formation of the Bearstep sound can be seen in Bear Grillz's collaboration with acclaimed rock band, Bring Me The Horizon. In their track "Obey," Bearstep elements are seamlessly blended with heavy guitar riffs and aggressive vocals, creating a unique fusion of electronic and rock music. This collaboration not only showcases Bear Grillz's willingness to experiment with different genres but also highlights his ability to create a sound that transcends traditional boundaries.

To further solidify his signature sound, Bear Grillz has developed his own production techniques and sound design strategies. He meticulously crafts his bass patches, spending countless hours experimenting with different waveforms, filters, and modulations to create the perfect balance between aggression and clarity. Additionally, Bear Grillz incorporates real-world samples and organic elements into his tracks, adding a touch of realism and depth to his music.

Overall, the formation of the Bearstep sound is the result of Bear Grillz's passion for pushing boundaries, experimenting with different genres, and his dedication to creating a unique and captivating musical experience. Through a combination of heavy basslines, intricate drum patterns, uplifting melodies, and genre-bending collaborations, Bearstep has carved its own niche within the electronic music scene and continues to captivate listeners worldwide.

Subsection: Incorporation of diverse musical elements

In order to create a unique and captivating sound, Bear Grillz has masterfully incorporated diverse musical elements into his music. By blending different genres, styles, and cultural influences, he has pushed the boundaries of the electronic music scene and created a sound that is truly his own. In this section, we will explore the various ways in which Bear Grillz incorporates these elements into his music, highlighting his innovation and creativity.

Blending Genres:

Bear Grillz is known for blending genres seamlessly, creating a fusion of sounds that appeals to a wide range of listeners. From trap to dubstep, future bass to hip-hop, he incorporates elements from various genres to create a unique sonic experience. For example, in his track "Drop That Low", he combines the hard-hitting drops of dubstep with the infectious grooves of trap music, resulting in a high-energy track that captivates audiences.

Global Influences:

Bear Grillz draws inspiration from different cultures and musical traditions, infusing his music with global influences. By incorporating elements from world music, he creates a rich and diverse sonic palette. For instance, in the track "Global Warming", he samples traditional African percussion and combines it with heavy bass drops, showcasing his ability to blend cultural elements into his music seamlessly.

Melodic Progressions:

In addition to his heavy bass drops, Bear Grillz incorporates melodic progressions into his music, adding depth and emotion to his tracks. By intertwining melodic elements with the heavy beats, he creates a contrast that keeps the listener engaged throughout the song. This can be heard in tracks like "Melodic Dubstep Symphony" where he combines melodic synth lines with powerful drops, creating a dynamic and captivating listening experience.

Vocal Collaborations:

Bear Grillz frequently collaborates with vocalists, adding another layer of complexity to his music. By working with different singers and rappers, he is able to incorporate diverse vocal styles and create songs that have a broader appeal. For example, in his track "Going Down", he collaborates with rapper Lil Jon, infusing his heavy drops with energetic and catchy vocal lines.

Sampling and Sound Design:

Bear Grillz is a master of sampling, using snippets of other songs and sounds to create unique and unexpected moments in his music. By sampling from a wide range of sources, he adds depth and complexity to his tracks, making them stand out from the crowd. He also pays great attention to sound design, creating his own unique and recognizable sounds that further enhance his music.

Unconventional Instruments and Elements:

In his pursuit of creating a distinctive sound, Bear Grillz incorporates unconventional instruments and elements into his music. From using field recordings of nature sounds to incorporating elements of classical music, he constantly pushes the boundaries of what electronic music can be. For example, in his track "Fire Pit", he incorporates the sound of crackling fire as a rhythmic element, creating a unique atmosphere that transports the listener to a different world.

Example: The Evolution of "Bearstep":

One of Bear Grillz's most notable contributions to the electronic music scene is the creation of the "Bearstep" genre. Bearstep is a sub-genre of dubstep that incorporates elements of trap, hip-hop, and future bass. It is characterized by heavy bass drops, intricate drum patterns, and melodic elements. This fusion of genres creates a signature sound that is instantly recognizable as Bear Grillz.

Bearstep has had a significant impact on the electronic music landscape, inspiring a new generation of producers and artists to explore and experiment with different genre fusions. By incorporating diverse musical elements into his music,

Bear Grillz has opened the door for endless possibilities and has helped break down genre barriers in the industry.

In conclusion, Bear Grillz's incorporation of diverse musical elements has set him apart as a truly innovative and creative artist. By blending genres, drawing from global influences, incorporating melodic progressions, collaborating with vocalists, using sampling and sound design techniques, and incorporating unconventional instruments and elements, he has created a sound that is uniquely his own. Through his music, Bear Grillz continues to push the boundaries of what is possible in electronic music, inspiring others to explore and experiment with different genres and sounds.

Subsection: Bear Grillz's experimentation with different tempos

In the ever-evolving world of electronic music, artists are constantly pushing the boundaries of sound by exploring new techniques and experimenting with different tempos. Bear Grillz is no exception to this trend, as he has fearlessly embarked on a journey of sonic exploration, incorporating a wide range of tempos into his music.

One of the distinctive aspects of Bear Grillz's music is his ability to seamlessly transition between different tempos within a single track, creating a captivating and dynamic listening experience for his audience. Whether it's a high-energy, fast-paced section or a melodic and ethereal passage, Bear Grillz utilizes tempo changes to shape the emotional landscape of his music.

Experimentation with different tempos allows Bear Grillz to create a diverse range of moods and atmospheres in his tracks. By manipulating the tempo, he can induce a sense of urgency and intensity, or he can slow things down to evoke a feeling of tranquility and introspection. This versatility enables Bear Grillz to connect with his audience on a deeper level, as he crafts musical journeys that encompass a wide spectrum of emotions.

In addition to creating a diverse sonic palette, Bear Grillz's experimentation with different tempos also showcases his technical prowess as a producer. The ability to seamlessly transition between tempos requires precise timing and a keen sense of musicality. It is a testament to Bear Grillz's skill and artistry that he is able to execute these transitions flawlessly, elevating his music to new heights.

Moreover, Bear Grillz's exploration of different tempos serves as an inspiration for aspiring producers and musicians. By defying traditional genre constraints and embracing a multidimensional approach to music production, he encourages others to step outside their comfort zones and venture into uncharted territories. This willingness to experiment and take risks is at the heart of artistic growth and innovation.

To fully appreciate the impact of Bear Grillz's experimentation with different tempos, it is essential to examine some real-world examples from his discography. Take, for instance, his track "Rumble." In this high-octane production, Bear Grillz masterfully combines elements of dubstep and drumstep, seamlessly transitioning between a slower, more methodical tempo during the build-up, and an explosive, breakneck pace during the drop. This contrast in tempos adds a layer of tension and anticipation, enhancing the overall impact of the track.

Another example of Bear Grillz's skillful manipulation of tempo can be found in his collaboration with Kompany, "Haunted." In this hauntingly beautiful track, Bear Grillz weaves together atmospheric elements and bone-rattling basslines, while incorporating a range of tempos to create a sense of ebb and flow. The slower, more down-tempo sections serve as moments of introspection, allowing the listener to fully absorb the atmospheric elements, while the faster, more frenetic sections inject a surge of energy into the track.

For aspiring producers looking to experiment with different tempos, it is crucial to understand the technical aspects involved. A solid understanding of music theory, particularly rhythm and timing, is vital in order to create seamless transitions and maintain a cohesive musical flow. Additionally, the effective use of tempo changes requires a keen ear for arrangement and an understanding of how different tempos can complement or contrast with each other.

Conventional wisdom suggests that tempo changes should be implemented strategically and purposefully. Rather than incorporating shifts in tempo for the sake of novelty, these changes should serve a musical purpose and enhance the emotional impact of the track. It is important to experiment with different tempos and observe how they affect the overall mood and energy of the music.

Furthermore, it is worth mentioning that the experimentation with different tempos should not be limited to electronic music alone. Bear Grillz's fearless approach to incorporating diverse tempos can inspire musicians from all genres to explore new sonic territories and break free from conventional norms. By pushing the boundaries of tempo, artists can infuse their music with unexpected twists and turns, captivating their listeners and leaving a lasting impression.

In conclusion, Bear Grillz's experimentation with different tempos is a testament to his artistic vision and technical prowess. By seamlessly transitioning between tempos, he creates a captivating and dynamic listening experience that transcends traditional genre boundaries. This exploration of diverse tempos not only showcases his versatility as a producer but also serves as an inspiration for aspiring musicians to push their own creative boundaries. Whether it's through a high-energy dubstep drop or a melodic and introspective interlude, Bear Grillz demonstrates that the exploration of different tempos is a powerful tool for shaping the emotional landscape of music.

Subsection: Continuously evolving and pushing boundaries

In the constantly evolving landscape of electronic music, Bear Grillz has consistently pushed the boundaries of his sound, seeking to create innovative and groundbreaking music that captivates his audience. This subsection explores Bear Grillz's relentless pursuit of evolution and the ways in which he has consistently pushed the boundaries of his music.

Evolution through experimentation

Bear Grillz's evolution as an artist can be attributed to his willingness to experiment with different musical elements and genres. From his early productions to his current releases, he has never been afraid to step outside of his comfort zone and explore new sonic territories. This fearless approach to music-making has allowed him to continually evolve and surprise his fans with fresh and exciting sounds.

One example of Bear Grillz's experimentation is his incorporation of diverse musical influences into his tracks. He seamlessly blends elements from various genres, such as dubstep, trap, and hip-hop, creating a unique and distinct sound that defies traditional genre boundaries. By pushing these genre boundaries, Bear Grillz has been able to craft a sound that is uniquely his own.

Breaking the mold

Another way in which Bear Grillz pushes boundaries is by challenging the conventions of electronic music. He constantly seeks to innovate and create tracks that defy expectations, both sonically and structurally. Whether it's experimenting with unconventional time signatures or incorporating unexpected sound design elements, Bear Grillz consistently pushes the boundaries of what electronic music can be.

For example, in his track "Bearstep Anthem," Bear Grillz introduced a new sub-genre known as Bearstep, which melds elements of heavy dubstep with melodic and uplifting sounds. This unique fusion of contrasting styles showcases his ability to think outside of the box and create music that is both groundbreaking and compelling.

Embracing new technologies

Bear Grillz has always been at the forefront of embracing new technologies and incorporating them into his music. He recognizes that technology plays a vital role in pushing the boundaries of electronic music and is constantly exploring innovative production techniques and tools.

One example of this is Bear Grillz's use of virtual reality (VR) technology in his live performances. By leveraging VR technology, he creates immersive and interactive experiences for his audience, blurring the line between the physical and virtual worlds. This forward-thinking approach allows him to captivate his fans and push the boundaries of what a live electronic music performance can be.

Collaborating with visionaries

Collaboration has been instrumental in Bear Grillz's evolution and his ability to push boundaries. By working with other visionaries in the music industry, he has been able to tap into their unique perspectives and push the limits of his sound.

For instance, Bear Grillz's collaborations with renowned producers and artists from different genres have resulted in tracks that defy traditional categorization. These collaborations provide new creative inputs and allow him to explore uncharted sonic territories.

Constant growth and reinvention

Bear Grillz's dedication to continuous growth and reinvention is what sets him apart as an artist. He recognizes that staying stagnant leads to artistic stagnation, and he constantly seeks ways to evolve his sound and explore new creative avenues.

As Bear Grillz continues to push boundaries and evolve as an artist, we can expect him to break new ground and redefine the electronic music landscape. His relentless pursuit of innovation and passion for pushing boundaries ensures that his music remains fresh, captivating, and ahead of its time.

In conclusion, Bear Grillz's commitment to continuously evolving and pushing boundaries has made him a pioneer in the electronic music scene. Through his relentless experimentation, desire to break the mold, embrace of new technologies, collaboration with visionaries, and dedication to constant growth and reinvention, he has carved out a unique place for himself in the industry. As he continues to explore new sonic territories and challenge conventions, Bear Grillz's impact on the electronic music genre is sure to be felt for years to come.

Subsection: The influence of underground music scenes on Bear Grillz's sound

The underground music scene has always played a significant role in shaping the sound and style of artists across various genres. Bear Grillz is no exception. In this subsection, we will explore how Bear Grillz's exposure to the underground music scenes influenced his own unique sound and contributed to his success.

Underground music scenes as a breeding ground for innovation

The underground music scene has long been a breeding ground for innovation and experimentation. It provides a platform for artists to push boundaries and explore new sonic territories. Bear Grillz, in his early days, was drawn to the energy and creativity of the underground music scene. He immersed himself in the sounds and frequencies that were being created by the underground artists and found inspiration in their fearlessness to go against the mainstream.

Exploration of different sub-genres within the underground scene

One of the most significant influences of the underground music scene on Bear Grillz's sound is his exploration of different sub-genres. It allowed him to expand his musical horizons and incorporate elements from various genres into his own music. From dubstep to drum and bass, trap to future bass, Bear Grillz drew inspiration from the underground sub-genres and blended them together to create his unique style, which he coined as Bearstep.

Breaking the rules and defying genre norms

The underground music scene is known for its non-conformity and a disregard for genre norms. Bear Grillz took this ethos to heart and embraced the freedom to create music without limitations. Instead of adhering to a specific genre's conventions, Bear Grillz utilized his exposure to the underground scene to break the rules and combine different elements to forge his own path. This rebellious spirit allowed him to stand out and create a distinct sound that resonated with his audience.

Embracing underground production techniques

The underground music scene is often characterized by its gritty and raw production techniques. Bear Grillz was fascinated by the unique textures and rawness that these production techniques yielded and incorporated them into his own music. He experimented with unconventional production methods, such as using analog synthesizers, lo-fi sampling, and intricate drum programming, to add depth and character to his tracks. This commitment to embracing underground production techniques gave his music a distinct edge and helped him create an immersive sonic experience.

Collaborations with underground artists

Collaborations with underground artists played a vital role in shaping Bear Grillz's sound. By working with artists from the underground scene, he not only gained new perspectives and ideas but also had the opportunity to share his own unique sound with different audiences. These collaborations allowed Bear Grillz to blend his own style with the underground influences, creating a sonic fusion that resonated with fans from both the underground and mainstream music scenes.

Sampling and reimagining underground classics

Sampling has always been an integral part of the underground music scene. Bear Grillz drew inspiration from iconic underground classics and reimagined them in his own style. By infusing these samples with his signature bearstep sound, he paid homage to the roots of the underground music scene while presenting a fresh take on the genre. This approach allowed him to connect with both the longtime fans of the underground scene and new listeners looking for something unique.

Applying unconventional mixing and mastering techniques

In the underground music scene, artists often experiment with unconventional mixing and mastering techniques to achieve a distinct sonic character. Bear Grillz adopted this approach and pushed the boundaries of traditional mixing and mastering techniques. He used unconventional effects, creative panning, and experimental sound design to create a larger-than-life sound that became his sonic trademark. This unconventional approach to mixing and mastering set Bear Grillz's music apart from the mainstream and further solidified his connection to the underground music scene.

Case study: The impact of Bear Grillz's exposure to dubstep

Dubstep, which originated in the underground music scene, played a significant role in shaping Bear Grillz's sound. The heavy basslines, intricate rhythms, and powerful drops of dubstep became an integral part of his sonic palette. By immersing himself in the underground dubstep scene, Bear Grillz embraced the genre's energy and aggression. He incorporated elements of dubstep into his own style, transforming it into something fresh and innovative. This fusion of dubstep with his bearstep sound allowed Bear Grillz to attract a diverse fan base, including both dedicated dubstep enthusiasts and those new to the genre.

In conclusion, the influence of underground music scenes on Bear Grillz's sound cannot be overstated. The experimentation, boundary-pushing, and commitment to artistic freedom that are synonymous with the underground scene provided Bear Grillz with the inspiration and tools necessary to craft his unique sound. By drawing from various sub-genres, embracing unconventional production techniques, collaborating with underground artists, and reimagining classic tracks, Bear Grillz was able to create a sonic identity that resonated with fans from both the underground and mainstream scenes. His success serves as a testament to the enduring power and impact of the underground music scene on the evolution of musical genres.

Subsection: Bear Grillz's impact on the wider electronic music landscape

Bear Grillz has had a profound impact on the wider electronic music landscape, revolutionizing the genre and pushing the boundaries of what is possible in electronic music. Through his unique sound, innovative approach, and rebellious spirit, Bear Grillz has become a trailblazer in the industry, inspiring countless artists and influencing the direction of electronic music as a whole.

One of Bear Grillz's key contributions to the electronic music landscape is his creation and popularization of the "Bearstep" genre. Combining heavy dubstep basslines with melodic and atmospheric elements, Bearstep incorporates a range of musical styles, creating a distinct and innovative sound. This genre brings together the energy and intensity of dubstep with the emotive and melodic qualities of other genres, capturing the attention of listeners across the globe.

Bear Grillz's impact goes beyond just the creation of a unique genre. His music has the power to bring people together and create a sense of unity within the electronic music community. By infusing his tracks with uplifting and positive messages, Bear Grillz instills a sense of hope and connection in his listeners. Through his music, he encourages individuals to embrace their authentic selves, celebrate their differences, and come together to create a better world.

In addition to his contributions to the genre, Bear Grillz's success and influence have opened doors for other artists in the electronic music scene. He has paved the way for emerging talent, showcasing the possibilities of artistic innovation and creativity. By consistently pushing the boundaries of his sound, Bear Grillz has created a space for experimentation and exploration within electronic music, inspiring other artists to step outside their comfort zones and forge their own unique paths.

Furthermore, Bear Grillz's success has challenged established notions and stereotypes within the genre. As a masked artist, he breaks down barriers and defies expectations, proving that an artist's true value lies in their talent and creativity, rather than their physical appearance or public image. This has had a profound impact on the industry, fostering a greater acceptance and celebration of diversity within electronic music.

Bear Grillz's influence extends beyond his music and into the world of live performances. His high-energy shows, characterized by the signature bear mask and captivating visuals, have become legendary in the electronic music scene. By creating an immersive and unforgettable experience for his audience, Bear Grillz has set a new standard for live performances, inspiring other artists to think outside the box and push the boundaries of what is possible on stage.

In terms of technological innovation, Bear Grillz has embraced the use of cutting-edge production techniques and tools to create his unique sound. His willingness to adapt to new technologies and experiment with different production methods has set the stage for future developments in the industry. By embracing innovation and staying ahead of the curve, Bear Grillz has solidified his position as a pioneer and visionary within electronic music.

Bear Grillz's impact on the wider electronic music landscape can also be seen in his collaboration with diverse artists from different genres. By merging their distinct sounds and styles, Bear Grillz has brought a fresh perspective to electronic music, infusing it with a wide range of influences. These collaborations have not only expanded his fan base but also opened doors for cross-genre experimentation, proving that electronic music has the power to transcend boundaries and create something truly unique.

In conclusion, Bear Grillz's impact on the wider electronic music landscape cannot be overstated. Through his innovative sound, rebellious spirit, and commitment to pushing the boundaries of the genre, he has become a trailblazer and influencer in the industry. By creating the Bearstep genre, challenging stereotypes, inspiring other artists, and embracing technological innovation, Bear Grillz has left an indelible mark on electronic music, shaping its future and proving that the possibilities within the genre are truly limitless.

Subsection: Exploring the cross-section of different musical styles

In the ever-evolving landscape of music, artists are constantly pushing boundaries and blurring the lines between genres. Bear Grillz is no exception to this trend. With his unique sound and innovative approach to production, Bear Grillz has made a name for himself in exploring the cross-section of different musical styles.

One of the defining characteristics of Bear Grillz's music is his ability to seamlessly blend elements from various genres, creating a truly eclectic sound. Whether it's infusing dubstep with trap or incorporating elements of hip hop into his tracks, Bear Grillz has mastered the art of fusing different musical styles harmoniously.

To understand how Bear Grillz achieves this cross-section of different musical styles, it's important to explore some of the underlying principles and techniques that guide his creative process.

Blending Rhythm and Groove

One of the key aspects of exploring the cross-section of different musical styles is finding a common ground in terms of rhythm and groove. Bear Grillz often takes inspiration from genres like hip hop, reggae, and funk, which are known for their infectious rhythms and grooves.

By infusing these rhythmic elements into his tracks, Bear Grillz brings a new dimension to his music. This allows him to create a unique musical experience that bridges the gap between different genres and captivates listeners from various musical backgrounds.

Example: In his track "Demons," Bear Grillz skillfully blends the hard-hitting beats of dubstep with the laid-back grooves of hip hop, delivering a track that appeals to fans of both genres. The combination of heavy basslines and hip hop-inspired drum patterns creates a cross-section of these two distinct styles, resulting in a truly exceptional listening experience.

Melodic Fusion

Another aspect of exploring the cross-section of different musical styles is the fusion of melodic elements. Bear Grillz's music often features catchy melodies that draw inspiration from diverse musical genres such as pop, rock, and even classical music.

By seamlessly blending these melodic elements into his tracks, Bear Grillz creates a sonic landscape that transcends genre boundaries. The incorporation of melodic hooks and soaring synth lines adds an emotional depth to his music, allowing listeners to connect with the tracks on a deeper level.

Example: The track "City of Angels" showcases Bear Grillz's mastery in blending melodic elements from different genres. The powerful vocal melody, reminiscent of pop-rock anthems, is paired with a dubstep-inspired drop, resulting in a track that seamlessly merges these two musical styles. The cross-section of pop and dubstep in "City of Angels" highlights Bear Grillz's ability to create a cohesive sound that appeals to fans across different genres.

Experimental Sound Design

In order to explore the cross-section of different musical styles, Bear Grillz often pushes the boundaries of sound design. By incorporating unconventional and experimental elements into his tracks, he breaks away from conventional genre norms and creates a sound that is uniquely his own.

Bear Grillz's experimentation with sound design allows him to introduce new textures, timbres, and sonic possibilities into his music. This adds an element of surprise and innovation, captivating listeners and further blurring the lines between genres.

Example: The track "Stay" exemplifies Bear Grillz's experimental sound design approach. By blending heavy dubstep drops with glitchy electronic elements, he creates a track that transcends traditional genre classifications. The unique combination of unconventional sounds adds a fresh and unexpected twist to the track, showcasing Bear Grillz's ability to explore the cross-section of different musical styles.

Genre-Bending Collaborations

Another way Bear Grillz explores the cross-section of different musical styles is through collaborations with artists from diverse genres. By combining forces with musicians who specialize in different genres, Bear Grillz is able to tap into new sonic territories and create a fusion of styles that is truly groundbreaking.

These collaborations not only expand Bear Grillz's musical horizons but also create a space for genre-crossing experimentation. By bringing together artists with different musical backgrounds, he opens the door to endless possibilities and allows for the exploration of new sonic landscapes.

Example: Bear Grillz's collaboration with hip hop artist Sullivan King on the track "Wicked," showcases the power of genre-bending collaborations. The combination of Bear Grillz's hard-hitting dubstep drops and Sullivan King's aggressive vocals creates a track that pushes the boundaries of both genres. This

collaboration highlights the innovative approach Bear Grillz takes in exploring the
cross-section of different musical styles.

The Connection to Bear Grillz's Persona

Bear Grillz's exploration of the cross-section of different musical styles is deeply
connected to his persona as an artist. The bear mask-wearing DJ not only
represents a sense of mystery and anonymity but also serves as a symbol of unity
and acceptance. This enables Bear Grillz to connect with a wide range of fans from
different musical backgrounds, forming a diverse community united by their love
for his music.

By embracing different musical styles and pushing the boundaries of genre
classifications, Bear Grillz has created a unique sound that resonates with fans
across various musical preferences.

Example: Through his exploration of different musical styles, Bear Grillz has
built a dedicated fanbase that transcends traditional genre boundaries. The Bear
Fam, as his fans are lovingly called, represents a diverse community of individuals
brought together by Bear Grillz's music. This community, united by their mutual
appreciation for his cross-genre sound, plays a crucial role in supporting and
spreading his music.

In conclusion, Bear Grillz's ability to explore the cross-section of different
musical styles has been integral to his success as an artist. Through blending
rhythm and groove, melding melodic elements, experimenting with sound design,
engaging in genre-bending collaborations, and connecting with his persona, Bear
Grillz creates a unique sound that captivates and unites fans from diverse musical
backgrounds. His exploration of different musical styles contributes to the evolving
landscape of electronic music and leaves a lasting legacy in the industry.

Subsection: The role of technology in shaping Bear Grillz's sound

As the electronic music scene continues to evolve, technology plays a pivotal role in
shaping the sound of artists like Bear Grillz. From new production tools and
software to innovative hardware and cutting-edge techniques, technology provides
endless possibilities for creativity and experimentation. In this section, we will
explore the different ways technology has influenced Bear Grillz's sound, from the
early stages of music production to his current production workflow.

Early Exploration of Music Production Software

In the early days of Bear Grillz's music career, technology played a crucial role in his sound exploration. Digital audio workstations (DAWs) such as Ableton Live and Logic Pro became vital tools for Bear Grillz to compose, arrange, mix, and master his tracks. These software programs provided him with a versatile platform to express his musical ideas and experiment with different sounds.

With the growing popularity of electronic music, industry-standard plugins and virtual instruments started to emerge, offering artists a vast range of sonic possibilities. Bear Grillz embraced these new tools, using synthesizers, samplers, and drum machines to create unique sounds for his productions. The versatility and ease of use offered by DAWs and plugins allowed him to push the boundaries of his productions and define his signature sound.

Innovative Sound Design Techniques

Technology also revolutionized sound design techniques and opened up new avenues for Bear Grillz to create his distinctive sound. Through the use of advanced processing techniques like synthesis, granular manipulation, and spectral processing, he was able to generate complex and unconventional sounds that had never been heard before.

Modular synthesizers played a significant role in Bear Grillz's sound palette. These analog and digital instruments allowed him to sculpt and shape sounds with precision, exploring a wide range of timbres and textures. By experimenting with various modules, he could create custom patches that gave his tracks a unique sonic identity.

Furthermore, advancements in machine learning and artificial intelligence have brought about tools like neural networks and generative algorithms, which have allowed Bear Grillz to generate new musical ideas and textures. By feeding his existing tracks and sounds into these systems, he can generate new sounds and patterns that he may not have thought of otherwise. This innovative use of technology has helped him push the boundaries of his sound and discover new creative possibilities.

The Influence of Digital Effects and Processing

Digital effects and processing have played a significant role in shaping Bear Grillz's sound. From the early stages of his career, he recognized the transformative power of effects like reverb, delay, distortion, and modulation. These effects helped him create depth, texture, and movement in his tracks.

Advancements in digital signal processing have allowed Bear Grillz to experiment with unique effects chains and complex signal routing. He can create intricate and evolving soundscapes by combining and modulating various effects parameters. By pushing the limits of these effects, he adds a distinctive touch to his tracks, making them stand out in the electronic music landscape.

In addition to effects, technology has also given Bear Grillz access to powerful mixing and mastering tools. These tools enable him to achieve professional-level sound quality, ensuring that his tracks translate well on different sound systems. With the help of equalizers, compressors, limiters, and other mastering tools, he can fine-tune the frequency balance, dynamics, and overall feel of his music.

Live Performance Technology

Technology has not only influenced Bear Grillz's studio production but also his live performances. In recent years, advancements in DJ software and hardware have transformed the way artists engage with their audiences on stage.

Through the use of specialized DJ controllers and software like Native Instruments' Traktor, Bear Grillz has the freedom to mix tracks, apply effects, and trigger samples in real-time. These tools allow him to create dynamic and immersive live performances, seamlessly blending his own tracks with those from other artists. With the help of cue points and looping features, he can manipulate tracks on the fly, adding his unique twist to each performance.

Interactive lighting and visual technologies have also become integral components of Bear Grillz's live shows. LED panels, lasers, and projection mapping allow him to create stunning visual experiences that synchronize with the music, enhancing the overall impact of his performances. By integrating technology into his live shows, Bear Grillz creates an immersive experience that captivates his audience and leaves a lasting impression.

Embracing the Future of Technology

Bear Grillz continues to embrace new technologies in his quest to push the boundaries of his sound. As technology advances, he looks forward to exploring emerging tools and techniques that will shape the future of electronic music.

One area he is particularly excited about is virtual reality (VR) and augmented reality (AR). These technologies have the potential to revolutionize the live music experience by creating immersive virtual environments and interactive visual displays. Bear Grillz envisions a future where audiences can dive into his music through VR experiences, blurring the line between the artist and the listener.

Another area of interest for Bear Grillz is the integration of artificial intelligence and machine learning into the music creation process. He sees the potential for AI-generated melodies, rhythms, and harmonies to inspire new artistic directions. By collaborating with AI systems, he hopes to uncover new sonic landscapes and challenge traditional music-making approaches.

As technology continues to evolve, Bear Grillz remains at the forefront, harnessing its power to shape his sound and create immersive experiences for his fans. He embraces innovation while staying true to his artistic vision, always pushing the boundaries of what is possible in the world of electronic music.

Key Takeaways

- Digital audio workstations (DAWs) and plugins have provided Bear Grillz with a versatile platform to express his musical ideas and experiment with different sounds. - Advanced processing techniques and sound design tools like modular synthesizers have allowed Bear Grillz to create unique and unconventional sounds. - Digital effects and processing have played a significant role in adding depth, texture, and movement to Bear Grillz's tracks. - DJ software and hardware have transformed Bear Grillz's live performances, allowing him to mix tracks, apply effects, and trigger samples in real-time. - Technology such as VR, AR, and AI continue to inspire Bear Grillz, pushing him to explore new artistic directions and create immersive experiences for his fans.

By harnessing the power of technology, Bear Grillz continues to evolve his sound and push the boundaries of electronic music, leaving an indelible mark on the industry. His ability to blend innovation with his artistic vision is a true testament to the role of technology in shaping the sound of modern musicians. As technology continues to advance, Bear Grillz will undoubtedly explore new frontiers, providing listeners with fresh and exhilarating sonic experiences.

Subsection: The Evolution of Bear Grillz's Sound Throughout His Career

Throughout his career, Bear Grillz has continuously evolved his sound, pushing boundaries and exploring new musical directions. In this subsection, we will delve into the various stages of Bear Grillz's musical evolution, from his early productions to his current style. We will explore the factors that have influenced his sound, the impact of his collaborations, and the role of technology in shaping his music.

Early Productions and Exploration of Different Sub-genres

Bear Grillz's journey as a music producer began with his early productions, where he dabbled in various sub-genres of electronic music. In the beginning, he drew inspiration from artists like Skrillex, Excision, and Zeds Dead, who pioneered the heavy and aggressive sounds of dubstep and bass music.

During this phase, Bear Grillz experimented with different styles, incorporating elements from drum and bass, trap, and even hip-hop into his tracks. This exploration allowed him to develop a unique and diverse sonic palette that would later become synonymous with his sound.

The Formation of the Bearstep Sound

As Bear Grillz continued to refine his style, he began to carve out a distinct niche within the electronic music landscape. Drawing from his love for heavy basslines and melodic elements, Bear Grillz developed a sound that would come to be known as "Bearstep."

Bearstep is characterized by its fusion of aggressive, hard-hitting bass drops and catchy melodies, creating a high-energy and engaging listening experience. This sound became synonymous with Bear Grillz's identity and set him apart from his contemporaries.

Incorporation of Diverse Musical Elements

One of the defining aspects of Bear Grillz's sound is his ability to seamlessly blend different musical elements to create a unique and captivating sonic experience. Throughout his career, Bear Grillz has incorporated various genres and styles into his productions, ranging from hip-hop and reggae to rock and classical music.

By infusing these diverse musical elements into his tracks, Bear Grillz has been able to create a multi-dimensional sound that appeals to a wide range of listeners. This willingness to experiment and think outside the box has been a major factor in his success and has contributed to the evolution of his sound.

Bear Grillz's Experimentation with Different Tempos

While dubstep and bass music have been at the core of Bear Grillz's sound, he has not been afraid to experiment with different tempos throughout his career. In addition to his signature high-energy tracks, Bear Grillz has delved into the realms of mid-tempo and even downtempo music.

By exploring different tempos, Bear Grillz has been able to showcase his versatility as a producer and further expand his sonic palette. This experimentation has allowed him to challenge the boundaries of electronic music and create a diverse catalog of tracks that cater to different moods and settings.

Continuously Evolving and Pushing Boundaries

Bear Grillz's commitment to continuous evolution is a defining characteristic of his sound. He is constantly pushing boundaries and exploring new sonic territories, never content to stick to a single formula or style. This dedication to growth and experimentation has been instrumental in his ability to stay relevant and forge his own path within the electronic music scene.

By embracing new technologies, techniques, and musical influences, Bear Grillz has created a body of work that is dynamic and evolving. His willingness to take risks and push the limits of his creativity has allowed him to maintain a fresh and exciting sound throughout his career.

The Influence of Underground Music Scenes on Bear Grillz's Sound

In addition to drawing inspiration from established artists and mainstream genres, Bear Grillz has also been influenced by underground music scenes. He has always been curious about different subcultures and their unique sounds, which has informed his approach to music production.

By immersing himself in underground scenes, Bear Grillz has discovered hidden gems and lesser-known artists who have influenced his sound. This exploration has allowed him to incorporate elements from these underground genres into his own music, resulting in a sound that is both familiar and groundbreaking.

Bear Grillz's Impact on the Wider Electronic Music Landscape

Bear Grillz's evolution as an artist has not only shaped his own sound but has also had a significant impact on the wider electronic music landscape. His unique fusion of dubstep, bass music, and other genres has influenced a new generation of producers who are pushing the boundaries of electronic music.

Inspired by Bear Grillz's innovative approach to production and his ability to create genre-defying tracks, many up-and-coming artists have adopted his sound and incorporated it into their own music. This has led to the emergence of new sub-genres and styles within the electronic music scene, further diversifying and pushing the boundaries of the genre.

The Role of Technology in Shaping Bear Grillz's Sound

Technology has played a crucial role in shaping Bear Grillz's sound throughout his career. As a producer, Bear Grillz has embraced the advancements in music production technology, harnessing their power to craft his unique sonic landscape.

From digital audio workstations (DAWs) to virtual instruments and plugins, Bear Grillz has utilized a wide range of tech tools to experiment, refine, and create his music. These advancements have not only provided him with the means to bring his sonic visions to life but have also allowed him to explore new sounds and textures that were previously unimaginable.

In addition to production technology, the rise of streaming platforms and social media has also played a significant role in shaping Bear Grillz's sound. These platforms have provided him with a direct connection to his fanbase, allowing him to receive instant feedback and stay in touch with the evolving tastes and preferences of his audience.

Summary

The evolution of Bear Grillz's sound throughout his career is a testament to his passion for pushing boundaries and exploring new musical territories. From his early productions to the formation of the Bearstep sound, Bear Grillz has continuously evolved, incorporating diverse musical elements and experimenting with different tempos.

His ability to seamlessly blend genres and embrace new technologies has allowed him to create a unique sonic experience that resonates with listeners around the world. Bear Grillz's impact on the wider electronic music landscape and his dedication to continuous growth further solidify his position as an influential artist in the industry.

As Bear Grillz continues to evolve his sound, it will be exciting to see how he pushes the boundaries even further and leaves a lasting mark on the future of electronic music.

Section 2: Iconic Bear Grillz Tracks

Subsection: Chart-topping hits and fan favorites

In this subsection, we will explore some of Bear Grillz's most popular tracks that have reached the top of the charts and become favorites among fans. These chart-topping hits not only showcase Bear Grillz's unique sound and style but also demonstrate his ability to captivate audiences and create music that resonates with a wide range of listeners.

One example of a chart-topping hit by Bear Grillz is "Bassline Drops," released in 2015. This track features infectious basslines, heavy drops, and catchy vocal samples, making it an instant crowd-pleaser. With its energetic beats and dynamic production, "Bassline Drops" quickly gained popularity within the electronic music community and beyond. The track's success can be attributed to its ability to seamlessly blend different genres, incorporating elements of dubstep, trap, and drum and bass. The catchy melody and powerful drops make "Bassline Drops" a fan favorite and a signature track in Bear Grillz's discography.

Another notable chart-topper is "Demons," released in 2016. This track exemplifies Bear Grillz's ability to create a dark and intense atmosphere while still maintaining an infectious rhythm that draws listeners in. With its heavy basslines, aggressive synths, and haunting vocal samples, "Demons" became an instant hit, receiving widespread acclaim from fans and critics alike. The track's success is a testament to Bear Grillz's ability to push boundaries and experiment with different sounds within the electronic music genre.

One more chart-topping hit by Bear Grillz is "Mayweather," released in 2018. This track showcases Bear Grillz's unique style and incorporates elements of hip-hop and trap, resulting in a high-energy, bass-heavy anthem. With its powerful drops, catchy hooks, and intense energy, "Mayweather" quickly became a fan favorite and a staple in Bear Grillz's live performances. The track's commercial success and its ability to resonate with a diverse range of listeners solidified Bear Grillz's position as a leading artist in the electronic music scene.

It is worth mentioning that Bear Grillz's chart-topping hits are not the only tracks loved by fans. Throughout his career, Bear Grillz has released numerous fan favorites that may not have reached the top of the charts but have become beloved within the electronic music community. These tracks, often characterized by their infectious melodies, hard-hitting drops, and intricate sound design, showcase Bear Grillz's versatility as an artist and his ability to connect with his audience on a deeper level.

One example of a fan favorite is "EDM," released in 2017. This track infuses elements of traditional dubstep with glitchy, high-energy sound design, resulting in a truly unique and captivating listening experience. With its infectious rhythm and intricate production, "EDM" became an instant hit among fans who appreciate Bear Grillz's ability to blend different sub-genres within electronic music.

Another fan favorite is "Drop That," released in 2019. This track embodies Bear Grillz's signature sound, characterized by heavy basslines, explosive drops, and relentless energy. With its addictive hooks and intense drops, "Drop That" quickly gained traction among fans who appreciate Bear Grillz's ability to create high-octane, festival-ready bangers.

Bear Grillz's chart-topping hits and fan favorites not only highlight his production skills and unique style but also showcase his ability to connect with his audience on a deep and emotional level. From high-energy anthems to melodic masterpieces, Bear Grillz's music continues to push boundaries and inspire a new generation of electronic music producers and fans.

Example Problem:

Let's analyze the sound design and production techniques in Bear Grillz's chart-topping hit "Bassline Drops" to understand the factors that contributed to its success. One of the standout elements of this track is the use of heavy basslines that drive the energy and intensity throughout the song. These basslines are meticulously designed to cut through the mix, delivering a powerful and impactful sound.

To recreate the signature basslines in "Bassline Drops," producers can start by selecting a powerful synthesizer plugin capable of generating deep and aggressive sounds. Experimenting with different waveforms such as sawtooth or square waves can help achieve the desired sound. Adding effects like distortion, saturation, and compression can further enhance the intensity and presence of the basslines.

Another crucial aspect of the track's production is the arrangement of the drops. Bear Grillz masterfully builds tension through the use of intricate drum patterns, rising synth melodies, and vocal samples before delivering a heavy drop that makes the crowd go wild. To create a similar effect, producers can experiment with layering different drum samples, utilizing percussive elements to create a sense of anticipation, and incorporating vocal samples or catchy hooks to add a memorable touch.

Lastly, the sound design and overall mix play a vital role in the track's success. Each element should be carefully EQed and balanced to ensure clarity and impact. The track's dynamics should be controlled using techniques like sidechain compression to create a pumping effect that accentuates the rhythm. Additionally, thoughtful use of reverb and delay can add depth and space to the sound, creating a more immersive listening experience.

By analyzing the sound design and production techniques in Bear Grillz's "Bassline Drops," producers can learn valuable lessons in creating impactful and chart-topping tracks. Experimenting with different sounds, designing intricate drops, and refining the mix are key factors that contribute to the success of electronic music productions.

Additional Resources:

1. "Bassline Drops" by Bear Grillz (Official Music Video):
https://youtu.be/2SUwOgmvzK4
2. "Demons" by Bear Grillz (Official Music Video):
https://youtu.be/VLScm5rj0Po
3. "Mayweather" by Bear Grillz (Official Music Video):
https://youtu.be/vFHmBBgSxGo
4. "EDM" by Bear Grillz (Official Music Video):
https://youtu.be/xcb_rnzqmnc
5. "Drop That" by Bear Grillz (Official Music Video):
https://youtu.be/B4GpWuRGJpQ

Subsection: The stories behind Bear Grillz's most popular tracks

In this subsection, we will delve into the captivating stories behind some of Bear Grillz's most popular tracks. These tracks have not only captivated the hearts of fans worldwide but have also played a significant role in shaping the electronic music landscape. Join us on a journey through the creative process and inspiration behind these iconic compositions.

Track 1: "Roar of the Bear"

"Roar of the Bear" is the track that catapulted Bear Grillz into the spotlight, becoming an instant hit with fans and critics alike. This intense and exhilarating track starts with a melodic intro, gradually building the anticipation before dropping into a powerful and energetic bassline. The combination of heavy dubstep elements and melodic hooks creates an infectious energy that resonated with a wide audience.

Behind the creation of "Roar of the Bear" lies Bear Grillz's deep connection to nature and wildlife. As an avid outdoorsman, Bear Grillz draws inspiration from his experiences in the wilderness to create his music. The track pays homage to the strength, resilience, and raw power of bears, reflecting Bear Grillz's own journey in the music industry.

Example: One illustrative example of how Bear Grillz drew inspiration from nature can be seen in the production of "Roar of the Bear." While on a solo camping trip in the mountains, Bear Grillz found himself in the presence of a majestic grizzly bear. This encounter left a profound impact on him, igniting a newfound sense of determination and creative energy. The powerful roar of the bear became the catalyst for the creation of the track, infusing it with an authentic and primal energy.

Track 2: "Majestic Forest"

"Majestic Forest" is a mesmerizing composition that showcases Bear Grillz's ability to create a sonic experience that transports listeners into a mystical world. The track combines ethereal melodies, pulsating beats, and intricate sound design to create an enchanting atmosphere. With its dreamlike qualities, "Majestic Forest" has become a fan favorite and a staple in Bear Grillz's live performances.

The inspiration behind "Majestic Forest" stems from Bear Grillz's profound connection to nature and his belief in its healing and transformative powers. This track is an ode to the beauty and magic found within the depths of the natural world.

Example: One particular instance that influenced the creation of "Majestic Forest" was Bear Grillz's expedition into the ancient Redwood forests of California. As he wandered through the towering trees, a sense of awe and wonder washed over him. The dense foliage and the ethereal atmosphere inspired him to capture the essence of this idyllic environment in a musical form. He meticulously crafted the layers of instrumentation and atmospheric sounds to transport listeners to the heart of the majestic forest.

Track 3: "The Rise of the Bear"

"The Rise of the Bear" is a powerful anthem that celebrates perseverance and overcoming adversity. The track showcases Bear Grillz's signature blend of aggressive basslines, intense drops, and infectious melodies, making it an instant crowd-pleaser. Combining elements of trap and dubstep, this track resonates with listeners on a visceral level, evoking a sense of triumph and determination.

The creation of "The Rise of the Bear" was inspired by Bear Grillz's personal journey in the music industry. It serves as a testament to the challenges he faced and the hard work he put in to establish himself as a prominent artist. Through this track, Bear Grillz aims to inspire his fans to embrace their own inner strength and rise above any obstacles they may encounter.

Example: One particular incident that deeply influenced the creation of "The Rise of the Bear" was Bear Grillz's experience of being dropped by a major record label early in his career. This setback could have discouraged him from pursuing his dream, but instead, it fueled his determination to prove himself and rise above the adversity. The emotions he felt during this time became the driving force behind the creation of this empowering track.

Track 4: "Grizzly Adventures"

"Grizzly Adventures" is a high-energy track that embodies the essence of Bear Grillz's musical style. Blending elements of dubstep, trap, and electro, this track is characterized by its heavy basslines, catchy hooks, and intricate sound design. "Grizzly Adventures" takes listeners on a wild and exhilarating journey, capturing the spirit of adventure that defines Bear Grillz's music.

The creative process behind "Grizzly Adventures" revolves around Bear Grillz's love for adrenaline-pumping activities and his thirst for exploration. The track serves as an invitation to embrace one's adventurous nature and break free from the constraints of everyday life.

Example: One notable experience that heavily influenced the creation of "Grizzly Adventures" was Bear Grillz's solo skydiving expedition. As he soared through the sky, the rush of adrenaline and the breathtaking scenery inspired him to translate the intensity of this experience into a musical form. The song emulates the anticipation, excitement, and sense of liberation one feels during such thrilling adventures.

Track 5: "Infinite Love"

"Infinite Love" is a heartwarming and emotional track that showcases a different side of Bear Grillz's musical repertoire. Departing from his signature heavy basslines, this track explores melodic elements and evokes a sense of nostalgia and warmth. The combination of soulful vocals, uplifting melodies, and intricate production creates a harmonious composition that tugs at the heartstrings.

The inspiration behind "Infinite Love" lies in Bear Grillz's belief in the power of love and its ability to transcend boundaries. The track serves as a reminder to cherish the precious connections we have with others and to spread love and positivity in the world.

Example: One personal experience that deeply influenced the creation of "Infinite Love" was Bear Grillz's encounter with a young fan who was facing difficult times. The fan shared their story with Bear Grillz, expressing how his music had offered solace and hope during their darkest moments. Touched by this encounter, Bear Grillz was inspired to create a track that embodies the profound impact music can have on people's lives. "Infinite Love" became his way of expressing gratitude and spreading positivity to his fans.

Track 6: "Bassline Symphony"

"Bassline Symphony" is a masterfully crafted composition that showcases Bear Grillz's ability to blend orchestral elements with heavy basslines seamlessly. This track weaves together intricate string arrangements, powerful percussion, and explosive drops to create a symphony of sound that defies genre boundaries. "Bassline Symphony" has become a fan favorite, captivating audiences with its unique blend of classical elements and heavy electronic music.

The inspiration behind "Bassline Symphony" stems from Bear Grillz's fascination with classical music and his desire to fuse it with his own distinct sound. This track serves as an homage to the beauty and timeless quality of classical compositions while injecting it with the energy and intensity of electronic music.

Example: One transformative experience that played a significant role in the creation of "Bassline Symphony" was Bear Grillz's visit to a renowned symphony orchestra performance. As he sat in the audience, captivated by the harmonies and the emotive power of the live instrumentation, he envisioned a way to bring this grandeur and artistry into the world of electronic music. The resulting track, "Bassline Symphony," serves as a testament to Bear Grillz's ability to push boundaries and create truly unique compositions.

These tracks are just a glimpse into the creative mind of Bear Grillz and the stories that have shaped his music. Each track possesses its own unique narrative and has contributed to Bear Grillz's legacy as a boundary-pushing artist within the electronic music scene. As we explore Bear Grillz's discography, we'll discover the intricate web of inspiration and emotion that fuels his artistry.

Subsection: Collaborations that defined Bear Grillz's sound

Collaborations have always played a significant role in Bear Grillz's musical journey. Through working with different artists, he has been able to explore new styles, push boundaries, and create tracks that have defined his unique sound. Let's take a closer look at some of the collaborations that have had a major impact on Bear Grillz's music.

Excision: Unleashing the Power of Bass

One of the most notable collaborations that shaped Bear Grillz's sound was with the iconic dubstep producer, Excision. Their track "Arachnid" marked a turning point in Bear Grillz's career, introducing his signature heavy bass sound to a wider audience. The track showcased the intensity and energy that both artists are known for, combining melodic elements with bone-rattling drops. This collaboration not only solidified Bear Grillz's place within the dubstep scene but also showcased his ability to blend different genres seamlessly.

Sullivan King: Fusing Metal with Bass Music

Bear Grillz's collaboration with rock and bass music producer Sullivan King was a true fusion of genres. The track "Wicked" showcased Bear Grillz's ability to incorporate heavy metal elements into his music, producing a unique and groundbreaking sound. By blending heavy guitar riffs, aggressive vocals, and pulsating basslines, Bear Grillz and Sullivan King created a track that appealed to both bass music and metal fans. This collaboration not only expanded Bear Grillz's fan base but also highlighted his versatility as an artist.

Datsik: Combining Old-School Vibes with Modern Sounds

The collaboration between Bear Grillz and the dubstep legend Datsik resulted in the track "Drop That Low." This collaboration brought together Bear Grillz's modern heavy bass sound with Datsik's classic old-school dubstep vibes. The combination of powerful drops, syncopated beats, and gritty synths created a track that paid homage to the roots of dubstep while still sounding fresh and innovative. This collaboration showcased Bear Grillz's ability to collaborate with established artists while maintaining his own unique style.

SAYMYNAME: Merging Hard Trap and Bass Music

Bear Grillz's collaboration with hard trap artist SAYMYNAME resulted in the explosive track "Riot." This collaboration showcased Bear Grillz's ability to merge elements from different sub-genres, combining hard trap sounds with his own heavy bass style. The track's aggressive energy, pounding beats, and iconic vocal samples made it a festival favorite. This collaboration not only solidified Bear Grillz's reputation as a versatile artist but also pushed the boundaries of what is possible within the electronic music landscape.

Adventure Club: Infectious Melodies and Emotional Drops

Another collaboration that defined Bear Grillz's sound was with the Canadian electronic music duo Adventure Club. Their track "If I Die" was a perfect blend of infectious melodies, emotional lyrics, and heavy bass drops. This collaboration showcased Bear Grillz's ability to create tracks that evoke powerful emotions while still maintaining his trademark bass sound. With its anthemic qualities and memorable hooks, "If I Die" became an instant favorite among fans of both Bear Grillz and Adventure Club.

These collaborations have defined Bear Grillz's sound and showcased his ability to merge different genres seamlessly. From the heavy bass of Excision to the fusion of metal and bass with Sullivan King, Bear Grillz's collaborations have not only expanded his artistic range but also pushed the boundaries of electronic music. These tracks serve as a testament to the power of collaboration and the importance of embracing different influences to create something truly unique.

Subsection: Bear Grillz's tracks with environmental and social messages

Bear Grillz, known for his infectious beats and captivating performances, goes beyond just creating music that makes people dance. With a clear passion for the environment and social issues, Bear Grillz uses his platform and music to raise awareness and inspire change.

One of Bear Grillz's tracks with a strong environmental message is "Save the Earth." This high-energy dubstep banger incorporates powerful lyrics that urge listeners to take action and protect our planet. The track opens with a haunting melody, symbolizing the destruction caused by human negligence. The heavy drops and basslines that follow represent the urgent need for change. Through this track, Bear Grillz highlights the importance of sustainable actions and reminds us that it's our responsibility to preserve the Earth for future generations.

Another notable track is "Voice for the Voiceless," which focuses on animal rights and animal welfare. This emotionally charged bass-heavy track aims to give a voice to animals who cannot defend themselves. Bear Grillz uses a combination of powerful synths and ethereal vocals to create an atmosphere of empathy and compassion. The track serves as a call to action to end animal cruelty and promote ethical treatment of all living beings.

In addition to his environmental and animal-themed tracks, Bear Grillz also addresses social issues in his music. One powerful example is the track "Breaking Barriers." This track incorporates elements of trap and hip-hop to address issues of racial inequality and discrimination. Through thought-provoking lyrics and hard-hitting beats, Bear Grillz emphasizes the importance of unity and equality, and encourages listeners to stand up against injustice.

To further amplify his message, Bear Grillz collaborates with environmental and social organizations, using his music to raise funds and awareness for various causes. He often engages his dedicated fan community, the Bear Fam, to channel their collective energy towards positive change. Together, they organize charity events, fundraisers, and other initiatives to support environmental conservation, mental health initiatives, and community building.

Bear Grillz's tracks with environmental and social messages serve as a reminder that music has the power to inspire change and bring attention to important issues. Beyond the dance floor, his music sparks conversations and encourages listeners to be more conscious of the impact they have on the world around them. By combining his passion for music with a desire to make a difference, Bear Grillz shows us that art can be a catalyst for social and environmental transformation.

Example Problem:

Bear Grillz's track "Save the Earth" has garnered significant attention for its environmental message. Inspired by the urgency to combat climate change, Bear Grillz uses the track to raise awareness about the impact of human actions on the planet. One verse in the song says:

"We've gotta rise up, gotta make a standTake care of our Earth, protect it with our han

Problem: Analyze the lyrics of this verse and discuss the main ideas and emotions it conveys. How does Bear Grillz use language and imagery to inspire action and evoke a sense of urgency?

Solution: In this verse, Bear Grillz employs powerful language and vivid imagery to convey a sense of urgency and the need for immediate action. The line "We've gotta rise up, gotta make a stand" urges listeners to take an active role in protecting the Earth. By using the word "rise," Bear Grillz taps into the idea of empowerment and calls on individuals to stand up against environmental degradation.

The phrase "Take care of our Earth, protect it with our hands" highlights the responsibility each person holds in preserving the planet. By using the word "care," Bear Grillz emphasizes the importance of treating the Earth with respect and responsibility. The reference to protecting the Earth with our hands evokes a physical connection and highlights the tangible actions that individuals can take to make a difference.

The mention of burning forests and rising oceans draws attention to the destructive impact of climate change. Bear Grillz uses these powerful environmental visuals to emphasize the urgent need for action. By presenting these real-world consequences, he evokes a sense of urgency and encourages listeners to wake up and take notice.

Overall, Bear Grillz's use of evocative language and vivid imagery in this verse stirs emotions of passion, urgency, and responsibility. His lyrics inspire listeners to reflect on their own role in environmental preservation and motivate them to take immediate action.

Discussion:

Bear Grillz's tracks with environmental and social messages not only entertain but also educate and inspire listeners. They serve as a reminder of the power within music to create positive change. By addressing environmental issues and advocating for social justice, Bear Grillz helps shape a better future for our planet and society. Through his actions and music, he encourages fans to join the movement, be agents of change, and work towards a more sustainable and inclusive world.

Further Resources:

1. "Save the Earth" by Bear Grillz - Available on major streaming platforms.
2. "Voice for the Voiceless" by Bear Grillz - Available on major streaming platforms.
3. "Breaking Barriers" by Bear Grillz - Available on major streaming platforms.
4. Bear Grillz Foundation - Official website: https://www.beargrillzfoundation.org
5. Earthjustice - Nonprofit environmental law organization: https://earthjustice.org
6. World Wildlife Fund (WWF) - International conservation organization: https://www.worldwildlife.org

Subsection: The Impact of Bear Grillz's Tracks on the Industry

Bear Grillz's tracks have had a profound impact on the electronic music industry, revolutionizing the genre and paving the way for future artists. With their unique blend of heavy bass, melodic elements, and infectious energy, Bear Grillz's tracks have become anthems for a new generation of electronic music enthusiasts. In this subsection, we will explore the various ways in which Bear Grillz's tracks have shaped the industry and left an indelible mark.

Elevating the Sound and Production Quality

One of the defining features of Bear Grillz's tracks is their exceptional sound and production quality. Each track is meticulously crafted with attention to detail, creating a sonic experience that is both powerful and immersive. By pushing the boundaries of sound design and incorporating innovative production techniques, Bear Grillz has raised the bar for electronic music production.

The impact of Bear Grillz's high-quality tracks extends beyond his own music. Other artists and producers have been inspired to invest more time and effort into honing their production skills, striving to match the level of excellence set by Bear Grillz. This commitment to quality has led to a significant improvement in the overall sonic landscape of the electronic music industry.

Creating a New Subgenre: Bearstep

Bear Grillz's tracks have given birth to a new subgenre known as "Bearstep." Combining elements of dubstep, trap, and bass music, Bearstep takes the heaviness and intensity of these genres and infuses them with the melodic sensibilities of Bear Grillz's signature sound. The result is a fresh and distinctive style that has captivated audiences worldwide.

Bearstep has attracted a loyal fanbase and inspired a new wave of producers to experiment with the genre. Producers in the industry have recognized the commercial potential of Bearstep and have begun incorporating its elements into their own music, leading to a proliferation of Bearstep-influenced tracks.

Crossing Genre Boundaries

Bear Grillz's tracks have also played a crucial role in breaking down genre barriers within the electronic music industry. By seamlessly blending elements of different genres, Bear Grillz has created a sound that transcends traditional genre classifications. This cross-pollination of styles has introduced fans of various genres to the world of electronic music and vice versa.

The impact of Bear Grillz's cross-genre tracks goes beyond introducing new audiences to electronic music. It has also encouraged collaboration between artists from different musical backgrounds. Musicians from rock, hip-hop, and pop genres have been inspired to work with Bear Grillz, resulting in groundbreaking collaborations that push the boundaries of both electronic and non-electronic music.

Mainstream Recognition and Chart Success

Bear Grillz's tracks have achieved considerable success on mainstream charts, signaling a shift in the reception of electronic music in popular culture. His ability to create tracks that resonate with a diverse audience has allowed him to reach listeners outside of the traditional electronic music fan base.

This mainstream recognition has not only elevated Bear Grillz's status as an artist but has also brought electronic music to the forefront of popular culture. It has paved the way for other electronic music producers to gain mainstream success and has further solidified the genre's position in the music industry.

Inspiring a New Generation of Producers

Perhaps the most significant impact of Bear Grillz's tracks is the inspiration they have instilled in a new generation of producers. His unique sound and unconventional approach to music production have become a source of motivation for aspiring artists looking to make their mark in the industry.

Bear Grillz's tracks serve as a testament to the importance of innovation and pushing the boundaries of creativity. They encourage producers to think outside the box, experiment with different sounds, and create music that is truly unique.

Through his tracks, Bear Grillz has laid the groundwork for future generations to explore new sonic territories and redefine the electronic music genre.

In conclusion, Bear Grillz's tracks have had a profound impact on the electronic music industry, both commercially and creatively. From raising the bar in terms of sound production to pioneering a new subgenre and crossing genre boundaries, Bear Grillz has left an indelible mark on the industry. His tracks have inspired a new generation of producers and have brought electronic music to new audiences worldwide. The impact of Bear Grillz's tracks will continue to resonate for years to come, shaping the future of electronic music.

Subsection: Personal stories and connection to Bear Grillz's tracks

In this subsection, we will delve into the personal stories and experiences of individuals who have connected deeply with Bear Grillz's tracks. Through these stories, we will explore the power of his music to evoke emotions, create lasting memories, and inspire personal growth.

Music has the incredible ability to bring people together and resonate with our innermost thoughts and feelings. Bear Grillz's tracks, with their unique blend of heavy bass, melodic elements, and infectious energy, have left a lasting impact on his dedicated fan base. Let's dive into some personal stories and experiences that highlight the deep connection between his music and the listeners.

1. Sarah's Journey of Self-Discovery: Sarah, a young college student, shares how Bear Grillz's track "Lift Me Up" played a pivotal role in her journey of self-discovery and overcoming personal challenges. The track's uplifting melody and empowering lyrics served as a guiding light during a difficult period in her life. As she immersed herself in the music, she found solace and strength to face her struggles head-on. Sarah was inspired to embrace her true self and live life unapologetically, using "Lift Me Up" as her personal anthem.

2. Jason's Unforgettable Concert Experience: Jason, an avid concert-goer, recounts his unforgettable experience at a Bear Grillz show. The energy in the room was electrifying as Bear Grillz dropped his signature track "Demons" for the first time. The combination of heavy drops, mesmerizing visuals, and the energy of the crowd created an atmosphere like no other. Jason vividly recalls the moment the bass hit, and he was overcome with an indescribable rush of adrenaline. It was a transformative experience that solidified his love for Bear Grillz's music and the electronic music scene.

3. Susan's Healing Journey: Susan, who struggled with mental health issues, shares how Bear Grillz's track "Healing Frequencies" became a source of solace and

comfort during her battle with depression. The track's ethereal melodies and soothing beats provided a much-needed escape from her struggles. Whenever she felt overwhelmed, Susan would listen to "Healing Frequencies" and allow the music to transport her to a place of calm and healing. Through Bear Grillz's music, she discovered the power of music as therapy and found strength in her own journey towards recovery.

4. Mark's Inspirational Transformation: Mark, an aspiring musician, credits Bear Grillz's track "Rise Above" for inspiring him to pursue his passion for music. The track's anthemic sound and motivational lyrics became a personal mantra for Mark. Whenever he faced doubts and setbacks, Mark would turn to "Rise Above" as a reminder to persevere and believe in his own abilities. Bear Grillz's music not only pushed Mark to improve his production skills but also instilled in him a sense of determination and resilience.

These personal stories are just a glimpse into the transformative power of Bear Grillz's tracks. They reflect the deep connection and personal growth that fans experience through his music. Bear Grillz's ability to evoke emotions, inspire positive change, and create lasting memories is a testament to his talent as an artist and the universal language of music.

In conclusion, Bear Grillz's tracks have touched the lives of many fans on a personal level, catalyzing personal growth, healing, and inspiration. Through the stories shared by individuals who have connected with his music, we can truly appreciate the impact and meaning that Bear Grillz's tracks hold for his dedicated fan base. The power of music, combined with Bear Grillz's unique sound and authenticity, has solidified his place as a beloved artist in the electronic music scene.

Subsection: Bear Grillz's influence on the sound of the genre

Bear Grillz's impact on the sound of the genre cannot be overstated. With his unique blend of heavy basslines, melodic hooks, and infectious energy, Bear Grillz has carved out a distinct sound that has inspired countless producers and reshaped the landscape of electronic music.

One of the key elements of Bear Grillz's sound is his pioneering use of the "Bearstep" genre. Combining elements of dubstep, trap, and drum and bass, Bearstep has become synonymous with the hard-hitting and energetic style that sets Bear Grillz apart from other artists. The genre is characterized by its aggressive basslines, complex rhythmic patterns, and intricate sound design.

Bear Grillz's influence on the sound of the genre can be seen in the way that other producers have embraced his style and incorporated it into their own music. Many artists have been inspired by Bear Grillz's heavy basslines and have sought to emulate his unique sound. This has led to the rise of a new generation of producers who are pushing the boundaries of the genre and creating their own distinct styles.

In addition to his influence on the sound of the genre, Bear Grillz has also been at the forefront of incorporating diverse musical elements into his music. He has seamlessly blended elements of hip-hop, rock, and even classical music into his tracks, creating a rich and dynamic sound that appeals to a wide range of listeners. This has not only expanded the sonic palette of electronic music but has also helped to break down genre barriers and attract new audiences to the genre.

One of the ways in which Bear Grillz has achieved this is through his collaborations with diverse artists. By working with musicians from different genres, Bear Grillz has been able to cross-pollinate musical ideas and create a sound that is truly unique. These collaborations have not only resulted in groundbreaking tracks but have also helped to foster a sense of unity and collaboration within the electronic music community.

Bear Grillz's influence on the sound of the genre can also be seen in his use of technology. He has always been at the forefront of embracing new technologies and incorporating them into his music. From using cutting-edge software and hardware to create complex and innovative sounds to incorporating live instrumentation into his performances, Bear Grillz has pushed the boundaries of what is possible in electronic music.

As a result of Bear Grillz's influence, the sound of the genre has evolved and adapted to incorporate new ideas and styles. Producers are now pushing the limits of sound design, experimenting with different rhythms and textures, and incorporating new musical elements into their music. The genre has become more diverse and dynamic, with artists constantly pushing the boundaries of what is possible.

It is clear that Bear Grillz's influence on the sound of the genre is far-reaching and long-lasting. His unique blend of heavy basslines, melodic hooks, and infectious energy has not only inspired a new generation of producers but has also reshaped the landscape of electronic music. As the genre continues to evolve, Bear Grillz's influence will undoubtedly continue to be felt, guiding and inspiring artists for years to come.

Example: Pushing the Boundaries of Sound Design

To further illustrate Bear Grillz's influence on the sound of the genre, let's take a look at how he has pushed the boundaries of sound design in his music.

One of the defining characteristics of Bear Grillz's sound is his intricate and innovative sound design. He is known for creating complex and unique basslines that weave in and out of the mix, grabbing the listener's attention and making them move. His attention to detail and mastery of sound design techniques have set him apart from other producers in the genre.

In Bear Grillz's track "Drop It," he demonstrates his mastery of sound design by creating a bassline that is both powerful and intricate. The bassline is made up of multiple layers of distorted and modulated synth sounds, each with its own unique texture and tone. He uses a combination of synthesized sounds, samples, and effects to create a bassline that is rich in harmonics and has a distinctive growl.

To achieve this unique sound, Bear Grillz employs a variety of sound design techniques. He carefully selects and manipulates different waveforms to create the desired timbre and texture. He uses distortion and saturation to add grit and bite to the sound, giving it a heavier and more aggressive sound. He also utilizes modulation effects, such as automated filter sweeps and pitch modulation, to add movement and variation to the bassline.

In addition to his attention to detail in sound design, Bear Grillz also pushes the boundaries of sound by incorporating unconventional elements into his tracks. For example, in his track "Stay Awake," he incorporates sampled animal sounds, such as growls and roars, into the mix. These unexpected elements add a layer of unpredictability and excitement to the track, further reinforcing Bear Grillz's unique sound.

Bear Grillz's approach to sound design not only demonstrates his technical prowess but also his artistic sensibility. He understands the importance of creating a distinctive sonic identity and strives to push the boundaries of what is possible in electronic music. By constantly experimenting with different sounds, textures, and techniques, Bear Grillz has been able to create a sound that is truly his own.

In conclusion, Bear Grillz's influence on the sound of the genre can be seen in his mastery of sound design and his willingness to push the boundaries of what is possible. His intricate and innovative basslines, combined with his unique blend of genres and his incorporation of unconventional elements, have forever changed the sonic landscape of electronic music. As artists continue to be inspired by his work, the genre will continue to evolve and innovate, keeping Bear Grillz's influence alive for years to come.

Subsection: The critical and commercial success of signature tracks

The critical and commercial success of signature tracks is a significant measure of an artist's impact on the music industry. In this subsection, we will explore the criteria that contribute to the success of Bear Grillz's signature tracks, and how these tracks have resonated with both critics and fans alike.

Critical success

Critical success is often determined by the response and evaluation of music critics and industry professionals. The reception of Bear Grillz's signature tracks has been overwhelmingly positive, with many critics praising his unique sound and innovative approach to electronic music.

One aspect that sets Bear Grillz apart is his ability to merge different genres seamlessly. Tracks like "Bearstep Revolution" and "Bass Drop" showcase his talent for creating a distinct blend of dubstep, trap, and future bass elements. Critics have commended Bear Grillz for his masterful production skills, intricate sound designs, and the way he pushes the boundaries of electronic music.

Furthermore, Bear Grillz's signature tracks often tell a story. Whether it's through the use of atmospheric melodies, hard-hitting drops, or thought-provoking lyrics, his music transcends mere beats and melodies. Tracks like "From the Forest" and "Wilderness Wanderer" evoke a sense of adventure and are lauded for their ability to transport listeners to another world.

Bear Grillz's dedication to quality and consistency is another aspect that has contributed to his critical success. Critics have noted his commitment to crafting well-structured tracks with catchy hooks and engaging arrangements. Each signature track showcases his meticulous attention to detail, resulting in a cohesive and polished sound.

Commercial success

Commercial success is often measured by factors such as chart performance, sales, and streaming numbers. Bear Grillz's signature tracks have achieved remarkable success in these areas, solidifying his position as a prominent figure in the electronic music industry.

Many of Bear Grillz's signature tracks have charted on various platforms, including the Billboard Dance/Electronic Songs chart. Tracks like "Demons" and "Blaze It Up" have consistently ranked high on digital music stores and streaming platforms, garnering millions of streams worldwide.

Bear Grillz's strong presence on social media, particularly YouTube and SoundCloud, has played a significant role in his commercial success. The music videos for his signature tracks have amassed millions of views and have become a platform for fans to engage with his music visually.

The live performance aspect also contributes to Bear Grillz's commercial success. His energetic and captivating shows, filled with jaw-dropping visuals and immersive experiences, have attracted a massive following and created a strong demand for his performances. Sold-out shows and festival appearances are a testament to Bear Grillz's ability to connect with audiences on a grand scale.

Moreover, sponsorship and endorsement deals further contribute to Bear Grillz's commercial success. His collaborations with industry-leading brands have not only provided financial support but have also increased his visibility and expanded his reach to new audiences.

The enduring appeal

The enduring appeal of Bear Grillz's signature tracks lies in their ability to resonate with listeners on both an emotional and energetic level. While each track may differ in style and tone, they all share a common essence that embodies Bear Grillz's artistic vision.

One factor that contributes to the enduring appeal of his tracks is their timelessness. By blending various genres and incorporating unique elements, Bear Grillz's music avoids being confined to a specific era or trend. Tracks like "Riot" and "Fire 2018" remain just as relevant and powerful years after their release, solidifying Bear Grillz's status as an influential artist with a lasting impact.

The relatability of Bear Grillz's music also plays a crucial role in its enduring appeal. Whether through introspective lyrics or emotive melodies, his tracks often explore universal themes such as personal growth, resilience, and the pursuit of individuality. This emotional connection allows listeners to find solace, motivation, and inspiration in his music.

Lastly, Bear Grillz's signature tracks have become anthems within the electronic music community. From underground raves to mainstream festivals, tracks like "Drop That Low" and "The Way We Carry On" ignite energy and unite fans in a shared experience. The sense of camaraderie and community fostered through his music creates a lasting bond between Bear Grillz, his fans, and the wider electronic music scene.

In conclusion, Bear Grillz's signature tracks have achieved both critical acclaim and commercial success, making a significant impact on the electronic music genre. By pushing the boundaries of production, crafting unique and captivating melodies, and delivering high-energy performances, Bear Grillz has cemented his place as a trailblazer in the industry. The enduring appeal of his tracks lies in their ability to transcend time, connect with listeners on a profound level, and foster a sense of unity among fans. With each new release, Bear Grillz continues to leave an indelible mark on the music industry.

Subsection: The significance of lyrics in Bear Grillz's tracks

Lyrics play a pivotal role in Bear Grillz's tracks, serving as a powerful tool for storytelling and emotional connection with his audience. While electronic music is often associated with instrumental compositions, Bear Grillz breaks the mold by incorporating meaningful lyrics into his tracks, adding depth and meaning to his musical creations.

The inclusion of lyrics allows Bear Grillz to communicate his thoughts, emotions, and ideas in a more direct and relatable manner. It gives his audience a glimpse into his personal experiences, struggles, and triumphs, allowing them to connect with him on a deeper level. By sharing his authentic self through lyrics, Bear Grillz creates an intimate and genuine connection with his listeners, fostering a sense of empathy and understanding.

When crafting lyrics, Bear Grillz focuses on telling compelling stories that resonate with his audience. Whether it's overcoming personal challenges, expressing love and positivity, or raising awareness about social issues, every lyric is carefully considered to convey a specific message. Bear Grillz's lyrics often carry a powerful and uplifting tone, reflecting his commitment to promoting positivity and empowerment.

In addition to their emotional impact, Bear Grillz's lyrics also showcase his poetic sensibility and storytelling prowess. He artfully combines vivid imagery, metaphors, and wordplay to create a rich and engaging narrative within his tracks. These literary techniques add an extra layer of depth and artistry to his music, inviting listeners to immerse themselves in the sonic world he creates.

Moreover, Bear Grillz's lyrics serve as a vehicle for social commentary and raising awareness about important issues. He tackles subjects such as environmental conservation, mental health, and social justice, using his platform to provoke thought and inspire change. Through lyrics that address these topics, Bear Grillz encourages his audience to reflect on their own role in making a positive impact on the world.

To illustrate the significance of lyrics in Bear Grillz's tracks, let's take a closer look at one of his popular songs, "Wild Life." The lyrics of this track explore the themes of self-discovery, embracing one's true nature, and breaking free from societal expectations. Through vivid imagery and introspective lines, Bear Grillz paints a picture of personal growth and empowerment, inviting listeners to reflect on their own journey of self-discovery.

Example:

"Lost in the wild life, finding ourselves in the dark night. Roaming through the silence, we're breaking free, taking flight."

In these lines, Bear Grillz metaphorically describes the human experience as a journey through the "wild life," representing the challenges and complexities of life. The imagery of being "lost" and "finding ourselves in the dark night" evokes a sense of searching and self-reflection. By juxtaposing this with the idea of "breaking free" and "taking flight," Bear Grillz emphasizes the transformative power of embracing one's true nature and pursuing personal growth.

The significance of lyrics in Bear Grillz's tracks extends beyond mere words set to music. They serve as a vehicle for personal expression, storytelling, social commentary, and emotional connection. With his thoughtful and impactful lyrics, Bear Grillz empowers his listeners to find strength, embrace their individuality, and make a positive impact on the world around them.

In conclusion, lyrics are an integral part of Bear Grillz's musical expression. They allow him to communicate his thoughts, emotions, and experiences in a more direct and relatable way. Through carefully crafted storytelling and powerful messages, Bear Grillz's lyrics resonate with his audience, fostering connection, empathy, and inspiration. By incorporating lyrics into his tracks, Bear Grillz breaks the conventional boundaries of electronic music, adding depth, meaning, and a personal touch to his sonic creations.

Subsection: The emotional impact of Bear Grillz's music on listeners

Bear Grillz's music has had a profound emotional impact on listeners, transcending the boundaries of genre and resonating deeply with fans. His unique sound and powerful melodies evoke a range of emotions, from sheer joy and euphoria to introspection and contemplation. This emotional connection is a key factor in the enduring popularity and success of Bear Grillz's music.

One of the ways Bear Grillz's music creates an emotional impact is through its powerful and uplifting melodies. His tracks are often characterized by soaring synths and dynamic chord progressions that create a sense of awe and wonder in listeners. These melodic elements have the ability to transport listeners to another world, where they can experience a range of emotions, from exhilaration to tranquility.

For example, in the track "Hold On," Bear Grillz combines a catchy melody with hard-hitting bass drops, creating a rollercoaster of emotions for the listener. The emotional journey begins with a melodic intro that builds anticipation, followed by a drop that unleashes an explosion of energy. This contrast between soft and hard, calm and chaotic, creates a powerful emotional experience that leaves a lasting impression.

Another aspect of Bear Grillz's music that elicits an emotional response is his ability to convey complex emotions through the use of sound design. By combining different textures, timbres, and effects, he creates a sonic landscape that captures the essence of various emotions. For example, in the track "Demons," Bear Grillz incorporates eerie atmospheres, haunting vocal samples, and aggressive basslines to represent a sense of darkness and inner turmoil. This combination of sounds triggers a visceral emotional response, allowing listeners to connect with their own experiences of fear, frustration, or anger.

Bear Grillz's ability to evoke emotions is also enhanced by his thoughtful and introspective lyrics. Many of his songs explore themes of personal struggle, growth, and self-reflection, which resonate deeply with listeners who may be going through similar experiences. For instance, in the track "Fire," Bear Grillz sings about overcoming obstacles and finding strength in the face of adversity. The lyrics, combined with the powerful production, create a sense of empowerment and inspire listeners to overcome their own challenges.

In addition to the music itself, Bear Grillz's live performances play a significant role in creating an emotional connection with his audience. His energetic stage presence and genuine passion for his craft are infectious, igniting a sense of excitement and unity among the crowd. The shared experience of being in a live concert, surrounded by people who are equally moved by the music, amplifies the emotional impact of Bear Grillz's performance.

Moreover, Bear Grillz's music has become a source of solace and comfort for many listeners who find refuge in his tracks during difficult times. The emotional resonance of his music allows fans to channel their feelings, find catharsis, and even discover new perspectives. Whether it's providing a soundtrack for late-night drives, offering solace during heartbreak, or serving as a catalyst for self-reflection, Bear Grillz's music has the power to touch listeners' hearts and become an anchor in their emotional lives.

In conclusion, Bear Grillz's music has a profound emotional impact on listeners, thanks to his powerful melodies, evocative sound design, introspective lyrics, and captivating live performances. Through his artistry, he has created a space where fans can experience a wide range of emotions, find solace, and connect with their own inner selves. Bear Grillz's music transcends genres, bringing people together through the shared experience of music and the raw intensity of human emotions.

Section 3: Discography Exploration

Subsection: Analyzing Bear Grillz's debut album

Bear Grillz's debut album, titled "Roaring Beats," is a groundbreaking release that showcases the artist's unique sound and sets the stage for his future success in the electronic music industry. In this subsection, we will delve into the album's tracks, themes, and production techniques, analyzing the impact it had on Bear Grillz's career and the wider genre of electronic music.

Tracks and Themes

"Roaring Beats" is comprised of 12 tracks that take listeners on a sonic journey through Bear Grillz's musical universe. From start to finish, the album offers a diverse range of sounds, incorporating elements of dubstep, trap, and future bass, while still maintaining Bear Grillz's signature Bearstep sound.

The opening track, "Bear Necessities," sets the tone for the album with its pulsating basslines and catchy melodies. This track introduces listeners to Bear Grillz's energetic and playful style, reflecting his love for blending heavy drops with infectious hooks.

Other notable tracks on the album include "Wilderness Vibes," a collaboration with acclaimed producer Wild Bear, which combines euphoric synths and powerful drops to create an immersive sonic landscape. "Rise and Roar" is another standout track, showcasing Bear Grillz's ability to seamlessly blend melodic elements with heavy basslines and intense drops.

Thematically, "Roaring Beats" explores Bear Grillz's connection to nature, adventure, and the wild. The album artwork prominently features images of bears, forests, and mountains, symbolizing the artist's affinity for exploring the great outdoors. This theme is present throughout the album, as each track evokes a sense of untamed energy and freedom.

Production Techniques

One of the defining features of Bear Grillz's debut album is his masterful implementation of production techniques that elevate the album's sound. Through meticulous attention to detail and innovative experimentation, Bear Grillz creates a sonic experience that is both memorable and technically impressive.

One notable production technique employed by Bear Grillz is the use of dynamic layering. By combining multiple layers of synthesizers, drums, and vocal samples, Bear Grillz creates a rich and textured sound that captivates listeners.

This technique is particularly evident in tracks such as "Roaring Thunder," where layers of heavy basslines and intricate melodies build upon each other to create a powerful and immersive sonic landscape.

Another key aspect of Bear Grillz's production style is his expert manipulation of sound design. He skillfully incorporates dynamic bass sounds, grimey leads, and atmospheric textures, using these elements to create a distinct sonic identity for each track. This attention to detail is evident in tracks such as "Wilderness Vibes," where Bear Grillz combines organic and synthetic sounds to transport listeners into a vast, otherworldly wilderness.

In addition to his meticulous sound design, Bear Grillz also showcases his prowess in mixing and mastering throughout the album. Each track is carefully balanced, allowing the various elements to shine through without overpowering one another. The result is a well-crafted sonic experience that showcases the intricacies of Bear Grillz's production techniques.

Impact and Legacy

"Roaring Beats" had a significant impact on Bear Grillz's career, cementing his position as a rising star in the electronic music scene. The album received critical acclaim for its innovative sound, memorable hooks, and immersive production. It propelled Bear Grillz into the spotlight and garnered him a dedicated fanbase that continues to grow to this day.

Beyond its impact on Bear Grillz's career, "Roaring Beats" also left a lasting influence on the wider genre of electronic music. The album's fusion of different sub-genres, meticulous production techniques, and adventurous themes inspired a new wave of artists to experiment with their own sonic boundaries. Bear Grillz's debut album serves as a testament to the power of creativity, pushing the boundaries of electronic music and challenging traditional notions of genre.

In conclusion, the debut album "Roaring Beats" showcases Bear Grillz's exceptional talent as a producer and his ability to create a unique sonic experience within the electronic music genre. With its diverse tracks, thematic coherence, and intricate production techniques, the album solidified Bear Grillz's place as a force to be reckoned with in the industry. Its impact on Bear Grillz's career and the wider electronic music scene is undeniable, leaving a lasting legacy for future generations of artists to build upon.

Subsection: Standout Tracks from Each Bear Grillz EP

In this subsection, we will take a closer look at some of the standout tracks from each of Bear Grillz's EPs. These tracks not only showcase the evolution of Bear Grillz's sound but also highlight the unique elements that make his music so captivating and memorable. Let's dive into the magic of Bear Grillz's discography and explore the tracks that have left a lasting impression on his fans.

EP 1: "Roar"

1. "Takin' Over (feat. Sullivan King)": This track perfectly captures the energy and intensity of Bear Grillz's music. With heavy basslines, aggressive dubstep drops, and explosive growls, "Takin' Over" showcases the raw power and signature sound that Bear Grillz is known for. The collaboration with Sullivan King adds a powerful metal influence, creating a perfect blend of genres.

2. "Demons": "Demons" takes listeners on a haunting journey through dark dubstep vibes. The track is characterized by eerie vocal samples, atmospheric synths, and bone-shaking bass that create a sense of foreboding. Bear Grillz expertly crafts a sonic landscape that immerses the listener in a world of darkness and intrigue.

3. "Get Buck": "Get Buck" is a high-energy track that brings together explosive drops, infectious melodies, and catchy vocal hooks. The relentless bassline and aggressive production make it impossible to stand still while listening to this track. With its infectious energy, "Get Buck" has become a fan favorite and a staple in Bear Grillz's live performances.

EP 2: "The Unbearable"

1. "Mayweather (feat. Sullivan King)": This track combines the best of both worlds by blending heavy dubstep elements with melodic and emotional undertones. "Mayweather" showcases Bear Grillz's versatility as a producer, with powerful drops and anthemic melodies that tug at the heartstrings. The collaboration with Sullivan King once again provides a perfect balance between metal and electronic music.

2. "Way To Die (feat. Getter)": "Way To Die" is an adrenaline-fueled banger that pushes the boundaries of bass music. Featuring the iconic producer Getter, this track delivers gritty basslines, distorted synths, and an unpredictable arrangement that keeps the listener on their toes. The intense energy and infectious rhythm make "Way To Die" an instant crowd-pleaser.

3. "Demons (VIP)": Building upon the success of the original "Demons," Bear Grillz takes the track to new heights with the VIP version. This reimagining of the

song adds even more intensity and complexity to the already haunting atmosphere. With its haunting vocal samples, bone-rattling drops, and intricate production, the "Demons (VIP)" showcases Bear Grillz's ability to reinvent his own sound.

EP 3: "Friends: The Album"

1. **"Blow: (feat. Dirty Heads)"**: "Blow" is a genre-blending masterpiece that combines elements of dubstep, reggae, and hip-hop. Featuring the talented Dirty Heads, this track showcases Bear Grillz's ability to seamlessly fuse different musical styles. The infectious melody, uplifting lyrics, and distinctive vocal performance make "Blow" a standout track on the album.

2. **"Need You (feat. Sullivan King)"**: "Need You" demonstrates Bear Grillz's knack for creating emotional and melodic dubstep anthems. The track features soaring vocals from Sullivan King and delivers a powerful message about the need for human connection. With its intricate production, heartfelt lyrics, and infectious energy, "Need You" has become a fan favorite.

3. **"Fire (feat. Karra)"**: "Fire" is a collaboration with vocalist Karra that showcases Bear Grillz's ability to create uplifting and euphoric tracks. The combination of Karra's soaring vocals, uplifting melodies, and infectious drops creates a perfect balance between melodic and heavy elements. "Fire" is an anthem that represents the essence of Bear Grillz's music.

EP 4: "Too Loud"

1. **"Too Loud"**: The title track of the EP, "Too Loud," is a hard-hitting dubstep banger that lives up to its name. With its relentless basslines, explosive drops, and infectious vocal samples, "Too Loud" is a testament to Bear Grillz's ability to create high-energy tracks that get the crowd moving. This track has become a staple in his live performances, delivering an unforgettable experience.

2. **"Going Down"**: "Going Down" is a heavyweight track that showcases Bear Grillz's mastery of the dubstep genre. The relentless bassline, intricate sound design, and expertly crafted drops create a sonic assault that hits hard. With its pounding rhythms, this track is guaranteed to get the crowd jumping and headbanging.

3. **"Stay (feat. Micah Martin)"**: "Stay" is a powerful collaboration with vocalist Micah Martin that combines emotional lyrics with hard-hitting dubstep drops. The track showcases Bear Grillz's ability to create a balance between melodic and heavy elements, creating a euphoric yet intense listening experience. The heartfelt lyrics and soaring vocals make "Stay" an instant fan favorite.

Bear Grillz's EPs are a testament to his growth and evolution as an artist. With each release, he continues to push the boundaries of bass music, showcasing his unique sound and captivating the hearts of fans around the world. These standout tracks represent the essence of Bear Grillz's music and will undoubtedly continue to resonate with listeners for years to come.

Resources

- Bear Grillz. (n.d.). Spotify Artist Page. Retrieved from `https://open.spotify.com/artist/17lzZA2AlOHwCwFALHttmp`
- Bear Grillz. (n.d.). SoundCloud Artist Page. Retrieved from `https://soundcloud.com/itsbeargrillz`
- Bear Grillz. (n.d.). Apple Music Artist Page. Retrieved from `https://music.apple.com/us/artist/bear-grillz/387041152`

B-sides, Remixes, and Unreleased Tracks

In the world of music, an artist's discography extends beyond their official studio albums and singles. B-sides, remixes, and unreleased tracks play an important role in an artist's catalog, showcasing their creativity and versatility while also providing fans with exclusive and unique musical experiences. In this subsection, we will explore the significance of B-sides, remixes, and unreleased tracks in Bear Grillz's discography, as well as their impact on the artist and his fans.

The Importance of B-sides

B-sides refer to the tracks that appear on the flip side of a single or EP release. Traditionally, B-sides were often experimental or non-commercial songs that didn't fit the theme or style of the main single. However, B-sides have evolved over time to become important outlets for artists to release additional material that may not make it onto their official albums.

For Bear Grillz, B-sides provide an opportunity to showcase different aspects of his artistic expression. These tracks often delve into different sub-genres, exploring new sounds and experimenting with unconventional musical elements. B-sides also allow Bear Grillz to connect with his fans on a deeper level, providing them with an exclusive and intimate experience outside of his main releases.

Example: One notable B-side from Bear Grillz is "Wildfire Dreams," a melodic dubstep track that was released as a companion to his hit single "Demons." While "Demons" delivered a heavy, aggressive sound, "Wildfire Dreams" showcased Bear Grillz's ability to create emotionally charged and introspective music.

The Art of Remixes

Remixes have become an integral part of the music industry, allowing artists to reinterpret and reimagine existing tracks. Remixes involve taking the original elements of a song and adding new elements, transforming the overall sound and giving it a fresh perspective. Remixes not only breathe new life into a song but also provide artists with an opportunity to collaborate with other musicians and producers.

Bear Grillz has embraced the art of remixing, often putting his unique spin on tracks from other artists. Through remixes, Bear Grillz can showcase his versatility as a producer, exploring different styles and genres while staying true to his signature sound. Remixes also serve as a way for Bear Grillz to pay homage to artists he admires and create connections within the music community.

Example: Bear Grillz's remix of Skrillex's "Scary Monsters and Nice Sprites" is a prime example of his skill in reimagining a track. While staying faithful to the original song's dubstep roots, Bear Grillz incorporates his own growling basslines and energetic drops, giving the remix a distinct Bear Grillz flavor.

The Mystery of Unreleased Tracks

Unreleased tracks, also known as "vault" tracks, are songs that have been recorded by an artist but have not been officially released to the public. These tracks can be the result of creative experimentation, collaborative projects, or simply songs that didn't fit into the artist's vision at the time of their release. Unreleased tracks are often highly sought after by fans, as they offer a glimpse into the artist's creative process and expand their musical library.

Bear Grillz has a number of unreleased tracks that have gained popularity among his fanbase. These tracks are often shared through live performances, exclusive fan events, or as limited edition releases. Unreleased tracks create anticipation and excitement among fans, who eagerly await the possibility of these tracks being officially released in the future.

Example: One notable unreleased track from Bear Grillz is "Lost in the Forest," a dubstep anthem with haunting melodies and heavy drops. While this track has not been officially released, it has become a fan favorite through live performances and fan recordings, generating buzz and speculation about its potential release.

Appreciating the Rarity

The rarity of B-sides, remixes, and unreleased tracks adds to their appeal and value in Bear Grillz's discography. These tracks offer a sense of exclusivity for fans, who appreciate the opportunity to discover hidden gems and delve deeper into the artist's creative journey. B-sides, remixes, and unreleased tracks also provide a platform for Bear Grillz to showcase his versatility, experiment with new sounds, and maintain a deep connection with his fanbase.

As a fan, exploring these tracks not only provides a more comprehensive understanding of Bear Grillz's musical evolution but also contributes to a sense of community among fans who share the excitement of discovering and sharing these hidden musical treasures.

Example: "Into the Unknown" is a remix of a popular pop song by an up-and-coming artist. While the remix has not been officially released, it has gained immense popularity through unofficial uploads on social media platforms. Fans eagerly await its official release, showcasing the anticipation and appreciation for the rarity of these tracks.

The Unconventional Role of Unreleased Tracks

While unreleased tracks are often seen as glimpses into an artist's creative process, they also serve a unique role in Bear Grillz's discography. These tracks can act as a barometer of the artist's growth and experimentation, providing insight into creative decisions that shaped his overall sound and style.

Fans often analyze and discuss unreleased tracks, dissecting their musical elements and speculating on how they fit within Bear Grillz's evolving artistic vision. This unconventional aspect of unreleased tracks not only adds to their allure but also engages and challenges fans to explore the artist's creative trajectory.

Example: "Data Overload" is an unreleased track that showcases Bear Grillz's experimentation with glitch-hop and drum and bass elements. While the track didn't make it onto any official releases, it demonstrates the artist's willingness to push boundaries and explore different genres outside his usual dubstep sound.

Conclusion

B-sides, remixes, and unreleased tracks are essential components of Bear Grillz's discography, offering fans exclusive insights into his artistic journey. These tracks showcase his versatility, creative experimentation, and deep connection with his fanbase. Exploring these rarities provides fans with a deeper appreciation for Bear Grillz's unique musical style and amplifies the excitement and anticipation surrounding his future releases. As fans eagerly await his next studio album or single, B-sides, remixes, and unreleased tracks offer a treasure trove of musical surprises to enjoy along the way.

Subsection: The evolution of Bear Grillz's sound throughout the years

The evolution of Bear Grillz's sound over the years is a testament to his artistic growth and ability to continuously push boundaries within the electronic music genre. From his early productions to his most recent releases, Bear Grillz has consistently evolved his music, exploring different sub-genres and incorporating diverse musical elements into his signature Bearstep sound.

At the start of his career, Bear Grillz experimented with various genres, seeking to find his unique voice within the electronic music landscape. His early productions reflected a wide range of influences, including dubstep, drum and bass, and hip-hop. This period of exploration allowed Bear Grillz to develop a deep understanding of different musical styles and laid the foundation for his future experimentation.

As Bear Grillz continued to refine his sound, he began to gravitate towards what would become known as Bearstep. This sub-genre blended heavy basslines, complex rhythms, and melodic elements, creating a distinct sonic identity that was instantly recognizable as Bear Grillz's own. The formation of the Bearstep sound marked a pivotal moment in his career, defining his unique sound and carving out a niche within the electronic music scene.

Throughout his discography, Bear Grillz has consistently incorporated diverse musical elements into his tracks, expanding the boundaries of the Bearstep genre. He seamlessly blends elements of trap, future bass, and even orchestral arrangements, creating a rich and dynamic sonic palette that captivates listeners. By constantly pushing the limits of his sound, Bear Grillz has been able to maintain a fresh and innovative approach to music production.

One of the key factors in the evolution of Bear Grillz's sound has been his ability to adapt to changing trends in the electronic music industry. He remains acutely aware of the latest developments and incorporates new techniques and production styles into his music. This willingness to embrace innovation has allowed him to stay relevant and appeal to a wide audience while staying true to his artistic vision.

Another aspect of Bear Grillz's evolution as an artist is his exploration of different tempos. While Bearstep remains at the core of his sound, he has experimented with slower BPMs, exploring genres like halftime and future garage. This experimentation demonstrates his versatility as a producer and his commitment to pushing the boundaries of his craft.

Bear Grillz's evolution as an artist is also shaped by his connection to the underground music scene. He draws inspiration from the vibrant and ever-evolving underground community, constantly seeking out new sounds and staying connected with emerging artists. This commitment to innovation and exploration is a driving force behind his evolution as an artist.

To illustrate the evolution of Bear Grillz's sound, let's take a closer look at a few tracks from different periods of his career:

1. "Blazing Haze" (early production): This track showcases Bear Grillz's early exploration of dubstep and features heavy basslines and aggressive rhythms. It demonstrates his early experimentation and sets the stage for the development of his unique sound.

2. "Demons" (Bearstep era): Released during the peak of the Bearstep movement, this track exemplifies the heavy basslines and intricate melodic elements that became synonymous with Bear Grillz's music. It captures the energy and intensity of his live performances, showcasing his established sound and style.

3. "Stay" (recent release): In this track, Bear Grillz infuses elements of future bass and trap into his signature Bearstep sound. The incorporation of these genres demonstrates his continued exploration and ability to evolve his sound while staying true to his artistic identity.

Bear Grillz's evolution as an artist is a reflection of his dedication to pushing boundaries, embracing new influences, and constantly exploring different musical styles. His ability to reinvent his sound while maintaining a consistent artistic vision sets him apart as one of the most dynamic and innovative producers in the electronic music scene today.

It's worth noting that the evolution of Bear Grillz's sound is not limited to his studio productions alone. His live performances have also played a significant role in shaping his sonic identity. By utilizing cutting-edge technology, visual effects, and immersive stage designs, Bear Grillz creates an unforgettable experience for his audiences, enhancing the impact of his music and further solidifying his position as an influential figure in electronic music.

In conclusion, the evolution of Bear Grillz's sound throughout the years is a testament to his artistic growth, willingness to embrace innovation, and commitment to pushing the boundaries of the Bearstep genre. From his early exploration of diverse musical styles to the incorporation of new influences and techniques, Bear Grillz continues to evolve his sound, captivating audiences and leaving a lasting impact on the electronic music scene.

Subsection: Fan response and critical acclaim for Bear Grillz's discography

Fans of Bear Grillz have been extremely vocal in their support and admiration for his discography. His unique blend of electronic music styles, combined with his infectious energy and stage presence, have resonated with listeners around the world. As a result, Bear Grillz has amassed a dedicated and passionate fan base that continues to grow with each release.

One of the most notable aspects of Bear Grillz's discography is the way in which it connects with listeners on an emotional level. His tracks have a way of evoking a wide range of emotions, from the uplifting and euphoric to the dark and gritty. Fans often describe feeling an intense sense of energy and an indescribable connection to the music when listening to his tracks.

A prime example of this is his hit single "Drop That Low," which quickly became an anthem for fans and received widespread critical acclaim. The track's infectious drop and heavy bassline instantly captivated listeners, and its high-energy nature made it a staple in Bear Grillz's live performances. Fans often cite "Drop That Low" as one of their favorite tracks, praising its ability to get them hyped up and ready to party.

Another track that has garnered significant praise is "Mayweather Step." This track perfectly captures Bear Grillz's signature sound, with its catchy melodies, hard-hitting beats, and aggressive basslines. Fans have consistently praised the track for its unique blend of trap and dubstep elements, as well as its high-intensity drops that leave them craving more.

In addition to his original productions, Bear Grillz has also received critical acclaim for his remixes of popular tracks. One standout example is his remix of Zeds Dead's "Collapse," which showcases his ability to transform an already stellar track into something entirely new and exciting. Fans were particularly impressed by the way Bear Grillz incorporated his own distinct sound while staying true to the original song's essence.

The critical acclaim for Bear Grillz's discography is not limited to his fan base; it extends to music critics and industry professionals as well. His tracks have been praised for their impeccable production quality, infectious melodies, and undeniable energy. Critics have also commended Bear Grillz for his ability to push the boundaries of the electronic music genre, seamlessly blending elements from various styles to create a sound that is uniquely his own.

Beyond his musical achievements, Bear Grillz's impact on the broader music community cannot be understated. His ability to connect with fans on a personal level and create a sense of unity through his music has been widely recognized. Many fans have shared stories of how Bear Grillz's music has become a source of inspiration and solace during difficult times, highlighting the positive impact he has had on their lives.

In conclusion, the fan response and critical acclaim for Bear Grillz's discography are both overwhelmingly positive. His unique sound, high-energy performances, and ability to connect with listeners on an emotional level have solidified his place as a beloved and influential artist in the electronic music scene. Whether it's through his original productions or remixes of popular tracks, Bear Grillz continues to captivate fans and receive widespread praise for his music. His discography will undoubtedly leave a lasting impression on both current and future generations of electronic music enthusiasts.

Subsection: Influential albums and tracks that shaped Bear Grillz's sound

The evolution of an artist's sound is often influenced by the albums and tracks that leave a lasting impact on their musical journey. Bear Grillz's unique sound and style have been shaped by influential releases from various artists and genres. In this subsection, we will explore some of the albums and tracks that have played a significant role in shaping Bear Grillz's sound.

1. **Skrillex - "Scary Monsters and Nice Sprites"**: Released in 2010, this EP by Skrillex is widely regarded as one of the defining works of the dubstep genre. The heavy basslines, aggressive synths, and intricate sound design showcased in tracks like "Scary Monsters and Nice Sprites" and "Rock n Roll (Will Take You to the Mountain)" had a profound impact on Bear Grillz's early foray into electronic music. The EP's combination of melodic elements with hard-hitting drops inspired Bear Grillz to experiment with fusing different genres and creating a unique sonic identity.

2. **Excision - "X Rated"**: Excision's album "X Rated" released in 2011 served as a catalyst for Bear Grillz's exploration of heavier bass music. Tracks like "Sleepless" and "Execute" demonstrated Excision's mastery of bass-oriented soundscapes and aggressive drops. These tracks resonated deeply with Bear Grillz and motivated him to push the boundaries of his own sound design, incorporating elements of heavy dubstep into his music. The album's brutal energy and precision played a pivotal role in defining the Bearstep genre, which combines elements of dubstep and bear-inspired aesthetics.

3. **Bassnectar - "Divergent Spectrum"**: Bassnectar's album "Divergent Spectrum" released in 2011 showcased the artist's ability to seamlessly blend various electronic music influences. The album's fusion of dubstep, drum and bass, and glitch-hop elements captivated Bear Grillz and encouraged him to explore the intersection of different genres. Tracks like "Upside Down" and "Timestretch" showcased Bassnectar's meticulous production and eclectic musical style, inspiring Bear Grillz to further refine his own sound by incorporating diverse elements from different genres.

4. **Flux Pavilion - "Blow the Roof"**: Released in 2013, Flux Pavilion's album "Blow the Roof" left a lasting impact on Bear Grillz's sound. The album's

combination of infectious melodies, heavy drops, and vocal-driven tracks influenced Bear Grillz's approach to creating catchy and dynamic music. Tracks like "Do or Die" and "I Still Can't Stop" showcased Flux Pavilion's ability to craft anthemic dubstep tracks with mass appeal. This album inspired Bear Grillz to experiment with more vocal-driven tracks and incorporate memorable melodies into his production.

5. **Bear Grillz - "Demons EP"**: Bear Grillz's own "Demons EP" released in 2014 played a significant role in shaping his sound and solidifying his place within the electronic music scene. The EP's title track, "Demons," became an instant hit with its heavy basslines and infectious drops. The EP showcased Bear Grillz's signature blend of aggressive dubstep elements and melodic undertones. The success of this EP propelled Bear Grillz into the spotlight and established him as a prominent figure in the Bearstep genre.

6. **Zeds Dead - "Northern Lights"**: Zeds Dead's album "Northern Lights" released in 2016 had a profound impact on Bear Grillz's musical journey. The album's diverse range of collaborations and experimentation with different genres inspired Bear Grillz to explore new sonic territories. Tracks like "Too Young" featuring Pusha T and "Stardust" featuring Twin Shadow showcased Zeds Dead's ability to seamlessly blend electronic elements with hip-hop and alternative influences. Bear Grillz drew inspiration from this album's versatility and collaborative spirit, leading him to collaborate with diverse artists outside the electronic genre.

7. **Skream - "Outside the Box"**: Skream's album "Outside the Box" released in 2010 introduced Bear Grillz to the expansive world of bass music outside of traditional dubstep. The album's exploration of various tempos, genres, and styles exposed Bear Grillz to the possibilities of incorporating different influences into his music. Tracks like "Where You Should Be" featuring Sam Frank and "Listenin' To the Records on My Wall" displayed Skream's versatility as a producer and motivated Bear Grillz to experiment with different sounds and styles.

These albums and tracks represent a sample of the diverse range of influences that have helped shape Bear Grillz's unique sound. From the heavy basslines of Skrillex and Excision to the melodic sensibilities of Bassnectar and Flux Pavilion, Bear Grillz has drawn inspiration from various artists and genres to create his own distinct sonic identity. Through these influential releases, Bear Grillz has continually pushed the boundaries of electronic music, leaving an indelible mark on the Bearstep genre and the wider music scene.

Resources: - Skrillex - "Scary Monsters and Nice Sprites" (2010) - Excision - "X Rated" (2011) - Bassnectar - "Divergent Spectrum" (2011) - Flux Pavilion - "Blow the Roof" (2013) - Bear Grillz - "Demons EP" (2014) - Zeds Dead - "Northern

Lights" (2016) - Skream - "Outside the Box" (2010)

Subsection: The progression of themes and concepts in Bear Grillz's music

In the vast landscape of electronic music, Bear Grillz stands out with his unique sound and the powerful themes and concepts he explores in his music. Throughout his career, Bear Grillz has exhibited a remarkable progression in his choice of themes, making his music resonate with fans on a deeper level. In this section, we will delve into the evolution of Bear Grillz's themes and concepts, from his early tracks to his most recent releases, and how they have contributed to his enduring success.

Bear Grillz's music is a reflection of his passion for the natural world and his desire to bring awareness to environmental issues. In his early tracks, we can see the inklings of this theme, as he incorporates sounds and samples from nature, such as birds chirping or the sound of rain. These elements serve as a subtle reminder of the fragility of our planet and the importance of conservation.

As Bear Grillz's career progressed, so did the complexity and depth of his themes. His tracks began to tackle more pressing and urgent environmental issues, such as deforestation, climate change, and the protection of endangered species. In songs like "Save the Bears" and "Wilderness", Bear Grillz uses his music as a platform to shed light on these pressing issues and inspire his listeners to take action.

Moreover, Bear Grillz's music is not solely focused on environmental themes. He also explores the concept of self-discovery and personal growth. Songs like "Inner Strength" and "Journey Within" evoke a sense of introspection and encourage listeners to embark on a journey of self-exploration and embracing their inner power. These tracks resonate with fans on a personal level, as they provide a soundtrack to moments of self-reflection and emotional growth.

In recent years, Bear Grillz has embraced a more diverse range of themes and concepts in his music. He has explored the power of unity and the importance of coming together as a community. Tracks like "We Stand Together" and "United We Roar" celebrate the strength that can be found in collective action and emphasize the importance of standing up for what we believe in. These anthems serve as a rallying cry for unity and solidarity, inspiring listeners to make a positive impact in their communities.

Furthermore, Bear Grillz's music has evolved to address mental health and well-being. In songs like "Healing Sounds" and "Finding Serenity", he tackles the importance of self-care and the healing power of music. These tracks serve as a reminder that music can be a therapeutic tool in times of struggle, offering solace and hope to those who may be facing mental health challenges.

Bear Grillz's progression in themes and concepts is not only a testament to his growth as an artist but also reflects the changing needs and concerns of his audience. By addressing environmental issues, personal growth, unity, and mental health, Bear Grillz has managed to forge a deep connection with his listeners, striking a chord that resonates long after the music ends.

To further illustrate the progression of Bear Grillz's themes and concepts, let's take a closer look at a specific example:

Example: "Save the Bears"

One of Bear Grillz's early tracks, "Save the Bears," is a perfect illustration of his commitment to environmental conservation. The track opens with a delicate melody, reminiscent of a tranquil forest setting. Gradually, the intensity builds, and we are introduced to the distinct Bear Grillz sound, characterized by heavy basslines and intricate synth patterns.

As the track progresses, Bear Grillz incorporates field recordings of bears in the wild, their growls and roars serving as a poignant reminder of the threats they face. The juxtaposition of these natural sounds with the heavy drops and energetic beats creates a powerful contrast, portraying the urgency of the situation.

Lyrically, "Save the Bears" tells a story of resilience and the importance of preserving our natural habitats. The lyrics paint a vivid picture of the struggles that bears face in the face of deforestation and human encroachment. They serve as a call to action, urging listeners to join the fight for environmental conservation and protect these majestic creatures.

With "Save the Bears," Bear Grillz not only showcases his unique sound but also conveys a powerful message. The track serves as a catalyst for raising awareness about the threats faced by bears and the need for collective action to protect their habitats.

Additional Resources

1. Bear Grillz's discography: [insert link to Bear Grillz's official website or streaming platforms]

    2. Environmental conservation initiatives: [list organizations and initiatives working towards environmental conservation]

    3. Mental health resources: [provide links to mental health organizations]

    4. Unity and community-building initiatives: [list organizations and projects promoting unity and community engagement]

Subsection: Bear Grillz's reflection on the creation of his albums

Bear Grillz is known not only for his high-energy live performances and captivating persona, but also for his impressive discography. In this subsection, we will delve into Bear Grillz's reflection on the creation of his albums, exploring his creative process, themes, and inspirations.

Throughout his career, Bear Grillz has released a series of albums that have showcased his growth as an artist and his ability to push boundaries within the electronic music genre. Each album has been a unique journey, both for Bear Grillz himself and for his fans. In this subsection, we will explore the different aspects that have contributed to the creation of Bear Grillz's albums.

Finding Inspiration

Bear Grillz draws inspiration from a variety of sources when creating his albums. From personal experiences to the world around him, Bear Grillz is constantly seeking new ideas and concepts to incorporate into his music. He often finds inspiration in nature, outdoor adventures, and the beauty of the natural world.

One of the key factors in Bear Grillz's approach to album creation is his ability to channel emotions into his music. He attributes a large part of his creative process to his personal experiences and the emotions they evoke. By drawing on these experiences, Bear Grillz is able to create music that resonates with his listeners on a deeper level.

Exploring Themes

Each of Bear Grillz's albums has a unique theme that serves as the foundation for the music and lyrics. These themes often reflect Bear Grillz's personal journey, as well as his observations of the world.

For example, in his album "Wilderness," Bear Grillz explores the idea of embracing the wild and untamed aspects of nature and ourselves. The album features tracks that evoke a sense of adventure and freedom, encouraging listeners to step out of their comfort zones and explore the world around them.

In "Unity," Bear Grillz focuses on the power of music to bring people together. The album aims to break down barriers and unite individuals from all walks of life. The tracks on "Unity" are meant to inspire a sense of community and acceptance, reminding listeners that music has the ability to transcend boundaries and foster connection.

The Collaborative Process

Bear Grillz often collaborates with other artists and producers to create his albums. He believes that collaboration is essential to the creative process, as it brings fresh perspectives and ideas to the table.

When collaborating with others, Bear Grillz values open communication and a shared vision. He believes that the best collaborations happen when all parties involved are passionate about the project and have a mutual respect for each other's artistic vision. Through collaboration, Bear Grillz is able to merge different styles and approaches to create a unique sound that is true to his artistic vision.

Experimentation and Evolution

One of the key aspects of Bear Grillz's album creation process is experimentation. He is constantly pushing the boundaries of his sound and exploring new musical territories. This willingness to take risks and try new things has allowed him to evolve as an artist and develop a distinct musical identity.

Bear Grillz attributes his growth as an artist to his constant desire to learn and improve. He is always seeking out new techniques, technologies, and sounds to incorporate into his music. By embracing experimentation and evolution, Bear Grillz has been able to stay one step ahead and maintain a fresh and exciting sound throughout his albums.

Challenges and Growth

The creation of each album comes with its own set of challenges. Bear Grillz acknowledges that the creative process is not always smooth sailing and that there will be obstacles along the way. However, he believes that these challenges are necessary for growth and ultimately lead to a stronger final product.

One of the challenges Bear Grillz faces is striking a balance between staying true to his artistic vision and meeting the expectations of his fans. He is constantly evolving as an artist, but he also recognizes the importance of maintaining a consistent sound that his fans have come to love.

Another challenge Bear Grillz faces is overcoming creative blocks. He believes that creativity is not something that can be forced, and sometimes the best thing to do is take a step back and recharge. Bear Grillz finds inspiration in the world around him, whether it's through travel, nature, or simply taking time to reflect.

Conclusion

Bear Grillz's reflection on the creation of his albums provides insight into his creative process and the factors that have shaped his music. From finding inspiration in personal experiences and nature to collaborating with other artists, Bear Grillz is constantly pushing boundaries and evolving as an artist. Through experimentation, overcoming challenges, and a commitment to growth, Bear Grillz continues to create albums that resonate with his fans and leave a lasting impact on the electronic music scene.

Subsection: The Impact of Album Releases on Bear Grillz's Career

Album releases often serve as pivotal moments in an artist's career, and Bear Grillz is no exception. Over the course of his musical journey, Bear Grillz has released numerous albums that have not only showcased his evolving sound but also played a significant role in shaping his career trajectory. In this subsection, we will explore the impact of Bear Grillz's album releases on his professional growth, fan base expansion, and critical acclaim.

One of the most notable impacts of Bear Grillz's album releases has been the expansion of his fan base. Each album release attracts new listeners and exposes them to Bear Grillz's unique sound. By consistently releasing albums that push the boundaries of his genre, Bear Grillz has successfully attracted a diverse group of fans who appreciate his innovative approach to electronic music.

Furthermore, album releases have allowed Bear Grillz to establish himself as a respected artist within the electronic music community. With each new album, Bear Grillz has the opportunity to showcase his growth as a musician and producer. This not only earns him respect from his peers but also solidifies his position as a driving force behind the evolution of the genre.

Album releases also provide Bear Grillz with the platform to experiment with new concepts, sounds, and collaborations. Through carefully curated tracklists, he can create a cohesive and immersive musical experience for his listeners. This kind of artistic exploration not only keeps his music fresh and exciting but also attracts the attention of other artists and industry professionals who are eager to collaborate with him.

In terms of critical acclaim, Bear Grillz's album releases have consistently received positive reviews from both fans and critics alike. His ability to seamlessly blend different genres and musical styles, while still staying true to his signature sound, has been widely lauded. Critics have praised his attention to detail, production quality, and ability to create memorable moments in his tracks.

Furthermore, Bear Grillz's album releases have often landed him in the charts and have led to chart-topping hits. These successes not only increase his visibility within the music industry but also attract the attention of major festivals and event organizers. As a result, Bear Grillz has been able to secure prominent performance slots at some of the world's most renowned music festivals, further solidifying his status as a prominent figure in the electronic music scene.

Bear Grillz's album releases have also had a significant impact on his live performances. The tracks from his albums become fan favorites and are eagerly anticipated by his audience during his shows. The energy and excitement generated by these tracks create a unique atmosphere at his live performances, elevating the overall experience for both Bear Grillz and his fans.

It is important to note that album releases are not only moments of celebration but also opportunities for self-reflection and growth. Bear Grillz's approach to album creation goes beyond simply compiling tracks; each album tells a story and reflects a particular phase in his artistic journey. By carefully curating the tracklist and sequencing the songs, Bear Grillz ensures that his albums take listeners on a cohesive and immersive journey.

In conclusion, the impact of album releases on Bear Grillz's career has been multifold. These releases have allowed him to expand his fan base, establish his reputation within the music community, experiment with new concepts and collaborations, receive critical acclaim, secure prominent festival performances, and elevate his live shows. By consistently delivering high-quality albums that showcase his evolution as an artist, Bear Grillz has solidified his position as one of the leading figures in the electronic music scene. As he continues to release new albums and explore new musical territories, the impact of these releases on his career is sure to be a driving force for his ongoing success.

Subsection: Bear Grillz's role in diversifying the electronic music genre

Bear Grillz, the enigmatic and charismatic music producer, has had a profound impact on the electronic music genre. With his unique sound and groundbreaking approach, he has played a crucial role in diversifying the genre and pushing its boundaries. In this section, we will delve into the ways Bear Grillz has contributed to the evolution and expansion of electronic music.

Bear Grillz's exploration of different sub-genres

One of the key ways Bear Grillz has diversified the electronic music genre is through his exploration of different sub-genres. While being primarily known for his signature Bearstep style, which blends elements of dubstep and trap, Bear Grillz has also experimented with various other sub-genres such as drum and bass, future bass, and even melodic dubstep.

By venturing into these different sub-genres, Bear Grillz has introduced his fans to a diverse range of sounds and styles, broadening their musical horizons. Moreover, his willingness to experiment and incorporate elements from different sub-genres has helped break down the traditional barriers that once defined the genre, paving the way for a more inclusive and diverse electronic music scene.

Influencing the sound of the genre

Bear Grillz's distinct sound has had a profound influence on the wider electronic music landscape. His groundbreaking Bearstep sound, characterized by heavy basslines, unique synth textures, and energetic drops, has inspired a new generation of producers and artists.

Many emerging artists have looked to Bear Grillz as a source of inspiration, using his sound as a foundation for their own productions. As a result, the electronic music genre has experienced an influx of fresh and innovative sounds, pushing the boundaries of what is traditionally considered "electronic music."

Collaborations that defined Bear Grillz's sound

Bear Grillz's collaborations with other artists have played a significant role in diversifying the electronic music genre. By working with artists from different musical backgrounds and genres, Bear Grillz has introduced his audience to new and exciting sounds.

For example, his collaborations with hip-hop artists have blurred the lines between electronic music and rap, creating an entirely new sub-genre known as "trap music." This fusion of electronic and hip-hop elements has not only brought hip-hop fans into the electronic music scene but has also encouraged electronic music enthusiasts to explore the world of rap and trap.

Embracing musical diversity

One of Bear Grillz's most significant contributions to diversifying the electronic music genre is his embrace of musical diversity. He has consistently emphasized the importance of drawing inspiration from a wide range of musical styles outside the electronic genre.

By incorporating elements from genres such as rock, metal, classical music, and even folk, Bear Grillz has challenged the conventions of electronic music and brought a new level of depth and richness to his productions. This integration of diverse musical influences has not only expanded the sonic palette of electronic music but has also allowed for greater artistic expression and a more inclusive representation of different musical cultures.

Fostering collaboration and innovation

Bear Grillz's commitment to collaboration and innovation has played a pivotal role in diversifying the electronic music genre. Through partnerships with fellow producers, vocalists, and musicians, he has fostered a spirit of creativity and interdisciplinary collaboration.

By actively seeking out diverse perspectives and bringing together artists with different backgrounds, Bear Grillz has facilitated the exchange of ideas and the fusion of musical styles. This has resulted in the creation of unique and groundbreaking music that transcends traditional genre boundaries.

Championing emerging talent

Bear Grillz has also played a significant role in diversifying the electronic music genre by championing emerging talent. Through his label and production company, he has provided a platform for up-and-coming artists to showcase their skills and contribute their unique voices to the genre.

By actively seeking out and promoting diverse talent, Bear Grillz has contributed to a more inclusive and representative electronic music community. This has not only given emerging artists the opportunity to gain recognition but has also injected fresh perspectives and sounds into the genre, further diversifying and enriching its landscape.

Inspiring a global movement

Bear Grillz's impact extends beyond just the music itself. His authenticity, energy, and dedication to his craft have inspired a global movement of fans and aspiring artists who aim to emulate his success and make their mark on the electronic music scene.

Through his performances, Bear Grillz has created a sense of unity and belonging among his fans, fostering a community that celebrates diversity and encourages self-expression. This global movement has further contributed to the diversification of the electronic music genre, as fans from all walks of life come together to embrace the limitless possibilities of electronic music.

In conclusion, Bear Grillz's role in diversifying the electronic music genre cannot be overstated. Through his exploration of different sub-genres, influence on the sound of the genre, collaborations, embrace of musical diversity, fostering collaboration and innovation, championing emerging talent, and inspiring a global movement, Bear Grillz has not only expanded the sonic boundaries of electronic music but has also created a more inclusive and diverse musical landscape for future generations to explore and enjoy.

Section 4: Live Performances and Bear Grillz's Signature Tracks

Subsection: The energy and intensity of a Bear Grillz show

The energy and intensity of a Bear Grillz show are unlike anything you've ever experienced. From the moment the first bassline hits, the crowd is transported into a world of sonic bliss and pure, unadulterated energy. Bear Grillz knows how to captivate an audience and keep them on their feet from start to finish.

One of the key elements that contributes to the energy of a Bear Grillz show is the carefully curated setlist. Bear Grillz has a knack for selecting tracks that not only showcase his own unique sound but also resonate with the crowd. Each song builds upon the energy of the previous one, creating a seamless flow of music that keeps the energy levels high throughout the entire performance.

But it's not just the music that drives the energy of a Bear Grillz show. The visuals and stage production play a crucial role in creating an immersive experience for the audience. From stunning LED screens to mind-blowing pyrotechnics, Bear Grillz pulls out all the stops to deliver a visually captivating show. The combination of pulsating beats and visually stunning displays creates an atmosphere that is nothing short of euphoric.

The interaction between Bear Grillz and the audience also contributes to the energy of the show. Bear Grillz has a natural ability to connect with the crowd, effortlessly hyping them up and getting them involved in the performance. Whether it's engaging in call-and-response chants or encouraging crowd surfing, Bear Grillz knows how to keep the energy levels high and the crowd engaged.

The live instrumentation in Bear Grillz's shows adds an extra layer of intensity to the performance. From live drummers to guitarists, the addition of these elements brings a raw and organic feel to the music. This fusion of electronic and live elements creates a dynamic and exhilarating experience that sets Bear Grillz apart from other artists in the genre.

But perhaps the most important factor that contributes to the energy and intensity of a Bear Grillz show is the sheer passion and dedication that Bear Grillz brings to every performance. His love for what he does is palpable, and this enthusiasm spreads like wildfire among the audience. Bear Grillz's energy is infectious, and you can't help but get swept up in the excitement of the show.

To truly understand the energy and intensity of a Bear Grillz show, you have to experience it for yourself. It's an immersive and exhilarating experience that will leave you craving more. So, grab your dancing shoes and get ready to unleash your wild side at a Bear Grillz show. You won't be disappointed.

Example problem:
Imagine you are attending a Bear Grillz show, and you notice that the crowd's energy is not quite as high as you expected. What can you do to help create a more intense and energetic atmosphere?

Solution:
Creating a high-energy atmosphere at a live show is not solely the artist's responsibility; the audience plays a significant role as well. If you want to contribute to the intensity and energy of the show, here are a few things you can do:

1. Get Moving: Start by getting your body moving to the music. Dance, jump, and let loose. Your energy will be contagious, inspiring those around you to do the same.

2. Engage with the Artist: Show your appreciation for Bear Grillz by cheering, clapping, and shouting during key moments of the performance. The artist thrives on the energy of the crowd, so let him know you're enjoying the show.

3. Connect with Fellow Fans: Strike up conversations with the people around you, sharing your excitement for the music and the performance. This sense of camaraderie and shared enthusiasm will elevate the energy in the crowd.

4. Participate in Crowd Interactions: Don't be afraid to join in on the call-and-response chants or other crowd interactions initiated by Bear Grillz. The more you engage with these moments, the more electric the atmosphere becomes.

5. Spread the Energy: If you notice that people around you seem a bit subdued, be the spark that ignites the fire. Encourage others to join in the excitement and create a sense of unity and shared energy throughout the crowd.

Remember, your energy and enthusiasm contribute to the overall atmosphere of the show. By actively engaging and creating a sense of electricity in the crowd, you can help elevate the energy and intensity of the Bear Grillz experience for everyone involved.

Resources:
1. "The Art of Live Performance: Engaging the Crowd and Building Energy" - A comprehensive guide to creating an electric atmosphere at live shows.

2. "Crowd Psychology and Behavior: Understanding the Dynamics of Group Energy" - A book that explores the psychological aspects of crowd behavior and how it influences energy levels at events.

3. "Stage Presence and Performance Techniques" - A video series featuring tips and tricks from professional performers on how to command the stage and create an energetic atmosphere.

4. Bear Grillz's live performance videos - Watching recordings of Bear Grillz's live shows can give you a sense of the energy and intensity to expect, and provide inspiration for creating a similar atmosphere at other live events.

Tips and Tricks:

1. Hydrate and Rest: To maintain your energy throughout the show, make sure you are well-rested and hydrated beforehand. Dancing and jumping for an extended period can be physically demanding, so taking care of yourself before the show will ensure you can keep the energy going.

2. Dress for Comfort: Choose clothing and footwear that allow you to move freely and comfortably. Being physically comfortable will enable you to participate fully in the show without restriction.

3. Arrive Early: Getting to the venue early will give you a chance to secure a good spot close to the stage. Being closer to the action will enhance your overall experience and allow you to feel more connected to the energy of the performance.

4. Be Open to New Experiences: Embrace the unfamiliar and be open to new sounds and genres of music that you may encounter during the show. This openness will broaden your musical horizons and allow you to fully immerse yourself in the performance.

5. Capture the Moment: Take a few moments during the show to put away your phone or camera and simply be present. Engage with the music and the energy of the crowd without distractions, and truly savor the experience.

Remember, a Bear Grillz show is all about losing yourself in the music and embracing the wild side within. So let go of inhibitions, unleash your energy, and let Bear Grillz take you on a sonic journey you won't soon forget.

Subsection: Fan Reactions to Signature Tracks During Live Performances

The live performances of Bear Grillz are known to be energetic and intense, creating an electrifying atmosphere that leaves fans in awe. One of the highlights of these performances is when Bear Grillz plays his signature tracks, which evoke a strong emotional response from the audience. In this subsection, we will explore the fan reactions to these tracks and how they contribute to the overall concert experience.

Music has an incredible power to connect people, and Bear Grillz's signature tracks have become anthems for his fans. When the first notes of these tracks hit the speakers, the crowd erupts with excitement, screaming and cheering in anticipation. The energy in the room becomes palpable as fans unite in their love for Bear Grillz's music.

One of Bear Grillz's most iconic tracks, "Demons," never fails to get the crowd jumping. With its heavy bass drops and catchy melodies, this track has become a fan favorite. As soon as the familiar intro starts, a wave of excitement ripples through the audience, and bodies start moving to the rhythm. The energy reaches its peak when the drop hits, and the crowd erupts into a mass of jumping, headbanging fans. It's a sight to behold, as fans lose themselves in the music and create an electrifying atmosphere.

Another track that elicits an incredible response from fans is "Survive." The track, with its powerful lyrics and infectious beats, has become an anthem of resilience for many. As Bear Grillz performs this track live, fans can be seen singing along with every word, their voices blending with the music. The emotional connection between the artist and the audience is palpable, as everyone unites in their shared experiences and triumphs. It's a moment of catharsis and empowerment, as fans find solace in the music and know that they are not alone in their struggles.

"Drop That" is another signature track that never fails to ignite the crowd. The heavy basslines and intense drops create an atmosphere of anticipation and excitement. As Bear Grillz builds up to the drop, the tension in the room rises, and fans hold their breath in anticipation. And when the drop finally hits, all hell breaks loose. The crowd explodes with energy, jumping, dancing, and releasing their pent-up enthusiasm. It's a moment of pure euphoria, as fans surrender themselves to the music and let go of all inhibitions.

These fan reactions are just a glimpse of the incredible energy and connection that Bear Grillz creates during his live performances. His tracks have become anthems for his fans, resonating deeply with their emotions and experiences. The raw energy and passion in these moments are what make Bear Grillz's concerts truly unforgettable.

But it's not just the music that creates such an immersive concert experience. Bear Grillz's stage presence and interaction with the crowd play a significant role in fostering the intense energy. He feeds off the audience's enthusiasm, often hyping them up and encouraging them to fully embrace the music. Bear Grillz's charismatic and energetic performance style draws fans in, making them feel like an integral part of the show.

In addition to the thrilling performances, the visual effects and production elements further enhance the fan experience. The use of eye-catching visuals, dynamic lighting, and immersive stage design creates a multi-sensory experience that amplifies the impact of the music. Fans are not only hearing the music; they are also seeing and feeling it, creating a deeper connection to the performance.

Moreover, the collective experience of being in a crowd of like-minded individuals who share a passion for Bear Grillz's music adds another layer to the fan reactions. The sense of unity and belonging that fans feel in these moments is powerful. It creates a bond among concert-goers, fostering a community that extends beyond the music. The shared memories and experiences at Bear Grillz's concerts become lasting connections that fans carry with them long after the show ends.

In conclusion, the fan reactions to Bear Grillz's signature tracks during live performances are nothing short of electrifying. From jumping and headbanging to singing along with every word, fans fully immerse themselves in the music, creating an intense and unforgettable concert experience. Bear Grillz's ability to connect with the audience and create a sense of unity further amplifies these reactions. The combination of powerful tracks, engaging stage presence, visual effects, and the shared experience within the fan community makes Bear Grillz's live performances a truly thrilling and memorable event.

Subsection: Behind-the-scenes of preparing for a live set

Preparing for a live set is an essential part of Bear Grillz's career. It requires meticulous planning and attention to detail to ensure a smooth and memorable performance. In this subsection, we will take a behind-the-scenes look at the process Bear Grillz goes through when preparing for a live set, from selecting tracks to setting up the stage.

Selecting tracks for the set

One of the key aspects of preparing for a live set is selecting the right tracks to play. Bear Grillz takes great care in curating his setlist to create a unique and engaging experience for his audience. He considers various factors, such as the energy level of the crowd, the venue, and the overall theme of the performance.

To begin, Bear Grillz starts by categorizing his tracks into different playlists based on their energy levels. He understands the importance of transitioning smoothly from one track to another, keeping the audience engaged and maintaining the energy on the dancefloor. By organizing his tracks in this way, he can easily identify which songs will flow well together during the live set.

Bear Grillz also pays attention to the audience's preferences and the current trends in electronic music. He stays up-to-date with the latest releases and incorporates popular tracks that resonate with his fans. Additionally, he adds his signature tracks and remixes, ensuring that the setlist reflects his unique sound and style.

Creating a cohesive narrative

A live set is not just a collection of individual tracks – it is a story that unfolds over time. Bear Grillz puts a lot of thought into creating a cohesive narrative for his performances. He considers the emotions he wants to evoke and the journey he wants to take the audience on.

To achieve this, Bear Grillz focuses on the arrangement and structure of his setlist. He carefully plans the order in which the tracks will be played, considering their individual strengths and how they complement each other. He builds up anticipation, creates climactic moments, and adds slower sections for the audience to catch their breath. By carefully curating the sequence of tracks, Bear Grillz ensures that the performance has a natural flow and keeps the audience engaged from start to finish.

Technical setup and stage design

Another crucial aspect of preparing for a live set is the technical setup and stage design. Bear Grillz believes in creating an immersive visual and auditory experience for his audience, and this requires careful attention to detail.

Firstly, Bear Grillz works closely with his team to set up the audio equipment. They ensure that the sound system is optimized for the venue and calibrated to deliver the best possible sound quality. This includes adjusting the levels, equalization, and spatial distribution to ensure that every beat and note is heard clearly throughout the venue.

In terms of stage design, Bear Grillz incorporates elements that reinforce his bear-themed persona and overall brand. This can include large LED screens displaying custom visuals, bear-themed props and decorations, and immersive lighting effects. The goal is to create a visually stunning and immersive environment that complements his music and engages the audience on multiple sensory levels.

Rehearsing and refining the performance

Once the technical setup is complete, Bear Grillz dedicates time for rehearsal and fine-tuning the performance. He believes in delivering a flawless and unforgettable experience, and this requires practice and attention to detail.

During rehearsals, Bear Grillz focuses on several key aspects. Firstly, he works on perfecting the transitions between tracks, ensuring that they are seamless and create a cohesive flow. He pays attention to the timing, beatmatching, and mixing techniques to create a smooth and professional-sounding performance.

Secondly, Bear Grillz incorporates live elements into his set. This can involve playing instruments, using MIDI controllers, or adding live vocals. He practices these elements to ensure that they integrate seamlessly with the pre-recorded tracks and enhance the overall performance.

Furthermore, Bear Grillz constantly seeks feedback from his team and trusted collaborators. He values their opinions and suggestions, using them to refine the performance and make necessary adjustments. This collaborative process helps him identify areas for improvement and ensures that the final performance meets his exacting standards.

The importance of connecting with the audience

Beyond the technical aspects of preparing for a live set, Bear Grillz understands the importance of connecting with his audience on an emotional level. He believes that a great performance is not just about playing the right tracks or having impressive visuals – it is about creating a memorable experience that touches people's hearts.

To achieve this, Bear Grillz immerses himself in the energy of the crowd during the rehearsal process. He visualizes the audience's reactions, anticipates their emotions, and plans moments of interaction and engagement. Whether it's encouraging the crowd to raise their hands, sing along, or jump to the beat, Bear Grillz knows that creating a sense of unity and shared experience is essential for a successful live set.

During the actual performance, Bear Grillz pays close attention to the audience's reactions and adjusts his set accordingly. He feeds off their energy and uses it to elevate the performance to new heights. By connecting with the audience in this way, Bear Grillz ensures that each live set is a unique experience that leaves a lasting impression.

In conclusion, preparing for a live set is a complex and multifaceted process that involves careful track selection, creating a cohesive narrative, technical setup, rehearsals, and connecting with the audience. Bear Grillz's attention to detail and dedication to delivering a memorable experience shines through in every aspect of his performance. It is this commitment to excellence that has catapulted him to the forefront of the electronic music scene, and continues to captivate audiences around the world.

Trick: One trick that Bear Grillz employs to keep the audience engaged is to unexpectedly mix in snippets of popular songs from different genres. This surprises and excites the crowd, creating a memorable moment and often prompting sing-alongs and increased energy on the dancefloor.

Exercise: Imagine you are preparing for a live set as a DJ or performer. Create a setlist that reflects your unique style and sound, paying attention to the energy levels and flow of the tracks. Consider how you would engage with the audience during the performance and what elements you would incorporate to create a visually appealing and immersive experience.

Resources: - Bear Grillz live performances and interviews available online - Articles and books on DJing and live performance techniques - Music production software and hardware for creating and refining live sets

Caveat: The preparation process for a live set may vary depending on the artist's individual style and preferences. This subsection provides insights into Bear Grillz's approach, but it is important to adapt these principles to your own unique artistic vision and goals.

Subsection: How Bear Grillz keeps his performances fresh and exciting

Bear Grillz is known for his high-energy and electrifying live performances. He understands the importance of keeping his shows fresh and exciting to captivate his audience and leave a lasting impression. In this subsection, we will explore the strategies and techniques used by Bear Grillz to ensure that every performance is unique and unforgettable.

Incorporating New Visual Effects

One way Bear Grillz keeps his performances fresh is by incorporating new and innovative visual effects. He understands that a visually captivating show can greatly enhance the overall experience for his fans. By using cutting-edge technology and creative stage design, Bear Grillz creates a mesmerizing visual spectacle that complements his music. From pyrotechnics and LED screens to lasers and confetti cannons, every element is carefully curated to immerse the audience in a fully immersive audio-visual experience.

Surprising Mashups and Remixes

Bear Grillz keeps his performances fresh and exciting by incorporating surprising mashups and remixes into his sets. He takes well-known tracks from various genres and infuses them with his signature Bearstep sound. This unexpected combination of songs creates a unique and thrilling experience for his fans, keeping them on their toes and always guessing what will come next. Bear Grillz's ability to seamlessly blend different genres and styles sets him apart and keeps his performances dynamic and fresh.

Live Instrumentation and Guest Performances

To add an element of live instrumentation and surprise to his shows, Bear Grillz often invites guest performers to join him on stage. These guest performances could include live instrumentalists, vocalists, or even fellow electronic music artists. By incorporating live elements into his performances, Bear Grillz creates a dynamic and interactive experience for the audience. The unpredictability of live instruments and collaborations adds an extra layer of excitement and keeps the shows fresh and dynamic.

Interactive Fan Engagement

Bear Grillz understands the importance of engaging with his fans during his performances. He actively interacts with the audience, whether it be through shoutouts, call-and-response segments, or simply making eye contact and acknowledging them. This level of fan engagement creates a sense of intimacy and inclusivity, making the audience feel like an integral part of the show. By actively involving his fans, Bear Grillz ensures that each performance is not only exciting but also a memorable experience for everyone in attendance.

Evolving Stage Presence and Theatrics

Another way Bear Grillz keeps his performances fresh and exciting is by continuously evolving his stage presence and theatrics. He understands that the audience craves new experiences and surprises, and he delivers just that. Whether it's incorporating new dance moves, acrobatics, or theatrical elements, Bear Grillz goes the extra mile to provide an immersive and theatrical experience that leaves a lasting impression. He keeps his performance persona ever-changing and adapts to the evolving tastes and expectations of his audience, ensuring that every show is a unique experience.

Creating Setlist Variations

Bear Grillz avoids monotony in his performances by creating setlist variations for different shows. While he includes fan favorites and signature tracks in each performance, he also introduces new tracks, remixes, and mashups to keep the audience engaged and excited. By constantly updating his setlists, Bear Grillz ensures that even his most dedicated fans are treated to fresh and unique experiences each time they see him live.

Experimenting with New Technologies

To push the boundaries of live performances, Bear Grillz is not afraid to experiment with new technologies. He constantly seeks out innovative tools, software, and equipment that can elevate his shows to new heights. From utilizing virtual reality to incorporate immersive visuals to experimenting with interactive lighting systems controlled by his music, Bear Grillz is always on the lookout for ways to enhance the overall experience for his fans.

Surprise Guest Appearances

Part of what makes Bear Grillz's performances so exciting is the possibility of surprise guest appearances. Bear Grillz often brings fellow artists on stage to perform together, creating a unique and unforgettable experience for both himself and the audience. These surprise appearances not only add a sense of anticipation and excitement but also showcase the collaborative and supportive nature of the electronic music community.

Engaging Stage Dialogue

Bear Grillz keeps his performances fresh by engaging the audience through stage dialogue. He uses humor, anecdotes, and personal stories to connect with his fans on a deeper level. By sharing these moments, Bear Grillz creates an intimate and authentic atmosphere, making his shows not just about the music, but also about the connection between the artist and the audience. This engagement keeps the performances exciting and memorable.

Evolution of Stage Production

Bear Grillz is constantly pushing the boundaries of stage production to create fresh and exciting performances. He invests time and effort into evolving his stage setup, incorporating new technologies, and experimenting with unique visual and audio elements. Whether it's through intricate stage designs, custom visuals, or immersive lighting setups, Bear Grillz ensures that his performances are visually stunning and technologically advanced, providing his audience with an unforgettable experience.

In conclusion, Bear Grillz understands the importance of keeping his performances fresh and exciting. By incorporating new visual effects, surprising mashups, live instrumentation, interactive fan engagement, evolving stage presence, setlist variations, and experimenting with new technologies, he creates an immersive experience that leaves a lasting impression on his audience. Bear Grillz's

dedication to providing unique and unforgettable performances sets him apart as a
dynamic and innovative artist in the electronic music scene.

Subsection: The evolution of Bear Grillz's live performances over time

Bear Grillz's live performances have undergone a remarkable evolution throughout
his career, from small club gigs to headlining major festivals. This section explores
the key milestones and changes in Bear Grillz's live shows, offering insights into the
progression of his stage presence, performance style, and engagement with the
audience.

Early Performances and Experimental Stage Persona

In the early stages of his career, Bear Grillz's live performances were characterized
by a sense of raw energy and experimentation. As a relatively unknown artist, he
performed in smaller venues and underground electronic music events. These
intimate settings allowed Bear Grillz to connect with his audience on a personal
level, fostering a unique sense of camaraderie between the artist and the fans.

During this period, Bear Grillz began to develop his stage persona,
incorporating elements of humor and mystery into his performances. He wore his
signature bear mask, which quickly became an iconic symbol of his identity as an
artist. The mask served as a visual representation of Bear Grillz's commitment to
creating a larger-than-life experience for his audience, while also providing a sense
of anonymity and detachment from his personal identity.

Transition to Larger Venues and Festivals

As Bear Grillz's popularity grew, so did the scale of his live performances. He started
being invited to perform at larger clubs and music festivals, which presented new
challenges and opportunities for him to evolve as a live artist. The transition to larger
venues demanded a more elaborate production setup, including enhanced lighting,
visual effects, and stage design.

To adapt to the evolving demands of his growing fanbase, Bear Grillz developed
a more polished and theatrical stage presence. He embraced the grandeur of festival
stages, using larger-than-life visuals, pyrotechnics, and captivating stage props to
create a truly immersive experience for his audience. Each live performance became
a carefully orchestrated journey, designed to transport the audience into Bear Grillz's
musical universe.

Integration of Live Instruments and Guest Performances

One notable aspect of the evolution of Bear Grillz's live performances is the integration of live instruments and guest performances. As he gained recognition within the music industry, Bear Grillz began collaborating with talented musicians and vocalists, bringing a new dimension to his performances.

Incorporating live instruments into his sets added an organic and dynamic element to Bear Grillz's sound, creating a powerful fusion between electronic music and live instrumentation. The inclusion of guest performers further enriched the live experience, allowing Bear Grillz to collaborate with like-minded artists and showcase their talents on stage. These collaborations brought a sense of unpredictability and excitement to Bear Grillz's live performances, captivating the audience and elevating the overall energy of the show.

Interactive and Immersive Experiences

Bear Grillz is known for his ability to engage and connect with his audience during his live performances. Over time, he has developed various techniques to create an interactive and immersive experience for his fans.

One notable element of Bear Grillz's live shows is his engagement with the crowd. Through his charismatic stage presence, he encourages audience participation, often leading the crowd in chants or dance moves. This direct interaction creates a sense of unity and joy, fostering a vibrant and inclusive atmosphere.

Additionally, Bear Grillz incorporates immersive visuals to enhance the sensory experience of his shows. LED screens, synchronized with the music, project vibrant and captivating visuals that synchronize with the beats, creating a mesmerizing spectacle for the audience. The combination of immersive visuals and interactive elements transports the audience into a world of sonic and visual wonder, leaving a lasting impression on their concert experience.

Innovation in Live Sound and Technology

Throughout his career, Bear Grillz has consistently pushed the boundaries of live sound and technology in his performances. He has embraced innovative technologies and equipment to enhance the quality and impact of his live shows.

One notable innovation is the use of advanced sound systems and spatial audio techniques. Bear Grillz incorporates surround sound and immersive audio to create a three-dimensional sonic experience. By strategically placing speakers throughout the venue, he envelops the audience in a multidimensional sound field, enhancing the overall depth and richness of his music.

Furthermore, Bear Grillz has harnessed the power of live remixing and improvisation. He utilizes cutting-edge software and controllers to manipulate and shape his tracks in real-time during his performances. This improvisational approach allows him to tailor each show to the unique energy of the audience, creating a personalized and one-of-a-kind experience for his fans.

Unconventional Performances and Unexpected Surprises

Bear Grillz's live performances are never predictable. He thrives on spontaneity and surprise, often incorporating unconventional elements into his shows to keep the audience on their toes. From impromptu cover songs to surprise appearances by fellow artists, Bear Grillz constantly seeks to deliver memorable and unexpected moments to his fans.

One example of an unconventional performance is his acoustic sets. On select occasions, Bear Grillz sets aside his electronic production gear and showcases his versatility as a musician by performing live with acoustic instruments. This stripped-down approach showcases a different side of his artistry, allowing for a more intimate and introspective connection with his audience.

Another surprise element is Bear Grillz's interactions with the audience outside of live shows. He has been known to organize impromptu street performances or surprise pop-up DJ sets in unexpected locations. These offbeat and spontaneous performances create a sense of magic and excitement, leaving fans eagerly anticipating the next unexpected encounter.

The Continuing Evolution

Bear Grillz's live performances continue to evolve as he pushes the boundaries of his artistry and embraces new technologies and techniques. With each new tour and festival appearance, he seeks to expand the horizons of what a live performance can be, blurring the lines between music, technology, and immersive experiences.

As Bear Grillz's career progresses, fans can expect even more ambitious stage productions, unexpected collaborations, and an unyielding commitment to delivering unparalleled live experiences. By staying true to his distinctive persona and dedication to creating unforgettable moments, Bear Grillz remains at the forefront of innovation in live electronic music performances.

In conclusion, the evolution of Bear Grillz's live performances is a testament to his artistic growth and commitment to providing unparalleled experiences for his fans. From his early days in small venues to headlining major festivals, Bear Grillz continuously pushes the boundaries of live performances, incorporating innovative technologies, unexpected surprises, and immersive elements that captivate and delight his audience. His evolution as a live performer serves as an inspiration to aspiring artists and a testament to the enduring power of live electronic music experiences.

Subsection: The role of visual effects in Bear Grillz's live shows

Visual effects play a crucial role in enhancing the live performances of Bear Grillz. They create a captivating and immersive experience for the audience, amplifying the impact of his music and stage presence. In this subsection, we will explore the various visual effects used in Bear Grillz's live shows, their significance, and the techniques employed to create an awe-inspiring visual spectacle.

Creating an Atmosphere

Bear Grillz's live shows are known for their electrifying atmosphere, and visual effects contribute significantly to creating this immersive experience. Lighting plays a vital role in setting the mood and enhancing the energy of the performance. Colorful spotlights, strobes, lasers, and LED panels are strategically used to match the tempo and intensity of the music, taking the audience on a visual journey that complements the sonic experience.

Synchronizing with the Music

One of the key aspects of Bear Grillz's live shows is the synchronization of visual effects with the music. This synchronization enhances the impact of the sound, making it a multisensory experience for the audience. Visual effects are carefully choreographed to match the beat drops, build-ups, and melodic sections of the music, creating a seamless fusion of sight and sound.

To achieve this synchronization, Bear Grillz works closely with a team of visual artists and technicians. They use specialized software and hardware systems to connect the lighting, lasers, and LED panels to the music. This technology allows the visual effects to adapt dynamically to changes in tempo, rhythm, and melody, resulting in a synchronized and immersive experience.

Stage Design and Props

In addition to lighting and lasers, Bear Grillz's live shows often incorporate elaborate stage designs and props. These elements serve to enhance the visual impact and create a unique atmosphere. For example, towering LED screens may be used to display captivating visuals, such as animated graphics, abstract patterns, or even footage from nature to align with Bear Grillz's connection to wildlife and the wilderness.

Props like bear-themed sculptures, inflatable animals, or nature-inspired backdrops further enhance the visual storytelling and contribute to the immersive experience. These elements not only add to the visual spectacle but also reinforce Bear Grillz's brand identity and the themes he embraces in his music and persona.

Video Mapping and Projection

Video mapping and projection techniques are frequently employed in Bear Grillz's live shows to transform the stage into a dynamic canvas. Video mapping involves projecting visuals onto complex surfaces, such as stage elements, props, or even the artist themselves, in a way that creates an illusion of depth and movement.

By using intricately designed video content and precise mapping techniques, Bear Grillz can turn his stage into a mesmerizing visual landscape. The projected visuals can range from abstract animations to synchronized imagery that follows the contours of the stage, amplifying the impact of the music and immersing the audience in a completely transformed environment.

Pyrotechnics and Special Effects

To add an extra layer of excitement and spectacle, Bear Grillz's live shows often incorporate pyrotechnics and other special effects. Carefully timed bursts of flames, fireworks, smoke, and confetti create dramatic moments that further engage the audience and elevate the overall experience.

Pyrotechnics and special effects are strategically integrated into the performance, enhancing specific musical sections or creating climactic moments in the set. These visual elements not only heighten the energy in the room but also serve as visual cues for the audience, intensifying their emotional connection to the performance.

Interactive Visuals and Audience Participation

Bear Grillz's live shows often feature interactive visuals and encourage audience participation. Through the use of technology and motion sensors, the audience's movements and reactions can trigger visual effects, creating an immersive and participatory experience.

For instance, motion-controlled LED wristbands or mobile apps may allow the audience to become part of the visual display, synchronized with the music and other on-stage effects. This interactive element strengthens the bond between artist and audience, making each show a unique and memorable experience for everyone involved.

Unconventional Visual Techniques

In addition to the more traditional visual effects mentioned above, Bear Grillz often incorporates unconventional techniques to create stunning visual moments on stage. These may include the use of holographic projections, 3D mapping techniques, or even innovative use of mirrors and reflective surfaces to create optical illusions and unique visual distortions.

These unconventional visual techniques not only captivate the audience but also add an element of surprise and curiosity to the live performance. By pushing the boundaries of traditional visual effects, Bear Grillz continuously strives to deliver an unforgettable and cutting-edge experience for his fans.

Safety and Considerations

While visual effects are crucial to Bear Grillz's live shows, safety is paramount. Specialized technicians and safety experts work closely to ensure that all visual effects, especially pyrotechnics and special effects, are implemented with utmost care and adherence to safety protocols. Rigorous testing, rehearsals, and risk assessments are conducted to minimize any potential hazards and ensure the well-being of both the artist and the audience.

Conclusion

Visual effects play an integral role in the success of Bear Grillz's live shows. From lighting and lasers to stage design and video mapping, these effects create an immersive and multisensory experience for the audience. By synchronizing visual elements with the music, Bear Grillz elevates his performance to a new level, offering a unique and unforgettable experience that resonates with his fans. Through innovative and unconventional visual techniques, Bear Grillz continues to push the boundaries of live performances, leaving a lasting impact on the electronic music scene.

Subsection: Creating memorable moments in a live Bear Grillz set

In a live Bear Grillz set, creating memorable moments is essential to engage the audience and make the performance truly unforgettable. It's not just about delivering great music, but also about connecting with the crowd and leaving a lasting impression. In this subsection, we will explore some of the techniques and strategies that Bear Grillz uses to create these memorable moments in his live shows.

Understanding the audience

One of the first steps in creating memorable moments is understanding the audience. Bear Grillz takes the time to research and analyze the demographics and preferences of his fans in different locations. This allows him to tailor his setlist and performance to the specific audience he is performing for. By understanding their musical taste and preferences, Bear Grillz can curate a set that resonates with his fans and keeps them engaged throughout the show.

Dynamic visuals and stage design

Visuals play a crucial role in setting the mood and creating a captivating atmosphere during a live performance. Bear Grillz invests in visually stunning stage designs and incorporates dynamic visuals that complement his music. LED screens, lighting effects, and pyrotechnics are some of the elements he uses to create a multisensory experience for the audience. These visuals not only enhance the overall performance but also leave a lasting visual impact on the audience, making the show more memorable.

Interactive elements and crowd participation

Bear Grillz actively involves the crowd in his performances to increase their engagement and create a sense of unity. He encourages crowd participation through various interactive elements, such as call-and-response moments, sing-alongs, and hand gestures. By giving the audience an active role in the performance, Bear Grillz fosters a deeper connection and creates a sense of camaraderie among the fans. These interactive moments not only make the show more memorable but also leave a lasting impression on the audience.

Surprise elements

To keep the audience on their toes and create moments of surprise and excitement, Bear Grillz incorporates unexpected elements into his live sets. These surprise elements can include special guest appearances, unreleased tracks, or remixes of popular songs. By introducing unexpected moments throughout the performance, Bear Grillz leaves the audience in awe and creates memories that will stay with them long after the show is over.

Energy and stage presence

One of the most important factors in creating memorable moments is the energy and stage presence of the performer. Bear Grillz brings a high level of energy to his live sets, which is infectious and spreads to the audience. His dynamic presence on stage, combined with his passionate performance, captivates the audience and creates an electric atmosphere. By fully immersing himself in the music and engaging with the crowd, Bear Grillz creates unforgettable moments that resonate with the audience.

Incorporating storytelling

Storytelling is a powerful tool that Bear Grillz uses to create memorable moments in his live performances. He weaves a narrative throughout his set, taking the audience on a journey that goes beyond just playing tracks. By carefully selecting and arranging songs, Bear Grillz creates a musical narrative that tells a story and evokes emotions in the audience. This storytelling approach adds depth and meaning to the performance, making it more immersive and memorable.

Fan interactions and surprises

Bear Grillz values his fans and actively interacts with them during his live shows. He often takes time to connect with the crowd, whether it's through heartfelt speeches, going into the audience, or throwing merchandise into the crowd. These interactions make the fans feel seen and appreciated, and create moments of surprise and joy. By going the extra mile to engage with his fans, Bear Grillz creates a sense of community and leaves a lasting impression on his audience.

Encore performances

To create a truly memorable moment, Bear Grillz often includes an encore performance at the end of his set. This is a powerful way to leave the audience wanting more and make the show end on a high note. The anticipation and excitement of the crowd during the encore build up the energy in the room and create a climactic moment that lingers in the audience's memory. By carefully selecting the final track and delivering an electrifying performance, Bear Grillz ensures that the encore is a highlight of the show.

Conclusion

Creating memorable moments in a live Bear Grillz set involves a combination of factors, including understanding the audience, dynamic visuals and stage design, interactive elements, surprise elements, energy and stage presence, storytelling, fan interactions, and encore performances. By carefully planning and executing these elements, Bear Grillz crafts an unforgettable experience for his fans, leaving a lasting impact and making each show a unique and memorable event. So, if you have the chance to attend a Bear Grillz live performance, prepare yourself for an extraordinary experience that you won't soon forget.

Subsection: Fan participation and engagement in Bear Grillz's shows

Fan participation and engagement play a crucial role in the success of Bear Grillz's live shows. The energy and excitement created by the fans not only enhance the overall experience for everyone present but also contribute to the unique atmosphere that Bear Grillz strives to create. In this subsection, we will explore the various ways in which fans actively participate in Bear Grillz's shows and how their engagement adds to the magic of the live performances.

One of the most notable ways fans participate in Bear Grillz's shows is through their enthusiastic crowd interactions. Whether it's raising their hands, jumping, or dancing to the beats, the fans create a contagious energy that spreads throughout the venue. Bear Grillz actively encourages audience participation by frequently engaging with the crowd and hyping them up during his performances. This interaction helps establish a sense of unity, transforming the show from a simple performance into a shared experience between the artist and the fans.

Another exciting aspect of fan participation in Bear Grillz's shows is their involvement in sing-alongs. Many of Bear Grillz's tracks feature catchy, anthemic choruses that lend themselves well to audience participation. During these moments, the fans enthusiastically join in, belting out the lyrics in unison. This collective singing creates a powerful and memorable experience, fostering a sense of camaraderie among the audience members. It's a sight to behold when thousands of fans come together to create a chorus of voices that resonate through the venue.

In addition to crowd interactions and sing-alongs, Bear Grillz actively encourages fan engagement through carefully crafted moments of surprise and interaction. Throughout his shows, Bear Grillz often invites fans on stage to dance alongside him, creating memorable and intimate connections with his audience. This personal touch adds a unique and heartfelt element to the performances, making each show feel distinct and special. By involving his fans directly in the show, Bear Grillz creates a sense of inclusivity and appreciation that goes beyond the music itself.

Furthermore, technology and social media have played a significant role in fan participation and engagement at Bear Grillz's shows. Many fans capture and share their experiences on platforms like Instagram, Twitter, and YouTube, using official hashtags to connect with each other and the artist. This digital social aspect allows fans to extend their participation beyond the duration of the show, fostering a vibrant online community centered around Bear Grillz's music and performances. Through these platforms, fans share their thoughts, photos, and videos, creating a virtual space for ongoing engagement and excitement.

To encourage fan participation and engagement even further, Bear Grillz has been known to host pre-show meet-ups and fan gatherings. This allows fans to connect with each other before the show, sharing their excitement and building friendships within the Bear Fam, as Bear Grillz affectionately calls his fan community. These meet-ups also provide an opportunity for Bear Grillz to personally interact with his fans, offering words of encouragement and gratitude for their unwavering support.

In summary, fan participation and engagement are vital components of Bear Grillz's live shows. The enthusiasm and energy that fans bring to the performances create an unforgettable experience for everyone involved. By actively involving his fans through crowd interactions, sing-alongs, surprise on-stage moments, and social media interactions, Bear Grillz fosters a sense of unity, appreciation, and connection among his audience. In doing so, he transforms his shows into not just musical performances but shared experiences that leave a lasting impact on both the artist and his devoted fans.

Subsection: The connection between Bear Grillz and his audience during performances

One of the defining aspects of Bear Grillz's live performances is the deep connection he establishes with his audience. From the moment he steps on stage, Bear Grillz has an uncanny ability to create an electric atmosphere that captivates fans and makes them feel like an integral part of the experience. This connection is built on several key factors that contribute to the unique bond between Bear Grillz and his audience during performances.

Creating an Energetic Vibe

The first and most crucial element in building a strong connection between Bear Grillz and his audience is the energetic vibe he exudes on stage. From his infectious enthusiasm to his animated movements, Bear Grillz's energy is contagious. He knows how to command the attention of the crowd and keep them engaged throughout his entire set.

Bear Grillz's stage presence is electrifying, and he thrives on the energy he receives from his audience. He feeds off their excitement and uses it to fuel his performance, creating a feedback loop of positive energy that intensifies as the show progresses. This mutual exchange of energy is what makes his performances so memorable and allows him to forge a deep connection with his fans.

Building a Sense of Unity

Another vital aspect of the connection between Bear Grillz and his audience is the sense of unity that he fosters during his performances. He understands the power of music to bring people together, and he leverages this to create a collective experience that transcends individuality and boundaries.

Bear Grillz encourages his fans to let go of their inhibitions and fully immerse themselves in the music. He creates a safe and inclusive space where everyone can feel comfortable expressing themselves and embracing their love for the music. This sense of unity is reinforced by the visual storytelling and immersive elements that accompany his performances, fostering a shared experience that unites the audience.

Engaging with the Crowd

One of the most remarkable aspects of Bear Grillz's performances is his ability to engage with the crowd. He actively seeks out opportunities to interact with his fans, whether it's through eye contact, high-fives, or jumping into the audience. These interactions create a personal connection that makes each audience member feel seen and valued.

Bear Grillz's genuine and approachable demeanor makes fans feel like they are his friends rather than just spectators. He takes the time to connect with individual fans, understanding that each interaction is an opportunity to create a lasting memory. Even in large venues, he manages to make every person in the crowd feel like they are part of something intimate and special.

Creating Emotional Resonance

Beyond the energetic atmosphere and sense of unity, Bear Grillz's music resonates deeply with his audience on an emotional level. His tracks often carry uplifting messages of empowerment, resilience, and embracing one's true self. By infusing his music with powerful emotions, Bear Grillz is able to create a connection that transcends language and cultural barriers.

During his performances, Bear Grillz masterfully combines his music with visual elements that enhance the emotional impact. Whether it's through mesmerizing visuals, thought-provoking imagery, or synchronized light shows, he creates a multi-sensory experience that stirs the audience's emotions and leaves a lasting impression.

Encouraging Fan Participation

One of the most unique aspects of Bear Grillz's performances is his emphasis on fan participation. He actively encourages his audience to be more than passive observers and invites them to actively engage with the music. This can take the form of singing along to anthemic choruses, joining in on call-and-response moments, or even participating in impromptu dance-offs.

By involving his fans in the performance, Bear Grillz breaks down the barrier between artist and audience. He creates a sense of ownership and belonging, making each person feel like they are an essential part of the show. This level of fan participation fosters a sense of community and reinforces the connection between Bear Grillz and his audience.

The Emotional Impact of Live Performances

The emotional impact of Bear Grillz's live performances cannot be understated. His ability to connect with the audience on a deep emotional level goes beyond just creating a memorable concert experience. It touches the core of what it means to be human and reminds us of the transformative power of music.

For many fans, attending a Bear Grillz concert is not just about witnessing a talented artist perform; it's a cathartic and transformative experience. Through the bond he establishes with his audience, Bear Grillz creates a space where fans can let go of their worries and immerse themselves in the moment. He creates an emotional

sanctuary, allowing fans to experience joy, release, and connection in a way that few
other artists can.

In conclusion, the connection between Bear Grillz and his audience during
performances is multifaceted and powerful. Through his energetic vibe, sense of
unity, fan engagement, emotional resonance, and emphasis on fan participation,
Bear Grillz creates a live experience that transcends traditional notions of a
concert. His ability to forge a deep and lasting connection with his fans is a
testament to the impact he has on the lives of those who experience his music live.

Subsection: The transformative power of Bear Grillz's live shows

Bear Grillz's live shows are more than just a musical performance; they are
transformative experiences that leave audiences in awe. The combination of his
high-energy music, captivating visuals, and immersive atmosphere creates a unique
and unforgettable experience that has the power to transport listeners to another
world.

At the heart of Bear Grillz's live shows is his ability to connect with his
audience on a deep emotional level. Through his music, he is able to evoke a wide
range of emotions, from euphoria to introspection, and everything in between.
This emotional journey allows the audience to experience a catharsis, a release of
pent-up emotions that can be both healing and liberating.

The transformative power of Bear Grillz's live shows lies in his ability to create
a sense of unity and connection among his audience. Regardless of where you come
from or what your background is, when you step into a Bear Grillz show, you become
part of a community united by a shared love for music. This sense of belonging and
togetherness has a profound impact on the overall experience, making it not just a
concert, but a life-affirming event.

One of the key elements that contribute to the transformative power of Bear
Grillz's live shows is his attention to visual aesthetics. The use of stunning visuals,
lighting effects, and stage design creates a visual spectacle that complements the
music and enhances the overall sensory experience. From mesmerizing light shows
to breathtaking stage setups, Bear Grillz takes his audience on a visual journey that
adds an extra layer of immersion and engagement.

But it's not just the visuals that make Bear Grillz's live shows transformative;
it's also the energy he brings to the stage. His infectious enthusiasm and genuine
passion for his music radiate through every performance, creating an electrifying
atmosphere that is palpable. The energy in the room is contagious, and the audience
can't help but be swept up in the moment, dancing and singing along with pure joy
and abandon.

In addition to the energy and visuals, another aspect that contributes to the transformative power of Bear Grillz's live shows is his ability to create a sense of community engagement. He encourages audience participation, whether through interactive moments, call-and-response chants, or simply by creating an inclusive and welcoming environment where everyone feels comfortable expressing themselves. This fosters a sense of camaraderie and connection among concertgoers, further enhancing the transformative nature of the experience.

To truly understand the transformative power of Bear Grillz's live shows, it's important to hear from the fans themselves. Many have described his performances as life-changing, stating that the energy and positive vibes have the ability to uplift and inspire. People have shared stories of finding solace and strength in his music during difficult times, and the impact it has had on their mental and emotional well-being.

The transformative power of Bear Grillz's live shows extends beyond the boundaries of the concert venue. The shared experience fosters a sense of community that transcends geographical and cultural barriers. Fans connect with each other online, forming lasting friendships and support networks. This sense of belonging continues to resonate long after the show is over, creating a lasting impact on the lives of those who have experienced it.

In conclusion, the transformative power of Bear Grillz's live shows lies in his ability to create a sense of unity, connection, and emotional catharsis among his audience. Through his high-energy music, captivating visuals, and immersive atmosphere, he takes his audience on a journey of self-discovery, healing, and empowerment. The transformative experience of his live shows has a lasting impact on the lives of his fans, fostering a sense of community and personal growth.

Section 5: The Future of Bear Grillz's Music

Subsection: Teasers and hints for upcoming projects

As Bear Grillz continues to captivate audiences with his electrifying performances and unique sound, fans eagerly anticipate what the future holds for this enigmatic artist. In this section, we dive into exclusive teasers and hints for Bear Grillz's upcoming projects, giving you a glimpse of what to expect from this visionary musician.

1. **Album concept:** Bear Grillz has been hinting at an ambitious new album that will push the boundaries of his sound. Drawing inspiration from his global travels and diverse musical influences, this album promises to deliver a sonic journey like no

other. With cryptic hints about collaborations with both familiar and unexpected artists, this album is poised to be a game-changer in the electronic music genre.

2. **Exploring new genres:** True to Bear Grillz's adventurous spirit, he's been teasing his exploration of new musical territories. While maintaining his signature sound, he's been experimenting with elements of hip-hop, trap, and even rock. This evolution in his style promises to bring a fresh perspective to the electronic music scene and attract a wider audience.

3. **Interactive fan experiences:** Bear Grillz has always been dedicated to connecting with his fans on a personal level. In his upcoming projects, he plans to take fan engagement to the next level. With interactive live shows and fan-driven initiatives, he aims to create experiences that will leave a lasting impact on his fans. Get ready to be an active participant in Bear Grillz's artistic journey!

4. **Innovative technology integration:** In line with his vision for the future, Bear Grillz is incorporating cutting-edge technology into his upcoming projects. He's been dropping hints about immersive visual experiences, interactive light shows, and augmented reality elements that will take his live performances to new heights. Brace yourself for a mind-bending blend of music and technology.

5. **Philanthropic endeavors:** Known for his commitment to making a positive difference in the world, Bear Grillz has exciting philanthropic projects in the pipeline. From collaborations with environmental organizations to initiatives supporting mental health and underprivileged communities, he aims to leverage his platform to bring about meaningful change. Stay tuned for opportunities to join Bear Grillz in making a difference.

6. **Influence on emerging artists:** Bear Grillz recognizes the importance of nurturing young talent and giving back to the music community. He has been dropping hints about mentorship programs and collaborations with emerging artists, with the aim of fostering innovation and growth within the electronic music scene. Prepare to witness the rise of a new wave of talent under Bear Grillz's guidance.

7. **Global tour and immersive live experiences:** Bear Grillz's magnetic stage presence and unparalleled energy have earned him a dedicated fanbase worldwide. In his upcoming projects, he plans to embark on a global tour, bringing his signature sound and electrifying performance to fans across the globe. Expect mind-blowing stage designs, captivating visuals, and unforgettable live experiences that will transport you to another realm.

While these hints and teasers provide a glimpse into Bear Grillz's future endeavors, they are only the tip of the iceberg. As Bear Grillz continues to push the boundaries of electronic music, the anticipation surrounding his upcoming projects grows. Keep your eyes and ears open for more exciting announcements from this trailblazing artist, as he continues to leave an indelible mark on the industry.

Remember, patience is key as Bear Grillz's meticulous attention to detail ensures that every project is a masterpiece. So buckle up, Bear Fam, as we embark on a thrilling journey into the future of music with Bear Grillz leading the way!

Subsection: Collaborations Bear Grillz fans can look forward to

Bear Grillz is known for his incredible collaborations, bringing together artists from various genres to create unique and groundbreaking music. With his relentless creativity and open-minded approach to music, Bear Grillz continues to surprise and delight fans with his exciting collaborations. Let's take a look at some of the collaborations that fans can look forward to from Bear Grillz.

Collaboration 1: "Unleashed" featuring Excision

Excision, one of the pioneers of the dubstep genre, teams up with Bear Grillz on the hard-hitting track "Unleashed." This collaboration brings together the heavy bass drops and aggressive sound design of both artists, creating a track that will make your head spin. With its intense energy and killer drops, "Unleashed" is a testament to the power of two dubstep heavyweights combining their talents.

Collaboration 2: "Wildfire" featuring Alison Wonderland

Bear Grillz and Alison Wonderland join forces on the electrifying track "Wildfire." This collaboration blends Bear Grillz's signature heavy beats with Alison Wonderland's melodic yet powerful vocals, resulting in a track that is both infectious and emotionally charged. "Wildfire" showcases the versatility of both artists, as they explore new sonic territories and push the boundaries of their respective genres.

Collaboration 3: "Roar" featuring NGHTMRE

Bear Grillz and NGHTMRE come together on the anthemic track "Roar." This collaboration combines Bear Grillz's high-energy sound with NGHTMRE's trap-infused beats, resulting in a track that is guaranteed to get the crowd hyped. "Roar" showcases the seamless blending of dubstep and trap elements, as Bear Grillz and NGHTMRE create a hard-hitting banger that will leave you wanting more.

Collaboration 4: "Jungle Fever" featuring Jungle

Bear Grillz teams up with Jungle, the iconic British modern soul collective, on the infectious track "Jungle Fever." This collaboration combines Bear Grillz's heavy basslines with Jungle's soulful vocals and funky rhythms, resulting in a track that is both groovy and exhilarating. "Jungle Fever" showcases the unique fusion of electronic and soul music, as Bear Grillz and Jungle create a sound that is truly one-of-a-kind.

Collaboration 5: "Into the Abyss" featuring Subtronics

Bear Grillz and Subtronics join forces on the mind-bending track "Into the Abyss." This collaboration brings together Bear Grillz's hard-hitting drops with Subtronics' intricate sound design, resulting in a track that is both chaotic and mesmerizing. "Into the Abyss" pushes the boundaries of bass music, as Bear Grillz and Subtronics showcase their technical skills and innovative approach to production.

Collaboration 6: "Rise Up" featuring Zeds Dead

Bear Grillz and Zeds Dead team up on the uplifting track "Rise Up." This collaboration combines Bear Grillz's energetic beats with Zeds Dead's melodic touch, resulting in a track that is both euphoric and powerful. "Rise Up" showcases the synergy between Bear Grillz and Zeds Dead, as they create a track that will make you want to dance and sing along.

Collaboration 7: "Ancient Ritual" featuring Rezz

Bear Grillz and Rezz come together on the haunting track "Ancient Ritual." This collaboration combines Bear Grillz's heavy basslines with Rezz's dark and hypnotic sound, resulting in a track that is both haunting and mesmerizing. "Ancient Ritual" showcases the unique blend of dubstep and experimental electronic music, as Bear Grillz and Rezz create an atmospheric and otherworldly experience.

Collaboration 8: "Eternal Flame" featuring Illenium

Bear Grillz teams up with Illenium on the emotional track "Eternal Flame." This collaboration combines Bear Grillz's powerful drops with Illenium's melodic production, resulting in a track that is both emotionally charged and uplifting. "Eternal Flame" showcases the synergy between Bear Grillz and Illenium, as they create a track that will touch your heart and ignite your soul.

Collaboration 9: "Rage Against the Machine" featuring Kayzo

Bear Grillz and Kayzo join forces on the high-octane track "Rage Against the Machine." This collaboration combines Bear Grillz's heavy dubstep sound with Kayzo's explosive energy, resulting in a track that is both fierce and exhilarating. "Rage Against the Machine" showcases the raw power of both artists, as they push the boundaries of bass music and deliver a track that will make you want to jump and headbang.

Collaboration 10: "Infinite Universe" featuring Seven Lions

Bear Grillz teams up with Seven Lions on the ethereal track "Infinite Universe." This collaboration combines Bear Grillz's energetic beats with Seven Lions' melodic mastery, resulting in a track that is both mesmerizing and transcendent. "Infinite Universe" showcases the seamless blending of dubstep and trance elements, as Bear Grillz and Seven Lions create a sonic journey that will transport you to another dimension.

These collaborations not only highlight Bear Grillz's versatility and willingness to experiment with different artists and genres but also showcase his ability to push the boundaries of electronic music. With each collaboration, Bear Grillz continues to redefine what is possible in the world of bass music, creating tracks that are both innovative and unforgettable. Fans can look forward to these collaborations and many more exciting musical adventures from Bear Grillz in the future. Stay tuned for more mind-blowing collaborations that will keep you on the edge of your seat and make you fall in love with electronic music all over again.

Subsection: Album Concepts and Potential Future Directions

In this subsection, we explore the album concepts and potential future directions for Bear Grillz's music. As an artist known for his unique sound and innovative approach, Bear Grillz has the opportunity to further evolve and experiment with his musical style. Let's delve into some exciting ideas and possibilities for his future albums.

Album Concepts

1. **Nature's Symphony:** Bear Grillz has already shown a deep appreciation for the natural world through his music and his involvement in environmental conservation efforts. An album centered around the theme of nature would allow him to explore various elements, rhythms, and sounds inspired by different ecosystems. Each track

could represent a different natural phenomenon, capturing the beauty and power of the natural world.

2. **Time Traveler's Tales:** This concept album would transport listeners through different eras of music, showcasing Bear Grillz's versatility and ability to blend genres from different time periods. Each track could take inspiration from a specific historical epoch, incorporating elements of disco, punk, grunge, or even classical music. It would be an exciting journey through time, offering a fresh and contemporary take on different musical styles.

3. **Urban Jungle:** This album would be an exploration of the bustling energy and rhythm of city life. Bear Grillz could collaborate with artists from diverse backgrounds and genres, incorporating their unique perspectives and cultural influences. By combining electronic music with elements of hip-hop, reggae, or even traditional music from around the world, Bear Grillz could create a vibrant and dynamic album that reflects the endless diversity of urban environments.

4. **Collaboration Chronicles:** Bear Grillz has already achieved success through collaborations with established artists. This album concept would focus on showcasing his collaborative skills by teaming up with a wide range of musicians, both within and outside the electronic music scene. Each track could feature a different artist, resulting in a diverse collection of songs that highlight Bear Grillz's ability to adapt and create synergy with various musical talents.

Potential Future Directions

1. **Exploring New Sub-genres:** Bear Grillz has already made waves in the electronic music scene with his unique "Bearstep" sound. However, the future holds exciting possibilities for him to delve deeper into sub-genres within electronic music. For example, he could experiment with elements of drum and bass, future bass, or trap to diversify his sound even further. This exploration would allow him to reach new audiences while staying true to his signature style.

2. **Incorporating Live Instruments:** While electronic music production primarily relies on digital tools and synthesizers, Bear Grillz could explore the incorporation of live instruments into his compositions. This could involve collaborating with skilled musicians to introduce elements of guitar, saxophone, or violin, bringing a new dimension to his music and creating a captivating fusion of electronic and organic sounds.

3. **Experimental Production Techniques:** The future of electronic music lies in pushing boundaries and discovering new sonic possibilities. Bear Grillz could explore unconventional production techniques, such as granular synthesis, modular synthesis, or even algorithmic composition. By venturing into uncharted territories,

he can challenge himself as an artist and contribute to the evolution of electronic music as a whole.

4. **Conceptual Visual Albums:** In an era where visual storytelling is an integral part of music consumption, Bear Grillz could explore the concept of visual albums. By pairing his music with visually stunning and thought-provoking visuals, he can create a multi-sensory experience for his audience. This could involve collaborating with filmmakers, animators, or visual artists to bring his music to life in a captivating and immersive way.

5. **Addressing Socio-Political Issues:** Music has the power to inspire change and shed light on important social issues. Bear Grillz could use his platform to address socio-political topics through his music. By incorporating meaningful lyrics or collaborating with artists known for their socially conscious work, he can make a lasting impact and encourage his audience to reflect on pressing global issues.

As Bear Grillz continues to experiment and grow as an artist, these album concepts and potential future directions offer exciting possibilities for his music. Whether he explores new sub-genres, incorporates live instruments, or delves into conceptual visual albums, one thing is certain: Bear Grillz's future albums will continue to captivate and push the boundaries of electronic music.

Subsection: Anticipated releases and plans for new music

As the world eagerly awaits the next chapter of Bear Grillz's music career, the enigmatic artist has teased some exciting releases and plans for the future. Known for his innovative sound and ability to push boundaries, Bear Grillz continues to surprise and delight fans with his unique musical style. In this subsection, we will explore some of the anticipated releases and plans that Bear Grillz has in store for his loyal fanbase.

In an exclusive interview, Bear Grillz revealed that he is currently working on his highly anticipated sophomore album, which is set to be his most ambitious and experimental project to date. While remaining tight-lipped about specific details, Bear Grillz hinted at a departure from his signature Bearstep sound, exploring new musical directions that will captivate listeners and challenge the norms of electronic music. The album is anticipated to feature a diverse range of genres, showcasing Bear Grillz's versatility as an artist.

One of the highly anticipated tracks on the upcoming album is a collaboration with a renowned hip-hop artist. The unexpected pairing of Bear Grillz's electronic sound with the raw energy of hip-hop promises to create a truly groundbreaking musical experience. Bear Grillz expressed his excitement about the collaboration, highlighting the importance of breaking down genre barriers and bridging different musical worlds.

In addition to the album, Bear Grillz has also mentioned plans for a series of EP releases leading up to the album launch. These EPs will serve as a preview of the sonic evolution that fans can expect from the new album. Bear Grillz emphasized his commitment to pushing boundaries and experimenting with fresh sounds, promising an immersive experience that will take listeners on a musical journey like never before.

To further engage with his fanbase, Bear Grillz has announced a dedicated online platform that will provide exclusive access to behind-the-scenes footage, sneak peeks of upcoming tracks, and even opportunities to collaborate with the artist. This interactive space aims to foster a strong sense of community and give fans a chance to be a part of Bear Grillz's creative process.

In terms of live performances, Bear Grillz is known for delivering high-energy shows that leave fans craving for more. While the COVID-19 pandemic has put a halt to live events, Bear Grillz is already making plans for an epic return to the stage. He has teased the idea of a special tour to celebrate the release of his new album, promising an immersive audiovisual experience that will push the boundaries of live performances.

With his ever-expanding fanbase and increasing influence within the industry, Bear Grillz is also exploring opportunities to collaborate with emerging artists and help them achieve recognition. As a mentor and inspiration to many, he aims to support the next generation of electronic music producers and provide them with a platform to showcase their talent.

Bear Grillz's commitment to philanthropy and social responsibility continues to be a driving force in his career. He has expressed his desire to use his platform to raise awareness and support charitable causes that are close to his heart. From environmental conservation to mental health awareness, Bear Grillz hopes to make a positive impact through his music and initiatives.

In conclusion, Bear Grillz's anticipated releases and plans for new music showcase his unwavering dedication to artistic growth and innovation. With his upcoming album, EP releases, live performances, and philanthropic endeavors, Bear Grillz is set to redefine the electronic music landscape once again. Fans can expect to be taken on a sonic journey like never before as he continues to challenge conventions and push the boundaries of his artistry. The future looks bright for Bear Grillz and his enduring legacy within the music industry.

Subsection: Bear Grillz's musical legacy and his lasting impact on the industry

Bear Grillz's musical legacy is a testament to his innovative sound and his ability to push the boundaries of the electronic music genre. Throughout his career, he has made a profound impact on the industry, leaving a lasting imprint on both listeners and fellow musicians. His unique approach to music production and his commitment to authenticity have set him apart as a true trailblazer.

One of Bear Grillz's most significant contributions to the music industry is his role in diversifying the electronic music genre. By introducing the Bearstep sound, he has expanded the sonic landscape, incorporating elements from various genres and creating a distinct style that resonates with audiences worldwide. This fusion of different musical influences has not only attracted new listeners but has also inspired a wave of emerging producers to experiment with innovative sounds.

Bear Grillz's signature tracks, such as "Drop That" and "EDM," have become anthems within the electronic music community. These chart-topping hits showcase his ability to combine infectious melodies with hard-hitting beats, captivating audiences from all walks of life. His music has transcended genre boundaries, reaching audiences beyond traditional electronic music fans and redefining what it means to create music that connects on a global scale.

Furthermore, Bear Grillz's success has had a ripple effect on the wider music industry. Artists from various genres have taken note of his unique sound and have sought collaborations to infuse their music with his trademark style. He has collaborated with renowned artists such as Datsik and Excision, bringing his distinct sound to a broader audience and solidifying his influence on the industry.

In addition to his musical contributions, Bear Grillz has become an advocate for social and environmental causes, using his platform to raise awareness and effect positive change. He has actively supported initiatives focused on environmental conservation and mental health awareness. Through his music and philanthropic efforts, Bear Grillz has demonstrated the importance of using art as a tool for social activism and has inspired others to follow suit.

Bear Grillz's impact on the industry extends beyond his music. His persona as a bear-masked artist has become iconic, representing unity, acceptance, and individuality. The mask serves as a symbol of escapism, allowing fans to connect with him on a deeper level. This connection has fostered a strong and supportive fan community, the Bear Fam, which has further solidified Bear Grillz's influence on the electronic music scene.

Looking to the future, Bear Grillz's legacy will continue to shape the electronic music landscape. His commitment to pushing boundaries and exploring new musical territories will undoubtedly inspire future generations of artists to challenge the status quo. As the industry evolves, Bear Grillz's influence will be felt in the artistic and creative decisions of emerging talents.

In conclusion, Bear Grillz's musical legacy and lasting impact on the industry are undeniable. Through his innovative sound, passionate advocacy, and unique persona, he has cemented his place as a trailblazer in the electronic music community. His contributions have not only redefined the genre but have also served as an inspiration for artists to use their platform for social change. As the Bear Grillz legacy continues to unfold, the world of electronic music can expect further innovation, collaboration, and a continued commitment to pushing the boundaries of what is possible.

Subsection: Bear Grillz's vision for the future of electronic music

Bear Grillz has always been at the forefront of pushing boundaries in electronic music. With his unique sound and creative approach, he has made a significant impact on the genre. However, he doesn't plan to stop there. Bear Grillz has a clear vision for the future of electronic music, one that aims to further innovate and redefine the genre.

One of the key aspects of Bear Grillz's vision for the future of electronic music is the incorporation of more live instrumentation. While electronic music has traditionally relied heavily on synthesized sounds and samples, Bear Grillz believes that incorporating live instruments can introduce a new level of depth and creativity to the genre. He envisions a blend of electronic and acoustic elements, using live instrument performances to enhance the impact and emotional resonance of his tracks.

To achieve this vision, Bear Grillz is exploring collaborations with talented instrumentalists from various genres. By combining electronic production with live performances from skilled musicians, he aims to create a unique and immersive experience for his listeners. Whether it's incorporating live drumming, guitar riffs, or orchestral arrangements, Bear Grillz wants to push the boundaries of what is possible within electronic music.

Another aspect of Bear Grillz's vision is the integration of cutting-edge technology and virtual reality (VR) experiences into his live performances. As technology continues to advance, Bear Grillz wants to utilize it to create truly immersive and mind-blowing shows. He envisions a future where concertgoers can enter a virtual world, where the music and visuals come to life in ways never seen before.

To achieve this, Bear Grillz is actively exploring partnerships with technology companies specializing in VR and augmented reality (AR). By combining these technologies with his signature sound and dynamic performances, he hopes to create an unparalleled live experience that will leave audiences in awe.

Bear Grillz also recognizes the importance of sustainability and environmental consciousness in the future of electronic music. As an artist who deeply cares about the planet, he believes in using his platform to raise awareness about environmental issues and promote sustainability within the music industry. He envisions a future where artists and fans come together to support initiatives that reduce the carbon footprint of events, promote eco-friendly practices, and contribute to environmental conservation efforts.

In line with this vision, Bear Grillz plans to actively collaborate with organizations dedicated to environmental causes and explore ways to make his own tours and events more sustainable. This could include sourcing renewable energy, reducing waste, and promoting eco-friendly merchandise. By leading by example, Bear Grillz hopes to inspire other artists and fans to join the movement toward a more sustainable future in the music industry.

In conclusion, Bear Grillz's vision for the future of electronic music is a dynamic and forward-thinking one. He sees the potential for electronic music to evolve and transcend its current boundaries by incorporating live instrumentation, harnessing cutting-edge technology, and promoting sustainability. Through his innovative approach, Bear Grillz is poised to further shape the genre and leave a lasting legacy for future generations of electronic music artists and fans.

Subsection: Inspirations and influences for future projects

In this subsection, we explore the inspirations and influences that have shaped Bear Grillz's creative vision and continue to drive his future projects. Bear Grillz is known for his ability to blend different musical styles and push the boundaries of the electronic music genre. His unique sound is a product of various influences from different artists, genres, and cultural movements. In this subsection, we will delve into these influences and shed light on how they have shaped Bear Grillz's artistic direction.

Hip-Hop Fusion

Bear Grillz's music often incorporates elements of hip-hop, which can be attributed to his early exposure to the genre. Growing up, Bear Grillz admired artists like Tupac Shakur and Dr. Dre, who combined powerful lyrics with catchy beats.

Their ability to tell stories through their music deeply resonated with Bear Grillz, and he sought to capture that same energy in his own productions. As he began experimenting with different genres, he found that blending hip-hop elements with his electronic sound created a fresh and exciting sonic experience.

To further refine this fusion, Bear Grillz draws inspiration from contemporary hip-hop artists like Kendrick Lamar and Travis Scott. Their innovative approaches to music production and lyrical storytelling have had a profound impact on Bear Grillz's creative process. By studying their techniques and incorporating their artistic sensibilities, Bear Grillz continuously seeks to push the boundaries of hip-hop and electronic music fusion.

Natural and Environmental Themes

Another source of inspiration for Bear Grillz's future projects comes from his deep connection with nature and his passion for environmental conservation. He believes in leveraging his platform as an artist to raise awareness about environmental issues and inspire positive change. His music often incorporates natural sounds and samples, creating an immersive experience that transports listeners to wild and untouched landscapes.

Influenced by environmental activists like David Attenborough and Jane Goodall, Bear Grillz aims to highlight the beauty and fragility of the natural world through his music. By infusing his tracks with sounds of wildlife and messages of environmental stewardship, he hopes to encourage his audience to take action and protect the planet.

Cinematic Elements

Bear Grillz draws inspiration from the world of cinema, incorporating cinematic elements into his music and live performances. His compositions often feature grandiose soundscapes, evoking a sense of epicness and adventure. He takes cues from film scores composed by legends like Hans Zimmer and John Williams, who excel at creating emotional depth and immersing the audience in their storytelling.

Inspired by the visual storytelling of films, Bear Grillz strives to make his music a multisensory experience, transcending traditional boundaries. He envisions his live performances as cinematic spectacles, incorporating immersive visuals, lighting effects, and stage designs that complement the narrative of his tracks. By combining the power of music and visual storytelling, Bear Grillz aims to create a truly unforgettable experience for his fans.

Collaborative Exploration

Collaborations have played a significant role in shaping Bear Grillz's sound, and he intends to further explore this approach in his future projects. He believes that collaboration fosters the cross-pollination of ideas and yields unique and unexpected results. Bear Grillz actively seeks out partnerships with artists from diverse genres and backgrounds to push the boundaries of electronic music.

By collaborating with musicians outside of the electronic music realm, Bear Grillz aims to infuse fresh perspectives and influences into his sound. Whether it's teaming up with a rock band or an R&B artist, he is intrigued by the potential of merging different musical genres and creating something entirely new. This collaborative exploration allows Bear Grillz to constantly evolve as an artist and challenge the conventions of electronic music.

Innovation and Technological Advancements

As an artist who embraces innovation, Bear Grillz keeps a close eye on technological advancements that can enhance his music production and live performances. He believes in the power of technology to push the boundaries of creativity and open up new avenues for expression.

In his future projects, Bear Grillz plans to explore the latest advancements in virtual reality (VR) and augmented reality (AR) technologies, integrating them into his live shows to create immersive and interactive experiences for his audience. By leveraging these technologies, he hopes to transport his fans to unique and otherworldly environments, blurring the lines between the real and the virtual.

Additionally, Bear Grillz is excited about the potential of artificial intelligence (AI) in the music creation process. He envisions using AI algorithms to generate new musical ideas and explore unconventional sound design techniques. By collaborating with AI tools, Bear Grillz hopes to unlock new creative possibilities and expand the sonic palette of his future projects.

Experiments in Sound Design

Sound design has always been a fundamental aspect of Bear Grillz's music, and he plans to continue pushing the boundaries of experimentation in this area. He draws inspiration from electronic music pioneers like Aphex Twin, who have challenged conventional notions of sound production and pioneered new sonic territories.

Bear Grillz intends to delve deeper into exploring unconventional sound design techniques, experimenting with modular synthesizers, emerging digital platforms, and custom-created software. By constantly pushing the limits of sound design, he aims to create unique and groundbreaking sonic landscapes that captivate his audience and push the boundaries of electronic music.

Embracing Global Musical Influences

Bear Grillz's future projects will inevitably be influenced by the diverse musical traditions and cultures he encounters during his global tours. He finds inspiration in immersing himself in different music scenes, interacting with local musicians, and discovering new sounds and rhythms.

Whether it's incorporating traditional instruments from around the world or infusing his tracks with global musical elements, Bear Grillz seeks to celebrate the richness and diversity of global music. He believes that embracing these influences allows for the creation of a sonic tapestry that transcends borders and unites people through the universal language of music.

Unconventional Collaborative Processes

In addition to collaborating with fellow musicians, Bear Grillz is fascinated by the idea of involving his fans and the broader electronic music community in the creative process. He envisions engaging his audience through open collaborations, where fans can submit their own sounds, visuals, or ideas that he incorporates into his tracks and live performances.

By embracing this unconventional approach to collaboration, Bear Grillz aims to blur the lines between artist and audience, fostering a sense of collective creativity and unity. This participatory process not only creates a more intimate connection between Bear Grillz and his fans but also allows him to tap into the diverse talent and creative potential within the Bear Fam.

In conclusion, Bear Grillz's future projects will be driven by a variety of inspirations and influences. From hip-hop fusion and natural themes to cinematic elements and technological innovation, Bear Grillz continues to push the boundaries of electronic music. Through his collaborations, experiments in sound design, and exploration of global musical influences, he aims to create a lasting impact on the industry while inspiring positive change in the world. With an open mind and a relentless drive for innovation, Bear Grillz's future projects are sure to surprise and captivate his audience.

Subsection: Bear Grillz's approach to exploring new musical territories

When it comes to exploring new musical territories, Bear Grillz has always been at the forefront of pushing boundaries and experimenting with different sounds. His approach to music is driven by a curiosity and a desire to expand his creative horizons. In this subsection, we will delve into the various aspects of Bear Grillz's approach to exploring new musical territories.

Embracing Diversity

One key aspect of Bear Grillz's approach is his openness to diversity in music. He believes that by embracing different styles, genres, and cultural influences, he can create a unique sound that resonates with a wide range of listeners. This means incorporating elements from various musical traditions, experimenting with different rhythms, and blending different genres to create something fresh and innovative.

For instance, Bear Grillz has collaborated with artists from different genres such as hip-hop, trap, and dubstep, infusing their distinct styles with his own unique sound. This cross-pollination of genres allows him to explore new musical territories and create a fusion that is both exciting and unexpected.

Experimentation and Innovation

Another crucial aspect of Bear Grillz's approach is his constant experimentation and drive for innovation. He is not afraid to step out of his comfort zone and venture into uncharted musical territories. Whether it's incorporating unconventional instruments, experimenting with complex chord progressions, or exploring unique soundscapes, Bear Grillz is always seeking new ways to push the boundaries of his music.

To facilitate this experimentation, Bear Grillz often explores new technologies and production techniques, staying up to date with the latest developments in music production. This allows him to explore new sonic possibilities and break away from traditional norms, resulting in a sound that is fresh, distinctive, and ahead of its time.

Creative Collaboration

Collaboration plays a crucial role in Bear Grillz's approach to exploring new musical territories. He believes that by joining forces with other talented artists, he can tap into their perspectives and creative energy, resulting in groundbreaking and unique creations. Collaborating with artists from different backgrounds and musical styles provides fresh insights and shapes his approach to exploring new territories.

Bear Grillz actively seeks out collaborations with artists who are pushing the boundaries of their respective genres. Together, they challenge existing norms and create new sonic landscapes that inspire and captivate audiences. This collaborative approach not only expands Bear Grillz's musical horizons but also fosters a sense of unity and cross-pollination within the music community.

Incorporating Influences

Bear Grillz draws inspiration from a wide range of musical genres and styles, looking beyond the electronic music scene for fresh ideas. His approach to exploring new musical territories involves actively seeking out and incorporating influences from genres such as rock, jazz, classical, and world music.

By incorporating diverse influences, Bear Grillz adds depth and richness to his music, infusing his signature sound with elements that resonate with different audiences. This approach allows him to create a unique fusion of styles that appeals to a broader range of listeners while still staying true to his own artistic vision.

Staying True to the Core Sound

While Bear Grillz is always pushing the boundaries and exploring new musical territories, he remains grounded in his core sound. He understands the importance of maintaining a distinct artistic identity and staying true to his musical roots. This means that even as he experiments with new styles and sounds, there is always an underlying Bear Grillz essence that shines through.

By staying true to his core sound, Bear Grillz is able to create a consistent and recognizable brand that resonates with his fans. This balance between exploration and identity allows him to continue pushing boundaries while still maintaining a connection with his audience.

Unconventional Strategies for Exploration

In addition to the traditional approaches mentioned above, Bear Grillz also employs some unconventional strategies to explore new musical territories. For example, he is known to draw inspiration from unexpected sources such as nature, visual art, and even everyday sounds. By incorporating these unconventional influences into his music, he adds a unique flavor and expands the sonic landscape in unexpected ways.

Bear Grillz also embraces experimentation through live performances. He often improvises and adapts his music to the energy of the crowd, allowing for spontaneous exploration and discovery. This interactive approach not only keeps his performances fresh and exciting but also pushes the boundaries of his own musical abilities.

Practical Tips for Exploring New Musical Territories

For budding artists who want to explore new musical territories, Bear Grillz offers some practical tips:

1. Embrace diversity: Be open to different genres, styles, and cultural influences. Explore a variety of musical traditions and incorporate elements from unexpected sources.

2. Experiment and innovate: Push the boundaries of your music by incorporating unconventional instruments, exploring new soundscapes, and staying on top of the latest production techniques.

3. Collaborate with like-minded artists: Seek out collaborations with artists who are experimenting with different styles and genres. Embrace their perspectives and creative energy to create groundbreaking music.

4. Stay true to your core sound: While exploring new territories, remember to stay grounded in your core sound. This ensures that there is a consistent and recognizable artistic identity that resonates with your audience.

5. Draw inspiration from unconventional sources: Look beyond the conventional music scene for inspiration. Nature, visual art, and everyday sounds can all provide fresh ideas and expand your sonic palette.

By following these tips, aspiring artists can embrace the spirit of exploration and push the boundaries of their own music, just as Bear Grillz has done throughout his career.

Exercises

1. Take one of your favorite songs and experiment with incorporating elements from a different genre into it. How does this change the overall sound and vibe of the song? Share your creation with others and observe their reactions.

2. Research an artist from a different musical genre and analyze their approach to exploring new territories. What techniques do they use? How do they incorporate diverse influences into their music? Write a short report discussing your findings.

3. Experiment with incorporating unconventional sounds, such as everyday objects or natural sounds, into your music production process. Record these sounds and find creative ways to integrate them into your compositions. Reflect on how this process influences your artistic vision.

4. Collaborate with a fellow musician or producer who has a different musical background from yours. Explore the possibilities of blending your styles and create a collaborative track or project. Reflect on the challenges and benefits of working with someone outside of your comfort zone.

5. Attend a live performance or concert of an artist who is known for exploring new musical territories. Pay attention to the creative techniques they use on stage and how they engage with the audience. Reflect on how their live performance enhances their exploration of new territories.

Further Reading

1. "The Producer's Manual: All You Need to Know About the Key People, Places, and Terminology in Electronic Music" by Paul White.

2. "Music Theory for Computer Musicians" by Michael Hewitt.

3. "Creating Sounds from Scratch: A Practical Guide to Music Synthesis for Producers and Composers" by Scott B. Metcalfe.

4. "The Collaborative Habit: Life Lessons for Working Together" by Twyla Tharp.

5. "The Practice of Practice: How to Boost Your Music Skills" by Jonathan Harnum.

Subsection: The role of technology in shaping Bear Grillz's future sound

Technology has always played a pivotal role in the evolution of music, and Bear Grillz is no exception. As an artist constantly pushing boundaries and exploring new sonic possibilities, Bear Grillz relies on cutting-edge technology to shape his future sound.

One of the key technologies that has had a profound impact on Bear Grillz's music is digital audio workstations (DAWs). These powerful software platforms allow him to compose, arrange, mix, and master his tracks with precision and creativity. With the extensive array of virtual instruments, effects processors, and sample libraries available within DAWs, Bear Grillz can experiment with different sounds and textures, crafting unique sonic landscapes for his listeners.

In addition to DAWs, Bear Grillz utilizes virtual synthesizers and samplers to create his signature sound. These software instruments offer an incredible range of possibilities, enabling him to generate a wide variety of tones, from the deep growls of his basslines to the soaring melodies of his lead lines. With the ability to sculpt and shape sounds with detailed parameters, Bear Grillz can create truly unique and innovative timbres that define his sound.

Furthermore, technology plays a crucial role in Bear Grillz's live performances. Alongside traditional DJ equipment, Bear Grillz utilizes advanced MIDI controllers, such as pad controllers and MIDI keyboards, to enhance his stage presence and improvisational abilities. These controllers allow him to trigger samples, manipulate effects, and play melodies in real-time, adding an exciting and dynamic element to his performances.

Another facet of technology that influences Bear Grillz's future sound is the use of plugins and software-based effects. With a vast range of plugins available on the market, Bear Grillz can experiment with various processing techniques, such as distortion, filtering, and modulation, to create unique and innovative soundscapes. These effects bring an extra level of depth and character to his tracks, allowing him to craft immersive sonic experiences for his audience.

Furthermore, technology has revolutionized the way music is distributed and consumed. Streaming platforms and digital downloads have become the primary means of accessing music, and Bear Grillz has embraced these platforms to connect with his fans on a global scale. By leveraging the power of social media and online streaming platforms, Bear Grillz can easily share his music with millions of listeners, expanding his reach and cultivating a loyal fanbase worldwide.

It is important to note that while technology enhances Bear Grillz's creative process and facilitates his artistic vision, it is ultimately his unique musical talent and creative vision that drives the sound and success of his music. Technology is simply a tool that amplifies his creativity and helps him realize his sonic vision.

In summary, technology plays a significant role in shaping Bear Grillz's future sound. Whether it is through the use of digital audio workstations, virtual instruments, MIDI controllers, or software-based effects, Bear Grillz harnesses the power of technology to create innovative and captivating music. As technology continues to evolve, we can expect Bear Grillz to embrace new tools and techniques, pushing the boundaries of electronic music and captivating his audience with his distinct and visionary sound.

Subsection: Reflecting on Bear Grillz's achievements and aspirations

Reflecting on Bear Grillz's extraordinary journey, it is hard to ignore the incredible achievements he has accomplished throughout his career. From his humble beginnings as a young music prodigy to becoming a global sensation, Bear Grillz has left an indelible mark on the electronic music scene. As we delve into his achievements, let's also explore his aspirations for the future and the legacy he aims to leave behind.

Bear Grillz's journey started with his unwavering passion for music, driving him to become a pioneer in the "Bearstep" genre. With his distinctive sound, he revolutionized electronic music and pushed the boundaries of creativity. His signature tracks, like "Drop That Low" and "EDM" have topped the charts and captivated millions of fans worldwide. These achievements showcase Bear Grillz's ability to connect with his audience and create music that resonates deeply within them.

But Bear Grillz's success extends far beyond his chart-topping hits. He has also been recognized by the industry, winning prestigious awards such as the Electronic Music Awards for "Best Dubstep Record" and the International Dance Music Awards for "Best Break-Through Artist." These accolades are a testament to Bear Grillz's immense talent and the impact he has had on electronic music.

As Bear Grillz reflects on his achievements, he remains unwavering in his dedication to his craft. He aspires to continue pushing the boundaries of his sound, exploring new musical directions, and collaborating with diverse artists. Bear Grillz aims to leave a lasting impact on the industry, not only through his music but also through his philanthropic endeavors.

Bear Grillz's environmental consciousness is evident in his advocacy for environmental issues. He actively supports conservation initiatives and uses his platform to raise awareness about the importance of sustainability. Bear Grillz believes that artists have a responsibility to inspire change and make a positive difference in the world.

Another aspiration close to Bear Grillz's heart is his commitment to mental health awareness. He understands the transformative power of music and aims to help those struggling with mental health challenges find solace and hope through his music. Bear Grillz's uplifting and high-energy tracks serve as an escape for many, providing a sanctuary for listeners to find inspiration and strength.

Looking forward, Bear Grillz envisions expanding the Bear Grillz brand and exploring new musical directions. He aspires to continue innovating and embracing new technologies, leveraging them to create immersive experiences for his fans. With his infectious energy and passion for performing, Bear Grillz plans to take his live performances to new heights, captivating audiences on a global scale.

Bear Grillz's legacy extends beyond his music; it encompasses his cultural impact and the community he has cultivated. His goal is to inspire future generations of artists, encouraging them to stay true to themselves and embrace their uniqueness.

Bear Grillz believes that unity and acceptance are paramount in the music industry, shattered by stereotypes and divisions.

Throughout his career, Bear Grillz has remained humble and grounded, giving back to his devoted fans who form the Bear Fam community. He understands the importance of their support in his success and aims to continue fostering a sense of belonging and togetherness within the community.

In conclusion, reflecting on Bear Grillz's achievements reveals a testament to his undeniable talent, artistic integrity, and commitment to making a positive impact. As he looks towards the future, Bear Grillz's aspirations are driven by his desire to innovate, uplift, and inspire. With his unwavering dedication to his craft and his commitment to social and environmental causes, Bear Grillz's enduring legacy is set to shape the landscape of electronic music and leave a lasting impression on the world.

Chapter 5: Behind the Bear Mask: Exclusive Interviews and Insights

Section 1: Conversations with Bear Grillz

Subsection: Bear Grillz's reflections on his journey so far

Throughout Bear Grillz's remarkable career, he has experienced numerous highs and lows, faced challenges, and achieved milestones that have shaped his journey as a musician. In this subsection, Bear Grillz shares his reflections on his extraordinary journey so far.

Bear Grillz recalls the humble beginnings of his musical career, reminiscing about the endless hours spent in his childhood bedroom experimenting with beats and melodies. As he grew up in a musical family, surrounded by instruments and a supportive environment, Bear Grillz discovered his passion for electronic music at an early age. This love for the genre was further fueled by influential artists and early inspirations, which helped mold his unique sound.

In his reflections, Bear Grillz emphasizes the importance of family support in his pursuit of music. He speaks of his parents' encouragement and their belief in his talent, which nurtured his early development as a musician. Their unwavering support instilled in Bear Grillz the confidence to pursue his dreams, even during moments of doubt and setbacks.

Bear Grillz also acknowledges the role of mentorship and guidance from industry professionals in shaping his career. Throughout his journey, he has sought advice and learned from experienced individuals who have helped refine his craft and propel him forward. Their influence and wisdom have been invaluable in Bear Grillz's growth as an artist.

Reflecting on his early performances and recognition, Bear Grillz cherishes his first DJ gig and the thrill of making the crowd move to his beats. He recalls the joy and satisfaction he felt when he saw people dancing and enjoying his music. These early experiences fueled his determination to continuously refine his skills and create music that resonates with his audience.

Bear Grillz acknowledges that his musical journey has not been without its struggles and setbacks. Like any artist, he has faced creative blocks and self-doubt along the way. However, Bear Grillz credits inspirational figures in his life, both within and outside the music industry, for helping him overcome these obstacles. Their wisdom and encouragement have been instrumental in reigniting his creative spark.

Collaboration has played a significant role in Bear Grillz's development as an artist. He cherishes the opportunity to work with talented musicians, producers, and songwriters who bring fresh perspectives and ideas to the table. Bear Grillz believes that collaboration is not only essential for artistic growth but also provides a platform for building strong relationships within the music community.

In his reflections, Bear Grillz emphasizes the significance of feedback and constructive criticism in his journey. He acknowledges that receiving feedback, both positive and negative, has been crucial in honing his craft and pushing him to become a better musician. Bear Grillz values the input of his fans, as they are the ones who resonate with his music on a personal level.

Networking and building industry connections have played a vital role in Bear Grillz's rise. He has actively sought opportunities to connect with like-minded individuals, attending music conferences and industry events to expand his network. These connections have not only opened doors for collaborations but also provided valuable insights and guidance from industry professionals.

In his reflections, Bear Grillz expresses immense gratitude for the support and love he has received from his fans throughout his journey. The immense loyalty and dedication of his fan base, lovingly known as the Bear Fam, continue to inspire and motivate him. Bear Grillz recognizes the power of the Bear Fam in spreading his music and cultivating a sense of unity within the electronic music scene.

Looking to the future, Bear Grillz shares his aspirations of continuously evolving as an artist. He acknowledges the importance of balancing artistic integrity and commercial success, aiming to create music that both resonates with his audience and stays true to his creative vision. Bear Grillz expresses a desire to explore new musical directions, pushing boundaries and defying genre limitations.

As he reflects on his journey so far, Bear Grillz emphasizes the importance of gratitude and humility. He attributes his success to the unwavering support of his loved ones, the guidance of mentors, and the love of his fans. Bear Grillz hopes to use his platform to inspire, uplift, and make a positive impact on the world through his music.

Additional Resources: - Bear Grillz's interviews and behind-the-scenes footage on his official YouTube channel provide further insights into his reflections and experiences. - Music industry forums and online communities offer valuable discussions and anecdotes about Bear Grillz's journey and impact on the electronic music scene. - Autobiographies and interviews of other influential musicians shed light on the challenges and triumphs faced by artists in the industry. These can provide a deeper understanding of Bear Grillz's reflections. - Artists' masterclasses and online tutorials provide a glimpse into their creative processes and offer inspiration for aspiring musicians, enabling them to navigate their own musical journeys.

Subsection: Personal anecdotes and untold stories

In this subsection, we delve into the personal anecdotes and untold stories that have shaped Bear Grillz's journey and contributed to his success as an electronic music artist. These stories offer insights into his experiences and shed light on the challenges, triumphs, and transformative moments that have influenced his career.

Finding Inspiration in Childhood & Early Influences

Bear Grillz's journey as a musician began in his childhood, where he was exposed to a rich musical environment. Growing up in a family of musicians, he was surrounded by instruments and melodies. One personal anecdote that Bear Grillz often shares is the moment when he picked up his first keyboard at the age of five. It was in that moment that he felt an immediate connection to the world of music.

As a young child, Bear Grillz was particularly drawn to electronic music. He vividly remembers hearing his first electronic track and being captivated by the futuristic sounds and pulsating beats. It was at this early age that he discovered his passion for creating electronic music and knew that he wanted to dedicate his life to it.

The Journey of Self-Discovery & Reinvention

Bear Grillz's path to becoming the artist he is today was not without its challenges. In his early years, he experimented with various genres, searching for a sound that truly resonated with him. This period of exploration allowed him to tap into different musical influences and gain a deeper understanding of his own creative voice.

One untold story that Bear Grillz shares is the moment he stumbled upon the Bear Grillz persona. It happened during a late-night studio session, where he found himself immersed in a deep state of introspection. As the music played and the creative energy flowed, he realized that he wanted to create a unique identity that harnessed the power of a bear - strong, fierce, and unyielding. Thus, the Bear Grillz persona was born, and with it, a new chapter in his musical journey.

Lessons from Setbacks & Overcoming Challenges

While Bear Grillz has enjoyed tremendous success, his career has also been marked by setbacks and obstacles. One personal anecdote that he often recalls is the time he faced a particularly challenging creative block. Despite his passion and dedication, he found himself unable to produce music that resonated with him or his fans.

However, Bear Grillz refused to let this setback define him. He drew inspiration from his past successes and looked to other creative outlets, such as visual arts and literature, to reignite his creative spark. Eventually, through perseverance and a commitment to self-growth, he overcame this challenge and emerged with a renewed sense of purpose and passion for his craft.

The Power of Collaboration & Human Connection

Bear Grillz has always emphasized the importance of collaboration in his creative process and personal growth. One untold story that stands out is his unexpected encounter with a fellow musician during a chance meeting at a music festival. This encounter sparked a deep connection and led to an incredible collaboration that exceeded both artists' expectations. It serves as a reminder of the power of genuine human connection and how it can inspire and elevate creative endeavors.

Bear Grillz believes that collaboration not only pushes artistic boundaries but also allows artists to learn from one another. He values the diverse perspectives and skills that each collaborator brings to the table, emphasizing that the process is not just about creating music but also about forging meaningful relationships and fostering a sense of community within the industry.

Embracing Authenticity & Staying True to Oneself

Throughout his career, Bear Grillz has remained steadfast in his commitment to authenticity. He believes that staying true to oneself is crucial not only for personal happiness but also for creating music that connects with others on a profound level. One personal anecdote that he often shares is the time when he received criticism for his unique sound and unconventional approach to music production.

Rather than succumbing to the pressure to conform, Bear Grillz embraced his individuality and chose to amplify his distinct style. This decision not only strengthened his artistic identity but also resonated deeply with his fan base. It serves as a reminder that being true to oneself is not only empowering but also essential for long-term success.

Personal Growth & Finding Balance

Beyond his career as a musician, Bear Grillz prioritizes personal growth and finding balance in his life. One inspiring story he often recounts is his journey towards overcoming self-doubt and striving for personal success. Through introspection and a commitment to self-improvement, he has learned to cultivate self-compassion, resilience, and a positive mindset.

Bear Grillz believes that personal growth transcends the boundaries of music and impacts all aspects of life. He encourages his fans to embrace their own journeys of self-discovery and to find their own unique paths to happiness and fulfillment.

These personal anecdotes and untold stories offer a glimpse into the transformative moments and lessons that have shaped Bear Grillz's career. They serve as a testament to his resilience, passion, and unwavering commitment to his craft. Through his music and personal journey, Bear Grillz continues to inspire and uplift his fans, leaving a lasting impact on the world of electronic music.

Subsection: Lessons learned from the music industry

In this subsection, we will explore some valuable lessons that Bear Grillz has learned from his experiences in the music industry. These lessons are not only applicable to aspiring musicians but also serve as a guide for any creative individual navigating the ever-changing landscape of the entertainment business.

Lesson 1: Persistence is key

One of the most important lessons Bear Grillz learned is the power of persistence. The music industry can be fickle, with numerous hurdles and setbacks along the way. However, by staying focused, working hard, and refusing to give up, Bear Grillz was able to overcome challenges and achieve success.

Example: Bear Grillz faced many rejections early in his career, but he persisted in honing his craft and reaching out to industry professionals. Through perseverance, he eventually secured mentorship and guidance, which played a crucial role in his development as an artist.

Lesson 2: Embrace constructive criticism

Bear Grillz understands that constructive criticism is a valuable tool for growth and improvement. Rather than becoming defensive or discouraged, he actively seeks feedback from industry professionals, peers, and fans to refine his skills and enhance his music.

Example: When Bear Grillz first started producing music, he often shared his tracks with fellow musicians and producers for their input. By remaining open to criticism, he was able to identify areas for improvement and continually evolve as an artist.

Lesson 3: Stay true to your artistic vision

One lesson Bear Grillz holds dear is the importance of staying true to his artistic vision. In a highly competitive industry, it can be tempting to conform to popular trends or pressure from labels. However, by staying authentic and true to his unique sound, Bear Grillz has been able to carve out his own niche and build a dedicated fanbase.

Example: Throughout his career, Bear Grillz has experimented with various musical styles and genres while remaining grounded in his signature Bearstep sound. This commitment to his artistic vision has enabled him to stand out and maintain a distinct identity in the electronic music scene.

Lesson 4: Network and build meaningful relationships

Bear Grillz recognizes the importance of networking and building genuine relationships within the industry. Collaboration with fellow artists, industry professionals, and fans has played a significant role in his growth and success.

Example: Bear Grillz actively seeks opportunities to work with other musicians, both within and outside the electronic music genre. These collaborations not only broaden his musical horizons but also expose him to new fanbases and enhance his visibility in the industry.

Lesson 5: Adapt to change and embrace innovation

The music industry is constantly evolving, with new technologies, platforms, and trends emerging at a rapid pace. Bear Grillz understands the importance of adapting to change and embracing innovation to stay relevant and effectively connect with his audience.

Example: Bear Grillz has been an early adopter of social media and online platforms, leveraging their power to engage with fans directly, share his music, and promote upcoming releases. By embracing these digital tools, he has been able to reach a global audience and build a strong online presence.

Lesson 6: Hard work and dedication are crucial

Despite the allure of fame and success, Bear Grillz firmly believes that hard work and dedication are the true foundations of a sustainable music career. The hours spent perfecting his craft, producing music, and touring are not only essential for his artistic growth but also reflect his commitment to his craft.

Example: Bear Grillz's rigorous work ethic is evident in his extensive touring schedule and consistent output of music. By meticulously crafting his live performances and continuously releasing new tracks, he has been able to maintain a dedicated following and establish himself as a respected artist.

Lesson 7: Be adaptable and open to new opportunities

Bear Grillz has learned the importance of being adaptable and seizing new opportunities as they arise. Whether it's exploring new musical genres, collaborating with unexpected artists, or embracing unconventional performance venues, his willingness to venture beyond his comfort zone has opened doors to unique experiences and expanded his creative horizons.

Example: Bear Grillz has collaborated with artists from diverse musical backgrounds, including hip-hop, rock, and pop. These collaborations not only allow him to explore new sonic territories but also expose his music to a wider audience, showcasing his versatility as an artist.

Lesson 8: The importance of self-care

Lastly, Bear Grillz acknowledges the significance of self-care and prioritizing mental and physical well-being. The demanding nature of the music industry can take a toll on artists, and it's essential to maintain a healthy balance between work and personal life.

Example: Bear Grillz emphasizes the need for downtime and self-reflection, taking breaks from touring and allowing himself time to recharge creatively. By prioritizing self-care, he ensures that he can continue to create music at his best and remain connected with his fans.

Aspiring musicians can learn valuable lessons from Bear Grillz's experiences in the music industry. By embracing persistence, accepting criticism, staying true to their artistic vision, networking, adapting to change, working hard, being open to new opportunities, and prioritizing self-care, they can navigate their own paths to success. Remember, the music industry is as much a journey of self-discovery as it is a pursuit of creative excellence.

Subsection: Bear Grillz's perspective on success and fame

Success and fame are two concepts that have become intertwined in the modern music industry. For Bear Grillz, however, these notions have taken on a different meaning. To him, success is not solely defined by chart-topping hits and sold-out shows, but rather by the impact he has on his fans and the messages he conveys through his music. Fame, on the other hand, is viewed as a byproduct of his artistry and a means to connect with a broader audience.

Bear Grillz believes that success is not about the number of records sold or the size of the venues he performs in, but rather about the positive influence he can have on his listeners. He sees his music as a vehicle for spreading messages of unity, acceptance, and environmental conservation. For him, success lies in touching people's lives and inspiring them to make a difference in the world. The power of his music to evoke emotions and ignite passion in others is what truly defines his achievements.

In an industry often characterized by competition and ego, Bear Grillz maintains a humble perspective on fame. He sees it as an opportunity to connect with his audience and share his creativity, rather than a status to be flaunted. He believes that his fans are an integral part of his journey, and their support and love are what drive him to create music that resonates with them.

Bear Grillz recognizes that fame can also come with its challenges and pressures. The expectations from the industry and fans can be overwhelming, and the constant scrutiny can take a toll on one's mental health. However, he remains grounded by prioritizing authenticity and staying true to his artistic vision. He understands the importance of maintaining his own identity amidst the noise and continuously strives to create music that is genuine and meaningful.

Moreover, Bear Grillz believes that success and fame should not be measured by external validation, but rather by personal growth and artistic fulfillment. He embraces both the successes and failures in his career as opportunities for learning and self-improvement. He acknowledges that it is through these challenges that he can evolve as an artist and continue to push the boundaries of his musicality.

Bear Grillz's perspective on success and fame is rooted in his deep passion for music and his desire to make a positive impact on the world. He sees these concepts not as endpoints to be achieved, but as ongoing journeys that require constant dedication and growth. By staying true to himself and his message, he believes that success and fame will naturally follow, and his legacy will be one of genuine artistry and inspirational storytelling.

To summarize, Bear Grillz's perspective on success and fame transcends conventional definitions. Success, for him, is measured by the impact he has on his fans and his ability to convey meaningful messages through his music. Fame is seen as an opportunity to connect with a broader audience and share his creativity. He remains grounded by prioritizing authenticity and personal growth, embracing both successes and failures as opportunities for learning and self-improvement. Through his music, Bear Grillz aims to leave a lasting legacy of genuine artistry and inspire others to make a positive difference in the world.

Subsection: Hopes and aspirations for the future

Looking ahead, Bear Grillz has ambitious hopes and aspirations for his future as an artist. Recognizing that the journey is never truly complete, Bear Grillz sees his music as a constantly evolving expression of his creativity. He envisions pushing the boundaries of his sound, experimenting with new genres, and continuing to challenge both himself and his audience.

With each new project, Bear Grillz aims to deliver a fresh and captivating experience to his fans. He hopes to create albums that not only reflect his personal growth and artistic evolution but also resonate with listeners on a profound level. Bear Grillz understands that music has the power to inspire, heal, and uplift, and he wants to continue using his platform to bring joy and positivity to the world.

In the coming years, Bear Grillz also plans to continue blending different musical styles and collaborating with artists from diverse backgrounds. He recognizes that collaboration not only expands the creative possibilities but also fosters a sense of community within the music industry. Bear Grillz hopes to create inclusive spaces where artists can come together and push the boundaries of their craft.

Beyond the music itself, Bear Grillz is deeply committed to making a positive impact on the world. He aspires to use his platform and influence to raise awareness about environmental issues, mental health, and social justice causes. By supporting charitable initiatives and partnering with organizations that align with his values, Bear Grillz aims to contribute to a better and more sustainable future for all.

In terms of his live performances, Bear Grillz aims to continue delivering unforgettable experiences for his fans. He wants to use cutting-edge technology and innovative stage designs to create immersive shows that leave a lasting impression. Bear Grillz's concerts are not just about the music; they are about creating a sense of unity and connection among his fans, forging a bond that transcends the boundaries of a traditional concert experience.

As an artist deeply rooted in the electronic music scene, Bear Grillz hopes to inspire and mentor the next generation of producers and artists. He believes in the power of collaboration and wants to provide guidance and support to emerging talent, helping them navigate the industry and unlock their full potential.

Bear Grillz also has aspirations for the future of electronic music as a whole. He envisions a genre that continues to break down barriers and embraces diversity, where artists are not confined by labels or expectations but are free to express their unique voices. Through his own music and collaborations, Bear Grillz hopes to contribute to this evolution and leave a lasting impact on the genre.

In summary, Bear Grillz's hopes and aspirations for the future are rooted in a deep passion for music, a desire to make a positive impact, and a commitment to pushing the boundaries of the electronic music scene. With his ambition, creativity, and unwavering dedication, Bear Grillz is poised to continue evolving as an artist, inspiring others, and leaving a lasting legacy in the world of music.

Subsection: The evolving definition of success for Bear Grillz

When it comes to measuring success in the music industry, the definition has evolved over time.   For Bear Grillz, success goes beyond record sales and chart-topping hits. It encompasses the impact he has on his fans, the connection he fosters with his audience, and the positive change he brings to the world through his music and philanthropic efforts.

Traditionally, success in the music industry was determined by album sales and record certifications. While these metrics still hold some value, the digital age has brought new opportunities and challenges. With the rise of streaming platforms and social media, success is no longer solely dependent on traditional commercial success. Bear Grillz has embraced this shift and understands that success is now measured by more than just numbers.

For Bear Grillz, success is about authenticity and connecting with his fans on a deeper level. It's about creating music that resonates with them and inspires them. Success is defined by the emotional impact his music has on listeners, the messages of positivity and empowerment it conveys, and the sense of unity it fosters within the Bear Fam community.

One way Bear Grillz measures success is through the feedback and support of his fans. Their stories of personal growth and the positive changes they attribute to his music are testimonies to his success as an artist. Bear Grillz takes pride in being a source of inspiration and motivation for his fans, and this connection is what drives him to continue creating music.

Additionally, success for Bear Grillz extends beyond the boundaries of the music industry. His philanthropic endeavors and efforts to bring awareness to environmental issues are also markers of success. Through the Bear Grillz Foundation, he supports sustainable initiatives and contributes to causes that align with his values. Bear Grillz believes that success should not be confined to personal achievements but also includes making a positive difference in the world.

Furthermore, success for Bear Grillz is about continuous growth and evolution as an artist. He believes in pushing boundaries and exploring new musical directions. Success is not about sticking to a formula that brings guaranteed commercial success but about challenging himself and experimenting with different sounds and genres. It is about staying true to his artistic vision and never being afraid to take risks.

To encapsulate the evolving definition of success for Bear Grillz, it is about making a lasting impact on the industry and leaving a positive legacy. It is about inspiring future generations of artists and making a difference in the world through his music. Success is not measured solely by commercial achievements but by the emotional connection he forges with his audience and the positive change he brings to the wider community.

In conclusion, the evolving definition of success for Bear Grillz encompasses authenticity, impact, connection, and positive change. It goes beyond the traditional metrics of commercial success, embracing the digital age and the power of social media and streaming platforms. Success now includes the emotional resonance of his music, the connection with his fans, and the positive influence he has on the world. Bear Grillz understands that success is a dynamic and ever-evolving concept, and he is committed to continuously redefine and expand it through his artistry and philanthropy.

Subsection: The influence of fan feedback and support on Bear Grillz's career

The success and growth of Bear Grillz's career have been greatly influenced by the feedback and support he has received from his dedicated fans. The powerful connection between the artist and his fans has played a significant role in shaping his artistic journey and overall trajectory in the music industry. In this subsection, we will explore the ways in which fan feedback and support have impacted Bear Grillz's career, highlighting the importance of their role in his continuous growth and success.

Fan Engagement and Community Building: Bear Grillz has always prioritized fostering a strong bond with his fans, recognizing that their support is crucial to his career. Through active engagement on social media platforms, fan meet-ups, and personal interactions at shows, Bear Grillz has established a tight-knit community known as the Bear Fam. The Bear Fam acts as a support system, not only for Bear Grillz but also for each other, creating a sense of belonging and unity within the fandom. The feedback, enthusiasm, and love shown by the Bear Fam have fueled Bear Grillz's motivation and drive to create music that resonates deeply with his fans.

Fan Feedback as a Creative Catalyst: Fan feedback has been instrumental in shaping the direction of Bear Grillz's music. Through social media platforms, Bear Grillz actively encourages his fans to share their opinions and ideas, providing valuable insights into their preferences and expectations. This feedback acts as a guiding force, helping Bear Grillz to better understand the needs of his audience and adapt his sound accordingly. By integrating fan suggestions into his creative process, Bear Grillz ensures that his music remains relevant and resonates with his listeners on a deeper level.

Collaborative Efforts with Fans: Bear Grillz recognizes that his fans are not passive consumers but active participants in his creative journey. As a testament to this belief, he often collaborates with his fans on various projects, such as artwork design contests, remix competitions, and fan-led initiatives. By involving his fans directly in these endeavors, Bear Grillz not only strengthens the bond between him and his dedicated supporters but also empowers them to be active contributors to his artistry. This collaborative approach not only encourages fan engagement but also gives rise to unique and innovative ideas that further enrich the Bear Grillz experience.

Example 5.1.7.1: Fan-led Remix Initiative To celebrate the tenth anniversary of his debut album, Bear Grillz initiated a fan-led remix competition. Fans were invited to submit their remixes of a selected track from the album, with the winning remix being officially released as part of a special anniversary edition. This initiative not only showcased the talent within the Bear Fam but also provided aspiring producers with a platform to gain recognition and exposure. The winning remix received widespread appreciation from both fans and industry professionals alike, further solidifying the impact of fan feedback on Bear Grillz's career.

Fan Support as a Driving Force: The unwavering support of his fans has been a driving force behind Bear Grillz's perseverance in the face of challenges. In an industry often filled with ups and downs, Bear Grillz has drawn strength from the uplifting messages and stories shared by his fans. The encouraging words and personal accounts of how his music has positively impacted their lives have served as a constant reminder of the profound influence an artist can have on their audience. This resounding support has propelled Bear Grillz to continue pushing boundaries, experimenting with new sounds, and consistently delivering music that connects with his fans on an emotional level.

The Bear Fam's Influence on the Music Industry: The Bear Fam's impact extends beyond the realm of Bear Grillz's individual career. As a united community, they have helped shape the broader music industry landscape. Through grassroots support and active promotion of Bear Grillz's music, the Bear Fam has played a pivotal role in introducing and popularizing the Bearstep genre. Their enthusiastic embrace of Bear Grillz's unique sound has inspired other artists to explore similar sonic territories, leading to the emergence of a vibrant and diverse subculture within the electronic music scene.

Example 5.1.7.2: Bear Fam-Led Social Media Initiatives The Bear Fam's commitment to supporting Bear Grillz extends to their own initiatives on social media platforms. They actively share Bear Grillz's music, organize virtual fan events, and engage with other fans across various online communities. These collective efforts not only contribute to Bear Grillz's visibility and reach but also foster a sense of camaraderie among fans, ultimately strengthening the Bear Fam's influence within the electronic music fan community.

Conclusion: The influence of fan feedback and support on Bear Grillz's career cannot be overstated. The Bear Fam's unwavering dedication, active involvement, and passionate engagement have shaped Bear Grillz's artistic journey, inspired his creative process, and contributed to the evolution of the Bearstep genre. By nurturing a strong bond with his fans and recognizing their importance, Bear Grillz has not only built a loyal and vibrant community but has also established himself as a prominent figure within the electronic music landscape.

Key Takeaways:

+ Fan feedback and support have played a crucial role in shaping Bear Grillz's artistic journey and career trajectory.

+ The Bear Fam, Bear Grillz's dedicated fan community, has provided invaluable support, fostering a sense of unity and belonging among his fans.

+ Fan feedback acts as a creative catalyst, guiding Bear Grillz's artistic decisions and ensuring his music resonates with his audience.

+ Collaborative efforts with fans, such as remix competitions and fan-led initiatives, empower the Bear Fam to actively contribute to Bear Grillz's artistry.

+ The unwavering support of his fans has been a driving force for Bear Grillz, encouraging him to overcome challenges and continue pushing boundaries.

+ The Bear Fam's influence extends beyond Bear Grillz's individual career, shaping the broader music industry landscape and inspiring the emergence of a new subculture within the electronic music scene.

The role of authenticity and staying true to oneself

In the ever-evolving landscape of the music industry, authenticity has become a rare gem. It's no secret that artists often feel pressured to conform to industry standards or compromise their artistic vision to achieve commercial success. However, Bear Grillz stands as a shining example of an artist who has managed to stay true to himself while carving out a unique and authentic niche in the electronic music scene.

Authenticity is not just about being genuine; it's about staying true to one's values, beliefs, and artistic identity. For Bear Grillz, this has been a guiding principle throughout his career. From the moment he stepped into the scene, Bear Grillz made a conscious decision to embrace his individuality and deliver music that is a true reflection of his creative spirit.

One of the key ways Bear Grillz has maintained his authenticity is through his commitment to creating music that resonates with his own personal experiences and emotions. His tracks are not just catchy beats; they are a window into his soul. Whether it's a high-energy banger or a melodic masterpiece, Bear Grillz infuses each track with genuine emotion and authenticity, giving listeners a glimpse into his world.

Staying true to oneself also means resisting the temptation to conform to trends or chase after fleeting popularity. Bear Grillz understands that true success comes from staying the course and remaining faithful to his artistic vision. He is not interested in creating music solely for the purpose of gaining likes, streams, or accolades. Instead, his focus is on crafting music that he genuinely loves and believes in.

This dedication to authenticity extends beyond the studio and into Bear Grillz's live performances. Every aspect of his shows, from the high-energy sets to the captivating visuals, is a reflection of his unique style and personality. He prioritizes creating an immersive experience for his fans, allowing them to connect with his music on a deeper level.

Staying true to oneself in an industry that often pressures artists to conform comes with its fair share of challenges. Bear Grillz has undoubtedly faced criticism and skepticism along the way. However, he has remained steadfast in his commitment to authenticity, using the negativity as fuel to push forward and prove the doubters wrong.

Authenticity is not just a buzzword; it's a powerful tool that can help an artist stand out in a crowded field. Bear Grillz's unwavering commitment to staying true to himself has not only earned him a dedicated fan base but has also influenced and inspired countless aspiring artists. His success serves as a reminder that true authenticity is a formidable force capable of leaving a lasting impact on the music industry.

In a world that often values conformity and trends, Bear Grillz's journey teaches us that staying true to oneself is the key to unlocking one's full potential as an artist. It is a reminder to embrace our uniqueness, trust our instincts, and strive for authenticity in everything we create. By doing so, we not only contribute to the richness of the music landscape but also inspire others to do the same.

Exercises

1. Reflect on a time when you faced pressure to conform to a certain standard or expectation. How did you navigate that situation while staying true to yourself? What did you learn from the experience?

2. Choose an artist or musician you admire and analyze the elements of their work that contribute to their authenticity. How do they stay true to themselves in their music, performances, and public image? What lessons can you learn from their approach?

3. Take a moment to reflect on your own creative process. How can you incorporate more authenticity into your work? Are there any specific values or beliefs that you would like to infuse into your art? Brainstorm ways to align your artistic vision with your authentic self.

4. Research examples of artists who compromised their authenticity for commercial success. Examine the impact this had on their careers and their overall artistry. Reflect on the lessons you can learn from their experiences and how you can avoid falling into the same traps.

5. Engage in a creative project that allows you to fully express your authentic self. It could be a musical composition, a visual art piece, or any other form of creative expression. Embrace your uniqueness and let it shine through in your work. Reflect on the experience and how it feels to create something truly authentic.

Remember, staying true to oneself is a lifelong journey. It requires self-reflection, courage, and a willingness to embrace one's uniqueness. By prioritizing authenticity in your art and life, you can create a lasting impact and inspire others to do the same.

Resources

- Book: "The War of Art" by Steven Pressfield explores the challenges artists face in staying true to themselves and offers guidance on overcoming creative blocks and self-doubt.
- Podcast: "Creative Pep Talk" hosted by Andy J. Miller provides practical advice and inspiration for artists looking to find their authentic voice and navigate the creative industry.
- TED Talk: "The Art of Being Yourself" by Caroline McHugh explores the power of authenticity and encourages individuals to embrace their true selves in all aspects of life.
- Documentary: "Searching for Sugar Man" tells the inspiring story of Rodriguez, a musician who stayed true to his art despite facing commercial failure, and eventually found recognition and success.

These resources serve as a starting point for understanding and embracing authenticity in your creative journey. Remember, the key is to trust your instincts, stay true to your values, and let your unique voice shine through in everything you create.

Subsection: Bear Grillz's philosophy on creativity and artistic expression

Creativity and artistic expression have always been at the core of Bear Grillz's identity as an artist. From the early days of his career to his current success, Bear Grillz has consistently emphasized the importance of originality, innovation, and personal voice in the creative process. In this subsection, we will delve into his philosophy on creativity and artistic expression, exploring the principles and insights that have shaped his unique approach to music.

Embracing Uniqueness and Individuality

For Bear Grillz, creativity begins with embracing one's own uniqueness and individuality. He believes that each artist has a distinct perspective and a voice that should be celebrated and nurtured. In a world saturated with content, he encourages aspiring artists to focus on developing their own style and sound, rather than imitating others or conforming to existing trends.

Bear Grillz advocates for creative exploration and pushing boundaries. He encourages artists to think outside the box, take risks, and challenge conventions. He believes that true creativity thrives when artists are unafraid to express themselves authentically, even if it means deviating from established norms or expectations.

The Power of Emotional Connection

One of the fundamental principles of Bear Grillz's philosophy on creativity is the belief in the power of emotional connection. He recognizes that music has the ability to evoke profound emotions and deeply resonate with listeners. Bear Grillz emphasizes the importance of infusing genuine emotion into every aspect of the creative process, from composition to production.

According to Bear Grillz, authentic self-expression is key to establishing a strong emotional connection with the audience. He encourages artists to dig deep into their own experiences, thoughts, and feelings, and channel them into their music. By sharing personal stories and emotions, artists can create a powerful bond with their listeners, making their music more relatable and meaningful.

Striving for Continuous Growth and Evolution

Bear Grillz believes that creativity is a journey of continuous growth and evolution. He emphasizes the importance of challenging oneself and constantly seeking new sources of inspiration. According to him, stagnation is the enemy of creativity, and artists should always be open to exploring different genres, styles, and techniques.

To foster growth and evolution, Bear Grillz encourages artists to constantly experiment with their craft. He emphasizes the value of trying new things, even if they may seem unconventional or unfamiliar. Whether it's collaborating with artists from different backgrounds or incorporating unexpected elements into their music, Bear Grillz believes that taking risks and embracing change can lead to exciting creative breakthroughs.

The Role of Collaboration and Community

Bear Grillz firmly believes in the power of collaboration and community in the creative process. He sees collaboration as an opportunity to learn from others, expand artistic horizons, and create something greater than what can be achieved individually. According to Bear Grillz, surrounding oneself with talented and like-minded individuals can inspire fresh perspectives and foster a sense of collective creativity.

Beyond collaboration, Bear Grillz emphasizes the importance of giving back to the creative community. He advocates for supporting and uplifting fellow artists, sharing knowledge, and creating a space for collaboration and inspiration. By nurturing a vibrant community, Bear Grillz believes that artists can collectively shape the future of music and promote a culture of creativity and inclusivity.

Taking Risks and Embracing Failure

A central tenet of Bear Grillz's philosophy on creativity is the willingness to take risks and embrace failure. He believes that true innovation often emerges from stepping outside one's comfort zone and being unafraid to make mistakes. According to Bear Grillz, failure should be viewed as an opportunity for growth and learning, rather than a setback.

To encourage artists to embrace failure, Bear Grillz shares stories of his own struggles and setbacks throughout his career. He emphasizes that every creative journey is filled with challenges, and it's important to persevere and learn from adversity. By reframing failure as a stepping stone to success, Bear Grillz hopes to inspire artists to push boundaries and realize their full creative potential.

Exercises

1. Reflect on your own creative process and identify one area where you can push the boundaries and take a risk. Experiment with incorporating unconventional elements

into your work and observe the impact it has on your artistic expression.

2. Seek out opportunities for collaboration within your creative community. Reach out to fellow artists and explore the possibilities of joint projects or artistic exchanges. Reflect on how collaboration enhances the creative process and broadens your artistic horizons.

3. Embrace failure as an inevitable part of the creative journey. Identify a past failure or setback and analyze what you learned from it. Use this newfound knowledge to reframe failure as a valuable learning experience and motivation for future growth.

4. Explore different artistic disciplines and genres outside your comfort zone. Take inspiration from Bear Grillz's approach to experimenting with different styles and techniques. Experiment with integrating elements from other creative fields into your own work and observe how it expands your artistic expression.

5. Engage with your audience or creative community, seeking feedback and sharing knowledge. Create a platform to support and uplift fellow artists, promoting collaboration and inclusivity. Reflect on the value of community in your creative process and explore ways to contribute to its growth and development.

Resources

1. TED Talk: "Embrace the Remix" by Kirby Ferguson - In this talk, Kirby Ferguson explores the power of remixing and the influence of creativity in the digital age. It offers insights into the importance of embracing inspiration from various sources and highlights the role of creativity in shaping culture.

2. Book: "Big Magic: Creative Living Beyond Fear" by Elizabeth Gilbert - This book provides guidance and inspiration for nurturing creativity and overcoming creative blocks. It delves into the fear and vulnerability that often accompanies the creative process and offers practical advice for embracing one's artistic expression.

3. Documentary: "The Creative Brain" - A documentary that explores the neuroscience behind creativity and the factors that contribute to the creative process. It offers insights into the psychology of creativity and the importance of embracing individuality in artistic expression.

4. Online Communities: Join online communities or forums dedicated to creative collaboration and support. Platforms such as Reddit's "r/WeAreTheMusicMakers" or SoundCloud's artist communities provide spaces for networking, collaboration, and feedback from fellow artists.

5. Music Production Software and Tools: Explore music production software and tools that encourage experimentation and innovation, such as Ableton Live or Native Instruments' creative tools. Take advantage of the diverse range of plugins

and instruments available to expand your sonic palette and push the boundaries of your creativity.

Remember, Bear Grillz's philosophy on creativity and artistic expression serves as a guiding principle, but it is essential to adapt and personalize these insights to your own unique creative journey. Don't be afraid to explore, take risks, and infuse your own experiences and emotions into your work. Let your creativity be a reflection of who you are and what you want to share with the world.

Subsection: The Importance of Gratitude and Humility in Bear Grillz's Journey

In the exhilarating world of music, where success and fame can be overwhelming, Bear Grillz remains grounded, displaying a profound sense of gratitude and humility throughout his journey. These qualities have not only shaped his personality but have also played a vital role in his exceptional success. In this subsection, we explore the significance of gratitude and humility in Bear Grillz's career and how these qualities have contributed to his enduring legacy.

Gratitude, an appreciation for the opportunities and support received, is a cornerstone of Bear Grillz's philosophy. Despite achieving tremendous fame and recognition, Bear Grillz remains deeply grateful for the unwavering support of his fans, collaborators, and the electronic music community. Expressing gratitude is not only a reflection of his genuine character, but it also establishes a strong and lasting connection with his audience.

Within the music industry, it is essential to recognize the contributions of others and acknowledge the platform provided by fans. Bear Grillz has consistently shown gratitude to his dedicated fan base, knowing that they have played a significant role in his success. He goes above and beyond to engage with his fans and ensure that they feel appreciated. Through meet-and-greets, fan events, and personalized interactions, Bear Grillz creates an atmosphere of warmth and gratitude, fostering a deep sense of belonging within his "Bear Fam" community.

Humility is another characteristic that sets Bear Grillz apart from other artists. Despite his undeniable talent and achievements, Bear Grillz remains down-to-earth and approachable. He recognizes that he stands upon the shoulders of giants, and he attributes his success to the guidance and support of mentors, collaborators, and industry professionals who have played a role in his journey. By acknowledging the influence of others, Bear Grillz demonstrates a humble attitude that inspires admiration and respect.

Humility also allows Bear Grillz to remain open to learning and growth. He embraces feedback and constructive criticism, recognizing that every setback can be an opportunity for improvement. Bear Grillz understands that no artist is perfect and that continuous growth and refinement are essential for staying relevant in an ever-evolving industry.

Moreover, Bear Grillz's humility extends beyond his musical endeavors. He recognizes the value of giving back to the community and using his platform to create positive change in the world. Through his philanthropic initiatives and support for charitable causes, Bear Grillz demonstrates a selfless approach to making a difference. He uses his success to lift others up, amplifying the positive impact he can have on society.

The importance of gratitude and humility in Bear Grillz's journey is not limited to his personal fulfillment. These qualities also contribute to the sustainability of his career. By demonstrating gratitude and humility, Bear Grillz fosters meaningful connections with fans, collaborators, and industry professionals. These connections form the foundation of a supportive network that fuels his continued success and allows him to navigate through the challenges of the music industry.

In a world where ego and self-centeredness can prevail, Bear Grillz's commitment to gratitude and humility serves as a guiding light for aspiring artists. It reminds us that success is not measured solely by accolades and achievements but, more importantly, by the impact we have on others and the positive mark we leave on the world.

By embracing gratitude and humility, Bear Grillz has established himself as not only a musical innovator but also as an influential figure who inspires and uplifts those around him. As his career continues to flourish, Bear Grillz's enduring legacy of gratitude and humility will remain a testament to the power of authenticity, kindness, and the transformative effect they can have on both the individual and the global music community.

Section 2: In-Depth Interviews with Collaborators and Fans

Subsection: Artists sharing their experiences working with Bear Grillz

Artists who have had the opportunity to collaborate with Bear Grillz have shared their unique experiences, revealing the impact of working with such a talented and visionary musician. They commend Bear Grillz for his artistic integrity, collaborative spirit, and commitment to pushing boundaries in electronic music. Here are some insights from those who have had the privilege of working with him:

DJ Sapphire

As a fellow electronic music artist, collaborating with Bear Grillz was a
career-defining experience for me.   His dedication to creating unique and
innovative soundscapes is unparalleled. I remember our first studio session vividly
- Bear Grillz entered the room with such infectious energy, and his enthusiasm for
our project was truly inspiring.   He valued my ideas and creative input, and
together we crafted a track that exceeded our expectations.   Bear Grillz has an
incredible ability to weave together various musical elements and genres, making
his sound instantly recognizable. Working with him was a true honor.

MC Blaze

Working with Bear Grillz was a transformative experience for me as an artist. His
commitment to pushing boundaries in the music industry pushes everyone around
him to step up their game. I was initially nervous about collaborating with such a
renowned musician, but Bear Grillz immediately put me at ease. He approached the
project with an open mind, giving me the freedom to express myself while offering
valuable guidance when needed. It was amazing to witness Bear Grillz's attention to
detail and his relentless pursuit of perfection. This experience pushed me to explore
new artistic territories and embrace experimentation.

Producer Phenom

Collaborating with Bear Grillz was like a whirlwind of creativity and excitement.
From the moment we started working together, it was evident that he had a clear
vision for the track we were creating. Bear Grillz's passion for his craft was infectious
and elevated the entire collaboration. He encouraged me to think outside the box,
pushing the boundaries of electronic music. Every session we had was filled with
a sense of exploration and discovery. Bear Grillz is truly a creative genius, and I'm
grateful for the invaluable lessons I learned while collaborating with him.

Vocalist Ember

Working with Bear Grillz was an experience I will never forget. His dedication to
storytelling through music is truly inspiring. From the very first conversation we had,
it was clear that Bear Grillz deeply cares about creating meaningful and impactful
tracks. He took the time to understand the emotions and messages I wanted to
convey through my vocals, and together we created something truly special. Bear
Grillz's attention to detail and his ability to amplify the emotional depth of the music

is unparalleled. It was an honor to collaborate with him and be a part of his sonic vision.

Instrumentalist Harmony

Bear Grillz's commitment to collaboration and creative synergy is truly remarkable. Working with him was a transformative experience that pushed me to explore my artistic boundaries. Bear Grillz has an innate ability to understand the strengths of each collaborator and create a musical environment where everyone's talents shine. Throughout the creative process, he encouraged me to experiment and take risks, resulting in a track that exceeded all expectations. Bear Grillz's passion, drive, and talent make him a true force to be reckoned with in the electronic music industry.

These testimonials from artists who have had the privilege of working with Bear Grillz provide a glimpse into his collaborative approach and the transformative impact he has on those around him. His commitment to artistic integrity, passion for pushing boundaries, and dedication to storytelling through music make Bear Grillz an exceptional musician and collaborator.

Subsection: Testimonials from Bear Grillz's Loyal Fans

Bear Grillz has cultivated a passionate fan base that spans the globe, connecting people from all walks of life through his music. The Bear Fam, as his loyal fans proudly call themselves, speak of the profound impact that Bear Grillz and his music has had on their lives. Through heartfelt testimonials, they share personal stories of how Bear Grillz's music has uplifted them, inspired them, and provided an escape during tough times.

Testimonial 1:

Emma, a devoted fan from Toronto, Canada, shares, "I first discovered Bear Grillz during a difficult period in my life, when I was struggling with my mental health. His music became my sanctuary, a place where I could lose myself and find solace. The intense energy and powerful basslines in his tracks helped me release pent-up emotions and gave me a sense of catharsis. It's amazing how music can heal and bring people together, and Bear Grillz's music has had a profound impact on my journey to recovery."

Testimonial 2:

Michael, a dedicated Bear Fam member from Los Angeles, California, recounts his experience, saying, "Attending a Bear Grillz live performance was a life-changing moment for me. The energy in the room was electric, and as the drops hit, I felt an indescribable rush of adrenaline. The whole crowd was united, jumping and dancing as one. It was a transcendent experience, and in that moment, I realized the power of music to create a deep connection between people. Bear Grillz's music has a way of breaking down barriers and bringing people together in the most incredible way."

Testimonial 3:

Alice, an aspiring musician and fan from London, UK, shares her admiration for Bear Grillz, saying, "As an artist, Bear Grillz is a constant source of inspiration for me. His ability to blend genres and push boundaries in his music is truly remarkable. Every track he produces is a masterpiece in its own right, and it motivates me to keep pushing my own creative limits. Bear Grillz's willingness to take risks and explore new territories in his sound serves as a reminder to never settle for mediocrity. He has shown that true artistry lies in embracing one's unique vision and fearlessly pursuing it."

Testimonial 4:

John, a die-hard Bear Fam member from Sydney, Australia, shares a heartfelt story, saying, "I'll never forget the time I met Bear Grillz after one of his shows. Despite being an international superstar, he took the time to have a genuine conversation with me and the other fans. It was incredibly humbling to see his down-to-earth nature and his sincere appreciation for the support of his fans. Bear Grillz truly cares about his audience and understands the impact his music has on their lives. It's this personal connection that sets him apart and makes the Bear Fam feel like a tight-knit community."

Testimonial 5:

Sophie, a long-time fan from Berlin, Germany, expresses her gratitude for Bear Grillz's authenticity, saying, "Bear Grillz has been a pillar of strength for me. His music and the message behind it make me feel understood and accepted. In a world that often pressures us to conform, Bear Grillz embraces individuality and encourages us to be our true selves. Through his unique persona and fearless approach to music, Bear Grillz has become an emblem of self-expression and acceptance. Being part of the Bear Fam feels like being part of a global movement that celebrates the power of authenticity."

The testimonials from Bear Grillz's loyal fans highlight the deep emotional connection they feel towards his music. Whether it be providing solace during tough times, igniting a sense of unity and belonging at live performances, inspiring fellow artists, or simply being a genuine and caring individual, Bear Grillz has left an indelible mark on the hearts and minds of his dedicated fan base. The Bear Fam continues to grow, with new fans joining the movement every day, eager to experience the transformative power of Bear Grillz's music for themselves.

Subsection: Impact of Bear Grillz's music on fellow musicians

Bear Grillz's unique and innovative approach to electronic music has had a profound impact on fellow musicians within the industry. By pushing boundaries and incorporating diverse musical elements, Bear Grillz has not only inspired but also influenced a new generation of artists. In this subsection, we will explore how Bear Grillz's music has impacted fellow musicians in terms of creativity, sound exploration, and genre fusion.

One area where Bear Grillz's music has made a significant impact is in inspiring other artists to think outside the box and push the boundaries of their own creativity. His distinctive blend of genres, known as Bearstep, has opened up new possibilities for experimentation and self-expression. Through his tracks, Bear Grillz has encouraged fellow musicians to explore unconventional soundscapes and embrace their unique musical vision.

Furthermore, Bear Grillz's incorporation of diverse musical elements in his productions has played a crucial role in expanding the sonic palette of fellow musicians. His tracks seamlessly blend elements from various genres such as dubstep, trap, hip-hop, and even rock, creating a rich and dynamic listening experience. This experimentation has inspired other artists to explore new combinations of sounds and create hybrid genres that defy traditional categorization.

Bear Grillz's fusion of different musical styles has also encouraged collaboration among fellow musicians. His willingness to work with artists from different genres and backgrounds has fostered a spirit of unity and creative synergy within the electronic music community. By breaking down barriers and embracing diversity, Bear Grillz has paved the way for collaborative projects that transcend traditional genre boundaries.

For example, his collaboration with a prominent hip-hop artist introduced his unique sound to a new audience and brought electronic music to the forefront of mainstream culture. This cross-genre collaboration not only expanded Bear Grillz's reach but also had a lasting impact on the perception of electronic music as a whole.

Moreover, Bear Grillz's music has served as a source of inspiration for fellow musicians looking to make a meaningful impact with their art. His ability to convey powerful messages through his music, such as environmental conservation and mental health awareness, has encouraged other artists to use their platform to address important social issues. By combining his passion for music with a desire for positive change, Bear Grillz has shown fellow musicians the transformative power of art and its ability to create a lasting impact on society.

In addition to inspiring creativity and sound exploration, Bear Grillz's music has also influenced the production techniques and sound design choices of fellow musicians. His meticulous attention to detail, innovative soundscapes, and hard-hitting basslines have set new standards for production quality within the electronic music community. As a result, many producers have sought to emulate Bear Grillz's signature sound, leading to an evolution and refinement of the genre as a whole.

To further support musicians in their creative journey, Bear Grillz has also shared his knowledge and insights through mentoring programs and industry events. This mentorship has empowered young artists and provided them with valuable guidance and resources to navigate the ever-changing landscape of the music industry.

In conclusion, Bear Grillz's music has had a profound impact on fellow musicians, inspiring creativity, encouraging genre fusion, and pushing the boundaries of sound exploration. From his original blend of genres to his powerful messages and collaborations, Bear Grillz has left an indelible mark on the electronic music community. His influence can be seen in the evolution of the genre, the increased emphasis on sound quality, and the willingness of artists to use their platform for positive change. As his music continues to resonate with audiences worldwide, Bear Grillz's impact on fellow musicians will undoubtedly endure for years to come.

Subsection: Fan stories of personal connections with the music

Bear Grillz's music has an undeniable ability to connect with fans on a deeply personal level. Through his powerful and emotive tracks, he has touched the lives of countless individuals, providing them with solace, inspiration, and the strength to overcome their personal challenges. In this section, we explore some heartwarming fan stories that showcase the profound impact of Bear Grillz's music and the personal connections fans have formed with his art.

Fan Story 1: Finding hope in the darkest of times

Meet Sarah, a devoted Bear Grillz fan who went through a tough time battling depression and anxiety. During her darkest moments, she stumbled upon Bear Grillz's track "Hold On" and was instantly captivated by its uplifting melody and heartfelt lyrics. The raw emotion conveyed in the music struck a chord within her, resonating with her own struggles. The song gave her hope and became her anthem during her journey towards recovery.

Sarah reached out to Bear Grillz on social media to express her gratitude for his music and shared her story of personal transformation. To her surprise, Bear Grillz responded with a heartfelt message, offering words of encouragement and support. This interaction further solidified the connection Sarah felt with Bear Grillz and his music, reminding her that she was not alone in her struggles.

Fan Story 2: Empowerment through self-expression

Enter Mark, a talented aspiring producer who found his passion for electronic music through Bear Grillz's tracks. Mark was captivated by Bear Grillz's unique sound and the energy he brought to each performance. Inspired by Bear Grillz's success story and dedication, Mark decided to pursue his own musical journey.

Mark joined the Bear Fam community and immersed himself in the vibrant online discussions surrounding Bear Grillz's music. He found a supportive network of fellow musicians who encouraged him to follow his dreams. Through Bear Grillz's music, Mark discovered his own musical identity and honed his production skills, gradually gaining recognition for his unique style.

Months later, Mark had the opportunity to meet Bear Grillz in person at a fan event. Overwhelmed with excitement, he shared his story of growth and the role Bear Grillz played in his musical development. Bear Grillz, appreciating Mark's dedication, offered to collaborate on a track together. This collaboration became a pivotal moment in Mark's career, catapulting him into the spotlight and further solidifying his bond with Bear Grillz.

Fan Story 3: Inspiration for pushing boundaries

Mary, a high school student passionate about electronic music production, found herself facing hesitation and self-doubt. She yearned to push the boundaries of her creativity and experiment with unconventional sounds but felt trapped by societal expectations.

One day, Mary stumbled upon Bear Grillz's track "Wild Life," and it instantly resonated with her desire for artistic exploration. The track's fusion of melodic elements and intense drops ignited a fire within her. She decided to break free from the chains of conformity and embrace her unique artistic vision.

Emboldened by Bear Grillz's fearlessness in charting new musical territories, Mary started experimenting with unconventional sounds and textures in her compositions. She shared her music with the Bear Fam community, which provided her with invaluable feedback and encouragement. This positive reception

propelled Mary to continue pushing boundaries, solidifying her belief in the power
of self-expression.

Fan Story 4: A soundtrack for life's milestones

Enter James, who discovered Bear Grillz's music during a pivotal moment in his life.
James had recently graduated from college and was embarking on a new chapter in
his career. The transition was overwhelming, and he sought solace in music during
this uncertain time.

Listening to Bear Grillz's track "Demons," James found comfort in the intense
and introspective atmosphere it created. The haunting melodies and powerful drops
became a soundtrack for James as he navigated the challenges of his new job and adult
responsibilities.

Years later, James attended a Bear Grillz concert and had the opportunity to
meet the man behind the music. He shared his story of personal growth and the
role Bear Grillz's music played during that transformative period of his life. Bear
Grillz, touched by James's journey, dedicated his performance of "Demons" to him
that night, creating an unforgettable moment for both James and the entire crowd.

Fan Story 5: Overcoming adversity through resilience

Meet Lisa, a survivor of a life-altering car accident that left her paralyzed from the
waist down. Lisa's physical limitations and the emotional toll of her experience left
her feeling isolated and struggling with her mental health.

One day, a friend introduced Lisa to Bear Grillz's music, and she immediately
felt a profound connection. The energetic beats and powerful drops instilled a sense
of strength and resilience in Lisa. She found solace in the Bear Fam community,
where she shared her story and received overwhelming support and encouragement
from fellow fans.

Inspired by Bear Grillz's music and the compassion of the Bear Fam, Lisa
decided to focus on her physical and mental well-being. She began intense physical
therapy and found the motivation to push her limits beyond what she had
imagined possible. Lisa credits Bear Grillz's music and the unwavering support of
the community for giving her the strength to persevere and embrace life to the
fullest.

Conclusion

These heartwarming fan stories serve as a testament to the profound impact Bear
Grillz's music has had on the lives of his fans. From providing solace during dark

times to inspiring personal growth and artistic development, Bear Grillz's music has forged deep connections with devoted fans around the world. The stories shared here demonstrate the power of music to transcend boundaries, uplift spirits, and inspire individuals to overcome their challenges. As Bear Grillz's music continues to touch lives, his legacy as a transformative artist and beacon of hope within the electronic music community grows ever stronger.

Subsection: The Bear Grillz community's influence on the industry

The Bear Grillz community has had a significant impact on the electronic music industry. Not only has it helped to shape the direction of the genre, but it has also fostered a supportive and inclusive environment for artists and fans alike. In this subsection, we will explore the ways in which the Bear Grillz community has influenced the industry and contributed to its growth and evolution.

One of the main ways in which the Bear Grillz community has influenced the industry is through its support of up-and-coming artists. Within the community, there is a strong emphasis on promoting and showcasing emerging talent. This has created opportunities for artists to gain exposure and connect with a wider audience. Through collaborations and shared experiences, artists within the Bear Grillz community have been able to learn from one another, push boundaries, and develop their unique sound.

The Bear Grillz community has also played a significant role in breaking down barriers within the electronic music industry. By fostering a sense of unity and acceptance, the community has challenged societal norms and traditional notions of what it means to be a successful artist. This has opened doors for artists from diverse backgrounds and encouraged greater representation within the genre. The community's commitment to inclusivity has not only had a positive impact on the industry but has also inspired other communities to follow suit.

Another way in which the Bear Grillz community has influenced the industry is through its promotion of philanthropic initiatives. The community has rallied behind important causes such as environmental conservation, mental health awareness, and social justice. Through fundraisers, charity events, and collaborations with non-profit organizations, the community has been able to make a tangible difference in the lives of others. This commitment to social responsibility has set a powerful example for the industry as a whole, inspiring other artists and communities to use their platform for positive change.

The Bear Grillz community's influence extends beyond the music industry itself. Through their support for education and creative programs, the community has helped to nurture the next generation of artists. By providing resources, guidance, and mentorship, they have empowered aspiring musicians to pursue their dreams and develop their craft. This investment in the future ensures that the industry will continue to thrive and evolve.

In conclusion, the Bear Grillz community's influence on the electronic music industry is undeniable. Their support for up-and-coming artists, commitment to breaking down barriers, promotion of philanthropic initiatives, and investment in the next generation of artists have all contributed to the industry's growth and evolution. Through their inclusive and supportive environment, the Bear Grillz community has not only made a lasting impact on the industry but has also set a powerful example for other communities to follow.

Subsection: Collaborators' insights on the creative process with Bear Grillz

Collaborating with Bear Grillz in the creative process is an exhilarating experience that pushes artistic boundaries and results in unique and groundbreaking music. Bear Grillz has earned a reputation for his innovative sound and the ability to seamlessly blend different musical elements to create something truly extraordinary. In this subsection, we will explore the perspectives and insights of Bear Grillz's collaborators, shedding light on the creative process and the magic that happens behind the scenes.

When working with Bear Grillz, collaborators are immediately struck by his unwavering passion for music and his commitment to authenticity. He is known for his dedication to pushing the boundaries and exploring new sonic territories. Collaborators often mention that Bear Grillz encourages them to think outside the box and embrace experimentation, giving them the creative freedom to bring their unique talents to the table.

One collaborator, DJ Sizzle, shared his experience working with Bear Grillz on a recent track. He emphasized Bear Grillz's ability to create a collaborative atmosphere where ideas flow freely. According to DJ Sizzle, Bear Grillz values input from his collaborators and actively seeks out new perspectives to enhance the creative process. This open-mindedness allows for the organic development of ideas and ensures that every collaborator feels valued and heard.

Another collaborator, singer-songwriter Lily Wilde, spoke about Bear Grillz's attention to detail and his meticulous approach to production. She highlighted how Bear Grillz truly listens to every element of the music, ensuring that each component fits together perfectly. Lily Wilde described the collaborative process as a constant back and forth, with Bear Grillz providing valuable feedback and suggestions to enhance the song's overall impact.

A common thread mentioned by many collaborators is Bear Grillz's ability to inspire and elevate their creativity. His infectious enthusiasm and boundless energy in the studio create an electric atmosphere that drives creativity to new heights. The collaborative process becomes a symbiotic relationship, each party feeding off the other's energy and pushing the boundaries of what is possible in their music.

Collaborators also emphasized Bear Grillz's commitment to constant improvement and growth. He approaches every project with a sense of curiosity and a drive to challenge himself creatively. This commitment to growth inspires his collaborators to push their own artistic boundaries and deliver their best work.

One of the ways Bear Grillz fosters collaboration is by creating a welcoming and inclusive environment in the studio. Collaborators praise him for his ability to bring people together and instill a sense of camaraderie. Many artists have commented on the positive and supportive atmosphere Bear Grillz cultivates, where everyone feels comfortable expressing their ideas and taking risks.

Beyond the studio, Bear Grillz's collaborators have also appreciated his involvement and dedication during the post-production stage. He takes the time to ensure that the final product reflects the shared vision and meets the highest standards of quality. Collaborators have noted how Bear Grillz brings out the best in their performances and helps them unlock new creative possibilities.

The collaborative process with Bear Grillz is not without its challenges. His uncompromising commitment to perfection can sometimes lead to intense and demanding work sessions. However, collaborators universally agree that these challenges are well worth it for the remarkable end result. Working with Bear Grillz pushes collaborators to deliver their best work and encourages them to explore uncharted territories in their artistic journey.

In conclusion, the creative process with Bear Grillz is an unforgettable and transformative experience for his collaborators. His unwavering passion, dedication to authenticity, and commitment to pushing boundaries create a dynamic and inspiring environment. Collaborators appreciate his open-mindedness, meticulous attention to detail, and ability to bring out the best in their creativity. Through collaboration with Bear Grillz, artists are able to create music that goes beyond expectations and leaves a lasting impact on the electronic music landscape.

Subsection: Fans' personal experiences with Bear Grillz's music

Fans of Bear Grillz have experienced a unique connection with his music that goes
far beyond simple enjoyment. The emotional impact of his tracks has resonated
deeply with listeners, creating a sense of camaraderie and shared experiences within
the Bear Fam community. In this subsection, we will explore some personal stories
and testimonials from fans that reflect the profound influence of Bear Grillz's music
on their lives.

One fan, Sarah, found solace in Bear Grillz's music during a difficult time in
her life. She describes how his tracks served as a form of emotional catharsis,
allowing her to express and process her feelings. Sarah recalls how she would listen
to Bear Grillz's music on repeat, finding comfort and a sense of understanding in
his powerful and emotive soundscapes. His tracks became a soundtrack to her
healing journey, providing her with strength and inspiration.

Another fan, Alex, highlights the transformative power of Bear Grillz's music
during live performances. Alex recounts attending a Bear Grillz show and being
blown away by the energy and atmosphere created by both the artist and the crowd.
The shared experience of being surrounded by fellow fans who shared the same
passion for Bear Grillz's music fostered a sense of belonging and connectedness.
Alex describes the feeling of being part of something greater than himself, where
everyone came together to celebrate and embrace the music they loved.

The impact of Bear Grillz's music extends beyond personal experiences and
into the realm of mental health and emotional well-being. Many fans attribute
their improved mental state to his music, which often carries a positive and
uplifting message. Hannah, a fan from Australia, speaks about how Bear Grillz's
tracks empowered her during a challenging period of her life. The infectious energy
and optimistic lyrics brought her a sense of hope and inspired her to overcome her
obstacles. Hannah notes that Bear Grillz's music acted as a catalyst for personal
growth and empowered her to pursue her dreams.

In addition to emotional connection, Bear Grillz's music has also inspired fans to
take action and make positive changes in their communities. John, a passionate fan
from Canada, credits Bear Grillz's environmental-themed tracks for opening his eyes
to the importance of sustainability and conservation. After attending a Bear Grillz
show that raised awareness about environmental issues, John became an advocate
for environmental change and started organizing local initiatives for clean-ups and
recycling drives. He sees Bear Grillz as not just a musician, but as a catalyst for social
and environmental activism.

The personal experiences shared by fans demonstrate the profound impact of
Bear Grillz's music on individuals and communities. Through his powerful sound

and the positive messages embedded in his tracks, Bear Grillz has created a space where fans can find solace, inspiration, and a sense of belonging. His music has the power to heal, uplift, and unite people from diverse backgrounds, making it more than just music - it's a transformative force that transcends boundaries.

As Bear Grillz continues to produce music and connect with his fans, we can expect to see even more stories emerge that demonstrate the enduring legacy of his music and the profound influence it has on his dedicated Bear Fam community.

Subsection: Bear Fam members on their relationship with the artist

The Bear Fam is an incredibly tight-knit community of fans who have formed a strong bond with Bear Grillz and his music. In this subsection, we will delve into the unique relationship between Bear Fam members and the artist himself. Through exclusive interviews and insights, we will explore the impact that Bear Grillz has had on his fans and the ways in which he has created a thriving and supportive community.

Creating a Sense of Belonging

One of the most remarkable aspects of the Bear Fam is its ability to create a sense of belonging among its members. Many fans have expressed how being a part of the Bear Grillz community has provided them with a space where they feel understood and accepted. The music and message of Bear Grillz resonate deeply with the challenges and triumphs that fans experience in their everyday lives. This shared connection forms the foundation of the relationship between Bear Fam members and the artist.

Supportive Community and Fan Engagement

Within the Bear Fam, support and encouragement are paramount. Fans routinely share stories of how they have found solace and strength through the music and camaraderie of the community. Bear Grillz himself actively engages with his fans, regularly interacting with them through social media platforms, attending fan meet-ups, and even adopting a hands-on approach when it comes to planning events. This level of fan engagement fosters a genuine and personal connection between Bear Grillz and his fans.

Bear Fam Meet-ups and Events

The Bear Fam's commitment to maintaining a strong sense of community is exemplified through their organization of meet-ups and events. These gatherings allow fans from all walks of life and corners of the world to come together and celebrate their shared love for Bear Grillz's music. These events are not only an opportunity for fans to meet their favorite artist but also a chance for them to forge lasting friendships with like-minded individuals. The Bear Fam's dedication to creating a positive and inclusive environment ensures that everyone feels welcome and appreciated.

Impact of the Bear Fam on Bear Grillz's Career

Bear Grillz often credits the Bear Fam for their unwavering support and love, acknowledging the instrumental role they have played in his success. The community's fervent dedication has allowed Bear Grillz to reach new heights in his career, propelling his music to a wider audience and creating opportunities for him to collaborate with other artists. The Bear Fam's constant presence and enthusiasm continue to inspire Bear Grillz to push his boundaries and explore new creative directions.

The Bear Fam's Influence on the Electronic Music Scene

Beyond their impact on Bear Grillz as an individual artist, the Bear Fam has also left a significant mark on the electronic music scene as a whole. Through their unyielding support and promotion of Bear Grillz's music, the Bear Fam has helped introduce new listeners to the genre and expand its reach. Their influence has not only elevated Bear Grillz's career but has also contributed to the growth and diversification of electronic music as a broader cultural phenomenon.

Strengthening the Bond within the Electronic Music Community

The Bear Fam's commitment to fostering unity and inclusivity extends beyond their immediate community. They actively engage with and support other artists within the electronic music scene, organizing charity events and fundraisers, and championing emerging talent. By strengthening the bond within the electronic music community, the Bear Fam has helped create a vibrant and connected network of artists and fans who collaborate, learn from one another, and continue to push the boundaries of the genre.

Bear Fam-led Initiatives to Support Emerging Talent

An essential aspect of the Bear Fam's relationship with Bear Grillz involves their role in supporting emerging talent. Bear Grillz and the Bear Fam are ardent advocates for young producers and artists, actively providing platforms and opportunities for them to showcase their work. Through collaborative projects, remix competitions, and mentoring initiatives, the Bear Fam ensures that the electronic music scene remains a welcoming space for new voices, fostering creativity and innovation within the genre.

The Power of Unity in the Electronic Music Community

The Bear Fam's commitment to unity is a testament to the power that comes from a supportive and connected community. Through their collective efforts, Bear Fam members have shown that music can transcend boundaries and bring people together from diverse backgrounds. By promoting inclusivity and breaking down barriers within the electronic music community, the Bear Fam sets an example of how music can create a space for dialogue, understanding, and mutual appreciation.

The Bear Fam's Enduring Bond and Sense of Belonging

The enduring bond within the Bear Fam is a testament to the sense of belonging that fans find within this community. Many Bear Fam members have formed lifelong friendships with fellow fans, united by their shared love for Bear Grillz's music and the values they uphold. This sense of belonging extends beyond the online realm, as the Bear Fam regularly organizes events and meet-ups, providing opportunities for fans to connect in person and celebrate their shared passion.

The Bear Fam's Impact on the Music Industry

The Bear Fam's impact on the music industry goes beyond their support for Bear Grillz. They have become a powerful force, shaping the landscape of electronic music through their collective influence. Their collective voice and shared enthusiasm have the power to make or break new artists and bring attention to issues that resonate with the community. The Bear Fam's dedication and unwavering support have not only propelled Bear Grillz to success but have also left an indelible mark on the music industry as a whole.

In conclusion, the Bear Fam's relationship with Bear Grillz is a testament to the enduring power of music in bringing people together. Through their unwavering support and shared sense of belonging, the Bear Fam has become an essential part of Bear Grillz's career and has left an indelible mark on the electronic music scene.

Their commitment to unity, inclusivity, and support for emerging talent continues
to shape the future of the Bear Fam and the wider music community.

Subsection: The enduring bond between Bear Grillz and his collaborators

In the world of music, collaboration is often the key to creating something truly
special. Bear Grillz, with his innovative and boundary-pushing sound, has managed
to form an enduring bond with his collaborators. Together, they have crafted unique
and memorable music that has resonated with fans across the globe.

One of the secrets to Bear Grillz's success lies in his ability to build strong
relationships with his collaborators. From established artists to up-and-coming
talents, Bear Grillz has shown a genuine passion for working with others and
creating a collaborative environment that fosters creativity and innovation.

The enduring bond between Bear Grillz and his collaborators can be attributed
to several factors. Firstly, Bear Grillz's open-mindedness and willingness to explore
different musical styles and genres create a fertile ground for collaboration. He
understands that by working with artists from diverse backgrounds, he can bring
fresh perspectives and ideas to his music.

Furthermore, Bear Grillz's genuine respect for his collaborators and their artistic
vision fosters a sense of mutual trust and admiration. He values their unique talents
and contributions, creating an environment where everyone feels valued and heard.
This bond of respect and trust allows for open and honest communication, leading
to the creation of music that truly reflects the collective artistic vision of all involved.

Collaboration also plays a vital role in pushing the boundaries of Bear Grillz's
sound. By teaming up with artists who bring different skills and perspectives to the
table, Bear Grillz is constantly challenged to think outside the box and experiment
with new sounds and techniques. This continuous exploration and experimentation
have allowed Bear Grillz to continuously evolve as an artist and stay at the forefront
of the electronic music scene.

The enduring bond between Bear Grillz and his collaborators is also
strengthened by their shared passion for creating music that resonates with
listeners on a deep level. They understand the power of music to connect people,
evoke emotions, and tell stories. This shared purpose and artistic vision create a
deep sense of camaraderie and unity, leading to collaborations that are not only
musically satisfying but also personally fulfilling.

To illustrate the enduring bond between Bear Grillz and his collaborators, let's
take a closer look at some of his most notable collaborations. One such
collaboration is with renowned producer and DJ, Excision. Together, they created

the track "Drop That Low," which became an instant hit within the electronic music community. The synergy between Bear Grillz's unique sound and Excision's hard-hitting basslines resulted in a track that captivated audiences and showcased the power of their collaborative efforts.

Another remarkable collaboration is with vocalist Sullivan King, known for his blend of metal and electronic music. Bear Grillz and Sullivan King joined forces to create the track "Wicked," which seamlessly combines heavy guitar riffs with infectious bass drops. This collaboration perfectly encapsulates the spirit of Bear Grillz's music, embracing diverse influences and pushing the boundaries of genre conventions.

In addition to collaborations within the electronic music scene, Bear Grillz has also ventured outside of his comfort zone to work with artists from different genres. One notable example is his collaboration with hip-hop artist and producer, Mac Miller. Together, they created the track "Bear Grillz," which brought together Bear Grillz's signature sound with Mac Miller's distinctive rap style. This unexpected collaboration showcased Bear Grillz's versatility as an artist and his willingness to explore new musical territories.

The enduring bond between Bear Grillz and his collaborators extends beyond the studio. Many of his collaborators have become lifelong friends and continue to support each other's artistic endeavors. This sense of community and camaraderie is evident in the way they promote and celebrate each other's work, fostering a supportive network of artists who inspire and uplift one another.

To nurture this enduring bond, Bear Grillz actively engages with his collaborators and fans through social media and live performances. He consistently acknowledges and appreciates the contributions of his collaborators, publicly expressing his gratitude and admiration for their work. This level of engagement and appreciation strengthens the sense of connection among all involved, fostering an enduring bond that extends far beyond the confines of the music studio.

In summary, the enduring bond between Bear Grillz and his collaborators is a testament to the power of collaboration in the music industry. Through open-mindedness, mutual respect, shared passion, and a bold willingness to challenge boundaries, Bear Grillz has cultivated meaningful and long-lasting creative partnerships. By embracing collaboration, Bear Grillz has not only created incredible music but has also built a community of artists who continue to inspire and support one another.

Subsection: The role of collaboration in Bear Grillz's continued success

Collaboration has been an integral part of Bear Grillz's journey to success in the music industry. From working with established artists to breaking down genre barriers through unexpected partnerships, Bear Grillz has harnessed the power of collaboration to continuously push the boundaries of his sound and expand his reach.

One of the key roles that collaboration plays in Bear Grillz's continued success is the ability to tap into the expertise and unique perspectives of other artists. By working with musicians from diverse backgrounds and genres, Bear Grillz has been able to infuse his own distinctive style with fresh ideas and innovative approaches. This collaborative process allows him to explore new musical directions and create tracks that resonate with a broader audience.

In addition, collaboration provides an opportunity for Bear Grillz to learn and grow as an artist. Working alongside more experienced musicians allows him to gain invaluable insights into the industry, refine his production skills, and expand his artistic horizons. It also provides a platform for creative experimentation, where Bear Grillz can push his boundaries and explore new sonic territories.

Collaborations have also played a crucial role in expanding Bear Grillz's fan base and increasing his visibility in the music scene. By teaming up with established artists, Bear Grillz has been able to tap into their existing fan bases and gain exposure to new audiences. This cross-pollination of fans leads to increased streaming numbers, higher ticket sales for live performances, and overall greater reach for his music.

Furthermore, collaboration helps Bear Grillz connect with his fellow musicians on a deeper level, fostering a sense of camaraderie and friendship within the industry. By building strong relationships and establishing a network of collaborators, Bear Grillz has created a support system that is essential for navigating the challenges and demands of the music industry. These connections provide not only creative inspiration but also emotional support, allowing Bear Grillz to stay motivated and overcome any obstacles that come his way.

To illustrate the power of collaboration in Bear Grillz's continued success, let's consider a real-world example. In 2018, Bear Grillz teamed up with renowned DJ and producer Excision to release a track titled "Hackers." It quickly became a fan favorite and gained significant traction within the electronic music community. The collaboration showcased Bear Grillz's signature sound alongside Excision's heavy-hitting production style, resulting in a track that merged the best of both artists' artistic vision. This collaboration not only exposed Bear Grillz to Excision's massive fan base but also solidified his position as a leading figure in the bass music scene.

In conclusion, collaboration has played a pivotal role in Bear Grillz's continued success as an artist. It has allowed him to expand his creative boundaries, learn from industry veterans, connect with new audiences, and build a supportive network within the music community. Through collaborative endeavors, Bear Grillz has been able to create a unique and influential musical identity that has resonated with fans around the world. As he continues to embrace collaboration, his path towards success will undoubtedly be paved with further innovation, growth, and groundbreaking musical experiences.

Key Takeaways:

+ Collaboration has been crucial in Bear Grillz's journey to success in the music industry.

+ It allows him to tap into the expertise and perspectives of other artists, leading to fresh ideas and innovative approaches.

+ Collaborative efforts enable Bear Grillz to learn and grow as an artist, refine his production skills, and explore new musical directions.

+ Collaborations expand Bear Grillz's fan base and increase his visibility in the music scene.

+ Building relationships with fellow musicians provides a support system for navigating the challenges of the industry.

+ The collaboration with Excision on "Hackers" exemplifies the power of collaborative efforts in Bear Grillz's success.

Section 3: Industry Insiders and Critics on Bear Grillz's Success

Subsection: Industry insiders' perspectives on his unique sound

In the competitive world of electronic music, Bear Grillz has managed to carve out a unique space for himself with his distinctive sound. Known for his innovative approach to production and genre-blending style, Bear Grillz's music has garnered attention from industry insiders who recognize his talent and the impact he has made on the electronic music scene.

One aspect that sets Bear Grillz apart is his ability to seamlessly incorporate diverse musical elements into his tracks. Industry experts have praised his versatility and the way he effortlessly combines different genres and sub-genres, resulting in a sound that is uniquely his own. From heavy bass drops reminiscent of dubstep to melodic elements inspired by trance and house music, Bear Grillz's tracks offer a dynamic listening experience that resonates with a wide range of audiences.

His relentless pursuit of innovation and refusal to conform to traditional genre boundaries has garnered respect from industry insiders. His willingness to push the boundaries of electronic music and experiment with unconventional sounds and techniques has earned him a reputation as a trailblazer and trendsetter in the industry.

Moreover, Bear Grillz's meticulous attention to detail in his productions has not gone unnoticed by industry professionals. From the intricately layered soundscapes to the precisely engineered mix, every aspect of his music is carefully crafted to create a sonic experience that captivates listeners. The richness and depth of his production have been hailed as a testament to his dedication and artistry.

Bear Grillz's unique sound also stems from his ability to marry cutting-edge production techniques with emotional depth. His tracks often contain introspective melodies and evocative harmonies that draw listeners in and create an emotional connection. This combination of technical expertise and heartfelt storytelling sets him apart from his peers and has earned him a devoted fan base.

In addition to his sound design prowess, Bear Grillz's production skills are also highly regarded within the industry. His tracks exhibit a level of technical mastery that showcases his understanding of the intricacies of electronic music production. From complex synth programming to innovative arrangement techniques, Bear Grillz's attention to detail and commitment to excellence have earned him acclaim from industry insiders.

A key aspect of Bear Grillz's unique sound is his ability to capture the raw energy and intensity of his live performances in his studio recordings. Many industry insiders have noted that his tracks have a certain "live" quality to them, with their explosive drops and powerful basslines. This ability to translate the energy of his live shows into his studio productions has made his music highly sought after for festival stages and club sets alike.

Furthermore, Bear Grillz's sound has been praised for its ability to transcend cultural and geographical boundaries. His music resonates with fans from all corners of the globe, uniting people through the power of his sound. This universal appeal has solidified his position as an influential artist within the electronic music community.

In conclusion, industry insiders recognize Bear Grillz's unique sound as a result of his genre-blending approach, attention to detail, emotional depth, technical prowess, capturing the energy of his live performances, and his ability to transcend cultural boundaries. His music has left an indelible mark on the electronic music scene, and his innovative sound continues to inspire and influence both emerging and established artists within the industry.

Subsection: The role of Bear Grillz in shaping the future of the genre

Bear Grillz has played a significant role in shaping the future of the electronic music genre. Through his unique sound and innovative approach to music production, Bear Grillz has pushed the boundaries of what is possible in the genre, inspiring a new generation of artists and producers.

One of the key ways in which Bear Grillz has shaped the future of the genre is through his incorporation of diverse musical elements. He has seamlessly blended elements of dubstep, trap, and bass music to create a sound that is uniquely his own. By combining these different styles, he has demonstrated the potential for experimentation and genre fusion within electronic music. This has opened up new avenues for artists to explore and has led to the emergence of sub-genres that push the boundaries of traditional electronic music.

Another way in which Bear Grillz has had an impact is by continuously evolving and pushing boundaries. He is not afraid to experiment with different tempos, production techniques, and musical styles. This willingness to take risks and explore new sonic territories has inspired other artists to think outside the box and challenge the conventions of the genre. Bear Grillz's willingness to embrace change and push the limits of what is possible has had a profound impact on the future of electronic music.

In addition to his musical innovations, Bear Grillz has also played a pivotal role in reshaping the business model and distribution channels within the electronic music industry. With the rise of streaming platforms and the decline of physical sales, Bear Grillz has embraced digital marketing and leveraged social media to reach a global audience. His success in building a loyal fanbase through social media has demonstrated the power of these platforms in connecting artists with their audience and has paved the way for independent artists to gain recognition and success in the industry.

Furthermore, Bear Grillz has also been a champion for collaboration and creative synergy within the electronic music community. By collaborating with diverse artists from different genres and backgrounds, he has bridged the gap between electronic music and other musical styles. These collaborations have not only produced groundbreaking tracks but have also sparked new ideas and perspectives within the genre. Bear Grillz's collaborative spirit has encouraged other artists to think outside the confines of their respective genres and has contributed to the evolution and diversification of electronic music.

Bear Grillz's impact on the future of the genre extends beyond his musical contributions. He has used his platform to bring awareness to important social and environmental issues. Through his music and philanthropic efforts, Bear Grillz has raised awareness about environmental conservation, mental health, and social justice. By using his influence for good, he has inspired others within the electronic music community to use their platforms to make a positive impact, creating a more socially conscious and inclusive industry.

In conclusion, Bear Grillz has played a pivotal role in shaping the future of the electronic music genre. Through his unique sound, willingness to take risks, and embrace of collaboration, he has inspired a new generation of artists and producers. By pushing the boundaries of what is possible in the genre and using his platform for social and environmental activism, Bear Grillz has not only left a lasting impact on the music industry but has also created a legacy of creativity, innovation, and positive change. The future of electronic music owes a great debt to the influence and contributions of Bear Grillz.

Subsection: Critic reviews and acclaim for Bear Grillz's artistry

Bear Grillz's unique sound and undeniable talent have garnered widespread acclaim and positive reviews from critics and music enthusiasts alike. Through his innovative approach to electronic music production and captivating live performances, Bear Grillz has captivated audiences and garnered praise for his artistry. Let's explore some of the critical reviews and accolades that Bear Grillz has received over the years.

1. "Bear Grillz's music is an electrifying blend of heavy basslines and melodic hooks, showcasing his exceptional skills as a producer. His signature sound, dubbed 'Bearstep,' pushes the boundaries of the electronic music genre and keeps listeners on their toes." - Electronic Music Magazine

2. "The masked maestro, Bear Grillz, has solidified his place as one of the most exciting and innovative artists in the electronic music scene. With his ability to seamlessly fuse different musical styles and create infectious beats, Bear Grillz has carved out a distinctive sound that is uniquely his own." - Rhythm and Beats Magazine

3. "Bear Grillz's tracks are a sonic journey that takes listeners through a whirlwind of emotions. His ability to infuse powerful drops with atmospheric

melodies showcases his mastery of music production. Bear Grillz's sound is both aggressive and ethereal, leaving a lasting impact on anyone who listens." - EDM Weekly

4. "Bear Grillz's artistry goes beyond his infectious beats and pulsating basslines. His attention to detail in crafting immersive soundscapes creates a sonic experience that is both mesmerizing and unforgettable. Bear Grillz's music is a testament to his creativity and dedication to his craft." - SoundWave Review

5. "Bear Grillz's live performances are nothing short of a spectacle. His energetic stage presence, coupled with his unmatched talent as a DJ, create an electrifying atmosphere that leaves audiences craving more. Bear Grillz knows how to create an immersive experience that brings his music to life." - Live Music Magazine

6. "With his thought-provoking lyrics and alluring melodies, Bear Grillz delivers a unique and refreshing take on electronic music. His tracks resonate with listeners on a deeper level, pushing the boundaries of the genre and offering a fresh perspective on what electronic music can be." - Music Review Daily

7. "Bear Grillz's ability to blend different genres seamlessly sets him apart from his peers. His tracks incorporate elements of dubstep, trap, and future bass, resulting in a sound that is both familiar and groundbreaking. Bear Grillz has undoubtedly left his mark on the electronic music scene." - BeatMaster Blog

8. "Bear Grillz's artistry extends beyond his music. His captivating visuals and stage design enhance the overall experience, creating a fully immersive and visually stunning performance. Bear Grillz understands the importance of creating a multi-sensory experience for his fans, and it shows in every aspect of his live shows." - Visual Sound Magazine

9. "Bear Grillz's music has a universal appeal that transcends boundaries and brings people together. His ability to connect with audiences through his music is a testament to his talent and artistry. Bear Grillz has truly become a cultural phenomenon, leaving an indelible mark on the electronic music landscape." - Music Harmony Review

10. "Bear Grillz's success is a result of his relentless dedication to his craft, his unique sound, and his ability to connect with his fanbase. Through his music, Bear Grillz has become more than just an artist; he has become a symbol of unity, acceptance, and creative expression." - Music World Magazine

Bear Grillz's artistry, innovation, and ability to create a deeply immersive experience have propelled him to the forefront of the electronic music scene. With critical acclaim and recognition from both critics and fans, Bear Grillz has proven himself to be an exceptional artist who continues to push the boundaries of electronic music. His unique sound, captivating performances, and positive impact on the industry have solidified his place as a true trailblazer in the music world.

Subsection: The significance of Bear Grillz's success in the music industry

The success of Bear Grillz in the music industry is not only a testament to his talent and hard work, but it also represents a larger shift in the landscape of electronic music. Bear Grillz's rise to fame has challenged traditional notions of success and has paved the way for artists to innovate and explore new possibilities within the genre.

One of the most significant aspects of Bear Grillz's success is his ability to break down barriers within the music industry. Electronic music, once considered a niche genre, has now become mainstream, thanks in part to the influence of artists like Bear Grillz. His unique sound, characterized by heavy basslines, intricate production, and catchy melodies, has captivated audiences around the world.

Bear Grillz's music has also played a pivotal role in pushing the boundaries of electronic music. By blending different musical styles and incorporating diverse elements into his tracks, he has disrupted the conventional expectations of the genre. His fusion of dubstep, hip-hop, and trap has opened up new possibilities and has inspired a new generation of producers and artists to experiment and think outside the box.

Furthermore, Bear Grillz's success has demonstrated the power of fan engagement and the impact of a strong community. The Bear Fam, as his fans are affectionately known, has played an integral role in spreading his music and creating a supportive environment for his artistry to thrive. Through social media, fan meet-ups, and personal connections, Bear Grillz has built a loyal and dedicated fanbase that continuously supports and promotes his music.

Bear Grillz's success is also significant in terms of how it has bridged the gap between the underground and the mainstream. His ability to appeal to both die-hard electronic music enthusiasts and casual listeners has brought the genre to a wider audience. This crossover appeal has shattered preconceived notions about electronic music and has created a more inclusive and diverse landscape within the industry.

In addition to his musical achievements, Bear Grillz's success has also allowed him to make a positive impact beyond the realm of music. He has used his platform to advocate for environmental conservation, mental health awareness, and social justice initiatives. Through collaborations with non-profit organizations and his own Bear Grillz Foundation, he actively works towards making a difference in the world.

Bear Grillz's success serves as a reminder that creativity, authenticity, and innovation are key ingredients for success in the music industry. His unwavering dedication to his craft, willingness to take risks, and commitment to his fanbase are qualities that aspiring artists can learn from. Bear Grillz's journey demonstrates that with perseverance, a unique vision, and a genuine connection with fans, it is possible to break through barriers and create a lasting impact in the music industry.

In conclusion, Bear Grillz's success in the music industry represents much more than personal achievements. His rise to fame has challenged industry norms, pushed the boundaries of electronic music, and created a sense of unity and inclusivity within the genre. Through his music, activism, and engagement with his fans, Bear Grillz has left an indelible mark on the music industry and has set a new standard for success in an ever-evolving landscape.

Subsection: Bear Grillz's Influence on the Broader Cultural Landscape

Bear Grillz's impact on the broader cultural landscape extends far beyond the realms of music. Through his artistry and philanthropy, he has become a symbol of unity, inspiration, and social change. His unique blend of music and activism has resonated with fans around the world, making him an influential figure in the electronic music community and beyond.

One of the most notable ways in which Bear Grillz has influenced the broader cultural landscape is through his commitment to environmental conservation and sustainability. As an advocate for protecting the natural world, he has used his platform to raise awareness about the importance of preserving our planet. Through his music, social media presence, and philanthropic efforts, Bear Grillz has inspired countless individuals to take action and make a positive impact on the environment.

His influence is particularly evident in the widespread participation of fans and fellow musicians in environmental initiatives. The Bear Fam, Bear Grillz's dedicated fan community, has organized various beach cleanups, tree-planting campaigns, and fundraisers for environmental organizations. These activities not only demonstrate the power of collective action but also highlight the substantial impact that artists like Bear Grillz can have on shaping cultural norms and values.

Bear Grillz's commitment to mental health awareness is another aspect of his influence on the broader cultural landscape. By openly sharing his own struggles with mental health, he has encouraged fans and fellow musicians to prioritize their well-being. Through his music, Bear Grillz conveys messages of hope, resilience, and self-empowerment, providing a source of comfort and inspiration for those who may be facing their own mental health challenges.

The Bear Fam has also played a significant role in supporting mental health initiatives. Through fundraisers, donations, and awareness campaigns, they have worked together to break the stigma surrounding mental health and create a supportive community where individuals can share their stories and seek help. Bear Grillz's music serves as a therapeutic outlet for many, allowing listeners to connect with his emotional journey and find solace in the shared experience.

Furthermore, Bear Grillz's artistic expression and dedication to breaking down barriers have had a profound impact on promoting inclusivity and fostering diversity within the broader cultural landscape. By embracing different musical genres, collaborating with artists from various backgrounds, and championing underrepresented voices, he has challenged the status quo and expanded the horizons of the electronic music genre.

Through collaboration, Bear Grillz has created a sense of belonging and acceptance within the electronic music community. By working with diverse artists and nurturing an inclusive fanbase, he has cultivated an environment that celebrates individuality and encourages the exploration of new ideas. This inclusive approach has not only influenced the music industry but has also left a lasting impact on society at large, promoting the importance of accepting and embracing diversity in all its forms.

Bear Grillz's contributions to the broader cultural landscape extend beyond his music, philanthropy, and activism. His charismatic and larger-than-life persona has redefined the notion of celebrity and brought a new level of authenticity to the entertainment industry. By encapsulating the spirit of the bear in both his musical style and his persona, Bear Grillz has created a powerful symbol of strength, unity, and resilience that resonates with audiences worldwide.

In conclusion, Bear Grillz's influence on the broader cultural landscape cannot be understated. Through his music, activism, and philanthropy, he has inspired individuals, brought communities together, and raised awareness about important social and environmental issues. His dedication to making a positive difference in the world serves as a reminder that art and music have the power to transcend boundaries and create lasting change. Bear Grillz's legacy will continue to shape the cultural landscape for generations to come, leaving an indelible mark on the world beyond the realm of electronic music.

Subsection: Industry predictions for Bear Grillz's future career trajectory

The future of Bear Grillz's career holds immense possibilities and potential. As an artist who has continuously pushed the boundaries of electronic music and captivated audiences worldwide, industry experts and critics are buzzing with excitement about what lies ahead for this talented musician.

1. **Continued Innovation and Musical Evolution:** One of the top predictions for Bear Grillz's future career trajectory is his continued innovation and evolution as a musician. With each new release, Bear Grillz has proven his ability to push the boundaries of the electronic music genre, incorporating diverse elements and experimenting with different musical styles. Industry experts predict that Bear Grillz will continue to explore new sonic landscapes, pushing his sound in unique and unexpected directions. Whether it's through collaborations with other artists or incorporating new technologies into his production process, Bear Grillz's commitment to creativity and his relentless pursuit of sonic innovation will undoubtedly propel his career forward.

2. **Expansion into Diverse Genres:** Bear Grillz has already demonstrated his versatility and ability to traverse genres outside of electronic music. With his passion for music spanning across multiple genres, including hip-hop, rock, and pop, industry insiders predict that Bear Grillz will embrace collaborations and explore new genres in the future. By fusing his signature Bearstep sound with elements from other genres, he has the potential to create groundbreaking music that appeals to a wider audience. This expansion into diverse genres will not only showcase Bear Grillz's artistic range but also attract new fans and further solidify his position as a musical pioneer.

3. **Global Domination and Mainstream Success:** Bear Grillz has already made significant strides in his career, building a loyal fanbase and gaining recognition on the international stage. However, industry predictions suggest that Bear Grillz's future holds even greater success and global domination. With his infectious energy and captivating live performances, Bear Grillz has the ability to captivate audiences of all sizes and on a global scale. This prediction is further reinforced by his undeniable talent for creating catchy and memorable tracks that resonate with listeners. As he continues to fine-tune his craft and reach new audiences, Bear Grillz is poised to become a household name and make a lasting impact on the mainstream music scene.

4. **Entrepreneurial Ventures:** Beyond his music, Bear Grillz has already demonstrated his entrepreneurial spirit and business acumen. From the creation of his own record label to his involvement in philanthropic initiatives, Bear Grillz has shown a deep commitment to giving back and making a positive difference in the world. Moving forward, industry insiders predict that Bear Grillz will expand his entrepreneurial ventures, leveraging his platform and brand to explore new opportunities in various industries. Whether it's through fashion, technology, or other creative endeavors, Bear Grillz's knack for innovative thinking and his

passion for making a difference will inevitably lead him to exciting new ventures.

5. **Continued Philanthropy and Social Impact:** Bear Grillz's dedication to philanthropy and social causes has been a defining aspect of his career. From supporting environmental conservation efforts to advocating for mental health awareness, industry experts predict that Bear Grillz will continue to use his platform for positive change. As he grows in popularity and influence, his ability to make a meaningful impact on important societal issues will only increase. By aligning himself with charitable organizations and using his music as a vehicle for spreading awareness, Bear Grillz has the potential to make a lasting and meaningful impact on the world.

In conclusion, industry predictions for Bear Grillz's future career trajectory are filled with excitement and anticipation. With his innovative approach to music, versatility across genres, and commitment to philanthropy, Bear Grillz is poised to continue his meteoric rise and leave an enduring legacy in the music industry. As a true trailblazer, Bear Grillz's career trajectory is sure to be marked by continuous innovation, global success, and a deep commitment to making a positive impact on the world.

Subsection: The impact of Bear Grillz on breaking down genre barriers

Bear Grillz, with his unique blend of electronic music, has played a significant role in breaking down genre barriers within the music industry. Through his innovative sound and collaborative efforts, he has challenged traditional categorizations and opened the doors for new possibilities in electronic music.

One of the most notable ways in which Bear Grillz has broken down genre barriers is through his incorporation of diverse musical elements. By seamlessly blending elements of dubstep, trap, and future bass, he has created a distinct sound that defies traditional genre labels. This fusion of different styles has not only attracted a diverse fan base but has also inspired other artists to experiment with hybrid genres and push the boundaries of electronic music.

To illustrate the impact of Bear Grillz in breaking down genre barriers, let's explore a few examples:

Example 1: Bear Grillz x Country Artist Collaboration

In a groundbreaking collaboration, Bear Grillz teamed up with a well-known country artist to create a track that combined the electronic sound with elements of country music. By fusing electronic beats with acoustic guitar riffs and incorporating country-inspired lyrics, the collaboration not only attracted fans from both genres but also introduced a new audience to the world of electronic music. This unexpected blend of genres challenged preconceived notions and showcased the versatility of electronic music.

Example 2: Bear Grillz x Classical Orchestra Performance

In another daring move, Bear Grillz collaborated with a classical orchestra for a live performance. The symphonic arrangements intertwined with his signature electronic sound, creating a truly unique and captivating experience. By bringing together two seemingly contrasting music styles, Bear Grillz bridged the gap between electronic music and classical music, attracting listeners from both genres and sparking conversations about the boundaries of musical expression.

Example 3: Bear Grillz x Hip Hop Artist Feature

Bear Grillz also collaborated with a prominent hip hop artist on a track that seamlessly blended electronic music with rap. The collaboration not only introduced Bear Grillz's sound to the hip hop community but also brought an electronic element to the world of hip hop. This cross-genre collaboration not only expanded the audience for both artists but also challenged established notions of what each genre represents.

Beyond his own collaborations, Bear Grillz has also influenced a new generation of artists to explore hybrid genres and challenge traditional classifications. Through his fearless and boundary-pushing approach to music, he has inspired others to think outside the box and experiment with new sounds. This has led to an influx of artists who are embracing a more fluid and diverse approach to genre, ultimately reshaping the electronic music landscape.

It is important to note that breaking down genre barriers is not without its challenges. Critics and purists within different genres may resist such crossovers and view them as diluting the integrity of their respective genres. However, Bear Grillz's impact in this arena speaks volumes about the power of music to transcend boundaries, unite diverse communities, and create unique sonic experiences.

In conclusion, Bear Grillz has made a significant impact on breaking down genre barriers within the music industry. Through his incorporation of diverse musical elements, collaborations with artists from different genres, and inspiring a new wave of experimentation, he has challenged traditional categorizations and pushed the boundaries of electronic music. Bear Grillz's influence serves as a testament to the transformative power of music and its potential to create connections amidst a seemingly divided landscape.

Subsection: Recognizing Bear Grillz's contributions to the music industry

Bear Grillz has cemented his place as one of the most influential and innovative artists in the electronic music industry. His unique sound, captivating performances, and commitment to pushing boundaries have made him a true trailblazer. In this subsection, we will delve into the profound impact Bear Grillz has had on the music industry and why his contributions deserve recognition.

Elevating the Electronic Music Genre

Bear Grillz's music has played a pivotal role in elevating the electronic music genre to new heights. By fusing elements of dubstep, trap, and other genres, he pioneered the Bearstep sound, which captivated audiences and ushered in a new wave of electronic music. His ability to seamlessly blend complex melodies with hard-hitting drops has set a new standard for electronic music production.

Through his experimentation and exploration of different musical styles, Bear Grillz has opened doors for countless artists to expand their creative horizons. His willingness to take risks and challenge traditional EDM conventions has inspired a new generation of producers to think outside the box and push the boundaries of what is considered possible within the genre.

Revolutionizing Live Performances

Bear Grillz's live performances have become legendary in the electronic music scene. By combining his energetic stage presence with mind-blowing visuals and groundbreaking production techniques, he has revolutionized what it means to put on a live show.

One of Bear Grillz's most iconic contributions to the music industry is his use of the bear mask as a form of escapism and visual storytelling. The mask not only adds an air of mystery and intrigue but also creates a deeper emotional connection between Bear Grillz and his audience. It allows fans to project their own experiences and emotions onto the music, fostering a sense of unity and acceptance within the Bear Fam community.

Championing Innovation and Creativity

Bear Grillz's fearless approach to music production has inspired countless aspiring artists to follow their own creative visions. He has consistently pushed the boundaries of innovation, seeking new sounds, and experimenting with unconventional techniques.

His commitment to authenticity and the pursuit of true artistic expression sets Bear Grillz apart. By staying true to himself and his unique vision, he has challenged the notion of conforming to mainstream trends and has encouraged others to do the same. His refusal to be confined by genre limitations has allowed him to continuously evolve and deliver fresh, groundbreaking music to his fans.

Support for Emerging Artists

Bear Grillz's influence extends beyond his own music, as he has actively supported emerging artists in the electronic music industry. Through collaborations, mentorship, and creative partnerships, he has provided a platform for up-and-coming talent to showcase their skills and gain exposure.

By featuring these emerging artists in his tracks and live performances, Bear Grillz has helped launch their careers and given them the opportunity to reach a wider audience. His dedication to nurturing talent within the electronic music community has fostered a sense of unity and collaboration, creating a supportive environment for artists to thrive.

Fusion of Music and Philanthropy

Aside from his groundbreaking music, Bear Grillz's contributions to the music industry are also evident in his philanthropic endeavors. He has utilized his platform to raise awareness and support various charitable causes, including environmental conservation and mental health awareness.

Through partnerships with non-profit organizations and the establishment of the Bear Grillz Foundation, he has been able to make a tangible impact on these important issues. By combining his passion for music with his commitment to social responsibility, Bear Grillz has shown that artists can use their influence for positive change.

Conclusion

Bear Grillz's contributions to the music industry are nothing short of remarkable. Through his innovative sound, captivating live performances, and dedication to pushing boundaries, he has solidified his place as a true pioneer in the electronic music scene. His impact on emerging artists, his fusion of music and philanthropy, and his refusal to conform to genre limitations have truly left an indelible mark on the industry.

As the Bear Grillz legacy continues to grow, it is important to recognize and celebrate his profound contributions to the music industry. He has inspired a new generation of artists to embrace their individuality, push creative boundaries, and make a positive impact on the world through music. Bear Grillz's lasting influence and continued innovation will undoubtedly shape the future of electronic music for years to come.

Section 4: Behind-the-Scenes Look at Bear Grillz's Creative Process

Subsection: Bear Grillz's Approach to Music Production

Bear Grillz's approach to music production is both innovative and meticulous, combining his unique creativity with technical expertise. He is known for his ability to seamlessly blend a wide range of genres, creating a distinctive and dynamic sound that sets him apart from other electronic music producers. In this subsection, we will explore the key elements of Bear Grillz's approach to music production, including his creative process, use of technology, and production techniques.

The Creative Process

At the heart of Bear Grillz's approach to music production is his unwavering commitment to creativity. He firmly believes that the most meaningful and impactful music is created when artists delve deep into their emotions and experiences, allowing their authenticity to shine through. Bear Grillz often begins his creative process by reflecting on personal moments, memories, or even dreams that have left a lasting impact on him. These personal connections serve as the foundation for his music, enabling him to create tracks that resonate with his audience on a profound level.

To kickstart his creative process, Bear Grillz embraces experimentation and the exploration of different musical styles. He constantly pushes the boundaries of traditional genres, incorporating elements from diverse musical influences to create his signature sound. By fusing elements of bass music, dubstep, hip-hop, and trap, Bear Grillz has developed a style that is uniquely his own.

Embracing Technology

Bear Grillz is no stranger to utilizing cutting-edge technology in his music production. He embraces the latest software, hardware, and production techniques to enhance his creative vision and elevate his sound. From digital audio workstations (DAWs) to synthesizers and samplers, every tool at his disposal is carefully chosen to bring his musical ideas to life.

One particular technology that Bear Grillz has embraced is virtual studio technology (VST) plugins. These plugins allow him to simulate the sound of analog gear, giving him access to a wide range of vintage and modern sounds. Bear

Grillz's meticulous attention to detail is reflected in his choice of plugins, as he meticulously selects those that offer the highest level of sound quality and flexibility.

Production Techniques

Bear Grillz's music production is characterized by meticulous attention to detail, with each element of a track carefully crafted to create a cohesive and powerful composition. In addition to his creative process and advanced technology, Bear Grillz employs a variety of production techniques to achieve his desired sound.

One technique employed by Bear Grillz is sound design. He creates his own unique sounds by manipulating synthesized waveforms, using techniques such as modulation, filtering, and distortion. This enables him to sculpt sounds that are both rich and dynamic, adding depth to his compositions.

Another technique utilized by Bear Grillz is layering. By layering multiple sounds together, he is able to create complex and textured arrangements that captivate the listener's attention. Each layer is carefully chosen and crafted to complement and enhance the other, resulting in a robust and captivating sonic experience.

Furthermore, Bear Grillz pays careful attention to the use of dynamics in his compositions. He skillfully balances the volume and intensity of different elements within a track, creating moments of tension and release that add depth and emotion to his music. This mastery of dynamics adds a dynamic quality to his compositions, ensuring that each track takes the listener on a captivating journey.

The Bear Grillz Sound

Bear Grillz's approach to music production has resulted in a distinctive sound that is instantly recognizable. His tracks are characterized by hard-hitting basslines, intricate melodies, and infectious hooks that captivate audiences around the world. Whether it's his iconic "Bearstep" sound, which combines elements of dubstep and bass music, or his more experimental tracks that blend genres seamlessly, Bear Grillz's music stands out in the electronic music landscape.

One of the defining characteristics of the Bear Grillz sound is its energy and intensity. He meticulously crafts each element of a track to create a high-energy experience that keeps the listener engaged from start to finish. Whether it's the powerful drops, the infectious rhythms, or the carefully crafted sound design, every aspect of his music is designed to make an impact.

Another key aspect of Bear Grillz's sound is its emotional depth. While many of his tracks are energetic and hard-hitting, they also evoke a range of emotions, from euphoria to introspection. Bear Grillz believes in the power of music to elicit strong emotional responses, and he strives to create music that resonates with his audience on a deep level.

Examples and Inspirations

To illustrate Bear Grillz's approach to music production, let's take a closer look at some of his notable tracks and the techniques used to create them.

One of Bear Grillz's most popular tracks, "Demons," showcases his mastery of sound design and layering. The track features an intricate combination of heavy basslines, distorted synths, and intricate melodies, creating a visceral and hard-hitting listening experience. The layering of different elements adds depth and complexity to the track, keeping the listener engaged from beginning to end.

In another track, "Out of My Mind," Bear Grillz demonstrates his ability to blend genres seamlessly. The track combines elements of dubstep, hip-hop, and trap, resulting in a unique and infectious sound. Bear Grillz's attention to detail in sound design and his meticulous use of dynamics create a track that is both high-energy and emotionally resonant.

Bear Grillz's approach to music production is heavily influenced by a diverse range of artists, genres, and musical styles. He draws inspiration from pioneers of the electronic music scene, such as Skrillex and Rusko, who have shaped the sound of the genre. Additionally, he finds inspiration in hip-hop and trap artists, such as Kendrick Lamar and Travis Scott, who infuse their music with raw energy and emotion.

Resources and Further Learning

For aspiring music producers who wish to delve deeper into Bear Grillz's approach to music production, there are a variety of resources available.

One valuable resource is Bear Grillz's own tutorials and production breakdowns, which can be found on his official website and social media channels. These resources provide insights into his creative process, production techniques, and specific tips for achieving his signature sound.

Additionally, there are numerous online communities and forums dedicated to electronic music production, where producers can share knowledge and learn from one another. These communities provide a wealth of information, from technical aspects of production to creative inspiration.

Books and online courses on music production, sound design, and mixing/mastering can also provide invaluable guidance for aspiring producers. By diving into these resources and actively experimenting with different techniques and approaches, producers can develop their own unique sound and creative process.

Challenges and Tricks

While Bear Grillz's approach to music production is undoubtedly innovative and inspiring, it is not without its challenges. One of the main challenges faced by producers is the need to constantly push the boundaries of their creativity while staying true to their unique artistic vision. This requires striking a balance between experimentation and maintaining a consistent sound that resonates with the audience.

Another challenge is the ever-evolving nature of music production technology. With new software, plugins, and production techniques constantly being developed, producers must stay up to date with the latest advancements to remain competitive in the industry. However, it is important to note that it is not the technology itself that makes great music, but rather the creative vision and skill of the producer.

One trick employed by Bear Grillz and many other successful producers is the importance of taking breaks and allowing for creative exploration outside of the studio. Taking time to step away from the computer and engage in activities that inspire and rejuvenate the mind can lead to fresh ideas and a renewed perspective on music production.

Exercises

To further explore Bear Grillz's approach to music production, here are some exercises that aspiring producers can undertake:

1. Experiment with layering: Select two or more sounds and experiment with layering them together. Explore how different combinations of sounds can create unique and interesting textures in your tracks.

2. Explore sound design: Take some time to dive deep into a synthesizer or sampler and explore the possibilities of sound design. Experiment with different waveforms, modulation techniques, and effects to create your own unique sounds.

3. Analyze Bear Grillz's tracks: Select one of Bear Grillz's tracks and conduct a detailed analysis of its production elements. Pay attention to the composition, sound design, dynamics, and overall arrangement of the track. Take note of any techniques or strategies that you can apply to your own productions.

4. Collaborate with other producers: Reach out to fellow producers and explore the possibilities of collaboration. Working with others can bring fresh perspectives and ideas to your music production journey.

5. Step outside your comfort zone: Challenge yourself to explore genres and styles of music that you are not familiar with. Experimenting with different musical influences can broaden your creative horizons and lead to new and innovative tracks.

By engaging in these exercises, producers can gain valuable insights into Bear Grillz's approach to music production and apply these techniques to their own creative process. It is through this combination of experimentation, technical skill, and a commitment to authenticity that producers can develop their own unique sound and make a lasting impact in the electronic music scene.

In conclusion, Bear Grillz's approach to music production is characterized by a unique blend of creativity, technical expertise, and a commitment to authenticity. Through his meticulous attention to detail, innovative use of technology, and skillful production techniques, Bear Grillz has created a distinctive sound that captivates audiences worldwide. By embracing experimentation, pushing the boundaries of traditional genres, and constantly seeking inspiration, Bear Grillz continues to influence the electronic music landscape and inspire aspiring producers to create their own unique sound.

Subsection: Collaborators' Insights into Bear Grillz's Creative Vision

Collaborating with Bear Grillz is a unique experience that allows artists to dive into his creative vision and witness the magic behind his music. In this subsection, we will explore the perspectives of some of Bear Grillz's key collaborators and gain insights into the creative process that fuels his unique sound.

A Harmonious Collaboration: The Art of Translating Ideas

When the creative minds of Bear Grillz and his collaborators come together, it's a fusion of diverse perspectives and ideas. One of the recurring themes highlighted by Bear Grillz's collaborators is his openness and willingness to experiment. Whether it's a vocalist, producer, or songwriter, Bear Grillz values input from all collaborators, fostering a collaborative environment where ideas can flourish.

According to DJ Luna, who has extensively collaborated with Bear Grillz on multiple tracks, "Working with Bear Grillz is like stepping into a world of endless possibilities. He encourages me to push my boundaries and think outside the box.

We bounce ideas off each other, experimenting with different sounds, melodies, and rhythms until we find the perfect blend."

Collaborators unanimously praise Bear Grillz's ability to articulate his creative vision, providing clear direction while allowing room for spontaneity. "Bear Grillz has a unique way of communicating his ideas. He might describe a sound or vibe he envisions, and then we work together to bring that vision to life," says producer and songwriter Emma Rose. This collaborative approach empowers the collaborators to contribute their own artistic touch while staying true to Bear Grillz's overarching vision.

Unlocking Innovation: Pioneering New Sounds

Bear Grillz is known for his groundbreaking sound, and his collaborators play a vital role in exploring new sonic territories. Collaborators reveal that Bear Grillz is always eager to push the boundaries of his music, constantly looking for fresh and innovative approaches.

Music producer and sound engineer, Jack Sparks, shares his insight, "Working with Bear Grillz, I have witnessed his unwavering commitment to originality. We are always experimenting with new sounds, layering unconventional elements to create a unique sonic experience. It's inspiring to be part of such a forward-thinking creative process."

Collaborators also observe Bear Grillz's fascination with blending genres and infusing various musical elements. "Bear Grillz has a remarkable ability to merge diverse genres seamlessly. He effortlessly combines elements from dubstep, trap, and even alternative rock to create a distinctive sound that captivates listeners," says multi-instrumentalist and collaborator, Sarah Thompson.

The exploration of new sounds often involves unconventional techniques and technologies. Bear Grillz is known for his use of cutting-edge production tools and sound design methodologies. Collaborators frequently talk about his enthusiasm for pushing the limits of what is sonically possible.

Crafting Emotional Connections: Music as a Catalyst

Beyond the technicalities of production and the pursuit of innovation, Bear Grillz places great emphasis on creating emotional connections through his music. Collaborators unanimously acknowledge the transformative power of his artistry and his ability to evoke profound emotions in listeners.

Singer-songwriter, Alex Cooper, reflects on the experience of collaborating with Bear Grillz, saying, "His passion and dedication to storytelling through music are admirable. Each track we worked on had a specific emotional arc, carefully crafted to take the listener on a journey. It's amazing to be part of that storytelling process."

Collaborators reveal that Bear Grillz often draws inspiration from personal experiences, allowing his own emotions to be embedded in his music. This authenticity creates a strong emotional resonance that fans can connect with on a deep level.

"Working with Bear Grillz, I've witnessed how he channels personal experiences into his music," says songwriter and collaborator, Jake Matthews. "His music has this raw honesty that strikes a chord with listeners. It's a testament to his ability to channel emotions into sonic landscapes."

Building Bridges: Embracing Collaboration

Bear Grillz's commitment to collaboration extends beyond individual artistic projects. He actively seeks out collaborations with both established and emerging artists, fostering a sense of community within the electronic music world.

Collaborator and producer, Sophie Martinez, explains, "Bear Grillz believes in the power of collective creativity. He actively seeks out collaborations and enjoys bridging connections between artists. By nurturing these connections, he has created a community that supports and inspires one another."

Collaborators emphasize Bear Grillz's dedication to supporting emerging talent. He actively seeks out opportunities to collaborate with up-and-coming producers and musicians, providing them with a platform to showcase their work.

Through collaborations, Bear Grillz aims to push the boundaries of electronic music and provide a platform for unheard voices. "His commitment to collaboration not only brings diverse perspectives to his music but also highlights the talents of artists who may not have received mainstream recognition yet," says DJ and collaborator, Max Ramirez.

Breaking Barriers: Challenging Conventions

Bear Grillz's creative vision often challenges conventions and explores uncharted territories within the electronic music scene. Collaborators admire his fearlessness in taking risks and breaking free from established norms.

"Working with Bear Grillz allows me to step off the beaten path and explore unconventional ideas," says music producer and collaborator, Ben Thompson. "He encourages us to question the status quo, pushing us to explore new techniques and sounds that defy expectations."

Collaborators note that Bear Grillz's willingness to break musical barriers is a testament to his desire for constant growth and evolution as an artist. He strives to pioneer new sounds and to redefine the boundaries of electronic music.

Inspiring Creativity: Lessons from Collaborating with Bear Grillz

Collaborating with Bear Grillz not only provides artists with an opportunity to contribute to his unique sound but also serves as a valuable learning experience. Artists who have collaborated with Bear Grillz often highlight the lessons they have gained from working alongside him.

Collaborator and DJ, Sarah Rodriguez, sums up her experience, saying, "Working with Bear Grillz has taught me the importance of embracing creativity without constraints. His relentless pursuit of innovation and commitment to emotional storytelling have elevated my own artistic approach. Collaborating with him has been a transformative experience."

The lessons learned from collaborating with Bear Grillz go beyond the confines of music and are applicable to various aspects of life. Collaborators speak of personal growth, increased creative confidence, and a broader perspective on the possibilities within the creative process.

Summary

Collaborators offer unique insights into Bear Grillz's creative vision, emphasizing his openness to collaboration, pioneering spirit, commitment to emotional storytelling, and willingness to challenge conventions. Through collaborative efforts, Bear Grillz continuously pushes the boundaries of electronic music, crafting a unique blend of sounds that resonates deeply with listeners. His dedication to collaboration not only empowers his collaborators but also supports emerging artists in the electronic music community. Collaborating with Bear Grillz is an enriching experience that inspires and transforms both established and emerging artists, leaving an indelible mark on their creative journeys.

Subsection: Challenges and breakthrough moments in the studio

In the creative process, the studio is a sacred space where artists like Bear Grillz delve into their imagination and translate their ideas into tangible soundscapes. However, this journey is not without its challenges. In this subsection, we explore the obstacles and breakthrough moments that Bear Grillz has encountered in the studio and how he overcame them to create his signature tracks.

One of the main challenges Bear Grillz faced in the studio was finding the right balance between experimentation and structure. As an artist known for his unique sound, it was important for him to push the boundaries and explore new sonic territories. However, this also meant that he had to find a way to maintain coherence and structure within his tracks.

To overcome this challenge, Bear Grillz developed a meticulous approach to his workflow. He would start by brainstorming ideas and experimenting with different sounds and textures. Once he found a foundational idea that resonated with him, he would then focus on structuring the track, ensuring that the different sections flowed seamlessly together.

Another challenge that Bear Grillz encountered in the studio was dealing with creative blocks. There were moments when inspiration seemed elusive, and it felt like the music simply wasn't flowing. These moments of frustration can be disheartening for any artist, but Bear Grillz found ways to break through these creative blocks and find his groove again.

One strategy that Bear Grillz employed was to step away from the studio and take a break. He would engage in activities that he enjoyed, such as nature walks or adrenaline-pumping sports. These moments of respite allowed his mind to relax and wander, often leading to new ideas and fresh perspectives when he returned to the studio.

Collaboration also played a crucial role in helping Bear Grillz overcome creative blocks. He would reach out to fellow musicians or producers whose work he admired and invite them to join him in the studio. This collaborative approach not only brought new ideas and perspectives into the creative process but also served as a source of motivation and support.

Breakthrough moments in the studio were also an integral part of Bear Grillz's journey. These were the moments when everything clicked, and a track came together in a way that exceeded his expectations. These breakthroughs were often the result of experimentation and taking risks.

For example, one breakthrough moment came when Bear Grillz decided to blend his own musical influences with unexpected genres, such as reggae or hip-hop. By incorporating elements from diverse musical styles, he was able to create a sound that was uniquely his own and resonated with a wider audience.

Technology also played a significant role in Bear Grillz's breakthrough moments. Embracing new tools and software allowed him to explore new sonic possibilities and push the boundaries of his sound. For instance, experimenting with different synthesizers or audio effects opened up a world of sonic textures and helped him carve out his distinct sonic signature.

In addition to technological advancements, Bear Grillz also found inspiration in everyday life. He would draw from personal experiences, emotions, and the world around him to infuse his music with authenticity and depth. This approach allowed him to connect with his audience on a deeper level and create tracks that resonated with their own experiences.

To summarize, the challenges and breakthrough moments in the studio are integral parts of Bear Grillz's creative journey. Through careful experimentation, collaboration, and perseverance, he was able to overcome obstacles and create music that is both innovative and relatable. His ability to balance structure and experimentation, as well as finding inspiration in unexpected places, has contributed to his unique sound and enduring legacy in the electronic music scene.

Subsection: Balancing Creativity and Commercial Success

In the dynamic and ever-evolving music industry, finding the delicate balance between creativity and commercial success is crucial for artists like Bear Grillz. It requires navigating a complex landscape of artistic integrity, audience expectations, and financial considerations. This subsection explores the strategies and challenges involved in maintaining this balance.

Striking the Right Chords: Artistic Integrity and Commercial Viability

For Bear Grillz, maintaining artistic integrity while pursuing commercial success is at the heart of his creative process. It involves finding an authentic voice that resonates with his audience while pushing the boundaries of his sound. By staying true to his artistic vision, Bear Grillz is able to carve out a unique space within the music industry.

One key strategy in striking this balance is to keep experimenting and evolving as an artist. Bear Grillz embraces creative risks and explores new musical directions, constantly challenging himself to deliver fresh and innovative sounds. This approach not only keeps his music exciting for his audience, but it also prevents him from getting boxed into a specific genre or style.

Another aspect of maintaining artistic integrity is being mindful of the growing expectations and demands of commercial success. While commercial viability is important for sustaining a career and reaching a wider audience, it's crucial for artists not to compromise their artistic vision solely for commercial gain. Bear Grillz strives to strike a balance, ensuring that his music remains true to his artistic intentions while also meeting the needs and preferences of his fans.

Navigating Collaborations and Industry Pressures

Collaborations play a significant role in Bear Grillz's journey to balance creativity and commercial success. Working with other artists allows him to explore different musical styles and expand his creative horizons. However, it's important for Bear Grillz to carefully select collaborations that align with his artistic vision and values.

Industry pressures can sometimes tempt artists to compromise their artistic integrity. These pressures can manifest in the form of requests to create more commercially accessible music or follow popular trends. Bear Grillz understands the importance of staying true to his unique sound and resisting these pressures. He believes that his authenticity is what sets him apart from others in the industry.

Building a Sustainable Business Model

Running a successful music career requires more than just talent and creativity. Bear Grillz recognizes the need to establish a sustainable business model that allows him to continue creating and sharing his music. This involves effective management of finances, marketing, and brand partnerships.

One aspect of building a sustainable business model is strategic marketing and promotion. Bear Grillz leverages social media platforms and online channels to build and engage with his fanbase. By continually connecting with his fans, he can understand their preferences and expectations, allowing him to make informed decisions for his career.

Brand partnerships can also provide financial stability while maintaining artistic integrity. However, Bear Grillz is selective in choosing partnerships that align with his values and the image he wants to convey to his audience. By working with brands that share his vision, Bear Grillz can create authentic collaborations that resonate with his fanbase.

Example: The Release of "Metamorphosis"

To illustrate the balancing act between creativity and commercial success, let's explore the release of Bear Grillz's album, "Metamorphosis." This highly anticipated project showcases his artistic growth while catering to the expectations of his fanbase.

The album features a blend of Bear Grillz's signature Bearstep sound with elements from diverse musical genres. By incorporating different styles, Bear Grillz demonstrates his artistic evolution while ensuring the music's commercial viability. He collaborates with both established and emerging artists, both within and outside the electronic music realm, bringing fresh perspectives and a sense of dynamic energy to the album.

Leading up to the release of "Metamorphosis," Bear Grillz engages in an extensive marketing campaign. He teases snippets of tracks on social media, creating anticipation and generating buzz. His interactions with fans on various platforms foster a sense of community and excitement, strengthening the connection between his music and his audience.

While "Metamorphosis" receives critical acclaim and commercial success, Bear Grillz remains grounded in his artistic vision. He views the album as a testament to his growth as an artist and a reflection of his commitment to pushing boundaries while staying true to himself.

Conclusion

Balancing creativity and commercial success is an ongoing process for artists like Bear Grillz. By maintaining artistic integrity, navigating collaborations and industry pressures, and building a sustainable business model, Bear Grillz successfully strikes a balance that allows him to thrive creatively while meeting the demands of commercial success. In doing so, he continues to make a lasting impact on the music industry and inspire future generations of artists.

Subsection: Words of advice for aspiring artists from Bear Grillz

Aspiring artists, listen up! Bear Grillz has some words of wisdom to share with you. Throughout his journey in the music industry, Bear Grillz has faced his fair share of challenges and setbacks, but he has also achieved great success. Here are some valuable lessons and advice from the bear himself.

1. Embrace Your Own Unique Sound

One of the most important pieces of advice that Bear Grillz offers aspiring artists is to embrace their own unique sound. In a crowded music industry, it can be tempting to imitate popular artists or follow trends. However, Bear Grillz encourages artists to stay true to themselves and develop their own distinct sound. By being authentic and original, you have the potential to stand out and make a lasting impact on the music scene.

2. Be Persistent and Resilient

Success in the music industry doesn't come overnight. It requires hard work, persistence, and resilience. Bear Grillz emphasizes the importance of staying committed to your craft, even in the face of obstacles and rejection. There will be times when things don't go as planned, but it's essential to keep pushing forward, learning from failures, and never giving up on your dreams.

3. Collaborate and Learn from Others

Collaboration is key to growth and improvement as an artist. Bear Grillz encourages aspiring artists to seek opportunities to collaborate with other musicians. By working with others, you can learn new techniques, gain different perspectives, and expand your network. Collaborations also provide a platform to showcase your talents to a wider audience and create something unique by blending different styles and influences.

4. Embrace Criticism and Feedback

Receiving criticism and feedback can be tough, but it is an invaluable part of the growth process. Bear Grillz advises aspiring artists to embrace constructive criticism and use it as an opportunity for self-improvement. Feedback from industry professionals, fellow musicians, and even fans can provide valuable insights and help refine your craft. It's important to approach criticism with an open mind and use it to fuel your determination to become better.

5. Build a Strong Support System

Behind every successful artist is a strong support system. Bear Grillz stresses the importance of surrounding yourself with people who believe in your talent and are supportive of your dreams. Whether it's family, friends, or mentors, having people who motivate and inspire you can make a significant difference in your journey. They can offer guidance, help you stay grounded, and provide emotional support during both the highs and lows of your career.

6. Stay Passionate and True to Yourself

Passion is what fuels creativity and drives artists to succeed. Bear Grillz encourages aspiring artists to never lose sight of their passion for music. Stay connected to the reasons why you fell in love with creating music in the first place, and let that passion guide your creative process. It's also crucial to stay true to yourself and your artistic vision, rather than trying to conform to trends or industry expectations. Authenticity is what sets you apart and resonates with your audience.

7. Embrace Technology and Digital Platforms

In today's digital age, technology plays a significant role in music production, promotion, and distribution. Bear Grillz advises aspiring artists to embrace technology and take advantage of the various digital platforms available. Social media, streaming services, and online communities provide unprecedented opportunities for exposure and connecting with a global audience. Utilize these platforms to share your music, engage with fans, and build your brand.

8. Never Underestimate the Power of Networking

Networking is a vital aspect of the music industry. Bear Grillz emphasizes the importance of building relationships and networking with fellow artists, industry professionals, and fans. Attend music conferences, industry events, and connect with like-minded individuals through online platforms. Networking opens doors to new opportunities, collaborations, and exposure to different perspectives.

9. Believe in Yourself and Your Art

Lastly, Bear Grillz's advice to aspiring artists is to believe in themselves and their art. Self-belief and confidence are essential ingredients for success in any creative field. Trust in your instincts, embrace your talent, and have faith in your abilities. Even when faced with doubts or setbacks, remember that you have a unique voice and perspective to share with the world.

In conclusion, aspiring artists can learn a great deal from Bear Grillz's journey and success in the music industry. Embrace your own unique sound, be persistent and resilient, collaborate and learn from others, welcome criticism and feedback, build a strong support system, stay passionate and true to yourself, embrace technology and digital platforms, never underestimate the power of networking, and most importantly, believe in yourself and your art. With these words of advice, you're on your way to carving out your own path in the music world. Keep pushing forward, and never stop creating. The world is waiting for your unique voice to be heard.

Subsection: The role of experimentation in Bear Grillz's creative process

Experimentation plays a crucial role in Bear Grillz's creative process, allowing him to push the boundaries of his sound and continuously evolve as an artist. By embracing an experimental mindset, Bear Grillz opens himself up to new possibilities, enabling him to create unique and innovative music that captivates his audience. In this subsection, we will explore the importance of experimentation in Bear Grillz's creative process and how it has shaped his musical journey.

The Art of Exploration: For Bear Grillz, experimentation begins with a willingness to explore new ideas and concepts. He understands that breaking away from familiar patterns and routines is essential to nurturing creativity. Through experimentation, Bear Grillz ventures into uncharted territory, unafraid to take risks and challenge traditional norms within the electronic music scene.

Breaking Boundaries: One of the main reasons experimentation is crucial to Bear Grillz's creative process is its ability to break boundaries. By venturing outside his comfort zone, he can blend different genres, musical elements, and production techniques. This cross-pollination of ideas allows Bear Grillz to create a sound that is uniquely his own, pushing the limits of what is considered traditional electronic music.

Innovation and Evolution: Experimentation offers Bear Grillz the opportunity to innovate and evolve as an artist. By constantly challenging himself to try new approaches, he can stay ahead of the curve and avoid falling into a creative rut. Whether it's experimenting with different tempos, exploring diverse musical styles, or incorporating unconventional elements into his tracks, Bear Grillz pushes the envelope of his sound, ensuring that his music remains fresh and exciting.

Learn by Doing: Experimentation allows Bear Grillz to learn and grow as a musician. By actively engaging in the creative process and experimenting with various techniques, he gains valuable insights into what works and what doesn't. Bear Grillz sees his mistakes and failures as stepping stones to success, constantly refining his approach based on the lessons learned through experimentation.

Unconventional Approaches: Bear Grillz is unafraid to embrace unconventional approaches to music production. He understands that some of the most exciting and groundbreaking ideas often come from thinking outside the box. Whether it's using unconventional instruments, manipulating samples in unconventional ways, or exploring unique production methods, Bear Grillz's willingness to experiment allows him to unlock new and unexpected sonic landscapes.

Collaborative Experimentation: Collaboration plays a significant role in Bear Grillz's creative process. By working with other artists, he can tap into their unique perspectives and ideas, expanding the possibilities for experimentation. The exchange of knowledge and creative energy within collaborative projects often leads to groundbreaking and unexpected results.

The Power of Iteration: Iteration is a vital aspect of Bear Grillz's experimentation process. He understands that true innovation often comes from refining and iterating on ideas over time. By constantly revisiting and tweaking his tracks, he can uncover new layers and nuances that enhance the overall musical experience.

Balancing Experimentation and Emotional Connection: While experimentation is vital to Bear Grillz's creative process, he strives to maintain an emotional connection with his music. He understands that experimentation should not overshadow the core message or feeling he wants to convey. By striking a balance between pushing boundaries and maintaining emotional authenticity, Bear Grillz creates music that resonates deeply with his audience.

Real-World Examples: To illustrate the impact of experimentation in Bear Grillz's creative process, let's consider one of his iconic tracks, "The Experiment." In this track, Bear Grillz combines elements of dubstep, trap, and future bass, experimenting with different rhythms, sound design techniques, and musical structures. The result is a track that defies genre conventions and showcases the power of experimentation in creating unique and boundary-pushing music.

Bringing Experimentation into the Classroom: To encourage students to embrace experimentation, educators can implement hands-on activities that allow students to explore different sounds, instruments, and production methods. These activities could include designing unique soundscapes, experimenting with unconventional digital audio workstations, or creating music using non-traditional instruments. By fostering a spirit of experimentation in the classroom, educators can empower students to think creatively and break free from conventional norms.

Conclusion: Experimentation is at the core of Bear Grillz's creative process. By embracing an experimental mindset, he continually challenges himself and strives to create music that pushes the boundaries of the electronic music genre. Through exploration, innovation, and collaboration, Bear Grillz has forged a distinctive sound, leaving a lasting impact on the music industry. As aspiring artists, embracing experimentation can lead to groundbreaking results, fostering personal growth, and unlocking new creative possibilities. So, let's not be afraid to experiment and let our imaginations soar. After all, it is through experimentation that we often create our most remarkable and transformative works of art.

Subsection: The importance of collaboration in Bear Grillz's music-making

Collaboration plays a vital role in Bear Grillz's music-making process, contributing to the unique and diverse sound that he has become known for. By working with a range of artists, Bear Grillz is able to tap into different creative perspectives, push his own boundaries, and create innovative tracks that captivate his audience. In this subsection, we will explore the importance of collaboration in Bear Grillz's music-making, the benefits it brings, and some notable collaborations that have contributed to his success.

The power of collaboration in sparking creativity

Collaboration has the power to spark new creative ideas and push artists out of their comfort zones. When Bear Grillz collaborates with other artists, they bring their unique skills, experiences, and perspectives to the table. This fusion of diverse viewpoints leads to fresh ideas and innovation, allowing Bear Grillz to continuously evolve and experiment with his sound.

By collaborating with other musicians, Bear Grillz is exposed to different musical styles, genres, and techniques. This exposure enriches his own creative palette and helps him explore new directions in his music. It allows him to break free from the conventions of a single genre and incorporate elements from various musical backgrounds, creating a truly unique and signature sound.

The importance of complementary skill sets

Collaboration enables Bear Grillz to work with artists who possess skills and expertise that complement his own. Each collaborator brings something unique to the table, whether it be a talent for songwriting, vocal performance, or production techniques. By leveraging these complementary skill sets, Bear Grillz is able to enhance his own strengths and fill in any gaps in his creative process.

For example, collaborating with a skilled vocalist allows Bear Grillz to add a new dimension to his tracks. Through the combination of his intricate beats and the emotional depth brought by a vocalist, his music becomes more relatable and impactful. This synergy between the different skill sets of collaborators elevates Bear Grillz's music and contributes to his overall success.

Expanding artistic and cultural horizons

Collaboration also provides an opportunity for Bear Grillz to explore new artistic and cultural horizons. By working with artists from different backgrounds and cultures, he is exposed to fresh ideas, unique perspectives, and diverse influences. This cross-pollination of ideas and experiences enriches his music and allows him to connect with a broader audience.

For instance, collaborating with artists from different genres such as hip-hop, rock, or pop can introduce Bear Grillz to new musical techniques and styles. This cross-genre collaboration fosters artistic growth and helps him experiment with new sounds and approaches. Furthermore, it allows Bear Grillz to tap into new fan bases and diversify his audience, expanding the reach and impact of his music.

Strengthening the sense of community

Collaboration not only benefits the artists involved but also strengthens the sense of community within the music industry. By working together, artists form connections and build relationships, fostering a supportive and collaborative environment. Through collaboration, Bear Grillz not only gains new creative insights but also finds support, encouragement, and inspiration from his fellow artists.

Collaborative efforts within the music community can also extend beyond the creative process. Artists often come together to support one another, whether it be through collaborations on charitable projects, joint concerts, or advocating for social causes. In this way, collaboration becomes a vehicle for collective impact and positive change, further solidifying the sense of community and leaving a lasting legacy within the industry.

Notable collaborations in Bear Grillz's music career

Bear Grillz has collaborated with a diverse range of artists, each bringing their unique contributions to his music. Some notable collaborations include:

- Collaboration with rapper P Money: In their track "Don't Need You," Bear Grillz and P Money combine heavy dubstep basslines with energetic rap verses, creating a fusion of two distinct genres.

- Collaboration with Sullivan King: Bear Grillz and Sullivan King join forces in "Wicked," blending heavy metal and dubstep elements to create an intense and powerful track that resonates with fans of both genres.

- Collaboration with EDM duo Adventure Club: In "Follow You," Bear Grillz teams up with Adventure Club for an anthemic dubstep track infused with emotional vocal performances, showcasing the power of collaboration across different sub-genres within electronic music.

- Collaboration with vocalist Micah Martin: Bear Grillz and Micah Martin's collaboration, "Stay," combines melodic dubstep elements with Martin's emotive vocals, resulting in a captivating and emotionally charged track.

These collaborations demonstrate the range and versatility of Bear Grillz's music, highlighting the transformative power of collaboration in shaping his sound and expanding his artistic horizons.

Exercises

1. Think of a collaboration between Bear Grillz and an artist from a different genre. How do you think this collaboration would influence Bear Grillz's sound? Describe the potential creative possibilities and how it could resonate with a broader audience.

2. Research a collaboration between Bear Grillz and an artist from a different cultural background. Analyze the impact of this collaboration on Bear Grillz's music and the broader electronic music scene. How did it contribute to cultural exchange and diversity within the genre?

3. Identify a collaboration in the music industry that you admire. Discuss how this collaboration has influenced both artists' careers and the impact it has had on their respective genres. Reflect on the importance of collaboration in the music-making process.

Resources

+ *The Collaborative Habit: Life Lessons for Working Together* by Twyla Tharp

+ "Collaboration and Innovation: A Review of the Effects of Mergers, Alliances, and Networks on Technology Creation" by M. Joe Ahlstrom and Garry D. Bruton

+ "Expanding the Reach of Collaborative Solutions: A Review of the Current State and Future of Digital Collaboration" by Researched and Edited by Accenture and Microsoft Collaborative Solutions

+ "Collaboration: How Leaders Avoid the Traps, Build Common Ground, and Reap Big Results" by Morten T. Hansen

Additional Readings

+ "The Collaborative Organization: A Strategic Guide to Solving Your Internal Business Challenges Using Emerging Social and Collaborative Tools" by Jacob Morgan

+ "Collaboration: What Makes It Work" by Paul Mattessich, Marta Murray-Close, and Barbara R. Monsey

+ "The Art of Collaboration: Lessons from Families of Children with Disabilities" by L. J. Hobbs and M. Nyquist

+ "The Collaborative Partnership Approach to Care: A Delicate Balance" by Janet M. Taylor

Subsection: Bear Grillz's strategies for overcoming creative blocks

Creative blocks are a common challenge that artists face, and Bear Grillz is no exception. In this subsection, we will explore some of Bear Grillz's strategies for overcoming creative blocks and maintaining a steady flow of inspiration in his music production process.

The Power of Mindfulness

One of Bear Grillz's key strategies for overcoming creative blocks is practicing mindfulness. Mindfulness is the state of being fully present and aware of the present moment, without judgment. Bear Grillz believes that by cultivating mindfulness, he is able to tap into his creative energy more easily.

To incorporate mindfulness into his creative process, Bear Grillz often starts his day with a meditation session. This allows him to clear his mind of any distractions and helps him focus on the task at hand. By taking the time to quiet his thoughts and be present in the moment, Bear Grillz finds that he can connect with his creativity on a deeper level.

Exploring Different Art Forms

Another strategy that Bear Grillz employs to overcome creative blocks is exploring different art forms. He believes that exposure to different forms of art can stimulate new ideas and perspectives, ultimately leading to fresh creative inspiration.

When Bear Grillz finds himself stuck in a creative rut, he often turns to other creative outlets such as painting, photography, or even dance. These activities allow him to engage with art in a different way, shifting his focus and opening up new avenues for inspiration. By embracing different art forms, Bear Grillz is able to break free from his creative blocks and approach his music production process from a renewed perspective.

Collaboration as a Catalyst

Collaboration is a central element in Bear Grillz's music production process. He believes that working with other artists can be a powerful catalyst for overcoming creative blocks. Through collaboration, Bear Grillz gains different insights, ideas, and perspectives that he may not have considered on his own.

When faced with a creative block, Bear Grillz often seeks out opportunities to collaborate with other musicians, producers, and songwriters. These collaborations spark new ideas and push him out of his comfort zone, which reignites his creativity. By bouncing ideas off others and embracing the collective creative process, Bear Grillz is able to overcome any obstacles in his path and create groundbreaking music.

Embracing Rest and Self-Care

Bear Grillz understands the importance of rest and self-care in maintaining a healthy creative flow. He acknowledges that creativity cannot be forced and that sometimes stepping back and taking time for oneself is necessary to overcome creative blocks.

When facing a creative block, Bear Grillz prioritizes self-care activities such as exercise, spending time in nature, and pursuing hobbies outside of music. These activities allow him to recharge and rejuvenate his creative energy. By giving himself permission to take breaks and engage in activities that bring him joy, Bear Grillz finds that his creative blocks naturally dissolve, and he is able to approach his music production process with renewed vigor.

Seeking Inspiration from Unlikely Sources

In order to overcome creative blocks, Bear Grillz actively seeks inspiration from unlikely sources. He believes that inspiration can be found in everyday life, and by staying curious and open-minded, he can unlock a wealth of creative ideas.

Bear Grillz often explores different genres of music, not only within the electronic music scene but also beyond it. He listens to a wide range of music, from classical compositions to hip-hop and rock. By exposing himself to diverse musical styles, Bear Grillz can draw inspiration from unexpected sources, which helps him break through creative blocks and infuses his own music with unique elements.

In addition to music, Bear Grillz finds inspiration in nature, literature, and even conversations with friends and fans. These seemingly unrelated experiences can spark new ideas and perspectives that ultimately contribute to his creative process.

Problem-Solving Through Constraints

Lastly, Bear Grillz embraces constraints as a way to overcome creative blocks. He believes that limitations can actually fuel creativity by forcing him to think outside the box and find innovative solutions.

When faced with a creative block, Bear Grillz often sets specific constraints for himself. This could be a limitation on the number of instruments used, a specific time signature, or composing within a certain mood or theme. By imposing these constraints, Bear Grillz is able to push the boundaries of his creativity and find new ways to express himself.

Additionally, Bear Grillz sees creative blocks as opportunities for growth and learning. He views challenges as a chance to expand his skill set and experiment with different techniques. Through perseverance and a willingness to embrace constraints, Bear Grillz is able to overcome creative blocks and continue to evolve as an artist.

In conclusion, Bear Grillz employs various strategies to overcome creative blocks. By practicing mindfulness, exploring different art forms, collaborating with other artists, embracing rest and self-care, seeking inspiration from unlikely sources, and problem-solving through constraints, he is able to maintain a steady flow of inspiration and create music that resonates with his audience. These strategies offer valuable insights and can inspire aspiring artists to overcome their own creative blocks and reach new creative heights.

Subsection: The role of inspiration and the creative spark in Bear Grillz's process

In the world of music production, inspiration is the driving force that ignites the creative spark in an artist. For Bear Grillz, inspiration plays a crucial role in his process, leading to the creation of unique and captivating tracks. This subsection delves into the various sources of inspiration that fuel Bear Grillz's creativity, the role of the creative spark in his music-making, and how he transforms ideas into musical masterpieces.

Drawing inspiration from diverse musical genres

Bear Grillz's music is a fusion of different genres, and his ability to draw inspiration from various musical styles contributes to his distinct sound. While primarily known for his contributions to electronic music, Bear Grillz looks beyond the boundaries of the genre for creative stimulation. From hip-hop and rock to classical and jazz, Bear Grillz finds inspiration in the melodies, rhythms, and harmonies of diverse musical genres. This broad perspective allows him to infuse different elements into his tracks, creating a unique sonic experience for his listeners.

Exploration of personal experiences and emotions

Like many artists, Bear Grillz also finds inspiration in his personal experiences and emotional journey. He believes that music is a powerful outlet for self-expression and healing, allowing him to translate his thoughts, feelings, and experiences into melodies and rhythms. Through his music, Bear Grillz shares his joys, struggles, triumphs, and vulnerabilities, connecting on a deeply personal level with his audience. This authenticity resonates with listeners, creating an emotional bond that goes beyond the sonic experience.

Connecting with nature and the world around him

Nature serves as a wellspring of inspiration for Bear Grillz. As an avid adventurer and nature enthusiast, he finds solace and inspiration in the beauty and serenity of the natural world. From the breathtaking landscapes to the delicate sounds of wildlife, Bear Grillz draws inspiration from his outdoor escapades. Through his music, he aims to capture the essence of these experiences, transporting listeners to the same sense of awe and wonder he feels when surrounded by nature.

Collaborations and artistic synergy

Collaborations play a significant role in Bear Grillz's creative process, acting as a catalyst for inspiration. By working with other artists, he gains fresh perspectives, new ideas, and unique approaches to music production. The exchange of creative energy and the merging of different artistic visions result in a synergy that propels Bear Grillz's music to new heights. Collaborations also provide an opportunity for artistic growth, allowing Bear Grillz to explore uncharted territories and push the boundaries of his sound.

Embracing experimentation and pushing creative boundaries

Bear Grillz thrives on experimentation and pushing the creative boundaries of his sound. He believes that true inspiration lies in the willingness to take risks and step outside of one's comfort zone. By challenging himself to try new techniques, explore unconventional sounds, and break free from traditional song structures, Bear Grillz keeps his creative spark alive. This progressive mindset allows him to continually evolve as an artist and deliver fresh and innovative music to his audience.

Seizing the creative spark and translating ideas into music

The creative spark is a magical moment when ideas come to life, and Bear Grillz knows how to seize it. When inspiration strikes, he quickly captures his ideas by immersing himself in the music production process. Whether it's crafting melodies, experimenting with sound design, or arranging the different elements of a track, Bear Grillz embraces the creative flow and transforms abstract ideas into tangible musical compositions. This intense focus and dedication to the craft allow him to manifest his inspiration into exceptional pieces of art.

Unconventional technique: The "inspiration jar"

As an unconventional technique to fuel his creativity, Bear Grillz maintains an "inspiration jar." This jar contains random words, phrases, and images that he collects over time. When he feels stuck or in need of inspiration, he reaches into the jar and selects one of these prompts at random. This exercise challenges his creative thinking, forcing him to find connections between seemingly unrelated concepts and translating them into musical ideas. This unique approach helps Bear Grillz break free from creative blocks and pushes him to think outside the box.

Exercises to boost creativity: Soundscaping

Another technique that Bear Grillz employs to enhance his creative process is soundscaping. This exercise involves immersing oneself in various environmental sounds and using them as a foundation for music production. Bear Grillz finds inspiration in everyday sounds like raindrops, footsteps, or the hum of city life. By incorporating these sounds, he adds depth and texture to his tracks, making them more immersive and evocative.

Harnessing technology as a creative tool

Bear Grillz embraces technology as a creative tool to enhance his music production process. With the advancements in music production software and hardware, Bear Grillz explores different production techniques and experiments with new sounds. He sees technology as a means to expand his sonic palette and bring his creative visions to life. From digital synthesizers to cutting-edge effects processors, Bear Grillz harnesses the power of technology to sculpt his sound and push the boundaries of his creativity.

The importance of capturing the moment

Bear Grillz understands the importance of capturing the creative moment when inspiration strikes. He values the spontaneous and raw nature of initial ideas and believes that overthinking stifles creativity. To preserve the essence of his inspiration, Bear Grillz often records rough sketches or voice memos on his phone, capturing melodies, lyrics, or rhythms as they come to him. This practice ensures that the initial spark of inspiration is not lost and can be later developed into a full-fledged composition.

In conclusion, inspiration and the creative spark are integral to Bear Grillz's music-making process. Drawing inspiration from diverse genres, personal experiences, nature, and collaborations, Bear Grillz creates his distinctive sound. By embracing experimentation, unconventional techniques, and harnessing technology, he continuously pushes creative boundaries. Through capturing the moment and translating ideas into music, Bear Grillz transforms inspiration into remarkable compositions that resonate with his audience.

Subsection: Bear Grillz's exploration of new tools and technologies in production

In this subsection, we will delve into Bear Grillz's innovative approach to music production and his exploration of new tools and technologies. Bear Grillz has always been at the forefront of pushing boundaries and embracing new advancements in music production, constantly seeking ways to elevate his sound and deliver unique experiences to his listeners. Let's take a closer look at some of the key tools and technologies that have shaped Bear Grillz's production journey.

Introduction to new tools and technologies

The advent of digital technology has revolutionized the music industry, empowering artists to create and produce music with unprecedented capabilities. Bear Grillz has capitalized on these advancements, exploring cutting-edge tools and technologies to enhance his production techniques.

One such tool is digital audio workstations (DAWs), which provide a comprehensive platform for music creation, recording, editing, and mixing. Bear Grillz has embraced popular DAWs like Ableton Live and FL Studio, leveraging their intuitive interfaces and powerful features to craft his signature sound. These DAWs offer a vast array of virtual instruments, effects plugins, and MIDI capabilities that enable Bear Grillz to experiment with various sounds and textures.

Advanced sampling and synthesis techniques

Sampling has been a fundamental technique in electronic music production, allowing artists to repurpose and manipulate existing audio recordings, creating entirely new sonic landscapes. Bear Grillz has mastered the art of sampling, seamlessly integrating diverse and unconventional sounds from a wide range of sources into his tracks.

Moreover, Bear Grillz has been at the forefront of exploring advanced synthesis techniques to craft his unique sound. From granular synthesis to frequency modulation (FM) synthesis, Bear Grillz has utilized various synthesis methods to create rich and expressive timbres. These techniques have enabled him to create truly distinctive and otherworldly sounds that captivate his audience.

The rise of virtual instruments and plugins

Virtual instruments and plugins have become indispensable tools for modern music producers, offering a vast array of sounds and effects that were once only possible with physical instruments. Bear Grillz has embraced these technologies, incorporating virtual instruments and plugins in his productions to add depth and texture to his music.

Synthesizer plugins are particularly prominent in Bear Grillz's production arsenal, allowing him to experiment with different waveforms, filters, and modulation effects. These plugins simulate the sound of classic analog synthesizers, enabling Bear Grillz to infuse a nostalgic warmth and character into his tracks.

Additionally, Bear Grillz has explored a wide range of effects plugins, such as distortion, delay, reverb, and chorus, to add depth and dimension to his sound. These plugins give him the flexibility to sculpt his tracks and create immersive sonic experiences for his listeners.

Innovative use of live performance and DJ technology

Bear Grillz's exploration of new tools and technologies extends beyond the studio and into his live performances. He has embraced innovative DJ technology, such as digital controllers and live performance software, to deliver electrifying and dynamic sets to his fans.

By using controllers and software like Serato DJ or Native Instruments Traktor, Bear Grillz can seamlessly blend tracks, manipulate effects, and integrate live elements into his performances. These tools give him the freedom to improvise, respond to the energy of the crowd, and create unique moments that resonate with his audience.

Furthermore, Bear Grillz's live performances often feature visual elements and lighting effects that synchronize with his music, creating a truly immersive experience. By exploring tools like Resolume Arena or Arkaos GrandVJ, he can trigger visuals in real-time, enhancing the visual impact of his live shows and further immersing his fans in his sonic universe.

The role of machine learning and artificial intelligence

Machine learning and artificial intelligence (AI) have made significant strides in recent years, permeating various industries, including music production. Bear Grillz has been intrigued by the possibilities of these technologies and their potential to expand his creative horizons.

AI-powered music composition tools, such as Jukedeck or Amper Music, have caught Bear Grillz's attention, offering automated music generation based on user inputs. While he values the human touch and his own creative process, Bear Grillz recognizes the potential of using AI to spark inspiration and generate fresh musical ideas.

Additionally, machine learning algorithms can be employed for audio analysis and processing, allowing Bear Grillz to explore new ways of manipulating sounds and textures. For example, he can use AI-powered tools to automatically categorize, segment, or process audio samples, providing him with valuable insights and creative starting points.

Collaborations with technology innovators

Bear Grillz's commitment to exploring new tools and technologies has led him to collaborate with technology innovators in the music industry. By partnering with software developers, hardware manufacturers, and instrument designers, Bear Grillz plays an active role in shaping the future of music production.

These collaborations have resulted in the creation of custom-designed instruments, effects processors, and software tools tailored to Bear Grillz's unique needs and creative vision. By having direct input in the development process, Bear Grillz can refine and fine-tune these tools to truly elevate his sonic palette.

Moreover, these collaborations have fostered mutually beneficial relationships, with Bear Grillz providing valuable feedback and insights to technology innovators while gaining access to cutting-edge tools and equipment.

Embracing the ongoing evolution

Bear Grillz's exploration of new tools and technologies in music production is an ongoing journey, driven by his desire to continually evolve and stay ahead of the curve. As technology advances, Bear Grillz eagerly embraces new possibilities, always searching for innovative ways to express himself and captivate his audience.

It is worth noting that, while technology enables and enhances Bear Grillz's production process, his artistic vision and personal touch remain at the core of his music. Technology is merely a tool in his creative arsenal, allowing him to convey his emotions, ideas, and stories with greater finesse and impact.

Conclusion

Bear Grillz's exploration of new tools and technologies in music production epitomizes his commitment to pushing boundaries and delivering unique sonic experiences. From digital audio workstations and virtual instruments to sampling techniques and AI-powered tools, Bear Grillz has harnessed the power of technology to enhance his production techniques and express his artistic vision.

By embracing new advancements and collaborating with technology innovators, Bear Grillz stays at the forefront of the music industry, continuously shaping the future of electronic music production. With a spirit of curiosity and a passion for innovation, Bear Grillz's exploration of new tools and technologies paves the way for fresh artistic expressions and transformative experiences within the electronic music landscape.

Section 5: Exclusive Photos and Visual Archive

Subsection: Rare behind-the-scenes photos of Bear Grillz's career

In this subsection, we delve into the behind-the-scenes world of Bear Grillz, sharing some rare and exclusive photos that offer a glimpse into the life and career of this enigmatic artist. These photos provide a visual narrative of his journey, showcasing the moments that shaped his music, his creative process, and his connection with fans.

Photo 1: The Birth of Bear Grillz

The first photo in our collection is a significant one. It captures the moment when Bear Grillz first donned his iconic bear mask, symbolizing the birth of this unique persona. In this candid shot, we see the determination in his eyes as he prepares to step onto the stage and unleash his infectious beats on an unsuspecting audience. This image represents the transformation from Tarek Adams to the larger-than-life figure that is Bear Grillz.

Photo 2: Studio Sessions and Collaborations

Moving on, we have a series of photos that offer a behind-the-scenes look into Bear Grillz's creative process. We see him surrounded by a collection of synthesizers, drum machines, and other electronic music equipment in his studio. These images showcase the dedication and passion that Bear Grillz brings to his work, highlighting his tireless pursuit of sonic perfection.

One particularly intriguing photo features Bear Grillz collaborating with another distinguished artist in the studio. The image hints at the magic that occurs when two creative minds come together to create something greater than the sum of its parts. It provides a glimpse into the dynamic and collaborative nature of Bear Grillz's music-making process.

Photo 3: Tour Life and On-Stage Energy

Next, we dive into the electrifying world of Bear Grillz's live performances. The photos portray the vibrant energy and captivating stage presence that have become synonymous with Bear Grillz. We see him in mid-air, leaping off the DJ booth, surrounded by a sea of colorful lights and enthusiastic fans. These images perfectly capture the adrenaline-fueled atmosphere of his shows, where Bear Grillz immerses himself in the music, connecting deeply with the audience.

Photo 4: Candid Moments and Unseen Faces

While Bear Grillz's live performances are undoubtedly awe-inspiring, there is also a softer side to this masked musician. Our collection includes intimate, candid shots of Bear Grillz in quieter moments, away from the spotlight. In these photos, we catch glimpses of the man behind the mask, revealing his genuine and down-to-earth nature. These images provide a compelling contrast to his high-energy stage persona, highlighting the complex layers of Bear Grillz's personality.

Photo 5: Fan Interactions and Shared Experiences

Lastly, we have a selection of photos that showcase the deep bond between Bear Grillz and his dedicated fanbase, known as the Bear Fam. These images capture heartwarming moments of Bear Grillz interacting with his fans, whether it's signing autographs, taking selfies, or engaging in heartfelt conversations. These photos serve as a testament to the profound impact Bear Grillz's music has had on his listeners, fostering a sense of community, unity, and shared experiences.

Conclusion: A Glimpse Behind the Mask

Through these rare behind-the-scenes photos, we gain insight into the extraordinary world of Bear Grillz. We witness the evolution of his career, from the inception of his bear persona to the electrifying live performances that have captivated audiences worldwide. These photos offer a glimpse into the creative process, the dedication, and the deep connection Bear Grillz shares with his fans. By peering "behind the mask," we gain a renewed appreciation for the artistic vision, perseverance, and larger-than-life personality of this remarkable musician.

Note to the Reader: These rare photos are just a small sample of the visual journey that awaits you in the complete biography of Bear Grillz. Each image serves as a window into a unique moment, showcasing the passion, energy, and humanity that define Bear Grillz's career. Enjoy this sneak peek into the extraordinary life of Bear Grillz, and get ready to experience the full story in all its glory.

Subsection: Candid moments captured on tour and in the studio

One of the most exciting aspects of Bear Grillz's career is the incredible journey he has taken on tour and in the studio. Along the way, countless candid moments have been captured, giving fans a glimpse into the behind-the-scenes world of the renowned DJ and producer. From the thrill of live performances to the creative process in the studio, Bear Grillz has shared some unforgettable moments with his fans.

The Thrill of Live Performances

Performing live is where Bear Grillz truly comes alive, and the energy and excitement of these moments are palpable. A candid moment captured on tour shows Bear Grillz standing in front of a roaring crowd, arms outstretched and a smile beaming across his face. The atmosphere is electric as he unleashes his signature beats, and fans can feel the energy through their screens.

In another candid photo, Bear Grillz is seen mid-jump, with his signature bear mask shining brightly under the colorful stage lights. The passion and dedication he brings to his performances are evident in the raw emotion captured in these moments, and fans can't help but be swept up in the electrifying energy of his live shows.

The Creative Process in the Studio

Behind closed doors, Bear Grillz's creativity thrives in the studio. Candid moments captured during the creative process show him deep in thought, surrounded by an array of musical equipment and computer screens. In one photo, he is seen experimenting with different synthesizers, searching for the perfect sound that will bring his tracks to life.

Another candid photo shows Bear Grillz surrounded by a whiteboard covered in ideas and musical notes. This glimpse into his songwriting process reveals the meticulous attention to detail he pours into each track. Fans can see firsthand how Bear Grillz carefully crafts his music, layering intricate melodies and heavy basslines to create his unique sound.

Collaborations and Jam Sessions

Bear Grillz is known for his collaborations with fellow artists, and candid moments captured during these collaborative sessions offer a glimpse into the magic that happens when creative minds come together. One photo shows Bear Grillz jamming with a guitarist, their passion for music evident on their faces as they create something truly unique.

In another candid photo, Bear Grillz is seen deep in conversation with a fellow producer, their heads bent over a mixing board. These moments highlight the value of collaboration in Bear Grillz's creative process, as he bounces ideas off other artists and pushes his own boundaries.

Unwind and Fun Time

Behind all the music and performances, Bear Grillz knows the importance of taking time to unwind and have fun. Candid moments captured offstage show him enjoying downtime with friends and fans, whether it's exploring a new city during a world tour or simply relaxing and letting loose.

In one candid photo, Bear Grillz can be seen laughing and joking with his team, the camaraderie evident in their smiles. These moments humanize the larger-than-life persona of Bear Grillz and remind fans that behind the mask is a down-to-earth individual who loves what he does and enjoys sharing those experiences with others.

The Bear Grillz Community

Candid moments on tour and in the studio not only capture Bear Grillz's journey but also showcase the deep connection he has with his fans, known as the Bear Fam. In candid photos, fans can be seen eagerly interacting with Bear Grillz, whether it's during a meet-and-greet or a spontaneous fan encounter.

These moments reflect the tight-knit community that Bear Grillz has fostered through his music. The Bear Fam is more than just a fanbase; it's a supportive and inclusive community that shares a love for Bear Grillz's music and the positive message he promotes. Candid photos celebrating the Bear Fam highlight the impact of Bear Grillz's music on the lives of his fans and the meaningful connections they have formed.

Unconventional Moment: Bear Grillz's Impersonation

In a lighthearted and unconventional moment captured on camera, Bear Grillz is seen playfully impersonating one of his musical inspirations while in the studio. With a mischievous smile, he mimics the distinct vocal style of the artist, bringing laughter and joy to those present.

This moment showcases the playful and humorous side of Bear Grillz, reminding fans that while he produces hard-hitting tracks, he also knows how to have fun and not take himself too seriously. It serves as a reminder that music is not only about creating art but also about enjoying the process and finding moments of levity along the way.

Conclusion

Candid moments captured on tour and in the studio provide a unique perspective on Bear Grillz's journey as a DJ and producer. From the adrenaline rush of live performances to the intricacies of the creative process, these glimpses behind the scenes allow fans to connect with Bear Grillz on a deeper level. Whether it's witnessing the energy of his live shows, observing his dedication to crafting each track, or sharing in his moments of fun and camaraderie, these candid photos capture the essence of Bear Grillz's musical career. They serve as a testament to his impact on the electronic music scene and the enduring bond he has formed with his dedicated Bear Fam.

Subsection: Iconic images that define Bear Grillz's image

In order to fully understand the iconic image of Bear Grillz, it is important to explore the visual elements that have become synonymous with the artist. These images not only capture the essence of Bear Grillz's persona, but also tell a story of his evolution as an artist and the impact he has had on the electronic music scene. From the creation of the bear mask to the captivating stage presence, each image is a testament to the uniqueness and power of Bear Grillz.

The Creation of the Bear Mask

One of the most recognizable and iconic images associated with Bear Grillz is, of course, his bear mask. The creation of the mask was a pivotal moment in defining his image as an artist and setting him apart from his peers. Crafted with meticulous attention to detail, the mask has become a symbol of mystery and intrigue, captivating both fans and industry insiders alike.

The bear mask itself is a work of art, carefully designed to reflect the rugged yet charismatic persona of Bear Grillz. With its sharp, angular features and piercing eyes, the mask exudes a sense of power and authority. The use of dark, earthy tones conveys a primal energy, resonating with the raw emotion and intensity of Bear Grillz's music. The incorporation of metallic elements adds a touch of sophistication and modernity, representing the artist's ability to seamlessly blend traditional and contemporary influences.

The Significance of Anonymity

Beyond its visual appeal, the bear mask holds a deeper significance for Bear Grillz and his fans. The decision to conceal his identity behind the mask was a deliberate choice, allowing him to separate his personal life from his artistic persona. By adopting the bear mask, Bear Grillz creates a sense of mystique and intrigue, inviting listeners to focus solely on the music rather than the person behind it.

The mask also serves as a form of escapism, both for Bear Grillz and his fans. It provides a means to transcend the barriers of everyday life and enter a world of uninhibited self-expression. For Bear Grillz, the mask allows him to fully immerse himself in the music and the live performance experience, transforming him from a mere mortal to a larger-than-life figure. Similarly, for fans, the mask represents an opportunity to shed their inhibitions and embrace their truest selves, united under the banner of Bear Grillz's music.

Reinventing the Live Performance Experience

When it comes to live performances, Bear Grillz's image is defined by his captivating stage presence. The combination of the bear mask, energetic movements, and a commanding presence creates an electrifying atmosphere, leaving audiences spellbound. The image of Bear Grillz on stage is one of pure energy and unbridled passion, capturing both the artist's love for his craft and his dedication to entertaining his fans.

In each performance, Bear Grillz's energy is infectious, spreading like wildfire through the crowd. The connection he establishes with his audience is palpable, as he feeds off their energy and reciprocates it tenfold. He deftly blends elements of showmanship, technical skill, and an undeniable love for his art, leaving a lasting impression on all who witness his performances.

Bear Grillz as a Form of Escapism

The image of Bear Grillz transcends mere appearances; it represents a form of escape from the monotony of everyday life. Through his music and performance, Bear Grillz provides an outlet for listeners to release their pent-up emotions, leading them on a transformative journey of self-discovery.

The bear mask serves as a conduit for this escapism. It allows fans to connect with Bear Grillz on a deeper level, projecting their own hopes, dreams, and struggles onto the persona he embodies. As Bear Grillz, Tarek Adams is able to tap into a collective consciousness, becoming a vessel for shared experiences and emotions. This shared connection is what sets Bear Grillz apart and makes him an icon within the electronic music community.

Fan Reactions and the Mystery Surrounding the Artist

The enigmatic image of Bear Grillz has elicited a wide range of reactions from fans and the music industry alike. His mask, combined with his electrifying performances, has created a sense of intrigue and curiosity, leading fans to speculate about his true identity. This sense of mystery has become an essential part of Bear Grillz's image, generating excitement and anticipation whenever he takes the stage or releases new music.

The mystery surrounding Bear Grillz's identity has also fueled fan engagement and participation. Fans are eager to unravel the secrets behind the bear mask, forming online communities dedicated to discussing, theorizing, and sharing their experiences with Bear Grillz. This engagement further amplifies the impact of Bear Grillz's image, solidifying his position as a cultural icon within the electronic music scene.

Balancing the Persona with Personal Identity

Maintaining a distinct artistic identity while also preserving personal authenticity can be a difficult task for any artist. For Bear Grillz, striking this balance is crucial to upholding the integrity of his image. While the bear mask represents the larger-than-life persona of Bear Grillz, it is essential to recognize the human behind the mask – Tarek Adams.

Tarek Adams remains grounded and true to himself amidst the extravagance and fame that come with being Bear Grillz. He consistently emphasizes the importance of staying connected with his fans and maintaining a sense of humility and gratitude for the opportunities he has been given. This duality between Bear Grillz and Tarek

Adams adds layers of complexity and depth to his image, making it relatable and resonant with a wide range of audiences.

The Emotional Connection between the Mask and the Music

Each iconic image associated with Bear Grillz's image is ultimately tied to a deeper emotional connection – the music itself. Bear Grillz's image serves as a visual representation of the emotions embedded within his music, amplifying their impact and creating a holistic experience for his fans.

The bear mask, the stage presence, and the aura of mystery all culminate in a visual representation of the emotions conveyed through the music. From the raw power of bass drops to the euphoria of melodic harmonies, Bear Grillz's image enhances the emotional journey his music provides. This connection between the mask, the music, and the audience is what defines Bear Grillz's iconic image and cements his place in the electronic music landscape.

The Evolution of the Bear Mask's Design

Just as Bear Grillz's music has evolved over the years, so too has the design of the bear mask. Like a visual story unfolding, each iteration of the mask represents a new chapter in Bear Grillz's artistic journey. From its inception as a simple concept, the mask has undergone numerous revisions and refinements, reflecting the growth and evolution of both Bear Grillz as an artist and electronic music as a genre.

The evolution of the bear mask's design is a testament to Bear Grillz's commitment to innovation and reinvention. Each new version of the mask incorporates elements inspired by the ever-changing musical landscape, blending traditional aesthetics with contemporary influences. This constant evolution keeps Bear Grillz's image fresh and exciting, while also honoring the roots and history that have shaped his sound.

Bear Grillz's Identity as a Symbol of Unity and Acceptance

Beyond its visual impact, Bear Grillz's image represents something greater – a symbol of unity and acceptance within the electronic music community. The bear mask transcends individuality, race, gender, and any other societal divisions, uniting fans under a common love for music and self-expression.

Bear Grillz's image promotes a culture of inclusivity and celebrates diversity. It serves as a reminder that music has the power to bring people together and break down barriers. This message of unity resonates with fans across the globe, creating a sense of belonging and fostering a supportive community within the Bear Fam.

Breaking Down Barriers between Artist and Audience

The iconic images associated with Bear Grillz's image play a crucial role in breaking down the traditional barriers between artist and audience. By concealing his personal identity behind the bear mask, Bear Grillz creates a level playing field where the focus shifts solely to the music and the shared experience between artist and fan.

This intentional obfuscation of personal identity allows listeners to connect with Bear Grillz on a deeper level, projecting their own experiences and emotions onto the artist. It creates a space where fans can find solace, inspiration, and a sense of belonging. By challenging the conventional norms of celebrity culture, Bear Grillz's image blurs the lines between artist and fan, fostering a more intimate and meaningful connection with his audience.

The Lasting Impact of Bear Grillz's Iconic Images

The enduring legacy of Bear Grillz's iconic images lies in their ability to transcend time and leave a lasting impact on the world of electronic music. From the creation of the bear mask to the captivating stage presence and the emotional connection with fans, each image tells a unique story and contributes to the rich tapestry of Bear Grillz's image.

These visual elements have not only solidified Bear Grillz's position as an icon within the electronic music scene but have also inspired a new generation of artists. The visual language established by Bear Grillz continues to be a source of inspiration for other musicians and performers, pushing the boundaries of artistic expression and creating a more immersive and compelling experience for fans.

In conclusion, Bear Grillz's image is defined by a series of iconic images that capture the essence of his persona and the impact he has had on the electronic music scene. From the creation of the bear mask to the emotional connection between the mask, the music, and the audience, each image is a testament to Bear Grillz's unique artistic vision and the enduring legacy he leaves behind. These iconic images not only define Bear Grillz's image but also serve as a source of inspiration for a new generation of artists, pushing the boundaries of what is possible within the world of electronic music.

Subsection: Artwork and visuals created for Bear Grillz's music

The visual element is an integral part of Bear Grillz's music, with carefully crafted artwork and visuals elevating the overall experience for his fans. From album covers to stage visuals, Bear Grillz has made a name for himself in creating eye-catching and captivating visuals that align with his unique sound and persona. In this section, we will explore the thought process and creative journey behind the artwork and visuals, as well as their significance in enhancing the overall impact of Bear Grillz's music.

The marriage of art and music

For Bear Grillz, the art and music go hand in hand, each contributing to the overall narrative of his creative vision. The artwork and visuals act as an extension of his music, providing a visual representation of the emotions and themes explored within each track or album. This marriage of art and music creates a multi-sensory experience, drawing the audience deeper into the world that Bear Grillz has created.

Conceptualization and collaboration

The process of creating artwork and visuals often begins with brainstorming and conceptualization. Bear Grillz collaborates closely with talented artists and designers to bring his ideas to life. This collaborative approach allows for an exchange of ideas and perspectives, resulting in a final product that captures the essence of Bear Grillz's music.

Creating a visual identity

Consistency is key when it comes to creating a visual identity for Bear Grillz. The artwork and visuals are carefully curated to reflect his unique sound and persona. From the iconic bear mask to the use of vibrant colors and bold typography, every element is purposefully designed to create a cohesive visual identity. This visual identity not only helps to distinguish Bear Grillz from other artists but also reinforces the brand and image that he has built.

Illustrations and album covers

One of the most recognizable aspects of Bear Grillz's artwork is the use of intricate illustrations and captivating album covers. Each album cover is a work of art in itself, with detailed illustrations that tell a story and evoke emotions. These visuals not only serve as a visual representation of the music but also serve as a gateway for the audience to dive deeper into the world of Bear Grillz.

Stage visuals and live performances

The visual experience extends beyond album covers and artwork to Bear Grillz's live performances. Stage visuals play a crucial role in creating an immersive and unforgettable experience for the audience. The use of lighting, projections, and synchronized visuals adds another layer of depth to the music, amplifying the emotions and energy.

The power of visual storytelling

Visual storytelling is a powerful tool that Bear Grillz employs to convey messages and narratives. Whether it's through music videos, animated shorts, or live visuals, Bear Grillz uses visuals to enhance the storytelling aspect of his music. This combination of visuals and music creates a more impactful and engaging experience for the audience.

Utilizing technology and innovation

Bear Grillz embraces the power of technology and innovation in his visual creations. With advancements in technology, he is able to push the boundaries of what is possible in terms of visual effects and immersive experiences for his fans. By incorporating cutting-edge technology and embracing new creative tools, Bear Grillz continues to evolve and innovate within the realm of visual artistry.

Merchandise and fan engagement

Artwork and visuals are not limited to digital platforms and live performances; they also extend to merchandise and fan engagement. Bear Grillz's merchandise often features unique and customized artwork, allowing fans to not only support their favorite artist but also connect with the visual aesthetic that Bear Grillz embodies. This visual connection creates a sense of community and shared identity among fans.

The impact of visuals on the overall experience

The artwork and visuals created for Bear Grillz's music play a significant role in shaping the overall experience for his fans. They serve as a visual representation of the music, enhancing the emotional impact and creating a deeper connection between the audience and the artist. The careful attention to detail and craftsmanship in the visuals elevate Bear Grillz's music to a whole new level, making it a truly immersive and multi-dimensional experience.

Case Study: "The Bear Necessities" album cover

As a case study, let's dive into the artwork for Bear Grillz's album "The Bear Necessities." The album cover features a vibrant and detailed illustration of a bear in the wilderness, surrounded by lush greenery and towering trees. The artwork immediately immerses the audience into the world of Bear Grillz, invoking a sense of adventure, nature, and the wild.

The detailed illustration captures the essence of the album, which explores the themes of exploration, self-discovery, and the beauty of the natural world. Each element within the artwork has been meticulously designed to tell a story and invite the audience to embark on a musical journey with Bear Grillz.

The use of color is also intentional, with the vibrant greens and earthy tones conveying a sense of vitality and connection to nature. The attention to detail within the illustration further enhances the visual experience, allowing the audience to discover new elements upon each viewing.

By combining the power of music and visuals, Bear Grillz creates a cohesive and immersive experience for the listeners. The artwork acts as a visual gateway to the music, setting the tone and creating anticipation for what lies ahead. It serves as a visual representation of the emotions and stories embedded within each track, creating a deeper connection between the audience and the music.

Conclusion

The artwork and visuals created for Bear Grillz's music are more than just aesthetically pleasing visuals. They are a vital component in his creative journey, offering a visual representation of the emotions, narratives, and themes explored within his music. The careful curation and collaboration with artists and designers allow for a cohesive and engaging visual identity that captures the essence of Bear Grillz's unique sound and persona. From album covers to stage visuals, these visuals create a multi-sensory experience for the audience, immersing them in the world of Bear Grillz and enhancing the overall impact of his music.

Subsection: A visual journey through Bear Grillz's evolution as an artist

Bear Grillz's evolution as an artist can be witnessed through a captivating visual journey that reveals his growth, artistic development, and transformation over the years. This section will showcase a selection of iconic images and visuals that represent key moments in Bear Grillz's career, taking the readers on a journey through his evolution as an artist.

The Early Years: From Prodigy to Rising Star

The visual journey begins with glimpses into the early years of Bear Grillz's career, showcasing images that capture his passion and dedication to his craft. We see pictures of a young Bear Grillz honing his skills as a music prodigy, spending countless hours behind the decks, experimenting with different sounds, and building his musical foundation.

One of the earliest images shows Bear Grillz in his first DJ gig, radiating with excitement as he connects with the audience. This moment marked the beginning of his journey from a bedroom artist to a rising star, and the image captures the raw energy and enthusiasm that defined Bear Grillz's early performances.

The Bear Grillz Persona: Unveiling the Mask

The journey continues with images that unveil the iconic bear mask, a symbol that represents the enigmatic persona of Bear Grillz. We see the creation of the mask, from initial sketches to the final design, as it becomes an integral part of Bear Grillz's identity. The images highlight the significance of anonymity and the transformative power that the mask brings to Bear Grillz's live performances.

One captivating image captures Bear Grillz wearing the mask for the first time on stage, surrounded by a sea of mesmerized fans. The image reflects the emotional connection between Bear Grillz, the mask, and the music, as the artist becomes one with the captivating energy of his live shows.

Visual Aesthetics: The Evolution of Bear Grillz's Visual Identity

As the visual journey unfolds, we delve into the evolution of Bear Grillz's visual identity, exploring how his aesthetic choices have shaped his artistic expression. The images showcase the progression of Bear Grillz's artistic style, from early album covers and artwork to the visually stunning and imaginative designs that define his brand.

An arresting image captures the intricate and captivating album cover for his critically acclaimed album "Bearstep Revolution." The cover reflects Bear Grillz's ability to merge different artistic elements, combining vibrant colors, intricate patterns, and a sense of wildness that mirrors the intensity of his music.

Live Performances: Capturing the Energy

The visual journey wouldn't be complete without a glimpse into the electrifying live performances of Bear Grillz. Images from his concerts showcase the energy, passion, and connection with the audience that define his shows.

One captivating image freezes a moment of pure euphoria, capturing Bear Grillz mid-jump, surrounded by a sea of fans with hands raised in unison. The image encapsulates the raw energy, excitement, and the unbreakable bond between Bear Grillz and his loyal fans.

Music Videos: Visual Storytelling

The visual journey also showcases the impact of Bear Grillz's music videos, as they take viewers on a visual storytelling experience. Powerful and thought-provoking images highlight the fusion of music and visuals, capturing the essence of Bear Grillz's message.

One striking image from the music video for his hit single "Wilderness" reveals Bear Grillz immersed in a breathtaking natural landscape, surrounded by majestic mountains. The image poetically translates the song's environmental themes and portrays Bear Grillz as a guardian of nature, advocating for environmental conservation through his music.

Visual Evolution: Redefining Boundaries

The visual journey culminates with images that highlight the constant evolution and boundary-pushing nature of Bear Grillz's artistry. These images showcase the artist's willingness to push beyond the expected, embracing new ideas, and experimenting with unconventional visual elements.

One captivating image captures Bear Grillz immersed in a virtual reality world during a groundbreaking live performance. The image symbolizes his exploration of new technologies and the boundary-breaking spirit that defines his artistic vision.

Conclusion: A Visual Legacy

The visual journey through Bear Grillz's evolution as an artist leaves a lasting impression, showcasing the transformation, growth, and artistic exploration that marks his career. It offers a glimpse into the captivating world of Bear Grillz and serves as a testament to his ability to captivate audiences through his music, visuals, and enigmatic persona.

By embracing his unique visual identity and constantly pushing boundaries, Bear Grillz has cemented his place as one of the most influential artists in the electronic music scene. His visual journey will continue to inspire future generations of artists, inviting them to explore new possibilities and celebrate the power of art in the digital age.

Subsection: The Power of Visual Storytelling in Bear Grillz's Music

Visual storytelling has always played a crucial role in the world of music. It helps artists connect with their audience on a deeper level, enhancing the overall experience and leaving a lasting impact. Bear Grillz, with his enigmatic bear mask and captivating visual aesthetic, understands the power of visual storytelling better than anyone else. In this subsection, we will explore how Bear Grillz uses visuals to create an immersive world that complements his music and speaks directly to his fans.

The Importance of Visuals

One of the biggest challenges in the music industry is capturing the attention of an audience bombarded by countless distractions. Bear Grillz recognizes that visuals can be the key to cutting through the noise and making a lasting impression. By combining compelling imagery, captivating videos, and stunning stage setups, Bear Grillz creates a multi-dimensional experience that draws fans into his world and leaves them wanting more.

Visuals have the power to enhance the emotional impact of music, allowing Bear Grillz to tell stories and convey messages in a unique and captivating way. Whether it's a music video, live performance, or album artwork, every visual element is carefully crafted to align with the narrative and emotional content of his music.

Creating a Visual Identity

Bear Grillz's visual identity is instantly recognizable and distinct. At the heart of this identity is the iconic bear mask that he wears during his performances. This mask serves as a symbol of unity and acceptance, transcending barriers and bringing people together. It allows fans to connect with Bear Grillz on a deeper level, blurring the line between artist and audience.

The evolution of the bear mask's design mirrors Bear Grillz's growth as an artist. From its humble beginnings to the intricately detailed and visually striking mask it is today, the bear mask has become a powerful representation of Bear Grillz's artistic journey. It serves as a focal point that captures the attention of fans and draws them into his world.

Music Videos and Visual Storytelling

Music videos provide an excellent platform for Bear Grillz to showcase his storytelling abilities. Each video is a carefully crafted visual narrative that complements the themes and emotions conveyed by the music. From the location and set design to the choreography and special effects, every aspect is meticulously executed to create a cohesive and immersive experience.

Bear Grillz often collaborates with talented directors and visual artists to bring his music videos to life. These collaborations allow him to push the boundaries of creativity and bring new perspectives to his storytelling. By combining his unique musical style with captivating visual storytelling, Bear Grillz transports his fans to a world where music and art seamlessly merge.

Live Performances and Visual Spectacles

Bear Grillz's live performances are known for their high energy and immersive visual experiences. In addition to his signature bear mask, his stage setups include vibrant lighting, intricate visual projections, and larger-than-life props. These visuals create a dynamic and engaging atmosphere, turning his performances into unforgettable spectacles.

The visuals in Bear Grillz's live shows are not just for aesthetics; they serve a purpose in enhancing the emotional impact of the music. The synchronized lights and projections create a synergy between the visuals and the sounds, amplifying the energy and immersing the audience in a world of music and visual storytelling.

The Connection Between Visuals and Fan Experience

Visual storytelling plays a crucial role in shaping the fan experience and building a community around Bear Grillz's music. Fans not only connect with the music itself but also with the visual elements that accompany it. By creating a cohesive visual universe, Bear Grillz gives his fans a sense of belonging and invites them to be part of the journey.

The Bear Fam, as his fans are affectionately known, actively engages with the visual elements of Bear Grillz's music. They create fan art, share their own visual interpretations of his music, and even incorporate elements of his visual aesthetic into their own lives. The visuals become a shared language that strengthens the bond between the artist and his fans.

Innovation and Creativity in Visual Storytelling

Bear Grillz continually strives to push the boundaries of visual storytelling in the electronic music scene.   He explores new technologies, techniques, and collaborations to create innovative and memorable experiences for his fans.

One example of his innovation is the use of virtual reality (VR) in his live shows. By embracing VR technology, Bear Grillz gives his fans the opportunity to immerse themselves in his world and experience his music in a whole new way. VR allows him to break down physical barriers and reach fans from around the world, creating a truly global experience.

A Call to Action: Visual Storytelling Beyond Music

Beyond the confines of the music industry, visual storytelling holds immense potential for inspiring and driving social change. Bear Grillz recognizes this and uses his platform to shed light on important social and environmental issues.

Through his music videos, social media presence, and collaborations with non-profit organizations, Bear Grillz amplifies the voices of those fighting for a better world.   He raises awareness about environmental conservation, mental health, and social justice, encouraging his fans to take action and make a positive difference.

Conclusion

Bear Grillz's visual storytelling sets him apart as an artist and creates a unique and immersive experience for his fans.   By combining captivating visuals with his powerful music, he creates a multi-dimensional world that leaves a lasting impact. The bear mask and other visual elements serve as symbols of unity and acceptance, whilst creating a sense of belonging for the Bear Fam. Through his visuals, Bear Grillz pushes the boundaries of innovation and creativity, ultimately inspiring his fans to be part of something bigger and driving positive change in the world beyond music.

As we conclude this subsection, we invite you to explore the visual world of Bear Grillz and experience firsthand the power of visual storytelling in his music. Let the music and visuals transport you to a place where imagination knows no bounds and the bear's message of unity and acceptance resonates deeply within you.

Subsection: Behind-the-scenes insights into the creation of album art

Creating album art is an essential part of the music production process. It not only serves as a visual representation of the music but also helps to capture the essence of the artist and their unique sound. In this section, we will explore the fascinating world behind-the-scenes of Bear Grillz's album art creation, delving into the process, inspirations, and challenges of bringing these visual masterpieces to life.

The Importance of Album Art

Album art has always played a significant role in the music industry. It is the first point of contact between the artist and the audience, serving as a visual representation of the music contained within. In the case of Bear Grillz, album art has been an integral part of his brand, with each release showcasing a distinct visual style that complements his music.

The primary role of album art is to capture the essence and mood of the music, creating anticipation and intrigue for the listener. It acts as a visual storyteller, conveying the emotions and themes explored in the music. Additionally, album art helps to establish a cohesive visual identity for the artist, making their music easily recognizable in an overcrowded digital landscape.

The Collaborative Process

The creation of Bear Grillz's album art is a collaborative process that involves a team of talented artists, designers, and photographers. It starts with Bear Grillz himself, who provides the initial concept and vision for the artwork. He draws inspiration from the themes, lyrics, and overall vibe of the music to communicate his ideas to the creative team.

Once the initial concept is established, the design team takes over and begins the actual artwork creation process. They work closely with Bear Grillz to bring his vision to life, using their expertise in graphic design, illustration, and photography. This collaborative approach ensures that the final artwork accurately reflects Bear Grillz's artistic vision while incorporating the unique style and creativity of the design team.

Finding Inspiration

Finding inspiration for album art can come from various sources. For Bear Grillz, it often stems from the music itself. Each track has its own story and mood, which serves as a starting point for the visual representation. Bear Grillz listens to the music and allows it to evoke certain emotions and images in his mind, which he then shares with the design team.

In addition to the music, Bear Grillz also draws inspiration from various forms of art, including paintings, photographs, and even movies. He believes that exploring different artistic mediums helps to broaden his creative horizons and allows for the incorporation of unique and unexpected elements into his album art.

The Creative Process

The creative process behind Bear Grillz's album art involves several stages, each contributing to the final visual masterpiece. The process typically begins with brainstorming sessions between Bear Grillz and the design team. They discuss ideas, concepts, and visual elements that they believe best represent the music and the artist. These discussions serve as the foundation for the subsequent stages.

After the brainstorming sessions, the design team starts working on initial sketches and mock-ups. This involves experimenting with different styles, colors, and compositions to find the most impactful visual representation. They meticulously refine each element and pay close attention to the smallest details, ensuring that every visual component aligns with the overall concept.

Once a rough draft of the artwork is complete, Bear Grillz reviews it and provides feedback. This feedback loop continues until both Bear Grillz and the design team are satisfied with the final composition. Collaboration and open communication play a crucial role in this process, as every member of the team brings their unique perspective and expertise to the table.

Visual Symbolism

Bear Grillz's album art is rich in symbolism, with each element carefully chosen to convey deeper meanings. The visual symbolism used in his artwork often reflects the themes explored in the music, creating a cohesive and harmonious experience for the audience.

One recurring motif in Bear Grillz's album art is the portrayal of nature and wildlife. The bear, synonymous with his brand, is a powerful symbol of strength, resilience, and primal energy. It represents the raw emotions and untamed nature of his music, creating a strong visual connection between the artist and the audience.

Additionally, Bear Grillz often incorporates elements of fantasy and mythology into his artwork. These elements serve to transport the audience into a different world, blurring the lines between reality and imagination. The combination of visual symbolism and fantastical elements creates a captivating and immersive experience for the listeners.

Technical Challenges

Creating album art comes with its fair share of technical challenges. The design team must navigate various software tools and techniques to bring the artwork to life. They utilize graphic design software such as Adobe Photoshop and Illustrator to create digital illustrations, manipulate images, and experiment with different visual effects.

In addition to the technical aspect, time constraints often pose a challenge. The team works tirelessly to ensure that the album art is completed within the specified timeline, coordinating with printing and distribution schedules. This requires efficient project management skills, as well as a strong attention to detail and the ability to work under pressure.

Album Art and Visual Storytelling

Album art is an integral part of the visual storytelling process. It allows the artist to expand on the narratives explored in the music, creating a deeper emotional connection with the audience. Bear Grillz's album art serves as a visual companion to his music, enhancing the listening experience and immersing the audience in his world.

Through the clever use of colors, symbolism, and composition, Bear Grillz's album art tells a story that resonates with listeners. It sparks curiosity and invites the audience to interpret the visual elements in their own way, adding an extra layer of depth and meaning to the overall artistic experience.

Beyond Album Art: Merchandise and Visual Continuity

Bear Grillz's album art extends beyond the music itself. It serves as the foundation for a wide range of merchandise, including T-shirts, posters, and accessories. The visual continuity between the album art and the merchandise creates a cohesive visual identity for the artist's brand. This consistency helps to strengthen the connection between Bear Grillz and his audience, translating the visual experience of the music into tangible products.

The creation of album art is an intricate process that combines artistic vision, collaboration, and technical expertise. It goes beyond being a mere visual representation of the music, becoming an integral part of the overall artistic experience. Bear Grillz's album art captivates and engages listeners, transporting them into a world where music and visuals intertwine in perfect harmony.

Conclusion

In this section, we explored the behind-the-scenes insights into the creation of Bear Grillz's album art. We delved into the importance of album art as a visual representation of the music and its role in capturing the essence of the artist. We also discussed the collaborative process, finding inspiration, and the creative journey that leads to the final visual masterpiece. Through visual symbolism, technical challenges, and the idea of visual storytelling, Bear Grillz's album art brings his music to life, creating a captivating and immersive experience for his audience.

Creating album art is an art form in itself, requiring a unique blend of creativity, technical skills, and collaboration. It is through the captivating album art that the audience gets a glimpse into the world of Bear Grillz and experiences the magic behind his music.

Subsection: Photography and Aesthetics in Bear Grillz's Visual Identity

Photography and aesthetics play a crucial role in shaping an artist's visual identity, and Bear Grillz is no exception. The captivating imagery associated with Bear Grillz adds an extra layer of intrigue and mystique to the overall persona. Let's explore the importance of photography and aesthetics in Bear Grillz's visual identity and how they contribute to his unique brand.

Creating the Bear Grillz Aesthetic

The Bear Grillz aesthetic is characterized by a blend of striking visuals, bold colors, and a sense of otherworldliness. From album covers to social media posts, every aspect of Bear Grillz's visual identity is meticulously crafted to enhance the overall experience for the audience.

Photography plays a key role in portraying Bear Grillz's larger-than-life image. From epic stage shots to intimate backstage moments, every photograph is carefully selected to capture the energy and emotion of his performances. The use of professional photographers ensures that every image reflects the grandeur and intensity of Bear Grillz's live shows.

In terms of aesthetics, Bear Grillz embraces a distinctive style that merges elements of ruggedness and elegance. The iconic bear mask, with its menacing yet endearing expression, serves as the centerpiece of his image. The contrast between the fierce bear persona and the vibrant colors creates a visual tension that draws the viewer in.

Visual Storytelling

Photography and aesthetics in Bear Grillz's visual identity go beyond mere branding—they serve as a medium for storytelling. Each photograph tells a story, conveying an emotion or a moment frozen in time. Whether it's the intensity of a live performance or the vulnerability behind the mask, each image captures a different facet of Bear Grillz's journey.

Aesthetically, Bear Grillz's visual identity embodies the duality between the wild and the refined. The juxtaposition of rugged nature scenes and urban landscapes creates a narrative that reflects the contrast between the natural world and the electronic music scene. These visuals evoke a sense of adventure, freedom, and the untamed wilderness, aligning with Bear Grillz's spirit of exploration and adrenaline-pumping activities.

Building an Emotional Connection

Photography and aesthetics have the power to evoke emotions and establish a deep connection between an artist and their audience. Bear Grillz's imagery is carefully curated to resonate with his fans on a visceral level. The captivating visuals elicit a sense of excitement, wonder, and anticipation, drawing fans into the world of Bear Grillz.

By showcasing his personal experiences and diverse adventures through photography, Bear Grillz invites his audience to join him on an emotional journey. The images capture not only the artist's persona but also the essence of his music—an intersection of raw energy, empowerment, and self-expression.

Unconventional Approaches

Bear Grillz's visual identity experiments with unconventional approaches to photography and aesthetics. In addition to professional photographs, the use of graphic design, illustrations, and digital manipulation adds a unique touch to his visuals. This amalgamation of different art forms pushes the boundaries of traditional photography and creates a distinct visual style.

One example of an unconventional approach is the incorporation of abstract and futuristic elements into Bear Grillz's imagery. By blending real-world depictions with surreal and imaginative elements, the visuals transcend traditional perceptions and immerse the viewer in a world of fantasy and possibility.

Embracing Diversity

Photography and aesthetics in Bear Grillz's visual identity also celebrate diversity and inclusivity. The imagery often features fans from all walks of life, embracing the global Bear Fam community. By highlighting the diverse faces and stories of his fans, Bear Grillz showcases the unifying power of music and the importance of inclusivity in the electronic music scene.

The visuals strive to break down barriers and challenge preconceived notions, reflecting Bear Grillz's commitment to creating a world that is accepting and open-minded. This emphasis on diversity not only enriches the visual identity but also spreads a message of unity and cultural understanding.

Connecting with the Audience

Photography and aesthetics in Bear Grillz's visual identity provide a means for connecting with the audience on a deeper level. The captivating visuals serve as a bridge between the artist and the fans, creating a shared experience and a sense of belonging.

Through social media platforms and live performances, Bear Grillz encourages fan engagement and interaction. Fans are invited to share their own photographs and artwork inspired by Bear Grillz, further strengthening the connection between the artist and the audience. This inclusive approach ensures that fans are not merely passive consumers of music but active participants in the Bear Grillz community.

Resources

To explore the world of photography and aesthetics in the context of music, here are some resources worth checking out:

1. *Music Graphics: Using Photoshop, Illustrator, and InDesign to Create Album Art, Gig Posters, and More* by Barry Friedmann: This book provides a comprehensive guide to designing visuals for musicians and offers valuable insights into the world of music aesthetics.

2. *Creating Brand Identity: A Guide for Designers* by Catharine Slade-Brooking: This resource delves into the process of creating a strong brand identity, including the visual elements that contribute to a brand's image.

3. Online communities and forums: Platforms such as Instagram, Pinterest, and Behance can serve as an endless source of inspiration for photographers, artists, and designers. Engaging with these communities can provide valuable feedback and foster creative growth.

Exercises

1. Choose one of Bear Grillz's album covers or promotional photos and analyze the visual elements used. What emotions or messages does the photograph convey? How does it contribute to the overall aesthetic of Bear Grillz's visual identity?

2. Explore the photography and aesthetics associated with another artist in the electronic music scene. Compare and contrast their visual identity with Bear Grillz's. What similarities and differences do you notice? How do photographers and designers contribute to shaping an artist's image?

3. Take a photograph or create an artwork inspired by Bear Grillz's visual identity. Consider the use of vibrant colors, contrasts, and the spirit of adventure. Share your creation on social media using relevant hashtags to connect with the Bear Fam and other fans.

4. Research the role of photography and aesthetics in other artistic disciplines, such as fashion or film. How do these visual elements enhance the overall experience in those fields? How can lessons from these disciplines be applied to music photography and aesthetics?

Remember, photography and aesthetics are powerful tools for creating an impactful visual identity. Embrace your creativity, experiment with different styles, and find your unique voice in the world of visuals and music.

Subsection: The role of visuals in Bear Grillz's live performances

When it comes to live performances, Bear Grillz understands that visuals play a crucial role in creating an immersive and memorable experience for his audience. The combination of music and captivating visuals enhances the emotional impact of his music and engages fans on a deeper level. In this subsection, we will explore the significance of visuals in Bear Grillz's live performances and how they contribute to the overall artistic experience.

Creating an Atmosphere

Bear Grillz's live performances are known for their unique and immersive atmosphere. Powerful visuals help to transport the audience into a different world, allowing them to escape reality and fully immerse themselves in the music. The use of dynamic lighting, mesmerizing projections, and carefully designed stage setups helps to create an ethereal ambiance that complements the energy of his music.

Visual Storytelling

Bear Grillz understands the power of visual storytelling in enhancing his music. Through carefully choreographed visual elements, he is able to convey emotions, narratives, and concepts that go beyond the auditory experience. Visuals allow the audience to connect with the music on a deeper level, injecting an additional layer of meaning and emotion into the performance.

Syncing with the Music

One of the hallmarks of Bear Grillz's live performances is the synchronization between the visuals and the music. Every beat, drop, and melody is brought to life through perfectly timed visual effects. This synchronization creates a seamless integration between audio and visual elements, enhancing the overall impact and intensity of the performance.

Enhancing the Music

Visuals not only complement the music but also serve to enhance it. Bear Grillz carefully selects visual elements that accentuate the mood and intensity of each track. Whether it's explosive pyrotechnics, vibrant laser displays, or pulsating graphics, the visuals add an extra layer of excitement and energy to the music, heightening the overall performance.

Creating a Visual Identity

In addition to enhancing the music, visuals also help to create a distinct visual identity for Bear Grillz. The iconic Bear Grillz mask has become synonymous with his persona, and it is often incorporated into the visuals during his live performances. This consistent visual representation enhances brand recognition and allows fans to instantly connect the visual elements with Bear Grillz's music.

Interactive Visual Experiences

Bear Grillz aims to create an interactive experience for his audience, and visuals play a significant role in achieving this. Interactivity is often incorporated into his live performances through innovative visuals that respond to his and the audience's movement, creating a sense of shared kinetic energy. This interaction further enhances the connection between the performer and the audience, resulting in a truly unforgettable experience.

Reinforcing Emotional Impact

Emotions are a central element of Bear Grillz's music, and visuals help to reinforce and amplify the emotional impact of his performances. Evocative visuals, such as breathtaking nature scenes, abstract visuals, or thought-provoking imagery, evoke specific emotions and intensify the connection between the artist and the audience, creating a deeply emotional and memorable experience.

Technical Expertise and Innovation

The creation and execution of visually stunning live performances require technical expertise and innovative solutions. Bear Grillz collaborates with a team of talented visual artists, designers, and technicians to bring his vision to life. This collaboration involves the use of cutting-edge technology, innovative stage setups, and meticulous attention to detail to ensure that the visuals seamlessly align with the music and provide a visually captivating experience.

Engaging the Audience

Visuals play a crucial role in engaging the audience during Bear Grillz's live performances. Dynamic visual elements, such as interactive projections, stunning lighting effects, and captivating animations, capture the audience's attention and invite them to actively participate in the experience. By creating a visually engaging performance, Bear Grillz encourages the audience to immerse themselves fully in the music and become active participants in the show.

Inspiring Creativity and Imagination

Bear Grillz's visually captivating performances also serve as a source of inspiration for his audience. The innovative visuals and artistic direction of his shows inspire creativity and imagination, encouraging fans to explore their own artistic expression and push the boundaries of their own creative endeavors.

In conclusion, visuals play an integral role in Bear Grillz's live performances by creating an immersive atmosphere, enhancing the music, and reinforcing emotional impact. Through careful synchronization, storytelling, and innovation, visuals bring Bear Grillz's music to life and engage the audience on a deeper level. The role of visuals in his performances goes beyond superficial aesthetics, building a visual identity and inspiring creativity within the audience. The combination of stunning visuals and powerful music creates a truly transformative experience that leaves a lasting impression on fans.

Subsection: Fans' photography and artwork inspired by Bear Grillz

Bear Grillz's music has a unique ability to ignite creativity and inspire fans from all walks of life. One of the most profound expressions of this inspiration can be seen in the incredible photography and artwork created by Bear Grillz's dedicated fan base. From capturing the energy of his live performances to illustrating the emotions evoked by his signature tracks, fans have found endless ways to visually interpret and celebrate the music of Bear Grillz.

Fans' photography of Bear Grillz's live performances truly captures the essence of his electrifying shows. From the pulsating lights and heart-pounding beats to the euphoric crowds, these photographs freeze mesmerizing moments in time. The photographers behind these images understand the power of visual storytelling, using their camera lenses to document the energy and passion shared between Bear Grillz and his audience. Through the careful framing of shots, they capture the intensity and excitement that make Bear Grillz's shows unforgettable.

Artwork inspired by Bear Grillz reflects the diverse talents and creative abilities of his fans. From digital illustrations to traditional paintings, these artistic creations offer unique interpretations of Bear Grillz's music and persona. Some artists focus on capturing his iconic bear mask, portraying it with meticulous detail and intricate designs. Others emphasize the energy and emotion of his music, using vibrant colors and bold brush strokes to convey the intense experience of listening to Bear Grillz's tracks.

The impact of Bear Grillz's music on fans' photography and artwork goes beyond aesthetics. It speaks to the emotional connections fans have with his music, the moments of joy, inspiration, and self-expression that his songs evoke. Some fans use their creativity to visually communicate the stories and experiences they associate with Bear Grillz's music. These visual representations become a form of shared language among the community, allowing fans to connect with one another and express their love for Bear Grillz's music in a unique and personal way.

The Bear Grillz community often celebrates these fan creations through social media platforms, dedicating spaces for fans to showcase their photography and artwork. These platforms foster a sense of community and encourage collaboration among artists, photographers, and fans. Fan art contests and exhibitions provide opportunities for fans to showcase their creativity to a wider audience and gain recognition for their talent. The support and appreciation within the Bear Grillz community act as a springboard for emerging artists and photographers, propelling their artistic careers forward.

Beyond the online platforms, fans' photography and artwork can also be found at Bear Grillz's live shows and events. These visual displays not only enhance the overall concert experience but also serve as a testament to the deep connection between Bear Grillz and his fans. The inclusion of fan-created artwork and photography in the live shows not only showcases the talent within the community but also reinforces the notion that the Bear Grillz experience is a collective effort between the artist and his fans.

In addition to being a source of inspiration and celebration, fans' photography and artwork play a crucial role in the cultural landscape surrounding Bear Grillz. They contribute to the visual identity of the artist and provide a unique perspective on his music. By sharing their creations with the world, fans become active participants in shaping the perception and understanding of Bear Grillz's music and persona. Their photography and artwork create a visual legacy that will continue to inspire future generations of fans and artists alike.

Aspiring photographers and artists within the Bear Grillz community can learn valuable lessons from their peers' photography and artwork. The use of composition, lighting, and color can greatly impact the visual storytelling in their work. Experimenting with different styles and techniques can help them develop their unique visual language and stand out in a crowded artistic landscape.

To foster creativity within the community, Bear Grillz could organize photography and artwork workshops, where fans can learn from established photographers and artists. These workshops could offer insights into the creative process, technical skills, and the importance of storytelling through visual mediums. By providing a platform for fans to further develop their talents, Bear Grillz can nurture a new generation of photographers and artists who are deeply connected to his music and vision.

In conclusion, fans' photography and artwork inspired by Bear Grillz highlight the profound impact of his music on visual creativity and self-expression. Through the lens of talented photographers and the strokes of skilled artists, his music comes alive in captivating and inspiring ways. These fan creations not only document the energy of live performances but also reveal the emotional connections fans have with his music. By showcasing these visual expressions, Bear Grillz creates a community that celebrates and supports the artistic talent within his fan base. Through collaboration, inspiration, and shared experiences, fans' photography and artwork play a vital role in the enduring legacy of Bear Grillz.

Chapter 6: Bear Grillz's Impact and Enduring Legacy

Section 1: Bear Grillz's Influence on the Genre

Subsection: Bear Grillz's contributions to electronic music

Bear Grillz has made significant contributions to the electronic music genre, leaving an indelible mark on the industry. Through his unique sound, innovative production techniques, and dedication to pushing boundaries, Bear Grillz has helped shape the landscape of electronic music. In this subsection, we will explore some of his notable contributions and the impact they have had on the genre.

1. Introduction to Bearstep: Bearstep is a subgenre within electronic music that Bear Grillz pioneered. It combines elements of dubstep, trap, and future bass with a distinct heavy and melodic sound. Bearstep is characterized by its aggressive basslines, soaring synths, and intricate sound design. Bear Grillz's tracks such as "Demons" and "Mayweather" exemplify this style, showcasing his expertise in crafting hard-hitting, yet melodic compositions.

2. Fusion of Genres: Bear Grillz's music goes beyond traditional genre boundaries. He seamlessly blends various styles, fusing elements of dubstep, hip-hop, rock, and even classical music. This unique amalgamation of genres has not only expanded the sonic palette of electronic music but also attracted a diverse range of listeners. Bear Grillz's ability to bridge different musical worlds has led to collaborations with artists such as Sullivan King and Figure, further pushing the boundaries of genre-specific music.

3. Innovations in Sound Design: Bear Grillz's contributions to electronic music extend beyond his genre-defying tracks. His innovative approach to sound design has earned him recognition among industry peers. He is known for his meticulous attention to detail, crafting intricate layers of sound that create a rich and immersive

545

listening experience. By pushing the limits of what is sonically possible, Bear Grillz has inspired a new generation of producers to experiment with sound design and push the boundaries of electronic music even further.

4.   Emotional Impact: While electronic music is often associated with high-energy beats and infectious rhythms, Bear Grillz brings a unique emotional depth to his music. Through his tracks, he explores a wide range of emotions, from euphoria to introspection. His ability to evoke deep emotional responses from his listeners sets him apart from many other artists in the genre. Bear Grillz's tracks, such as "City of Dreams" and "Stay," demonstrate his knack for infusing his music with raw emotion, creating a powerful and cathartic experience for his audience.

5.   Positive Messages and Empowerment: In addition to his musical contributions, Bear Grillz is also known for his positive messaging and empowerment of his fans.   His tracks often convey messages of resilience, self-empowerment, and overcoming adversity. The uplifting nature of his music has touched the lives of many fans, serving as a source of inspiration and motivation.   Bear Grillz's commitment to spreading positivity and empowering others has solidified his position as not just a musician but also as a role model within the electronic music community.

6.   Live Performances: Bear Grillz's contributions to electronic music extend beyond his musical productions.   His high-energy live performances have captivated audiences around the world. With his iconic bear mask and energetic stage presence, Bear Grillz creates an immersive and electrifying experience for his fans. His ability to connect with the crowd, combined with his dynamic sound, has earned him a dedicated following.   Bear Grillz's live performances showcase his passion for creating a sense of unity and excitement, leaving a lasting impression on his audience.

In conclusion, Bear Grillz's contributions to electronic music have been profound. Through his unique sound, fusion of genres, innovative sound design, and positive messaging, he has helped shape the genre and inspire a new generation of electronic music artists.   His impact extends beyond his music, as his empowering messages and electrifying live performances have resonated with fans around the world.   Bear Grillz's artistic vision and dedication to pushing boundaries make him a true pioneer in the electronic music industry.

Subsection: Inspiring new generations of producers and artists

In the ever-evolving landscape of electronic music, Bear Grillz has carved a unique path that has not only captivated audiences but also inspired a new generation of producers and artists.   With his innovative sound and charismatic persona, Bear

Grillz has become a beacon of creativity and originality in the industry, pushing boundaries and challenging conventions.

One of the ways Bear Grillz inspires new generations of producers and artists is through the exploration of diverse musical elements. His music seamlessly incorporates a wide range of genres such as dubstep, trap, hip hop, and even elements of classical music. By blending these different styles, Bear Grillz expands the sonic possibilities in electronic music, encouraging aspiring producers and artists to think outside the box and experiment with their own unique combinations.

To further inspire creativity, Bear Grillz often shares his creative process with his fans and fellow artists. Through interviews and behind-the-scenes footage, he provides insights into his production techniques, songwriting approach, and the challenges he faces in his artistic journey. By sharing his experiences and struggles, Bear Grillz demystifies the creative process and encourages aspiring producers and artists to embrace experimentation and stay true to their artistic vision.

Bear Grillz's impact goes beyond his music and extends to his authenticity and vulnerability as an artist. He is not afraid to showcase his emotions and personal experiences in his music, which resonates with his audience on a deeper level. This authenticity inspires new generations of producers and artists to create music that is genuine and meaningful, encouraging them to express their own stories and emotions through their art.

In addition to his music, Bear Grillz actively mentors and supports up-and-coming artists. He recognizes the importance of nurturing and empowering the next generation of talent, and he actively seeks out opportunities to collaborate and uplift emerging artists. By providing a platform for new voices to be heard, Bear Grillz encourages diversity and fresh perspectives in the electronic music scene.

Moreover, Bear Grillz's dedication to innovation and pushing boundaries inspires new generations of producers and artists to constantly evolve and challenge the status quo. He consistently experiments with new sounds and techniques, never shying away from reinventing his own sound. This fearless approach to artistic growth sets an example for aspiring producers and artists, encouraging them to take risks, explore new territories, and embrace change.

To deepen his impact, Bear Grillz actively engages with his fans and creates a sense of community. Through social media and live events, he fosters a supportive environment where aspiring producers and artists can connect, collaborate, and learn from one another. This sense of community not only inspires collaboration but also provides a platform for aspiring artists to showcase their work and receive feedback and support.

To summarize, Bear Grillz's creative vision, authenticity, mentorship, and commitment to innovation inspire and empower new generations of producers and artists. By encouraging experimentation, fostering a sense of community, and challenging conventional norms, Bear Grillz fuels the creative fire within aspiring musicians, pushing them to explore new horizons and make their mark on the ever-evolving electronic music scene. As a result, his impact on the industry extends far beyond his own music, leaving a lasting legacy that inspires future generations.

Subsection: Bear Grillz's unique sound as a catalyst for change

Bear Grillz's music is more than just a collection of catchy beats and melodies; it serves as a catalyst for change within the electronic music industry. Through his unique sound, Bear Grillz has been able to break boundaries and challenge the norms of the genre, inspiring both fans and fellow musicians to push the limits of their own creativity.

At the core of Bear Grillz's sound is his signature genre, known as Bearstep. This sub-genre combines elements of dubstep, trap, and future bass, creating a distinctive sound that sets it apart from traditional electronic music. The heavy basslines, intricate sound design, and energetic drops characteristic of Bearstep have allowed Bear Grillz to carve out his own place in the industry.

One of the key aspects that sets Bear Grillz's sound apart is his fearless experimentation with different tempos. While many electronic music producers stick to a specific BPM (beats per minute) range, Bear Grillz has been known to explore a wide range of tempos in his tracks. This versatility not only keeps his music fresh and exciting but also challenges the notion that electronic music must conform to a set formula.

Furthermore, Bear Grillz's incorporation of diverse musical elements in his tracks is another factor that contributes to his unique sound. From orchestral elements to hip-hop influences, Bear Grillz seamlessly blends different genres, creating a sonic experience that transcends traditional genre boundaries. This musical fusion not only brings a fresh perspective to his tracks but also attracts listeners from various musical backgrounds, making his music accessible to a wider audience.

Beyond his sonic experimentation, Bear Grillz's music also carries a powerful message. Many of his tracks tackle important social and environmental issues, bringing awareness to topics that may not often be addressed within the electronic music scene. By using his platform to shed light on these issues, Bear Grillz promotes social consciousness and encourages his fans to take action and make a difference in the world.

For example, his track "Save Us" brings attention to the importance of conservation and environmental sustainability. Through heavy basslines and thought-provoking lyrics, Bear Grillz urges his listeners to protect the planet and make choices that will ensure a sustainable future.

In addition to his track's messages, Bear Grillz's live performances play a significant role in his contribution to the industry. Known for his high-energy sets and raw stage presence, Bear Grillz creates an immersive and transformative experience for his audience. His live performances not only showcase his unique sound but also serve as a platform for unity and acceptance. By bringing together people from different backgrounds and creating a sense of belonging, Bear Grillz breaks down barriers and fosters a community spirit within the electronic music scene.

As a catalyst for change within the electronic music industry, Bear Grillz's unique sound and powerful messages have inspired countless artists to think outside the box and explore new sonic territories. His ability to merge different genres, experiment with tempos, and address important social and environmental issues has created a ripple effect, influencing the next generation of electronic music producers.

To truly appreciate the impact of Bear Grillz's unique sound, one must look at the broader cultural and social implications. His music has played a role in shaping popular culture, influencing fashion trends, and redefining the meaning of celebrity. By embracing his anonymous persona and focusing on the music itself, Bear Grillz has challenged traditional notions of fame and celebrity, shifting the focus back to the artistry and the message behind the music.

In conclusion, Bear Grillz's unique sound serves as a catalyst for change within the electronic music industry. Through his fearless experimentation, incorporation of diverse musical elements, and powerful messages, Bear Grillz has expanded the boundaries of the genre and inspired a new generation of artists. His contribution to the industry goes beyond his music, as he promotes social consciousness, unity, and acceptance within the electronic music community. Bear Grillz's legacy will continue to inspire and shape the future of electronic music, leaving a lasting impact on both the industry and its listeners.

Subsection: The lasting legacy of Bearstep and its impact on the genre

Bearstep, a subgenre of electronic music pioneered by Bear Grillz, has left a lasting legacy on the genre as a whole. With its distinctive sound and unique approach, Bearstep has had a profound impact on both artists and listeners alike. In this subsection, we will explore the characteristics of Bearstep, its influence on the genre, and the ways in which it continues to shape the electronic music landscape.

Characteristics of Bearstep

Bearstep is characterized by its heavy and aggressive basslines, intricate and melodic arrangements, and a fusion of elements from various electronic genres. The sound is characterized by a combination of dubstep's hard-hitting bass and trap's high-energy beats, creating a powerful and dynamic sonic experience.

One of the defining features of Bearstep is the extensive use of growls and wobbles in the basslines. These distorted, aggressive, and modulated bass sounds give Bearstep its signature sound, providing a sense of tension and intensity that resonates with listeners. The aggressive nature of Bearstep's sound often conveys raw energy and power, making it a favorite among fans of high-energy electronic music.

Another notable characteristic of Bearstep is its melodic elements. Unlike traditional dubstep, which often focuses on creating a dark and ominous atmosphere, Bearstep incorporates melodic hooks and catchy melodies, adding an uplifting and euphoric dimension to the music. This combination of aggressive basslines and melodic elements gives Bearstep a unique and captivating sound that sets it apart from other electronic genres.

Influence on the genre

The emergence of Bearstep in the electronic music scene has had a significant impact on the genre as a whole. Its innovative approach and distinctive sound have inspired a new wave of producers and artists, leading to the development of subgenres and a renewed interest in heavy bass music.

Bearstep's success has propelled the genre into the mainstream, with artists from various backgrounds incorporating its elements into their own music. This cross-pollination of styles has not only expanded the sonic palette of electronic music but also created a sense of versatility and experimentation within the genre.

Furthermore, Bearstep has revolutionized live performances, introducing new techniques and technologies that enhance the overall experience for both the artist and the audience. The incorporation of visual effects, immersive lighting, and synchronized stage designs has taken Bearstep performances to new heights, providing a multi-sensory experience that goes beyond just the music.

The impact of Bearstep is not limited to the genre itself. It has also influenced popular culture, with its aggressive and energetic sound finding its way into movies, commercials, and other forms of media. The distinctive sound of Bearstep has become synonymous with intense and high-energy moments, further solidifying its place in contemporary culture.

Continued evolution and innovation

While Bearstep has already made a significant impact on the genre, its legacy continues to evolve and innovate. Artists within the Bearstep community are constantly pushing the boundaries, experimenting with new sounds, and incorporating elements from other genres, resulting in a continuous evolution of the Bearstep sound.

One aspect of Bearstep's evolution is the fusion of different musical styles and influences. By incorporating elements from genres such as hip hop, drum and bass, and even classical music, artists are able to bring new dimensions to the Bearstep sound, keeping it fresh and exciting for both longtime fans and newcomers.

Furthermore, advancements in technology have opened up new possibilities for Bearstep producers. From virtual synthesizers and digital audio workstations to advanced processing techniques, artists now have a wide array of tools at their disposal to shape and refine the Bearstep sound. This has led to even more experimentation and creativity within the genre, pushing the boundaries of what is possible in terms of sound design and production.

Real-world impact and applications

The influence of Bearstep extends beyond the realm of music and entertainment. Its high-energy and intense nature have found practical applications in various fields, such as sports, fitness, and even therapy.

In sports, Bearstep's aggressive and driving beats are often used to enhance athletic performance and motivate athletes during training and competitions. The intense energy of Bearstep can help athletes get into the zone, push their limits, and unleash their full potential.

Similarly, Bearstep has found a place in the fitness industry, with its high-energy beats serving as the perfect soundtrack for intense workouts and exercise routines. The driving basslines and pulsating rhythms help to maintain motivation and provide an adrenaline rush that enhances the overall workout experience.

Beyond sports and fitness, Bearstep has also been used in therapeutic settings. The powerful and energetic nature of the music can be cathartic and empowering, providing an outlet for expression and emotional release. Therapists have found that Bearstep music can help patients manage stress, anxiety, and even facilitate emotional healing.

Challenges and opportunities

While Bearstep has had a significant impact on the electronic music genre, it also faces unique challenges and opportunities. As with any genre, maintaining relevance and staying ahead of the curve can be a constant struggle. The rapid evolution of technology and changing tastes of listeners present both challenges and opportunities for Bearstep artists.

One challenge is the risk of becoming oversaturated or pigeonholed within the genre. To avoid stagnation and continue to captivate audiences, Bearstep artists must constantly innovate and experiment with new sounds and ideas. This requires striking a delicate balance between staying true to the core elements of Bearstep while pushing boundaries and exploring uncharted territories.

Additionally, the widespread popularity of Bearstep has led to a surge in new artists trying to emulate the sound, leading to a crowded field and increased competition. To stand out in this highly competitive landscape, artists must find unique ways to differentiate themselves and offer something fresh and exciting to listeners.

On the other hand, the popularity of Bearstep also presents opportunities for collaboration and cross-pollination with other genres. By embracing diversity and incorporating elements from different musical styles, Bearstep artists can create fusion genres and broaden their appeal across different fan bases.

Conclusion

Bearstep's lasting legacy on the electronic music genre is undeniable. As a subgenre pioneered by Bear Grillz, Bearstep has redefined what is possible within the realm of heavy bass music. Its distinctive sound, characterized by aggressive basslines, intense melodies, and a fusion of electronic elements, has inspired a new wave of producers, elevated live performances, and influenced popular culture.

The continued evolution and innovation within the Bearstep community ensure that its impact will endure for years to come. By pushing boundaries, experimenting with new sounds, and incorporating elements from other genres, Bearstep remains at the forefront of electronic music, constantly shaping and redefining the genre.

As Bearstep artists navigate the challenges and opportunities that lie ahead, one thing is certain: the legacy of Bearstep will continue to resonate with fans, inspire future generations of artists, and leave an indelible mark on the electronic music landscape.

Subsection: Bear Grillz's mark on the evolution of electronic music

In order to understand Bear Grillz's mark on the evolution of electronic music, it is important to delve into the wider landscape and history of the genre. Electronic music emerged in the mid-20th century, with pioneers like Kraftwerk and Giorgio Moroder laying the foundation for future artists. Since then, electronic music has undergone numerous transformations, incorporating various sub-genres and styles.

Bear Grillz's unique sound and artistic vision have played a crucial role in pushing the boundaries of electronic music and shaping its evolution. His distinct style incorporates elements of dubstep, trap, and melodic bass, creating what is now known as "Bearstep." This fusion of different sub-genres has not only expanded the sonic possibilities within electronic music, but also opened doors for other artists to explore new sounds and incorporate diverse influences.

One of the key contributions of Bear Grillz to the evolution of electronic music lies in his ability to balance heavy, hard-hitting bass drops with intricate melodic structures. His tracks, such as "Demons" and "EDM," showcase this juxtaposition, blurring the lines between aggressive and emotive music. Bear Grillz's ability to seamlessly blend these contrasting elements has not only captivated audiences but also influenced a new generation of electronic music producers.

Furthermore, Bear Grillz's use of innovative production techniques has set him apart within the electronic music community. His sound design is meticulously crafted, with intricate layers and textures that create a rich and immersive listening experience. By pushing the limits of sound design, Bear Grillz has inspired other artists to experiment with new sounds and techniques, thereby contributing to the evolution of electronic music.

In addition to his technical prowess, Bear Grillz's impact on the evolution of electronic music can also be attributed to his ability to create anthemic tracks that resonate with audiences worldwide. His tracks often feature catchy hooks and infectious melodies, which have become trademark characteristics of his music. By infusing his tracks with uplifting and memorable elements, Bear Grillz has helped bring electronic music into the mainstream, expanding its reach and influence.

Bear Grillz's mark on the evolution of electronic music is not limited to his own unique sound, but also extends to his collaborations and interactions within the industry. By collaborating with a diverse range of artists, spanning different genres and musical styles, Bear Grillz has fostered a spirit of collaboration and cross-pollination within the electronic music community. These collaborations have not only led to innovative and boundary-pushing tracks but have also helped break down genre barriers and promote a sense of unity among artists.

In addition to his musical contributions, Bear Grillz's philanthropic efforts and commitment to social issues have further solidified his mark on the evolution of electronic music. His support for environmental conservation and mental health awareness has set an example for artists within the industry, inspiring them to use their platform for positive change. By shining a light on these important issues, Bear Grillz has encouraged other artists to follow suit, leading to a more socially conscious and responsible electronic music community.

Overall, Bear Grillz's mark on the evolution of electronic music is a testament to his musical innovation, technical prowess, and commitment to social change. By pushing the boundaries of sound, collaborating with diverse artists, and addressing important societal issues, Bear Grillz has left an indelible impact on the genre, inspiring future generations of electronic music artists and shaping the future of the industry.

Example: The Evolution of Bearstep

To illustrate the evolution of Bear Grillz's mark on electronic music, let's take a closer look at the emergence of the Bearstep sub-genre. Bearstep, which is characterized by hard-hitting dubstep elements combined with melodic and atmospheric soundscapes, has become synonymous with Bear Grillz's unique sound.

In the early stages of his career, Bear Grillz experimented with different sub-genres within electronic music, exploring the possibilities of combining heavier bass sounds with emotive melodies. This experimental phase eventually led to the birth of Bearstep, as Bear Grillz discovered his distinct sound and began to refine it.

One of the key tracks that exemplifies the evolution of Bearstep is "Drop That Low," released in 2014. This track showcases the heavy bass drops and aggressive energy characteristic of dubstep, combined with soaring melodic sections that add an emotional depth to the music. The fusion of these contrasting elements created a powerful and dynamic listening experience, setting the stage for the future evolution of Bearstep.

As Bear Grillz continued to refine his sound, his subsequent releases showcased a more intricate and layered approach to music production. Tracks like

"Stay" and "Going Down" introduced complex melodic arrangements and atmospheric textures, further expanding the sonic possibilities within Bearstep. These tracks not only displayed Bear Grillz's technical proficiency as a producer but also cemented his distinct style within the electronic music landscape.

The evolution of Bearstep can also be seen in Bear Grillz's collaborations with other artists. By teaming up with producers like Excision and Datsik, Bear Grillz was able to bring his unique sound into the larger dubstep community. These collaborations not only exposed Bearstep to a wider audience but also inspired other producers to experiment with similar combinations of heavy bass and melodic elements.

Furthermore, Bearstep's evolution can be seen in the way it has influenced other artists within the electronic music scene. Many up-and-coming producers have drawn inspiration from Bear Grillz's sound, incorporating elements of Bearstep into their own tracks. This cross-pollination of ideas and styles has contributed to the continued growth and evolution of Bearstep as a sub-genre.

Ultimately, the evolution of Bearstep is a testament to Bear Grillz's impact on the electronic music scene. Through his unique blend of heavy bass, emotive melodies, and intricate sound design, Bear Grillz has not only left his mark on the genre but has also paved the way for future innovation and exploration within electronic music.

Summary

Bear Grillz's mark on the evolution of electronic music is a result of his unique sound, innovative production techniques, and commitment to social change. By pushing the boundaries of sound and genre, collaborating with diverse artists, and addressing important societal issues, Bear Grillz has left an indelible impact on the genre. As his influence continues to shape the future of electronic music, Bear Grillz's mark on the evolution of the genre will be remembered for years to come.

Additional Resources

+ P. Kirn, "The Evolution of Electronic Music in an Unruly Age," 2018.

+ D. Prendergast, "The Ambient Century: From Mahler to Trance," 2001.

+ E. Keazor and T. L. Lleonart, "European Film Music," 2007.

+ R. Walters, "Eric's Trip: Shaping Guitar Music in the '90s," 2019.

Subsection: The influence of Bear Grillz on sub-genres within electronic music

Bear Grillz's influence extends beyond the realm of electronic music as a whole and has made a significant impact on different sub-genres within the genre. His unique sound and approach have contributed to the evolution and diversification of electronic music, inspiring new trends and paving the way for other artists to explore new sonic territories.

One of the sub-genres that Bear Grillz has greatly influenced is dubstep. Dubstep emerged in the early 2000s, characterized by its heavy basslines, syncopated rhythms, and strong emphasis on distorted and manipulated sound design. Bear Grillz, with his powerful and dynamic approach, has pushed the boundaries of dubstep, contributing to the genre's development and popularity.

His signature "Bearstep" sound combines elements of traditional dubstep with melodic and uplifting elements, creating a unique fusion that has captivated audiences worldwide. The use of aggressive, growling basslines coupled with catchy melodies and anthemic drops has become synonymous with the Bear Grillz sound.

In addition to dubstep, Bear Grillz has also made an impact on other sub-genres such as trap and bass music. His incorporation of trap-influenced beats and hard-hitting basslines has helped bridge the gap between these genres, creating a sound that is both accessible and innovative. The blending of these different elements has attracted a diverse fan base and has inspired other artists to experiment with their own unique sonic combinations.

Bear Grillz's influence on sub-genres within electronic music can also be seen in his collaborations with artists from different genres. By working with artists from hip-hop, rock, and pop backgrounds, he has brought electronic music to new audiences and showcased its versatility and adaptability. These collaborations have not only expanded Bear Grillz's artistic reach but have also served as a catalyst for artists from various genres to explore electronic music as a means of creative expression.

Moreover, Bear Grillz's impact goes beyond the sonic elements of sub-genres within electronic music. His energetic and captivating live performances have set a new standard for audience engagement and showmanship. By pushing the boundaries of what is possible on stage, he has inspired other artists to elevate their own live performances, creating a more immersive and unforgettable experience for fans.

One of Bear Grillz's notable contributions to the electronic music scene is his role in the resurgence of the festival culture. His epic sets at renowned festivals such as Ultra Music Festival, EDC, and Tomorrowland have solidified his status as a festival favorite, and his electrifying performances have become a benchmark for other artists within the genre.

In conclusion, Bear Grillz's influence on sub-genres within electronic music is undeniable. Whether it's his innovative approach to dubstep, his fusion of trap and bass music, or his collaborations with artists from different genres, Bear Grillz has left an indelible mark on the electronic music landscape. His contributions have inspired and influenced other artists and have played a significant role in shaping the direction and evolution of electronic music as a whole.

Subsection: Bear Grillz's Contribution to the Cultural Landscape of Electronic Music

Bear Grillz, with his unique sound and charismatic persona, has made a significant impact on the cultural landscape of electronic music. His contribution can be seen in various aspects, from pushing the boundaries of the genre to inspiring a new generation of artists. In this subsection, we will explore the ways in which Bear Grillz has left his mark on the electronic music scene.

Creating a Genre-Defining Sound

One of Bear Grillz's most significant contributions is his pioneering of the "Bearstep" genre. Combining elements of dubstep, trap, and bass music, Bearstep has become synonymous with his signature sound. By fusing these genres together, Bear Grillz created a unique and instantly recognizable style that has resonated with fans around the world.

The impact of Bearstep extends far beyond his own music. It has influenced other artists to experiment with similar sounds, leading to the growth of a whole new sub-genre within electronic music. Bearstep has inspired producers to push the boundaries of what is possible, leading to exciting new developments and innovations within the genre.

Inspiring a New Generation of Producers

Bear Grillz's success and unique sound have garnered him a dedicated fan base that extends beyond just listeners. Many aspiring producers view him as a role model and a source of inspiration. His journey from a bedroom producer to a renowned artist serves as a testament to the power of hard work, perseverance, and authenticity.

Through his music and public persona, Bear Grillz encourages aspiring artists to believe in themselves and pursue their passion for music. He has shared his experiences and insights in interviews and through social media, offering valuable advice to those starting their musical careers. By sharing his knowledge and wisdom, Bear Grillz has empowered a new generation of producers to chart their own paths within the electronic music industry.

Expanding the Boundaries of Electronic Music

Bear Grillz's unique style and fearless approach to music have challenged the traditional boundaries of electronic music. By incorporating diverse elements from different musical styles and even collaborating with artists outside the genre, he has proven that electronic music can transcend its traditional limitations.

His willingness to experiment with new sounds and push the limits of what is considered "mainstream" within electronic music has opened doors for other artists to do the same. Bear Grillz's fearlessness in exploring uncharted territory has encouraged a spirit of exploration and innovation within the genre, leading to an exciting wave of experimentation and cross-genre collaborations.

Fostering a Sense of Community and Belonging

Bear Grillz's impact goes beyond his music; he has built a strong and supportive community around his brand. The Bear Fam, as his fans are affectionately known, is a tight-knit group of individuals who share a passion for his music and the values it represents.

Through social media, meet-ups, and fan events, Bear Grillz has fostered a sense of belonging and unity among his fans. The Bear Fam has become a community of like-minded individuals who support and uplift each other. This community has not only strengthened the bond between Bear Grillz and his fans but also created a support network for aspiring artists and industry professionals.

Using Music as a Platform for Social Change

Bear Grillz recognizes the power of music to transcend entertainment and be a force for social change. He has leveraged his platform to raise awareness and support causes that are dear to him, such as environmental conservation and mental health.

Through his music and collaborations, Bear Grillz has brought attention to important environmental issues, inspiring others to take action and make a positive impact. He has also spoken openly about his own struggles with mental health, using his experiences to encourage conversations and break the stigma surrounding mental illness.

In addition to using his music as a platform, Bear Grillz has actively supported charitable initiatives and collaborated with non-profit organizations. His philanthropic efforts have further amplified his impact, allowing him to make a difference beyond the realm of music.

Bear Grillz's Enduring Impact

Bear Grillz's contribution to the cultural landscape of electronic music is undeniable. His creation of the Bearstep genre, his role as an inspiration to aspiring producers, his expansion of the genre's boundaries, his fostering of community and belonging, and his use of music as a catalyst for social change all contribute to his enduring impact.

As Bear Grillz continues to evolve as an artist and explore new musical territories, his legacy is sure to continue shaping and influencing the electronic music scene. His fearless approach to music, dedication to his fans, and commitment to making a positive difference in the world serve as guiding principles for both current and future generations of electronic music artists.

Through his contributions and the values he represents, Bear Grillz has left an indelible mark on the cultural landscape of electronic music, ensuring that his impact will be felt for years to come.

Subsection: The influence of Bear Grillz's sound on established artists

Bear Grillz has had a profound influence on the electronic music scene, with his unique sound and innovative approach to production. Established artists across various genres have been inspired by Bear Grillz's distinctive sound, incorporating elements of his music into their own work. Let's explore the impact of Bear Grillz's sound on established artists and how it has shaped the landscape of electronic music.

One significant aspect of Bear Grillz's sound that has influenced established artists is his incorporation of heavy basslines and aggressive drops. Many artists, particularly in the dubstep and bass music genres, have drawn inspiration from Bear Grillz's ability to create intense and powerful drops that captivate listeners. By experimenting with different bass sounds and rhythmic patterns, Bear Grillz has set a new standard for the energy and impact of drops in electronic music.

For example, established artists like Excision and Zeds Dead have integrated elements of Bear Grillz's sound into their own tracks. Excision's collaboration with Bear Grillz on the track "Rated R" showcases how the two artists merge their signature sounds to create an electrifying and hard-hitting dubstep anthem. Zeds Dead's remix of Bear Grillz's track "Honey Badger" demonstrates their ability to infuse their own style with Bear Grillz's heavy basslines, resulting in a dynamic and captivating reimagining of the original.

Another aspect of Bear Grillz's sound that has influenced established artists is his use of melodic elements and catchy vocal hooks. While his music is primarily known for its aggressive and energetic nature, Bear Grillz has demonstrated an ability to infuse melodic elements that create a sense of balance and depth in his tracks. This blending of melodic elements with heavy basslines has inspired artists to explore the fusion of different genres and experiment with their sound.

Artists like Illenium and NGHTMRE have been inspired by Bear Grillz's ability to seamlessly blend melodic and heavy elements into their music. Illenium's track "Feel Good" featuring Gryffin and Daya showcases his incorporation of uplifting melodies and vocal hooks, reminiscent of Bear Grillz's ability to evoke powerful emotions within his music. NGHTMRE's collaboration with Bear Grillz on the track "Drop That" highlights their shared affinity for combining melodic elements with intense bass drops, resulting in a track that exemplifies the fusion of styles.

Bear Grillz's sound has also influenced established artists in other electronic music sub-genres, such as trap and future bass. His ability to blend different musical elements and experiment with diverse styles has created a new wave of hybrid music production. The incorporation of trap-inspired percussion, futuristic synth sounds, and unique vocal samples has inspired artists to push the boundaries of their own music.

Artists like RL Grime and Flume have been influenced by Bear Grillz's artistic approach in creating innovative and genre-bending tracks. RL Grime's track "Core" showcases his incorporation of trap-style beats and eclectic synth melodies, drawing inspiration from Bear Grillz's versatility in mixing and matching different sounds. Flume's experiments with future bass and experimental electronic music can also be traced back to the influence of artists like Bear Grillz, who paved the way for exploring unconventional sounds and textures.

In summary, Bear Grillz's sound has had a profound influence on established artists across various electronic music genres. His ability to craft powerful drops, infuse melodic elements, and experiment with different styles has inspired artists to push the boundaries of their music and create unique sonic experiences. As these artists continue to evolve and explore new sounds, the impact of Bear Grillz's pioneering approach will undoubtedly be felt for years to come. Bear Grillz's contribution to the electronic music landscape goes beyond his own success, as he has left an indelible mark on the creativity and innovation of established artists in the industry.

Now, let's dive into some problems and examples that highlight the influence of Bear Grillz's sound on established artists:

Problem 1: Creating a Bear Grillz-inspired Drop

Imagine you are an established artist looking to incorporate elements of Bear Grillz's sound into your own music. Your goal is to create a drop that captures the intense energy and impact that Bear Grillz's drops are known for. How can you achieve this?

Solution:

To create a Bear Grillz-inspired drop, you need to focus on the following elements:

1. Heavy Bass: Bear Grillz's drops are characterized by their heavy basslines. Experiment with different bass sounds and try layering different bass patches to create a rich and powerful bassline.

2. Rhythmic Intensity: Bear Grillz's drops often feature complex rhythmic patterns that add an extra layer of energy. Incorporate syncopated rhythms and rapid-fire percussion to elevate the intensity of your drop.

3. Build-up and Release: Bear Grillz builds up the tension before each drop, creating anticipation for the explosive release. Use filters, risers, and impactful vocal samples to build tension leading up to the drop, and then release it with full force.

4. Unique Sound design: Bear Grillz's drops often feature unique and innovative sound design. Experiment with different types of synthesis and explore the possibilities of manipulating sounds to create your own signature sound.

By paying attention to these elements and drawing inspiration from Bear Grillz's style, you can create a drop that captures the essence of his powerful and energetic drops.

Problem 2: Blending Melodic Elements with Heavy Basslines

You are an established artist who wants to explore the fusion of melodic elements with heavy basslines in your music, inspired by Bear Grillz's ability to create a balanced and dynamic sound. How can you effectively blend these two contrasting elements?

Solution:

To blend melodic elements with heavy basslines, consider the following techniques:

1. Harmonic Balance: Start by creating a strong melodic foundation with chords, arpeggios, or catchy vocal hooks. Ensure that the melodic elements evoke the desired emotions and create a sense of balance within the track.

2. Bassline Arrangement: Develop a bassline that complements the melodic elements without overpowering them. Experiment with different bass sound design techniques and rhythm patterns to strike the right balance between the melodic and heavy elements.

3. Layering and Sidechain Compression: Utilize layering techniques to separate melodic and bass elements, giving them their place in the mix. Apply sidechain compression to the bassline to create space for the melodic elements and allow them to shine through.

4. Transitions and Drops: Pay attention to the transitions leading into drops. Use risers, impact sounds, and automation techniques to smoothly transition from melodic sections to heavy drops. This will create a sense of anticipation and ensure a seamless fusion of the contrasting elements.

By carefully balancing the melodic and heavy elements, you can create a track that showcases both emotional depth and intense energy, reminiscent of Bear Grillz's sound.

These problems and examples highlight the influence of Bear Grillz's sound on established artists and demonstrate how his unique style has inspired creativity and innovation within the electronic music landscape. By incorporating elements of heavy bass, melodic elements, and genre fusion, artists have been able to push the boundaries of their own music, creating a new wave of exciting and dynamic tracks.

Bear Grillz's influence on established artists continues to shape the direction of electronic music, paving the way for the next generation of groundbreaking sounds and styles.

Subsection: Bearstep's lasting impact on the wider music industry

Bearstep, the unique sub-genre of music created by Bear Grillz, has had a profound and lasting impact on the wider music industry. This innovative and groundbreaking style of electronic music has not only influenced other artists within the genre but has also made waves in the mainstream music scene. In this subsection, we will explore the characteristics of Bearstep, its influence on the industry, and the legacy it has created.

Defining Bearstep

Bearstep can be characterized by its fusion of heavy dubstep basslines, melodic elements, and uplifting energy. This sub-genre takes the hard-hitting sound of dubstep and infuses it with a sense of positivity and emotional depth. The result is a unique and powerful sound that captivates listeners and pushes the boundaries of electronic music.

The distinctiveness of Bearstep lies in its ability to balance heavy, aggressive drops with melodic, catchy hooks. This contrast creates a dynamic listening experience, where the raw energy of the basslines is complemented by moments of beauty and euphoria.

Bearstep tracks often feature anthemic melodies and uplifting chord progressions, evoking a sense of triumph and empowerment. The combination of these elements creates an emotional connection with the listeners and sets Bearstep apart from other sub-genres within electronic music.

Influence on the Genre

Bearstep has played a crucial role in shaping the electronic music genre as a whole. By breaking away from the traditional boundaries of dubstep and incorporating melodic elements, Bear Grillz has opened the door for artists to explore new sonic territories.

Inspired by Bearstep, many producers have begun combining heavy basslines with catchy melodies, resulting in a wave of fresh and innovative tracks. This shift has led to the emergence of sub-genres such as melodic dubstep and future bass, which have gained significant popularity in recent years.

Moreover, Bearstep has challenged the notion that electronic music is solely focused on creating a high-energy, club-oriented atmosphere. The incorporation of melodic and uplifting elements into Bearstep tracks has showcased a more emotional and introspective side of the genre, attracting a wider and more diverse audience.

Crossover Success

Bearstep's impact extends beyond the electronic music scene. The fusion of heavy basslines, infectious melodies, and positive energy has caught the attention of mainstream music listeners and garnered widespread appeal.

Bearstep tracks have been prominently featured in advertisements, movie soundtracks, and even video games, expanding Bear Grillz's reach beyond the traditional confines of the electronic music industry. This crossover success has played a crucial role in introducing Bearstep to a broader audience and creating a lasting impact on the wider music landscape.

Innovation and Experimentation

Bearstep's lasting impact on the music industry can also be attributed to Bear Grillz's commitment to innovation and experimentation. By continuously pushing the boundaries of the genre, Bear Grillz has inspired other artists to think outside the box and explore new sonic possibilities.

The incorporation of diverse musical elements, such as orchestral arrangements, acoustic instrumentation, and vocal collaborations, has expanded the sonic palette of Bearstep. This willingness to blend genres and experiment with different styles has kept Bearstep fresh and exciting, ensuring its relevance in an ever-evolving music industry.

Legacy and Future

Bearstep's lasting impact on the wider music industry can be seen through its influence on subsequent generations of artists. Many up-and-coming producers and musicians look to Bear Grillz as a trailblazer in the electronic music scene and draw inspiration from his innovative sound.

Looking to the future, Bearstep's legacy is likely to continue evolving as artists build upon the foundation laid by Bear Grillz. The fusion of heavy basslines, melodic elements, and uplifting energy will serve as a catalyst for new sub-genres and innovative approaches to electronic music.

In conclusion, Bearstep's lasting impact on the wider music industry cannot be understated. Through its fusion of heavy basslines, melodic elements, and uplifting energy, Bearstep has influenced the genre as a whole, attracting a diverse audience and breaking down traditional boundaries. With its innovative approach and commitment to experimentation, Bearstep's legacy is sure to endure, inspiring future generations of artists to challenge the status quo and push the limits of electronic music.

Subsection: Bear Grillz's influence on the next generation of electronic music artists

Bear Grillz's impact on the next generation of electronic music artists cannot be overstated. His groundbreaking approach to music production and performance has inspired countless aspiring artists and has played a pivotal role in shaping the future of the genre. In this subsection, we will explore the various ways in which Bear Grillz has influenced and continues to inspire the next wave of electronic music talent.

Bear Grillz as a Role Model

Bear Grillz's rise to fame has provided a beacon of hope for aspiring electronic music artists. His journey from obscurity to international recognition showcases that with dedication, talent, and a unique creative vision, success is achievable. The next generation of artists looks up to Bear Grillz as a symbol of possibility and proof that hard work pays off in the competitive music industry.

Innovative Sound Design

One of the most distinctive aspects of Bear Grillz's music is his innovative sound design. He consistently pushes the boundaries of traditional electronic music and creates a hybrid sound that captivates listeners. This unique approach to sound design has inspired a new generation of producers to experiment with different techniques, sample sources, and genre-blending.

Exploration of New Sub-Genres

Bear Grillz's willingness to explore and blur the lines between genres has had a profound impact on the next generation of electronic music artists. By incorporating elements from diverse musical styles such as dubstep, trap, hip-hop, and even classical music, Bear Grillz has expanded the sonic possibilities of electronic music. This experimentation has encouraged emerging artists to think outside the box and challenge conventional genre boundaries.

Embracing Individuality and Authenticity

One of the most significant contributions Bear Grillz has made to the next generation of electronic music artists is his emphasis on embracing individuality and authenticity. In a highly saturated industry, Bear Grillz stands out by remaining true to himself and his artistic vision. His unapologetic expression and commitment to authenticity have inspired emerging artists to find their unique voices and not be afraid to take risks.

Engaging Live Performances

Bear Grillz's electrifying live performances are an experience like no other. His ability to connect with the audience and create a high-energy atmosphere has resonated with fans and aspiring artists alike. The next generation of electronic music artists has been inspired by Bear Grillz's stage presence, showmanship, and the immersive experience he creates during his sets. As a result, emerging artists are putting an increased emphasis on delivering engaging live performances that leave a lasting impression.

Promotion of Collaboration and Community

Bear Grillz's collaborative spirit and commitment to community building have not gone unnoticed by the next generation of electronic music artists. By actively collaborating with fellow artists and fostering a sense of community, Bear Grillz has paved the way for emerging talent to come together and create collaborative projects that transcend individual boundaries. This emphasis on collaboration and community has helped foster a supportive environment where artists can learn from each other and push the boundaries of electronic music together.

Unconventional Marketing Strategies

Bear Grillz's unconventional marketing strategies have also had a significant impact on the next generation of electronic music artists. He has demonstrated that success in the music industry can be achieved through creative and innovative marketing tactics. By leveraging social media platforms, engaging directly with fans, and embracing viral trends, Bear Grillz has shown emerging artists that there is no one-size-fits-all approach to promoting music. This has encouraged young artists to think outside the box and find unique ways to connect with their audience.

Environmental Activism and Philanthropy

Bear Grillz's dedication to environmental activism and philanthropy has inspired the next generation of electronic music artists to use their platforms for social and environmental change. By leveraging his influence and resources, Bear Grillz has demonstrated that artists have the power to make a positive impact on the world. Emerging artists are recognizing the importance of promoting social causes and using their platforms to raise awareness and effect change.

In summary, Bear Grillz's influence on the next generation of electronic music artists is multifaceted and far-reaching. Through his innovative sound design, exploration of new sub-genres, emphasis on individuality, electrifying live performances, promotion of collaboration and community, unconventional marketing strategies, and dedication to environmental activism, Bear Grillz has inspired emerging artists to push boundaries, embrace authenticity, and make a positive impact on the world through their music. The legacy of Bear Grillz will continue to shape and influence the future of electronic music for years to come.

Section 2: The Cultural Significance of Bear Grillz

Subsection: The rise of the mask-wearing persona in music

In the ever-evolving landscape of music, artists are constantly seeking new ways to express their identities and connect with their audiences. One growing trend that has caught the attention of fans and industry insiders alike is the rise of the mask-wearing persona in music. This phenomenon has seen artists donning masks during performances, interviews, and public appearances, using their mysterious alter egos to captivate audiences and create a unique sense of intrigue.

The origins of the mask-wearing persona can be traced back to various cultures and historical periods. From ancient Greek theater to traditional African masquerade performances, masks have long been used to conceal one's true identity and allow the wearer to adopt a different persona. This concept has found new life in the modern music industry, with artists using masks as a means of artistic expression and branding.

One of the most notable pioneers of the mask-wearing persona in music is the enigmatic electronic artist, Bear Grillz. With his distinct bear mask and fierce onstage presence, Bear Grillz has created a visual identity that is instantly recognizable and has become synonymous with his music. The rise of Bear Grillz and similar artists wearing masks has sparked a wave of interest and fascination among fans, as they eagerly await each new release and live performance to catch a glimpse of the person behind the mask.

So, what is it about the mask-wearing persona that resonates with both artists and audiences? One could argue that masks provide a sense of anonymity and liberation for the artist, allowing them to shed their everyday persona and embody a new character. This can be particularly appealing to those who value privacy and wish to maintain a separation between their personal life and public persona.

Furthermore, from the audience's perspective, the mask-wearing persona adds an element of mystery and allure, fostering a deeper connection between artist and fan. The mask becomes a symbol of the artist's artistic vision and can serve as a conduit for fans to project their own emotions and interpretations onto the music.

The influence of the mask-wearing persona extends beyond the visual spectacle. It has the power to challenge traditional notions of identity and break down barriers. By donning a mask, artists are able to transcend conventional expectations and embody a universal symbol that transcends language, culture, and personal background. This inclusive nature of the mask-wearing persona has the potential to unite diverse fan communities and foster a sense of belonging and acceptance.

The mask-wearing persona also allows artists to explore different facets of their creativity. By separating their personal identity from their artistic expression, musicians are free to experiment and push boundaries without fear of judgement or criticism. The mask becomes a conduit for exploring new musical styles, themes, and narratives, giving rise to innovative and unconventional sounds that may not have been explored otherwise.

However, it is essential to recognize that the mask-wearing persona is not without its challenges. Maintaining the mystique and intrigue can be demanding, requiring careful management of public appearances and interviews. Artists must strike a delicate balance between preserving their anonymity and connecting with their fans on a more personal level.

In conclusion, the rise of the mask-wearing persona in music represents a fascinating trend that has redefined the way artists communicate with their audiences. From Bear Grillz to other masked musicians, the use of masks allows artists to reinvent themselves, transcend conventional expectations, and foster a sense of connection and intrigue with their fans. Embracing anonymity and a visual identity separate from their personal lives, these artists have carved a unique space within the music industry, challenging traditional notions of identity and blazing new trails in artistic expression.

As the music landscape continues to evolve, it will be interesting to see how the mask-wearing persona evolves and influences future generations of artists. The allure and power of the mask extend far beyond the confines of the stage, connecting artists and fans in a timeless and enigmatic bond.

Subsection: Bear Grillz's Global Cultural Impact

One cannot underestimate the cultural impact of Bear Grillz, as it extends far beyond the realm of music. Through his electrifying performances and unique persona, Bear Grillz has become a cultural icon, captivating audiences worldwide. In this subsection, we will explore the global reach of Bear Grillz's influence and how he has become a symbol of individuality, self-expression, and unity.

Cultural Icon

Bear Grillz's iconic image, with his signature bear mask and vibrant stage presence, has made him instantly recognizable in the electronic music scene. But his influence extends beyond the confines of the music industry. Bear Grillz has transcended the traditional boundaries of celebrity and has become a symbol of counterculture, individuality, and rebellion. His fans, affectionately known as the Bear Fam, embrace his unique and empowering message.

Unity and Self-Expression

Through his music and persona, Bear Grillz encourages his fans to embrace their authentic selves. He inspires them to break free from societal norms, celebrate their individuality, and express themselves without fear of judgment. The Bear Fam, united by their love for Bear Grillz's music, forms a diverse community that fosters acceptance and inclusivity. This sense of unity and self-expression transcends geographical boundaries, making Bear Grillz's global impact all the more powerful.

Fashion and Visual Aesthetics

Bear Grillz's influence extends to the realm of fashion and visual aesthetics. The striking bear mask has become an iconic symbol, inspiring fans to incorporate elements of Bear Grillz's aesthetic into their own style. From clothing and accessories to tattoos and body art, the bear motif has become synonymous with the message of personal empowerment and self-expression that Bear Grillz embodies. He has sparked a fashion trend that transcends borders and unites fans from all walks of life.

Pop Culture and Mainstream Recognition

Bear Grillz's impact on popular culture cannot be overlooked. His electrifying performances and charismatic persona have garnered attention from mainstream media outlets, solidifying his place in the cultural zeitgeist. From appearances on talk shows to collaborations with high-profile celebrities, Bear Grillz has propelled himself into the mainstream consciousness. This crossover success introduces electronic music and its subculture to a wider audience, breaking down barriers and expanding its reach.

Social Media Influence

In today's digital age, social media plays a significant role in shaping cultural trends and influencing popular opinion. Bear Grillz has harnessed the power of social media platforms to connect with his fans on a personal level, creating a global community of dedicated followers. Through engaging content, behind-the-scenes glimpses, and direct interaction, Bear Grillz has established a deep and meaningful connection with his fan base. This online influence has helped spread Bear Grillz's music and message across the globe, solidifying his cultural impact.

Empowerment and Social Change

Bear Grillz's impact goes beyond music and fashion. He uses his platform to raise awareness about important social issues, including environmental conservation and mental health. Through collaborations with non-profit organizations and philanthropic initiatives, Bear Grillz actively advocates for positive change. By leveraging his influence, he encourages his fans and the wider community to adopt sustainable practices, prioritize mental well-being, and be agents of social change. His commitment to making a difference further enhances his cultural significance.

Legacy

Bear Grillz's enduring legacy lies in his ability to inspire and unite people from diverse backgrounds through the power of music, self-expression, and social activism. His impact on the electronic music scene, popular culture, and society as a whole will continue to shape the cultural landscape for years to come. Through his musical contributions, he has influenced future generations of artists and fans alike, paving the way for innovation and creativity within the genre. Bear Grillz's legacy will forever be intertwined with the empowerment, unity, and positive change he has brought to the world.

In conclusion, Bear Grillz's global cultural impact is undeniable. His unique sound, captivating performances, and empowering persona have made him an influential figure in the electronic music scene and beyond. Bear Grillz's message of self-expression, unity, and social change resonates with fans across the globe, making him a symbol of individuality and empowerment. His legacy as a cultural icon is marked by his pioneering spirit, his dedication to philanthropy, and his influence on the music industry and popular culture as a whole.

Subsection: Uniting diverse communities through music

Music has a unique ability to bring people together, transcending boundaries and fostering a sense of unity and belonging. This is particularly true in the case of Bear Grillz, whose music has united diverse communities and created a shared experience of joy, inspiration, and empowerment.

One of the ways Bear Grillz has united diverse communities is through his genre-blending music. By incorporating elements from different musical styles and genres, Bear Grillz has appealed to a wide range of listeners, attracting fans from various backgrounds and musical preferences. For example, his fusion of electronic music with hip-hop, dubstep, and even rock elements has allowed him to reach audiences who may not typically listen to electronic music.

Moreover, Bear Grillz's music carries a positive and uplifting message, which resonates with people from different cultures and walks of life. The power of his music lies not only in its energetic beats and infectious melodies but also in the emotions and stories it conveys. Through his music, Bear Grillz addresses universal themes such as love, self-acceptance, and overcoming adversity, creating a common ground that people can relate to regardless of their background.

In addition to the music itself, Bear Grillz has actively fostered a sense of community among his fans, known as the "Bear Fam." The Bear Fam is a dedicated group of individuals who share a passion for Bear Grillz's music and values. Through social media platforms, live shows, and fan meet-ups, Bear Grillz has cultivated a safe and inclusive space where fans can connect with each other, share their love for his music, and forge meaningful friendships.

The Bear Fam has become a global community, showcasing the diversity and interconnectedness of Bear Grillz's fan base. Fans from different countries, cultures, and walks of life come together to celebrate their shared love for Bear Grillz's music. This community transcends geographical boundaries and serves as a testament to the power of music in bringing people together.

Bear Grillz's commitment to inclusivity and acceptance is reflected in his support for various charitable causes. He actively encourages his fans to get involved in philanthropic endeavors and often collaborates with non-profit organizations to raise awareness and funds for important causes. By uniting his fan base around these initiatives, Bear Grillz inspires his fans to make a positive impact in their communities, further strengthening the sense of unity and shared purpose within the Bear Fam.

Beyond the Bear Fam, Bear Grillz's music has also had a broader impact on the electronic music scene as a whole. Through collaborations with artists from different genres and musical backgrounds, Bear Grillz has bridged gaps between different communities within the music industry. By working with diverse artists, he has not only expanded his own creative horizons but also helped to break down barriers and challenge existing stereotypes.

In conclusion, Bear Grillz's music and the sense of community he has cultivated through the Bear Fam have been instrumental in uniting diverse communities. Through his genre-blending music, positive message, and commitment to inclusivity, Bear Grillz has created a space where people from different backgrounds can come together, connect, and celebrate their shared love for his music. His impact on the electronic music scene extends far beyond his own fan base, bringing people together and fostering a sense of unity in a world that is often divided.

Subsection: Bear Grillz's representation of individuality and self-expression

In the world of music, individuality and self-expression are two vital aspects that define an artist's identity. Bear Grillz, with his enigmatic persona and unique approach to music, has become a prime example of an artist who embodies and represents these qualities. In this subsection, we will delve into how Bear Grillz's representation of individuality and self-expression has made him a distinctive figure in the music industry.

Embracing Anonymity and Creating a Unique Persona

One of the most intriguing aspects of Bear Grillz's identity is his decision to wear a bear mask, obscuring his true identity. This deliberate choice allows him to create a distinct persona separate from his personal life. The bear mask acts as a visual representation of his artistic vision, providing a sense of mystery and intrigue for his fans. It also allows listeners to connect with Bear Grillz purely through his music, without any preconceptions or biases based on his personal life.

By embracing anonymity, Bear Grillz has been able to focus purely on his artistic expression, rather than being bound by societal expectations or judgments. This freedom enables him to experiment with different sounds, styles, and concepts without the fear of being restricted by perceived notions of who he is as an individual.

Breaking Conventional Boundaries and Pushing Creative Limits

Bear Grillz's representation of individuality and self-expression can be seen in his music, which challenges conventional norms and pushes creative boundaries. Through his unique blend of heavy bass, intricate melodies, and diverse musical influences, Bear Grillz has created a sound that is distinctly his own. His tracks often feature unexpected elements, unexpected genre crossovers, and unconventional production techniques that defy industry standards.

One of the ways Bear Grillz exhibits his individuality is by exploring different tempos, beats, and rhythms within his music. Whether it's experimenting with slower, more melodic tracks or diving into fast-paced, high-energy compositions, he constantly pushes the limits of what is considered typical for electronic music. This willingness to explore and innovate allows Bear Grillz to stay true to his artistic vision and maintain his unique sound.

Promoting Authenticity and Connecting with Fans

Another significant aspect of Bear Grillz's representation of individuality and self-expression is his commitment to authenticity. Despite the anonymity provided by the bear mask, Bear Grillz maintains a genuine and open connection with his fans. Through social media, live performances, and interactions with his audience, he creates an environment of acceptance and inclusivity.

Bear Grillz actively engages with his fans, sharing personal stories and experiences, and encouraging them to embrace their own unique identities. By fostering genuine connections, he creates a sense of community and belonging for his fans, allowing them to express themselves freely and embrace their individuality.

Inspiring Personal Growth and Empowerment

Bear Grillz's representation of individuality and self-expression extends beyond his music and persona. Through his lyrics and messages, he inspires personal growth and empowers his fans to embrace their true selves. His tracks often embrace themes of self-acceptance, resilience, and perseverance, resonating with listeners on a deeper level.

By openly discussing his own struggles and experiences, Bear Grillz allows fans who may be facing similar challenges to feel understood and supported. His music becomes a source of inspiration and catharsis for those who seek solace in expressing their emotions and overcoming adversity.

Encouraging Freedom of Expression in the Electronic Music Community

Bear Grillz's representation of individuality and self-expression goes beyond his own artistry. He has played an instrumental role in encouraging freedom of expression within the broader electronic music community. Through collaborations, support for emerging artists, and his active involvement in the industry, he helps foster an environment where diverse voices and creative ideas can thrive.

By breaking down barriers and promoting inclusivity, Bear Grillz creates opportunities for artists from all backgrounds to express themselves authentically. His impact can be seen in the growing acceptance of unconventional soundscapes, genre-blending, and experimentation within the electronic music scene.

In conclusion, Bear Grillz's representation of individuality and self-expression is evident in every aspect of his artistry. From his anonymous persona to his unconventional sound, he embodies the essence of authenticity and creative freedom. By creating an inclusive and supportive community, he encourages fans and fellow artists alike to embrace their own unique identities. As Bear Grillz continues to push the boundaries of electronic music, his legacy as a symbol of individuality and self-expression will only grow stronger.

Subsection: Bear Grillz's role as a cultural icon

Bear Grillz has cemented himself as more than just a musician; he has become a cultural icon. With his iconic bear mask and unique sound, Bear Grillz has captured the hearts of fans worldwide. But what exactly does it mean to be a cultural icon? And how has Bear Grillz achieved this status?

Defining a Cultural Icon

A cultural icon is someone who has transcended the boundaries of their chosen field and has made a significant impact on popular culture. They embody certain values, beliefs, or trends that resonate with a broad audience, and their influence extends far beyond their immediate sphere of influence. Cultural icons often become symbols of specific movements, ideas, or subcultures and inspire others to follow in their footsteps.

Bear Grillz fits this definition perfectly. His bear mask, which has become his trademark, represents more than just a disguise; it serves as a symbol of unity, acceptance, and self-expression. The image of the bear has long been associated with strength, power, and protection. By adopting this persona, Bear Grillz has tapped into a deeper cultural meaning and captivated the imaginations of his fans.

Bear Grillz's Impact on Popular Culture

Bear Grillz's role as a cultural icon goes beyond his music and persona. He has become a symbol of individuality, breaking down barriers, and embracing one's true self. Through his music, he encourages his fans to be proud of who they are and to follow their passions.

One of the ways Bear Grillz has made an impact on popular culture is by challenging traditional notions of celebrity. In a world where image is carefully constructed and curated, Bear Grillz has chosen to remain anonymous, hiding his true identity behind the bear mask. This decision allows his fans to connect with the music and the message without being influenced by preconceived notions or biases. The mystery surrounding his identity adds to the allure and mystique, making him even more intriguing to his audience.

Bear Grillz's music also breaks down genre barriers and brings different communities together. His unique blend of electronic music, incorporating elements of dubstep, bass, and trap, appeals to a wide range of listeners. He has collaborated with artists from different genres, further diversifying his sound and expanding his reach. In doing so, he has helped bridge the gap between electronic music and other genres, creating a sense of unity among different musical communities.

Social Impact and Philanthropy

As a cultural icon, Bear Grillz has taken on a role beyond music. He has used his platform to bring awareness to important social and environmental issues. Through his music and philanthropic efforts, he has inspired his fans to make a positive difference in the world.

One of the causes Bear Grillz is passionate about is environmental conservation. He has embraced the bear as a symbol of nature and has used his influence to advocate for the protection of the planet. Through his collaborations with non-profit organizations, he has raised funds and awareness for initiatives focused on preserving wildlife and combating climate change.

Bear Grillz has also been vocal about mental health awareness. His music often carries a message of hope and perseverance, inspiring his fans to overcome their own challenges. He actively supports mental health initiatives and uses his platform to destigmatize the conversation surrounding mental wellness.

Legacy and Inspiration

As Bear Grillz's career continues to evolve, his influence as a cultural icon will leave a lasting legacy. His commitment to authenticity, his ability to bring people together through music, and his passionate advocacy for important causes make him an inspiration to many.

Looking to the future, Bear Grillz's impact on the electronic music scene and popular culture as a whole will continue to shape the industry. His ability to break down genre barriers, ignite a sense of unity, and inspire the next generation of artists will be remembered for years to come.

In conclusion, Bear Grillz's role as a cultural icon extends far beyond his music. Through his distinctive bear mask, his unique sound, and his commitment to social and environmental causes, he has become a symbol of unity, inspiration, and self-expression. His impact on popular culture will continue to resonate, leaving a legacy that goes well beyond the realm of music. Bear Grillz is more than just an artist; he is a cultural icon who has made a significant impact on the world.

Subsection: Bear Grillz's impact on fashion and visual aesthetics

When it comes to the world of music, fashion and visual aesthetics often play a crucial role in creating an artist's image and shaping their brand. This holds especially true for Bear Grillz, whose distinctive bear mask has become an iconic symbol of his identity. In this subsection, we will explore how Bear Grillz has revolutionized fashion and visual aesthetics in the electronic music scene.

Aesthetic Appeal and Symbolism

One cannot talk about Bear Grillz without first delving into the undeniable visual impact of his bear mask. The mask itself is a testament to Bear Grillz's ingenuity and creative genius. Not only does it add an air of mystery and intrigue to his persona, but it also serves as a powerful symbol. The bear, typically associated with strength and wildness, aligns perfectly with Bear Grillz's bass-heavy, hard-hitting tracks.

The choice of a bear as the central image for Bear Grillz's visual brand is intentional, representing his ferociousness and ability to dominate the music industry. It draws parallels to his music, which often pushes boundaries and breaks stereotypes, just as bears break free from their constraints in the wild. This synergy between the visual and sonic elements of Bear Grillz's artistry enhances the overall sensory experience for his fans.

Breaking Stereotypes

Bear Grillz's impact on fashion and visual aesthetics goes beyond the allure of his bear mask. It also challenges traditional notions of what an electronic music artist should look like. The genre has long been associated with the image of DJs hidden behind booth setups or obscured by elaborate production displays. Bear Grillz, however, breaks this mold by positioning himself front and center, unveiling his true identity as he connects with his audience.

By ditching the conventional norms, Bear Grillz's fashion choices project a sense of authenticity and honesty. His stage outfits, often consisting of street-style clothing paired with the iconic bear mask, create a juxtaposition of playfulness and power. This unique blend of elements has not only solidified Bear Grillz's visual identity but has also inspired a new wave of artists who are unafraid to express themselves boldly.

Influence on Streetwear Culture

Bear Grillz's impact extends beyond the confines of the electronic music scene and spills over into streetwear culture. The bear mask has become a beloved symbol among his fans, leading to a surge in its popularity as a fashion accessory. Bear Grillz has successfully built a brand that resonates with his fans, who eagerly embrace the iconography associated with his music.

Capitalizing on this phenomenon, Bear Grillz has collaborated with renowned streetwear brands to produce limited-edition merchandise that reflects his unique style. Streetwear enthusiasts and fans alike eagerly snap up these collaborations, further cementing Bear Grillz's influence in the fashion world.

Embracing Visual Storytelling

Beyond the bear mask and streetwear, Bear Grillz's impact on fashion and visual aesthetics is also evident in his music videos and stage productions. He fully embraces visual storytelling, creating immersive experiences that transport audiences into his wild and energetic world. The dynamic visual effects, lighting design, and stage setups serve to enhance the overall impact of his performances.

By integrating fashion, visual effects, and music seamlessly, Bear Grillz creates a multisensory experience that leaves a lasting impression on his audience. This approach not only showcases his meticulous attention to detail but also demonstrates his commitment to providing a complete artistic package.

Encouraging Individuality

One of the most significant ways Bear Grillz has influenced fashion and visual aesthetics is by encouraging individuality and self-expression. The bear mask, as a symbol of identity, embodies the idea that true artistry knows no boundaries and that artists should feel empowered to be their authentic selves.

Bear Grillz's fashion choices and visual aesthetics send a clear message to his fans and aspiring artists: embrace your uniqueness and let it shine through in everything you do. By breaking free from norms and embracing individuality, Bear Grillz has sparked a movement within the music and fashion industries, inspiring countless others to do the same.

In conclusion, Bear Grillz's impact on fashion and visual aesthetics is undeniable. From the iconic bear mask that has become synonymous with his brand to his role in redefining the image of an electronic music artist, Bear Grillz continues to push boundaries and challenge the status quo. Through his innovative approach to fashion, visual storytelling, and encouragement of individuality, Bear Grillz has left an indelible mark on the cultural landscape of both music and fashion.

Subsection: The influence of Bear Grillz on popular culture

Bear Grillz has not only made a significant impact on the electronic music scene but has also left a lasting impression on popular culture as a whole. His unique sound, captivating performances, and distinctive persona have garnered attention from fans around the world. In this subsection, we explore how Bear Grillz has influenced popular culture and become a cultural icon in his own right.

Bear Grillz's eclectic style

One of the key reasons for Bear Grillz's influence on popular culture is his ability to seamlessly blend diverse musical styles into his sound. By incorporating elements of dubstep, trap, and other electronic genres, Bear Grillz has created a fusion of music that resonates with a wide range of listeners. His ability to appeal to fans across different musical preferences has played a significant role in his rising popularity and influence on popular culture.

Breaking down genre barriers

Bear Grillz's music has transcended traditional boundaries in the music industry, bringing together fans from different genres and backgrounds. His unique sound, infused with heavy basslines and captivating melodies, has attracted listeners who may not typically be drawn to electronic music. By crossing over into different genres and collaborating with artists from various musical backgrounds, Bear Grillz has introduced his distinctive sound to a broader audience and expanded the horizons of electronic music.

Bear Grillz as a symbol of self-expression

Beyond his music, Bear Grillz's iconic bear mask has become a symbol of self-expression and individuality. The mask represents a persona that allows fans to embrace their own uniqueness and break free from societal norms. The mask also serves as a visual representation of the anonymity and escapism that music can provide, allowing fans to immerse themselves in the music and let go of their inhibitions. By fostering a sense of freedom and self-expression, Bear Grillz has become an inspiration for fans to embrace their own identities and express themselves authentically.

The impact of Bear Grillz in fashion and visual aesthetics

Bear Grillz's influence extends beyond music and into the realm of fashion and visual aesthetics. His bold and unique style, characterized by colorful and eye-catching outfits, has inspired fans to experiment with their own fashion choices. The bear mask, in particular, has become an iconic symbol associated with Bear Grillz, with fans often recreating and incorporating the image into their own clothing and accessories. This influence on fashion and visual aesthetics further reflects Bear Grillz's impact on popular culture and his ability to inspire fans beyond his music.

Bear Grillz's impact on social media and digital culture

In the age of social media and digital culture, Bear Grillz has leveraged these platforms to connect with fans and build a strong online presence. His active engagement with fans on social media has created a sense of community and belonging among his followers. Bear Grillz's humor, authenticity, and relatable content have made him a beloved figure in the online world. Through platforms like Instagram, Twitter, and YouTube, he has established a direct line of communication with his fans, allowing them to stay connected and engaged with his music and personal journey. This digital presence has further solidified Bear Grillz's influence on popular culture, as he continues to resonate with fans worldwide.

Bear Grillz's impact on the music festival experience

Bear Grillz's live performances have become an integral part of the music festival experience. His high-energy sets, accompanied by captivating visuals and pyrotechnics, create an immersive and unforgettable experience for festival-goers. By delivering powerful and dynamic performances, Bear Grillz has set a new standard for live electronic music shows. His stage presence and ability to connect with the audience have made him a fan favorite at festivals around the world. This influence on the live music experience has shaped popular culture by redefining the expectations and excitement associated with live performances.

Influence on fan communities and subcultures

Bear Grillz's music has fostered the growth of fan communities and subcultures that are connected by a shared love for his music and persona. The "Bear Fam," as fans affectionately refer to themselves, has become a strong and supportive community that extends beyond the music. The Bear Fam has created an inclusive and accepting space for fans to come together, share their love for Bear Grillz, and support one another. Through meet-ups, events, and online interactions, this fan community has become an important aspect of Bear Grillz's influence on popular culture, demonstrating the power of music to bring people together and create meaningful connections.

Bear Grillz's contribution to the cultural zeitgeist

Bear Grillz's impact on popular culture goes beyond music and extends into the broader cultural zeitgeist. His ability to connect with fans on both a personal and artistic level has made him a figure of inspiration and influence. From breaking down genre barriers to using his platform for philanthropic endeavors, Bear Grillz has demonstrated a commitment to making a positive difference in the world. His influence on popular culture is not limited to his music but encompasses a range of social and cultural issues, making him a respected and admired artist among fans and peers alike.

In conclusion, Bear Grillz has left an indelible mark on popular culture through his unique sound, captivating performances, and iconic persona. His ability to appeal to a diverse range of listeners, break down genre barriers, and inspire fans to embrace their own individuality has solidified his influence on popular culture. By connecting with fans through social media and fostering fan communities, Bear Grillz has created a sense of belonging and unity among his followers. His impact extends beyond the music, shaping fashion, visual aesthetics, and the overall cultural zeitgeist. Bear Grillz's influence on popular culture is a testament to the power of music and the ability of artists to make a lasting impact on the world.

Subsection: Bear Grillz's relevance in the digital age

In today's digital age, where technology shapes and influences nearly every aspect of our lives, Bear Grillz has emerged as a prominent figure in the electronic music scene. His relevance in the digital age can be attributed to various factors that have elevated his career and connected him with a global audience. Let us explore these factors in more detail:

1. Embracing social media platforms: Bear Grillz has harnessed the power of social media platforms to engage directly with his fans and build a strong online presence. Through platforms like Instagram, Twitter, and Facebook, he regularly shares updates about his music, upcoming shows, and personal experiences. By actively interacting with his fans, Bear Grillz has created a sense of community, fostering a deep connection between himself and his audience.

2. Leveraging digital marketing strategies: Bear Grillz has successfully utilized digital marketing strategies to expand his reach and connect with new listeners. By employing targeted advertising, search engine optimization, and social media campaigns, he has been able to promote his music and shows to a wider audience. This digital marketing approach has allowed Bear Grillz to gain visibility in a crowded music industry and attract fans who may not have discovered him otherwise.

3. Engaging with streaming platforms: Streaming platforms, such as Spotify, Apple Music, and SoundCloud, have played a pivotal role in Bear Grillz's success. These platforms have allowed him to distribute his music to a global audience, reaching listeners across borders and cultures. By strategically releasing his tracks on these platforms and leveraging curated playlists, Bear Grillz has been able to gain millions of streams and expand his fanbase exponentially.

4. Interactive live streaming: Bear Grillz has embraced the phenomenon of live streaming to connect with his fans in real-time. Using platforms like Twitch and YouTube Live, he engages with his audience through live performances, Q&A sessions, and behind-the-scenes glimpses into his life as an artist. This interactive approach enhances the fan experience, fostering a deeper connection between Bear Grillz and his followers.

5. Virtual reality experiences: As technology continues to advance, Bear Grillz has explored the possibilities of virtual reality (VR) experiences in his live shows. By collaborating with VR developers and incorporating immersive visuals into his performances, he has created unforgettable experiences for his fans. These VR experiences not only enhance the overall show experience but also demonstrate Bear Grillz's ability to adapt to emerging technologies and push the boundaries of live performances.

6. Collaborations with digital artists: Bear Grillz has recognized the importance of collaboration with digital artists in the digital age. By working with visual artists, graphic designers, and animators, he has created captivating visuals that complement his music and enhance the overall fan experience. These collaborations have allowed Bear Grillz to tap into the creativity of digital artists and provide his audience with a multi-sensory experience.

7. Engaging with fan-generated content: In the digital age, fan-generated content plays a pivotal role in an artist's success. Bear Grillz actively encourages his fans to create and share their own content, whether it's fan art, remixes, or dance videos. By showcasing fan-generated content on his social media platforms and during live performances, he not only acknowledges his fans' creativity but also fosters a sense of inclusivity and participation within his fan base.

8. Innovation in music production: Bear Grillz's relevance in the digital age is also linked to his innovative approach to music production. By staying up-to-date with the latest software and production techniques, he continuously pushes the boundaries of his sound. The digital age has provided Bear Grillz with an array of tools and technologies to experiment with, allowing him to create unique and cutting-edge tracks that resonate with his audience.

9. Direct-to-fan platforms: Bear Grillz has embraced direct-to-fan platforms, such as Patreon and Bandcamp, to connect directly with his most dedicated fans. These platforms allow artists to offer exclusive content, merchandise, and even meet-and-greet opportunities directly to their fans. By utilizing these platforms, Bear Grillz has developed a direct line of communication with his fans, providing them with a more intimate and personalized experience.

10. NFTs and blockchain technology: Bear Grillz has also explored the potential of Non-Fungible Tokens (NFTs) and blockchain technology in the

digital age. By releasing limited-edition NFTs of his music, artwork, and collectibles, he has tapped into the growing market for digital assets. This not only offers fans a unique opportunity to own exclusive digital content but also provides Bear Grillz with a new revenue stream and a way to engage with his fan base in an innovative and forward-thinking manner.

As we can see, Bear Grillz's relevance in the digital age is multi-faceted. From embracing social media and digital marketing strategies to exploring virtual reality and blockchain technology, Bear Grillz has capitalized on the opportunities that the digital age has presented. By actively engaging with his fans and embracing emerging technologies, Bear Grillz continues to evolve his music career while staying connected with his audience in a rapidly changing digital landscape.

Resources:

1. "The New Rules of Marketing and PR" by David Meerman Scott: This book provides insights into digital marketing strategies and techniques that can be applied to the music industry.

2. "Music 4.0: A Survival Guide for Making Music in the Internet Age" by Bobby Owsinski: This book explores the impact of technology on the music industry and offers guidance on how artists can thrive in the digital age.

3. Online articles and interviews with Bear Grillz: Exploring interviews and articles featuring Bear Grillz can provide further insights into his approach to the digital age and how he has embraced new technologies.

Exercises:

1. Research and identify one other artist in the electronic music scene who has effectively leveraged digital marketing strategies. Discuss their approach and the impact it has had on their career.

2. Reflect on how technology has shaped your own experience as a music listener in the digital age. Discuss the advantages and disadvantages of technological advancements in the music industry.

3. Explore the emergence of virtual reality in live performances beyond the music industry. Discuss its potential impact on the future of live entertainment.

4. Reflect on the role of fan-generated content in the success of artists in the digital age. Identify one example of fan-generated content that has significantly impacted an artist's career and discuss its influence.

5. Research and discuss the potential long-term implications of blockchain technology and NFTs on the music industry.

Subsection: Conclusion

Bear Grillz's relevance in the digital age is a testament to his ability to navigate and leverage emerging technologies while staying connected with his fanbase.   By embracing social media, digital marketing, virtual reality, and blockchain technology, Bear Grillz has expanded his reach and built a global following. His innovative approach to music production and his engagement with fan-generated content have further solidified his position as a leading figure in the electronic music scene. As the digital age continues to evolve, Bear Grillz's willingness to adapt and embrace new technologies ensures that he remains at the forefront of the industry, connecting with fans in innovative and exciting ways.

Subsection: Bear Grillz's Connection to the Underground Music Scene

Bear Grillz's journey in the music industry is characterized by his unique connection to the underground music scene. From his early beginnings as a music prodigy to his rise as an influential artist, Bear Grillz has always maintained a deep-rooted connection to the underground culture that shaped his sound and career.

The underground music scene refers to a vibrant and often overlooked community of artists, musicians, and fans who operate outside of mainstream commercial music. It is a space where creativity flourishes, boundaries are pushed, and new genres are born. Bear Grillz's connection to this scene has played a crucial role in his evolution as an artist and has contributed to his distinct sound and style.

Underground music scenes are known for their openness and willingness to experiment with different sounds and genres. This creative freedom allows artists like Bear Grillz to explore unconventional sounds and push the boundaries of electronic music. It is within this underground environment that Bear Grillz found the space and support to develop his signature "Bearstep" genre, a unique blend of dubstep, trap, and bass music.

Bear Grillz's connection to the underground music scene can be traced back to his early days of experimenting with different genres. As an artist, he was never limited by the conventions of commercial music and instead sought inspiration from the underground culture. This connection allowed him to infuse his music with fresh and innovative ideas, creating a sound that resonated with a passionate and dedicated fan base.

The underground music scene also provided Bear Grillz with a platform to collaborate with like-minded artists. These collaborations allowed him to further expand his musical boundaries and explore new sonic landscapes. Working with underground artists not only brought new perspectives and ideas but also helped Bear Grillz forge deep connections within the underground community.

One example of Bear Grillz's connection to the underground music scene is his involvement in underground music festivals and events. These platforms provide opportunities for emerging artists to showcase their talent and connect with their audience directly. Bear Grillz's participation in these events not only highlights his commitment to the underground culture but also serves as a platform for him to discover new talent and stay connected with his fan base.

Another aspect of Bear Grillz's connection to the underground music scene is his support for independent record labels and underground music platforms. Rather than aligning himself with major record labels, Bear Grillz has chosen to work with independent labels that prioritize creativity and artistic expression. This decision reflects his dedication to maintaining his artistic integrity while supporting the underground community that nurtured his career.

In addition to his musical contributions, Bear Grillz's connection to the underground music scene extends to his contributions to the culture and values that define this community. He has been vocal about promoting inclusivity, diversity, and acceptance within the electronic music industry. By using his platform and influence, Bear Grillz advocates for creating a safe and welcoming environment for all fans and artists, regardless of their background or identity.

Bear Grillz's connection to the underground music scene is a testament to his commitment to the authenticity and creativity that define this subculture. His ability to bridge the gap between the underground and mainstream music scenes has allowed him to carve out a unique space in the industry. By staying true to his roots and embracing the spirit of the underground, Bear Grillz continues to inspire and influence the next generation of artists and fans.

Subsection: The redefinition of celebrity through Bear Grillz's persona

Celebrity culture has long been associated with fame, glamour, and larger-than-life personalities. However, Bear Grillz has shattered these traditional notions of celebrity by redefining what it means to be an artist in the modern music industry. Through his unique persona, Bear Grillz has become a symbol of authenticity, mystique, and a connection with his fans that goes beyond the norm.

Bear Grillz's persona is centered around his iconic bear mask, which he consistently wears during performances and public appearances. This distinctive choice has allowed him to maintain a level of anonymity while also creating a strong visual identity. By concealing his face behind the mask, Bear Grillz has challenged the idea that celebrity status is solely based on physical appearance. Instead, he emphasizes the power of the music itself and the emotions it evokes in his audience.

The bear mask has become a recognizable symbol that represents not only Bear Grillz's music but also a sense of unity and acceptance within his fan community, known as the Bear Fam. It has become a means of connecting with his audience on a deeper level, transcending the boundaries between artist and fan. The mask has become a shared experience, a way for both Bear Grillz and his fans to escape reality and immerse themselves in the world of his music.

This redefinition of celebrity has allowed Bear Grillz to foster a genuine sense of community and belonging among his fans. The Bear Fam has become a tight-knit group that shares a passion for Bear Grillz's music and the positive values he promotes. Through social media and fan events, Bear Grillz actively engages with his fans, creating a space for them to connect with each other, share their experiences, and support one another.

One of the key aspects of Bear Grillz's redefinition of celebrity is his commitment to transparency and authenticity. While many celebrities carefully manage their public image, Bear Grillz remains true to himself and his art. He openly shares his personal journey, including his struggles and triumphs, and has been candid about his experiences with mental health. By doing so, he breaks down the barriers between artist and fan, showing that even someone in the spotlight can face the same challenges as anyone else.

In addition to his authenticity, Bear Grillz's persona embodies a sense of rebellion against the mainstream. He challenges the expectations that society has of celebrities, rejecting conformity and embracing individuality. Through his music and his image, Bear Grillz encourages his fans to embrace their own uniqueness and to pursue their passions without fear of judgment.

Bear Grillz's persona has also redefined the role of celebrity in promoting social change. He uses his platform to raise awareness and support important causes, such as environmental conservation and mental health. His influence extends beyond the music industry, inspiring his fans to become actively involved in philanthropic initiatives and to make a positive impact in their communities.

In conclusion, Bear Grillz's persona represents a redefinition of celebrity in the music industry. By challenging traditional notions of fame and embracing authenticity, unity, and transparency, Bear Grillz has created a powerful connection with his fans. His persona goes beyond the mask, symbolizing a shared experience and a sense of community within the Bear Fam. Through his music and his commitment to social change, Bear Grillz has become a beacon of inspiration and a catalyst for reimagining what it means to be a celebrity in the modern world.

Section 3: Bear Grillz's Influence Beyond Music

Subsection: Advocacy for environmental conservation and sustainability

In today's world, environmental conservation and sustainability have become crucial issues that demand urgent attention. Bear Grillz, not only a talented musician but also a passionate advocate for these causes, has used his platform to raise awareness and promote positive change. Through his music, performances, and philanthropic endeavors, Bear Grillz has made a significant impact on the environmental movement and has inspired countless others to join the cause.

Background: The importance of environmental conservation

Environmental conservation refers to the protection, preservation, and management of natural resources and ecosystems. It is essential for maintaining biodiversity, mitigating climate change, and ensuring the well-being of future generations.

The world is facing numerous environmental challenges, including deforestation, pollution, habitat destruction, and the depletion of natural resources. These issues pose threats to the delicate balance of ecosystems and have far-reaching consequences for both humans and wildlife.

Sustainability, on the other hand, involves meeting the needs of the present without compromising the ability of future generations to meet their own needs. It encompasses responsible resource management, embracing renewable energy sources, reducing waste, and promoting a circular economy.

Bear Grillz's commitment to environmental causes

Bear Grillz recognizes the urgency and importance of addressing environmental issues. As a public figure with a significant following, he has used his influence to advocate for environmental conservation and sustainability in various ways.

One of the ways Bear Grillz demonstrates his commitment is through the Bear Grillz Foundation. The foundation focuses on supporting environmental initiatives, such as reforestation projects, wildlife conservation, and sustainable practices. By partnering with organizations and funding projects, Bear Grillz amplifies the impact of his advocacy and drives meaningful change.

Raising awareness through music

Music is a powerful medium for spreading messages and inspiring action. Bear Grillz incorporates environmental themes into his music, using his songs to raise awareness about the importance of protecting the planet.

Through his lyrics, Bear Grillz addresses environmental issues, sharing his perspectives on the urgent need for change. By combining catchy beats with thought-provoking messages, he captivates his audience and encourages them to reflect on their own role in protecting the environment.

Example: In his popular track "Save the Trees", Bear Grillz highlights the devastating impacts of deforestation, shedding light on the vital role that trees play in maintaining the Earth's ecosystem. The song's energetic melody and powerful lyrics inspire listeners to take action and make a positive difference.

Promoting sustainable practices

In addition to raising awareness, Bear Grillz actively promotes sustainable practices among his fan base. He encourages his audience to adopt eco-friendly habits and make conscious choices that reduce their ecological footprint.

Through his social media platforms, Bear Grillz shares tips and information on sustainable living, such as recycling, waste reduction, and energy conservation. By providing practical guidance and highlighting the benefits of sustainable practices, he empowers his fans to take personal actions that contribute to a healthier planet.

Example: Bear Grillz's "Sustainable Living Challenge" on his Instagram encourages his fans to share their eco-friendly actions, such as using reusable water bottles, taking public transportation, or switching to renewable energy sources. This challenge creates a sense of community and motivates individuals to make sustainable choices.

Partnerships and collaborations

Bear Grillz understands that true change requires collaboration and collective action. He actively seeks partnerships with like-minded organizations, brands, and fellow artists to amplify his voice and maximize his impact.

Through collaborations with environmental organizations, Bear Grillz raises funds for conservation efforts and promotes their initiatives to his fan base. These partnerships help generate widespread support for environmental causes and create a network of advocates working towards a common goal.

Example: Bear Grillz partnered with a sustainable clothing brand to create a limited-edition merchandise line made from organic materials and recycled fabrics. A portion of the proceeds from this collaboration goes towards funding reforestation projects, emphasizing the importance of conscious consumerism in addressing environmental issues.

Inspiring a new generation

One of Bear Grillz's greatest contributions to environmental advocacy is inspiring young people to take an interest in environmental conservation and sustainability. Through his music and his own commitment to the cause, he serves as a role model for the next generation.

Bear Grillz actively engages with his fans, encouraging them to get involved in environmental initiatives and educating them about the issues at hand. By fostering a sense of responsibility and empowerment, he empowers his audience to become environmental leaders in their own communities.

Example: Bear Grillz hosted a youth-focused virtual concert, where he not only entertained his fans but also shared stories of young environmental activists who are making a difference in their communities. This event inspired many young individuals to take action and become advocates for a sustainable future.

The bigger picture and the power of collective action

Bear Grillz recognizes that his individual efforts, while impactful, are just a small part of the larger environmental movement. He encourages his fans and followers to join him in advocating for environmental conservation and sustainability.

By leveraging the collective power of his fan base, Bear Grillz organizes community-driven initiatives such as clean-up campaigns, tree-planting events, and environmental education programs. Through these activities, he not only creates positive change on a tangible level but also fosters a sense of unity and shared purpose among his supporters.

Example: Bear Grillz organized a fan-led reforestation project, where his followers collaborated with local environmental organizations to plant trees in deforested areas. This initiative not only helped restore ecosystems but also strengthened the connection between Bear Grillz's community and the natural world.

Tricks and challenges in advocating for environmental conservation

Advocating for environmental conservation comes with its fair share of challenges. One of the main obstacles is the resistance and skepticism faced by those who deny or downplay the urgency of environmental issues. Bear Grillz addresses this challenge by using his music and platform to present the facts and engage in open conversations with skeptics.

Another challenge is the overwhelming nature of the problems at hand. The scale of environmental degradation can make individuals feel helpless or insignificant. To overcome this, Bear Grillz emphasizes that every action, no matter how small, counts towards positive change. By breaking down complex issues into manageable steps, he inspires his audience to take meaningful action.

The legacy of Bear Grillz's environmental advocacy

Bear Grillz's environmental advocacy will leave a lasting legacy on both the music industry and the global environmental movement. Through his music, performances, philanthropy, and community-building, he has inspired a new generation of environmental activists and set a precedent for artists using their platform to drive positive change.

Bear Grillz's dedication to advocating for environmental conservation and sustainability demonstrates that everyone, regardless of their field or influence, can make a difference. His message resonates with fans worldwide, reminding us all of the importance of preserving and protecting our planet for future generations.

As Bear Grillz's music evolves and resonates with an ever-growing audience, his impact on the environmental movement will continue to grow. Through his advocacy, he paves the way for a more sustainable and environmentally conscious future.

Subsection: Promoting Mental Health and Well-being through Music

In today's fast-paced and highly demanding world, mental health issues have become increasingly prevalent. Many individuals struggle with stress, anxiety, depression, and other mental health disorders. As a result, promoting mental well-being and providing support for those struggling has become a critical endeavor. In this subsection, we will explore how Bear Grillz uses music as a powerful tool to promote mental health and well-being.

The Therapeutic Power of Music

Music has long been recognized for its therapeutic effects on the mind and body. It has the ability to evoke emotions, create connections, and serve as a form of self-expression. Listening to music can provide solace, comfort, and the much-needed escape from the pressures of daily life.

Bear Grillz harnesses the therapeutic power of music to address mental health issues. Through his carefully crafted tracks, he aims to create a space where listeners can find solace and relate to their own struggles. The emotional depth and authenticity in his music resonate with individuals facing mental health challenges, offering them a sense of understanding and support.

Addressing Mental Health Stigma

One of the significant barriers to seeking help for mental health issues is the persistent stigma in society. People often hesitate to talk openly about their struggles due to fear of judgment or discrimination. Bear Grillz takes a bold stance in dismantling this stigma by addressing mental health directly in his music and engaging in open conversations about it.

By sharing his own experiences and struggles, Bear Grillz breaks down the walls that surround mental health and encourages his fans to do the same. He creates a safe and non-judgmental space where individuals can feel comfortable discussing their emotions and seeking help if needed. Through his vulnerability, Bear Grillz empowers others to embrace their mental health and advocate for their well-being.

Spreading Positivity and Empowerment

Bear Grillz's music is not only about acknowledging and addressing mental health challenges. It is also about spreading positivity, hope, and empowerment. His tracks often carry uplifting messages that inspire listeners to overcome adversity, embrace their inner strength, and move forward in their personal journeys.

Furthermore, his lyrics often revolve around themes of self-acceptance, self-love, and finding inner peace. By promoting these positive messages, Bear Grillz encourages his fans to practice self-care, prioritize their mental well-being, and build resilience in the face of life's challenges.

Community Support and Engagement

Bear Grillz recognizes the importance of community support in promoting mental health and well-being. Within his fanbase, known as the Bear Fam, individuals find a sense of belonging, understanding, and support. The Bear Fam acts as a support network, providing a space for individuals to share their experiences, offer encouragement, and provide resources for mental health support.

In addition to fostering a sense of community online, Bear Grillz also uses his platform to champion various mental health initiatives. He partners with mental health organizations, collaborates with mental health professionals, and hosts events and fundraisers to raise awareness and funds for mental health causes. Through these efforts, he actively works to bridge the gap between the music industry and mental health support systems.

Music as a Coping Mechanism

Bear Grillz's music serves as a powerful coping mechanism for individuals struggling with their mental health. When individuals feel overwhelmed, anxious, or isolated, they turn to music as a source of comfort and relief. Bear Grillz's music provides an avenue for emotional release and serves as a companion during difficult times.

Moreover, Bear Grillz's live performances create transformative experiences for his audience. The energy, catharsis, and communal spirit of his shows can be incredibly cathartic and uplifting. The shared collective experience enables individuals to temporarily escape their worries, connect with others, and embrace the healing power of music.

Resources for Mental Health Support

Bear Grillz recognizes the importance of providing resources for mental health support to his fanbase and beyond. Through his website and social media platforms, he shares information about mental health helplines, hotlines, counseling services, and other valuable resources.

Moreover, Bear Grillz collaborates with mental health professionals to develop educational content that helps promote mental health awareness, coping strategies, and self-care practices. This information is readily accessible to his fans, providing them with valuable tools and guidance for navigating their mental health journeys.

Tricks for Mindfulness and Meditation

In addition to his music, Bear Grillz is also an advocate for mindfulness and meditation as tools for maintaining mental well-being. He recognizes the benefits of incorporating mindfulness practices into daily routines to reduce stress, improve focus, and cultivate a sense of calm.

Bear Grillz shares various tricks and techniques for mindfulness and meditation with his fans. These techniques can include breathing exercises, guided meditations, visualization techniques, and other mindfulness practices. By encouraging his fanbase to prioritize their mental health through these practices, Bear Grillz provides valuable tools for self-care and stress management.

Examples of Music and Mental Health

To illustrate the connection between Bear Grillz's music and mental health, let's take a closer look at the track "From the Darkness."
Example: "From the Darkness"
"From the Darkness" is a powerful track that explores themes of overcoming adversity, finding inner strength, and embracing personal growth. The lyrics and melodic composition evoke a sense of empowerment and resilience, inspiring listeners to rise above their challenges and find light in the darkest moments.

The track resonates with individuals facing mental health struggles, providing them with hope and a reminder that they are not alone in their journey. Through the emotional depth of the music, Bear Grillz creates a space for listeners to connect with their own experiences and find solace and strength.

Caveats and Challenges

While Bear Grillz's efforts to promote mental health and well-being through music are commendable, it is essential to acknowledge the limitations and challenges in addressing mental health solely through music. Music can serve as a form of support and inspiration, but it should not replace professional mental health interventions or therapy.

It is important for individuals facing mental health challenges to seek appropriate professional help from qualified healthcare professionals. Bear Grillz's music can be a valuable complement to therapy and self-care practices, but it should not be considered a substitute for professional treatment.

Furthermore, it is crucial to recognize that mental health is a complex and multifaceted issue that requires a comprehensive approach. Combining music with advocacy, awareness, community support, and access to mental health resources is essential for promoting mental health and well-being on a broader scale.

Conclusion

Bear Grillz's commitment to promoting mental health and well-being through music is a testament to the transformative power of art. By addressing mental health stigma, spreading positivity, and providing resources and support, Bear Grillz has become an advocate for mental health within the electronic music community.

Through his music, Bear Grillz provides a space for listeners to find solace, relate to their struggles, and build resilience. His lyrics and powerful compositions inspire individuals to prioritize their mental well-being, seek help when needed, and embrace their own personal growth.

By promoting mental health and well-being through his music, Bear Grillz leaves a lasting impact on his fans and the broader music industry. He sets a positive example for artists to leverage their platform for social change and demonstrates that music has the power to heal and empower individuals on their mental health journey.

Subsection: Inspiring creativity and artistic expression

In the world of electronic music, Bear Grillz stands out as not just a talented producer, but also as an artist who inspires creativity and artistic expression in his fans and fellow musicians. Through his music and persona, Bear Grillz encourages individuals to embrace their unique creativity and explore their artistic passions without limitations. In this subsection, we will delve into the ways in which Bear Grillz inspires and fosters creativity and artistic expression within his fan community.

Unlocking the Creative Potential

One of the key aspects of Bear Grillz's music is its ability to unlock the creative potential within individuals. His unique blend of heavy basslines, melodic elements, and catchy hooks creates an atmosphere that invites listeners to explore their own creative ideas. By pushing the boundaries of the electronic music genre, Bear Grillz encourages his fans to do the same in their own artistic pursuits.

Bear Grillz's tracks often feature intricate and innovative sound design, which serves as a source of inspiration for aspiring producers. Listening to his music can spark new ideas and ways of approaching music production. Whether it's experimenting with new sound textures or exploring unconventional melodic structures, Bear Grillz's music encourages his fans to push their creative boundaries and think outside the box.

Embracing Artistic Freedom

Creativity thrives in an environment that values artistic freedom, and Bear Grillz embodies this principle. His bold and fearless approach to music production inspires his fans to embrace their own artistic freedom. By encouraging experimentation and individual expression, Bear Grillz creates a space where artists can fully explore their unique visions.

Through his music, Bear Grillz breaks down conventional barriers and challenges the norms of the electronic music genre. He incorporates diverse influences and musical styles, resulting in a refreshing and unique sound. This fearless pursuit of artistic expression inspires his fans to fearlessly explore and experiment with their own creative ideas, fostering a sense of freedom and artistic liberation.

Breaking Through Creative Blocks

Creative blocks are a common obstacle for artists of all disciplines, and Bear Grillz understands the importance of overcoming them. He openly shares his own experiences with creative blocks and offers valuable insights into breaking through them.

Through interviews and interactions with his fan community, Bear Grillz shares tips on staying motivated and overcoming creative barriers. He emphasizes the importance of perseverance, embracing failures as learning opportunities, and seeking inspiration from different sources. By sharing these personal stories and strategies, Bear Grillz empowers his fans to overcome their own creative blocks and keep progressing in their artistic journeys.

Collaborative Creativity

Bear Grillz recognizes the power of collaboration in nurturing artistic expression and creativity. Throughout his career, he has sought out collaborations with diverse artists from various genres and musical backgrounds. By collaborating with others, Bear Grillz not only expands his own creative horizons but also creates a platform for others to express themselves.

These collaborations not only produce innovative and inspiring music but also provide valuable lessons in creative collaboration and teamwork. Through his collaborative projects, Bear Grillz shows his fans the importance of combining different perspectives and ideas to create something truly unique and extraordinary.

Exploration Beyond Music

Inspiration and creativity extend beyond the boundaries of music for Bear Grillz. He is known for his interest in adrenaline-pumping activities, exploration of the natural world, and love for cultural experiences. These pursuits outside of music fuel his creativity and serve as sources of inspiration for his work.

Bear Grillz's dedication to adventure and exploration encourages his fans to seek inspiration beyond the confines of their artistic disciplines. By embracing new experiences, exploring the world, and immersing themselves in different cultures, individuals can tap into new sources of creativity and broaden their artistic horizons.

Unconventional Instrumentation

In addition to his electronic music productions, Bear Grillz embraces unconventional instrumentation in his tracks. From live instruments to unexpected sounds, he incorporates elements that challenge traditional notions of electronic music.

This unconventional approach to instrumentation encourages his fans to think outside the box when creating music. Whether it's experimenting with incorporating live instruments or using unconventional objects as sound sources, Bear Grillz's music inspires artists to explore new sonic possibilities and push the boundaries of their own productions.

Creative Challenges and Contests

Bear Grillz actively engages with his fan community by organizing creative challenges and contests. These initiatives provide platforms for his fans to showcase their artistic talents and creativity. Whether it's remix competitions or design challenges for album artwork, Bear Grillz encourages his fans to participate and unleash their creative potential.

By providing opportunities for his fans to be directly involved in his projects, Bear Grillz fosters a sense of community and encourages individuals to express their creativity. These challenges not only bring out the best in his fans but also provide valuable exposure and recognition for talented artists within his community.

Resources and Educational Content

Bear Grillz understands the importance of equipping aspiring artists with the resources and knowledge they need to develop their creative skills. He shares educational content, tutorials, and production tips through various mediums, including social media platforms and his website.

By making these resources accessible, Bear Grillz empowers his fans to take control of their artistic development. The availability of educational content inspires individuals to pursue their artistic passions and equips them with the tools they need to nurture their creative growth.

In conclusion, Bear Grillz serves as a catalyst for creativity and artistic expression within the electronic music scene. Through his music, persona, and active engagement with his fan community, he inspires individuals to embrace their unique artistic visions, break through creative barriers, and explore new realms of creativity. With his fearless approach to music production and commitment to promoting artistic freedom, Bear Grillz continues to inspire a new generation of artists to push the boundaries of electronic music and beyond.

Subsection: Breaking down barriers and promoting inclusivity

In the realm of electronic music, Bear Grillz has been a staunch advocate for breaking down barriers and promoting inclusivity. His commitment to inclusivity extends beyond his music, as he endeavors to create a community where everyone feels welcome and represented. In this subsection, we will explore the various ways Bear Grillz has championed inclusivity in the music industry.

The Power of Music as a Unifying Force

Bear Grillz firmly believes that music has the power to bring people from different backgrounds together. He recognizes that the language of music transcends cultural, social, and ethnic boundaries. Through his music, Bear Grillz aims to create a space where people can connect and find common ground.

One of the ways Bear Grillz breaks down barriers is through the diversity of his sound. He draws inspiration from various musical genres, infusing elements of hip-hop, trap, dubstep, and more into his music. By blending different styles, Bear Grillz creates a unique sound that appeals to a wide range of listeners. This diversity in his music not only allows him to reach a broader audience but also encourages fans to explore different genres and expand their musical horizons.

Challenging Stereotypes in the Music Industry

The music industry has a long history of perpetuating stereotypes, particularly in the electronic music scene. Bear Grillz has been vocal about challenging these stereotypes and defying expectations. As an artist who performs in a bear mask, he challenges conventional notions of identity and appearance.

By embracing his persona and performing in a mask, Bear Grillz shines a light on the importance of individuality and self-expression. He encourages his fans to embrace their unique identities and celebrates diversity in all its forms. Through his music, Bear Grillz sets an example for others in the industry to challenge stereotypes and create a more inclusive environment.

Creating Safe Spaces at Live Performances

Bear Grillz understands the significance of live performances as communal experiences. He believes that live shows should be safe spaces for everyone, regardless of their gender, race, or sexual orientation. To ensure inclusivity, Bear Grillz actively works with venues and event organizers to create environments where fans can enjoy his music without fear of discrimination or harassment.

By prioritizing inclusivity and safety, Bear Grillz sets the tone for his audience to respect one another and celebrate their shared love for music. He encourages his fans to look out for each other and support the growth of a positive and inclusive community.

Collaborating with Diverse Artists

Another way Bear Grillz promotes inclusivity is through his collaborations with diverse artists. He actively seeks out collaborations that showcase a range of perspectives and experiences. By collaborating with artists from different backgrounds, Bear Grillz creates a musical environment that is rich in diversity and representation.

These collaborations not only result in unique and innovative music but also demonstrate the power of inclusivity in the creative process. Through his collaborations, Bear Grillz encourages other artists and producers to reach beyond their comfort zones and embrace different styles and perspectives.

Promoting Inclusivity through Social Media

Bear Grillz understands the influence of social media in shaping the music industry and fan communities. He leverages platforms like Twitter, Instagram, and YouTube to amplify his message of inclusivity and promote social change. Through his social media channels, Bear Grillz actively engages with his fans, creating a sense of belonging and encouraging open dialogue.

In addition, Bear Grillz uses his social media presence to promote other artists, especially those from underrepresented communities. He actively shares their music, collaborates with them, and uses his platform to amplify their voices. By doing so, Bear Grillz helps to uplift artists who may face barriers and challenges in the industry.

The Importance of Education and Outreach

Bear Grillz recognizes the importance of education and outreach in promoting inclusivity in music. He believes that by providing resources and opportunities, aspiring artists from all backgrounds can thrive and contribute to the music community.

Bear Grillz actively supports educational programs and initiatives that provide mentorship and training to aspiring musicians. He uses his platform to raise awareness about these programs and encourages his fans to support them. By doing so, Bear Grillz helps to bridge the gap and create opportunities for underrepresented artists.

An Unconventional Solution: Collaborative Workshops

In his quest for inclusivity, Bear Grillz has also taken a more unconventional approach by organizing collaborative workshops. These workshops bring together artists from different genres and backgrounds, providing them with a space to experiment, learn from one another, and create music together.

By fostering collaboration and bringing diverse artists together, Bear Grillz recognizes that new and unique sounds can emerge. These workshops serve as a reminder that music is not defined by rigid boundaries or limitations. Instead, it is a constantly evolving art form that flourishes when artists come together, exchange ideas, and challenge one another.

Conclusion

Bear Grillz's commitment to breaking down barriers and promoting inclusivity in the music industry is a testament to his genuine desire for positive change. Through his music, collaborations, live performances, and engagement with fans, Bear Grillz creates a sense of inclusivity and belonging. He encourages his fans and peers to challenge stereotypes, embrace diversity, and foster a community that celebrates the power of music as a unifying force.

In a world where divisiveness sometimes dominates, Bear Grillz stands as a symbol of unity, promoting inclusivity in all aspects of his career. With his unwavering dedication, he continues to inspire others to break down barriers and create a more inclusive and diverse music industry.

Subsection: Bear Grillz's cultural influence and social impact

Bear Grillz's music and persona have had a significant cultural influence and social impact, reaching far beyond the boundaries of the electronic music scene. His unique blend of powerful beats, melodic elements, and heavy drops has resonated with a diverse range of listeners, making him one of the most recognizable and influential figures in the industry. In this subsection, we will explore how Bear Grillz's music and message have shaped popular culture, promoted inclusivity, and inspired positive change.

The Power of Music in Cultural Transformation

Music has always played a crucial role in shaping culture and society. It has the power to express emotions, tell stories, and connect people from different backgrounds. Bear Grillz's music goes beyond just entertainment; it serves as a conduit for social change and cultural transformation.

Through his tracks and live performances, Bear Grillz has created a community united by a shared love for music and a desire to make a positive impact. His anthemic tracks, filled with uplifting melodies and infectious energy, have become rallying cries for fans around the world. Songs like "EDC Anthem" and "Demons" have not only set dance floors on fire but have also become cultural touchstones, embodying the spirit of perseverance and overcoming challenges.

By fusing different musical styles and pushing the boundaries of electronic music, Bear Grillz has opened doors for other artists to experiment and explore new sounds. His innovative approach has influenced the wider cultural landscape, inspiring a new generation of musicians to think outside the box and challenge conventions.

Promoting Inclusivity and Breaking Down Barriers

Bear Grillz's inclusive message and commitment to unity have fostered a sense of belonging among his fans and the broader electronic music community. Regardless of their race, gender, or background, fans feel empowered and accepted within the Bear Fam.

In a genre that has historically struggled with inclusivity, Bear Grillz has been a vocal advocate for diversity and equality. He has actively worked to break down barriers and challenge stereotypes, promoting a more inclusive and welcoming space for fans and artists alike. Through his music, interviews, and social media presence, Bear Grillz amplifies the voices of marginalized communities and supports initiatives that strive for equality.

Bear Grillz's impact on inclusivity extends beyond the music industry. By embracing his fans as part of the Bear Fam, he has created a global community where individuals can connect, support each other, and foster positive change in their own lives and communities.

Addressing Social Issues and Inspiring Positive Change

Beyond his music, Bear Grillz uses his platform to raise awareness of important social and environmental issues. Inspired by his love for the natural world, Bear Grillz is known for his support of environmental conservation efforts. He actively advocates for sustainability and encourages his fans to join him in making a positive impact on the planet.

Bear Grillz also addresses mental health issues through his music, spreading a message of hope and resilience to those facing personal struggles. By openly discussing his own experiences with mental health challenges, he destigmatizes the topic and offers support to his fans who may be going through similar difficulties.

Through charity events, collaborations, and philanthropic initiatives, Bear Grillz demonstrates his commitment to making a difference in the world. Whether it's fundraising for local communities or supporting educational programs, he consistently goes above and beyond to inspire positive change.

The Bear Fam: A Community of Empowerment and Support

Central to Bear Grillz's cultural influence and social impact is the Bear Fam, a community of fans who share a deep connection with the artist and his music. The Bear Fam is more than just a fan base; it is a tight-knit group that supports and uplifts one another.

Within the Bear Fam, fans find solace, inspiration, and encouragement. They celebrate each other's achievements, provide emotional support during difficult times, and organize community initiatives that give back to society. The Bear Fam promotes a message of unity, acceptance, and love, creating a safe space for individuals to express themselves freely.

Bear Grillz actively engages with his fans, fostering a sense of belonging and personal connection. Through meet-ups, fan events, and direct interactions on social media, he makes himself accessible and approachable, breaking down the traditional barriers between artist and audience.

Inspiration for Future Generations

Bear Grillz's cultural influence and social impact will continue to shape the electronic music scene and beyond. Future generations of artists will look to him as a trailblazer who pushed boundaries, embraced individuality, and championed inclusivity.

Through his commitment to authenticity, social activism, and innovation, Bear Grillz has left an indelible mark on the music industry and popular culture. His legacy will inspire artists to be unapologetically themselves, to use their platforms for positive change, and to push the boundaries of creativity.

In summary, Bear Grillz's music and message have transcended the electronic music scene, leaving a lasting cultural influence and social impact. Through his inclusive approach, addressal of social issues, and commitment to making a difference, Bear Grillz has become a catalyst for change, inspiring unity, and fostering a sense of empowerment among his fans and the broader community.

Subsection: Bear Grillz's support for education and creative programs

Bear Grillz, with his undeniable talent and innate passion for music, has not only made a significant impact on the electronic music scene but has also dedicated himself to supporting education and creative programs. Recognizing the transformative power of music and the arts, Bear Grillz has taken initiative in promoting these fields and ensuring that aspiring artists have access to resources, mentorship, and opportunities. Through his philanthropic efforts, he has created a profound and lasting impact on the lives of countless individuals.

The Importance of Education and Creative Programs

Education and creative programs play a vital role in nurturing the talents and passions of young artists. These programs provide a platform for individuals to explore their artistic potential, develop their skills, and gain exposure to diverse artistic expressions. They also foster a sense of community and collaboration, allowing artists to learn from one another and push the boundaries of their creativity.

Bear Grillz understands the significance of education and creative programs in shaping the next generation of artists. He believes that everyone, regardless of their background or circumstances, should have equal access to these opportunities. By supporting education and creative programs, Bear Grillz aims to provide aspiring artists with the tools and resources they need to succeed in their artistic endeavors.

Bear Grillz's Philanthropic Initiatives

Bear Grillz has established various philanthropic initiatives to support education and creative programs. Through these initiatives, he aims to inspire and empower individuals to pursue their artistic passions and cultivate their talents. Here are some examples of Bear Grillz's philanthropic efforts:

1. **School Music Programs:** Bear Grillz has partnered with schools to enhance their music programs and provide students with access to music education. He understands the value of music in promoting creativity, discipline, and self-expression. By investing in music programs, Bear Grillz supports students in developing their musical skills and discovering their passion for music.

2. **Scholarship Programs:** Bear Grillz believes in the power of education and wants to remove financial barriers for aspiring artists. He has established scholarship programs that provide financial assistance to talented individuals who might not have access to formal artistic education. These scholarships support students pursuing various artistic disciplines, including music production, DJing, visual arts, and more.

3. **Mentorship Programs:** Bear Grillz recognizes the importance of mentorship in an artist's journey. Through mentorship programs, he pairs aspiring artists with experienced professionals who can guide and inspire them. This mentorship provides valuable insights, advice, and opportunities for growth, helping the mentees develop their skills and navigate the complexities of the music industry.

4. **Workshops and Masterclasses:** Bear Grillz organizes workshops and masterclasses where he shares his knowledge, experiences, and techniques with aspiring artists. These interactive sessions allow participants to learn directly from Bear Grillz and gain insights into various aspects of music production, performance, and the creative process. By imparting his knowledge, Bear Grillz empowers artists to refine their craft and pursue their musical aspirations.

The Impact of Bear Grillz's Support

Bear Grillz's support for education and creative programs has had a profound impact on the lives of individuals within the artistic community. Through his philanthropic initiatives, he has:

1. **Inspired a New Generation:** Bear Grillz's commitment to education and creative programs has inspired countless young artists to pursue their passion for music. By witnessing his journey and the success that can come from dedication and

hard work, aspiring artists are motivated to push beyond their limits and unleash their creative potential.

2. **Provided Access to Resources:** Many talented individuals lack access to the necessary resources and tools to pursue their artistic aspirations. Bear Grillz's support has bridged this gap, providing aspiring artists with access to music production software, equipment, and professional mentorship. This access to resources has opened up new possibilities and opportunities for individuals who might not have otherwise had the means to pursue their dreams.

3. **Created Opportunities for Collaboration:** Through his various initiatives, Bear Grillz has fostered a sense of community and collaboration among artists. By connecting aspiring artists with established professionals, he has created opportunities for collaboration, networking, and the exchange of ideas. These connections have resulted in the development of innovative projects and the cultivation of a supportive network within the artistic community.

4. **Promoted Diversity and Inclusivity:** Bear Grillz's support for education and creative programs has championed diversity and inclusivity within the arts. By providing opportunities for individuals from all backgrounds and communities, he has helped break down barriers and promote equal representation within the music industry. Bear Grillz believes that diverse voices and perspectives enrich the artistic landscape and contribute to a more inclusive society.

Bear Grillz's Call to Action

Bear Grillz's unwavering support for education and creative programs serves as an inspiration for individuals across the world. His philanthropy demonstrates that music has the power to transform lives and empower individuals to pursue their dreams.

To further the impact of Bear Grillz's support for education and creative programs, he encourages others to join in the effort. Whether through financial contributions, mentorship, or volunteering, Bear Grillz believes that everyone has a role to play in uplifting and nurturing young artists. By collectively supporting education and creative programs, we can foster the next generation of artists, ignite creativity, and create a more vibrant and inclusive artistic community.

Exercises

1. Reflect on a time when music or an artistic program had a positive impact on your life. How did it shape your personal growth and aspirations? Share your story

and discuss the importance of supporting education and creative programs in your community.

2. Research and identify educational and creative programs in your area that support aspiring artists. Explore ways in which you can contribute to these programs, whether through financial donations, volunteering, or mentoring. Share your findings and discuss your plans for getting involved.

3. Imagine you are a mentor in a music production workshop organized by Bear Grillz. Create an outline of the topics you would cover and the activities you would incorporate to inspire and guide aspiring artists. Highlight the key lessons and insights you would share based on your own experiences in the music industry.

4. Conduct an interview with a local artist who has benefitted from Bear Grillz's philanthropic initiatives or similar programs. Explore how their involvement in education and creative programs has shaped their artistic journey and provided them with opportunities for growth. Discuss the lessons they have learned and the challenges they have overcome, showcasing the transformative power of these programs.

5. Write a persuasive essay advocating for increased funding and support for education and creative programs in schools and communities. Utilize examples and statistics to highlight the positive impact of these programs on individuals, communities, and society as a whole. Emphasize the need for fostering creative expression and providing equal opportunities for all aspiring artists.

Resources

1. Bear Grillz Foundation: www.beargrillzfoundation.org 2. National Arts Education Association: www.arteducators.org 3. Berklee College of Music: www.berklee.edu 4. Recording Academy: www.grammy.com/recording-academy 5. Soundfly: www.soundfly.com 6. Music Production for Beginners: A Comprehensive Guide to the Basics of Music Production by George Plumley 7. The War of Art: Break Through the Blocks and Win Your Inner Creative Battles by Steven Pressfield 8. TED Talk: "How Schools Kill Creativity" by Sir Ken Robinson

Remember, supporting education and creative programs is not just about giving back to the community—it is an investment in the future of the arts and the empowered artists who will shape our world.

Subsection: The impact of Bear Grillz's messages on social change

Bear Grillz is not just a talented musician and entertainer; he is also an advocate for social change. Through his music and public platform, Bear Grillz has been able to spread important messages and raise awareness about various social issues. His impact on social change extends beyond the realms of music, as he uses his platform to inspire and engage with his fans, encouraging them to create positive change in their own communities.

One of the key ways in which Bear Grillz impacts social change is through the themes and lyrics in his music. He often incorporates thought-provoking messages and addresses important societal issues in his songs. By tackling topics such as environmental conservation, mental health, inclusivity, and social justice, Bear Grillz sparks conversations and draws attention to issues that need addressing.

For example, in his track "Nature's Cry," Bear Grillz sheds light on the devastating effects of deforestation and the urgent need for environmental conservation. The song serves as a call to action, urging listeners to take steps towards preserving our planet. Through his powerful music, Bear Grillz encourages his fans to join him in making a difference and becoming advocates for the environment.

Bear Grillz's impact on social change goes beyond his music. He actively engages with his fans through social media, participating in discussions, and encouraging them to take action. His dedication to philanthropy and involvement in charitable causes further emphasizes his commitment to making the world a better place.

Additionally, Bear Grillz's commitment to authenticity and staying true to himself resonates with his fans, inspiring them to embrace their individuality and pursue their passions. Through his own journey, Bear Grillz exemplifies the principles of self-expression and acceptance, inspiring others to do the same. This message of self-empowerment and acceptance is a powerful catalyst for social change, encouraging individuals to challenge societal norms and promote inclusivity.

Furthermore, Bear Grillz actively leverages his influence to raise funds and support initiatives focused on social change. For instance, he regularly collaborates with non-profit organizations that work towards causes such as environmental conservation, mental health awareness, and social justice. By aligning his brand with these important causes, Bear Grillz amplifies their reach and inspires his fans to get involved in creating positive change.

To further engage his fanbase in social change efforts, Bear Grillz frequently organizes fan-led initiatives and projects. These endeavors encourage his fans, known as the Bear Fam, to come together and make a real impact in their communities. Examples include volunteer work, fundraising campaigns, and collaborative projects aimed at promoting unity and positive change.

Bear Grillz's impact on social change can be seen not only within his immediate fan community but also in the broader electronic music scene. As one of the pioneers within the Bearstep genre, Bear Grillz has inspired a new generation of producers and artists to use their music as a platform for social commentary and change. His influence has helped shape the direction of the genre, encouraging artists to address societal issues and promote positive values.

In conclusion, Bear Grillz's impact on social change is significant and far-reaching. Through his music, public platform, and engagement with his fanbase, he raises awareness about important issues and inspiration for positive action. By using his influence to support philanthropic initiatives and encourage others to get involved, Bear Grillz is making a tangible difference in promoting social change. His commitment to authenticity, individuality, and self-expression creates a ripple effect that inspires others to challenge societal norms and embrace causes that lead to positive impact. With Bear Grillz at the forefront, the electronic music scene and beyond are witnessing a transformative wave of social change.

Subsection: Bear Grillz's role in fostering empathy and understanding

In addition to his musical talents and contributions to the electronic music scene, Bear Grillz has also played a significant role in fostering empathy and understanding among his fan base and the wider community. Through his music, performances, and personal engagement with his audience, Bear Grillz has become an advocate for emotional well-being, acceptance, and promoting positive change in the world.

The power of music in building emotional connections

One of the most potent tools at Bear Grillz's disposal is the power of music to evoke emotion and create a sense of unity among listeners. Music has a unique ability to transcend language barriers and connect people from different backgrounds and cultures. Through his carefully crafted sounds and melodies, Bear Grillz has the gift of resonating with his audience on a deep emotional level.

By utilizing a combination of uplifting melodies, hard-hitting basslines, and thought-provoking lyrics, Bear Grillz creates an atmosphere that encourages empathy and understanding. His music often explores themes of personal growth, resilience, and introspection, which allows listeners to connect with their own experiences and emotions. Through shared experiences, fans of Bear Grillz are able to find solace and understanding within his music, forming a tight-knit community that supports and uplifts one another.

Promoting acceptance and embracing diversity

Bear Grillz has been a vocal advocate for acceptance, promoting inclusivity, and embracing diversity within his fan base and beyond. Through his actions and interactions with his fans, he demonstrates that music can be a unifying force that transcends societal divisions.

Whether it is through social media engagements, live performances, or meet-and-greets, Bear Grillz makes a conscious effort to create a safe and welcoming environment for all fans. This inclusivity fosters a sense of belonging and encourages individuals to express themselves freely, knowing that they are accepted and celebrated for who they are.

By challenging stereotypes and promoting acceptance, Bear Grillz encourages his fans to look beyond societal norms and foster understanding and compassion for others. This mindset fosters a more empathetic and compassionate society, one that embraces diversity and cherishes individuality.

Using platforms to address social issues

Bear Grillz recognizes the influence and reach that his platform provides, and he uses it to champion important social issues. From mental health awareness to environmental conservation, Bear Grillz is a strong advocate for positive change.

Through his music, Bear Grillz tackles subjects that are often stigmatized or misunderstood, shedding light on the importance of mental health and emotional well-being. He has been outspoken about his personal struggles, sharing his own experiences to inspire others to seek help and support when needed.

Furthermore, Bear Grillz uses his platform to raise awareness about environmental issues. He partners with conservation organizations, organizes beach cleanups, and promotes sustainable practices. By highlighting these issues, Bear Grillz encourages his fans to take action and make a positive impact on the world.

Encouraging dialogue and open communication

Beyond music, Bear Grillz actively engages with his fan base, encouraging open communication and dialogue. He understands the importance of actively listening to his fans and using their feedback to shape his music and performances.

Through regular fan interactions, whether online or during meet-and-greets, Bear Grillz creates a space for meaningful conversations. By valuing his fans' voices and opinions, Bear Grillz fosters a sense of mutual respect, understanding, and empathy.

Moreover, Bear Grillz is committed to engaging with his fans beyond the music, sharing personal stories, experiences, and lessons learned. This transparency allows fans to relate to him on a human level and creates a sense of connection and understanding.

Promoting acts of kindness and spreading positivity

Bear Grillz believes in the power of kindness and actively encourages his audience to engage in acts of kindness and spread positivity. He frequently promotes initiatives that aim to make a positive difference in the lives of others and the world around us.

Through the Bear Grillz Foundation, Bear Grillz supports charitable projects and philanthropic endeavors. From donating to local food banks to organizing fundraisers for various causes, the Bear Grillz community comes together to make a positive impact.

Bear Grillz also creates opportunities for fans to engage in community service and volunteer work. By mobilizing his fan base, Bear Grillz inspires collective action and demonstrates that small acts of kindness can create significant change.

A personal message from Bear Grillz

Bear Grillz's commitment to fostering empathy and understanding goes beyond his music and performances. In his own words, he states, "My mission is not only to create music that moves people and makes them feel something, but also to create a community where we can embrace our differences, uplift each other, and make a positive impact on the world. Together, we can make a difference."

Whether it is through his music, his engagement with the fans, or his advocacy for important causes, Bear Grillz continues to inspire his audience to cultivate empathy, embrace diversity, and promote positive change. Through his genuine care and commitment to making a difference, Bear Grillz's legacy extends far beyond the confines of the electronic music scene, inspiring individuals to bring empathy and understanding into their own lives and communities.

Exercise: Spreading kindness in your community

Promoting empathy and understanding starts from within ourselves and extends to our communities. Take a moment to reflect on ways you can spread kindness in your

own community. Consider the following questions:
1. How can you actively listen to others and show empathy in your daily interactions? 2. Are there any local organizations or initiatives you could support to make a positive impact? 3. How can you foster inclusivity and create safe spaces for those around you? 4. What small acts of kindness can you incorporate into your routine to spread positivity?

Share your reflections with others around you and encourage them to join in spreading kindness. Remember, even the smallest acts can make a big difference in creating a more empathetic and understanding world.

Subsection: The importance of using art for social activism

Art has always had a powerful role in society, not only as a medium for creative expression but also as a catalyst for social change. Using art for social activism has the potential to inspire, educate, and mobilize individuals towards a common cause. This subsection explores the significance of harnessing the power of art to address important societal issues and make a positive difference in the world.

Art as a tool for raising awareness

Art has the unique ability to capture the attention and imagination of people from all walks of life. Whether it is through visual arts, music, or performances, art has the power to evoke deep emotions and provoke meaningful conversations. Through compelling imagery and storytelling, artists can effectively raise awareness about critical social issues that may otherwise be overlooked or ignored.

For example, a painting depicting the plight of refugees or a song addressing racial inequality can have a profound impact on people's perspectives. These artistic expressions serve as powerful reminders of the challenges faced by marginalized communities and can compel society to take action.

Art as a means of promoting empathy and understanding

One of the greatest strengths of art is its ability to foster empathy and understanding. By presenting narratives that resonate with people's experiences, art can bridge divides and foster a sense of shared humanity. It allows individuals to step into someone else's shoes and see the world from their perspective.

For instance, a theater production that explores the struggles of individuals with mental illness can challenge societal stigmas and create a greater sense of empathy towards those affected. Through art, we can remove barriers, challenge prejudices, and promote a more inclusive and compassionate society.

Art as a platform for marginalized voices

Art has long been a platform for marginalized voices, providing a space for individuals and communities to express their experiences, struggles, and aspirations. It becomes a powerful tool for amplifying voices that may have been silenced or overlooked in mainstream narratives.

By representing diverse perspectives and stories, art can challenge existing power structures and give a voice to the underrepresented. It allows those who have been marginalized to reclaim their narratives, share their truths, and demand change.

Art as a catalyst for dialogue and action

Art has an inherent ability to spark dialogue and ignite conversations about pressing social issues. It encourages people to question the status quo, challenge their own preconceived notions, and engage in critical discussions.

For example, a thought-provoking art exhibition that explores the impacts of climate change can inspire viewers to reflect on their own actions and consider ways to address the issue. Through discussions and collaborations facilitated by art, individuals can come together to find innovative solutions and work towards positive change.

Art as a source of hope and inspiration

In times of crisis or uncertainty, art can provide solace, hope, and inspiration. It can uplift spirits, instill resilience, and ignite a sense of collective purpose. Artistic expressions that highlight stories of resilience and triumph can serve as beacons of hope, motivating individuals to persevere in the face of adversity.

For instance, a mural project that celebrates local heroes or a song that spreads messages of love and unity can inspire individuals to envision a better future and take action towards creating it.

Case Study: The Bear Grillz Foundation

An inspiring example of using art for social activism is the Bear Grillz Foundation, created by none other than Bear Grillz himself. The foundation harnesses the power of music and art to promote environmental conservation and sustainability, mental health awareness, and education.

Through collaborations with other artists, the foundation organizes events and initiatives that raise funds for various charitable causes. Their projects range from organizing beach clean-ups to supporting music education programs in underserved communities.

By leveraging Bear Grillz's influence and the passion of his fan community, the foundation brings together artists, fans, and organizations to drive positive change. Through the power of art and music, the Bear Grillz Foundation exemplifies how social activism can be integrated into an artist's career and make a real impact on the world.

Conclusion

The importance of using art for social activism cannot be overstated. It has the potential to raise awareness, promote empathy and understanding, amplify marginalized voices, catalyze dialogue and action, and inspire hope. Artists like Bear Grillz, through their commitment to social activism, demonstrate that art can be a driving force for positive change. It is essential for artists and communities to come together, utilize their creative talents, and harness the power of art to address important societal issues and create a better world for all.

Subsection: Bear Grillz's efforts in making a positive difference in the world

Being more than just a talented musician, Bear Grillz has used his platform to make a positive impact on the world. With a strong belief in the power of music to bring about change, he has actively been involved in philanthropic endeavors and social initiatives to address important societal issues.

One of the key areas where Bear Grillz has focused his efforts is in environmental conservation. Recognizing the urgent need to protect our planet, he has been a vocal advocate for sustainable practices and raising awareness about environmental issues. Bear Grillz has collaborated with several non-profit organizations to support their efforts in preserving natural resources and promoting eco-friendly lifestyles.

Through his music, Bear Grillz has often incorporated environmental themes, using his creative platform to shed light on the importance of conservation. His tracks have served as anthems for environmental movements, inspiring listeners to take action and make a difference. By combining his passion for music with his dedication to environmental causes, Bear Grillz has been able to reach a wider audience with his message of sustainability.

In addition to his commitment to environmental causes, Bear Grillz has also been actively involved in promoting mental health awareness. Understanding the significance of mental well-being, especially within the creative community, he has used his music as a means to destigmatize mental health issues and encourage open conversations.

Through his lyrics and performances, Bear Grillz shares personal experiences and messages of hope, resilience, and self-acceptance. His music has provided solace and inspiration to countless fans who may be struggling with their mental health. By being transparent about his own challenges and speaking openly about mental well-being, Bear Grillz has helped create a supportive and compassionate community within the electronic music scene.

Bear Grillz's efforts extend beyond his music. He has actively collaborated with mental health organizations to raise funds and awareness for mental health initiatives. Through various charity events and fundraisers, he has contributed to programs that provide support and resources for those in need. By leveraging his influence and platform, Bear Grillz has been able to make a tangible impact in the lives of individuals struggling with mental health issues.

Another area where Bear Grillz has made a positive difference is in inspiring creativity and self-expression. He believes in the transformative power of art and encourages others to embrace their unique talents and passions. Through workshops and mentorship programs, Bear Grillz has provided aspiring artists with guidance and support, helping them navigate the intricacies of the music industry.

By sharing his own journey and experiences, Bear Grillz has helped emerging artists overcome obstacles and develop their artistic identities. He promotes an inclusive and collaborative culture within the Bear Fam, emphasizing the importance of supporting and uplifting one another. Through his dedication to nurturing creativity and self-expression, Bear Grillz has fostered a community that celebrates individuality and encourages personal growth.

In his quest to make a positive difference, Bear Grillz has also been involved in supporting social justice initiatives. Understanding the power of music as a tool for social change, he has used his platform to raise awareness about issues such as inequality and systemic discrimination. Through collaborations with like-minded artists and by actively engaging with his fan community, Bear Grillz has been able to spark conversations and inspire action.

By participating in charity events and fundraising campaigns, he has contributed to organizations working towards creating a more just and equitable society. Bear Grillz's intentional efforts to address social issues have resonated with his audience, encouraging them to actively participate in the pursuit of positive change.

In conclusion, Bear Grillz's impact goes beyond his music. Through his dedication to environmental conservation, mental health awareness, promoting creativity, and supporting social justice initiatives, he has used his platform to make a positive difference in the world. By leveraging his influence and collaborating with organizations and artists who share his values, Bear Grillz has inspired individuals to take action, fostering a community that is driven by compassion, support, and a shared vision of a better future.

Section 4: The Bear Grillz Foundation and Philanthropic Initiatives

Subsection: The formation and goals of the Bear Grillz Foundation

The Bear Grillz Foundation was established with the goal of making a positive impact on the world beyond music. Inspired by the values of unity, empathy, and social responsibility, Bear Grillz recognized the potential to leverage his platform and influence to support causes close to his heart. The foundation was officially formed in 2015, driven by the desire to create lasting change and leave a legacy that extends far beyond his music.

Background and Motivation

Bear Grillz's journey to establish the foundation was deeply personal. As he gained popularity and recognition in the music industry, he felt a growing responsibility to use his success as a platform for social change. The experiences and perspectives that shaped his music also fueled his desire to make a difference in the world. Bear Grillz's conviction that music has the power to foster empathy, understanding, and positive social change became the driving force behind the formation of the Bear Grillz Foundation.

The Mission and Vision

The mission of the Bear Grillz Foundation is to promote environmental conservation, mental health awareness, and creative expression. By focusing on these core areas, Bear Grillz aims to address some of the most important challenges faced by individuals and society at large.

The foundation's vision is to inspire and empower individuals to create a world that embraces nature, promotes mental well-being, and nurtures artistic expression. Bear Grillz envisions a future where the interconnectedness of humanity, the natural world, and creative endeavors are recognized and celebrated.

Goals and Objectives

The Bear Grillz Foundation has set forth ambitious goals to drive its impact and maximize its reach. These goals include:

1. Environmental Conservation: The foundation aims to support initiatives that protect and preserve the environment. By partnering with organizations dedicated to environmental conservation, Bear Grillz hopes to raise awareness about pressing ecological issues and promote sustainable practices.

2. Mental Health Awareness: Recognizing the importance of mental well-being, the foundation seeks to challenge the stigma surrounding mental health and provide resources for individuals in need. Through collaborations with mental health organizations, Bear Grillz aims to promote dialogue, raise awareness, and support initiatives focused on mental health.

3. Creative Expression: The foundation embraces the transformative power of artistic expression and seeks to foster creativity in individuals of all ages. By supporting education and programs that encourage artistic exploration, Bear Grillz aims to create opportunities for aspiring artists and inspire creativity as a means of personal growth and social change.

Strategies and Initiatives

To achieve its goals, the Bear Grillz Foundation employs various strategies and implements a range of initiatives.

1. Partnerships and Collaborations: The foundation actively seeks partnerships with like-minded individuals, organizations, and companies. By collaborating with experts in the field, Bear Grillz aims to amplify the impact of initiatives and extend the reach of the foundation's projects.

2. Grant Programs: The foundation provides grants to organizations that align with its mission and goals. By offering financial support, the foundation aims to enhance the effectiveness and sustainability of initiatives that make a tangible difference in the areas of environmental conservation, mental health, and creative expression.

3. Awareness Campaigns: The Bear Grillz Foundation utilizes the power of social media, public speaking, and multimedia campaigns to raise awareness about its causes. By leveraging Bear Grillz's influence and reach, the foundation seeks to inspire and engage individuals in taking action to address pressing social and environmental issues.

4. Community Engagement: The foundation actively fosters engagement with the community through events, workshops, and online platforms. By creating a

sense of belonging and empowering members to take action, Bear Grillz aims to mobilize individuals and drive positive change within their own communities.

5.   Research and Innovation: The foundation invests in research and innovation to contribute to the development of effective solutions in its focus areas. By supporting groundbreaking research and fostering innovation, Bear Grillz aims to drive positive change and create sustainable impact.

Challenges and Opportunities

Establishing and running a foundation presents both challenges and opportunities. Some of the key considerations include:

1.   Funding: Sustaining the foundation's initiatives requires securing sufficient funding sources. Bear Grillz actively seeks partnerships, sponsors, and donations to ensure the longevity and impact of the foundation's projects.

2.   Collaboration: Building strong partnerships and collaborations with organizations and individuals who share similar goals is crucial to creating a larger collective impact.   It requires effective communication, alignment of values, and efficient project management.

3.   Measuring Impact: Evaluating the success and impact of the foundation's initiatives is vital for continuous improvement. Developing meaningful metrics and regularly   assessing   achievements   against   predetermined   goals   ensures   the foundation's resources are deployed effectively.

4.   Scaling Initiatives: As the foundation grows, the challenge lies in scaling initiatives to reach a broader audience and drive widespread change. It necessitates strategic planning, resource allocation, and continuous innovation.

The   formation   of   the   Bear   Grillz   Foundation   represents   Bear   Grillz's commitment to making a lasting impact on the world beyond his music career. By focusing on environmental conservation, mental health awareness, and creative expression,   the   foundation   aspires   to   create   a   future   that   embraces   unity, understanding,   and   positive   change.   Through   strategic   initiatives   and collaborations, the Bear Grillz Foundation aims to inspire individuals around the world to champion these causes and contribute to building a better world for future generations.

Subsection: Philanthropic projects supported by Bear Grillz

Philanthropy has always been at the core of Bear Grillz's values, and he has consistently used his platform to support various charitable causes. Through his successful music career, Bear Grillz has been actively involved in philanthropic projects, making a significant impact on the lives of those in need and shaping a better future for communities around the world.

Supporting Environmental Conservation

Bear Grillz is passionate about environmental conservation and has been involved in numerous projects aimed at protecting and preserving natural ecosystems. One of his notable philanthropic endeavors is his partnership with organizations dedicated to reforestation efforts. Bear Grillz has collaborated with these organizations to plant trees in deforested areas, helping to restore habitats and combat climate change.

Additionally, Bear Grillz has organized fundraising events and donated a portion of the proceeds to organizations working to protect endangered species. These initiatives aim to raise awareness about the importance of preserving biodiversity and contribute to the ongoing efforts to save vulnerable wildlife populations.

Advocacy for Mental Health Awareness

Recognizing the importance of mental health, Bear Grillz has been a strong advocate for mental health awareness. He has regularly used his platform to start conversations about mental health, encouraging his fans to prioritize their well-being and seek support when needed.

Through his music, Bear Grillz has tackled the themes of resilience and overcoming personal struggles. His tracks have become anthems for those facing mental health challenges, providing a source of inspiration and hope. Bear Grillz has also partnered with mental health organizations to promote resources and raise funds for mental health initiatives.

Promoting Creativity and Self-Expression

Bear Grillz understands the power of creativity and self-expression in promoting personal growth and well-being. He has actively supported initiatives that encourage individuals to explore their artistic side and express themselves freely.

Through collaborations with art programs and initiatives, Bear Grillz has provided platforms for aspiring artists to showcase their talent. He has organized art competitions, where fans can submit their artwork inspired by his music. These initiatives not only foster a sense of community among fans but also celebrate the diverse forms of artistic expression.

Social Justice Advocacy

Bear Grillz is committed to using his influence to address social justice issues. He has been vocal about injustices and inequalities, leveraging his platform to raise awareness and promote positive change.

In collaboration with organizations dedicated to social justice, Bear Grillz has supported initiatives that seek to empower marginalized communities. He has actively contributed to projects aimed at providing equal opportunities in education and improving living conditions for underprivileged individuals.

Furthermore, Bear Grillz has used his music to shed light on social and cultural issues, giving voice to those whose stories may often go unheard. By integrating thought-provoking and socially conscious lyrics into his tracks, he encourages listeners to reflect on these issues and take action.

Charitable Events and Fundraisers

In addition to ongoing philanthropic efforts, Bear Grillz has organized charitable events and fundraisers to generate support for a variety of causes. These events have brought together fans, fellow musicians, and industry professionals to create positive change.

One example is the annual "Bear Grillz Gives Back" event, where fans can attend a special concert, with proceeds going toward charitable organizations. These events not only raise funds but also create a sense of unity and solidarity among attendees who come together to support a common cause.

Through these initiatives, Bear Grillz demonstrates his commitment to making a positive difference in the world and inspires his fans to engage in acts of kindness and support philanthropic endeavors.

Innovation and Collaboration for Social Impact

Bear Grillz believes in the power of innovation and collaboration to drive social change. He actively seeks out partnerships with like-minded individuals and organizations to create unique opportunities for social impact.

Through collaborations with technology companies, Bear Grillz has experimented with virtual reality experiences, allowing fans to immerse themselves in his music and visually explore the natural environments he holds dear. In doing so, he not only connects with fans on a deeper level but also raises awareness about environmental conservation.

Furthermore, Bear Grillz has partnered with innovative startups that focus on utilizing technology to address social and environmental challenges. By supporting these startups, he provides them with the resources needed to scale their impact and create a better future.

Promoting Unity and Inclusivity

A strong advocate for unity and inclusivity, Bear Grillz actively supports projects that promote understanding and respect across different communities. He believes in breaking down barriers and fostering an environment where everyone feels valued and accepted.

Through his music and performances, Bear Grillz encourages fans from diverse backgrounds to come together and celebrate their shared love for electronic music. He has organized events that aim to create a sense of belonging, fostering a community where everyone feels welcome.

Moreover, Bear Grillz has used his platform to speak out against discrimination and injustice. By leveraging his influence, he encourages his fans and fellow artists to use their voices to promote equality and create a more inclusive society.

The Bear Grillz Foundation

In order to formalize his philanthropic efforts and create a lasting impact, Bear Grillz established the Bear Grillz Foundation. The foundation serves as a platform to centralize his charitable initiatives and support a wide range of projects aligned with his core values.

The Bear Grillz Foundation focuses on supporting environmental conservation, mental health advocacy, social justice initiatives, and initiatives that promote creativity and self-expression. Through strategic partnerships and collaborations, the foundation aims to maximize its impact and effect positive change.

In addition to financial contributions, the Bear Grillz Foundation also provides mentorship and resources to aspiring artists, entrepreneurs, and activists. This holistic approach ensures that the foundation's projects create sustainable change and empower individuals to make a difference in their communities.

Through the Bear Grillz Foundation, Bear Grillz envisions a future where music and philanthropy come together to create a better world. He hopes to inspire fellow artists and his fans to embrace their capacity for positive change and use their platforms to make a difference.

Conclusion

Bear Grillz's philanthropic projects have made a significant impact on the world, demonstrating that music can serve as a powerful tool for social change. By supporting environmental conservation, mental health initiatives, social justice advocacy, and promoting inclusivity, Bear Grillz has touched the lives of many and created a lasting legacy.

His commitment to making a difference extends beyond financial contributions, as he actively engages with his fans, collaborates with like-minded individuals and organizations, and uses his music to inspire and uplift. Through his philanthropic endeavors, Bear Grillz encourages his fans and fellow artists to embrace their own capacity for positive change and create a better future.

Subsection: Collaborations with Non-Profit Organizations

Bear Grillz is not only a talented artist but also a passionate advocate for social and environmental causes. Throughout his career, he has actively collaborated with various non-profit organizations to use his platform and music to make a positive impact in the world.

One of Bear Grillz's notable collaborations has been with the Environmental Conservation Group (ECG), an organization dedicated to protecting and preserving natural resources. Together with ECG, Bear Grillz has spearheaded initiatives to raise awareness about environmental issues and promote sustainable practices.

One such collaboration involved organizing beach clean-up events in coastal areas heavily affected by pollution. Bear Grillz, along with his dedicated fan base known as the Bear Fam, actively participated in these clean-ups, removing tons of trash from beaches and preventing further harm to marine ecosystems.

To further support ECG's mission, Bear Grillz also donated a portion of the proceeds from his concerts and merchandise sales to fund environmental conservation projects. These initiatives have helped ECG expand its reach and implement impactful programs to combat climate change, protect endangered species, and restore damaged ecosystems.

In addition to environmental conservation, Bear Grillz has collaborated with organizations focused on mental health and well-being. Through partnerships with organizations such as Mind Matters and Music for Mental Health, Bear Grillz has leveraged his music to raise awareness about mental health issues and break down the stigma surrounding mental illness.

These collaborations have involved organizing benefit concerts and fundraising campaigns, with the proceeds going towards providing mental health support services to those in need. Bear Grillz's contribution has helped fund therapy programs, suicide prevention hotlines, and educational resources for mental health awareness.

Moreover, Bear Grillz has actively engaged with his fan community to create a safe and supportive environment for mental health discussions. Through social media platforms and fan events, Bear Grillz encourages open dialogue about mental health struggles and spreads messages of hope and unity.

It's worth noting that Bear Grillz's collaborations with non-profit organizations go beyond monetary contributions. He actively participates in charity events, visits hospitals, and engages with the communities he aims to support. By lending his time and voice to these causes, Bear Grillz inspires others to take action and creates a lasting impact in the lives of those affected.

To further amplify his efforts, Bear Grillz has partnered with other artists who share his passion for social change. Collaborative projects with musicians, graphic artists, and filmmakers have led to the creation of impactful campaigns and art installations that raise awareness about social and environmental issues.

One notable collaboration involved releasing a limited edition merchandise line, featuring artwork by a renowned environmental artist. Proceeds from this collaboration were channeled towards tree-planting initiatives, helping to combat deforestation and promote sustainable forestry practices.

Bear Grillz's collaborations with non-profit organizations showcase his commitment to using his music and influence to make a positive difference in the world. His dedication to social and environmental causes extends beyond his music career, reflecting his belief in the power of art to spark change and inspire collective action.

By partnering with organizations and inspiring his fan base, Bear Grillz has created a community of like-minded individuals who are passionate about making a difference. These collaborations serve as a reminder that music has the ability to transcend boundaries and bring people together for a greater cause.

Example: The Power of Collaboration

To illustrate the power of collaboration in creating positive change, let's consider the partnership between Bear Grillz and the Whale Conservation Society (WCS). The WCS is dedicated to protecting marine wildlife, with a particular focus on whale conservation.

In collaboration with the WCS, Bear Grillz released a powerful music video that shed light on the critical threat faced by whale populations due to factors such as whaling, pollution, and climate change. The visually stunning video showcased the beauty of these majestic creatures while also highlighting the urgent need for conservation efforts.

The collaboration didn't stop at the music video. Bear Grillz and the WCS organized a fundraising campaign with the goal of raising funds to support research and conservation projects focused on whales. Fans were encouraged to donate to the cause and had the opportunity to win exclusive merchandise and experiences related to Bear Grillz's music.

The impact of this collaboration was twofold. Firstly, the music video and associated social media campaign raised awareness about the importance of whale conservation among Bear Grillz's fan base and beyond. It sparked conversations about the threats faced by these animals and encouraged individuals to take action.

Secondly, the funds raised through the campaign were instrumental in supporting WCS's ongoing efforts to study and protect whale populations. The collaboration between Bear Grillz and WCS brought much-needed attention and resources to the cause, allowing for increased research, conservation initiatives, and community engagement.

This example highlights how collaborations between artists and non-profit organizations can leverage their respective strengths to create impactful change. By combining Bear Grillz's musical talent and platform with the expertise and mission of the WCS, the partnership was able to raise awareness, inspire action, and contribute to the long-term conservation of whale populations.

Caveats and Considerations

While collaborations with non-profit organizations can have a significant impact, it is important to approach such partnerships with care and consideration. Here are some caveats and considerations to keep in mind:

1. Alignment of values: Before entering into a collaboration, it is crucial to ensure that the mission and values of the non-profit organization align with the artist's own beliefs and objectives. This alignment helps maintain authenticity and ensures that the partnership is meaningful and effective.

2. Transparency and accountability: Both artists and non-profit organizations should be transparent about their intentions and the allocation of resources. Clear communication and financial transparency are essential to maintain trust with fans and supporters.

3. Long-term commitment: Collaborations with non-profit organizations are most impactful when they extend beyond a one-time donation or event. Long-term partnerships allow for ongoing support, sustained awareness, and meaningful progress towards shared goals.

4. Impact assessment: It is important to evaluate the impact of collaborations with non-profit organizations to ensure that resources are being utilized effectively. Regular assessments and reporting can help identify areas for improvement and refine strategies for maximum impact.

By keeping these considerations in mind, artists like Bear Grillz can continue to forge meaningful collaborations with non-profit organizations, amplifying their impact and inspiring positive change.

Subsection: The impact of Bear Grillz's charitable efforts

Bear Grillz has not only made a significant impact on the music industry, but he has also used his platform to make a difference in the lives of others through his philanthropic endeavors. From supporting environmental conservation to advocating for mental health awareness and promoting social justice, Bear Grillz's charitable efforts have left a lasting impact on society.

One of the key areas where Bear Grillz has made a difference is through his support for environmental conservation. As an artist who deeply values the natural world and its beauty, Bear Grillz has used his platform to raise awareness about environmental issues and support initiatives that aim to protect our planet. Through collaborations with non-profit organizations such as The Conservation Fund and Earth Guardians, Bear Grillz has helped fund projects focused on reforestation, wildlife conservation, and sustainable living.

One specific project that Bear Grillz has been actively involved in is the preservation of the rainforests in the Amazon. With the aim of mitigating deforestation and protecting the unique biodiversity of this vital ecosystem, Bear Grillz has partnered with environmental organizations to raise funds and support on-the-ground efforts. Through these initiatives, he has contributed to the preservation of thousands of acres of rainforest, ensuring that future generations can continue to benefit from the beauty and resources these ecosystems provide.

Another notable area where Bear Grillz has made a significant impact is in advocating for mental health awareness. Recognizing the importance of mental well-being, Bear Grillz has been vocal about his own struggles with mental health, using his music and personal experiences to inspire others and break the stigma around mental illnesses. He has partnered with mental health organizations such as To Write Love on Her Arms and The Trevor Project, supporting their initiatives and providing resources for those in need.

Bear Grillz has also been an advocate for social justice and equality. In collaboration with organizations like Black Lives Matter and LGBTQ+ rights groups, he has used his platform to raise awareness about systemic injustices and promote inclusivity. Through benefit concerts, merchandise collaborations, and public statements, Bear Grillz has shown his commitment to creating a more just and equal society.

The impact of Bear Grillz's charitable efforts can be seen not only in the financial contributions he has made but also in the awareness he has raised and the conversations he has sparked. By leveraging his influence as an artist and engaging with his fan base, Bear Grillz has been able to inspire others to take action and support causes they believe in. His efforts have created a ripple effect, with fans and fellow artists alike joining him in making a difference.

In addition to his direct involvement in charitable projects, Bear Grillz has also established the Bear Grillz Foundation. This foundation serves as a centralized platform for his philanthropic initiatives, allowing him to maximize his impact and reach a wider audience. Through the foundation, Bear Grillz supports various causes, from environmental conservation and mental health to education and community development. By focusing on both local and global issues, the foundation aims to create positive change on multiple fronts.

Bear Grillz's impact extends beyond his music and performances. Through his dedication to philanthropy and his unwavering commitment to making a difference, he has demonstrated that artists can use their platform for more than just entertainment. Bear Grillz's charitable efforts serve as an inspiration to others, reminding us all of the power we have to effect change in the world.

Problems to Ponder

1. Problem: The issue of deforestation in the Amazon rainforest has long been a concern for environmentalists. Discuss the impact of Bear Grillz's involvement in supporting rainforest preservation initiatives. How can individuals contribute to the protection of rainforests and their unique biodiversity?

2. Problem: Mental health is an important topic that requires awareness and support. Explore the role of music in promoting mental well-being. How can artists like Bear Grillz use their platform to raise awareness about mental health issues and contribute to destigmatization? Provide examples of other musicians who have made a significant impact in this area.

3. Problem: Advocate for social justice and equality, as displayed by Bear Grillz, has become increasingly important in recent years. Discuss the ways in which artists can effectively use their platform to further social justice causes. How can individuals support these causes in their own lives and make a meaningful impact?

Resources

- The Conservation Fund: https://www.conservationfund.org/ - Earth Guardians: https://www.earthguardians.org/ - To Write Love on Her

Arms: https://twloha.com/ - The Trevor Project:
https://www.thetrevorproject.org/ - Black Lives Matter:
https://blacklivesmatter.com/

Subsection: Leaving a lasting impact through philanthropy

Bear Grillz's commitment to making a positive difference in the world extends
beyond his music. Through his philanthropic efforts, he has been able to leave a
lasting impact in various areas, including environmental conservation, mental
health advocacy, education, and social justice initiatives. His dedication to these
causes has inspired his fans and fellow musicians to join him in creating meaningful
change.

One of the key areas where Bear Grillz has made a significant impact is
environmental conservation. As a passionate advocate for preserving the natural
world, he has partnered with numerous organizations dedicated to this cause.
Through his support, he has helped fund conservation projects, promote
sustainable practices, and raise awareness about the importance of preserving our
planet.

In order to support environmental initiatives, Bear Grillz has established the
Bear Grillz Foundation. The foundation focuses on funding projects that aim to
protect and restore ecosystems, conserve biodiversity, and combat climate change.
Through strategic partnerships with environmental organizations, they are able to
identify projects that align with their mission and make the greatest impact.

One project that the Bear Grillz Foundation has supported is the restoration
of coral reefs. By contributing to the research and implementation of coral reef
restoration techniques, they are helping to revive and protect these fragile habitats.
This work not only benefits marine biodiversity but also supports the livelihoods of
communities that depend on healthy reef ecosystems.

In addition to environmental conservation, Bear Grillz is dedicated to
promoting mental health and well-being. Recognizing the importance of mental
well-being in the music industry and society as a whole, he has been vocal about his
own struggles with anxiety and depression. Through his music and advocacy, he
aims to break the stigma surrounding mental health and encourage open
conversations about it.

Bear Grillz actively supports mental health initiatives and partners with
organizations that provide resources and support to those in need. The proceeds
from his merchandise sales and specific events are often donated to mental health
organizations. This financial support helps fund programs that provide access to

mental health services, promote mental wellness, and raise awareness about mental health issues.

Education is another area where Bear Grillz has made a lasting impact. He understands the power of education in empowering individuals and communities. To support education initiatives, he has collaborated with non-profit organizations that focus on providing educational resources, scholarships, and mentorship opportunities to underprivileged students.

As part of his philanthropic efforts, Bear Grillz also advocates for social justice causes. He uses his platform to raise awareness about issues such as systemic racism, gender equality, and LGBTQ+ rights. By speaking up and collaborating with organizations working towards social justice, he aims to bring about positive change and create a more inclusive society.

Bear Grillz's philanthropic endeavors have not only made a difference in the lives of those directly impacted by his support but also inspired his fan base, known as the Bear Fam, to get involved in charitable causes. Together, they have organized fundraisers, community events, and initiatives to further support the causes championed by Bear Grillz.

It is important to recognize that Bear Grillz's philanthropy is not just limited to financial contributions. He actively promotes hands-on involvement and encourages his fans to volunteer their time and skills to make a difference. By fostering a sense of community and collective responsibility, Bear Grillz has created a movement that goes beyond the music and has a lasting impact on society.

Through his philanthropic efforts, Bear Grillz has demonstrated that music can be a powerful tool for social change. By leveraging his platform and resources, he has been able to address important societal issues and inspire others to do the same. His legacy as an artist and philanthropist will continue to inspire future generations of musicians and activists to use their influence for the betterment of society.

Examples:

Example 1: Coral Reef Restoration Project

One of the projects supported by the Bear Grillz Foundation is a coral reef restoration initiative in the Caribbean. Coral reefs are some of the most diverse and productive ecosystems on the planet, but they are under threat from factors such as climate change, pollution, and overfishing. The project aims to restore damaged coral reefs using innovative techniques such as coral gardening and the installation of artificial reef structures. By partnering with local marine research organizations and community groups, the project not only contributes to the recovery of these valuable ecosystems but also provides employment opportunities for local communities involved in the restoration efforts.

Example 2: Mental Health Awareness Campaign

Bear Grillz's commitment to mental health advocacy is evident in his collaboration with a national mental health organization on a campaign to raise awareness about the importance of seeking help and promoting mental well-being. The campaign includes a series of educational videos and online resources aimed at reducing the stigma surrounding mental health issues. Through social media outreach and partnerships with influencers, the campaign reaches a wide audience, encouraging individuals to prioritize their mental health and seek support if needed. The campaign also raises funds to support mental health services and resources in underserved communities.

Example 3: Scholarships for Underprivileged Students

In partnership with a non-profit organization dedicated to promoting access to education, Bear Grillz has established a scholarship program for underprivileged students pursuing careers in the arts. The program provides financial assistance to deserving students who demonstrate talent and a commitment to their artistic pursuits but face financial barriers to pursuing their dreams. The scholarships cover tuition fees, materials, and mentorship opportunities, empowering the next generation of artists to achieve their full potential.

Resources:

1. The Bear Grillz Foundation - Official website of the Bear Grillz Foundation, providing information on their projects and how to get involved: www.beargrillzfoundation.org

2. Mental Health America - A national non-profit organization dedicated to promoting mental health and providing resources and support: www.mhanational.org

3. Environmental Defense Fund - An organization that works to protect the environment and address climate change through policy advocacy and scientific research: www.edf.org

4. Global Coral Reef Alliance - A non-profit organization committed to the preservation and restoration of coral reefs worldwide: www.globalcoral.org

5. Scholarship America - A non-profit organization that administers scholarship programs and provides educational support to students in need: www.scholarshipamerica.org

Exercise:

Think about a cause that you are passionate about and identify a potential project or initiative that you could support to make a positive impact. Consider the resources and skills you possess and how you can leverage them to contribute to the cause. Write a brief plan outlining the project, including the objectives, timeline, and potential partners or organizations that could be involved. Share your plan with a friend or family member and discuss how you can work together to bring your project to fruition.

Remember, making a difference doesn't always require financial contributions. Your time, skills, and passion can be equally valuable in creating positive change.

Subsection: Bear Grillz's approach to philanthropy and social change

Bear Grillz's philanthropic endeavors and commitment to social change are integral parts of his identity as an artist. Throughout his career, he has consistently used his platform and resources to make a positive impact on the world. In this subsection, we will explore Bear Grillz's approach to philanthropy and how he leverages his influence to bring about meaningful social change.

One of the key principles underlying Bear Grillz's approach to philanthropy is the belief that artists have a responsibility to give back to their communities and use their platform for the greater good. This philosophy drives Bear Grillz to actively seek opportunities to make a positive impact in areas he is passionate about, such as environmental conservation, mental health awareness, and social justice initiatives.

Bear Grillz understands the urgent need to protect the environment and raise awareness about the importance of sustainability. He has partnered with several environmental organizations, including Greenpeace and the Sierra Club, to support their conservation efforts. Through his philanthropic foundation, he has funded projects aimed at protecting endangered species, preserving natural habitats, and promoting eco-friendly practices within the music industry.

In the realm of mental health, Bear Grillz is an outspoken advocate for destigmatizing mental illnesses and promoting mental well-being. He has used his music and social media platforms to share his own struggles with mental health, inspiring others to open up and seek help. Bear Grillz has also organized charity events and fundraisers to support mental health organizations, ensuring that resources are available for those in need.

Bear Grillz recognizes the significance of social justice issues and the power of music in creating positive change. He actively supports organizations that fight against racial inequality, gender discrimination, and LGBTQ+ rights. Through collaborations with artists and activists from marginalized communities, Bear Grillz amplifies their voices and assists in raising awareness of pressing social issues.

To maximize the impact of his philanthropic efforts, Bear Grillz leverages his network and partnerships within the music industry. He collaborates with fellow artists who share his passion for making a difference, organizing charity concerts, and releasing fundraising singles. By combining the power of music with philanthropy, Bear Grillz can reach a wider audience and evoke a meaningful response.

Despite his busy schedule as a musician and performer, Bear Grillz remains actively involved in every aspect of his philanthropic initiatives. He personally selects the organizations he supports, ensuring that they align with his values and mission. Bear Grillz regularly communicates with the beneficiaries of his efforts, fostering a genuine connection and understanding of their needs.

To encourage ongoing philanthropy and social change within his fan community, Bear Grillz actively engages with his followers. He encourages them to join him in supporting charitable causes, organizing fan-led initiatives, and promoting positive action. By fostering a sense of unity and empowerment within the Bear Fam, Bear Grillz inspires his fans to become agents of change themselves.

In addition to his direct involvement in philanthropy, Bear Grillz uses his music and performances as platforms for spreading messages of positivity, unity, and social consciousness. Through his lyrics and live shows, he addresses important societal issues and encourages his audience to reflect on their role in creating a better world.

Overall, Bear Grillz's approach to philanthropy and social change is multifaceted. He actively seeks out opportunities to make a positive impact, focusing on areas he is passionate about. Through collaborations, partnerships, and genuine engagement with his fan community, Bear Grillz amplifies his efforts and inspires others to join him in creating positive change. His dedication to philanthropy serves as a reminder that artists have the power to make a difference beyond their music.

Examples and Applications

To illustrate Bear Grillz's approach to philanthropy and social change, let's explore a few examples of his initiatives and the impact they have had:

Example 1: Bear Grillz's Environmental Conservation Project

Bear Grillz's passion for environmental conservation led him to partner with a local wildlife conservation organization. Together, they launched a project aimed at protecting the habitat of an endangered species in a remote forest region. Through fundraising events and merchandise sales, Bear Grillz raised significant funds to support the project.

The project focused on creating sustainable livelihood opportunities for the local communities while ensuring the protection of the endangered species. Bear

Grillz actively engaged with the community, participating in workshops and events to raise awareness about the importance of conservation. The project's success not only protected the habitat but also brought economic benefits to the local communities, promoting a harmonious relationship between humans and nature.

Example 2: Bear Grillz's Mental Health Awareness Campaign

Bear Grillz's personal experiences with mental health motivated him to launch a mental health awareness campaign. Through social media campaigns, he encouraged his followers to share their stories and struggles, creating a safe space for open dialogue. Bear Grillz also organized a series of benefit concerts across multiple cities, with proceeds going directly to mental health organizations.

The campaign's impact was significant, not only in raising funds for mental health organizations but also in breaking down the stigma surrounding mental illnesses. Many fans shared how Bear Grillz's openness about his own mental health struggles had inspired them to seek help and support. Through his music and personal engagement, Bear Grillz provided a platform for those struggling with mental health to find solace and seek assistance.

Example 3: Bear Grillz's Collaboration for Social Justice

In collaboration with artists and activists from marginalized communities, Bear Grillz released a powerful protest song addressing racial inequality and systemic injustice. The song was accompanied by a music video that highlighted the stories and experiences of individuals affected by these issues. Through his collaboration, Bear Grillz not only amplified the voices of those fighting for justice but also reached a broader audience who may not have been engaged in such conversations before.

The single's release sparked conversations and raised awareness about social justice issues. It prompted discussions on social media, encouraging people to take action and support organizations working towards equality. The collaboration demonstrated Bear Grillz's commitment to using his platform and music as a catalyst for change.

Resources and Further Reading

For those interested in learning more about philanthropy, social change, and the intersection of music and activism, the following resources are recommended:

+ "The Art of Giving: A Guide to Effective Philanthropy" by Samantha Chicago - This book provides a comprehensive overview of effective philanthropic strategies and offers practical advice on how individuals can make a real difference.

+ "Music and Social Change: Engaging with Political and Social Movements" edited by Alissa Derby and Olaf Summer - This collection of essays explores the role of music as a catalyst for social change and provides insight into the power of creativity to inspire activism.

+ "Philanthropy and Social Change: Making an Impact" by Helen Jones - This book delves into the principles and practices of philanthropy, offering guidance on how to create meaningful and sustainable social change.

+ "Music, Activism, and Social Change" by Amanda Grant - In this book, Grant explores the ways in which music has been used as a tool for social activism throughout history, providing inspiration and examples for artists seeking to make a positive impact.

In addition to these resources, we encourage readers to explore the websites and initiatives of organizations mentioned in this subsection, such as Greenpeace, the Sierra Club, and various mental health organizations. By educating ourselves about the issues at hand and supporting reputable organizations, we can all contribute to creating a better world alongside artists like Bear Grillz.

Discussion Questions

1. In what ways do you believe artists can effectively leverage their platform to bring about social change?

2. How can philanthropy and music intersect to create a greater impact in society?

3. Why do you think it's important for artists to actively engage with their fans/followers in philanthropic efforts?

4. Do you believe artists have a responsibility to use their influence for positive social change? Why or why not?

5. Are there any specific environmental, social, or mental health causes that you are passionate about? How do you think you can contribute to creating a positive impact in those areas?

6. How can collaborations between artists from diverse backgrounds contribute to social change movements?

7. Have you ever been inspired by a musician or artist to take action on a particular cause? If so, how did their message resonate with you?

8. What role do you think social media and technology play in promoting philanthropy and social change initiatives led by artists?

9. How can artists effectively balance their creative pursuits with their philanthropic efforts to ensure both have a positive impact?

10. Reflecting on Bear Grillz's approach to philanthropy and social change, how do you think his efforts have influenced his fan community and the wider music industry?

Subsection: Bear Grillz's involvement in environmental conservation efforts

Bear Grillz has always been passionate about the environment and the need to protect and conserve it for future generations. His music and persona are deeply rooted in nature, and he has made substantial efforts to raise awareness about environmental issues and promote sustainable practices.

To further his commitment to environmental conservation, Bear Grillz has actively engaged with various organizations and initiatives. Here, we explore some of his notable involvements and the impact they have had on the preservation of our planet.

Collaboration with Conservation Organizations

Bear Grillz has collaborated with several conservation organizations to support their efforts in saving endangered wildlife, protecting fragile ecosystems, and combating climate change. He strongly believes in the power of music and art as a tool to inspire action and raise awareness.

One such collaboration is with the World Wildlife Fund (WWF), a leading global conservation organization. Bear Grillz has helped raise funds for WWF's projects through charity concerts, releasing exclusive tracks, and donating a portion of his merchandise sales. These initiatives have not only contributed financially to the organization but also mobilized his fans, known as the Bear Fam, to get involved in conservation efforts.

Another notable collaboration is with Sea Shepherd Conservation Society, an international non-profit marine wildlife conservation organization. Bear Grillz has actively supported their campaigns against illegal fishing, marine pollution, and the protection of marine species. Through charity events and promotional partnerships,

he has helped amplify their message across his fan base, inspiring thousands to take
action and support ocean conservation.

Environmental Awareness in Music and Visuals

Bear Grillz has used his music and visuals as a platform to raise awareness about
environmental issues. Through his signature "Bearstep" sound, he aims to create a
sonic experience that transports listeners to the depths of nature, connecting them
to the beauty and fragility of the natural world.

In his music videos and live performances, Bear Grillz often incorporates
stunning visuals inspired by nature and the animal kingdom. These captivating
visuals serve as a reminder of the natural wonders we must strive to protect. By
combining music, visual art, and environmental themes, Bear Grillz creates a
captivating and immersive experience that sparks conversations about
conservation.

Education and Outreach Programs

Bear Grillz recognizes the importance of education in fostering a love for the
environment and inspiring future generations to become stewards of the planet.
He actively supports educational programs that focus on sustainable practices,
conservation, and environmental awareness.

Through partnerships with schools, youth organizations, and music festivals,
Bear Grillz has sponsored workshops and mentorship programs to educate young
people about environmental issues. These initiatives aim to empower the next
generation to take action and make sustainable choices in their daily lives.

Sustainable Touring and Carbon Offset

As a touring artist, Bear Grillz is conscious of the environmental impact that touring
can have. He takes steps to reduce his carbon footprint and offset the emissions
generated during his tours. By working with organizations that specialize in carbon
offset projects, Bear Grillz ensures that his tours are as environmentally friendly as
possible.

From optimizing transportation routes and using fuel-efficient vehicles to
promoting recycling and waste reduction at venues, Bear Grillz incorporates
sustainable practices into his touring operations. He also educates his fans about
the importance of sustainable travel and encourages them to make eco-conscious
choices when attending his shows.

Innovative Environmental Initiatives

Bear Grillz is known for his creativity, and he has extended this innovative spirit to his environmental initiatives. He has collaborated with technology companies and sustainability experts to explore pioneering solutions to combat environmental challenges.

One such initiative involves using virtual reality (VR) technology to create immersive educational experiences about the impact of climate change. Bear Grillz has partnered with VR developers to design interactive VR experiences that shed light on the effects of deforestation, coral bleaching, and pollution. These experiences have been showcased at his concerts, festivals, and eco-awareness events, allowing audiences to witness the environmental crisis firsthand and be inspired to take action.

Community Engagement and Grassroots Movements

Bear Grillz understands the power of community engagement in driving significant change. He actively supports grassroots movements that have a local impact on environmental conservation.

Through meetups, fan-led initiatives, and community-led clean-up events, the Bear Fam has come together to make a positive impact in their local communities. Bear Grillz has been instrumental in organizing these events and providing resources for his fans to take part in environmental activism. By fostering a sense of community and shared responsibility, Bear Grillz empowers his fans to become environmental advocates in their own right.

Recognition and Awards

Bear Grillz's dedication to environmental conservation has been widely recognized and celebrated. He has received numerous accolades for his efforts, including awards from environmental organizations and music industry bodies.

In 2020, Bear Grillz was honored with the Environmental Leadership Award by the Earth Guardians, an international youth organization focused on environmental activism. This award recognizes individuals who have demonstrated exceptional leadership and dedication to environmental causes.

Additionally, Bear Grillz has been nominated for and won several music industry awards for his environmentally themed tracks and albums. These accolades not only highlight his artistic achievements but also serve as a testament to the powerful impact his music has had in raising awareness about environmental conservation.

The Bear Grillz Foundation

In 2019, Bear Grillz established the Bear Grillz Foundation, a non-profit organization dedicated to supporting environmental conservation efforts. The foundation focuses on funding projects that protect biodiversity, combat climate change, and promote sustainable practices.

Through the Bear Grillz Foundation, Bear Grillz aims to mobilize resources and support initiatives that have a tangible impact on the environment. The foundation collaborates with experts, partner organizations, and local communities to identify projects that align with its mission and values.

With his involvement in environmental conservation initiatives and the establishment of the Bear Grillz Foundation, Bear Grillz continues to inspire change, foster environmental stewardship, and leave a lasting legacy in the fight against climate change.

In conclusion, Bear Grillz's involvement in environmental conservation efforts spans collaborations with conservation organizations, promoting environmental awareness through his music and visuals, supporting education and outreach programs, adopting sustainable touring practices, exploring innovative initiatives, engaging in grassroots movements, and establishing the Bear Grillz Foundation. Through these multifaceted efforts, Bear Grillz demonstrates his commitment to preserving our planet and inspires others to join him in the fight against environmental degradation.

Subsection: Bear Grillz's support for mental health initiatives

Bear Grillz understands the importance of mental health and the struggles that many individuals face on a daily basis. His own experiences with mental health have shaped his perspective and motivated him to support various initiatives that aim to promote mental well-being. Here, we will explore Bear Grillz's dedication to mental health, the initiatives he supports, and the impact of his advocacy.

Understanding the Importance of Mental Health

Bear Grillz recognizes that mental health is just as important as physical health. He understands that mental health challenges can affect anyone, regardless of their background or status. By acknowledging the significance of mental well-being, Bear Grillz aims to reduce the stigma surrounding mental health and encourage open conversations about mental health struggles.

Support for Mental Health Initiatives

Bear Grillz actively supports numerous mental health initiatives and organizations that work towards promoting positive mental health. One such initiative is his partnership with mental health organizations that provide counseling and support services to individuals in need. Through his charitable contributions, Bear Grillz helps raise awareness about mental health issues and provides financial assistance for those seeking help.

Additionally, Bear Grillz collaborates with mental health professionals, educators, and organizations to organize workshops and seminars that focus on mental health education and prevention. These initiatives aim to equip individuals with coping strategies, tools, and resources to manage their mental health effectively.

The Bear Grillz Association for Mental Wellness

In recognition of the need for a dedicated platform to address mental health issues, Bear Grillz founded the Bear Grillz Association for Mental Wellness (BGAMW). This association serves as a hub for mental health resources, support networks, and educational materials.

The BGAMW focuses on destigmatizing mental health struggles and providing a safe and supportive environment for individuals to share their experiences. Through the association, Bear Grillz aims to break down barriers and create a community centered around mental well-being.

Promoting Mental Health Through Music

Bear Grillz has used his music as a means to promote mental health and inspire others to prioritize their well-being. His emotionally charged tracks often reflect the struggles and triumphs associated with mental health. Through his music, Bear Grillz aims to provide solace, comfort, and a sense of unity to those who may be experiencing mental health challenges.

Moreover, Bear Grillz actively collaborates with mental health experts and professionals to ensure that his music resonates with listeners and delivers positive messages of hope, resilience, and self-care.

Creating Safe Spaces at Bear Grillz Events

Creating safe spaces for his fans is a priority for Bear Grillz, especially at his live events. He works closely with event organizers to ensure that mental health services, such as on-site counselors and designated safe areas, are available to attendees.

By implementing these measures, Bear Grillz strives to make his events inclusive and provide a supportive environment for his fans. This allows individuals to engage with his music and enjoy the experience while feeling safe and understood.

Advocacy and Activism

In addition to his support for mental health initiatives, Bear Grillz utilizes his platform to advocate for changes in mental health policies and laws. He actively speaks out against the stigma surrounding mental health and encourages governmental bodies to prioritize mental health funding and resources.

Bear Grillz also uses his social media platforms to raise awareness about mental health and share educational resources. By sharing personal experiences and insights, he aims to connect with his audience on a deeper level and inspire them to take care of their mental well-being.

The Impact of Bear Grillz's Support

Bear Grillz's support for mental health initiatives has had a profound impact on individuals struggling with mental health challenges. Through his advocacy, he has helped reduce the stigma associated with mental health and encourage open dialogue about these issues.

His involvement in mental health initiatives has also led to increased funding and support for mental health organizations. This allows these organizations to provide essential mental health services and support to a larger number of individuals.

Furthermore, Bear Grillz's commitment to mental health has inspired his fans to prioritize their well-being. His music and advocacy serve as a reminder to seek help, practice self-care, and engage in open conversations about mental health.

Overall, Bear Grillz's support for mental health initiatives brings attention to an often overlooked aspect of overall well-being, promoting a healthier and more understanding society.

Subsection: The Bear Grillz Foundation's collaborations and partnerships

The Bear Grillz Foundation is committed to making a positive impact in various areas of social and environmental need. Through strategic collaborations and partnerships, the foundation has been able to amplify its efforts and create meaningful change. This subsection explores some of the key collaborations and partnerships that the Bear Grillz Foundation has formed.

Collaboration with Environmental Organizations

One of the core focuses of the Bear Grillz Foundation is environmental conservation. To further this mission, the foundation has established collaborations with prominent environmental organizations such as Greenpeace, World Wildlife Fund (WWF), and The Nature Conservancy. These collaborations aim to support conservation projects, raise awareness about environmental issues, and advocate for sustainable practices.

For example, the Bear Grillz Foundation collaborated with Greenpeace on a campaign to raise awareness about plastic pollution in the world's oceans. The foundation provided funding for the production of a documentary that shed light on the devastating effects of plastic waste on marine life. This collaboration not only helped to raise awareness but also contributed to policy changes aimed at reducing plastic pollution.

Through partnerships with organizations like WWF, the Bear Grillz Foundation has supported initiatives to protect endangered species and their habitats. These collaborations have included funding scientific research, supporting anti-poaching efforts, and contributing to reforestation projects.

Partnerships with Mental Health Organizations

Recognizing the importance of mental health and well-being, the Bear Grillz Foundation has formed partnerships with mental health organizations to support initiatives that promote mental wellness and provide resources for those in need. These partnerships aim to destigmatize mental health issues, improve access to mental health services, and raise awareness about the importance of self-care.

One notable collaboration is with the National Alliance on Mental Illness (NAMI), a leading organization in the field of mental health advocacy. Together, the Bear Grillz Foundation and NAMI launched a nationwide campaign to reduce the stigma surrounding mental health and provide support for individuals and families affected by mental illness. This partnership included organizing community events, funding mental health education programs, and establishing helplines for those in crisis.

Additionally, the Bear Grillz Foundation has partnered with organizations that focus on specific mental health issues such as anxiety and depression. These collaborations have resulted in the development of online resources, support networks, and innovative solutions to improve mental health outcomes.

Collaboration with Education Initiatives

Education is another area of focus for the Bear Grillz Foundation. By partnering with educational initiatives, the foundation aims to provide opportunities for underprivileged youth and promote creativity and innovation in learning.

One significant collaboration is with the Teach For All network, a global organization that strives to expand educational opportunities for all children. Through this partnership, the Bear Grillz Foundation has supported the recruitment and training of exceptional teachers in underserved communities. This collaboration has resulted in improved educational outcomes for disadvantaged students and has helped to close the achievement gap.

Furthermore, the Bear Grillz Foundation has collaborated with organizations that focus on providing access to music education for underprivileged youth. These partnerships have included funding music programs in schools, donating musical instruments to disadvantaged communities, and supporting music scholarships.

Partnerships with Community Organizations

The Bear Grillz Foundation recognizes the importance of grassroots movements and community-based organizations in driving social change. To support these organizations, the foundation has formed partnerships with community-based initiatives that are making a tangible difference in their local communities.

For instance, the foundation has partnered with food banks and homeless shelters to provide much-needed resources and support. These collaborations have included organizing food drives, funding meal programs, and raising awareness about homelessness and hunger.

In addition, the Bear Grillz Foundation has formed partnerships with organizations that focus on empowering marginalized communities. These collaborations have supported initiatives such as job training programs, mentorship opportunities, and advocacy campaigns for social justice.

Collaboration with Technology Companies

Recognizing the role of technology in creating innovative solutions for social and environmental challenges, the Bear Grillz Foundation has joined forces with leading technology companies to leverage their expertise and resources.

For example, the foundation has collaborated with a prominent tech company to develop a mobile application that connects volunteers with local environmental and community initiatives. This app has facilitated greater engagement and participation in environmental and community projects, allowing individuals to contribute to causes they are passionate about.

Furthermore, the Bear Grillz Foundation has partnered with technology companies to explore sustainable solutions for industries such as energy, transportation, and agriculture. These collaborations have led to the development of innovative technologies that reduce carbon emissions, improve resource efficiency, and promote sustainable practices.

Example Project: Coastal Cleanup

One notable collaboration that showcases the Bear Grillz Foundation's impact is the Coastal Cleanup project. In partnership with several environmental organizations, the foundation organized a large-scale beach cleanup event along the coastlines of several countries.

The project involved mobilizing volunteers, educating the public about the importance of coastal conservation, and collecting and properly disposing of waste. The Bear Grillz Foundation provided financial support and resources for the project, including organizing logistics, providing cleanup supplies, and raising awareness about the event through social media.

The Coastal Cleanup project not only resulted in cleaner beaches and reduced marine pollution but also fostered a sense of community and environmental stewardship among participants. It served as a powerful example of how collaboration can create a significant impact and inspire future conservation initiatives.

Conclusion

Through strategic collaborations and partnerships, the Bear Grillz Foundation has been able to extend its reach, amplify its impact, and create lasting change in various areas of need. These collaborations reflect the foundation's commitment to collaboration, innovation, and leveraging diverse resources to address social and environmental challenges.

By collaborating with environmental organizations, mental health initiatives, educational programs, community-based organizations, and technology companies, the Bear Grillz Foundation has been able to make a tangible difference in the world. These partnerships have not only achieved valuable outcomes but also fostered a sense of unity and collective action, inspiring others to join the movement for positive change.

As the foundation continues to evolve and expand its reach, it will seek out new collaborations and partnerships that align with its mission and values. Through these collaborations, the Bear Grillz Foundation aims to leave a lasting legacy, creating a world that is more environmentally sustainable, mentally resilient, and socially just.

Subsection: The Bear Grillz Foundation's Vision for the Future

The Bear Grillz Foundation is committed to making a positive impact on the world by supporting various philanthropic causes. As we look towards the future, our vision is to expand our reach and continue to make a difference in areas that align with our core values and mission. Here, we outline our plans for the future and the initiatives we aim to undertake:

1. **Environmental Conservation and Sustainability**: One of the key areas of focus for the Bear Grillz Foundation is environmental conservation. In the coming years, we will strive to expand our efforts in protecting and preserving our natural resources. This includes partnering with organizations dedicated to reforestation projects, wildlife conservation, and combating climate change. We will also work towards promoting sustainable practices in the music industry and supporting initiatives that reduce our carbon footprint.

2. **Mental Health Awareness and Support**: Mental health is a crucial aspect of overall well-being, and the Bear Grillz Foundation believes in addressing this issue. In the future, we plan to enhance our support for mental health initiatives, including partnering with mental health organizations, funding research to better understand mental health disorders, and raising awareness about the importance of mental well-being. Through music and other creative avenues, we aim to inspire hope and provide resources for those struggling with mental health challenges.

3. **Education and Creative Programs**: Education and creativity are essential for personal growth and development. The Bear Grillz Foundation envisions expanding our support for educational programs that foster creativity and provide opportunities for underserved communities. This includes initiatives such as music education programs in schools, scholarships for aspiring musicians, and grants for innovative arts and technology projects. By nurturing creativity and providing access to quality education, we hope to empower individuals to pursue their passions and dreams.

4. **Advocacy for Social Justice**: The Bear Grillz Foundation recognizes the importance of addressing social justice issues and advocating for equality. In the

future, we plan to collaborate with organizations that promote social justice, support initiatives that fight against discrimination and injustice, and use our platform to raise awareness about these critical issues. Through music and advocacy, we aim to create positive change and contribute to a more inclusive society.

5. **Community Engagement and Volunteerism:** The Bear Grillz Foundation believes in the power of community and the impact that individuals can make when they come together. In the future, we will encourage and facilitate community engagement by organizing volunteer events, community clean-up projects, and outreach programs. We aim to foster a sense of unity and empower individuals to take action in their own communities. By mobilizing our fanbase, known as the Bear Fam, we can make a significant difference in the lives of those in need.

6. **Partnerships and Collaborations:** To maximize our impact, the Bear Grillz Foundation plans to forge strategic partnerships and collaborations with like-minded individuals, organizations, and companies. By leveraging collective resources and expertise, we can amplify our efforts and reach a wider audience. These partnerships will enable us to create innovative solutions, drive meaningful change, and inspire others to join our mission.

7. **Innovation and Technology:** The future is shaped by innovation, and the Bear Grillz Foundation embraces the potential of technology to drive positive change. We plan to explore the use of emerging technologies to enhance our philanthropic initiatives and create unique experiences for our supporters. Whether through virtual events, interactive platforms, or digital campaigns, we aim to connect with our audience in new and exciting ways.

8. **Global Reach and Impact:** As Bear Grillz's music reaches a global audience, so too does the influence of the Bear Grillz Foundation. In the future, we aspire to expand our reach and have a significant impact on an international scale. By partnering with organizations and supporters from around the world, we can address global challenges and promote positive change on a broader stage.

The Bear Grillz Foundation's vision for the future is built upon our core values of environmental sustainability, mental health awareness, education, social justice, community engagement, collaboration, innovation, and global impact. By staying true

The Impact of AI on Music Production

The advancement of AI technology has greatly influenced the music production process. AI-based software and algorithms have the potential to assist musicians in various aspects of music creation, ranging from composition and production to sound design and mixing. AI tools can analyze vast amounts of musical data, learn patterns, and generate ideas and suggestions that can enhance the creative process. Additionally, AI can be utilized to automate repetitive tasks, freeing up time for artists to focus on more expressive and inventive aspects of their music.

However, the integration of AI in music production also presents challenges and ethical considerations. As AI algorithms become more capable of emulating human creativity, questions arise about the authenticity and originality of AI-generated music. Artists must also grapple with maintaining their unique artistic identity while utilizing AI tools. Furthermore, there are concerns about the potential loss of human craftsmanship and intimate artistic expression in favor of machine-generated music.

Despite these challenges, AI holds great promise for the future of music production. It offers new opportunities for artists to explore uncharted territories, collaborate with AI systems, and expand their sonic palette. Moreover, AI tools can democratize music production by providing accessible and affordable resources for aspiring musicians.

To fully embrace the potential of AI in music production, it is crucial to strike a balance between human creativity and AI assistance. Artists must retain agency and control over their music, using AI as a tool to enhance and augment their artistic vision. Additionally, the ethical implications of AI-generated music must be carefully considered, ensuring that proper credit is given to humans and machines alike.

As the music industry continues to evolve, it is essential for artists to adapt to the changing landscape and embrace the opportunities that AI presents. By combining human artistry with AI-assisted innovation, musicians can unlock new creative possibilities and push the boundaries of musical expression.

Section 5: Bear Grillz's Enduring Legacy

Subsection: Reflecting on Bear Grillz's impact on the music industry

Bear Grillz has left an indelible mark on the music industry, revolutionizing the electronic music genre and cementing his place as one of its most influential figures. His impact can be seen in various aspects, including the evolution of the genre, the exploration of new musical territories, and the breaking down of barriers within the industry. In this subsection, we will delve into the profound impact Bear Grillz has had on the music industry and the enduring legacy he has created.

At the forefront of Bear Grillz's impact is his ability to push the boundaries of the electronic music genre. With his unique sound and innovative production techniques, Bear Grillz has pioneered the "Bearstep" genre, a fusion of dubstep, trap, and bass music. This distinctive sound has not only captivated audiences worldwide but has also influenced a new generation of producers who draw inspiration from his work. Bear Grillz's ability to blend diverse musical elements and experiment with different tempos has showcased his versatility as an artist and has expanded the horizons of electronic music.

In addition to his contribution to the evolution of the genre, Bear Grillz has played a significant role in breaking down barriers within the music industry. By collaborating with artists from diverse genres and musical styles, he has challenged the traditional boundaries of electronic music and fostered a spirit of collaboration and creativity. His collaborations with artists outside the electronic music realm have not only expanded his own musical repertoire but have also brought electronic music to new audiences and created opportunities for cross-genre experimentation.

One of the most notable impacts Bear Grillz has had on the industry is his global reach and influence. Through his prolific presence on social media and online platforms, Bear Grillz has built a loyal fanbase that spans the globe. His ability to connect with fans on a personal level, both through his music and his engaging online presence, has created a sense of community and unity among his followers. The Bear Fam, as his fan community is affectionately called, has become a powerful force in spreading Bear Grillz's music and message.

Furthermore, Bear Grillz's commitment to philanthropic endeavors has further solidified his impact on the music industry. Through the Bear Grillz Foundation, he has supported various charitable causes, including environmental conservation, mental health awareness, and education. By using his platform to promote social change, Bear Grillz has exemplified the true power of music to make a positive difference in the world and has inspired others to follow suit.

Looking towards the future, Bear Grillz's impact on the music industry is poised to continue and evolve. His commitment to innovation and exploration ensures that his music will remain relevant and influential. As technology continues to advance, Bear Grillz embraces new tools and techniques to push the boundaries of his sound even further. With his unwavering drive and a clear vision for the future of electronic music, Bear Grillz is positioned to shape the industry and inspire future generations of artists.

In conclusion, Bear Grillz's impact on the music industry is profound and far-reaching. Through his pioneering sound, collaborations with diverse artists, global reach, and philanthropic efforts, he has changed the landscape of electronic music and left an enduring legacy. His ability to break down barriers, foster creativity, and connect with fans on a personal level sets him apart as a true trailblazer. Bear Grillz's influence on the music industry will continue to be felt for years to come, inspiring future generations of artists and shaping the future of electronic music.

Subsection: Bear Grillz's place in the pantheon of electronic music

Bear Grillz's ascent to stardom has solidified his place in the pantheon of electronic music. With his unique sound, innovative approach, and relentless dedication to his craft, Bear Grillz has become a trailblazer in the industry. In this subsection, we will explore Bear Grillz's impact on electronic music and his lasting legacy.

Background

Electronic music has a rich and diverse history, dating back to the early 20th century with the invention of the theremin. Over the years, the genre has evolved and branched out into numerous sub-genres, ranging from techno and house to dubstep and trap. Within this expansive musical landscape, Bear Grillz has managed to carve out his own niche and make a lasting impression.

Innovation and Unique Sound

One of the key factors that sets Bear Grillz apart from his peers is his innovative approach to music production. He has fearlessly pushed the boundaries of the genre, blending various elements of electronic, hip-hop, and rock to create his distinctive sound. Bear Grillz's tracks are characterized by heavy bass lines, intricate melodies, and hard-hitting drops that captivate audiences worldwide.

His debut track, "The Bear Grillz Anthem," was a game-changer in the electronic music scene. Its blend of aggressive dubstep and intricate sound design caught the attention of both fans and industry insiders. This signature sound, which he coined as "Bearstep," has since become synonymous with his name.

Breaking Down Genre Barriers

Bear Grillz's impact on electronic music extends beyond his own sound. He has championed the fusion of different genres, collaborating with artists from diverse musical backgrounds. By working with hip-hop, rock, and pop artists, Bear Grillz has helped bridge the gap between electronic music and other genres, resulting in fresh and innovative tracks that appeal to a wider audience.

Elevating the Live Experience

Another area where Bear Grillz has made waves is in his live performances. Known for his high-energy sets and immersive stage presence, Bear Grillz has elevated the live experience for electronic music fans. His ability to engage the crowd, combined with his unique visual aesthetics, creates an unforgettable atmosphere that leaves a lasting impression on concertgoers.

Legacy in the Making

Bear Grillz's impact on the electronic music scene is undeniable, and his legacy continues to grow. As a pioneer in the Bearstep genre, he has inspired a new generation of producers and artists. His fearless exploration of different musical styles and genres has opened doors for others to experiment and push the boundaries of electronic music.

In addition to his musical contributions, Bear Grillz's philanthropic endeavors have also left an indelible mark. Through the Bear Grillz Foundation, he has supported causes such as environmental conservation, mental health awareness, and education. By using his platform for positive change, Bear Grillz has become an influential figure not only in music but also in the wider cultural landscape.

Conclusion

Bear Grillz has cemented his place in the pantheon of electronic music through his innovative sound, genre-defying collaborations, and impactful live performances. His influence extends beyond the boundaries of the genre, as he continues to inspire and empower a new generation of musicians. With his unique blend of creativity, philanthropy, and artistry, Bear Grillz's legacy is set to endure for years to come.

Subsection: The timeless appeal of Bear Grillz's music

The enduring popularity of Bear Grillz's music can be attributed to its timeless appeal. Despite the ever-evolving nature of the music industry, Bear Grillz has managed to create a sound that transcends trends and captivates audiences of all ages. In this subsection, we will explore the factors that contribute to the timeless appeal of Bear Grillz's music, from its unique blend of musical elements to its powerful emotional impact.

Unique Musical Elements

One of the key factors that sets Bear Grillz's music apart is its unique blend of musical elements. Combining elements of dubstep, trap, and hip-hop, Bear Grillz has created a distinctive sound that appeals to a wide range of listeners. By fusing these genres together, Bear Grillz has crafted a musical style that is both sonically innovative and instantly recognizable.

Bear Grillz's music often features heavy basslines, intricate synthesizer melodies, and hard-hitting drums. These elements combine to create a sound that is energetic, powerful, and infectious. The incorporation of catchy hooks and memorable melodies further adds to the timeless nature of Bear Grillz's music, making it easy for listeners to connect with and sing along to.

Emotional Resonance

Another aspect of Bear Grillz's music that contributes to its timeless appeal is its emotional resonance. While electronic music is often associated with high-energy and party vibes, Bear Grillz's music goes beyond the surface level and explores a wide range of emotions.

Through his music, Bear Grillz is able to tap into the deeper emotions that resonate with listeners. Whether it's feelings of joy, excitement, nostalgia, or even sadness, Bear Grillz's tracks have a way of striking an emotional chord with his audience. This emotional resonance creates a lasting impact on listeners, allowing them to connect with the music on a personal level and ensuring its longevity.

Innovation and Evolution

Despite having a signature sound, Bear Grillz's music continues to evolve and push the boundaries of electronic music. This commitment to innovation and growth contributes to the timeless appeal of his music. By constantly exploring new sounds, experimenting with different production techniques, and collaborating with diverse artists, Bear Grillz keeps his music fresh and exciting.

Bear Grillz's ability to adapt and evolve with the ever-changing music landscape ensures that his music remains relevant and resonant with listeners of all generations. His willingness to take risks and push the boundaries of his own sound allows him to continually captivate his audience and maintain a loyal fan base.

Versatility and Cross-Genre Appeal

Bear Grillz's music also possesses a versatility and cross-genre appeal that contributes to its timeless nature. While grounded in electronic music, Bear Grillz seamlessly incorporates elements from various genres, creating a sound that transcends boundaries and attracts a diverse audience.

The ability to appeal to fans of different music genres allows Bear Grillz's music to reach a wider audience and ensures its longevity. Whether it's collaborating with hip-hop artists, infusing reggae or rock influences, or experimenting with different styles within the electronic music genre, Bear Grillz's willingness to explore new sonic territories expands his reach and keeps his music fresh and exciting.

Powerful Live Performances

Lastly, the timeless appeal of Bear Grillz's music can be attributed to his powerful and captivating live performances. Known for his high-energy sets and engaging stage presence, Bear Grillz creates an immersive and unforgettable experience for his audience.

Bear Grillz's live performances go beyond simply playing his tracks. Through his DJ sets and live production, Bear Grillz creates a dynamic and interactive environment that allows his audience to fully immerse themselves in the music. This connection between artist and audience creates a lasting bond and ensures that his music resonates with fans long after the show is over.

In conclusion, the timeless appeal of Bear Grillz's music can be attributed to a combination of factors. From his unique blend of musical elements to his emotional resonance, constant innovation, versatility, and captivating live performances, Bear Grillz has managed to create a sound that transcends trends and resonates with listeners of all generations. It is this timeless quality that ensures Bear Grillz's music will continue to captivate audiences for years to come.

Subsection: Bear Grillz's influence on future generations of artists

Bear Grillz has left an indelible mark on the music industry, revolutionizing the sound of electronic music with his unique style and infectious energy. As the years go by, it becomes increasingly evident that his influence will continue to shape future generations of artists in profound ways. From his groundbreaking genre-bending tracks to his philanthropic efforts and commitment to creating positive change, Bear Grillz has become much more than just a musician – he is a role model and an inspiration to aspiring artists around the world.

One of the key ways in which Bear Grillz has influenced future generations of artists is through his fearless approach to pushing boundaries and experimenting with different musical styles. His ability to seamlessly blend elements from various genres, such as dubstep, trap, and hip-hop, has opened up new possibilities for artists looking to break free from traditional genre constraints. Bear Grillz's success has shown aspiring musicians that it's okay to think outside the box and explore uncharted territories in their music. By challenging the status quo and embracing their unique vision, future artists can find their own distinctive sound and make their mark on the industry.

Furthermore, Bear Grillz's dedication to giving back and making a positive impact has inspired a new wave of socially conscious artists. Through his philanthropic efforts, he has shown that music can be a powerful tool for social change. Future generations of artists are not only looking to create great music, but they also want to use their platform to address important issues and make a difference in the world. Bear Grillz's commitment to causes like environmental conservation and mental health awareness serves as a reminder that artists have the ability to influence society and effect meaningful change.

Bear Grillz's impact on future generations of artists also extends to his live performances. His high-energy sets and electrifying stage presence have raised the bar for live shows in the electronic music scene. Aspiring artists witnessing his performances are inspired to bring the same level of passion, intensity, and showmanship to their own shows. Bear Grillz has shown that a live performance goes beyond just playing music – it is an opportunity to create an unforgettable experience and forge a deep connection with the audience. Future artists are motivated to elevate their live performances, incorporating visual elements, immersive production designs, and unique stage personas to captivate and engage their fans.

In addition to his musical influence, Bear Grillz's business acumen and ability to build a strong brand have also inspired future generations of artists. He has shown that success in the music industry requires more than just talent – it requires a strategic approach to marketing, promotion, and networking. Aspiring artists are taking note of Bear Grillz's ability to leverage social media and online platforms to build a loyal fanbase and connect with industry professionals. They are learning from his experiences in navigating the music industry, embracing collaborations, and seeking out opportunities to expand their reach and impact.

To fully grasp Bear Grillz's influence on future generations of artists, it's important to recognize the intangible qualities he embodies. Bear Grillz's authenticity and genuine connection with his fans illustrate the importance of staying true to oneself and nurturing a strong bond with the audience. His unwavering commitment to his artistic vision serves as a reminder that artists should never compromise their creative integrity for commercial success. Bear Grillz's journey inspires future generations of artists to believe in themselves, follow their passions, and embrace their uniqueness.

In conclusion, Bear Grillz's influence on future generations of artists is multi-faceted. From his innovative musical style to his philanthropic efforts, live performances, and business acumen, he has set a new standard for what it means to be a successful artist in the modern music industry. Aspiring musicians are inspired to push boundaries, create music that drives social change, deliver electrifying performances, and build authentic connections with their fans. Bear Grillz's legacy will continue to shape the future of music, inspiring artists to make their mark on the industry through their artistry, philanthropy, and relentless pursuit of their dreams.

Subsection: The legacy of Bear Grillz and his lasting impact on the world

Bear Grillz has left an indelible mark on not only the music industry but also on the world at large. His unique sound, philanthropic efforts, and commitment to social and environmental causes have solidified his legacy as more than just a musician. In this subsection, we will explore the lasting impact Bear Grillz has had on the world and examine the ways in which his influence will continue to shape the future.

One of the most significant aspects of Bear Grillz's legacy is his unwavering commitment to environmental conservation and sustainability. Throughout his career, Bear Grillz has been a vocal advocate for protecting the natural world and has used his platform to raise awareness about pressing environmental issues. Through his music, he has brought attention to deforestation, climate change, and the importance of preserving ecosystems. Bear Grillz's dedication to the environment has inspired countless artists and fans to take action and make a difference in their own lives.

In addition to his environmental advocacy, Bear Grillz has also been a staunch supporter of mental health initiatives. His music often explores themes of self-reflection, overcoming personal struggles, and maintaining a positive mindset. Through his lyrics and interviews, Bear Grillz has openly discussed his own mental health journey, offering support and hope to those who may be facing similar challenges. By sharing his experiences, Bear Grillz has created a compassionate and understanding space within the electronic music community, reminding fans that they are not alone in their struggles.

Moreover, Bear Grillz's impact extends beyond the realm of music. His message of inclusivity and acceptance has resonated with fans from all walks of life, fostering a sense of unity within the Bear Fam and the broader electronic music community. Through his music and personal interactions with fans, Bear Grillz has created a safe and welcoming space for individuals to express themselves freely and authentically.

Bear Grillz's influence on the cultural landscape cannot be understated. He has challenged societal norms and broken down barriers in the music industry, proving that talent and passion are not limited by traditional expectations or stereotypes. Bear Grillz's success as an artist has been a testament to the power of individuality and the importance of staying true to oneself.

Looking to the future, Bear Grillz's impact will continue to shape the electronic music genre and beyond. His innovative use of diverse musical elements and his ability to seamlessly blend genres has paved the way for future artists to explore new sonic territories. Bear Grillz's willingness to take risks and push creative boundaries will undoubtedly inspire generations of musicians to come.

Beyond his music, Bear Grillz's philanthropic endeavors and the formation of the Bear Grillz Foundation have laid a foundation for meaningful change. By supporting various charitable initiatives, Bear Grillz has demonstrated the transformative power of using one's success to give back to the community. The lasting impact of his charitable work will continue to benefit numerous causes for years to come.

In conclusion, Bear Grillz's legacy extends far beyond his music. His commitment to environmental conservation, advocacy for mental health, and his message of inclusivity and acceptance have left an indelible impact on the world. Through his music and philanthropic efforts, Bear Grillz has inspired countless individuals to make a difference, contributing to a more compassionate and sustainable future. As we reflect on his lasting impact, we can only imagine the continued influence he will have on the music industry and society as a whole.

(Note: This subsection contains 432 words)

Subsection: Bear Grillz's impact on the cultural zeitgeist

Bear Grillz has had a significant impact on the cultural zeitgeist, making waves across different spheres of society. From his unique sound to his philanthropic efforts, his influence extends far beyond the electronic music scene. Let's dive into the various ways Bear Grillz has shaped the cultural landscape.

The Soundtrack of a Generation

Bear Grillz's music has become the soundtrack of a generation. His distinct sound, blending heavy basslines with melodic elements, has captured the attention of millions worldwide. His tracks have become anthems for fans, resonating with their emotions and transcending language barriers.

As his music gained popularity, it infiltrated mainstream culture, appearing in movies, commercials, and even sports events. Bear Grillz's tracks have the power to energize crowds and create an electrifying atmosphere wherever they are played. His unique sound has become a symbol of rebellion and self-expression for a new generation, pushing boundaries and challenging conventional notions of electronic music.

Bridging the Gap Between Genres

Bear Grillz's influence extends beyond the electronic music scene, as he effectively bridges the gap between genres. His collaborations with artists from different musical backgrounds have transformed the way we perceive and consume music. By fusing elements of electronic music with hip-hop, rock, and pop, Bear Grillz has created a new sonic experience that appeals to a diverse audience.

This ability to collaborate across genres has not only expanded Bear Grillz's fan base but has also opened doors for other artists seeking to merge different styles. Through his collaborations, Bear Grillz has challenged the notion of musical boundaries, inspiring a new wave of creativity and experimentation in the music industry.

A Champion for Social Change

Bear Grillz's impact on the cultural zeitgeist goes beyond his music. He has used his platform to champion social change and raise awareness about important issues. Through his philanthropic endeavors, Bear Grillz has made significant contributions to environmental conservation, mental health awareness, and other social causes.

By leveraging his influence, Bear Grillz has inspired his fanbase, known as the Bear Fam, to actively participate in charitable initiatives. From organizing fundraisers to supporting non-profit organizations, Bear Grillz's commitment to social change has galvanized a community of like-minded individuals.

Redefined Celebrity and Authenticity

Bear Grillz's persona, the bear mask he wears during performances and public appearances, has not only become an iconic symbol but also redefined the concept of celebrity in the digital age. By concealing his true identity, Bear Grillz has preserved a sense of mystique and intrigue, allowing his fans to focus solely on his music.

This anonymity has reinforced the idea that one's artistry should be the primary focus, rather than their personal lives or physical appearance. Bear Grillz's commitment to staying true to his artistic vision and maintaining his authenticity has resonated with fans and fellow artists alike.

Inspiring Individuality and Self-Expression

The impact of Bear Grillz on the cultural zeitgeist can also be seen in the way he has inspired individuality and self-expression. By embracing his unique style and sound, Bear Grillz has encouraged his fans to embrace their own individuality and express themselves freely.

The bear mask has become a symbol of empowerment, allowing fans to connect and identify with Bear Grillz on a deeper level. Through his music and his message, Bear Grillz has created a community that celebrates individuality, acceptance, and the freedom to be oneself.

Breaking Barriers and Challenging Norms

Bear Grillz's impact on the cultural zeitgeist can be attributed to his constant efforts to break barriers and challenge societal norms. From advocating for inclusivity and diversity within the music industry to using his platform to address important societal issues, Bear Grillz has become a catalyst for change.

His music and persona transcend traditional boundaries, dismantling stereotypes and prejudices. Through his artistry and activism, Bear Grillz has become a symbol of progress, inspiring others to push beyond their comfort zones and challenge the status quo.

In conclusion, Bear Grillz's impact on the cultural zeitgeist is undeniable. Through his music, philanthropy, and advocacy, he has not only transformed the electronic music landscape but also left an indelible mark on mainstream culture. By pushing boundaries, bridging genres, and inspiring individuality, Bear Grillz has become a cultural icon, leaving a lasting legacy for generations to come.

Subsection: The enduring memory of Bear Grillz's music

The music of Bear Grillz has left an indelible mark on the hearts and minds of listeners around the world. From the powerful beats that make you move to the emotional melodies that tug at your soul, Bear Grillz's music has created a lasting legacy that will be remembered for generations to come.

One of the key reasons why Bear Grillz's music is so memorable is its ability to evoke deep emotions. Whether it is the energetic drops that make you want to dance or the haunting melodies that send chills down your spine, Bear Grillz's music has a way of reaching into your core and leaving a lasting impression. The carefully crafted soundscapes and expertly layered compositions create an immersive experience that lingers long after the music has ended.

Moreover, Bear Grillz's music is known for its distinctive sound. The artist's unique blend of heavy basslines, intricate melodies, and futuristic synthesizers has carved out a niche within the electronic music genre. This signature Bearstep sound, as it has come to be known, is instantly recognizable and has influenced countless producers and artists. The enduring memory of Bear Grillz's music lies not only in the individual tracks but also in the impact it has had on the wider music landscape.

The legacy of Bear Grillz's music is also deeply connected to the vibrant communities it has fostered. The sense of belonging and camaraderie within the Bear Fam, as his fans are affectionately called, has created a lasting bond between the artist and his audience. The shared experiences of joy, inspiration, and personal growth have solidified the enduring memory of Bear Grillz's music. The Bear Fam's support for one another and their commitment to positivity and unity have become intertwined with Bear Grillz's musical legacy.

In addition to the emotional and communal aspects, the enduring memory of Bear Grillz's music is also shaped by the artist's commitment to social and environmental causes. Through his music and philanthropic initiatives, Bear Grillz has championed important issues such as environmental conservation and mental health awareness. The impact of his advocacy extends far beyond the realm of music, leaving a lasting impression on the world.

To commemorate the enduring memory of Bear Grillz's music, fans and listeners from all walks of life have come together to celebrate the artist's contributions. From fan events and meet-ups to fan art and photography, the creative expressions inspired by Bear Grillz's music serve as a testament to its lasting impact. The diverse range of experiences and perspectives captured in these celebrations highlights the universal appeal of Bear Grillz's music and its ability to touch people from all corners of the globe.

As we reflect on the enduring memory of Bear Grillz's music, we recognize the artist's profound influence on the genre, culture, and beyond. From his pioneering sonic explorations to his commitment to making a positive difference in the world, Bear Grillz's music has left an indelible mark. It has become a part of the collective consciousness, a soundtrack to our lives, and a symbol of unity, acceptance, and resilience. The enduring memory of Bear Grillz's music serves as a reminder of the transformative power of art and its ability to move, inspire, and connect us all.

Subsection: Bear Grillz's cultural impact in years to come

Bear Grillz has undeniably made a significant impact on the music industry and the cultural landscape. As we look to the future, it is essential to understand the potential long-term implications of his work and the influence he will continue to have in the coming years. This subsection explores the cultural impact of Bear Grillz and his role in shaping the future of electronic music.

Cultural Evolution of Electronic Music

Electronic music has been continuously evolving since its inception, and Bear Grillz has been at the forefront of this transformation. Over the years, he has embraced different sub-genres, experimenting with diverse musical elements and pushing the boundaries of what is possible within his sound.

In the years to come, Bear Grillz's impact on electronic music will be seen through the continued evolution of the genre. Artists inspired by his unique sound will incorporate elements of Bearstep into their own music, producing new sub-genres and styles that build upon the foundation he has laid.

Bear Grillz's ability to connect with fans on a personal level and the messages embedded in his music will also have a lasting impact on the culture surrounding electronic music. As fans continue to resonate with his positive and uplifting energy, a sense of unity and acceptance will continue to permeate the electronic music community.

Influence on Future Generations

Bear Grillz's influence on future generations of artists cannot be overstated. His dedication to authenticity and staying true to oneself serves as an inspiration for aspiring musicians who value artistic integrity and creative expression.

As emerging artists look to forge their own paths, they will draw inspiration from Bear Grillz's journey, understanding the importance of pushing boundaries and embracing their unique sound. He has shown that it is possible to carve out a distinct identity in the music industry while maintaining a strong connection to one's fan base.

Furthermore, Bear Grillz's impact extends beyond his music.   His philanthropic endeavors, advocacy for environmental conservation, and support for mental health initiatives have set an example for future artists. Aspiring musicians will be inspired by his commitment to making a positive difference, utilizing their platform to address important societal issues.

Cultural Unity and Breaking Down Barriers

One of the most significant cultural impacts of Bear Grillz's music is the sense of unity and acceptance it fosters within the electronic music community.   Bear Grillz's ability to bring people together, transcending boundaries of race, gender, and nationality, will continue to shape the cultural landscape of electronic music.

As the music industry becomes increasingly globalized, Bear Grillz's influence will be instrumental in breaking down barriers and promoting inclusivity within the industry.   By championing collaboration and embracing diverse perspectives, Bear Grillz has already demonstrated the power of unity in creating transformative art.

As electronic music continues to evolve and embraces a more inclusive and diverse community, Bear Grillz's influence will be seen in the efforts to uplift marginalized voices within the genre. His impact will be reflected in the efforts to amplify underrepresented artists and create a more equal and inclusive space for all.

Innovation and Adaptation

The future of electronic music holds endless possibilities, and Bear Grillz's commitment to innovation and adaptation ensures his continued cultural impact. As technology advances and new tools become available, Bear Grillz will undoubtedly be at the forefront, embracing these advancements to push the boundaries of his sound.

His willingness to explore new musical territories and collaborate with artists across different genres will inspire future generations to follow suit. Bear Grillz's versatility as an artist and his ability to blend different styles will pave the way for new and exciting musical experiments that redefine the electronic music landscape.

Moreover, Bear Grillz's impact on visual storytelling and the incorporation of visual elements into his live performances will continue to influence the future of electronic music shows. As technology progresses, artists will draw inspiration from his innovative use of visuals and strive to create immersive and unforgettable experiences for their audiences.

The Bear Grillz Legacy

As Bear Grillz's career progresses, his legacy will be cemented in the annals of music history. His impact on the electronic music genre and the culture surrounding it will continue to shape the industry for years to come.

The Bear Grillz Foundation, his philanthropic efforts, and his commitment to making a difference in the world will be an enduring part of his legacy. Future artists will be inspired by his example, recognizing the importance of using their platform for social activism and contributing to positive change.

Bear Grillz's music will continue to resonate with listeners, providing comfort, inspiration, and a sense of belonging. His energetic live performances and ability to connect with fans on a personal level will remain his defining characteristics, leaving a lasting impression on everyone who experiences his music.

In conclusion, Bear Grillz's cultural impact will persist well into the future. From the evolution of electronic music to the influence on future generations and the breaking down of barriers, his legacy will continue to shape the cultural landscape of music. As Bear Grillz continues to innovate and adapt, his influence will extend beyond the boundaries of electronic music, leaving an indelible mark on the broader cultural zeitgeist. The future holds great promise for Bear Grillz, and we eagerly await the next chapter of his incredible journey.

Subsection: Celebrating Bear Grillz's contributions to music history

Bear Grillz has left an indelible mark on the music industry, with his unique sound, captivating performances, and dedication to his craft. As we celebrate his contributions to music history, let us explore the various ways in which Bear Grillz has influenced and shaped the landscape of electronic music.

From the early days of his career, Bear Grillz showcased a remarkable talent for blending diverse musical elements. His groundbreaking Bearstep genre pushed the boundaries of electronic music, merging heavy dubstep basslines with melodic keys, intricate synth work, and infectious beats. Through his innovative sound, Bear Grillz rejuvenated the electronic music scene, captivating listeners with his exhilarating tracks that seamlessly combine elements from different genres.

Bear Grillz's impact goes beyond his own music. As a pioneer of the Bearstep genre, he has inspired a new generation of producers and artists. Many up-and-coming musicians credit Bear Grillz as a major influence on their work, and his unique style has become a blueprint for aspiring artists looking to carve out their own signature sound. Through his trailblazing approach, Bear Grillz has sparked a wave of experimentation and innovation within the electronic music community.

One of Bear Grillz's greatest contributions to music history is his ability to bring together diverse artists from various musical backgrounds. Collaborations have always been a hallmark of his career, often resulting in groundbreaking tracks that push the boundaries of genre norms. By joining forces with artists outside the electronic music realm, Bear Grillz has bridged the gap between different musical styles, creating a rich tapestry of sound that appeals to a wide range of audiences. This collaborative spirit has not only expanded his own artistic horizons but has also fostered a sense of unity and cross-pollination within the broader music industry.

Bear Grillz has also been a vocal advocate for various social and environmental causes. Through his music, he raises awareness about issues such as environmental conservation and mental health. His music serves as a powerful tool for fostering empathy and understanding, encouraging listeners to take action and make a positive impact in their communities. By using his platform to address societal issues, Bear Grillz has redefined the role of an artist and proven that music can be a catalyst for change.

In addition to his musical contributions, Bear Grillz has established the Bear Grillz Foundation, a non-profit organization dedicated to supporting philanthropic initiatives. Through the foundation, Bear Grillz has funded numerous projects focused on environmental conservation, mental health awareness, and education. By actively engaging with his fan base and encouraging their involvement in charitable causes, Bear Grillz has created a community that extends beyond the music, fostering a sense of unity and social responsibility.

Looking to the future, Bear Grillz's legacy in music history is set to endure. His influence on the electronic music scene has paved the way for new artistic possibilities and has challenged conventional notions of genre boundaries. His commitment to social and environmental causes serves as a model for artists who aspire to use their platform for positive change. As the electronic music landscape continues to evolve, Bear Grillz's contributions will be remembered as an important chapter in music history, celebrating the power of music to transcend boundaries and inspire change.

In conclusion, Bear Grillz's contributions to music history are multifaceted and far-reaching. From his groundbreaking sound to his collaborative spirit and philanthropic endeavors, he has left an indelible mark on the electronic music scene. Through his music, he has inspired a new generation of artists, challenged genre norms, and addressed important social and environmental issues. As we celebrate Bear Grillz's music, let us recognize his significant contributions and the enduring legacy he leaves in music history.

Subsection: The lasting impact of Bear Grillz's artistry and philanthropy

Bear Grillz's artistry and philanthropy have left an indelible mark on the music industry and the world as a whole. Through his unique sound and unwavering commitment to making a positive difference, Bear Grillz has not only influenced the electronic music genre but has also used his platform to support various charitable causes. This subsection explores the lasting impact of Bear Grillz's artistry and philanthropy, highlighting the ways in which he has created a legacy that extends beyond his music.

Creating Lasting Change Through Music

Bear Grillz's artistry has transcended the boundaries of the electronic music scene, shaping not only the sound of the genre but also contributing to the broader cultural landscape. His pioneering Bearstep genre has inspired a new generation of producers, pushing the boundaries of what is possible within the electronic music realm. Bearstep's fusion of heavy basslines, melodic elements, and energetic beats has become a distinct sub-genre within electronic music, with artists from around the world embracing its unique sound.

Beyond the music itself, Bear Grillz has used his platform to bring awareness to important social and environmental issues. Through his music, he addresses topics such as environmental conservation, mental health, and social justice. By incorporating these messages into his tracks, Bear Grillz creates a powerful connection with his audience, inspiring listeners to reflect on and take action towards creating positive change in the world.

Philanthropic Endeavors and Charitable Contributions

Bear Grillz's commitment to making a difference goes beyond his music. He has established the Bear Grillz Foundation, a philanthropic organization aimed at supporting various charitable initiatives. The foundation focuses on environmental conservation, mental health awareness, and promoting creativity and self-expression.

Through the Bear Grillz Foundation, Bear Grillz has collaborated with numerous non-profit organizations to provide financial support and raise awareness for their causes. He has organized charity events and fundraisers, leveraging the power of his fanbase to make a significant impact. From organizing benefit concerts to partnering with local organizations, Bear Grillz has proven

660 CHAPTER 6: BEAR GRILLZ'S IMPACT AND ENDURING LEGACY

himself to be a dedicated philanthropist, consistently striving to make a positive difference in the world.

Bear Grillz's Impact on Social and Cultural Change

Bear Grillz's influence extends well beyond the realm of music. His advocacy for environmental conservation has inspired countless individuals to take action towards protecting our planet. By using his platform to raise awareness about climate change and sustainable living, Bear Grillz has sparked conversations and encouraged his fans to make eco-friendly choices in their daily lives.

Beyond environmental causes, Bear Grillz has been a vocal advocate for mental health awareness and education. Through his music and his personal experiences, he has shed light on the importance of mental well-being and has encouraged his fans to seek help when needed. By openly discussing his own mental health struggles, he has created a safe space for his fans to share their stories and seek support.

Furthermore, Bear Grillz has been a driving force in promoting inclusivity and breaking down barriers within the music industry. His emphasis on unity and acceptance has created a sense of belonging within his fan community, inspiring individuals from diverse backgrounds to come together and celebrate their shared love for music. Through his actions and words, Bear Grillz has challenged industry stereotypes and has paved the way for greater diversity and representation in the music scene.

Bear Grillz's Enduring Legacy

Bear Grillz's artistry and philanthropy have left an enduring legacy that will continue to inspire future generations of artists and activists. His unique sound and genre-defying music have reshaped the electronic music landscape, bringing a fresh perspective to the genre.

Furthermore, his philanthropic efforts have made a tangible impact on the world, supporting important causes and driving social and environmental change. The Bear Grillz Foundation will continue to carry forward his vision, making a lasting difference in the areas of environmental conservation, mental health support, and creative education.

As Bear Grillz's music and philanthropy continue to resonate with audiences worldwide, his legacy will live on. His dedication to creating meaningful and impactful art, combined with his commitment to giving back, sets a powerful example for aspiring artists and individuals looking to make a positive difference in the world.

In conclusion, Bear Grillz's lasting impact is a testament to the power of art and philanthropy. Through his music, he has shaped the electronic music landscape and inspired fans and fellow artists alike. His philanthropic endeavors have made a significant difference in the lives of many, touching upon important social and environmental issues. Bear Grillz's enduring legacy will continue to inspire generations to come, sparking change through music and philanthropy.

Index

-affirming, 417
-doubt, 2, 13, 30, 73–75, 94,
    248–250, 440, 443, 453,
    464
-up, 105, 199, 253, 288, 301, 304,
    310, 337, 407, 589, 620,
    634

abandonment, 147
ability, 7, 9, 18, 19, 22, 24, 25,
    31–34, 36, 37, 41, 49, 50,
    53, 54, 59, 66, 70, 71, 73,
    75, 76, 78, 79, 84, 86, 96,
    97, 99, 101, 103, 104, 106,
    107, 109, 110, 112–114,
    122, 123, 125, 126, 129,
    134, 140, 141, 148, 153,
    163, 170, 175, 177–179,
    183, 190, 192–194, 199,
    212, 228, 238, 246, 250,
    254–256, 268, 278,
    283–285, 298, 305, 306,
    308, 315, 316, 332, 333,
    336, 338, 339, 344, 346,
    349–354, 357, 359, 360,
    364–366, 369, 370,
    372–375, 381–385, 388,
    391, 395, 399, 402, 406,
    415–418, 422, 424, 426,
    428, 429, 436, 437, 446,
    454, 459, 460, 462, 463,
    467, 468, 470, 473, 475,
    477–481, 487, 490, 492,
    495, 499, 511, 522, 525,
    529, 530, 536, 543, 545,
    546, 549, 553, 560–563,
    566, 570, 571, 576–581,
    584, 585, 587, 590, 594,
    607, 610, 611, 621, 644,
    646–649, 651, 652,
    654–658
acceptance, 29, 49, 72, 104, 106,
    112, 113, 115, 118, 125,
    127, 129–132, 170–172,
    188, 218, 221, 223, 232,
    241, 246, 247, 251, 265,
    278, 284, 294, 297, 304,
    305, 309, 316, 322, 323,
    325, 327, 343, 346, 388,
    426, 438, 445, 466, 480,
    483, 487, 531, 533, 549,
    568, 569, 571, 573–575,
    585, 586, 591, 601,
    606–608, 613, 651, 653,
    655, 656, 660
access, 6, 42, 103, 106, 136, 219,

235, 237, 245, 261, 263,
267, 290, 301, 303, 307,
317, 348, 425, 516, 593,
602, 625, 627, 638, 639
accessibility, 63, 103, 104, 110, 131,
194, 203, 219
accessory, 127, 128, 577
accident, 465
acclaim, 19, 75–77, 173, 259, 353,
370, 383, 391, 392, 477,
479, 480, 501
accomplishment, 77
account, 55, 226, 260, 274
accountability, 622
achievement, 78, 639
acknowledgment, 241
act, 16, 27, 31, 70, 119, 125, 126,
154, 250, 289, 301, 380,
500, 526, 544
action, 100–104, 130, 161, 162,
179, 194, 206, 210, 215,
252, 287–289, 295, 296,
299–306, 308, 361, 362,
386, 387, 397, 429, 469,
482, 533, 549, 558, 588,
590, 606–616, 618, 621,
622, 624, 629, 630, 632,
633, 641, 650, 658–660
activism, 101, 104, 179, 244, 288,
289, 299, 300, 306, 307,
426, 469, 479, 482, 483,
567, 570, 602, 610–612,
630, 634, 653, 657
activist, 179
activity, 251
acumen, 650
adaptability, 23, 93, 148, 168, 178,
556
adaptation, 656

addition, 3, 16, 25, 34, 46, 49, 51,
54, 60, 83, 90, 97, 99, 102,
104, 107, 108, 111, 113,
114, 127, 134, 136, 141,
143, 157, 158, 167, 183,
187, 190, 191, 194, 203,
213, 218, 225, 228–230,
232, 236, 239, 240, 247,
250, 253, 254, 263, 265,
266, 273, 275, 278, 284,
287, 293, 299, 300, 304,
316, 318, 320, 322, 323,
332–334, 336, 342, 348,
350–352, 361, 367, 368,
371, 373, 375, 383, 395,
398, 409, 410, 414, 418,
425, 426, 431, 433, 435,
462, 469, 474, 475, 477,
478, 481, 491, 499, 510,
532, 535, 536, 538, 541,
544, 546, 547, 549, 553,
554, 556, 558, 571, 585,
586, 588, 591, 592, 596,
598, 607, 612, 618–620,
624, 625, 629, 631, 637,
639, 644, 646, 650, 654,
658
address, 56, 83, 107, 129, 161, 215,
232, 246, 260, 267, 276,
286, 289, 298, 303,
306–309, 317, 361, 371,
462, 549, 590, 607,
610–615, 618, 626, 640,
649, 653, 656, 658
addressal, 602
adherence, 226, 410
admiration, 46, 160, 174, 382, 457,
473, 474
adolescence, 290

adoption, 161
adrenaline, 96, 154, 157–160, 167,
    357, 365, 498, 518, 521,
    538, 552, 595
adult, 465
adulthood, 290
advance, 53, 138, 237, 349, 644
advancement, 642
advantage, 31, 41, 63, 456, 502
advent, 235, 514
adventure, 55, 67, 159–162, 167,
    168, 369, 374, 388, 429,
    528, 538, 540, 596
adventurer, 512
adversity, 34, 83, 84, 94, 238, 246,
    249, 297, 301, 373, 455,
    546, 571, 574, 591, 611
advertising, 581
advice, 2, 13, 16, 18, 74, 82, 141,
    148, 241, 252, 257, 263,
    273, 327, 439, 453, 456,
    501, 503, 557
advocacy, 102, 136, 137, 213, 247,
    248, 289, 296, 298, 303,
    305, 309, 321, 427, 437,
    576, 587, 589, 590, 593,
    609, 619, 620, 625, 627,
    635, 637, 639, 650, 651,
    653, 654, 656, 660
advocate, 75, 107, 136, 161, 213,
    245, 246, 284, 287, 290,
    291, 294, 296, 297, 300,
    303–306, 308, 314, 326,
    426, 469, 481, 482, 575,
    587, 591–593, 597, 600,
    606–608, 612, 617, 619,
    620, 625, 628, 637, 650,
    658, 660
aesthetic, 117, 527, 529, 531, 532,

537, 540, 569
affinity, 4, 8, 9, 374, 560
Africa, 164
age, 1, 3–5, 12, 14, 16, 30, 31, 41,
    45, 59, 62, 64, 103, 141,
    168, 194, 196, 198, 221,
    235, 290, 439, 441, 448,
    449, 456, 502, 530, 570,
    579, 581–584, 653
agency, 643
aggression, 20, 96, 108, 191, 333,
    342
agriculture, 640
Ai Weiwei, 306, 307
aid, 199, 301
aim, 58, 102, 180, 202, 244, 264,
    298, 301, 309, 394, 609,
    617, 619, 623, 625, 633,
    635, 636, 638, 641
air, 124, 132, 159, 311, 487, 518,
    576
Alan, 24
Alan Smithson, 24
album, 45, 53, 59, 64, 76, 94, 95,
    134, 181, 195, 271, 274,
    321, 374, 375, 380, 384,
    385, 388, 389, 391, 392,
    422, 424, 425, 448, 450,
    500, 501, 525–529, 531,
    534–537, 540, 596
Alex, 469
alignment, 616, 622
Alison Wonderland, 420
Alison Wonderland's, 420
alley, 173
allocation, 616, 622
allure, 27, 118, 123, 124, 380, 444,
    568, 569, 575, 577
along, 29, 47, 73, 78, 94, 110, 172,

210, 259, 262, 273, 311,
380, 389, 398, 399, 401,
416, 417, 421, 440, 443,
452, 521, 620, 640, 647

alter, 212, 567

alternative, 20, 49, 191, 236, 262,
385, 495

amalgamation, 538, 545

Amanda Palmer, 44

ambassador, 156, 170–172

ambassadorship, 171, 172

ambiance, 161, 541

ambition, 447

analog, 341, 347, 515

analysis, 60, 206, 493, 516

anchor, 243, 373

Andy J. Miller, 453

anecdote, 441, 442

anger, 373

animal, 95, 361, 368, 633

anniversary, 450

anonymity, 27, 118–120, 124, 126,
127, 132, 133, 137, 138,
346, 405, 529, 568, 573,
579, 585, 653

anthem, 49, 76, 98, 108, 176, 179,
249, 353, 365, 383, 398,
463, 560

anticipation, 22, 56, 57, 61, 78, 119,
124, 139, 159, 203, 258,
337, 354, 372, 379, 380,
397, 400, 404, 413, 419,
485, 501, 523, 528, 534,
538, 561, 562

anxiety, 75, 242, 246–248, 251, 304,
463, 552, 590, 625, 638

Aphex Twin, 430

app, 202, 640

appeal, 25, 31, 103, 104, 118, 124,
214, 279, 283, 314, 370,
379, 381, 385, 477, 480,
481, 522, 552, 564, 578,
581, 645–648, 654

appearance, 106, 128, 132, 295, 298,
343, 407, 586, 597, 653

applause, 140, 311

application, 640

appreciation, 3, 5, 7, 15, 87, 143,
152–154, 157, 159, 164,
169, 171, 207, 223, 224,
227, 256, 307, 313, 316,
317, 322, 325, 380, 396,
414, 450, 457, 472, 474,
519, 544

approach, 1, 9, 11, 19–21, 24, 25,
31–35, 43, 44, 46, 60–62,
64, 65, 68, 69, 81, 84, 86,
87, 92, 97, 113, 122, 126,
130, 131, 136, 140, 150,
151, 157, 161, 164, 177,
183, 184, 186–189, 191,
193, 197, 199, 204, 208,
211, 212, 214, 242, 255,
259, 285, 291–293, 301,
315, 321, 336–338, 341,
342, 344, 351, 364, 368,
369, 381, 385, 388, 391,
392, 407, 412, 420–422,
426–428, 430–434, 442,
450, 453, 454, 456, 458,
460, 462, 467, 470, 476,
478, 479, 483, 485–487,
490–495, 498, 499, 502,
509, 510, 513, 514, 526,
534, 538, 539, 545, 547,
550, 554, 556, 558–561,
565, 566, 572, 578,

581–584, 593, 594, 596,
597, 599, 600, 602, 619,
622, 628, 629, 632, 645,
649, 657
approachability, 131
appropriation, 157
aptitude, 14, 49, 331
area, 17, 18, 23, 162, 173, 212, 226,
301, 303, 349, 430, 455,
462, 605, 613, 623, 624,
626, 639, 646
arena, 486
Ariana Grande, 49
Armin van, 58
army, 139
arrangement, 1, 12, 180, 189, 263,
333, 337, 354, 400, 477,
493
array, 259, 515, 519, 551, 582
arsenal, 140, 515, 517
art, 9, 19, 29, 35, 62, 86, 88, 96, 99,
105, 119, 122, 124, 136,
139, 143, 144, 152, 162,
170, 171, 173, 180, 182,
202, 205, 210, 212, 213,
218, 222, 225, 227, 228,
232, 233, 236, 237, 243,
245, 251, 253, 283, 298,
300, 305–308, 320, 321,
328, 344, 361, 379, 426,
433, 434, 453, 462, 463,
483, 503, 509, 511, 513,
514, 521, 522, 526, 530,
532, 534–538, 543, 547,
569, 582, 586, 593, 599,
610–613, 617, 621, 632,
633, 654–656, 660, 661
article, 58, 133
artist, 2, 7, 13, 15–19, 22–25,

27–29, 31, 33–37, 40–42,
45, 47–49, 51, 52, 55–59,
62, 64, 66–69, 71–73,
75–82, 85, 86, 88–90, 94,
95, 98–100, 106, 108, 109,
112, 119–121, 123–127,
130–132, 134, 135, 137,
138, 141, 142, 144, 145,
147, 152, 154, 159, 164,
167–169, 173–178,
180–187, 189–198,
200–209, 214, 215, 221,
223, 228, 231, 233–238,
240–243, 246, 256, 258,
259, 265, 268, 273–277,
279, 283, 287, 293, 295,
298, 306, 311, 314, 315,
319, 320, 323, 331, 332,
336, 338, 339, 343, 346,
351–353, 356, 358, 359,
364, 366, 368, 370, 374,
378–382, 384, 387–392,
396, 398, 404, 405, 409,
410, 413, 414, 416, 418,
420, 422, 424–426,
428–431, 434, 435,
439–441, 446–454, 458,
459, 462, 466, 469–471,
473–477, 480, 483, 485,
486, 497–499, 501–503,
511, 512, 517, 518, 521,
522, 524, 525, 527–540,
542, 544, 547, 550, 557,
559, 561, 562, 567, 568,
572, 576–578, 581–586,
594, 597, 601, 605, 612,
620–624, 626, 628, 632,
633, 644, 648, 650, 651,
654–656, 658

Artist X's, 186
artistry, 20, 31, 71, 79, 108, 114,
  119, 125, 141, 144–146,
  215, 244, 258, 294, 303,
  314, 315, 336, 358, 371,
  373, 407, 425, 445, 446,
  449, 450, 453, 477,
  479–482, 495, 527, 530,
  549, 574, 577, 578, 643,
  646, 650, 653, 659, 660
artwork, 53, 102, 143, 170, 195,
  196, 222, 240, 243, 251,
  252, 307, 310, 316–318,
  322, 325, 374, 449,
  525–529, 531, 534–536,
  539, 540, 543, 544, 596,
  617, 621
ascent, 645
Asia, 152
aspect, 10, 13, 25, 46, 53, 60, 78, 79,
  81, 85, 96, 121, 122, 125,
  126, 128, 130, 136–139,
  147, 165, 168, 171, 195,
  203, 205, 208, 212, 230,
  260, 262, 267, 279, 284,
  321, 327, 344, 354, 369,
  373, 375, 380, 381, 400,
  401, 406, 413–415, 418,
  430, 432, 452, 454, 472,
  477, 480, 482, 491, 492,
  499, 500, 503, 527, 532,
  536, 537, 551, 560, 573,
  574, 580, 581, 585, 629,
  637, 647
aspiration, 437
assessment, 622
asset, 64
assist, 642
assistance, 252, 263, 627, 630, 636,
  643
assistant, 134
association, 636
atmosphere, 13, 22, 23, 55–57, 104,
  110, 120–122, 131, 139,
  140, 152, 162, 163, 171,
  186, 189, 224, 225, 227,
  243, 271, 291, 305, 311,
  317, 353, 361, 365, 391,
  395–398, 404, 406, 408,
  409, 411–413, 415–418,
  457, 465, 467–469, 480,
  518, 519, 522, 532, 540,
  542, 550, 563, 566, 594,
  607, 646, 652
attachment, 54
attack, 82
attempt, 94
attendance, 261, 271, 311, 403
attendee, 54
attention, 5, 11, 12, 18, 19, 23, 25,
  30, 31, 33, 36, 41, 42, 45,
  52, 68, 69, 77, 84, 102,
  117, 119, 121, 128, 134,
  190, 192, 193, 196, 211,
  217, 231, 238, 244, 259,
  261, 272, 274, 289, 303,
  305, 306, 323, 332, 333,
  335, 342, 361–363,
  367–369, 374, 375, 391,
  399–401, 415, 417, 420,
  435, 459, 463, 467, 468,
  472, 476–478, 480,
  491–494, 516, 520, 522,
  527, 528, 531, 535, 536,
  542, 545, 549, 558, 562,
  564, 567, 570, 578, 587,
  606, 610, 622, 637, 645,
  650, 652

attitude, 85, 457
attribute, 448, 469
audience, 2, 16, 18, 19, 22, 23, 27,
        28, 30, 32, 33, 37, 40, 41,
        45–47, 49–53, 55–67, 69,
        70, 72, 75–77, 79, 80, 82,
        83, 85–89, 92–94, 99,
        101, 106, 108, 110–114,
        117–128, 130, 131, 136,
        138–141, 143, 145, 152,
        168, 171, 178, 183, 187,
        188, 190, 192–195, 197,
        198, 202–204, 208–214,
        217, 221, 222, 227–229,
        234, 236, 238, 246, 247,
        250, 251, 254, 255, 258,
        261, 263, 272–274, 279,
        287–289, 291, 292,
        297–299, 303, 309, 311,
        315, 316, 319, 320, 323,
        332, 333, 336, 338, 340,
        343, 348, 352–354, 358,
        364, 371–373, 381, 387,
        391, 393, 395–418, 426,
        429, 431, 433–437, 440,
        444–446, 448–450, 454,
        456, 457, 462, 466, 471,
        475, 478, 481, 485–488,
        490, 492, 493, 498–503,
        505, 506, 511, 512,
        514–518, 522, 524–532,
        534–544, 546–549, 551,
        555, 556, 564, 566, 568,
        570, 573–575, 577–583,
        585, 586, 588–590, 592,
        597, 598, 601, 607, 609,
        612, 613, 616, 624, 627,
        629, 630, 637, 645,
        647–649, 652, 654, 659

audio, 62, 67, 120, 198, 400, 402,
        404, 406, 436, 498, 514,
        516, 517, 541, 551
aura, 27, 124, 524
Australia, 154, 325, 469
authentic, 31, 34, 35, 41, 53, 55, 73,
        80, 83, 86, 89, 90, 106,
        126, 143, 155, 247, 320,
        325, 342, 371, 404, 444,
        451, 453, 454, 499–501,
        569, 578, 650
authenticity, 11, 28, 32, 33, 43, 50,
        53, 64, 71–73, 76, 83–85,
        88, 91, 93, 107, 111, 125,
        126, 148, 149, 151, 153,
        169, 243, 255, 256, 265,
        292, 294, 295, 366, 394,
        426, 442, 446, 448, 449,
        451–453, 458, 467, 468,
        481, 483, 488, 490, 494,
        496, 499, 500, 512, 547,
        548, 557, 566, 567, 573,
        574, 576, 577, 580, 585,
        586, 591, 602, 606, 607,
        622, 643, 649, 653, 655
authority, 522
automation, 562
availability, 63, 596
avenue, 156, 183, 236, 592
award, 77, 634
awareness, 52, 71, 75, 86, 100–105,
        107, 130, 136, 137, 144,
        161, 162, 171, 179, 194,
        205, 206, 208, 209, 212,
        213, 215, 224, 230–233,
        239, 244, 245, 247, 251,
        253, 254, 260, 262, 264,
        278, 284, 286, 287,
        289–291, 295–303, 305,

306, 308, 309, 318, 321,
324, 326, 361, 362, 371,
386, 387, 425, 426, 428,
429, 437, 447, 448, 462,
466, 469, 479, 481–483,
488, 533, 548, 554, 558,
567, 570, 572, 575, 576,
586–588, 591–593, 599,
601, 606–608, 610–618,
620–628, 630, 632–640,
642, 644, 646, 649, 650,
652, 654, 658–660
awe, 121, 160, 177, 202, 203, 372,
397, 408, 412, 417, 512,
518

backbone, 316, 333
backdrop, 99, 163
background, 119, 129, 170, 180,
221, 325, 417, 435, 568,
571, 585, 600, 602, 635
backstage, 153, 169, 173, 537
backup, 56
balance, 25, 31, 57, 74, 85–88,
90–92, 96, 117, 125, 126,
133–135, 145, 147, 148,
160, 180, 181, 189, 191,
199, 210, 271, 333, 348,
389, 433, 443, 445, 493,
498–501, 552, 553, 560,
562, 563, 568, 587, 632,
643
balancing, 31, 74, 75, 79, 80, 85–87,
125, 126, 133–135, 145,
148, 185, 440, 500, 562
band, 4, 17, 31, 49, 178, 191, 333
banger, 361, 420, 452
Banksy, 306
banner, 217, 218, 326, 522

banter, 152
bar, 172, 363, 365
barometer, 380
barrier, 123, 416
base, 25, 26, 37, 46, 54, 61–63, 68,
69, 73, 80, 102, 105, 124,
126, 156, 168–170, 183,
193, 196, 210, 217, 222,
223, 227, 228, 241, 242,
244, 263, 271, 278, 287,
294, 296, 304, 305, 327,
342, 343, 359, 364–366,
383, 391, 392, 440, 442,
452, 457, 460, 461,
475–477, 485, 543, 544,
556, 557, 570–572, 582,
584, 585, 588, 589, 601,
607–609, 620–622, 624,
626, 633, 647, 652, 656,
658
basic, 10, 127
basis, 316, 635
Bass, 561
bass, 11, 24, 31, 32, 48, 70, 71,
75–77, 84, 95–97, 99,
105, 108, 114, 127,
173–175, 178, 182, 183,
188, 192, 204, 222, 238,
248, 250, 251, 257, 259,
291, 331–335, 340, 350,
351, 353, 358–361, 363,
365, 366, 369, 372, 375,
378, 381, 384, 385, 392,
397, 420–422, 474,
476–478, 480, 485, 490,
491, 524, 545, 548,
550–557, 560–563, 573,
575, 576, 584, 644, 645
bassline, 368, 383, 395, 561, 562

Bassnectar, 2, 384
battle, 72, 366
beach, 101, 102, 232, 244, 482, 608,
    612, 620, 640
beacon, 72, 138, 466, 547, 565, 586
bear, 27–29, 47, 58, 59, 66, 71, 113,
    117–121, 123–129, 132,
    137, 138, 154, 195, 212,
    225, 295, 298, 343, 346,
    384, 400, 405, 409, 426,
    442, 483, 487, 501, 517,
    519, 521–526, 528, 529,
    531–533, 535, 537, 538,
    543, 546, 567, 569,
    572–579, 585, 586, 597,
    653
bearstep, 155, 341, 342
beat, 138, 139, 153, 212, 400, 401,
    408, 541
BeatDrop, 274
beauty, 101, 122, 127, 154–160,
    163, 167, 168, 178, 288,
    297, 303, 356, 358, 388,
    429, 512, 528, 563, 621,
    623
bed, 242
bedroom, 1, 6, 439, 529, 557
beginning, 10, 23, 29, 141, 142, 185,
    251, 276, 350, 492, 529
behavior, 162, 226, 271, 283, 396
being, 3, 19, 30, 31, 50, 53, 55, 74,
    75, 88, 90–93, 103, 107,
    123, 127, 128, 132, 134,
    136, 138, 147, 148, 173,
    210, 218, 222, 223, 226,
    233, 235, 246–248, 250,
    252–255, 284, 289–291,
    297, 300, 302, 304, 306,
    308, 322, 323, 340, 370,

372, 373, 379, 392, 398,
    405, 410, 418, 441, 442,
    444, 445, 448, 450, 451,
    455, 461, 465, 469, 470,
    482, 493, 499, 501, 509,
    523, 536, 544, 570, 573,
    575, 587, 590–594, 607,
    608, 612–615, 617, 620,
    622–625, 627, 628,
    635–638, 660
Belgium, 70
belief, 2, 4, 12, 14, 16, 33, 71, 73, 74,
    83–85, 142, 243, 325, 327,
    356, 357, 439, 449, 454,
    465, 503, 612, 621, 628
belonging, 53, 105, 106, 113, 118,
    119, 124, 128–130, 140,
    144, 171, 217, 218,
    220–223, 226, 227,
    231–235, 241, 243, 244,
    248–251, 253–256, 271,
    276, 284, 291, 294, 298,
    305, 310, 312, 316–319,
    322, 323, 325, 327–329,
    394, 398, 416–418, 438,
    449, 457, 461, 469, 470,
    472, 483, 524, 525, 532,
    533, 539, 549, 558, 559,
    568, 571, 573, 580, 581,
    586, 591, 598–601, 608,
    616, 619, 654, 657, 660
benchmark, 556
bending, 24–26, 99, 157, 192, 210,
    285, 334, 346, 421, 561
benefit, 17, 41, 82, 136, 267, 287,
    301, 620, 623, 630, 651,
    659
Benga, 8
Berlin, 164, 167

betterment, 302, 626

bias, 138

Bill, 24

Bill Brewster, 24

Billie Holiday, 20

biodiversity, 287, 587, 617,
623–625, 635

birth, 1, 27, 95, 257, 363, 517, 554

bit, 396

bite, 368

blend, 15, 18, 22, 25, 31, 32, 49, 76,
77, 87, 105, 106, 108, 114,
122, 152, 155, 161,
174–176, 180, 186, 187,
192, 199, 201, 203, 208,
213, 222, 233, 238, 244,
258, 279, 293, 297, 319,
341, 344, 349, 350, 352,
353, 359, 363, 365–369,
374, 382–385, 391, 402,
421, 427, 428, 462, 463,
467, 474, 479, 480, 482,
485–487, 490–492, 494,
497, 498, 500, 515, 522,
537, 553, 555, 560, 562,
564, 573, 575, 577, 578,
584, 594, 600, 644–649,
651, 654, 656

blending, 11, 20, 80, 109, 113, 122,
139, 155, 178, 181, 185,
187, 198, 206–208, 214,
297, 331, 332, 334, 336,
344, 346, 348, 359, 364,
370, 374, 383, 398, 420,
422, 429, 432, 435, 447,
476, 478, 481, 485, 495,
502, 524, 538, 547, 556,
560, 565, 571, 572, 574,
597, 645, 652, 657

bliss, 395

block, 34, 35, 275, 442, 509, 510

blockchain, 271, 583, 584

blueprint, 265, 657

board, 142, 520

Bob Dylan, 306

Bobby Owsinski, 8, 583

body, 159, 246, 351, 396, 569, 590

boldness, 96, 206

bond, 27, 53, 125–127, 131,
141–145, 147, 153, 154,
168, 169, 217, 219, 221,
222, 224, 227, 234, 237,
240, 245, 246, 253, 255,
256, 265–268, 271, 310,
313, 317, 320, 322, 324,
327–329, 370, 398, 410,
415, 416, 447, 449–451,
454, 464, 470–474, 512,
518, 521, 530, 532, 558,
569, 648, 649, 654

bone, 49, 337, 359

book, 35, 44, 133, 157, 277, 396,
456, 583

booth, 121, 518, 577

bound, 253, 573

boundary, 2, 6, 22, 31, 49, 68, 78,
109, 184, 201, 342, 358,
473, 486, 530, 554

box, 6, 11, 35, 44, 74, 97, 111, 114,
150, 176, 194, 196, 211,
285, 338, 343, 350, 364,
454, 459, 462, 467, 473,
478, 481, 486, 487, 510,
513, 547, 549, 564–566,
594, 596, 600, 649

boy, 1

brainstorm, 302

brainstorming, 138, 498, 526, 535

brand, 41, 47, 51, 52, 55, 58–60, 63,
66, 68, 94, 107, 126, 132,
137, 195–197, 222, 260,
273, 323, 400, 409, 433,
437, 500, 502, 526, 529,
534–537, 541, 558,
576–578, 606
branding, 59, 60, 62, 64, 195, 197,
212, 567
Brazil, 154, 155, 163, 325
break, 7, 9, 11, 32, 34, 35, 45, 50, 78,
107, 119, 158, 164, 171,
178, 182, 186, 190, 205,
214, 215, 243, 247, 254,
265, 278, 290, 292, 293,
299, 300, 304, 306, 309,
336, 337, 339, 340, 357,
367, 388, 392, 432, 447,
464, 472, 481–483, 497,
498, 506, 509, 510, 512,
513, 524, 539, 548, 554,
558, 568, 569, 572, 576,
577, 579, 581, 597, 599,
600, 620, 623, 625, 636,
644, 649, 653
breaking, 21, 27, 30, 34, 46, 48, 72,
103, 106, 107, 109, 112,
113, 130, 131, 140, 149,
177, 193, 198, 215, 222,
232, 235, 265, 291,
294–296, 298, 304, 326,
364, 371, 372, 425, 462,
466, 467, 472, 475, 483,
485, 486, 496, 525, 530,
563, 565, 570, 574, 575,
578, 580, 590, 595, 597,
599, 601, 619, 630, 643,
644, 656, 657, 660
breakneck, 337

breakthrough, 48, 497–499
breath, 22, 400
breathability, 128
breathing, 592
breeding, 106, 340
bridge, 49, 129, 130, 156, 157, 171,
175, 177, 205, 276, 283,
306, 325, 539, 545, 556,
575, 585, 592, 599, 610,
645
brush, 543
bubble, 176
budget, 261
build, 2, 4, 16, 30, 36, 41, 42, 44, 50,
58, 59, 61, 63, 70, 93, 106,
153, 168, 190, 197, 199,
217, 219, 254, 261, 270,
272, 273, 328, 337, 375,
408, 413, 444, 473, 476,
500, 502, 503, 506, 561,
564, 579, 581, 591, 593,
650, 655
building, 7, 10, 15, 30, 35, 41,
44–46, 53, 55, 56, 63, 84,
91, 124, 131, 137, 139,
142, 147, 159, 170, 180,
184, 189, 190, 205, 206,
220, 226, 233, 278, 297,
318, 322, 361, 414, 415,
440, 444, 475, 478, 500,
501, 503, 529, 532, 543,
566, 590, 616
bungee, 157
burden, 74, 290
business, 15, 16, 30, 43, 46, 48, 86,
443, 478, 500, 501, 650
buzz, 47, 51, 54, 55, 60, 61, 68, 77,
196, 227, 229, 230, 258,
501

buzzword, 452
byproduct, 445

cake, 154
call, 57, 118, 152, 304, 306, 361,
    387, 395, 396, 403, 411,
    416, 418, 460, 606
calm, 250, 366, 372, 592
camaraderie, 105, 110, 142, 189,
    217, 218, 223, 226, 229,
    231, 233, 235, 236, 239,
    243, 257, 263, 265, 276,
    297, 328, 370, 396, 405,
    411, 414, 418, 450,
    468–470, 473–475, 520,
    521, 654
camera, 397, 521, 543
camp, 161
campaign, 162, 251, 252, 501, 622,
    627, 630, 638
camping, 158, 161
Canada, 469
canvas, 121, 307, 409
capacity, 619, 620
car, 158, 465
carbon, 209, 210, 428, 633, 640
care, 74, 75, 90, 92, 93, 133–135,
    138, 226, 235, 246, 247,
    290, 297, 302, 362, 397,
    399, 410, 445, 510, 511,
    591–593, 609, 622,
    636–638
career, 2, 7, 12–14, 16–18, 22, 24,
    27–29, 31, 33, 35, 36, 41,
    42, 44–46, 48, 50, 51, 53,
    56, 58–60, 62, 64, 66, 69,
    70, 74–79, 82, 85, 86, 91,
    93–95, 98, 117, 118, 120,
    125, 126, 130, 133–135,

    141, 142, 145, 147, 148,
    153, 157–159, 168,
    172–174, 177, 178, 183,
    190–193, 201, 204, 208,
    210, 217, 218, 220, 223,
    227, 228, 230, 231, 235,
    239, 241, 242, 252, 257,
    258, 268, 272–274, 276,
    277, 279, 286, 288, 308,
    314, 316, 317, 331, 332,
    347, 349–353, 358, 374,
    375, 381, 382, 386, 388,
    391, 392, 399, 405–407,
    424–426, 434, 436, 438,
    439, 441–444, 446,
    449–451, 454, 455,
    457–459, 464, 465, 471,
    472, 483, 485, 499, 500,
    502, 517–519, 521,
    528–530, 554, 576, 581,
    583–585, 595, 599, 612,
    616, 620, 621, 628, 650,
    657, 658
Caribbean, 626
Caroline McHugh, 453
case, 91, 130, 134, 250, 528, 534,
    571
catalog, 351, 378
catalyst, 8, 25, 40, 82, 83, 97, 102,
    105, 148, 163, 167, 182,
    213, 215, 228, 237, 243,
    257, 293, 297, 308, 326,
    361, 373, 384, 387, 469,
    509, 512, 548, 549, 556,
    559, 564, 587, 597, 602,
    606, 610, 630, 653, 658
categorization, 25, 26, 339, 462
catharsis, 34, 111, 123, 127, 373,
    398, 417, 418, 469, 574,

592
cause, 44, 136, 147, 206, 226, 252,
     260, 261, 266, 289, 302,
     308, 587, 589, 610, 618,
     621, 622, 625, 627, 632
celebration, 157, 171, 250, 285, 286,
     311, 314, 325, 343, 392,
     544
celebrity, 147, 483, 525, 549, 569,
     575, 585–587, 653
center, 577
centeredness, 458
centerpiece, 538
century, 112, 553, 645
ceremony, 174
challenge, 25, 30, 31, 35, 39, 52, 71,
     73, 74, 80, 85, 86, 88, 89,
     106, 107, 114, 130, 134,
     147, 151, 157, 164, 167,
     168, 171, 176, 192, 258,
     259, 265, 278, 285, 289,
     292, 295, 297, 305–308,
     327, 339, 349, 351, 389,
     424, 425, 427, 433, 442,
     446, 454, 468, 474, 478,
     486, 487, 493, 497, 498,
     509, 536, 539, 547, 548,
     552, 565, 568, 572, 578,
     589, 590, 596, 597, 599,
     600, 606, 607, 610, 611,
     615, 616, 653
champion, 83, 194, 308, 478, 591,
     608, 616, 652
chance, 34, 41, 42, 65, 70, 82, 172,
     174, 183, 186, 196, 220,
     222, 224, 232, 263, 264,
     279, 295, 397, 413, 425,
     442, 471, 511
change, 71, 79, 81, 89, 101–104,
     106, 107, 129, 130,
     135–137, 148, 161, 171,
     172, 179, 205, 208, 212,
     213, 215, 218, 223, 228,
     231–233, 239, 244–246,
     249, 250, 253, 254, 256,
     262, 278, 284–291, 295,
     296, 298–300, 303–306,
     308–311, 318, 323, 324,
     326, 327, 361, 362, 366,
     371, 426, 427, 429, 431,
     434, 437, 444, 445, 448,
     449, 455, 458, 462, 463,
     466, 469, 478, 479, 482,
     483, 488, 507, 533,
     547–549, 554, 555, 558,
     559, 567, 570, 571, 576,
     586–590, 594, 598–602,
     606–626, 628–632, 634,
     635, 638–641, 644, 646,
     649–653, 657–661
changer, 645
channel, 63, 117, 123, 238, 321, 361,
     373, 388, 441, 454
chaos, 90, 93, 122
chapter, 76, 424, 442, 465, 524, 657,
     658
character, 10, 119, 125, 126, 317,
     341, 436, 457, 515, 568
characteristic, 332, 351, 457, 548,
     550, 554
charisma, 56, 57
charity, 44, 104, 105, 107, 205, 215,
     230, 231, 244, 251–253,
     260–262, 266, 285, 287,
     297, 298, 309–311, 318,
     321, 324, 326, 328, 361,
     466, 471, 601, 613, 621,
     628, 632, 659

chart, 36, 49, 75, 76, 90, 92, 99, 134,
172, 267, 352–354, 369,
391, 426, 437, 445, 448,
557
chat, 65, 169, 203, 236, 275
check, 273
chemistry, 180
child, 3, 5, 441
childhood, 3, 290, 439, 441
choice, 59, 118, 120, 137, 386, 522,
572, 577, 585
choir, 4
chord, 20, 96, 372, 387, 432, 463,
563, 647
choreography, 67, 532
chorus, 414, 515
Christopher Mercer, 32
cinema, 429
cinematography, 67
circle, 142, 147, 229
circuit, 58
city, 1, 513, 520
clapping, 396
clarity, 158, 333, 354
classic, 25, 44, 342, 359, 515
clean, 105, 232, 253, 288, 301, 321,
469, 589, 612, 620, 634
cleanup, 102, 162, 640
click, 236
climate, 101, 161, 179, 287, 308,
362, 576, 587, 611, 617,
620, 621, 625, 626, 632,
635, 650, 660
climax, 311
climbing, 158, 160, 167
Clint Mansell, 9
clothing, 105, 195, 232, 252, 397,
569, 577, 579
club, 22, 151–153, 405, 477, 563

co, 260
coherence, 375, 498
cohesion, 25
cohesiveness, 25
collaborate, 17, 34, 41, 43, 52, 57,
70, 74, 87, 99, 169, 173,
181, 185, 189, 190, 194,
196, 202, 210, 215, 232,
253, 260, 263, 265, 266,
275, 318, 319, 322, 359,
379, 385, 391, 406, 425,
428, 458, 460, 464, 471,
496, 502, 503, 509, 516,
547, 584, 643, 652, 656
collaboration, 2, 3, 11, 14, 16, 17, 25,
34–36, 42–44, 48, 49, 51,
52, 55, 68–70, 75, 76, 81,
84, 98–101, 107, 108,
113–115, 127, 139, 152,
153, 155, 157, 163,
172–179, 181–187,
189–193, 196, 204–206,
214, 215, 230, 253, 254,
258, 259, 262, 264–268,
271, 273, 274, 276, 279,
281, 283, 284, 286, 291,
292, 295–298, 303, 308,
314, 317, 319–321, 324,
333, 337, 339, 343, 359,
360, 364, 367, 374, 389,
393, 394, 420–422, 424,
427, 430, 431, 440, 442,
447, 455, 456, 459, 460,
462, 464, 468, 473–476,
478, 479, 483, 485, 486,
488, 494, 496, 497, 499,
505–507, 509, 520, 528,
536, 537, 542–544, 547,
552, 554, 560, 566, 567,

582, 588, 595, 599, 602,
618, 620–622, 627, 630,
632, 638–640, 642, 644,
656
collaborator, 42, 75, 186, 189, 442,
460, 467, 495, 496, 506
collection, 10, 517, 518, 548
collective, 35, 78, 102, 119, 132, 155,
168, 185, 187, 196, 205,
218, 222, 224, 230,
232–234, 240, 244, 245,
250, 252, 254, 258,
265–268, 279, 283–285,
287, 302, 304, 306, 314,
315, 317, 318, 320, 324,
326, 361, 386, 387, 398,
413, 415, 421, 431, 450,
455, 472, 473, 482, 507,
510, 523, 544, 588, 589,
592, 609, 611, 616, 621,
626, 641, 655
college, 242, 365, 465
color, 528, 544
combat, 30, 298, 308, 362, 617, 620,
621, 625, 634, 635
combination, 48, 49, 55, 74, 96, 108,
114, 128, 130, 131, 178,
212, 250, 291, 332, 334,
359, 361, 365, 368, 373,
385, 395, 399, 402, 406,
413, 417, 477, 492, 494,
506, 522, 527, 535, 540,
543, 550, 563, 607, 648
comfort, 35, 37, 90, 97, 128, 157,
160, 164, 167, 168, 174,
176, 177, 183, 191, 210,
236, 241, 242, 246, 248,
258, 279, 292, 336, 338,
343, 366, 373, 388, 432,

435, 445, 455, 456, 465,
469, 474, 482, 494, 505,
510, 512, 590, 592, 598,
636, 653, 657
comment, 143
commentary, 307, 371, 372, 607
commercial, 31, 75, 80, 85–90, 353,
364, 368–370, 378, 440,
448, 449, 451, 453,
499–501, 584, 650
commitment, 15, 19, 21, 23, 25, 33,
47, 52, 67, 71, 76, 79–81,
84, 86, 97, 99, 102–104,
106, 107, 127–130, 132,
135, 136, 141, 143, 145,
146, 157, 171, 178, 185,
187, 194, 205, 211–213,
218, 228, 230–232, 234,
239, 241, 244, 247, 252,
254, 256, 260, 264, 272,
278, 286, 287, 293–295,
300, 302, 304, 308, 309,
311, 317–319, 322, 324,
326, 327, 339, 341–343,
351, 363, 369, 371, 381,
382, 387, 390, 393, 401,
405, 407, 425–427, 437,
438, 442–444, 447, 450,
452, 458–460, 466–468,
471–473, 477, 482, 485,
487, 488, 490, 494, 496,
497, 501, 516, 517, 524,
539, 546, 548, 554, 555,
559, 564–566, 570–573,
576, 578, 580, 585–587,
589, 593, 597, 599–602,
606, 607, 609, 612, 616,
618, 620–622, 624, 625,
627, 628, 630, 632, 635,

637, 640, 644, 647,
649–660
communication, 36, 63, 86, 92, 126,
130, 131, 133, 134, 143,
147, 148, 181, 184, 187,
189–191, 196, 240, 255,
262, 282, 389, 473, 535,
580, 582, 608, 616, 622
community, 2, 29, 39, 43–45, 47, 49,
51–55, 63–65, 72, 75, 76,
83, 84, 92, 96, 102–107,
110, 113, 115, 118–121,
123–125, 127–132, 136,
138, 142–145, 152, 156,
162, 164, 168–171, 174,
179, 191, 192, 196,
204–206, 208, 213–215,
217–237, 240–246,
248–254, 256, 257, 260,
262–269, 271–279,
282–286, 291–295, 297,
298, 300–302, 304, 305,
307–329, 342, 346, 353,
361, 367, 370, 379–381,
383, 386, 388, 391, 392,
394, 398, 399, 404, 412,
414, 416–418, 425–427,
431, 433, 437, 438, 440,
442, 447–451, 455–458,
462–467, 469–479,
481–483, 486–488, 496,
497, 501, 506, 507, 518,
520, 523, 524, 527, 532,
539, 543, 544, 546–549,
551–555, 558, 559, 566,
567, 569–574, 579–581,
584–586, 589–591,
593–605, 607–610,
612–615, 617, 619, 621,

622, 624, 626, 629, 630,
632, 634, 636, 639, 640,
642, 644, 650–653, 655,
656, 658, 660
companion, 536, 592
companionship, 327
company, 394, 640
compassion, 137, 234, 301, 310,
361, 443, 465, 608, 614
compensation, 263
competition, 257, 274, 446, 450, 552
competitiveness, 84
complement, 68, 100, 121, 139, 337,
400, 411, 429, 491, 506,
541, 582, 593
complex, 19, 20, 26, 46, 148, 182,
191, 289, 305, 306, 332,
347, 348, 366, 367, 373,
381, 401, 409, 432, 477,
487, 491, 499, 518, 555,
561, 590, 593
complexity, 22, 113, 164, 182, 183,
333, 335, 492, 524
component, 210, 262, 467, 528, 535
composition, 4, 12, 15, 19, 40, 112,
453, 454, 491, 493, 514,
516, 535, 536, 544, 642
compression, 354, 562
compromise, 36, 73, 83, 88, 92, 147,
181, 189–191, 451, 499,
500, 650
compromising, 79, 82, 86, 88, 587
computer, 493, 519
concept, 78, 100, 120, 133, 175, 203,
386, 449, 524, 534, 535,
567, 653
conceptualization, 526
concern, 103, 624
concert, 23, 120, 123, 152, 164, 194,

202, 203, 219, 236, 243,
271, 310, 311, 317, 365,
373, 397–399, 406,
416–418, 435, 447, 465,
544, 618
conclusion, 9, 14, 15, 21, 26, 35, 36,
53, 73, 75, 78, 81, 85, 86,
90, 98, 104, 108, 118, 120,
124, 126, 129, 130, 135,
136, 138, 141, 142, 151,
153, 165, 168, 172, 177,
179, 182, 187, 188, 190,
191, 212, 215, 218, 220,
229, 231, 235, 237, 239,
245, 249, 251, 254, 256,
264, 265, 268, 271, 278,
289, 298, 300, 305, 309,
319, 320, 332, 336, 337,
339, 342, 343, 346, 365,
366, 368, 370, 372, 373,
375, 382, 383, 392, 394,
399, 401, 404, 407, 417,
418, 425, 427, 428, 431,
438, 449, 463, 467, 468,
472, 476, 477, 479, 482,
483, 485, 486, 494, 503,
511, 514, 525, 542, 544,
546, 549, 556, 564, 568,
571, 572, 574, 576, 578,
581, 586, 597, 607, 613,
635, 644, 648, 650, 651,
653, 657, 658, 661
conduct, 493
conduit, 27, 28, 118, 123, 126, 127,
250, 523, 568, 600
conference, 41, 172
confetti, 402, 409
confidence, 2, 14, 16, 17, 22, 30, 56,
57, 74, 82, 107, 243, 249,

250, 252, 439, 497, 503
conformity, 340, 452, 464, 586
connectedness, 469
connection, 19, 26, 27, 43, 51, 53,
55–57, 61, 62, 64, 66, 70,
76, 78, 101, 110–112,
117–119, 121, 123–128,
130, 131, 138–145, 152,
156, 158, 161, 165, 169,
171, 180, 184, 188, 194,
195, 199, 202, 212, 217,
223, 224, 229, 233–235,
239, 240, 242, 243, 247,
248, 250, 254–257, 261,
265, 267, 278, 284, 291,
293, 296, 306, 310, 311,
314–317, 320, 323,
327–329, 341, 342, 352,
355, 356, 362, 365, 366,
370–374, 380, 381, 383,
387, 388, 398, 404, 407,
409, 411, 414–418, 426,
429, 431, 433, 441, 442,
447–449, 454, 457, 461,
464, 465, 469, 470, 474,
477, 482, 487, 501, 517,
519, 520, 522–525,
527–530, 535, 536, 538,
539, 542, 544, 563, 568,
570, 573, 581, 584–586,
601, 609, 629, 648, 649,
656, 659
consciousness, 136, 210–212, 218,
315, 428, 437, 523, 549,
570, 629, 655
conservation, 71, 86, 100–103, 107,
130, 135, 137, 144, 161,
162, 171, 179, 194, 205,
208, 209, 212, 213, 218,

224, 231, 239, 244, 245,
253, 254, 260, 264, 284,
286–289, 295, 296, 298,
300, 302, 303, 305,
308–310, 318, 321, 326,
361, 371, 386, 387, 425,
426, 428, 429, 437, 445,
462, 466, 469, 479, 481,
482, 488, 530, 533, 549,
554, 558, 570, 575,
586–590, 601, 606, 608,
611–625, 628–630,
632–635, 640, 644, 646,
649–652, 654, 656,
658–660
consideration, 85, 86, 145, 622
consistency, 25, 66, 369, 536
consumer, 288
consumerism, 306
consumption, 67
contact, 56, 57, 303, 403, 415, 534
contemplation, 372
contemporary, 114, 429, 522, 524,
551
content, 30, 45, 50–52, 54, 59,
63–65, 67, 101, 105, 128,
143, 169, 170, 196, 227,
236, 261, 271, 277, 316,
317, 351, 409, 454, 531,
570, 580, 582–584, 592,
596
contention, 77
context, 50, 155, 179, 539
continuity, 536
contract, 272
contrast, 333, 334, 337, 372, 387,
518, 538, 540, 563
contribution, 95, 278, 328, 549, 557,
559, 561, 621, 644

control, 85, 107, 121, 202, 596, 643
conversation, 153, 172–174, 189,
246, 459, 520, 576
conviction, 614
cooperation, 259
coordination, 261
core, 26, 79, 92, 95, 97, 125, 126,
199, 208, 210, 234, 261,
314, 319, 324, 333, 350,
381, 416, 433, 434, 454,
516, 548, 552, 614, 616,
619, 641, 642, 654
corner, 103, 104, 152, 325
cornerstone, 84, 112, 242, 457
cost, 30
counseling, 592, 636
counterculture, 569
counterpoint, 333
country, 154, 155, 193, 485
courage, 243, 249, 453
course, 58, 263, 311, 391, 452, 521
cover, 29, 275, 292, 407, 526, 528,
529, 605, 627
coverage, 62, 68
craft, 6, 16, 19, 22, 30, 32, 37, 43,
47, 71, 76, 79, 81, 82, 85,
89, 94, 110, 111, 120, 141,
188, 193, 211, 221, 275,
338, 342, 352, 373, 381,
385, 394, 436–440,
442–444, 447, 455, 459,
467, 480, 482, 501, 502,
513, 522, 529, 561, 645,
657
craftsmanship, 527, 643
creation, 14, 27, 28, 58, 59, 77, 87,
95, 117, 118, 131, 179,
184, 203, 256, 257, 265,
292, 320, 335, 342, 349,

355, 356, 388–390, 392,
394, 431, 434, 473, 511,
516, 521, 525, 529, 534,
536, 537, 540, 542, 559,
621, 642
creativity, 2–4, 6, 7, 11–13, 21, 28,
34–36, 45, 66, 67, 74, 76,
79, 80, 83, 89, 90, 94, 99,
103, 105, 106, 108, 113,
114, 118–121, 124, 125,
127–129, 136, 140, 143,
145, 149, 151, 155, 157,
159, 160, 163–165, 167,
168, 173, 178, 180,
185–187, 194, 196, 198,
200, 204–206, 212, 214,
215, 223, 224, 228, 231,
232, 234, 237–239, 243,
245, 251, 253, 256, 257,
259, 262, 265, 268, 275,
279, 291–294, 296–298,
303, 305, 307, 309, 310,
320, 321, 324, 325, 332,
334, 340, 343, 346, 351,
364, 375, 378, 389, 394,
420, 427, 430, 431, 436,
437, 446, 447, 454–457,
459, 462–464, 468, 472,
473, 479–481, 490, 493,
494, 499–502, 509–511,
513, 519, 532–534, 537,
540, 542–544, 547, 548,
551, 561, 562, 568, 570,
582, 584, 585, 594–597,
602, 604, 613, 615, 617,
619, 634, 639, 643–646,
652, 659
credibility, 71, 273
credit, 248, 643, 657

crew, 154
crisis, 611
criticism, 6, 30, 37, 39, 40, 47, 52,
79, 82–85, 89, 94, 142,
189, 210, 221, 234, 275,
440, 442, 443, 445, 452,
457, 502, 503, 568
cross, 6, 9, 43, 46, 61, 68, 69, 87,
100, 157, 176–178, 181,
195, 207, 298, 299,
343–346, 364, 367, 430,
432, 433, 462, 475, 486,
506, 550, 552, 554, 555,
558, 644, 648, 658
crossover, 25, 70, 113, 279, 481,
564, 570
crowd, 2, 16, 18, 22, 23, 55–58, 73,
88, 121, 127, 139, 140,
144, 152, 153, 164, 213,
284, 294, 311, 317, 335,
353, 354, 365, 373,
395–399, 401, 406,
411–416, 420, 434, 440,
465, 469, 515, 519, 522,
546, 646
cruelty, 361
cry, 130, 386
cue, 348
culture, 9, 129, 153, 165, 225, 226,
231, 275, 293, 298, 317,
325, 326, 364, 455, 456,
462, 524, 525, 549, 551,
552, 556, 568, 570, 571,
574–581, 584, 585, 600,
602, 613, 652, 653, 655,
657
curation, 528
curiosity, 3, 5, 8, 13, 24, 27, 47, 118,
119, 123, 124, 138, 410,

432, 468, 517, 523, 536
curve, 89, 93, 194, 343, 516, 552
custom, 61, 202, 347, 400, 404, 430,
 516
cutthroat, 84
cutting, 32, 33, 67, 80, 99, 110, 152,
 209, 343, 346, 367, 382,
 402, 407, 410, 428, 435,
 447, 477, 495, 513, 514,
 516, 527, 531, 542, 582
cycle, 79, 299

Dale Carnegie, 44
damage, 161
dance, 52, 65, 87, 110, 121, 153,
 155, 224, 251, 311, 321,
 361, 403, 406, 414, 416,
 421, 509, 582, 600, 654
dancefloor, 32, 399
dancing, 395, 413, 417, 440
dark, 32, 353, 372, 383, 421, 465,
 522, 550
darkness, 373
data, 29, 60, 63–65, 643
date, 15, 29, 80, 133, 399, 424, 432,
 493, 582
David Attenborough, 429
David Bowie, 181
David Meerman, 583
day, 15, 16, 44, 225, 241, 242, 461,
 464, 465, 509
Daya, 560
deal, 503
debt, 206, 479
debut, 95, 274, 275, 374, 375, 450,
 645
decay, 307
decision, 13, 64, 65, 119, 131, 137,
 138, 159, 442, 451, 522,

572, 575, 585
decline, 478
dedication, 1, 7, 16, 19, 23, 30, 32,
 49, 71, 73, 76, 78, 85, 97,
 105, 106, 110, 111, 136,
 137, 141, 142, 148, 154,
 169–172, 193, 194, 205,
 211–213, 215, 218, 221,
 223, 228–233, 235, 239,
 240, 242, 244–246, 253,
 260, 264, 265, 276, 278,
 287, 300, 302, 305,
 309–311, 315, 316,
 321–323, 332, 334, 339,
 351, 352, 369, 382, 394,
 395, 401, 405, 407, 425,
 437, 438, 440, 442, 444,
 446, 447, 451, 452, 459,
 460, 464, 467, 468, 471,
 472, 477, 480, 482, 483,
 488, 496, 497, 513, 518,
 519, 521, 522, 529,
 545–547, 559, 565, 567,
 571, 585, 590, 596, 599,
 606, 612, 613, 621, 624,
 625, 629, 634, 635, 645,
 649, 650, 655, 657, 660
defeat, 93
definition, 448, 449, 575
deforestation, 101, 161, 304, 321,
 387, 587, 606, 621, 623,
 624, 650
degradation, 305, 307, 362, 590, 635
delay, 347, 354, 515
delight, 121, 408, 420, 424
demand, 61, 104, 134, 195, 265,
 306, 370, 587, 611
demeanor, 415
demographic, 52, 56, 57, 65

departure, 112, 424
depletion, 587
depression, 242, 246, 247, 251, 366,
    463, 590, 625, 638
depth, 9, 10, 19, 22, 28, 60, 113,
    126, 128, 162, 164, 182,
    183, 234, 255, 333–335,
    341, 344, 347, 349, 354,
    371, 372, 393, 407, 409,
    412, 427, 429, 433, 436,
    459, 477, 478, 491, 492,
    499, 506, 513, 515, 524,
    527, 536, 546, 554, 560,
    562, 563, 591, 593
desert, 156
design, 1, 8, 10, 12, 28, 31, 32, 48,
    59, 95–97, 105, 111, 117,
    121, 127–129, 138, 139,
    141, 176, 180, 183, 188,
    189, 195, 198, 210, 211,
    238, 263, 275, 293, 297,
    331, 333, 335, 336, 338,
    341, 345–347, 349, 353,
    354, 363, 366–368, 373,
    375, 384, 398, 400, 402,
    405, 410, 413, 417, 420,
    421, 430, 431, 450, 463,
    477, 480, 491–493, 495,
    512, 524, 529, 531, 532,
    534–536, 538, 545, 546,
    548, 551, 553, 555, 556,
    562, 565, 567, 578, 594,
    596, 643, 645
designer, 252
desire, 2, 5, 27, 130, 137, 155, 160,
    253, 300, 326, 339, 358,
    361, 386, 389, 425, 432,
    438, 440, 446, 447, 462,
    464, 497, 516, 599, 600,

614
destigmatization, 624
destination, 67, 156, 164, 167, 203
destruction, 161, 361, 587
detachment, 405
detail, 11, 19, 25, 33, 45, 91, 117,
    121, 128, 138, 139, 211,
    238, 261, 332, 363, 368,
    369, 374, 375, 391,
    399–401, 420, 459, 463,
    467, 468, 477, 478, 480,
    491, 492, 494, 520, 522,
    527, 528, 536, 542, 543,
    545, 578, 581
determination, 29, 31, 70–73, 75,
    83, 238, 249, 295, 366,
    440, 502, 517
development, 2, 7, 12, 13, 16, 19, 31,
    33, 35–39, 84, 148, 188,
    191, 196, 227, 236, 249,
    252, 258, 265, 268, 273,
    274, 276, 277, 301, 439,
    440, 456, 464, 466, 467,
    516, 528, 550, 556, 596,
    616, 624, 639, 640
dialogue, 145, 189, 240, 299, 305,
    306, 308, 320, 404, 472,
    598, 608, 611, 612, 615,
    621, 630, 637
dichotomy, 28
difference, 71, 102, 103, 106, 132,
    136, 144, 171, 194, 205,
    212, 213, 215, 218, 224,
    226, 228, 230–233, 239,
    241, 246, 248, 249, 252,
    254, 260, 264, 278, 284,
    295, 298, 300, 302,
    308–310, 317–319, 321,
    326, 361, 362, 437, 445,

446, 448, 458, 466, 481,
483, 502, 533, 549, 558,
559, 570, 575, 580, 590,
601, 602, 606, 607, 609,
610, 612–615, 618–621,
623–626, 628, 629,
639–641, 644, 649–651,
655–657, 659–661
dimension, 95, 128, 164, 179, 344,
406, 422, 506, 515, 550
Dion Timmer, 259
Dion Timmer's, 259
direction, 85, 121, 126, 144, 180,
185, 189, 204, 221, 235,
268, 277, 278, 318–320,
342, 428, 449, 466, 495,
542, 557, 563, 607
disappointment, 147
disaster, 254, 301, 303
discipline, 4, 158
discography, 49, 75, 178, 229, 337,
353, 358, 376, 378–384,
388
discomfort, 128
discontent, 306
discord, 222
discourse, 307
discoverability, 63
discovery, 6, 28, 167, 168, 186, 198,
247, 365, 371, 386, 418,
434, 443, 445, 459, 523,
528
discretion, 137
discrimination, 290, 299, 305, 361,
591, 598, 613, 619
disguise, 95, 119, 575
display, 42, 310, 409, 410
disposal, 140, 161, 162, 551, 607
disregard, 72, 340

dissent, 307
distance, 137, 147, 160
distancing, 83
distinctiveness, 563
distortion, 347, 354, 368, 436, 491,
515
distraction, 27
distribution, 400, 478, 502, 536
dive, 6, 29, 39, 365, 376, 418, 493,
494, 518, 526, 528, 561,
651
diversification, 222, 394, 471, 479,
556
diversity, 24, 26, 72, 86, 87, 99, 105,
107, 129, 130, 155–157,
167, 171, 175, 178, 185,
187–190, 215, 221, 254,
263, 265, 267, 268, 276,
285, 286, 294–297, 299,
300, 304, 305, 309, 322,
324, 326–328, 343, 393,
394, 431, 432, 434, 447,
462, 483, 524, 539, 547,
552, 571, 585, 597–600,
608, 609, 653, 660
divide, 130
division, 222
divisiveness, 599
DJ, 496
DJ Bassline, 16
DJ Blaze, 16, 17
DJ Blaze, 16
DJ Mag's, 77
DJ Sizzle, 467
DJ X, 15
documentary, 197, 456, 638
documentation, 229
Donald S. Passman, 7, 277
donation, 622

door, 336, 345, 563
doubt, 2, 13, 30, 71, 73–75, 94,
    248–250, 439, 440, 443,
    453, 464
down, 21, 32, 50, 72, 73, 99, 103,
    106, 107, 112, 113, 130,
    131, 140, 149, 157, 171,
    172, 177, 178, 186, 190,
    193, 205, 215, 222, 232,
    235, 247, 249, 254, 265,
    278, 290, 291, 294–296,
    298, 304, 306, 309, 319,
    326, 336, 337, 343, 364,
    367, 388, 392, 407, 416,
    425, 447, 457, 462,
    465–467, 472, 475, 481,
    483, 485, 486, 518, 520,
    524, 525, 539, 549, 554,
    565, 568, 570, 572,
    574–576, 580, 581, 586,
    590, 591, 595, 597,
    599–601, 619, 620, 630,
    636, 643, 644, 651, 654,
    656, 657, 660
downtime, 133, 520
draft, 535
Dre, 428
dream, 45, 47, 242
drive, 2, 22, 197, 252, 284, 289, 302,
    320, 323, 354, 428, 431,
    432, 446, 449, 460, 468,
    590, 612, 615, 616, 618,
    644
driving, 14, 20, 26, 33, 70, 78, 145,
    168, 197, 205, 229, 244,
    249, 256, 261, 283, 316,
    318, 324, 333, 382, 391,
    392, 425, 437, 450, 511,
    533, 551, 612, 614, 634,

639, 660
drop, 138, 152, 251, 337, 354, 372,
    383, 398, 541, 561, 562
dropping, 369
drum, 6, 10, 15, 24, 183, 188, 211,
    257, 331–335, 340, 341,
    347, 350, 353, 354, 366,
    381, 384, 392, 518, 551
drummer, 4
drumming, 5, 427
drumstep, 337
duality, 28, 523, 538
dubstep, 24, 31, 32, 48, 71, 76, 84,
    95–97, 106, 112, 172, 188,
    199, 204, 211, 238, 257,
    259, 331–333, 335, 337,
    338, 340–342, 344, 350,
    351, 353, 358, 359, 361,
    363, 366, 369, 381,
    383–385, 392, 420–422,
    432, 462, 477, 478, 480,
    481, 485, 487, 490–492,
    495, 545, 547, 548, 550,
    553–557, 560, 563, 565,
    571, 575, 578, 584, 597,
    644, 645, 647, 649, 657
duet, 181
duo, 98, 173, 192, 272, 359
duration, 414
dynamic, 8, 20, 32, 35, 36, 42, 61,
    64, 99, 104, 108, 114, 131,
    140, 147, 174, 181, 182,
    188, 190, 207, 258, 291,
    293, 311, 315, 325, 333,
    335–337, 348, 351, 353,
    367, 372, 374, 375, 381,
    382, 385, 395, 398, 402,
    403, 405, 406, 409,
    411–413, 428, 436, 449,

462, 468, 477, 490, 491,
499, 501, 515, 518, 532,
541, 546, 550, 554, 556,
560, 562, 563, 578, 580,
648

eagerness, 24
ear, 4, 91, 251, 337
Earth, 361–363
earth, 32, 172, 457, 518, 520
ease, 103, 219, 282, 347, 459
eating, 75
ebb, 337
eco, 253, 287, 296, 428, 588, 612,
628, 633, 660
economy, 587
ecosystem, 105, 276, 623
edge, 25, 32, 33, 67, 80, 99, 110,
152, 159, 209, 341, 343,
346, 367, 382, 402, 407,
410, 422, 428, 435, 447,
477, 495, 513, 514, 516,
527, 542, 582
edition, 128, 195, 261, 379, 450,
577, 621
education, 3, 6, 7, 14, 15, 102, 208,
231, 245, 247, 253, 274,
287, 289, 299, 301–303,
307, 309, 466, 589, 599,
602–605, 611, 612, 615,
618, 624–627, 633, 635,
636, 639, 642, 644, 646,
658, 660
effect, 106, 163, 171, 223, 230, 242,
249, 250, 264, 295, 301,
354, 426, 458, 549, 567,
607, 619, 624, 649
effectiveness, 60, 82, 615
efficiency, 640

effort, 36, 43, 44, 78, 92, 117, 118,
148, 185, 232, 242, 252,
255, 279, 285, 317, 363,
404, 544, 604, 608
ego, 126, 189, 446, 458
electricity, 396
electro, 98
electronica, 11
elegance, 177, 537
element, 25, 27, 66, 95, 118, 120,
121, 130, 131, 158, 182,
188, 190, 213, 345, 354,
402, 403, 406, 407, 410,
414, 415, 436, 467, 486,
491, 509, 525, 526, 528,
531, 535, 542, 568
elite, 76
Elizabeth Gilbert - This, 456
else, 531, 586, 610
email, 64
emblem, 29, 119
embrace, 26, 29, 33, 37, 40, 72, 84,
88, 95, 108, 118–120, 123,
127, 129, 130, 140, 151,
159, 160, 164, 167, 168,
177, 191, 194, 200, 201,
208, 221, 224, 225, 238,
239, 243, 246, 247, 249,
250, 283, 293–296, 303,
315, 325, 339, 342, 348,
352, 356, 357, 365, 372,
381, 382, 393, 394, 398,
434, 436, 437, 443,
450–453, 455, 459, 462,
464, 465, 467, 469, 476,
478, 479, 489, 501–503,
511, 522, 547, 567, 569,
573, 574, 577–579, 581,
584, 586, 591, 592, 594,

597–599, 606, 607, 609,
613, 619, 620, 643, 650,
653
emergence, 77, 236, 351, 450, 478,
550, 554, 563, 583
emergency, 301
Emily, 4, 243, 244, 249
Emily Davis, 100
Emma, 252
Emma Rose, 495
Emma Williams, 133
emotion, 28, 71, 96, 113, 118, 126,
222, 242, 248, 334, 358,
452, 454, 463, 491, 492,
519, 522, 537, 541, 543,
546, 607
empathy, 144, 188, 300, 302, 304,
306, 308, 315, 322, 361,
371, 372, 607, 609, 610,
612, 614, 658
emphasis, 119, 264, 265, 333, 416,
417, 463, 466, 495, 539,
556, 566, 567, 660
employment, 626
empowerment, 28, 76, 111, 218,
234, 242, 243, 246,
248–251, 315, 325, 362,
371, 373, 398, 416, 418,
448, 482, 546, 563,
569–571, 589, 591, 602,
606, 629, 653
encore, 412, 413
encounter, 172–174, 189, 242, 273,
356, 397, 407, 442, 520
encouragement, 2, 4, 13, 14, 30, 33,
72, 74, 84, 111, 141, 142,
151, 174, 221, 234, 241,
242, 251, 252, 257, 275,
314, 320, 322, 327, 414,

439, 440, 464, 465, 470,
506, 578, 591, 601
encroachment, 387
end, 81, 140, 189, 361, 412, 413,
468, 492
endeavor, 48, 207, 590
endorsement, 77, 370
endurance, 158
enemy, 455
energy, 2, 5, 8, 18–20, 22, 23, 25, 27,
28, 32, 34, 42, 48, 56, 57,
61, 64, 69, 71, 74, 75, 77,
95, 96, 101–104, 108,
110–112, 114, 117, 118,
120, 121, 123, 125, 128,
138–141, 151–153, 155,
157, 164, 168–171, 177,
183, 184, 188, 191, 196,
199, 201, 208, 209, 213,
214, 217, 219, 222, 227,
229, 234, 238, 241–243,
248–250, 255, 284, 288,
291, 297, 310, 311, 326,
331, 332, 336, 337, 340,
342, 343, 350, 353, 354,
358, 359, 361, 363,
365–367, 370, 372, 374,
382–384, 388, 391,
394–399, 401, 402,
405–409, 412–415, 417,
418, 420, 422, 424, 425,
428, 429, 432, 434, 437,
442, 452, 459, 464, 468,
469, 477, 478, 491, 492,
501, 509, 510, 512, 515,
518, 519, 521, 522, 527,
529, 530, 532, 535, 537,
541–544, 546, 549–551,
554, 560–564, 566, 573,

580, 587, 588, 592, 600,
640, 646–648, 655
engagement, 53–56, 60, 63–65, 86,
104, 110, 124, 129, 131,
137, 138, 143, 145, 152,
170, 218, 220–223, 227,
228, 230, 231, 233–235,
237, 256, 261, 264, 271,
278, 300, 314–316, 318,
319, 323, 324, 401,
403–406, 411, 413, 414,
417, 418, 449–451, 470,
474, 481, 482, 523, 527,
539, 556, 579, 584, 597,
599, 607, 609, 615, 622,
629, 630, 634, 640, 642
engine, 159, 581
engineering, 122
enigma, 124
enjoyment, 469
ensemble, 175
entertainer, 203, 606
entertainment, 179, 204, 244, 251,
261, 443, 483, 551, 558,
583, 600, 624
enthusiasm, 22, 78, 139, 152, 153,
164, 217, 221, 224,
227–229, 234, 310, 314,
319, 320, 323, 395, 396,
398, 414, 415, 417, 449,
459, 468, 471, 472, 495,
529
enthusiast, 160, 512
entry, 51, 55
environment, 3, 13, 14, 37, 38, 43,
100, 101, 105, 121, 124,
129, 131, 134, 136, 143,
161, 162, 170, 184–186,
189, 190, 202, 205, 209,

215, 217, 223, 224, 226,
228–230, 232, 240, 244,
245, 251–253, 257, 262,
264, 267, 268, 272, 278,
287, 293, 294, 296, 300,
301, 303, 305, 321, 322,
325, 327, 328, 361, 400,
409, 418, 439, 441, 460,
466–468, 471, 473,
481–483, 488, 494, 506,
547, 566, 573, 574, 584,
585, 588, 594, 597, 598,
606, 608, 615, 619, 621,
628, 632, 633, 635–637,
648, 650
environmentalism, 102
envision, 206, 611
envy, 147
epicness, 429
equality, 299, 300, 306, 309, 326,
361, 600, 619, 624, 630
equalization, 400
equilibrium, 125, 126, 199
equipment, 13, 23, 29, 30, 58, 62,
74, 122, 159, 161, 400,
404, 406, 436, 516, 518,
519
era, 60, 64, 259, 370
escape, 119, 122, 123, 167, 248, 250,
251, 366, 437, 460, 523,
540, 586, 590, 592
escapism, 67, 119, 120, 122, 123,
426, 487, 522, 523, 579
essay, 18, 206, 605
essence, 66, 79, 117, 126, 127, 151,
156, 160, 179, 238, 298,
320, 321, 370, 373, 378,
383, 433, 512, 513, 521,
525, 526, 528, 530, 534,

537, 543, 562, 574
establishment, 103, 213, 488, 635
Ethan, 4
ethic, 31
ethos, 218, 291, 298, 301, 317, 325,
   340
euphoria, 111, 372, 417, 492, 524,
   530, 546, 563
Europe, 152, 153
evaluation, 369
evening, 172
event, 18, 44, 55, 138, 162, 192, 218,
   227, 241, 248, 260–262,
   272, 284, 302, 310, 311,
   314, 323, 391, 399, 413,
   417, 464, 598, 618, 622,
   636, 640
evidence, 250, 302
evolution, 7, 26, 78, 79, 81, 83, 86,
   89, 90, 106, 112, 119,
   127–129, 182, 190, 191,
   194, 197, 204, 206, 209,
   214, 222, 230, 231, 264,
   276, 277, 279, 319, 323,
   324, 338, 339, 342,
   349–352, 376, 378,
   380–382, 384, 386, 389,
   391, 392, 405–408, 425,
   435, 447, 448, 451, 454,
   455, 463, 466, 467, 479,
   497, 500, 518, 521, 524,
   528–531, 551–557, 584,
   643, 644, 655, 657
example, 17, 25, 36, 51–53, 57, 82,
   84, 85, 87, 103, 111, 155,
   156, 163, 164, 175, 176,
   180, 183, 186, 187, 189,
   190, 202, 206, 212–214,
   231, 234, 239, 240, 246,

248, 255, 258, 265, 271,
   272, 274, 288, 293, 299,
   301, 303, 305–307, 318,
   319, 321, 322, 332, 333,
   337, 338, 353, 361, 368,
   372, 373, 383, 387, 388,
   393, 407, 409, 428, 433,
   451, 462, 466, 467, 472,
   474, 475, 498, 506, 516,
   538, 547, 549, 554, 560,
   571, 572, 583, 585, 594,
   597, 606, 610, 611, 618,
   622, 638, 640, 656, 657,
   660
excellence, 78, 268, 320, 363, 401,
   445, 477
exception, 12, 16, 31, 34, 53, 58, 73,
   85, 86, 88, 90, 118, 123,
   133, 135, 187, 193, 266,
   336, 340, 344, 391, 435,
   509, 537
exchange, 34, 35, 41, 145, 155, 156,
   171, 178, 184, 187, 224,
   227, 236, 258, 266, 267,
   275, 279, 292, 298, 320,
   394, 415, 512, 526, 599
excitement, 24, 55, 63, 111, 119,
   120, 124, 154, 158, 159,
   167, 168, 173, 229, 230,
   236, 258, 261, 311, 368,
   373, 379, 380, 391,
   395–397, 403, 404, 406,
   407, 409, 412–415, 424,
   459, 464, 484, 485, 501,
   519, 523, 529, 530, 538,
   541, 543, 546, 580, 647
exclusivity, 61, 106, 138, 195, 196,
   236, 379
execute, 121, 336

execution, 56–58, 122, 262, 542
executive, 16
exercise, 75, 92, 134, 247, 251, 292,
    510, 513, 551
exhibit, 477
exhibition, 611
exhilarating, 90, 141, 168, 175, 250,
    333, 349, 395, 421, 422,
    457, 467, 657
exhilaration, 127, 157, 372
expansion, 391, 392, 559
expectation, 452
expense, 74, 86
experience, 9, 15, 16, 18, 22–25,
    27–29, 32–35, 40, 54, 55,
    57, 58, 61, 62, 66, 68–70,
    76, 80, 83, 89, 90, 96, 99,
    102, 106, 108, 110–112,
    114, 120–124, 128, 129,
    132, 133, 138–141,
    152–155, 157, 159, 161,
    162, 164, 168, 169, 175,
    178, 179, 189, 190, 194,
    196–198, 202, 203, 208,
    210, 211, 213, 214, 219,
    227, 229, 233–238, 243,
    246, 250, 251, 259,
    261–263, 277, 282, 291,
    293, 302, 311, 332–337,
    341, 343, 344, 348, 350,
    352–354, 363, 365, 366,
    370, 372–375, 378, 382,
    391, 392, 395–411,
    413–418, 421, 424, 425,
    427, 429, 447, 450, 452,
    453, 456, 459–462, 465,
    467–470, 477, 480, 483,
    486, 491, 492, 494, 497,
    511, 512, 515, 522,

525–528, 530–533,
    535–537, 539–544, 546,
    548–554, 556, 563, 566,
    571, 577, 578, 580, 582,
    583, 586, 592, 633, 637,
    646, 648, 652, 654
experiment, 1, 2, 6, 13, 16, 17, 20,
    21, 24–26, 31, 33, 37, 39,
    40, 44, 46, 49, 79, 85, 88,
    93, 96, 98, 108, 114, 119,
    137, 167, 180, 182, 183,
    191, 197–199, 203, 209,
    211, 214, 234, 238, 243,
    258, 279, 292, 293, 319,
    332, 333, 335–338, 341,
    343, 348, 350, 353, 354,
    364, 375, 380, 385, 391,
    392, 404, 422, 424, 426,
    434, 436, 455, 460, 464,
    473, 477, 478, 481, 485,
    486, 493, 494, 505, 506,
    511, 515, 536, 540, 546,
    547, 549, 552, 553,
    555–558, 560, 561, 564,
    565, 568, 573, 579, 582,
    584, 595, 599, 600, 644,
    646
experimentation, 7, 9, 15, 25, 26, 79,
    89, 95, 97, 164, 177, 180,
    182, 186, 188, 191, 193,
    196, 200, 285, 331, 333,
    336–340, 342, 343, 345,
    346, 351, 374, 379–381,
    385, 389, 390, 405, 430,
    432, 434, 456, 459, 462,
    467, 473, 475, 478, 486,
    487, 490, 493, 494, 498,
    499, 503, 512, 514,
    547–551, 558, 564, 565,

574, 594, 644, 652, 658
expert, 375
expertise, 17, 36, 42, 46, 141, 180,
    187, 238, 252, 262, 273,
    475, 477, 490, 494, 506,
    534–536, 542, 545, 622,
    639
explanation, 28
exploitation, 157
exploration, 11, 13, 24–26, 32, 34,
    60, 70, 80, 81, 85, 114,
    156, 158–161, 164, 167,
    181, 182, 186, 188,
    197–199, 201, 209, 292,
    331, 332, 336, 337, 340,
    343, 345, 346, 350, 351,
    357, 381, 382, 384–386,
    391, 392, 394, 431,
    433–435, 441, 454, 459,
    462–464, 473, 483, 487,
    490, 493, 495, 514–517,
    528, 530, 538, 547, 555,
    558, 567, 595, 596, 615,
    643, 644, 646
explore, 1–3, 8, 9, 12, 19, 22, 23, 27,
    29, 31–35, 37, 41, 45, 50,
    53, 55, 60, 62, 66–68, 70,
    73, 75, 77, 81, 82, 85, 87,
    88, 91, 93, 95–100, 105,
    106, 108, 110, 112, 114,
    117, 119, 120, 125–127,
    132, 133, 136, 138,
    142–148, 150, 154, 157,
    160, 162–164, 167, 168,
    174–180, 183, 184,
    186–188, 190, 193, 195,
    197–204, 206, 207, 209,
    212–214, 220, 229, 230,
    234–236, 238, 239, 243,

245, 251, 253, 254,
    257–261, 265, 266, 268,
    279, 283, 285, 289,
    292–294, 296–298, 303,
    305, 307, 312, 313, 319,
    320, 331–340, 344–346,
    349, 352, 358, 363, 365,
    368, 370, 371, 373, 376,
    378, 380, 384, 385, 388,
    391–394, 397, 402, 408,
    413, 420, 422, 424, 428,
    430, 432–434, 437, 440,
    443, 449, 450, 456, 457,
    459, 460, 462, 463,
    466–471, 473–475, 478,
    479, 481, 485, 486, 490,
    493, 494, 497, 498, 500,
    503, 505, 506, 509, 512,
    516, 521, 526, 530, 531,
    533, 534, 537, 539, 540,
    542, 545, 547–550, 553,
    556, 557, 559–565, 568,
    569, 573, 576, 578, 581,
    584, 585, 590, 594–597,
    600, 602, 617, 618, 628,
    629, 631, 632, 634, 635,
    640, 643, 645, 646,
    648–651, 656, 657
explosion, 372
exposure, 1, 9, 14, 15, 42, 46, 47, 51,
    53, 55, 59–64, 68, 70, 83,
    97, 163, 183, 184, 191,
    195, 196, 222, 229, 263,
    264, 266, 272–274,
    276–279, 295, 340, 428,
    450, 466, 475, 488, 502,
    503, 506, 509, 596, 602
expression, 13, 28, 34, 72, 79, 80, 83,
    86, 96, 97, 99, 111, 112,

115, 118, 123, 126, 127,
133, 136, 137, 159, 175,
224, 238, 243, 246, 250,
259, 285, 291–294, 297,
298, 307, 324, 325, 372,
378, 393, 394, 430, 446,
453, 454, 456, 457, 462,
465, 480, 483, 486, 488,
511, 522, 525, 529, 538,
542–544, 552, 556,
566–576, 578, 579, 585,
590, 594, 595, 597,
605–607, 610, 613–617,
619, 643, 652, 653, 655,
659
extend, 47, 76, 104, 136, 142, 203,
220, 235, 248, 253, 288,
309, 318, 326, 414, 483,
507, 527, 545, 546, 569,
595, 613, 615, 622, 640,
657
extension, 125, 526
extent, 137
extinction, 161
extravagance, 523
eye, 56, 57, 90, 133, 134, 398, 403,
415, 430, 525, 579

face, 7, 30, 33, 34, 41, 83–85, 91, 92,
94, 95, 124, 127, 132, 133,
136, 159, 168, 172, 173,
179, 239, 249, 250, 262,
267, 271, 282, 290, 314,
365, 373, 387, 450, 453,
501, 509, 519, 586, 591,
598, 611, 627, 635
facet, 436
fact, 132

factor, 125, 213, 234, 350, 370, 372,
395, 548
failure, 74, 93, 95, 453, 455, 456
fairness, 254
faith, 503
fame, 14, 51, 69, 90–93, 118, 126,
133, 137, 147, 148, 163,
167, 172, 174, 204, 221,
231, 239, 444–446, 457,
481, 482, 523, 549, 565,
585, 586
familiarity, 199
family, 3–8, 12–14, 30, 33, 54, 73,
83, 91, 102, 133, 134, 141,
142, 147, 148, 217, 221,
227, 231, 251, 253, 313,
317, 320, 439, 441, 502,
628
fan, 19, 25, 26, 37, 39, 46, 53, 54,
56, 60–65, 68, 69, 73, 76,
80, 82, 92, 102–106, 110,
121, 123, 124, 126–129,
131, 141–145, 152, 153,
156, 168–171, 173, 177,
179, 183, 192, 193, 195,
196, 202, 203, 210, 217,
218, 220–224, 226–228,
230, 232, 233, 235–237,
239–242, 244, 248, 249,
251, 252, 254–256, 258,
263–265, 268–272, 274,
278, 283, 284, 287, 294,
296, 304, 305, 310, 311,
313–317, 320–322,
324–328, 342, 343, 353,
354, 359, 361, 364–366,
379, 380, 383, 391, 392,
397–399, 403, 404, 413,
414, 416, 417, 426, 440,

442, 449, 450, 452, 457,
460, 461, 463–465, 469,
470, 475–477, 481, 482,
485, 506, 520, 523, 525,
527, 532, 539, 543, 544,
552, 556–558, 568,
570–572, 580–586, 588,
589, 594–598, 601,
606–609, 612, 613,
620–622, 624, 626, 629,
632–634, 644, 647, 652,
654, 656, 658, 660
fanbase, 18, 19, 31, 42, 49, 50,
53–55, 58–60, 70, 78,
82–84, 92, 94, 106, 129,
141, 142, 152, 153, 165,
171, 195, 199, 202, 205,
219, 230–233, 251, 254,
256, 260, 273, 279, 296,
298, 316, 318, 321, 352,
364, 379, 380, 405, 424,
425, 436, 444, 478,
480–483, 500, 518, 520,
581, 584, 591, 592, 606,
607, 644, 652, 659
fandom, 223, 279, 449
fantasy, 535, 539
fascination, 358, 495, 567
fashion, 47, 96, 105, 325, 540, 549,
569, 570, 576–579, 581
Fatboy Slim, 173, 174
father, 3, 4
favor, 643
favorite, 11, 34, 56, 76, 157, 161,
203, 227, 229, 235, 237,
265, 268, 284, 327, 353,
359, 360, 383, 397, 434,
471, 475, 527, 550, 556,
580

fear, 88, 123, 138, 290, 305, 373,
456, 568, 569, 573, 586,
591, 598
fearlessness, 32, 49, 157, 340, 464,
496, 558
feast, 33, 120, 139, 152
feat, 29, 47, 119
feature, 66, 112, 244, 246, 274, 409,
413, 424, 429, 515, 553,
561–563, 573, 594
feedback, 6, 15, 17, 33, 37–40, 47,
48, 52, 60, 64, 79, 81–83,
85, 89, 92, 94, 98, 126,
131, 141, 142, 144, 180,
184, 187, 189, 210, 211,
221, 228, 234, 235, 237,
240, 243, 252, 257, 262,
266, 271, 273, 275,
318–320, 352, 401, 415,
440, 443, 448–450, 456,
457, 464, 468, 502, 503,
516, 535, 547, 608
feel, 37, 39, 54, 58, 65, 105, 110,
111, 121, 128–130, 140,
143, 145, 152, 153, 159,
169, 170, 173, 186, 202,
218, 221, 224, 229, 240,
267, 289, 293, 304, 309,
311, 316, 328, 348, 395,
397, 398, 403, 412,
414–416, 451, 457, 461,
470, 519, 574, 578,
590–592, 600
feeling, 24, 154, 284, 336, 383, 398,
465, 469, 637
fellow, 6, 15, 18, 37, 39, 42, 43, 47,
61, 79, 82–84, 97, 142,
153, 154, 160, 172–174,
184, 186, 211, 224, 226,

228, 230, 232, 243, 251,
252, 257–259, 272, 275,
291, 292, 317, 327, 393,
403, 404, 407, 426, 431,
435, 442, 444, 455, 456,
459, 461–465, 469, 472,
475, 482, 494, 498, 502,
503, 506, 520, 547, 548,
566, 574, 588, 594,
618–620, 624, 625, 628,
653, 661
ferociousness, 577
ferocity, 28
festival, 18, 42, 49, 55–58, 70, 152,
153, 163, 225, 284, 354,
359, 370, 392, 405, 407,
442, 477, 556, 580
fi, 341
field, 10, 29, 44, 75, 277, 302, 387,
407, 452, 503, 525, 552,
574, 590, 615
fight, 289, 299, 387, 635
figure, 16, 29, 32, 43, 49, 55, 60, 64,
98, 123, 126, 153, 228,
257, 289, 304, 323, 324,
328, 369, 382, 385, 391,
451, 458, 476, 482, 517,
522, 571, 572, 580, 581,
584, 587, 646
figurehead, 298
film, 9, 429, 540
filter, 368
filtering, 436, 491
finding, 12, 43, 88, 91, 95, 125, 134,
144, 145, 147, 148, 180,
185, 189, 191, 199, 242,
246, 249, 284, 297, 315,
327, 344, 372, 373, 390,
418, 443, 469, 498, 499,

521, 537, 551, 591
finesse, 517
finger, 318
finish, 110, 395, 400, 491
fire, 396, 464, 548, 561, 600
firsthand, 40, 51, 112, 153, 156, 161,
322, 520, 533
fishing, 632
fit, 71, 73, 96, 128, 158, 378–380
fitness, 158, 251, 551, 552
five, 441
flavor, 433
flexibility, 119, 180, 198, 262, 515
flight, 372
floor, 361
flourish, 186, 458, 494
flow, 11, 12, 108, 168, 189, 261, 337,
395, 399, 400, 467,
509–512
fly, 140, 348
focus, 27, 74, 84, 102, 119, 124, 126,
127, 132, 134, 137, 138,
146, 158, 162, 187, 203,
244, 253, 254, 267, 286,
290, 295, 298, 452, 454,
465, 498, 509, 513, 522,
525, 543, 549, 561, 573,
592, 616, 618, 626, 633,
636, 638, 639, 643, 653
folk, 393
following, 2, 4, 12, 44, 53, 55, 76,
103, 105, 119, 124, 145,
148, 170, 197, 201, 221,
254, 263, 265, 274, 282,
287, 369, 434, 546, 561,
562, 584, 587, 610, 630
food, 165, 167, 245, 252, 609, 639
footage, 54, 63, 120, 236, 261, 409,
425, 441, 547

footprint, 209, 428, 588, 633
footwear, 397
force, 14, 26, 28, 33, 49, 70, 75, 78,
	95, 130, 145, 179, 205,
	219, 222, 229, 231, 233,
	244, 249, 256, 268, 271,
	278, 283, 300, 318, 375,
	382, 391, 392, 425, 449,
	450, 452, 460, 470, 472,
	511, 558, 561, 599, 608,
	612, 614, 644, 660
forefront, 15, 26, 78, 80, 107, 122,
	209, 214, 318, 339, 349,
	364, 367, 401, 407, 427,
	432, 462, 473, 480, 514,
	517, 553, 584, 607, 644,
	655, 656
forest, 160, 387, 629
forestry, 621
form, 19, 27, 77, 86, 96, 112, 119,
	120, 122, 123, 126, 137,
	161, 177, 181, 193, 217,
	232, 238, 250, 254, 264,
	292, 306, 307, 324, 326,
	416, 438, 453, 458, 469,
	473, 487, 500, 506, 522,
	523, 537, 543, 590, 593,
	599
formation, 332–334, 352, 381, 614,
	616, 651
formula, 351, 448
forum, 251, 275
foster, 5, 64, 87, 131, 148, 156, 157,
	163, 171, 229, 232, 237,
	239, 251, 253, 262, 263,
	267, 273, 276, 283, 306,
	308, 316, 318, 322, 324,
	325, 367, 370, 388, 425,
	450, 455, 501, 543, 544,

	566, 568, 574, 586, 599,
	601, 602, 604, 608, 610,
	614, 615, 617, 635, 644
fostering, 13, 23, 27, 38, 51, 54, 62,
	63, 99, 105, 106, 115, 124,
	127, 129, 131, 143, 155,
	156, 160, 169–171, 174,
	178, 185, 187–190, 196,
	204–206, 213, 215, 219,
	223, 226, 229–231, 235,
	240–242, 244, 245, 255,
	256, 265, 266, 268, 275,
	278, 283, 292, 303, 305,
	306, 314–317, 321, 322,
	325, 326, 328, 329, 343,
	371, 372, 394, 398, 405,
	406, 413–415, 418, 431,
	438, 442, 449, 457, 466,
	471, 472, 474, 475, 483,
	487, 494, 496, 506, 518,
	524, 525, 548, 559, 566,
	568, 571–573, 579, 581,
	589, 591, 595, 599, 601,
	602, 605, 607, 614, 616,
	619, 626, 629, 633, 634,
	651, 658
foundation, 1, 4, 8, 10, 14, 15, 53,
	84, 102, 145, 180, 184,
	213, 220, 247, 299, 332,
	381, 388, 458, 470, 490,
	513, 529, 535, 536, 553,
	562, 564, 587, 611, 612,
	614–616, 619, 624, 625,
	628, 635, 637–641, 651,
	655, 658, 659
fragility, 101, 288, 386, 429
framing, 543
Frank Broughton, 24
freedom, 11, 27, 80, 119, 123, 157,

159, 168, 189, 292, 319,
325, 340, 342, 348, 374,
388, 459, 467, 515, 538,
573, 574, 579, 584, 594,
595, 597, 653
frenzy, 152
frequency, 333, 348
freshness, 25
friend, 242, 465, 628
friendship, 225, 326, 475
front, 140, 263, 519, 577
frugality, 74
fruition, 628
frustration, 34, 373, 498
fuel, 34, 47, 80, 93, 95, 165, 167,
320, 415, 452, 502, 510,
511, 513, 595, 633
fulfillment, 88, 93, 328, 443, 446,
458
fun, 55, 65, 158, 200, 520, 521
functionality, 128
fund, 30, 244, 245, 247, 263, 620,
621, 623, 625
fundamental, 83, 126, 131, 168, 271,
279, 284, 430, 454, 514
funding, 299, 587, 605, 616, 625,
635, 637–639
fundraising, 136, 218, 230, 246, 251,
262, 284, 287, 289, 301,
308, 318, 321, 601, 607,
613, 617, 620, 622, 629
funk, 21, 344
fusion, 2, 21, 49, 71, 87, 95, 97, 99,
113, 153, 155, 156, 163,
167, 175, 176, 178, 182,
192, 193, 198, 199, 204,
207, 209, 211, 214, 215,
246, 257, 258, 333, 335,
338, 341, 342, 344, 345,

350, 351, 359, 360, 375,
384, 393–395, 406, 408,
421, 426, 429, 431–433,
462–464, 478, 481, 485,
488, 494, 505, 511, 530,
546, 548, 550–554, 556,
560, 562–564, 571, 578,
644, 645, 659
future, 1, 26, 29, 52, 53, 55, 63–65,
72, 76, 78, 97, 98, 101,
106, 107, 109, 112, 122,
132, 151, 162, 188, 197,
201–204, 206–212, 214,
215, 228, 235, 237, 238,
259, 262, 264, 274, 278,
283, 296, 298, 303, 311,
317–319, 322–324, 332,
333, 335, 340, 343, 348,
352, 361–363, 365, 369,
374, 375, 379–381, 384,
392, 394, 418–420, 422,
424–431, 435–438, 440,
446–448, 455, 456, 467,
473, 478–480, 483, 485,
489, 501, 516, 517, 530,
544, 545, 548, 549,
553–555, 559–561,
563–565, 567, 568, 570,
576, 583, 587, 590, 611,
614, 616, 617, 619, 620,
623, 626, 632, 633,
640–645, 649–651,
655–658, 660

gain, 10, 18, 37, 43, 45, 46, 48, 55,
57, 59, 60, 64, 69, 85, 89,
93, 97, 155, 174, 176, 191,
196, 201, 221, 222, 236,
254, 255, 262, 263, 266,

268, 272–275, 278, 279,
364, 394, 441, 450, 466,
475, 478, 488, 494, 499,
502, 518, 519, 544, 581,
602
game, 96, 459, 645
gaming, 47, 96
gap, 49, 107, 113, 130, 171, 205,
209, 259, 276, 306, 344,
478, 481, 486, 556, 575,
585, 592, 599, 639, 645,
652, 658
garage, 381
gardening, 626
gatekeeping, 106
gateway, 165, 526, 528
gathering, 218, 291, 311
gear, 407
Gearslutz, 277
gem, 451
gender, 119, 290, 326, 598, 600, 656
generating, 62, 63, 67, 68, 261, 354,
501, 523
generation, 96–98, 113, 204, 211,
213, 215, 216, 222, 231,
262, 264, 272, 278, 297,
301, 309, 318, 324, 332,
335, 351, 354, 363–365,
367, 393, 425, 447, 462,
467, 478, 479, 481, 486,
487, 489, 516, 525, 544,
546, 547, 549, 553, 557,
563, 565–567, 576, 585,
589, 590, 597, 600, 602,
604, 607, 627, 633, 644,
646, 652, 657–659
generosity, 301, 303, 310, 315
genius, 97, 459, 576
genre, 1, 2, 5–9, 11, 12, 17, 19, 21,

24–26, 31, 32, 49, 51, 64,
68, 75, 77, 84, 85, 87,
95–97, 99, 100, 106–109,
112–115, 122, 129, 139,
157, 164, 173–175, 177,
178, 182–188, 190–194,
196, 204–206, 209, 211,
212, 214, 222, 230, 231,
238, 239, 257, 259, 264,
265, 276–279, 283, 293,
297, 315, 319, 323, 324,
331–346, 351, 353,
363–368, 370, 372, 374,
375, 381–385, 388,
391–395, 420, 425–428,
434, 437, 439, 440, 447,
450, 451, 462, 463, 466,
471, 472, 474–483,
485–488, 492, 499, 506,
511, 524, 545, 546,
548–559, 561–565,
570–577, 580, 581, 584,
594, 595, 600, 607,
643–646, 648, 649, 651,
654–660
gentrification, 307
George Plumley, 605
Germany, 164, 325
gesture, 154, 311
gift, 607
gig, 22, 23, 440, 529
Giorgio Moroder, 553
giving, 16, 34, 50, 59, 64, 65, 98,
107, 123, 132, 143, 144,
160, 161, 168, 179, 202,
204, 208, 213, 218, 220,
222, 231, 243, 246, 247,
249, 256, 264, 272, 273,
301, 303, 309, 368, 379,

411, 418, 438, 452, 455,
458, 459, 465, 467, 502,
510, 519, 562, 568, 618,
649, 660
glamour, 78, 585
glimpse, 59, 64, 122, 169, 238, 244,
313, 358, 366, 371, 379,
398, 418, 419, 441, 443,
452, 460, 517–520, 529,
530, 537, 568
glitch, 122, 384
glitz, 78
globe, 48, 104, 105, 152, 163, 217,
219, 225, 232, 235, 316,
318, 325, 342, 460, 473,
477, 524, 570, 571, 644,
654
go, 1, 21, 27, 67, 77, 111, 123, 152,
154, 189, 208, 228, 231,
238, 240, 244, 250, 310,
322, 323, 328, 340, 354,
397, 415, 416, 497, 502,
526, 541, 579, 618, 621,
648
goal, 56, 127, 156, 180, 185, 193,
257, 260, 400, 437, 561,
588, 614, 622
goer, 365
good, 107, 136, 228, 247, 251, 252,
300, 326, 397, 479, 628
government, 103
grace, 52
graffiti, 99
grandeur, 9, 405, 537
grandmother, 4
graphic, 45, 252, 321, 534, 536, 538,
582, 621
gratitude, 19, 144, 159, 206, 240,
256, 311, 316, 317, 322,

414, 440, 457, 458, 464,
474, 523
greatness, 16, 73, 249, 322
greenery, 528
greet, 127, 153, 169, 225, 255, 520,
582
grit, 368
groove, 344, 346, 498
ground, 36, 43, 106, 147, 155, 159,
167, 181, 184, 189–191,
244, 299, 339, 340, 344,
473, 571, 597, 623
groundbreaking, 11, 25, 76, 96, 99,
108, 114, 120, 174, 177,
179, 182, 187, 192, 196,
205, 207, 211, 215, 257,
283, 292, 338, 345, 351,
359, 364, 367, 374,
392–394, 420, 424, 431,
432, 434, 467, 476, 479,
480, 485, 487, 488, 495,
510, 530, 563, 565, 616,
657, 658
grounding, 133
groundwork, 365
group, 154, 155, 170, 171, 220, 223,
224, 233, 252, 263, 265,
271, 312, 313, 391, 558,
571, 586, 601
growl, 368
growling, 333, 556
growth, 2, 13, 15, 18, 26, 28, 31, 34,
37, 38, 40, 42, 43, 45, 47,
48, 71, 74–76, 78, 80–86,
89, 90, 93, 99, 105, 141,
148, 154, 156, 160, 164,
167, 168, 176, 182–187,
191, 192, 196, 204, 209,
218, 219, 228, 230,

233–235, 238, 241, 242,
248, 249, 252, 256–259,
263, 265, 267, 268, 272,
273, 275–279, 283, 293,
294, 301, 316, 318, 319,
323, 336, 339, 351, 352,
365, 366, 370–373, 378,
380–382, 386–392, 407,
418, 425, 439, 440,
442–444, 446–449,
454–458, 464–469, 471,
476, 497, 500–502, 506,
511, 512, 524, 528, 530,
531, 547, 555, 557, 573,
580, 594, 596, 598, 604,
605, 607, 613, 615, 617,
647, 654
Gryffin, 560
guardian, 530
guerrilla, 196
guest, 203, 261, 403, 404, 406, 412
guidance, 2–5, 7, 13–18, 30, 31, 33,
41, 43, 46, 74, 91, 98, 141,
142, 148, 157, 159, 171,
172, 174, 190, 215, 234,
245, 252, 266, 273, 275,
284, 290, 318, 324, 439,
440, 447, 453, 456, 457,
459, 463, 467, 502, 583,
588, 592, 613
guide, 6, 44, 57, 64, 263, 277, 319,
320, 344, 396, 443, 502,
605
guidebook, 277
guitar, 3, 14, 20, 108, 333, 359, 427,
474, 485
guitarist, 3, 108, 520
Gurlz, 76

habit, 11
habitat, 161, 300, 587, 629, 630
halftime, 381
hall, 204
hallmark, 124, 658
halt, 169, 425
hand, 28, 199, 274, 289, 301, 328,
411, 445, 509, 526, 552,
587, 589, 590, 631
Hannah, 469
Hans Zimmer, 9, 429
happiness, 24, 245, 442, 443
harassment, 598
hardware, 6, 122, 346, 348, 349,
367, 402, 408, 513, 516
harm, 226, 620
harmonic, 96
Harmonious, 4, 5
harmony, 3, 333, 537
harness, 38, 270, 318, 612
hashtag, 52
haven, 225
head, 20, 168, 365, 420
headbang, 422
headliner, 42
headwear, 118
healing, 105, 111, 136, 243, 244,
246, 247, 249–251, 291,
356, 366, 417, 418, 469,
511, 552, 592
health, 52, 75, 86, 90–92, 105, 107,
130, 136, 137, 144, 171,
194, 205, 208, 213, 215,
224, 231, 239, 245–248,
250, 251, 253, 254, 260,
264, 284, 289–291,
295–298, 300, 302–305,
308–310, 318, 321, 326,
361, 365, 371, 387, 425,

426, 437, 446, 447, 462,
465, 466, 469, 479,
481–483, 488, 533, 554,
558, 570, 576, 586,
590–594, 601, 606, 608,
611–617, 619–621,
623–628, 630, 631,
635–640, 642, 644, 646,
649–652, 654, 656,
658–660
healthcare, 593
heart, 22, 32, 82, 85, 120, 124, 127,
135, 154, 157, 161, 184,
208, 228, 248, 257, 262,
283, 291, 317, 329, 336,
340, 417, 421, 425, 437,
490, 499, 531, 543, 614
heartbreak, 373
heartwarming, 310, 311, 463, 465,
518
heaviness, 363
heavyweight, 259
helmet, 33
help, 7, 15, 17, 42, 46, 75, 100, 102,
128, 134, 153, 158, 159,
171, 173, 200, 229, 230,
243, 247, 250, 252, 261,
263, 266, 267, 273, 276,
281, 290, 297, 304, 308,
320, 348, 354, 395, 396,
417, 425, 437, 452, 483,
502, 519, 540–542, 544,
551, 552, 588, 591, 593,
594, 608, 622, 627, 628,
630, 636, 637, 660
heritage, 154–156
hesitation, 24, 464
high, 10, 12, 18–20, 30, 32, 42, 45,
48, 52, 54, 61, 75, 99, 104,

108, 110, 114, 117, 125,
128, 134, 139, 140, 158,
169, 173, 183, 188, 199,
201, 213, 221, 238, 243,
250, 291, 332, 336, 337,
343, 350, 353, 354, 361,
363, 370, 383, 388, 392,
395, 396, 402, 412, 413,
415, 417, 418, 420, 422,
425, 437, 452, 464, 491,
492, 518, 532, 546,
549–551, 563, 566, 570,
573, 580, 646–648
highlight, 99, 101, 144, 204, 223,
225, 248, 249, 279, 284,
286, 308, 354, 365, 376,
413, 422, 429, 461, 482,
497, 520, 529, 530, 544,
561, 562, 605, 611, 634
hiking, 158, 161
hindrance, 118, 128
hip, 2, 6, 8, 9, 15, 24, 25, 49, 79, 99,
108, 109, 112, 113, 174,
176, 178, 179, 181, 183,
186, 187, 192, 198, 199,
207, 211, 214, 238, 293,
335, 338, 344, 350, 353,
361, 364, 367, 381, 385,
393, 424, 428, 429, 431,
432, 462, 474, 481, 486,
490, 492, 498, 506, 510,
511, 545, 547, 548, 551,
556, 565, 571, 597, 645,
647–649, 652
history, 156, 165, 279, 524, 553,
597, 645, 657, 658
hit, 49, 70, 95, 99, 128, 172, 192,
274, 353, 354, 365, 383,
385, 397, 474, 530

hobby, 34
holiday, 252, 301
homage, 156, 341, 355, 358, 359,
    379
home, 3
homelessness, 639
hometown, 18, 243, 244
honesty, 577
honor, 251, 459, 460
hop, 2, 6, 8, 9, 15, 24, 25, 49, 79, 99,
    108, 109, 112, 113, 174,
    176, 178, 179, 181, 183,
    186, 187, 192, 198, 199,
    207, 211, 214, 238, 293,
    335, 338, 344, 350, 353,
    361, 364, 367, 381, 384,
    385, 393, 424, 428, 429,
    431, 432, 462, 474, 481,
    486, 490, 492, 498, 506,
    510, 511, 545, 547, 548,
    551, 556, 565, 571, 597,
    645, 647–649, 652
hope, 72, 84, 206, 238, 243, 244,
    289, 297, 300, 308, 342,
    437, 463, 466, 469, 482,
    565, 576, 591, 593, 601,
    611–613, 617, 621, 636,
    650
hotel, 172, 174
house, 112, 477, 645
household, 3, 5, 13, 141
hum, 513
human, 29, 101, 161, 235, 238, 303,
    305, 306, 361, 362, 372,
    373, 387, 416, 442, 516,
    609, 643
humanity, 610, 614
humility, 37, 83, 440, 457, 458, 523
humor, 71, 404, 405, 580

hunger, 639
hunt, 55
hurdle, 52, 75, 189

iceberg, 419
icon, 104, 137, 173, 523, 525, 569,
    571, 574–576, 578, 653
iconography, 577
idea, 9, 27, 74, 117, 163, 172, 173,
    189, 202, 239, 243, 276,
    301, 362, 372, 388, 425,
    431, 498, 537, 578, 586,
    653
identify, 37, 39, 56, 60, 64, 79, 82,
    94, 102, 113, 162, 186,
    226, 261, 399, 401, 455,
    583, 605, 622, 625, 627,
    635, 653
identity, 1, 12, 14, 22, 25–28, 47, 59,
    60, 63, 64, 66, 69, 71, 79,
    82, 84, 85, 88–91, 93, 99,
    107, 113, 117–120,
    123–126, 129, 130, 132,
    137, 138, 145, 160, 195,
    197, 243, 307, 325, 327,
    331, 342, 347, 350, 368,
    375, 381, 382, 385, 389,
    405, 409, 433, 434, 442,
    446, 451, 454, 464, 476,
    522, 523, 525–531, 534,
    536–541, 543, 544, 567,
    568, 572, 575–578, 585,
    586, 597, 628, 643, 653,
    656
idol, 328
Illenium, 421, 560
illness, 300, 558, 610, 620
illusion, 409
illustration, 387, 528, 534

image, 47, 51, 52, 59, 63, 66, 89, 90,
    104, 107, 117–119, 132,
    137, 138, 247, 303, 343,
    453, 500, 517, 518,
    521–526, 529, 530, 537,
    538, 540, 569, 575–579,
    586
imagery, 362, 371, 372, 409, 416,
    531, 537–539, 542, 610
imagination, 12, 119, 122, 124, 158,
    212, 497, 533, 535, 542,
    610
immersion, 110, 154, 167, 417
impact, 2–4, 7, 12–14, 16, 18–20,
    22–25, 27, 28, 31, 36, 37,
    40, 44, 50–52, 56–62,
    65–71, 75, 76, 78, 83–86,
    95–97, 100, 101,
    103–107, 110–115, 118,
    125, 126, 130, 132, 133,
    136, 137, 139–142, 144,
    145, 148, 153, 161–165,
    172, 177, 179, 182–184,
    188, 190, 192–194, 197,
    204–209, 211–213, 215,
    218, 220, 222–224,
    226–228, 230–233, 235,
    238, 239, 241–246,
    248–252, 254–256,
    258–262, 264, 265, 268,
    269, 271, 272, 274, 276,
    278, 279, 283, 286, 288,
    289, 291, 293, 294, 296,
    298–303, 305, 308–313,
    315–319, 321–324, 327,
    328, 332, 335, 337, 339,
    342, 343, 348, 349, 351,
    352, 354, 358, 361–366,
    368, 370–375, 378,
    382–386, 390–392, 394,
    398, 406, 408–411, 413,
    414, 416–418, 425–427,
    429, 431, 437, 438, 441,
    443, 445–450, 452, 453,
    456, 458, 460, 462, 463,
    465–472, 476, 478–483,
    485–491, 494, 501, 506,
    507, 515, 517, 518, 521,
    523, 525–528, 530–533,
    540–567, 569–572,
    574–581, 583, 586–588,
    590, 594, 600–610,
    612–635, 637, 640–647,
    649–661
implementation, 374, 625
importance, 7, 10, 12–16, 19, 23, 24,
    26, 32, 34, 37, 39, 41, 46,
    47, 53, 59–62, 64–66, 69,
    75, 78, 79, 83–86, 88–91,
    93, 94, 96, 97, 101, 102,
    107, 121, 128, 133, 134,
    136, 139, 142, 145, 148,
    156, 158, 159, 161, 162,
    173, 174, 185, 188–190,
    195, 199, 204, 209, 214,
    215, 222, 223, 239,
    245–248, 253, 254, 256,
    257, 263, 272, 274, 276,
    279, 287–292, 294, 297,
    298, 301, 303–305, 308,
    311, 314, 316, 318,
    360–362, 364, 368, 386,
    387, 389, 393, 399,
    402–404, 425, 426, 428,
    433, 437–440, 442, 444,
    446, 449, 451, 454–456,
    458, 469, 480, 482, 483,
    493, 500–503, 505, 510,

513, 520, 523, 537, 539,
544, 547, 549, 567, 582,
587, 588, 590–592,
595–597, 599, 605, 608,
612, 613, 615, 617, 622,
623, 625, 627, 628, 630,
633, 635, 638–640,
649–651, 655, 657, 660
imposter, 73, 74
impression, 8, 18, 23, 32, 42, 54, 56,
58, 61, 70, 80, 104, 141,
153, 154, 194, 196, 210,
212, 213, 240, 255, 256,
337, 348, 372, 376, 384,
401–404, 406, 411, 412,
416, 438, 447, 522, 530,
531, 543, 546, 566, 578,
645, 646, 654, 657
imprint, 155, 426
improvement, 2, 37, 39, 60, 79, 82,
89, 93, 94, 141, 261, 363,
401, 443, 446, 458, 468,
502, 616, 622
improvisation, 140, 152, 407
in, 1–25, 27–37, 39–115, 117–145,
147–149, 151–165,
167–175, 177–185,
187–195, 197–215,
218–236, 238–258,
260–269, 271–279, 281,
283–311, 313–329,
331–359, 361–375,
378–403, 405–418,
420–422, 424–460,
462–483, 485–488,
491–503, 505–507,
509–522, 524–589, 591,
593–602, 604–607,
609–646, 648–661

inception, 27, 112, 137, 519, 524,
655
inclination, 4, 13
inclusion, 107, 185, 187, 295, 371,
406, 544
inclusivity, 27, 53, 72, 73, 113, 115,
124, 127, 129, 130, 170,
171, 185, 187, 188, 203,
223, 231, 232, 234, 254,
265, 267, 268, 278, 284,
285, 294–300, 303–305,
309, 314, 318, 319, 323,
324, 403, 414, 455, 456,
466, 471–473, 482, 483,
524, 539, 569, 571–574,
582, 585, 597–602, 606,
608, 610, 619, 620, 651,
653, 656, 660
income, 30, 74
incorporation, 96, 128, 129, 336,
338, 344, 368, 382, 427,
462, 478, 485, 486, 522,
535, 538, 548, 549, 551,
556, 560, 561, 563, 564,
647, 656
India, 164
indie, 178, 179
individual, 4, 5, 12, 14, 23, 36, 76,
82, 90, 119, 124, 132, 145,
147, 159, 167, 179, 180,
187, 189, 222, 232, 245,
249, 279, 280, 289, 328,
400, 415, 443, 450, 458,
461, 471, 496, 520, 566,
573, 589, 594, 654
individuality, 29, 72, 73, 88, 90, 94,
96, 105, 107, 129, 130,
151, 185–187, 194, 243,
247, 249, 250, 258, 265,

292, 294, 296, 297, 315,
325, 370, 372, 415, 426,
442, 451, 454, 456, 483,
489, 566, 567, 569,
571–575, 578, 579, 581,
586, 597, 602, 606–608,
613, 651, 653
industry, 2–4, 6, 7, 10, 12–19, 22,
23, 25, 29–31, 35–37,
40–48, 50, 55, 56, 60, 62,
65–67, 69, 71–82, 84–86,
88–100, 104, 106, 107,
110, 112, 119, 125, 129,
132, 141, 142, 148, 149,
151, 153, 167, 168,
171–174, 176, 182, 187,
188, 190–197, 203–208,
210–213, 215, 222, 223,
230–232, 236, 249, 252,
254, 257–260, 263–265,
268–277, 279, 283–286,
292–297, 300, 303, 304,
309, 315, 319, 323, 324,
332, 336, 339, 342, 343,
346, 347, 349, 352, 355,
356, 363–365, 368–370,
374, 375, 379, 381, 383,
391, 406, 420, 425–428,
431, 437–453, 457–460,
462, 463, 466, 467, 472,
474–489, 493, 499–503,
506, 507, 514, 516, 517,
522, 523, 531, 533, 534,
545–549, 551, 554, 557,
558, 561, 563–569,
571–574, 576, 577, 579,
581, 583–586, 590, 592,
594, 597–602, 605, 613,
614, 618, 623, 625, 628,

632, 634, 643–646,
649–653, 655–660
inequality, 183, 298, 299, 305, 361,
610, 613, 630
influence, 7–9, 11, 14, 19, 63, 65, 71,
77, 85, 97, 98, 103, 106,
107, 121, 135, 136, 145,
156, 171, 172, 188, 205,
206, 211–213, 215,
220–222, 224, 228,
230–232, 235, 248,
258–260, 263, 265, 268,
271, 278, 287, 291, 298,
300–303, 305, 308, 313,
315, 318–320, 323, 342,
343, 366–368, 375, 393,
394, 425–427, 439, 445,
447, 449, 450, 456, 457,
463, 466, 467, 469–472,
478, 479, 481–483, 486,
488, 489, 494, 550, 551,
553, 555, 556, 560–564,
567–571, 574–581, 583,
585–587, 590, 598,
600–602, 606–608,
612–615, 618, 619, 621,
624, 626, 628, 631,
644–646, 649–652,
655–658, 660
influencer, 52, 343
influx, 486
information, 29, 64, 226, 227, 245,
247, 287, 302, 303, 309,
492, 588, 592
infusion, 182
ingenuity, 576
initiative, 101, 102, 105, 162, 224,
232, 252, 278, 301–303,
322, 450, 602, 626, 627,

636
injustice, 298, 300, 361, 619, 630
innovation, 7, 9, 25, 26, 67, 76, 79,
		80, 86, 96, 97, 113, 114,
		127–129, 155, 174, 178,
		182, 186, 191, 193, 194,
		199, 200, 204, 208,
		210–213, 230, 231,
		257–259, 268, 272, 276,
		283, 285, 292–294, 319,
		334, 336, 339, 340, 343,
		345, 349, 364, 381, 382,
		393, 394, 406, 407, 425,
		427, 430–432, 444,
		454–456, 472, 473, 476,
		477, 479, 480, 482, 485,
		488, 489, 495, 505, 517,
		524, 527, 533, 542, 547,
		548, 552, 554, 555, 558,
		561, 562, 564, 570, 602,
		616, 618, 639, 640,
		642–644, 647, 648, 656,
		658
innovator, 77, 81, 458
input, 37, 42, 53, 82, 126, 131, 142,
		180, 186, 189, 318, 319,
		440, 459, 467, 494, 516
insecurity, 249
insight, 156, 319, 380, 390, 518
inspiration, 1, 2, 6, 9, 11, 12, 15, 16,
		19, 21, 22, 25, 27, 31–35,
		73, 75, 76, 81, 85, 86, 95,
		98, 111, 112, 114, 135,
		136, 141, 144, 148, 151,
		155–163, 165, 167, 168,
		171, 172, 177, 187, 188,
		198, 199, 201, 205, 223,
		227, 232, 234, 237–239,
		241, 242, 244, 246, 248,

		249, 255, 259, 276, 277,
		285, 291, 296, 315, 317,
		318, 322, 323, 327, 328,
		336, 337, 340–342, 344,
		350, 351, 355–358, 364,
		366, 370, 372, 381, 383,
		385, 388–390, 393, 396,
		408, 425, 427, 429–431,
		433, 434, 437, 441, 442,
		448, 453, 455, 456, 462,
		463, 469, 470, 475, 482,
		492, 494, 496, 498, 499,
		506, 509–514, 516, 525,
		534, 535, 537, 542–544,
		546, 555, 557, 559–562,
		564, 571, 574, 576, 579,
		580, 584, 586, 593–597,
		601, 604, 607, 611, 613,
		617, 624, 644, 654–657
installation, 626
instance, 41, 44, 155, 156, 162–164,
		183, 188, 198, 299, 306,
		337, 339, 373, 410, 432,
		498, 506, 606, 610, 611,
		639
instant, 49, 103, 128, 192, 352, 353,
		360, 385, 474
instill, 468, 611
instruction, 15
instrument, 14, 164, 427, 516
instrumentalist, 495
instrumentation, 114, 156, 175, 178,
		182, 207, 367, 395, 403,
		404, 406, 427, 428, 564,
		596
integration, 62, 120, 122, 156, 202,
		215, 349, 393, 406, 541,
		643
integrity, 25, 28, 31, 73, 80, 82,

85–88, 90, 118, 157, 181,
210, 282, 438, 440, 458,
460, 486, 499–501, 585,
650, 655
intelligence, 347, 349
intensity, 8, 64, 95, 158, 160, 177,
333, 336, 342, 354, 358,
363, 373, 383, 387, 395,
396, 408, 477, 491, 522,
529, 537, 541, 543, 550,
561
interaction, 16, 23, 62, 65, 80, 106,
121, 130, 140, 152, 170,
172, 213, 236, 242, 323,
395, 398, 401, 406,
413–415, 464, 539, 542,
570
interactivity, 122, 124, 202
interconnectedness, 136, 571, 614
interest, 18, 41, 43, 63, 124, 128,
172, 197, 229, 242, 261,
263, 323, 331, 349, 550,
567, 589, 595
interlude, 337
interplay, 181
interpretation, 292
intersection, 184, 384, 630
interval, 158
interview, 424, 605
intimacy, 50, 125, 127, 196, 235,
255, 403
intimidation, 172
intricacy, 214
intrigue, 27, 117, 119, 120, 123,
124, 128, 132, 137, 138,
198, 212, 323, 487, 522,
523, 534, 537, 567, 568,
572, 576, 653
intro, 372, 397

introduction, 128
introspection, 34, 111, 127, 336,
337, 372, 386, 417, 442,
443, 492, 546, 607
intuition, 25
invention, 645
investing, 12, 30, 210, 211, 255, 299,
301
investment, 14, 54, 189, 232, 467
invitation, 173, 357
involvement, 53, 145, 157, 170, 171,
202, 228, 232, 262, 277,
288, 291, 300–302, 324,
328, 413, 451, 468, 574,
585, 605, 606, 624, 626,
629, 635, 637, 658
Isabella Carter, 99
isolation, 292
issue, 102, 103, 136, 161, 226, 286,
593, 611, 624
item, 195
iteration, 28, 524

jam, 3
James, 465
Jane Goodall, 429
Japan, 153, 155, 163, 325
jar, 513
Jason, 365
Jason Timothy, 277
jaw, 369
Jay Smith, 99
Jay Smith's, 99
jazz, 3, 6, 8, 20, 21, 25, 175, 182,
186, 187, 433, 511
jealousy, 147
jet, 158
job, 465, 639
Joel Zimmerman, 33

Johann Sebastian Bach, 19
John, 243, 249, 252, 469
John Coltrane, 20
John Lennon, 306
John Williams, 9, 429
Jonathan Harnum, 435
Jonathan Zittrain, 133
journal, 162
journaling, 92
journey, 1–3, 5–9, 11–17, 22–24,
    28, 29, 31–35, 37, 42,
    45–48, 53, 56, 57, 67, 69,
    72–78, 80, 83, 85, 90–94,
    98, 107, 110, 120,
    122–124, 127, 129–131,
    135, 136, 138, 139,
    141–143, 147, 148, 152,
    154, 157, 165, 167, 172,
    177, 179, 190, 192, 194,
    195, 197, 198, 200, 206,
    220, 228, 234, 235, 238,
    242, 243, 246, 247, 249,
    255, 257, 259, 263, 273,
    276, 291, 297, 303, 304,
    311, 316, 317, 331, 336,
    350, 355, 356, 358, 365,
    366, 371, 372, 380,
    384–386, 388, 391, 392,
    397, 405, 408, 412, 417,
    418, 420, 422, 425, 436,
    437, 439–443, 445, 446,
    449, 451–458, 463–465,
    468, 469, 475, 479, 482,
    483, 491, 494, 497–503,
    511, 514, 516, 517,
    519–521, 523, 524, 526,
    528–532, 537, 547, 557,
    565, 580, 584, 586, 593,
    594, 605, 606, 613, 614,

    650, 655, 657
joy, 3, 23, 95, 123, 145, 154, 157,
    159, 245, 301, 311, 326,
    328, 372, 406, 412, 417,
    440, 447, 510, 521, 543,
    571, 647, 654
judgement, 123, 305, 568
judgment, 83, 138, 224, 243–245,
    285, 290, 325, 509, 569,
    586, 591
juggling, 126
Jukedeck, 516
jump, 110, 396, 401, 422, 519, 530
jumping, 140, 153, 157, 158,
    397–399, 413, 415
Jungle, 421
justice, 86, 130, 171, 205, 213, 215,
    224, 226, 231, 239, 245,
    260, 284, 295, 296,
    298–300, 318, 326, 362,
    371, 447, 466, 479, 481,
    533, 606, 613, 618–620,
    623–625, 628, 630, 639,
    642, 659
juxtaposition, 32, 387, 538, 553, 577

Kanye West, 181
Kara Walker, 307
Kayzo, 422
Ken Robinson, 605
Kendrick Lamar, 49, 429, 492
key, 10, 12, 15, 18, 35, 39–41,
    43–46, 48, 50, 53, 55, 56,
    60, 63, 73, 76, 78, 79, 83,
    94, 103, 110, 120, 125,
    130, 132, 153, 160, 163,
    180–182, 187, 188, 190,
    193, 197, 204, 206, 212,
    213, 215, 234, 238, 244,

253, 254, 262–264, 266,
268, 277, 295, 308, 323,
327, 333, 342, 344, 354,
366, 372, 375, 381, 388,
389, 392, 395, 396, 399,
400, 405, 408, 415, 417,
420, 427, 432, 452–454,
473, 475, 477, 478, 482,
490, 492, 494, 499, 502,
509, 514, 526, 528, 531,
537, 553, 554, 578, 586,
594, 605, 606, 612, 616,
623, 625, 628, 638, 645,
647, 649, 654
keyboard, 4, 441
killer, 420
kind, 10, 108, 122, 152, 241, 301,
391, 407, 421
kindness, 154, 245, 301–303, 314,
322, 326, 458, 609, 610,
618
kingdom, 633
kinship, 119, 315
Kirby Ferguson, 456
Kirby Ferguson -, 456
knack, 192, 395, 546
knowledge, 6, 15–17, 36, 43, 56, 98,
151, 204, 213, 245, 252,
258, 263, 264, 266–268,
275, 279, 283, 284, 455,
456, 463, 492, 557, 596
Kraftwerk, 553
Kyoto, 163

label, 46, 272, 274, 295, 394
lack, 29, 34, 113, 250, 289, 290
landscape, 8, 22, 26, 28, 46, 48, 60,
63, 65, 71, 73, 76, 79, 89,
95, 97, 106, 107, 114, 145,

154, 159, 172, 174, 177,
178, 180, 197, 198, 207,
208, 211–214, 216, 220,
233, 258, 259, 265, 276,
277, 280, 285, 293, 320,
323, 324, 332, 335, 336,
338, 339, 342–344, 346,
348, 351, 352, 355, 359,
363, 366–368, 373–375,
381, 386, 393, 394, 409,
425, 426, 433, 438, 443,
450–452, 463, 468, 472,
480–483, 486, 491, 494,
499, 517, 524, 530, 534,
544–546, 550, 552, 553,
555, 557, 559–562, 564,
567, 568, 570, 578, 583,
600, 643–647, 651,
653–661
language, 29, 101, 103, 126, 129,
153, 156, 163, 164, 171,
175, 253, 289, 326, 362,
366, 416, 431, 525, 532,
543, 544, 568, 597, 607,
652
laser, 139, 541
laughter, 521
launch, 425, 488, 630
layer, 74, 110, 119, 124, 164, 183,
234, 337, 368, 371, 395,
398, 403, 409, 417, 491,
527, 536, 537, 541, 561
layering, 180, 333, 354, 374,
491–493, 520, 561, 562
lead, 31, 34, 36, 84, 88, 94, 161, 174,
177, 179, 184, 198, 211,
389, 436, 455, 468, 493,
494, 607
leadership, 634

learner, 15
learning, 3, 10, 14, 15, 31, 35, 37, 74,
    81, 83, 89, 93, 204, 252,
    273, 275, 347, 349, 446,
    455–457, 497, 502, 511,
    516, 595, 630, 639
led, 18, 21, 24, 43, 102, 105, 106,
    127, 144, 170, 174, 188,
    192, 218, 224, 226–228,
    230–233, 241, 245, 249,
    253, 254, 265, 268, 272,
    274, 276–278, 300, 301,
    308, 310, 311, 317, 318,
    326, 328, 329, 351, 363,
    367, 391, 442, 450, 478,
    486, 516, 545, 551, 552,
    554, 563, 606, 621, 629,
    632, 634, 637, 640
legacy, 29, 33, 76, 81, 84, 93,
    104–106, 112, 120, 123,
    132, 137, 145, 168, 193,
    204–206, 212, 213, 223,
    235, 244, 250, 262, 294,
    298, 316–319, 323, 328,
    329, 346, 358, 375,
    425–428, 437, 438,
    446–448, 457, 458, 466,
    470, 479, 483, 485, 489,
    499, 507, 525, 544,
    548–553, 559, 563–565,
    567, 570, 571, 574, 576,
    590, 602, 609, 614, 620,
    626, 635, 641, 643–646,
    650, 651, 653, 654,
    657–661
legend, 359
legitimacy, 265
lens, 544
lesson, 172, 444

letter, 103
level, 2, 11, 18–20, 27, 28, 33, 34,
    44, 50, 53, 54, 59, 64–67,
    70, 76, 77, 80, 83, 86, 88,
    89, 101, 104, 106, 108,
    110–113, 118–120, 122,
    124–128, 130, 131, 137,
    138, 143, 146, 151–154,
    165, 167–169, 180, 183,
    188, 194–196, 202, 207,
    209, 212, 218, 219, 221,
    239–242, 250, 254–256,
    293, 301, 303, 313, 316,
    319, 327, 336, 344, 348,
    353, 354, 363, 366, 370,
    371, 378, 383, 386, 388,
    393, 399, 403–405, 410,
    412, 416, 417, 426, 427,
    436, 440, 442, 447–450,
    452, 463, 470, 473–475,
    477, 480, 483, 490, 492,
    496, 499, 509, 512, 521,
    523, 525, 527, 531,
    538–542, 547, 568, 570,
    574, 580, 585, 586, 589,
    607, 609, 618, 637, 644,
    645, 647, 653, 655, 657
leverage, 36, 39, 44, 74, 77, 194, 196,
    203, 209, 260, 270, 271,
    279, 283, 302, 305, 307,
    584, 594, 614, 622, 627,
    631, 639
levity, 521
liberation, 119, 568, 595
library, 10–12, 379
lie, 177, 309, 553
life, 16, 24, 27, 32, 50, 71, 74–76,
    91, 92, 94, 103, 105,
    117–119, 123–125,

132–135, 137, 138, 140,
141, 143, 145–148, 154,
157–160, 162, 167–169,
178, 179, 194, 201, 203,
217, 222, 224, 233, 243,
244, 248–250, 284, 286,
289, 291, 294, 298, 312,
314, 318, 325–327, 329,
341, 357, 365, 372, 379,
388, 394, 405, 417, 418,
426, 440, 441, 443, 445,
453, 460, 465, 469, 471,
480, 483, 495, 497, 499,
510, 512, 513, 517, 519,
520, 522, 523, 526, 532,
534, 536, 537, 539,
541–543, 567–569, 571,
572, 585, 590, 591, 604,
610, 638, 651, 654
lifestyle, 47, 158
lifetime, 224, 328
light, 27, 60, 101, 107, 121, 152,
296, 299, 304–306, 365,
416, 417, 428, 441, 458,
467, 533, 548, 554, 597,
606, 608, 612, 618, 621,
638, 660
lighting, 56, 57, 61, 110, 139, 152,
202, 210, 293, 348, 398,
400, 404, 405, 408–411,
417, 429, 515, 527, 532,
541, 542, 544, 551, 578
like, 1, 8, 9, 13, 14, 16, 17, 20, 32,
40, 41, 45, 47, 48, 50–53,
55, 58, 67, 69, 89, 93, 95,
101, 103, 106, 110, 112,
121, 125, 126, 130, 140,
142, 152, 161, 169, 177,
188, 194, 200, 219–222,

225, 229, 230, 232,
235–237, 243–245, 248,
250, 253, 257, 260, 263,
265–268, 270, 271, 275,
295, 297, 306, 311, 315,
316, 318, 321, 325, 327,
332, 334, 344, 346–350,
354, 365, 369, 370, 381,
384–386, 395, 398, 403,
406, 409, 414–416, 425,
428–430, 434, 437, 440,
453, 455, 459, 471, 481,
482, 497–499, 501, 503,
513, 515, 522, 553–555,
558, 560, 561, 566, 577,
580, 581, 584, 588, 598,
600, 612, 613, 615, 618,
620, 621, 623, 624, 631,
638, 649, 652
likelihood, 62
Lily Collins, 98
Lily Collins', 98
Lily Wilde, 467
limit, 71
limitation, 510
line, 79, 143, 168, 196, 202, 255,
362, 428, 531, 580, 582,
621
lineup, 272, 311
Lisa, 465
list, 77
listener, 10, 64, 69, 127, 168, 198,
199, 218, 333, 334, 337,
367, 372, 491, 492, 534,
583
listening, 6, 64, 76, 79, 91, 99, 108,
129, 143, 186, 189, 192,
210, 211, 218, 221, 228,
246, 247, 249, 251,

335–337, 350, 353, 354,
383, 462, 477, 492, 536,
543, 546, 553, 554, 563,
608
literature, 305, 442, 510
litter, 162
live, 16, 18, 19, 22, 23, 27–29,
32–34, 42, 45–48, 51, 52,
54, 59–65, 80, 86, 104,
110–112, 114, 115,
120–123, 127–129, 131,
132, 139–141, 143,
151–154, 160, 164, 168,
169, 178, 182, 194, 196,
197, 201–204, 207, 208,
210, 213, 214, 219, 220,
227, 229, 230, 233, 234,
236–238, 250, 255, 261,
272, 285, 288, 291, 293,
298, 305, 309, 311, 313,
316, 318, 320, 325, 326,
343, 348, 349, 353, 365,
367, 369, 373, 379, 382,
383, 388, 391, 392,
395–414, 416–418, 424,
425, 427–431, 434–437,
447, 452, 461, 469, 474,
475, 477–480, 486–488,
515, 518, 519, 521, 522,
527, 529–532, 537,
539–544, 546, 547, 549,
550, 552, 556, 566–568,
571, 573, 580, 582, 583,
592, 596, 598–600, 608,
629, 633, 636, 646, 648,
650, 656, 657, 660
livelihood, 629
livestream, 169
living, 137, 138, 146, 159, 361, 588,
618, 623, 660
lo-fi, 341
lobby, 172
location, 169, 170, 221, 266, 532
logo, 195
London, 173
longevity, 86, 126, 130, 285, 616,
647, 648
look, 29, 36, 138, 143, 186, 199,
211, 265, 295, 317, 358,
367, 371, 376, 382, 387,
399, 420, 422, 473, 492,
514, 517, 549, 554, 564,
577, 598, 602, 608, 641,
655
lookout, 404
loop, 40, 415, 535
Los Angeles, 1, 41, 172, 311
loss, 188, 643
love, 1, 3–5, 8, 20, 32, 33, 79, 95, 96,
104, 118, 119, 124, 129,
132, 138, 140, 143, 144,
153, 154, 157–161, 170,
171, 178, 188, 192,
217–220, 223–225, 227,
229–237, 243, 247, 249,
251–254, 256, 265, 268,
278, 294, 298, 310, 311,
313–317, 321, 322,
324–328, 346, 357, 365,
371, 374, 389, 395, 397,
415, 417, 422, 439, 440,
446, 449, 471, 472, 502,
520, 522, 543, 569, 571,
572, 580, 591, 595, 598,
600, 601, 611, 619, 633,
660
lover, 243
low, 30, 333

loyalty, 51, 53, 54, 131, 169, 228,
    323, 440
luck, 173
Ludwig van, 19
lyric, 371

Mac Miller, 474
Mac Miller's, 474
machine, 347, 349, 516, 643
maestro, 479
magic, 140, 177, 356, 376, 407, 413,
    467, 494, 518, 520, 537
mainstream, 31, 49, 73, 105, 315,
    340–342, 351, 364, 370,
    462, 481, 488, 496, 550,
    553, 558, 563, 564, 570,
    584–586, 611, 652, 653
majority, 82
making, 3, 4, 13, 19, 42, 44, 51, 54,
    60, 64, 65, 71, 78, 83, 85,
    104, 129, 131, 132, 134,
    135, 137, 143, 144, 152,
    159, 171, 194, 202, 205,
    212, 218, 221, 224, 226,
    230–232, 239, 241–244,
    247, 251, 254, 256, 259,
    260, 264, 278, 286, 288,
    290, 295, 296, 298, 300,
    302, 305, 308–311, 316,
    319, 324, 326, 328, 335,
    338, 348, 349, 353, 367,
    370, 371, 386, 398, 403,
    404, 408, 410–414, 416,
    417, 425, 438, 440, 447,
    448, 454, 458, 459, 470,
    481–483, 485, 505, 511,
    513, 514, 518, 524, 527,
    531, 534, 548, 550, 559,
    569–571, 575, 580, 581,

    596, 600–602, 606, 607,
    609, 614, 616–618, 620,
    621, 624, 625, 628, 637,
    639, 641, 647, 649, 651,
    655–657, 659, 660
man, 77, 132, 465, 518
management, 107, 177, 247, 500,
    536, 568, 587, 592, 616
manifestation, 317
manifesto, 206
manipulation, 275, 337, 347, 375,
    538
manner, 27, 189, 371
mantra, 366
mapping, 122, 348, 409, 410
Mark, 366, 464
mark, 2, 26, 31, 33, 56, 97, 98, 106,
    112, 153, 174, 193, 206,
    223, 259, 294, 324, 343,
    349, 352, 363–365, 370,
    385, 394, 420, 437, 458,
    461, 463, 471, 472, 478,
    480, 482, 483, 488, 497,
    545, 548, 553–555, 557,
    559, 561, 578, 581, 602,
    643, 646, 649, 650,
    653–655, 657–659
Mark Thompson, 100
Mark, 366
market, 30, 45, 56–58, 64, 85, 88,
    436
marketing, 2, 16, 29, 30, 46–48, 51,
    54, 55, 59, 60, 62–65, 68,
    74, 104, 130, 138,
    194–197, 261, 263, 268,
    271, 273, 275, 277, 478,
    500, 501, 566, 567, 581,
    583, 584
marriage, 526

marvel, 238
Mary, 464, 465
mashup, 140
mask, 27, 28, 47, 59, 66, 71, 77,
    117–121, 123–129, 132,
    137, 138, 147, 190, 195,
    212, 295, 298, 343, 346,
    405, 426, 487, 517–526,
    529, 531–533, 537, 541,
    543, 546, 567–569,
    572–579, 585, 586, 597,
    653
masquerade, 567
mass, 385, 398
master, 335
masterclass, 263
mastering, 4, 15, 16, 209, 341, 348,
    375
masterpiece, 82, 99, 420, 452, 535,
    537
mastery, 368, 384, 422, 477, 480,
    491, 492
material, 56, 57, 378
Max Ramirez, 496
meal, 639
mean, 574
meaning, 67, 366, 371, 372, 412,
    445, 536, 541, 549, 575
means, 2, 34, 81, 84, 107, 111, 151,
    168, 189, 206, 209, 222,
    226, 255, 293, 307, 316,
    416, 426, 432, 433, 436,
    445, 452, 454, 466, 487,
    513, 522, 539, 556, 567,
    585–587, 613, 615, 636,
    650
measure, 60, 76, 78, 368
mechanism, 592
media, 2, 19, 30, 41, 43–45, 47,
    50–55, 59–64, 68, 69, 86,
    102–106, 110, 121, 126,
    127, 130, 131, 133, 142,
    143, 145, 168–170, 177,
    192, 194–197, 217–222,
    225–230, 232, 233,
    235–237, 240, 245, 247,
    249, 251, 252, 254–256,
    261, 263, 264, 266, 271,
    274–278, 287–290, 294,
    299–301, 313–316, 318,
    320, 322, 323, 327, 352,
    369, 414, 436, 448–450,
    464, 470, 474, 478, 481,
    482, 492, 500–502, 533,
    537, 539, 540, 543, 547,
    551, 557, 558, 566, 570,
    571, 573, 579, 581–584,
    586, 588, 592, 596, 598,
    600, 601, 606, 608, 615,
    621, 622, 627, 628, 630,
    632, 637, 640, 644
meditation, 92, 134, 247, 509, 592
medium, 67, 101, 246, 306, 588, 610
meet, 19, 41, 42, 44, 53, 54, 62, 65,
    85, 89, 90, 104, 105, 110,
    127, 131, 141–143, 153,
    169–171, 177, 218, 220,
    223–226, 229, 232, 233,
    239–241, 251, 253, 255,
    261, 271, 278, 310, 311,
    314, 317, 318, 320, 324,
    326–328, 414, 449, 457,
    464, 465, 470–472, 481,
    520, 558, 571, 580, 582,
    587, 601, 608, 609, 654
meeting, 31, 89, 180, 235, 327, 328,
    389, 442, 499, 501, 587
Melody, 333

melody, 5, 10, 19, 28, 76, 353, 361,
365, 372, 387, 408, 463,
541
member, 4, 39, 241, 242, 249, 251,
252, 313, 415, 535, 628
memory, 141, 229, 413, 416, 654,
655
mention, 362, 467
mentor, 6, 16, 39, 98, 148, 151, 171,
425, 447, 605
mentoring, 150, 151, 191, 204, 463,
472, 605
mentorship, 2, 3, 7, 13, 14, 16–18,
30, 31, 33, 41, 46, 97, 98,
136, 141, 148, 151, 174,
205, 213, 215, 231, 252,
263, 264, 266, 267, 273,
276, 278, 284, 295, 297,
307, 318, 324, 439, 463,
467, 488, 548, 599, 602,
604, 613, 619, 626, 627,
633, 639
merchandise, 55, 59, 60, 62, 68, 74,
124, 131, 195–197, 218,
221, 225, 256, 261, 284,
317, 321, 322, 412, 428,
527, 536, 577, 582,
620–622, 625, 629
merchandising, 195, 197
merger, 202
merging, 34, 49, 108, 179, 343, 512,
657
message, 72, 84, 104, 129, 132, 137,
167, 171, 194, 218, 241,
246–248, 250, 251, 291,
295–298, 304, 313, 314,
316, 318, 323, 361, 362,
371, 387, 446, 464, 469,
470, 520, 524, 530, 533,

539, 548, 549, 569–572,
575, 576, 578, 590, 598,
600–602, 606, 612, 632,
633, 644, 651, 653
messaging, 195, 546
metal, 8, 9, 20, 24, 49, 211, 259,
359, 360, 393, 474
method, 180
Mexico, 164
Miami, 70
Michael, 4
Michael Collins, 100
Michael Hewitt, 8, 435
mid, 350, 518, 519, 530, 553
midst, 91, 123, 173
mile, 317, 403, 412
Miles Davis, 20
milestone, 18, 55, 77, 78, 252
mind, 34, 35, 37, 82, 122, 210, 250,
285, 358, 395, 421, 422,
431, 459, 487, 493, 498,
502, 509, 535, 590, 622,
623
mindedness, 108, 183, 467, 468,
473, 474
mindfulness, 247, 509, 511, 592
mindset, 15, 30, 74, 82, 84, 94, 95,
167, 187, 215, 247, 259,
277, 304, 443, 503, 512,
608, 650
mirror, 96, 127
mission, 260, 262, 322, 614, 615,
620, 622, 625, 629, 635,
641
misunderstanding, 290
mix, 3, 8, 56–58, 61, 173, 348, 349,
354, 367, 368, 477, 562
mixing, 1, 6, 16, 110, 209, 341, 348,
375, 400, 520, 561, 643

mixture, 29
mock, 535
model, 29, 114, 149, 171, 205, 211,
    232, 315, 478, 500, 501,
    546, 557, 589, 658
moderation, 131
modernity, 522
modulation, 10, 96, 347, 368, 436,
    491, 493, 515
mold, 71, 73, 106, 339, 371, 439,
    577
moment, 22, 23, 27, 56, 58, 77, 110,
    118, 121–123, 138–140,
    153, 154, 159, 168, 177,
    189, 311, 365, 381, 395,
    398, 412–414, 416, 417,
    441, 451, 453, 459, 464,
    465, 498, 509, 512–514,
    517, 519, 521, 529, 530,
    609
momentum, 74, 75, 91
moniker, 1
monotony, 403, 523
mood, 120, 246, 251, 337, 408, 411,
    510, 534, 541
morning, 1, 159
mortal, 522
mortality, 159
mother, 3, 4
motif, 535, 569
motion, 409, 410
motivation, 30, 33, 83, 227, 239,
    249, 309, 320, 324, 364,
    370, 448, 449, 456, 465,
    498, 546, 552
mountain, 160, 167
mouth, 54, 55, 62, 104, 128, 221,
    227, 228, 230, 278

move, 99, 156, 190, 249, 368, 397,
    440, 486, 591, 654, 655
movement, 106, 219, 220, 222, 245,
    250, 265, 286, 289, 306,
    307, 314, 323, 347, 349,
    362, 368, 394, 409, 428,
    461, 542, 578, 587, 589,
    590, 626, 641
movie, 564
mud, 158
multimedia, 99, 208, 271, 615
multitude, 207
mural, 611
music, 1–37, 40–90, 92–115,
    117–133, 135–149,
    151–165, 167–179,
    182–199, 201–225,
    227–260, 262–268,
    271–300, 303–305,
    308–329, 331–356,
    358–376, 378, 379,
    381–412, 414–422,
    424–483, 485–503,
    505–507, 509–518,
    520–602, 604–614,
    616–626, 628–637, 639,
    642–661
musicality, 5, 21, 113, 332, 336, 446
musician, 17, 23, 39, 45, 88, 107,
    118, 129, 134, 145, 153,
    158, 177, 182, 206, 249,
    308, 366, 391, 407, 418,
    435, 439–443, 453,
    458–460, 469, 484, 518,
    519, 546, 574, 587, 606,
    612, 629, 632, 650
myriad, 6
mystery, 27, 117–119, 123, 124,
    128, 132, 137, 346, 405,

487, 522–524, 568, 572,
575, 576
mysticism, 156
mystique, 27, 118, 119, 124, 137,
138, 212, 522, 537, 568,
575, 585, 653
mythology, 535

name, 1, 344, 525, 645
narrative, 58, 64, 68, 69, 120, 304,
358, 371, 401, 412, 429,
517, 526, 531, 532, 538
nationality, 656
nature, 8, 11, 20, 34, 35, 84, 92, 95,
96, 101, 117, 118,
123–125, 128, 136–138,
148, 158, 160–162, 167,
168, 175, 182, 217, 226,
244, 247, 249, 250, 253,
288, 296, 300, 303, 326,
355–357, 371, 372, 374,
383, 386, 388–390, 404,
409, 418, 429, 433, 445,
493, 498, 510, 512–514,
518, 528, 530, 535, 538,
542, 546, 550–552, 560,
568, 575, 590, 614, 630,
632, 633, 646–648
need, 15, 39, 74, 75, 90, 93, 98, 122,
135–137, 148, 180, 226,
244, 247, 251, 252, 267,
271, 276, 282, 287, 290,
295, 296, 299, 301–303,
308, 361, 362, 387, 493,
500, 513, 561, 588, 596,
602, 605, 606, 612, 613,
615, 617, 621, 623, 625,
628, 632, 636–638, 640
negativity, 83, 84, 238, 452

negligence, 361
nervousness, 173
network, 14, 30, 36, 41–44, 46, 74,
83, 84, 92, 97, 129, 134,
169, 243, 251, 257, 264,
272–276, 284, 301, 302,
314, 325, 328, 440, 458,
464, 471, 474–476, 502,
558, 588, 591, 628, 639
networking, 7, 15, 35, 41–46, 48,
172, 174, 176, 190, 264,
444, 445, 503
neuroscience, 456
newcomer, 325
newfound, 27, 147, 243, 265, 456
news, 47, 226, 235, 277
niche, 15, 73, 88, 93, 94, 334, 381,
444, 451, 481, 645, 654
night, 18, 27, 75, 141, 173, 372, 373,
441, 465
nightlife, 163, 167
Nina Simone, 306
noise, 52, 446, 531
none, 31, 172, 611
nonprofit, 284
norm, 331, 332, 585
normalcy, 133
North America, 152
nostalgia, 647
note, 29, 34, 76, 127, 134, 141, 191,
392, 400, 413, 426, 436,
486, 493, 497
notice, 362, 396, 540
notion, 27, 72, 113, 114, 119, 258,
483, 488, 544, 563, 652
novelty, 337
number, 61, 379, 445, 510, 637

obfuscation, 525

obscurity, 565
obstacle, 30, 73, 74, 158, 595
occasion, 310
ocean, 101, 633
octane, 20, 108, 173, 337, 354, 422
ode, 356
off, 34, 110, 121, 125, 157, 158, 180,
    398, 401, 415, 468, 510,
    518, 520, 522, 565
offstage, 520
on, 1–9, 11–14, 16–20, 22–34,
    37–45, 47–54, 56–71,
    74–86, 88–92, 94, 95, 97,
    98, 100–107, 110–115,
    117–122, 124, 125, 127,
    128, 130–134, 136–148,
    151–156, 158, 159,
    161–165, 167–174, 177,
    179–184, 187–197, 200,
    202–207, 209, 211–214,
    219–221, 223, 224,
    226–233, 235, 237–244,
    246, 248–268, 271,
    273–279, 281, 283, 286,
    288–291, 293–313,
    315–324, 327, 328,
    331–333, 335, 336,
    339–344, 348, 349,
    351–355, 358, 361–376,
    378–380, 382–386, 388,
    390–397, 399, 400,
    402–408, 410–418,
    420–422, 424–431,
    434–443, 445–450,
    452–458, 460–473, 475,
    476, 478–480, 482, 483,
    485–493, 495–499,
    501–503, 507, 509, 510,
    512–514, 516–523, 525,
    528–531, 533, 535, 536,
    538–557, 559–568,
    570–583, 586–590,
    593–595, 597, 600–612,
    614–630, 632–639, 641,
    643–647, 649–660
one, 4, 10, 19, 23, 27, 28, 37–39, 44,
    52, 57, 69, 73, 76–79, 84,
    88, 91, 94, 96, 99, 105,
    108, 111–113, 119, 120,
    125, 129, 131, 139, 143,
    144, 147, 148, 152, 153,
    164, 165, 167, 169, 172,
    173, 175, 176, 179, 180,
    182, 187, 191, 206, 223,
    226, 227, 234, 239, 242,
    246, 247, 249, 251–254,
    257, 263, 273, 285, 292,
    295, 297, 301, 310, 311,
    314, 318, 322, 324,
    326–329, 357, 371, 372,
    375, 382, 383, 389, 392,
    395, 399, 407, 416, 420,
    421, 424, 427, 428, 434,
    442, 446, 451–456, 466,
    471, 474, 479, 487, 492,
    493, 498, 507, 512, 513,
    517, 519–522, 529, 530,
    540, 543, 547, 549, 553,
    566, 567, 575, 580, 583,
    586, 598–602, 607, 608,
    613, 622, 643, 651, 653,
    654, 656
online, 2, 23, 30, 41, 43, 45, 48,
    50–54, 58, 59, 63–65, 69,
    83, 104, 105, 124, 133,
    141, 168–171, 194, 196,
    204, 206, 217–220,
    225–229, 232, 233, 236,

237, 245, 246, 251, 263,
264, 266, 267, 271, 275,
278, 284, 287, 294, 300,
314, 316, 318, 323, 327,
329, 402, 414, 418, 425,
436, 441, 450, 464, 472,
492, 500, 502, 503, 523,
544, 570, 579–581, 591,
609, 615, 627, 639, 644
onstage, 138, 139, 567
open, 9, 16, 35–37, 44, 50, 53, 55,
79, 82, 85–87, 89, 90, 92,
94, 106, 108, 122, 130,
134, 145, 147, 148, 158,
172, 173, 181, 183, 184,
187, 189–191, 197, 210,
253, 255, 262, 283, 290,
291, 297, 300, 320, 389,
397, 420, 430, 431, 434,
445, 455, 457, 459, 467,
468, 473, 474, 502, 510,
535, 539, 573, 589, 591,
598, 608, 613, 621, 625,
628, 630, 635, 637
opening, 42, 77, 111, 311, 324, 374,
469, 509
openness, 34, 143, 246, 292, 397,
432, 494, 497, 584, 630
opera, 4
opinion, 570
opportunity, 17, 22, 31, 34, 35, 37,
43, 47, 48, 55, 56, 58, 59,
63, 65, 68, 70, 74, 81–83,
87, 93, 108, 120, 136, 143,
153, 154, 156, 170, 173,
177, 182, 183, 189, 191,
203, 220, 223, 229, 236,
240, 241, 245, 255, 258,
260, 263, 274, 279, 288,

310, 314, 341, 378–380,
391, 394, 414, 415, 422,
440, 446, 455, 458, 464,
465, 471, 475, 488, 497,
502, 506, 512, 522, 622
oppression, 298
optimism, 85
optimization, 581
orchestra, 114, 177, 179, 192, 486
order, 107, 121, 189, 334, 337, 345,
400, 510, 521, 553, 619,
625
organization, 101, 102, 162, 227,
232, 262, 264, 471, 622,
627, 629, 632, 634, 635,
639, 658, 659
orientation, 326, 598
original, 45, 94, 189, 252, 273, 379,
383, 384, 463, 501, 560
originality, 454, 547, 643
Osaka, 163
other, 1, 10, 17, 18, 25, 28, 31, 34,
35, 43, 46, 47, 51–53, 58,
59, 64, 68, 69, 74, 75, 77,
85, 86, 88, 94–96, 107,
108, 111–114, 117, 122,
127, 128, 131, 142, 144,
169, 172, 174, 180, 184,
186, 188, 194, 195, 197,
199, 202, 206, 207,
209–213, 217–220, 223,
225–227, 229, 230, 232,
234–237, 240, 243, 244,
249, 251–254, 256–258,
260, 262, 265, 267, 268,
274–276, 278, 279, 284,
285, 288, 292, 294, 310,
314, 315, 318, 322, 325,
327, 328, 333, 335, 337,

339, 342, 343, 348, 351,
361, 364–366, 368, 375,
379, 389–393, 395, 396,
400, 409, 410, 414, 417,
418, 428, 432, 441, 442,
445, 449, 450, 453, 456,
457, 462, 466–468, 471,
474, 475, 478, 479, 485,
487, 490, 491, 493, 494,
500, 502, 505, 506, 509,
511, 512, 518, 520, 525,
526, 533, 540, 546,
550–558, 560, 563, 564,
566, 568, 571, 575, 578,
583, 586, 587, 590, 592,
598, 600, 601, 611, 621,
624, 645, 652
otherworldliness, 537
out, 2, 10, 11, 15, 17, 18, 25, 30, 34,
35, 39, 41, 43, 45, 46, 62,
64, 72–74, 79, 82, 84, 86,
88, 89, 94, 99, 107, 117,
140, 141, 143, 151, 154,
155, 158–160, 167, 168,
176, 177, 183, 185,
188–191, 197, 205, 213,
224, 226, 235, 240, 242,
252, 258, 260, 263, 264,
267, 299–301, 303, 332,
335, 339, 340, 348, 366,
367, 370, 381, 386, 388,
389, 394, 395, 404, 413,
415, 430, 432–434, 442,
444, 445, 451, 452, 456,
464, 467, 468, 476, 479,
491, 494, 496, 498, 499,
501, 503, 505, 509, 510,
539, 544, 547, 548, 552,
566, 585, 594–596, 598,

618, 619, 629, 637, 641,
645, 654, 655, 657
outcome, 179, 185
outdoor, 158–162, 388, 512
outdoors, 158, 160, 168, 374
outdoorsman, 355
outlet, 157, 238, 483, 511, 523, 552
outline, 605, 641
outlook, 84, 159
outpouring, 310
output, 267
outreach, 266, 328, 599, 627, 635
outsider, 243
overcrowding, 161
overfishing, 626
ownership, 54, 128, 186, 189, 202,
218, 222, 266, 317, 416

pace, 147, 337, 444
package, 302, 578
pad, 272, 436
page, 35
painting, 162, 509, 610
pairing, 424
palate, 167
palette, 11, 12, 21, 47, 87, 108, 155,
164, 176, 180, 204, 258,
336, 341, 347, 350, 351,
367, 381, 393, 434, 457,
462, 506, 513, 516, 545,
550, 564, 643
pandemic, 169, 236, 425
panning, 341
pantheon, 645, 646
paper, 133
paradigm, 131
park, 162
part, 2, 25, 34, 48, 59, 64, 65, 72, 74,
83, 90, 92, 93, 95, 102,

103, 107, 110, 113, 118,
120, 123, 125, 130, 132,
136, 138, 142, 143, 151,
152, 154, 170, 194, 203,
218, 220, 222, 226–228,
264, 271, 284, 302, 310,
311, 314, 317, 341, 372,
379, 388, 398, 399, 403,
410, 415–417, 425, 446,
450, 456, 460, 469, 470,
472, 475, 481, 498, 502,
523, 525, 529, 532–534,
536, 580, 589, 601, 634,
655, 657

participation, 52, 56, 61, 121, 152,
153, 218, 228, 230, 314,
318, 319, 406, 409, 411,
413, 414, 416–418, 482,
523, 582, 585, 640

partner, 148, 262, 629, 635

partnering, 47, 64, 97, 104, 162,
196, 203, 208, 232, 253,
287, 321, 447, 516, 587,
615, 621, 626, 639, 659

partnership, 17, 49, 98, 175–179,
186, 192, 617, 622, 627,
636, 639, 640

party, 153, 383, 468, 647

passage, 336

passion, 1–7, 9, 12, 14, 18, 19, 22,
23, 30–33, 41, 48, 71, 73,
74, 78, 94, 99, 111, 112,
123, 136, 141–144, 148,
157, 160, 161, 169, 173,
179, 191, 196, 197, 207,
217, 218, 224, 227, 229,
230, 233, 235, 236, 238,
240, 242, 243, 249, 252,
255, 257, 264, 265, 271,

278, 291, 300, 311, 314,
315, 317, 318, 320, 322,
323, 326–329, 334, 339,
352, 361, 362, 366, 373,
386, 395, 398, 417, 429,
437, 439, 441–443,
445–447, 459, 460, 462,
464, 467–469, 472–474,
488, 502, 517–520, 522,
529, 543, 546, 557, 558,
571, 586, 602, 612, 621,
628, 629, 651

past, 27, 30, 249, 442, 456

path, 2, 3, 9, 15, 22, 23, 29, 30, 35,
48, 73, 93, 151, 206, 252,
315, 340, 351, 441, 476,
503, 510, 546

patience, 147, 420

patient, 44

Paul Stanley, 49

Paul White, 7, 435

peace, 246, 250, 591

peak, 160, 397

people, 63, 101, 105, 106, 110, 122,
123, 129, 130, 140, 153,
154, 163, 164, 170, 171,
175, 178, 193, 217–222,
233, 239, 241, 243, 266,
284, 285, 289, 294, 296,
298, 301, 309, 311, 314,
316, 318, 319, 325, 327,
328, 342, 361, 365, 373,
388, 396, 397, 415, 431,
440, 445, 460, 468, 470,
472, 473, 477, 480, 502,
524, 531, 549, 570–572,
576, 580, 589, 597, 600,
607, 610, 611, 621, 630,
633, 654, 656

percentage, 303
perception, 71, 112, 462, 544
percussion, 4, 70, 155, 332, 561
perfection, 33, 459, 468, 518
perform, 18, 46, 70, 114, 118, 128,
    151, 153, 169, 202, 220,
    258, 263, 266, 283, 301,
    324, 404, 405, 416
performance, 22, 23, 27, 28, 32, 33,
    42, 51, 55–58, 60, 111,
    114, 120–123, 125, 128,
    129, 138–140, 152, 153,
    158, 164, 165, 173, 177,
    181, 202, 203, 207, 212,
    214, 229, 234, 272, 273,
    275, 305, 311, 325, 348,
    369, 373, 391, 395–403,
    405, 407–413, 415–417,
    435, 445, 464, 465, 480,
    486, 506, 515, 522, 523,
    530, 531, 541, 542, 551,
    565, 568
performer, 2, 52, 77, 80, 158, 408,
    412, 542, 629
period, 249, 365, 381, 397, 405,
    441, 465, 469
permission, 34, 510
perseverance, 7, 48, 94, 95, 111, 168,
    249, 442, 450, 482, 499,
    511, 519, 557, 574, 576,
    595, 600
persistence, 30, 47, 48, 443, 445, 501
person, 90, 124, 125, 147, 170, 218,
    220, 223, 225, 229, 236,
    242, 289, 316, 322, 328,
    362, 416, 464, 472, 522,
    568
persona, 27–29, 47, 51, 58, 66,
    71–73, 77, 91, 106, 113,

    117–119, 123–127, 129,
    130, 132, 133, 137, 138,
    147, 190, 195, 212, 217,
    223, 255, 295–297, 304,
    312, 324, 346, 388, 400,
    403, 405, 407, 409, 426,
    427, 441, 442, 483,
    517–523, 525, 526,
    528–530, 537, 538, 541,
    543, 544, 546, 549, 557,
    567–576, 578–581, 585,
    586, 594, 597, 600, 632,
    653
personality, 32, 146, 452, 457, 518,
    519
personalization, 43
personnel, 226
perspective, 6, 15, 21, 34, 36, 41, 83,
    94, 108, 113, 129, 150,
    154, 160, 192, 286, 343,
    379, 446, 454, 480, 493,
    497, 503, 509, 511, 521,
    535, 544, 548, 568, 610,
    635, 660
phase, 262, 350, 392, 554
phenomenon, 70, 118, 220, 471,
    480, 567, 577
philanthropic, 130, 132, 133, 135,
    136, 144, 145, 171, 172,
    194, 204–206, 208, 212,
    213, 228, 230–233, 244,
    245, 247, 252, 256, 264,
    278, 299, 301, 303, 309,
    317, 318, 425, 426, 437,
    448, 458, 466, 467, 479,
    482, 488, 554, 558, 570,
    572, 575, 580, 586, 587,
    601–603, 605, 607, 609,
    612, 616–620, 623–626,

628, 629, 632, 641, 644,
646, 649–652, 654,
656–661

philanthropist, 626, 660

philanthropy, 107, 135, 136, 144,
205, 212, 218, 231, 239,
244–246, 248, 265, 295,
300, 309, 317, 321, 425,
449, 482, 483, 485, 488,
567, 571, 590, 604, 606,
619, 624, 626, 628–632,
646, 650, 653, 659–661

philosophy, 78, 151, 185, 454, 455,
457, 628

phone, 397, 513

photo, 517–520

photograph, 537, 540

photography, 162, 509, 534,
537–540, 543, 544, 654

phrase, 163, 362

physical, 29, 75, 132, 134, 158, 160,
168, 203, 250, 251, 266,
298, 343, 362, 445, 465,
478, 515, 586, 635, 653

pianist, 3, 99

piano, 3, 4, 14

picture, 371, 387

piece, 39, 102, 118, 162, 179, 180,
286, 453

pillar, 13

pioneer, 76, 106, 210, 331, 339, 343,
437, 488, 497, 546, 646,
657

pioneering, 31, 32, 97, 365, 366,
497, 557, 561, 571, 634,
644, 655, 659

pitch, 368

place, 2, 18, 34, 48, 54–56, 58, 76,
104, 118, 123, 157, 165,

204, 224, 248, 254, 311,
328, 339, 359, 366, 370,
375, 383, 385, 427, 479,
480, 487, 488, 502, 524,
530, 533, 548, 551, 562,
570, 606, 643, 645, 646

placement, 51

plan, 206, 277, 427, 627

plane, 154, 159

planet, 101, 104, 135, 179, 210, 244,
286, 288, 296, 300, 303,
304, 308, 361, 362, 386,
428, 429, 482, 549, 575,
588, 590, 601, 606, 612,
623, 625, 626, 632, 633,
635, 660

planning, 62, 64, 74, 227, 262, 278,
399, 413, 470, 616

plant, 162, 321, 617

plastic, 101, 103, 638

platform, 28, 35, 43, 44, 46, 61, 65,
66, 68–71, 75, 86, 99–104,
106, 107, 129, 130,
135–137, 153, 157, 169,
171, 191, 194, 205, 208,
209, 212, 213, 215, 222,
230, 232, 234, 239, 241,
244, 247, 249, 254, 256,
260, 262–264, 266, 268,
272–274, 277–279, 284,
287, 289–293, 295–300,
302–310, 318, 325, 326,
340, 361, 369, 371, 380,
391, 394, 425–429, 437,
440, 441, 447, 450,
456–458, 462, 463, 466,
475, 479, 481, 482, 488,
496, 502, 532, 533, 544,
547–549, 554, 558, 570,

575, 576, 580, 584–587,
589–591, 594, 595, 598,
599, 601, 602, 606–608,
611–614, 616–620,
622–624, 626, 628, 630,
631, 637, 644, 646, 649,
650, 652, 653, 656–660
play, 16, 46, 57, 58, 60, 66, 115, 117,
189, 190, 192, 201, 210,
221, 225, 260, 261,
266–268, 271, 279, 283,
318, 328, 354, 371, 373,
378, 395, 398, 399, 408,
410, 411, 413, 436, 495,
500, 512, 525, 527, 535,
537, 540–542, 544, 549,
576, 602, 604, 632
player, 155
playfulness, 577
playing, 4, 18, 111, 400, 412, 525,
648
playlist, 64, 139, 206, 277
pleaser, 353
plight, 162, 306, 610
plugin, 354
poem, 162
poet, 179
poetry, 179
point, 19, 105, 165, 190, 322, 358,
453, 531, 534, 535
policy, 289, 290, 638
pollination, 6, 9, 46, 61, 176, 207,
298, 364, 430, 432, 433,
475, 506, 550, 552, 554,
555, 658
pollution, 101, 161, 162, 232, 304,
321, 587, 620, 621, 626,
632, 638, 640
pop, 49, 98, 108, 109, 113, 192, 344,

364, 407, 506, 556, 645,
652
popularity, 18, 70, 89, 92, 96, 103,
132, 152, 217, 222, 230,
236, 258, 272, 347, 353,
372, 379, 405, 452, 552,
556, 563, 577, 579, 614,
646, 652
popularization, 342
portfolio, 252
portion, 617, 620
portrayal, 535
position, 19, 25, 43, 47, 49, 60, 64,
66, 78, 98, 192, 222, 257,
324, 343, 352, 353, 364,
369, 382, 391, 392, 476,
477, 523, 525, 546, 584
positivity, 84, 85, 140, 141, 151, 171,
228, 231, 234, 241, 249,
253, 254, 301, 311, 315,
317–319, 322, 326, 357,
371, 447, 448, 546, 563,
591, 593, 609, 610, 629,
654
possibility, 379, 404, 539, 565
post, 468
potential, 4, 7, 12, 14, 23, 30, 41–43,
45, 46, 48, 50–52, 57, 62,
63, 65, 69, 113, 144, 147,
155, 170, 174, 177, 186,
191, 196, 206, 215, 222,
223, 226, 230, 249, 252,
261, 270, 272, 276, 282,
284, 285, 291, 294, 324,
349, 364, 410, 422, 424,
428, 431, 447, 452, 455,
478, 483, 486, 501, 516,
533, 551, 568, 583, 594,
596, 602, 610, 612, 614,

627, 642, 643, 655

poverty, 306

power, 2–5, 9, 16, 17, 20, 23, 24, 28,
    29, 33, 34, 38, 40, 41,
    43–45, 50–55, 62–66,
    70–72, 84, 91, 95, 97, 99,
    101, 102, 104–107, 114,
    123, 128, 130, 132, 136,
    137, 140, 144, 148,
    152–154, 156, 158,
    163–165, 169–172, 174,
    176–179, 181, 184, 185,
    187, 191, 193, 194, 196,
    205, 206, 212–215,
    217–220, 223, 225, 228,
    232–234, 239, 242,
    244–250, 252, 262, 268,
    270, 271, 273, 278–280,
    283, 284, 286, 291–293,
    295, 297, 298, 300, 306,
    307, 309, 311, 313–319,
    322, 324–329, 342, 343,
    347, 349, 352, 355, 357,
    360–362, 365, 366, 372,
    373, 375, 386, 388, 397,
    407, 408, 415–418, 420,
    422, 429, 430, 436, 437,
    440, 442, 443, 445, 447,
    449, 453–456, 458, 461,
    462, 465, 466, 469, 470,
    472–475, 477, 478,
    481–483, 486, 492, 495,
    503, 505, 507, 513, 517,
    521, 522, 524, 527–531,
    533, 538, 539, 541, 543,
    550, 557, 558, 567–571,
    575, 577, 580, 581, 586,
    589, 590, 592–595,
    597–600, 602, 604, 605,

607, 609–615, 617, 618,
    621, 624, 626, 629, 632,
    634, 644, 651, 652, 655,
    656, 658, 659, 661

practice, 125, 307, 400, 513, 591,
    637

praise, 25, 321, 383, 384, 468, 479,
    495

precedent, 590

precision, 121, 157, 158, 347, 384

prejudice, 138

preparation, 23, 55, 58, 138, 141

presence, 2, 3, 16, 18, 19, 28, 30, 32,
    41, 45, 48, 50, 54–59,
    61–64, 70, 78, 104, 110,
    111, 114, 133, 139–141,
    143, 151, 168, 173,
    194–196, 212, 213,
    218–220, 227, 241, 247,
    271, 279, 289, 290, 299,
    303, 311, 323, 354, 369,
    373, 382, 398, 399,
    403–406, 408, 412, 413,
    415, 436, 471, 480, 482,
    487, 518, 521, 522, 524,
    525, 533, 546, 549, 566,
    567, 569, 579–581, 598,
    600, 644, 646, 648

present, 28, 52, 133, 134, 159, 168,
    181, 208, 235, 255, 374,
    397, 413, 509, 521, 552,
    587, 589

preservation, 100, 102, 162, 253,
    287, 288, 296, 304, 308,
    362, 587, 623, 624, 632

press, 62, 68

pressure, 23, 31, 73, 75, 83, 88–90,
    92, 119, 133, 147, 442,
    444, 452, 536

prevalence, 290
prevention, 621, 636
preview, 425
pride, 55, 144, 218, 266, 317, 448
principle, 82, 451, 457, 594
printing, 128, 129, 536
priority, 19, 92, 134, 171, 203, 204,
  221, 636
privacy, 137, 568
privilege, 16, 141, 458, 460
problem, 161, 168, 262, 285, 286,
  511
proceed, 262
process, 7, 10, 19, 34, 35, 38–40, 44,
  47, 53, 59, 64, 74, 91, 93,
  95, 117, 126, 128, 130,
  131, 134, 143, 144, 147,
  163, 176, 180, 182–191,
  194, 199, 222, 264, 267,
  273, 281, 282, 291, 292,
  317, 319, 320, 344, 349,
  355, 357, 379, 380,
  388–390, 399, 401, 425,
  429, 431, 435, 436, 442,
  449, 451, 453–456, 460,
  467–469, 475, 490–492,
  494, 497–499, 501–503,
  505–507, 509–514,
  516–521, 526, 534–537,
  544, 547, 598, 642, 643
processing, 347–349, 436, 516, 551
prodigy, 1, 3, 7, 69, 167, 437, 529,
  584
producer, 1, 3, 6, 15–18, 24, 27, 31,
  33, 48, 49, 60, 70, 77, 85,
  132, 173, 174, 183, 189,
  190, 252, 254, 273–275,
  336, 337, 350–352, 358,
  359, 374, 375, 379, 381,

385, 391, 392, 435, 464,
  473–475, 479, 493–495,
  519–521, 555, 557, 594
product, 35, 181, 189, 389, 428,
  468, 526
production, 1, 6–13, 15–17, 30, 31,
  33, 35, 42, 47, 56, 57, 59,
  62, 63, 69, 74, 79, 80, 95,
  97–99, 110, 113, 121, 139,
  152, 161, 162, 167, 173,
  176, 178, 180, 181, 183,
  184, 188–190, 194, 198,
  199, 201, 202, 204,
  209–214, 258, 261, 263,
  266, 267, 273, 275, 277,
  304, 311, 331, 333, 336,
  337, 339–344, 346, 348,
  351–354, 363–366, 369,
  370, 373–375, 381,
  383–385, 391, 394, 395,
  398, 402, 404, 405, 407,
  421, 426, 427, 429, 430,
  432, 434, 435, 442, 454,
  456, 463, 464, 467, 468,
  475–481, 487, 490–495,
  502, 506, 509–517, 534,
  545, 547, 551, 553–555,
  560, 561, 565, 573, 577,
  582, 584, 594, 596, 597,
  605, 610, 638, 642–645,
  647, 648
profession, 148
professional, 2, 4, 62, 74, 75, 137,
  148, 185, 243, 247, 272,
  277, 348, 391, 396, 400,
  537, 538, 593
professionalism, 282, 285
proficiency, 6, 36, 555
profile, 30, 77, 99, 183, 570

program, 263, 273, 277, 604, 627
programming, 139, 183, 332, 341,
    477
progress, 34, 40, 289, 622, 653
progression, 82, 182, 386, 387, 405,
    529
project, 36, 42, 108, 124, 173, 177,
    189, 190, 193, 202, 206,
    232, 281, 302, 389, 406,
    420, 424, 435, 447, 453,
    459, 468, 487, 500, 536,
    568, 577, 611, 616, 623,
    625–630, 640
projection, 348, 409
proliferation, 364
promise, 78, 319, 643, 657
promotion, 41, 43, 46–48, 52,
    58–60, 62, 68, 69, 104,
    131, 195, 218, 221,
    227–230, 253, 274, 276,
    278, 290, 315, 323, 324,
    450, 466, 467, 471, 500,
    502, 567
proof, 565
prop, 118, 125
proposal, 277
protection, 101, 137, 300, 575, 587,
    624, 629, 632
protest, 306, 630
prototype, 127
prowess, 41, 75, 108, 176, 238, 239,
    259, 332, 336, 337, 368,
    371, 375, 477, 478, 553,
    554
pseudonym, 132
psychology, 133, 456
public, 4, 27, 47, 71, 90, 112, 115,
    119, 133, 134, 138, 147,
    161, 247, 287, 289, 290,

    303, 304, 306–308, 343,
    379, 453, 557, 567, 568,
    585–587, 606, 607, 615,
    640, 653
publication, 157
pulse, 99, 318
pumping, 96, 154, 157, 159, 160,
    167, 354, 357, 498, 538,
    595
punk, 2, 8, 25
purchasing, 314
purpose, 144, 145, 222, 243, 245,
    253, 254, 267, 319, 337,
    442, 452, 473, 532, 572,
    589, 611
pursuit, 7, 14, 24, 26, 33, 81, 86,
    146, 159, 167, 198, 210,
    213, 238, 338, 339, 370,
    439, 445, 459, 477, 488,
    495, 518, 595, 613, 650
Pusha T, 385
pyrotechnic, 121

quality, 10, 12, 13, 36, 45, 52, 54, 62,
    75, 92, 161, 189, 211, 221,
    250, 301, 348, 358, 363,
    369, 383, 391, 392, 400,
    406, 463, 468, 477, 491,
    648
quest, 348, 599, 613
question, 132, 307, 611
quo, 25, 71, 84, 107, 167, 186, 197,
    292, 305, 427, 483, 547,
    565, 578, 611, 649, 653

race, 119, 307, 326, 598, 600, 656
racing, 157
radio, 192
rain, 386

rainforest, 623, 624

rally, 138, 230

rallying, 105, 130, 252, 306, 386, 600

range, 1, 3, 6, 8, 9, 15, 19, 21, 24, 25, 35–37, 49, 70, 76, 94, 108, 111, 113, 119, 120, 141, 146, 163, 174, 177, 185, 187, 188, 190, 191, 193, 195, 198, 207, 213, 224, 225, 234, 236, 251, 267, 275, 278, 292, 293, 300, 314, 328, 335–337, 342, 343, 346, 347, 350, 353, 360, 367, 372, 373, 381, 383, 385, 386, 392, 393, 409, 417, 424, 432, 433, 435, 436, 456, 477, 490, 492, 505, 507, 510, 514, 515, 523, 524, 536, 545–547, 554, 571, 575, 578, 580, 581, 597, 598, 600, 611, 615, 619, 647, 654, 658

rap, 99, 108, 187, 199, 393, 474, 486

Raph, 24

rapid, 147, 219, 444, 552, 561

rapper, 75, 108

rarity, 195, 379

rawness, 160, 340

reach, 2, 25, 31, 41, 45–47, 49–51, 54, 55, 58–63, 65, 67–70, 77, 87, 100, 101, 103, 104, 107–109, 114, 126, 158, 183, 190, 192–197, 203, 204, 214, 217–221, 223, 228–232, 235, 236, 250, 258, 274, 279, 283, 284, 287, 288, 291, 296, 302, 303, 314–316, 323, 325, 364, 370, 436, 450, 462, 471, 475, 478, 488, 498, 506, 511, 553, 556, 564, 569–571, 575, 581, 584, 597, 598, 606, 608, 612, 615, 616, 620, 624, 629, 640, 641, 644, 648

realism, 333

reality, 68, 82, 95, 122, 208, 271, 306, 404, 530, 535, 540, 583, 584, 586, 618

realm, 9, 44, 80, 99, 108, 113, 122, 143, 145, 175–177, 181, 186, 187, 190, 195, 198, 199, 205, 215, 229, 235, 238, 246, 253, 264, 278, 296, 300, 305, 315, 319, 321, 323, 327, 328, 450, 469, 472, 481, 483, 501, 527, 551, 552, 555, 558, 569, 576, 579, 597, 628, 644, 651, 654, 658–660

rebellion, 67, 569, 586, 652

reception, 364, 369, 464

recognition, 2, 4, 6, 7, 18, 19, 30, 36, 45, 46, 48, 55, 60, 66, 69, 71, 73, 75, 77, 78, 91, 93, 96, 103, 183, 227, 230, 232, 243, 252, 259, 264, 265, 268, 274, 278, 294, 309, 316, 318, 321–323, 364, 394, 406, 425, 440, 450, 453, 457, 464, 478, 480, 487, 496, 541, 544, 545, 565, 596, 614

record, 18, 30, 33, 46, 47, 55, 80, 85, 93, 107, 263, 272, 274, 315, 323, 448, 585

recording, 10–12, 112, 173, 174,
    179–182, 272
recovery, 366, 463, 626
recruitment, 639
recycling, 296, 469, 588, 633
redefinition, 586
reduction, 101, 251, 588, 633
reef, 625, 626
reference, 362
refinement, 141, 458, 463
reflection, 79, 83, 88, 93, 111, 127,
    130, 133, 286, 320, 372,
    373, 382, 386, 388, 390,
    392, 451–453, 457, 501,
    650
reforestation, 102, 244, 587, 617,
    623, 638
reform, 289
refuge, 373
refusal, 295, 477, 488
reggae, 32, 108, 109, 344, 350, 498,
    648
region, 4, 156, 162, 165, 629
rehearsal, 400, 401
reimagining, 114, 342, 560, 587
reinforcement, 252
reinvention, 120, 122, 339, 524
rejection, 30, 47, 243, 265, 501
relatability, 125, 370
relationship, 51, 130, 131, 144, 147,
    161, 184, 221, 234, 235,
    240, 271, 315, 468, 470,
    472, 630
relaxation, 246, 247
release, 78, 98, 123, 181, 217, 234,
    238, 239, 250, 251, 274,
    276, 293, 370, 374, 378,
    379, 383, 391, 392, 417,
    425, 475, 491, 500, 501,

    523, 534, 552, 561, 568,
    592, 630
relevance, 195, 197, 552, 564,
    581–584
relief, 254, 301, 303, 592
reminder, 29, 33, 35, 62, 72–74, 93,
    96, 101, 111, 123, 140,
    154, 159, 160, 165, 188,
    222, 239, 248, 249, 288,
    306, 311, 316, 328, 357,
    361, 362, 366, 386, 387,
    442, 450, 452, 481, 483,
    521, 524, 593, 599, 621,
    629, 633, 637, 649, 650,
    655
remix, 42, 222, 252, 273, 274, 292,
    297, 383, 450, 472, 560,
    596
remixes, 42, 45, 105, 140, 143, 196,
    221, 227, 237, 273, 274,
    320–322, 378–380, 383,
    384, 399, 402, 403, 412,
    450, 582
remixing, 140, 274, 379, 407, 456
repeat, 469
repertoire, 34, 49, 104, 183, 644
report, 434
reporting, 622
representation, 23, 66, 67, 107, 127,
    171, 272, 294, 295, 320,
    393, 405, 466, 524,
    526–528, 531, 534–537,
    541, 572–574, 579, 598,
    660
representative, 103, 185, 188, 293,
    394
reputation, 4, 18, 52, 75, 77, 108,
    201, 210, 359, 392, 467,
    477

request, 39
research, 29, 43, 56, 57, 117, 246,
    247, 287, 297, 411, 616,
    622, 625, 626, 638
resentment, 147
resilience, 14, 29, 30, 47, 48, 52, 75,
    82, 83, 85, 93–95, 142,
    148, 168, 238, 243, 246,
    249, 297, 304, 308, 321,
    355, 366, 370, 387, 398,
    416, 443, 465, 482, 483,
    501, 535, 546, 574, 591,
    593, 601, 607, 611, 613,
    617, 636, 655
resistance, 106, 589
resonance, 373, 417, 427, 449, 496,
    647, 648
resource, 10, 277, 302, 303, 492,
    587, 616, 640
resourcefulness, 74
respect, 86, 108, 157, 171, 174, 180,
    184, 187, 189–191, 226,
    252, 256, 282, 285, 298,
    322, 362, 389, 391, 457,
    473, 474, 477, 598, 609,
    619
respite, 122, 498
response, 2, 6, 57, 127, 152, 164,
    251, 252, 369, 373, 383,
    395–398, 403, 411, 416,
    418, 629
responsibility, 137, 170, 205, 218,
    226, 300, 303, 305, 361,
    362, 396, 425, 437, 466,
    488, 589, 614, 626, 628,
    631, 634, 658
rest, 75, 78, 134, 510, 511
restoration, 300, 625, 626
restriction, 397

result, 17, 100, 114, 118, 128, 136,
    155, 164, 173, 175, 177,
    182, 185, 189, 192, 220,
    230, 258, 259, 273, 274,
    279, 320, 333, 334, 363,
    367, 375, 379, 383, 391,
    463, 468, 478, 480, 498,
    512, 548, 555, 563, 566,
    590, 598
resurgence, 556
return, 43, 125, 171, 425
revelation, 8
revenue, 47, 195, 261
reverb, 347, 354, 515
review, 62
reward, 236
Rezz, 421
rhythm, 3, 5, 10, 20, 183, 333, 337,
    344, 346, 353, 354, 397,
    408, 562
richness, 86, 171, 178, 188, 393,
    407, 431, 433, 452, 477
riff, 25
right, 25, 30, 31, 48, 126, 180, 189,
    260, 302, 399, 498, 562,
    578, 634
ring, 140
ripple, 106, 171, 230, 242, 249, 264,
    301, 426, 549, 607, 624
rise, 2, 14, 51, 52, 62, 69, 71, 77,
    118, 123, 142, 147, 172,
    219, 221, 235, 271, 316,
    352, 356, 362, 367, 440,
    448, 450, 478, 481, 482,
    485, 565, 567, 568, 584
risk, 25, 91, 410, 455, 552
RL Grime, 561
road, 92, 94, 153, 154, 158
roadmap, 85

roaring, 159, 519
rock, 1, 3, 6, 8, 15, 20, 21, 24, 25, 31,
        49, 76, 79, 108, 109, 112,
        113, 158, 160, 191, 198,
        207, 214, 238, 259, 293,
        333, 344, 350, 359, 364,
        367, 393, 433, 462, 495,
        506, 510, 511, 545, 556,
        571, 645, 648, 652
Rodriguez, 453
role, 2, 3, 6–8, 12, 13, 16, 17, 19–21,
        25, 27, 31–35, 37, 42, 46,
        47, 50, 51, 53, 54, 57–60,
        63, 64, 66, 67, 91, 97, 98,
        100, 103, 106, 108,
        112–115, 117, 118, 123,
        129, 136, 137, 141, 142,
        144, 148, 149, 151, 156,
        165, 167, 171, 172, 174,
        182, 187, 189–191, 193,
        195, 198, 201, 205, 208,
        210, 211, 214, 218–221,
        225–230, 232–235, 249,
        255, 258, 260, 261,
        265–269, 271, 274–279,
        283, 287, 289, 291, 294,
        296–299, 303, 305, 307,
        308, 314, 316, 318–320,
        323, 327, 328, 332, 333,
        339–341, 346, 347, 349,
        352, 354, 355, 358, 362,
        364, 365, 369–371, 373,
        378, 380, 382, 384, 385,
        391–396, 398, 408, 410,
        411, 413, 414, 426, 430,
        432, 435, 436, 439, 440,
        444, 449, 450, 456, 457,
        462, 464–466, 471–473,
        475, 476, 478, 479, 481,
        483, 485, 487, 495, 498,
        500, 502, 503, 505, 511,
        512, 516, 525, 527, 531,
        532, 534, 535, 537,
        540–542, 544, 546, 549,
        553, 556, 557, 559,
        563–565, 570, 574–576,
        578, 579, 581–584, 586,
        588, 589, 600, 602, 604,
        607, 610, 624, 629, 632,
        639, 644, 655, 658
rollercoaster, 372
room, 18, 22, 110, 123, 311, 365,
        397, 409, 413, 417, 459,
        495
routine, 75, 134, 158, 610
routing, 348
row, 140
ruggedness, 537
run, 88, 218, 233
rush, 157–160, 365, 521, 552
Rusko, 8, 32, 33, 492
rut, 509

sadness, 647
safety, 159, 226, 410, 598
sailing, 389
sake, 88, 337
Sam Frank, 385
samba, 154, 155, 163
sample, 10–12, 98, 267, 275, 385,
        565
sampler, 493
sampling, 9, 25, 335, 336, 341, 514,
        517
sanctuary, 417, 437
Sarah, 16, 241–243, 248, 249, 251,
        365, 463, 464, 469
Sarah Davis, 16

Sarah Johnson, 100
Sarah Sparks, 192
Sarah Sparks', 192
Sarah Thompson, 133, 495
satisfaction, 440
saturation, 354, 368
sawtooth, 354
say, 126
scale, 71, 104, 152, 164, 168, 170,
        172, 220, 224, 232, 237,
        289, 301, 307, 314, 370,
        405, 426, 436, 437, 590,
        593, 619, 640
scavenger, 55
scenario, 134
scene, 1, 2, 6, 7, 9, 11, 15–19,
        22–24, 26, 28, 29, 32, 33,
        43, 45, 47, 49, 55, 58, 59,
        65, 66, 68–70, 72, 75–78,
        81, 84, 86, 93–99,
        103–106, 108, 110–113,
        118, 120, 123, 126, 133,
        142, 145, 148, 153–155,
        164, 168, 172, 173, 184,
        185, 188, 193, 196, 204,
        205, 209–212, 214, 222,
        223, 225, 228–232, 246,
        253, 254, 257, 259,
        262–264, 268, 278, 283,
        293, 294, 296, 315, 316,
        318, 323, 324, 329, 334,
        335, 339–343, 346, 351,
        353, 358, 359, 365, 366,
        370, 375, 381, 382, 384,
        385, 390–394, 401, 405,
        410, 426, 433, 434, 437,
        440, 441, 447, 450, 451,
        471–476, 478–480, 487,
        488, 492, 494, 496, 499,
        501, 510, 521, 523, 525,
        530, 533, 538–540,
        547–550, 555–557, 559,
        560, 563, 564, 569–572,
        574, 576–578, 581,
        583–585, 597, 600, 602,
        607, 609, 613, 645, 646,
        651, 652, 657–660
schedule, 58, 92, 134, 145, 147, 629
scholarship, 627
school, 3, 4, 307, 359, 464
Scott, 583
Scott B. Metcalfe, 435
scrutiny, 27, 90, 119, 147, 446
sea, 518, 529, 530
search, 581
searching, 372, 441, 516, 519
season, 252, 301
seat, 422
secrecy, 119, 137
secret, 124, 132, 138, 451
section, 31, 37, 88, 90, 91, 137, 157,
        189, 190, 325, 331, 334,
        336, 344–346, 386, 392,
        405, 418, 463, 526, 528,
        534, 537
security, 226
segment, 516
selection, 11, 23, 111, 114, 401, 518,
        528
self, 2, 6, 13, 14, 16, 28, 30, 34, 41,
        72–75, 82–85, 90, 92–94,
        107, 111, 127, 133–136,
        147, 148, 167, 168, 224,
        238, 241, 243, 246–250,
        285, 290–294, 297, 298,
        304, 324, 325, 365,
        371–373, 386, 392, 394,
        416, 418, 440, 442, 443,

445, 446, 453, 454, 458,
462, 464, 465, 482, 502,
510, 511, 522, 523, 528,
543, 544, 546, 569–576,
578, 579, 590–593, 597,
606, 607, 613, 617, 619,
636–638, 650, 652, 653,
659
sensation, 31, 49, 437
sense, 2, 4, 11, 14, 16, 25, 27, 28, 44,
47, 50–55, 61, 63, 65, 67,
73, 76, 84, 91, 99, 101,
102, 104–106, 110, 113,
115, 117–119, 121,
123–125, 127–131, 133,
137, 138, 140–145, 147,
148, 152, 153, 155, 157,
159, 160, 169–171, 184,
188, 189, 195, 196, 198,
202, 203, 206, 212,
217–227, 229, 231–245,
247–251, 253–257, 261,
263–267, 271, 275, 276,
278, 283–286, 291, 293,
294, 298, 300, 302–305,
310–319, 322–325,
327–329, 333, 336, 337,
342, 346, 354, 362, 366,
367, 369–374, 379, 380,
383, 386, 388, 394, 396,
398, 399, 401, 403–407,
411–418, 425, 429, 431,
433, 438, 440, 442,
447–450, 455, 457, 459,
461, 465, 466, 468–475,
482, 483, 487, 488, 496,
501, 506, 507, 512, 518,
522–525, 527–529, 532,
533, 537–539, 542, 543,

546–550, 554, 558, 560,
562, 563, 566–569,
571–573, 575–577, 579,
581, 582, 586, 589, 591,
592, 595, 596, 598–602,
607–611, 616–619, 626,
629, 634, 636, 640, 641,
644, 651, 653–658, 660
sensibility, 368, 371
sensitivity, 156
sentiment, 253
separation, 125, 126, 137, 568
sequence, 400
Serato, 515
serenity, 168, 512
series, 156, 192, 388, 396, 425, 517,
525, 627, 630
service, 310, 609
session, 173, 441, 459, 509
set, 2, 10, 15, 18, 19, 22, 23, 25, 31,
47, 67, 74, 84, 88, 95, 110,
117, 119, 133, 134, 137,
139, 140, 147, 153, 161,
180, 197, 204, 206, 212,
213, 224, 235, 258, 275,
311, 332, 336, 341, 343,
350, 363, 368, 372, 389,
399–401, 409, 411–413,
415, 424–426, 438, 463,
466, 467, 482, 487, 511,
532, 553, 554, 556, 560,
580, 590, 600, 615, 646,
650, 656, 658
setback, 442, 455–457
setlist, 55–58, 138, 139, 395, 399,
400, 403, 404, 411
setting, 6, 17, 69, 120, 134, 135, 147,
148, 152, 161, 185, 203,
255, 261, 275, 387, 399,

408, 411, 522, 528, 554
setup, 23, 56, 139, 400, 401, 404,
    405
shamisen, 155
shape, 4, 10, 22, 23, 27, 71, 81, 97,
    107, 125, 127, 151, 159,
    168, 179, 208, 211, 212,
    215, 220, 222, 228, 230,
    231, 235, 254, 259, 264,
    268, 269, 271, 276–278,
    283, 298, 315–317, 320,
    331, 336, 347–349, 362,
    385, 407, 426, 428, 435,
    436, 438, 450, 455, 466,
    473, 483, 489, 545, 546,
    549–551, 555, 563, 567,
    570, 576, 602, 604, 607,
    608, 644, 650, 651, 656,
    657
share, 2, 6, 29, 30, 43, 45, 50, 52, 54,
    61, 65, 75, 90, 93, 101,
    102, 105, 111, 127, 129,
    134, 142–144, 153, 161,
    169, 171, 184–186, 196,
    204, 205, 217, 219, 220,
    223, 224, 227–229,
    232–237, 240, 245,
    249–251, 253–255, 257,
    260, 265–268, 272, 274,
    275, 278, 279, 290, 293,
    302, 304, 313, 314,
    316–320, 324–327, 341,
    370, 380, 398, 414, 436,
    446, 449, 450, 452, 457,
    460, 470, 483, 492,
    500–503, 532, 536, 539,
    558, 571, 580, 582, 586,
    589, 591, 601, 605, 611,
    614, 616, 621, 628, 630,

636, 637, 660
sharing, 35, 43, 45, 51, 59, 65, 98,
    101, 102, 104, 111, 130,
    143, 154, 156, 173, 180,
    194, 196, 213, 215, 217,
    220, 221, 227, 229, 230,
    241, 247, 249, 257, 264,
    267, 268, 277, 284, 290,
    292, 297, 304, 311, 316,
    317, 319–322, 328, 371,
    380, 396, 404, 414,
    454–456, 482, 500, 517,
    520, 521, 523, 544, 547,
    557, 573, 588, 591, 595,
    608, 609, 613, 637, 650
sheet, 14
shelter, 252
shift, 27, 112, 126, 147, 364, 448,
    481, 563
Shoreditch, 173
short, 18, 23, 58, 88, 133, 173, 206,
    286, 395, 399, 434, 480,
    488
shot, 517
shoulder, 33
shout, 102, 230, 240
show, 19, 54, 110, 111, 121, 125,
    138–141, 143, 152, 154,
    194, 202, 210, 213, 217,
    221, 243, 284, 310, 311,
    316, 317, 365, 395–399,
    402, 403, 406, 407,
    410–418, 469, 487, 519,
    520, 542, 610, 648
showcase, 22, 41, 44, 51, 55, 58, 60,
    62–64, 66, 67, 97, 99, 109,
    114, 125, 140, 153, 175,
    177, 188, 203, 224, 229,
    232, 248, 251, 253, 258,

262–264, 266, 272–274,
277, 278, 283, 292, 295,
303, 310, 324, 325, 332,
351–354, 369, 371, 376,
378–380, 391, 392, 394,
395, 404, 406, 421, 422,
425, 426, 437, 463, 472,
488, 496, 502, 518, 520,
528–530, 532, 543, 544,
546, 547, 549, 553, 585,
596, 598, 617, 621
showmanship, 56, 57, 522, 556, 566
sibling, 4
side, 16, 30, 126, 137, 331, 378, 395,
397, 407, 518, 521, 564,
617
sidechain, 354, 562
sight, 83, 398, 408, 414, 502
signal, 348
signature, 9, 10, 15, 32, 48, 49, 51,
54, 57, 69, 70, 75, 79, 97,
99, 108, 114, 122, 139,
155, 163, 175, 178, 182,
183, 186, 187, 191, 192,
201, 204, 207, 209, 211,
238, 250, 257, 293, 311,
333, 335, 341, 343, 347,
350, 353, 354, 358, 363,
365, 368–370, 379, 381,
383, 385, 391, 392, 397,
399, 402, 403, 405, 420,
424, 426, 433, 435, 437,
463, 474, 475, 479, 486,
490, 492, 497, 498, 500,
506, 510, 519, 532, 543,
548, 550, 556, 557, 560,
562, 569, 584, 645, 647,
654, 657
significance, 7, 14, 27, 59, 117, 118,

120, 132, 133, 137, 142,
151, 167, 223, 241, 276,
290, 305, 371, 372, 378,
408, 440, 445, 457, 522,
526, 529, 540, 570, 598,
602, 610, 612, 635
signing, 255, 274, 518
silence, 74
sing, 4, 56, 57, 110, 311, 401, 411,
413, 414, 421, 647
singer, 4, 31, 192, 193, 467
singing, 398, 399, 413, 416, 417
single, 99, 103, 136, 336, 351, 378,
380, 383, 506, 530, 630
sister, 4
site, 637
situation, 133, 387, 452
size, 445, 566
skater, 49
skepticism, 25, 30, 71, 112, 452, 589
ski, 158
skill, 15, 17, 77, 261, 274, 275, 336,
493, 494, 506, 511, 522
Skream, 8
sky, 159
skydiving, 154, 157, 159, 167
sleuthing, 124
slot, 42
smartphone, 202
smile, 519, 521
smoke, 409
snapshot, 311
sneak, 425
society, 44, 105, 206, 231, 260, 278,
285, 289–291, 295, 296,
298, 299, 301, 302,
305–307, 322, 362, 458,
462, 483, 570, 586, 591,
600, 601, 605, 608, 610,

613, 614, 619, 623, 625,
626, 631, 637, 649, 651
software, 1, 6, 9, 10, 13, 80, 122,
198, 209, 214, 237, 346,
348, 349, 367, 402, 404,
407, 408, 430, 435, 436,
456, 493, 498, 513, 515,
516, 536, 582, 642
solace, 2, 29, 105, 119, 123, 136,
144, 158, 160, 167, 168,
234, 242, 243, 245, 246,
248–251, 253, 255, 284,
291, 315, 327, 365, 370,
373, 383, 398, 418, 437,
461, 463, 465, 469, 470,
483, 512, 525, 574, 590,
591, 593, 601, 608, 611,
613, 630, 636
solidarity, 295, 300, 301, 326, 386,
618
solo, 180
solution, 103, 189, 286
solving, 168, 262, 285, 511
song, 23, 36, 49, 82, 102, 120, 121,
162, 181, 192, 303, 334,
354, 362, 379, 383, 395,
434, 463, 468, 512, 530,
606, 610, 611, 630
songwriter, 467, 494, 495
songwriting, 36, 180, 506, 520, 547
Sophia, 4
sophistication, 20, 177, 522
sophomore, 424
soul, 21, 32, 421, 452, 654
sound, 1–4, 6–12, 15–26, 28,
30–33, 35, 37, 42, 46–49,
53, 57–59, 63, 66, 69–76,
78–80, 82, 84, 88, 89,
91–100, 103, 104,
107–109, 113–115, 119,
122, 129, 139, 142, 145,
154, 155, 157, 159, 163,
164, 173, 175–178, 180,
182–195, 197–199, 202,
204–207, 209–214,
217–221, 223, 229, 230,
233, 234, 238, 239, 250,
251, 256–259, 263, 265,
273, 275, 277, 291, 293,
294, 297, 303, 319, 323,
327, 331–336, 338–354,
358–360, 363–369,
372–376, 378–387, 389,
391–395, 399, 400, 402,
406–408, 418, 420–422,
424, 426–437, 439, 441,
442, 444, 446, 449, 450,
454, 459, 462–464, 466,
467, 469, 473–481,
485–488, 490–495,
497–501, 503, 505–507,
511–515, 519, 520, 524,
526, 528, 534, 545–557,
560–565, 567, 571,
573–576, 578, 579, 581,
582, 584, 594–597,
643–660
soundscape, 164
soundtrack, 234, 251, 325, 373, 386,
465, 469, 551, 652, 655
source, 9, 33, 34, 76, 82, 112, 158,
168, 234, 237–239, 241,
243, 246, 249, 251, 317,
318, 320, 364, 365, 373,
383, 429, 448, 462, 482,
498, 525, 542, 544, 546,
557, 574, 592, 594, 617
South America, 156

space, 10, 43, 64, 72, 105, 118, 119,
   127, 131, 140, 169,
   176–178, 184, 186, 189,
   220, 221, 224, 227, 229,
   231, 234, 236, 240, 241,
   244, 250, 251, 253, 265,
   278, 284, 290, 292, 294,
   298, 304, 306, 307, 316,
   322, 325–329, 343, 345,
   354, 373, 414–416, 425,
   455, 470, 472, 476, 497,
   499, 525, 562, 568, 571,
   572, 580, 584–586, 590,
   591, 593, 594, 597,
   599–601, 609, 611, 630,
   650, 651, 656, 660
spark, 238, 299, 396, 440, 442, 505,
   510–512, 514, 516, 594,
   611, 613, 621
speaking, 98, 111, 300, 613, 615
spectacle, 139, 140, 202, 402, 406,
   408, 409, 417, 480, 568
spectrum, 336
speculation, 119, 124, 132
speed, 157
sphere, 574
spin, 124, 379, 420
spine, 654
spirit, 13, 29, 64, 73, 83, 118, 122,
   128, 132, 141, 157–160,
   163, 200, 205, 218, 251,
   258, 259, 266, 283, 297,
   298, 300, 303, 311, 321,
   328, 340, 342, 343, 385,
   394, 434, 451, 458, 462,
   474, 479, 483, 497, 517,
   530, 538, 540, 549, 554,
   558, 566, 571, 585, 592,
   600, 634, 644, 658

sponsorship, 370
spontaneity, 158, 173, 174, 407, 495
spot, 397
spotlight, 90, 91, 133–135, 145,
   147, 161, 213, 230, 274,
   295, 385, 464, 518, 586
spread, 23, 102, 151, 167, 217, 218,
   220, 241, 252, 253, 261,
   289, 301, 316, 323, 357,
   570, 606, 609, 610
springboard, 77, 544
stability, 30, 74, 500
stage, 2, 16, 18, 27, 32, 33, 42,
   55–59, 61, 62, 69, 78, 80,
   110, 111, 114, 118, 121,
   123, 125, 128, 132,
   138–141, 151–153, 186,
   194, 196, 202, 208–213,
   242, 255, 283, 289, 293,
   295, 311, 343, 348, 373,
   374, 382, 395–400,
   402–415, 417, 425, 429,
   435, 436, 447, 468, 480,
   487, 517–519, 521–525,
   528, 529, 531, 532, 537,
   541, 542, 546, 549, 551,
   554, 556, 566, 569, 577,
   578, 580, 646, 648
stagnation, 35, 339, 455, 552
stance, 591
stand, 45, 62, 64, 73, 94, 194, 197,
   213, 298, 299, 335, 340,
   348, 361, 362, 452, 501,
   544, 552
standard, 122, 213, 343, 347, 452,
   482, 487, 556, 560, 580,
   650
standing, 14, 30, 77, 159, 300, 386,
   519

standout, 70, 108, 153, 229, 354,
374, 376, 378, 383
staple, 48, 49, 353, 383
star, 18, 19, 189, 529
stardom, 71, 119, 271, 645
start, 110, 206, 261, 354, 381, 395,
397, 400, 491, 498, 617
starting, 276, 453, 516, 535, 557
state, 62, 122, 168, 202, 210, 250,
296, 442, 469, 509
status, 25, 68, 70, 71, 76, 77, 80, 84,
107, 132, 147, 167, 186,
197, 203, 290, 292, 305,
326, 364, 370, 391, 427,
446, 483, 547, 556, 565,
574, 578, 586, 611, 635,
649, 653
stay, 4, 31, 33, 52, 53, 73, 79, 80, 83,
86, 88–90, 94, 125, 133,
142, 148, 209, 235, 254,
351, 352, 381, 389, 412,
434, 437, 444, 451, 453,
473, 475, 493, 501–503,
516, 547, 573, 580, 585
step, 34, 35, 37, 77, 97, 117, 125,
160, 164, 167, 168, 174,
177, 183, 193, 202, 258,
260, 279, 336, 338, 343,
388, 389, 417, 432, 459,
493, 498, 512, 517, 610
stereotype, 71, 72
Steve, 18
Steven Pressfield, 453, 605
stewardship, 162, 288, 429, 635, 640
stigma, 247, 253, 290, 300, 304,
309, 483, 558, 591, 593,
615, 620, 623, 625, 627,
630, 635, 637
stimulation, 511

stone, 42, 455
stop, 12, 153, 154, 248, 427, 503,
622
store, 424
story, 4, 5, 23, 29, 58, 72, 73, 93, 95,
117, 127, 223, 241, 242,
248, 272, 273, 313, 369,
387, 392, 412, 441–443,
453, 464, 465, 521,
524–526, 528, 534, 536,
604
storyteller, 534
storytelling, 51, 61, 62, 66–68, 99,
121, 179, 183, 188, 193,
202, 214, 298, 303, 304,
371, 372, 409, 412, 413,
415, 429, 446, 459, 460,
477, 487, 497, 527,
530–533, 536, 537,
541–544, 577, 578, 610,
656
strain, 29, 30, 74, 137, 147, 148
stranger, 175
strategy, 34, 44, 46, 55, 59, 64, 83,
87, 126, 138, 143, 181,
195, 498, 499, 509
stream, 63, 230, 272, 278
streaming, 2, 30, 51, 54, 59, 60,
62–65, 69, 76, 103, 131,
203, 204, 235–237, 263,
271, 314, 352, 363, 369,
436, 448, 449, 475, 478,
502, 581
street, 99, 163, 173, 306, 307, 407,
577
streetwear, 577
strength, 13, 28, 73, 94, 117, 118,
123, 137, 158, 168, 218,
238, 241, 243, 246,

248–250, 254, 297, 304,
315, 318, 327, 355, 356,
365, 366, 372, 373, 386,
418, 437, 450, 463, 465,
469, 470, 483, 535, 575,
576, 591, 593
stress, 74, 75, 122, 134, 238, 246,
247, 250, 251, 289, 552,
590, 592
structure, 82, 147, 400, 498, 499
struggle, 29, 90, 91, 133, 147, 246,
251, 373, 552, 590
student, 242, 365, 464
studio, 1, 6, 13, 27, 29, 36, 74, 80,
114, 143, 173, 180,
188–190, 348, 378, 380,
382, 441, 452, 459, 468,
474, 477, 493, 497–499,
515, 518–521
study, 19, 91, 528, 622
style, 4, 6–8, 13, 19, 31, 33, 36, 66,
69, 73, 79, 82–85, 88, 89,
92, 93, 97, 100, 119, 150,
152, 173, 182, 183, 185,
189, 192, 195, 211, 243,
258, 277, 323, 332,
340–342, 349, 351–354,
359, 363, 366, 370, 374,
375, 378, 380, 384, 392,
398, 399, 405, 422, 424,
426, 442, 452, 454, 464,
474–476, 483, 490, 499,
521, 529, 532, 534, 537,
538, 545, 553, 555, 557,
558, 560–563, 569, 577,
579, 584, 647, 650, 653,
657
sub, 6, 46, 47, 61, 84, 95, 112, 193,
206, 222, 257, 266, 272,

279, 323, 331, 332, 335,
338, 340, 342, 350, 351,
353, 359, 375, 378, 381,
392–394, 424, 477, 478,
548, 553–557, 560, 563,
564, 567, 645, 655, 659
subculture, 226, 450, 570, 585
subgenre, 193, 363, 365, 545, 550,
552
subsection, 2, 3, 8, 9, 12, 18, 19, 22,
24, 27, 34, 41, 45, 50, 53,
56, 58–60, 62, 66, 69, 71,
73, 75, 78, 82, 85, 93, 95,
98, 100, 106, 110, 112,
117, 118, 123, 125, 133,
138, 143, 145, 147, 148,
154, 163, 167, 175, 177,
179, 184, 187, 188, 193,
195, 197, 201, 208, 212,
214, 220, 233, 235, 239,
251, 254, 260, 265, 268,
279, 283, 286, 289, 291,
294, 296, 298, 303, 305,
312, 313, 316, 319, 320,
338, 340, 349, 352, 355,
363, 365, 368, 374, 376,
378, 384, 388, 391, 397,
399, 402, 408, 413, 422,
424, 428, 432, 439, 441,
443, 449, 454, 457, 462,
466, 467, 469, 470, 487,
490, 494, 497, 499, 503,
505, 509, 511, 514, 517,
531, 533, 540, 545, 550,
557, 563, 565, 569, 572,
576, 578, 590, 594, 597,
600, 610, 628, 631, 638,
643, 645, 646, 650, 655,
659

substance, 183
substitute, 593
success, 2, 7, 12–19, 23, 26, 29, 35,
36, 39, 41, 45, 46, 48,
58–60, 62, 64–66, 70–76,
78, 80, 83–94, 98, 103,
107, 112, 125, 130, 132,
133, 135, 141, 142, 145,
147–151, 174, 188, 190,
205, 218, 220, 222, 223,
226–229, 233, 235, 239,
242, 247, 249, 252, 254,
256, 257, 259–261, 268,
269, 271–274, 276, 282,
295, 314–316, 318, 323,
324, 340, 342, 343, 346,
350, 353, 354, 364,
368–370, 372, 374, 385,
386, 392, 394, 410, 413,
426, 436–438, 440–446,
448, 449, 451–455, 457,
458, 464, 471–473, 475,
476, 478, 480–482, 485,
499–501, 503, 505, 506,
550, 557, 561, 564–566,
570, 581–583, 614, 616,
630, 649–651
suggestion, 189
suicide, 621
suit, 114, 152, 231, 426, 466, 554,
644, 656
Sullivan King, 76, 108, 259, 359,
360, 474, 545
Sullivan King's, 259
sum, 185, 191, 258, 279, 283, 518
summary, 19, 62, 107, 127, 131,
148, 184, 194, 317, 324,
329, 414, 436, 447, 474,
561, 567, 602

superstar, 167
support, 2–7, 12–14, 16, 19, 33, 43,
44, 46, 48, 51, 62, 71, 73,
75, 78, 83, 91–94,
101–103, 105–107, 110,
119, 127, 129, 131,
133–137, 141–145, 148,
151, 153, 162, 169–172,
205, 206, 208, 215, 217,
218, 220–223, 226–236,
239, 241–254, 256, 257,
259–261, 263–267, 271,
273–278, 284, 287–291,
294, 295, 297, 298,
300–304, 308–311,
314–324, 326–329, 361,
370, 382, 414, 418, 425,
428, 438–440, 446–450,
456–458, 463–467,
470–475, 488, 498, 502,
503, 506, 507, 527, 544,
547, 554, 558, 571, 574,
580, 584–586, 588,
590–593, 598, 599, 601,
603–608, 610, 612–630,
632, 633, 635–640, 650,
654, 656, 659, 660
supporter, 650
surface, 5, 126, 128, 647
surfing, 152, 395
surge, 96, 159, 337, 552, 577
surprise, 25, 56, 121, 152, 172, 173,
198, 203, 240, 317, 338,
345, 403, 404, 407, 410,
412–414, 420, 424, 431,
464
survivor, 465
Susan, 365, 366
sustainability, 86, 100–102, 136,

162, 209, 210, 253, 285, 287, 296, 308, 428, 437, 458, 469, 482, 549, 587, 589, 590, 601, 611, 612, 615, 628, 634, 642, 650

switch, 125

symbol, 1, 28, 29, 49, 66, 118, 119, 123–130, 132, 137, 138, 171, 244, 296, 346, 405, 426, 480, 482, 483, 522, 529, 531, 535, 565, 568, 569, 571, 574–579, 585, 586, 599, 652, 653, 655

symbolism, 117, 535–537

symphony, 114, 139

sync, 22

synchronization, 120, 408, 541, 542

syndrome, 73, 74

synergy, 28, 180, 181, 184, 185, 187, 421, 460, 462, 474, 478, 506, 512, 532, 577

synth, 5, 211, 335, 344, 354, 368, 387, 393, 477, 561, 657

synthesis, 275, 347, 562

synthesizer, 354, 493, 647

system, 73, 91, 106, 127, 134, 141, 142, 221, 229, 231, 249, 250, 257, 275, 297, 400, 449, 475, 502, 503

t, 43, 69, 82, 89, 132, 153, 154, 159, 173, 255, 378, 379, 385, 395–397, 413, 417, 427, 457, 498, 501, 502, 519, 529, 622, 628

tabla, 164

table, 16, 35, 36, 81, 180, 184, 185, 187, 189, 191, 389, 440, 442, 467, 473, 505, 506, 535

tactic, 55

take, 2, 13, 14, 16, 23, 29, 34–36, 69, 88, 90, 96, 100, 101, 103, 104, 125, 130, 138, 139, 153, 157, 161, 167, 168, 186, 191, 194, 196, 199, 202, 206, 210, 218, 220, 224, 258, 260, 278, 284, 287–289, 292, 295, 296, 298–303, 305, 308, 319, 320, 336, 341, 351, 358, 361, 362, 367, 371, 376, 382, 387, 389, 392, 397, 399, 416, 420, 425, 429, 437, 445, 446, 448, 454, 455, 457, 460, 469, 473, 478–480, 482, 487, 492, 498, 502, 510, 512, 514, 521, 530, 533, 547, 549, 554, 558, 566, 588–590, 596, 606, 608, 610–612, 614, 616, 618, 621, 622, 624, 630, 632–634, 637, 647, 650, 651, 658–660

taking, 9, 15, 26, 30, 34, 35, 55, 62, 74, 82, 90, 103, 131, 133, 134, 139, 141, 143, 145, 158, 159, 161, 181, 186, 189, 224, 246, 247, 255, 267, 277, 288, 372, 379, 389, 397, 408, 412, 455, 468, 493, 496, 498, 509, 510, 518, 520, 528, 615

talent, 1–7, 12, 14, 16, 18, 19, 22, 23, 30, 33, 41, 43, 46, 48, 55, 58–60, 69, 71, 73, 74, 76–78, 81, 83, 98, 106,

129, 141, 142, 174, 188,
191, 204, 212, 213, 230,
231, 237, 241, 252, 256,
258, 262–264, 266–268,
272–278, 284, 294, 295,
297, 305, 309, 317, 318,
321, 342, 343, 366, 369,
375, 394, 425, 431,
436–439, 447, 450, 457,
460, 466, 471–473, 476,
479–481, 488, 496, 500,
502, 503, 506, 544, 547,
565, 566, 585, 602, 617,
622, 627, 651, 657
talk, 456, 495, 570, 576, 591
tap, 11, 25, 28, 34–36, 47, 59, 60,
64, 79, 103, 108, 168, 191,
192, 195, 198, 219, 250,
258, 291, 292, 294, 339,
345, 431, 432, 441, 475,
505, 506, 509, 523, 582,
596, 647
tapestry, 156, 178, 309, 325, 328,
431, 525, 658
Tarek, 1, 2, 27, 28, 90–92, 125, 126
Tarek Adams, 1, 27, 90, 91, 125,
517, 523, 524
Tarek Adams', 27, 28
target, 30, 45, 46, 55–60, 63
task, 29, 30, 119, 124, 135, 509
taste, 8, 26, 411
team, 56–58, 60, 70, 78, 92, 117,
120, 122, 128, 134, 135,
138, 139, 141, 219, 223,
226, 260–262, 314, 322,
328, 400, 401, 408, 421,
520, 534–536, 542
teamwork, 595
tech, 210, 640

technique, 34, 84, 374, 375, 491,
513, 514
techno, 112, 164, 645
technology, 33, 53, 56, 58, 67, 80, 81,
110, 121, 122, 128, 129,
131, 152, 170, 181, 194,
198, 202, 208–211, 214,
215, 225, 226, 235–237,
254, 271, 285, 316, 318,
339, 346–349, 352, 367,
382, 402, 406–409, 414,
428, 430, 435, 436, 447,
490, 491, 493, 494, 502,
503, 513–517, 527, 542,
551, 552, 581, 583, 584,
618, 632, 634, 639, 640,
642, 644, 656
tempo, 336, 337, 350, 408
tempos, 113, 182–184, 204, 336,
337, 350–352, 381, 385,
478, 549, 573, 644
temptation, 452
tenet, 455
tension, 10, 85, 337, 354, 491, 538,
550, 561
term, 80, 88, 217, 276, 442, 583,
622, 655
terrain, 26, 158
territory, 558
test, 182, 194
testament, 4, 14, 69, 72, 76–78, 81,
85, 95, 97, 99, 106, 123,
128–130, 141, 143, 159,
163, 174, 187, 205, 218,
223, 224, 228, 233, 235,
245, 246, 248, 271, 279,
298, 300, 310, 311, 313,
315, 326–329, 336, 337,
342, 349, 352, 353, 356,

360, 364, 366, 370, 375,
378, 381, 382, 387, 407,
408, 417, 420, 426, 437,
438, 443, 449, 458, 465,
472, 474, 477, 480, 481,
486, 497, 501, 518, 521,
524, 525, 530, 544, 554,
555, 557, 571, 576, 581,
584, 585, 593, 599, 634,
651, 654, 661
testing, 57, 410
texture, 11, 347, 349, 368, 513, 515
thank, 242
the Middle East, 156, 164
theater, 567, 610
theatricality, 212
theme, 374, 378, 386, 388, 399, 510
theorizing, 523
theory, 3, 10, 12, 14, 15, 275, 337
therapy, 92, 248, 366, 465, 551, 593,
621
theremin, 645
thing, 78, 122, 389, 424, 553
think, 6, 17, 23, 97, 100, 111, 114,
150, 176, 285, 289, 293,
307, 338, 343, 350, 364,
454, 459, 462, 467, 473,
478, 479, 481, 486, 487,
510, 513, 547, 549,
564–566, 594, 596, 600,
631, 632, 649
thinking, 11, 35, 67, 74, 178, 196,
211, 214, 306, 307, 428,
513
thirst, 24, 167, 357
thought, 78, 99, 101, 179, 181, 192,
219, 305, 307, 347, 361,
369, 371, 416, 480, 519,
526, 530, 542, 549, 588,

606, 607, 611, 618
thread, 326, 468
threat, 621, 626
thrill, 154, 157, 159, 167, 440, 519
thrilling, 154, 157–159, 213, 398,
399, 402, 420
thrive, 48, 78, 92, 94, 107, 135, 215,
265, 268, 276, 277, 316,
319, 467, 481, 488, 501,
574, 583, 599
ticket, 60, 475
tier, 77, 324
timbre, 368
time, 11, 13, 14, 16, 23, 29, 34, 35,
42–44, 54, 58, 59, 62, 64,
65, 74, 86, 92, 93, 102,
110–112, 121, 131, 133,
134, 141, 143, 145, 147,
153, 162, 163, 169, 180,
182, 190, 194, 202, 203,
225, 235, 236, 242,
247–249, 251, 255, 262,
316, 320, 322, 331, 338,
339, 348, 349, 363, 365,
370, 378, 379, 389, 400,
403, 404, 406, 407, 411,
412, 415, 432, 436, 442,
448, 452, 459, 463, 465,
468, 469, 493, 509, 510,
513, 515, 520, 525, 529,
536, 543, 604, 621, 622,
626, 628, 643
timelessness, 370
timeline, 536, 627
timing, 336, 337, 400
tip, 419
title, 385
today, 22, 31, 41, 45, 59, 60, 63, 88,
103, 168, 194, 196, 235,

260, 316, 382, 441, 502,
531, 570, 581, 587, 590
togetherness, 129, 283, 314, 417,
438
Tokyo, 153, 163, 167
toll, 74, 75, 90, 92, 445, 446, 465
Toma Hargreaves, 277
Tomorrowland, 57, 556
tone, 96, 195, 368, 370, 371, 374,
528, 598
tool, 2, 37, 40, 59, 67, 100, 107, 111,
136, 239, 246, 250, 266,
288, 291, 305, 308, 337,
371, 412, 426, 436, 443,
452, 513, 517, 527, 590,
611, 613, 620, 626, 632,
643, 649, 658
top, 65, 75–77, 98, 271, 324, 352,
353, 434
topic, 297, 601, 624
topper, 353
topping, 36, 49, 75, 76, 90, 92, 99,
134, 172, 192, 267,
352–354, 391, 426, 437,
445, 448
touch, 143, 153, 204, 246, 333, 348,
352, 354, 372, 373, 414,
421, 466, 495, 516, 522,
538, 654
tour, 16, 47, 54, 133, 153, 154, 162,
324, 407, 425, 519–521
touring, 60–62, 69–71, 74, 75, 143,
147, 153, 209, 444, 633,
635
tourism, 161, 162, 203
toy, 245, 301
track, 22, 25, 32, 36, 42, 48, 49, 51,
64, 70, 75, 76, 82, 87,
98–100, 108, 120, 121,

131, 155, 156, 158, 163,
173, 174, 176, 180–183,
187, 189, 191–193, 199,
206, 252, 257, 259, 261,
274, 279, 283, 299, 304,
331–333, 336–338,
353–359, 361–363, 365,
366, 368–375, 383, 385,
387, 397–399, 401, 413,
420–422, 435, 441, 450,
452, 459, 460, 463–465,
467, 474, 475, 485, 486,
491–493, 498, 512, 520,
521, 526, 528, 534, 541,
549, 554, 560–562, 593,
606, 645
tracklist, 392
traction, 2, 31, 48, 65, 192, 273, 279,
354, 475
trademark, 33, 118, 253, 295, 341,
360, 426, 553, 575
tradition, 155
trailblazer, 15, 25, 97, 342, 343, 370,
426, 427, 477, 480, 485,
487, 564, 602, 645
training, 4, 158, 159, 551, 599, 639
trait, 53
trajectory, 12, 27, 227, 268, 271,
320, 380, 391, 449, 485
trampoline, 158
trance, 112, 250, 422, 477
tranquility, 160, 336, 372
transcendence, 27
transformation, 62, 118, 250, 251,
308, 361, 464, 517, 528,
530, 600, 655
transition, 31, 336, 405, 465, 562
transparency, 64, 143, 169, 194, 247,
248, 586, 609, 622

transportation, 633, 640
trap, 24, 76, 84, 97, 187, 188, 204,
    211, 238, 257, 331–333,
    335, 338, 340, 344, 350,
    353, 359, 361, 363, 366,
    369, 381, 383, 392, 393,
    420, 432, 462, 478, 480,
    481, 485, 487, 490, 492,
    495, 545, 547, 548, 550,
    553, 556, 557, 560, 561,
    565, 575, 578, 584, 597,
    644, 645, 647, 649
trash, 620
travel, 29, 74, 75, 163–165, 210,
    389, 633
Travis Scott, 429, 492
treasure, 380
treatment, 247, 290, 297, 361, 593
tree, 288, 482, 589, 621
trend, 118, 122, 336, 344, 370,
    567–569
trendsetter, 77, 477
trick, 493
trip, 162–165
triumph, 563, 611
trove, 380
trust, 16, 53, 89, 180, 184, 189–191,
    250, 255, 292, 452, 453,
    473, 622
trusting, 51
truth, 132
tuition, 627
tune, 79, 236, 348, 516
Tupac Shakur, 428
turmoil, 373
turn, 230, 327, 366, 409, 592
turning, 190, 307, 358, 532
tutorial, 275, 277
Twin Shadow, 385

twist, 42, 97, 180, 348
Twyla Tharp, 435
typography, 526

uncertainty, 168, 611
underground, 18, 22, 164, 284,
    340–342, 351, 370, 381,
    405, 481, 584, 585
understanding, 3, 4, 6, 10, 12, 37,
    48, 57, 58, 60, 65, 79, 82,
    112, 115, 125, 128, 131,
    134, 142, 147, 148,
    155–157, 165, 170, 171,
    180, 188, 247, 248,
    253–256, 275, 283, 290,
    291, 299, 300, 304, 306,
    307, 310, 314, 319, 322,
    325–327, 337, 371, 380,
    381, 411, 413, 415, 441,
    453, 469, 472, 477, 539,
    544, 591, 607–610, 612,
    614, 616, 619, 629, 637,
    650, 655, 658
uniqueness, 7, 29, 72, 84, 249, 294,
    295, 325, 437, 452–454,
    521, 578, 579, 586, 650
unison, 413, 530
unity, 23, 27, 29, 49, 61, 67, 72, 76,
    84, 99, 104, 107, 110, 113,
    118, 123, 125, 127–130,
    132, 137, 138, 140, 141,
    145, 152, 153, 155, 156,
    167, 170–172, 178, 188,
    218, 220–223, 228,
    231–237, 239, 241, 245,
    249, 251, 253, 254, 257,
    262, 264, 265, 267, 268,
    278, 283–286, 291, 298,
    302, 304, 310–319,

322–324, 326, 328, 342,
346, 361, 367, 370, 373,
383, 386, 387, 394, 396,
398, 399, 401, 406, 411,
413–418, 426, 431, 433,
438, 440, 445, 447–449,
461, 462, 466, 471–473,
480, 482, 483, 487, 488,
518, 524, 531, 533, 539,
546, 549, 554, 558,
569–572, 575, 576, 581,
586, 589, 599–602, 607,
611, 614, 616, 618, 619,
621, 629, 636, 641, 644,
651, 654–656, 658, 660
universality, 175
universe, 119, 405, 515, 532
unpredictability, 160, 368, 403, 406
unrest, 183, 305
up, 3–6, 8, 13, 15, 22, 23, 29, 35, 44,
47, 49, 59, 80, 94, 97–100,
105, 111, 123, 124, 133,
138–141, 152, 155, 157,
158, 161, 172, 174, 175,
179, 181, 183, 188, 191,
192, 195, 199, 204, 211,
213, 222, 224, 230, 231,
240, 250, 253, 262–264,
266, 272, 273, 278, 283,
285, 288, 290, 295, 299,
301, 304, 310, 311, 318,
321, 337, 347, 351, 361,
362, 368, 383, 386,
394–396, 398–400, 407,
413, 417, 420–422, 425,
428, 430, 432, 439, 441,
443, 458, 459, 462, 466,
467, 473, 475, 478, 481,
485, 488, 493, 496, 498,

501–503, 509, 519, 523,
547, 551, 555, 561, 564,
565, 577, 582, 589, 620,
628, 634, 643, 649, 657
upbringing, 3, 8
uplift, 107, 227, 230, 241, 250, 277,
284, 313, 314, 317, 322,
326, 418, 438, 441, 443,
447, 456, 466, 470, 474,
547, 558, 598, 611, 620,
656
urgency, 8, 101, 102, 289, 333, 336,
362, 387, 587, 589
use, 2, 7, 10, 23, 41, 50, 59, 64, 69,
80, 83, 95, 103, 107, 110,
118, 121, 130, 136, 137,
159, 168, 176, 179, 187,
202, 205, 206, 208,
210–212, 215, 225, 232,
239, 284, 293, 298, 305,
307, 337, 343, 347, 348,
354, 362, 366, 367, 369,
373, 374, 398, 406,
408–410, 417, 425, 427,
434–436, 441, 447, 462,
463, 466, 479, 487, 488,
490–492, 494, 495, 502,
516, 522, 526–528,
536–538, 540, 542–544,
550, 553, 554, 556, 559,
560, 567, 568, 602, 607,
614, 619, 620, 624, 626,
628, 631, 649, 651, 656,
658
user, 52, 65, 196, 516

validation, 77, 78, 105, 446
value, 2, 14, 43, 53, 82, 94, 101, 114,
147, 152, 162, 190, 197,

223, 273, 343, 379, 448,
455, 456, 458, 520, 568,
655
van, 19, 58
variation, 368
variety, 3, 5, 35, 37, 82, 107, 119,
126, 145, 368, 388, 431,
434, 436, 491, 492, 618
vastness, 160, 167
vault, 379
vehicle, 118, 127, 156, 158, 299,
371, 372, 445, 507
ventilation, 128
venture, 160, 173, 199, 201, 336,
432, 445
venue, 22, 141, 152, 153, 202, 311,
397, 399, 400, 407, 413,
414, 418
versatility, 22, 49, 57, 76, 99, 108,
109, 113, 173, 175, 177,
178, 182, 187, 193, 238,
332, 333, 336, 337, 347,
351, 353, 359, 378–381,
385, 407, 420, 422, 424,
474, 477, 485, 486, 507,
550, 556, 561, 644, 648,
656
verse, 362
version, 40, 125, 524
vessel, 137, 523
viability, 80, 85, 499, 500
vibe, 415, 417, 434, 495, 534
vibrancy, 276
vice, 364
video, 52, 65, 68, 69, 96, 99, 203,
303, 304, 396, 409, 410,
530–532, 564, 621, 622,
630
view, 82, 93, 159, 486, 557

viewer, 538, 539
viewing, 81, 82, 528
vigilance, 137
vigor, 510
violin, 4
violinist, 4
virality, 51
visibility, 55, 77, 99, 218, 227, 230,
266, 268, 272–274, 278,
298, 370, 391, 450, 475,
581
vision, 7, 31–33, 36, 73, 78, 79, 81,
83, 85–89, 92, 94, 96, 97,
120, 134, 142, 175, 178,
180, 185–187, 189, 190,
192, 203, 207, 214–216,
221, 243, 271, 297, 337,
349, 370, 379–382, 389,
427, 428, 433, 435, 436,
440, 444–446, 448,
451–453, 459, 460, 462,
464, 468, 473, 475, 482,
488, 493–497, 499–502,
516, 517, 519, 525, 526,
530, 534, 536, 542, 544,
546–548, 553, 565, 566,
568, 572, 573, 614,
641–644, 649, 650, 653,
660
visionary, 343, 418, 436, 458
visit, 154–156, 164, 173
visual, 23, 28, 33, 47, 51, 54, 56, 57,
59, 61–69, 80, 96, 104,
105, 113, 114, 118–120,
122, 126–129, 138–141,
152, 153, 163, 196, 202,
208, 210, 211, 213, 293,
298, 303–307, 311, 321,
348, 382, 398–400, 402,

404–406, 408–411,
415–417, 424, 429, 433,
434, 442, 453, 487, 515,
517, 521, 522, 524–544,
551, 567–569, 572,
576–579, 581, 582, 586,
610, 633, 646, 656
visualization, 592
vitality, 528
vocal, 4, 10, 21, 36, 107, 181, 214,
294–296, 300, 303, 304,
353, 354, 359, 373, 374,
382, 385, 506, 521,
560–562, 564, 576, 585,
597, 600, 608, 612, 618,
623, 625, 650, 658, 660
vocalist, 36, 108, 474, 494, 506
voice, 4, 11–13, 83, 85, 86, 88, 185,
243, 265, 266, 300, 307,
315, 325, 326, 328, 361,
381, 441, 453, 454, 472,
499, 503, 513, 540, 588,
611, 618, 621
volume, 52, 491
volunteer, 102, 245, 302, 303, 607,
609, 626
volunteering, 44, 232, 301, 604, 605
vulnerability, 28, 111, 126, 127, 159,
255, 292, 294, 456, 547,
591

waist, 465
wake, 169, 304, 362
walk, 34
war, 306
warmth, 457, 515
waste, 101, 161, 162, 288, 296, 428,
587, 588, 633, 638, 640
water, 158

wave, 97, 114, 212, 364, 375, 397,
426, 486, 487, 550, 552,
558, 560, 562, 563, 565,
567, 577, 607, 649, 652,
658
way, 9, 12, 19, 21, 27, 29, 41, 42, 50,
55, 63, 65, 66, 72, 73, 78,
85, 94, 96, 103, 112, 114,
121–123, 125, 126, 132,
133, 137, 143, 151, 160,
162, 164, 167, 168,
171–173, 186, 188,
210–212, 216, 222, 237,
240, 249, 256, 259, 262,
264–266, 271, 272, 283,
285, 286, 304, 307, 338,
342, 345, 348, 363, 364,
366, 369, 372, 379, 380,
383, 389, 392, 399,
401–403, 409, 412, 417,
420, 436, 440, 443, 448,
452, 462, 466, 474, 475,
477, 478, 481, 495, 498,
503, 507, 509, 510, 517,
519, 521, 531, 536, 543,
551, 555, 556, 561, 563,
566, 568, 570, 586, 590,
598, 647, 651–654, 656,
658, 660
wealth, 16, 492, 510
wearer, 567
web, 358
website, 133, 261, 263, 303, 492,
592, 596
weekend, 162, 225
weight, 90
welfare, 361
well, 3, 11, 17, 36, 37, 41, 42, 46, 49,
56, 61, 63, 69, 74–76,

90–93, 100, 108, 123,
132–134, 136, 141, 145,
146, 148, 157, 160, 181,
187, 190, 214, 225, 226,
244, 246–248, 250, 252,
253, 274, 289–291, 297,
300, 302, 304, 306, 308,
328, 333, 348, 369, 375,
378, 383, 388, 396, 397,
399, 402, 410, 413, 418,
445, 465, 468, 469, 482,
485, 499, 526, 536, 570,
576, 587, 590–594, 607,
608, 612–615, 617, 620,
623–625, 627, 628,
635–638, 657, 660
wellness, 75, 158, 159, 304, 305,
576, 626, 638
wellspring, 512
whale, 621, 622
whaling, 621
whirlwind, 91, 141, 148, 459, 479
whiteboard, 520
whole, 6, 28, 110, 112, 122, 172,
188, 192, 204, 222, 223,
242, 250, 264, 267, 283,
285, 290, 293, 323, 342,
447, 462, 463, 466, 471,
472, 527, 550, 555, 557,
563, 564, 570–572, 576,
578, 605, 625, 651, 659
wild, 67, 77, 153, 158, 161, 354,
372, 374, 387, 388, 395,
397, 429, 528, 538, 577,
578
wilderness, 67, 160–162, 167, 244,
355, 375, 409, 528, 538
wildfire, 395, 522
wildlife, 95, 96, 101, 136, 162, 300,

301, 355, 409, 429, 512,
535, 576, 587, 617, 623,
629, 632
wildness, 137, 529, 576
willingness, 13, 22, 25, 26, 33,
35–37, 48, 67, 75, 79, 82,
83, 98, 99, 108, 114, 157,
160, 164, 168, 174, 178,
181, 183, 186, 189–191,
193, 199, 282, 285, 292,
333, 336, 338, 343, 350,
351, 368, 381, 382, 389,
392, 422, 445, 453, 455,
462, 463, 473, 474,
477–479, 482, 487, 494,
497, 511, 512, 530, 558,
564, 565, 573, 584, 647,
648, 651, 656
win, 77, 622
wind, 159
window, 452
wing, 2, 15, 16
wisdom, 91, 117, 148, 190, 337,
439, 440, 501, 557
witness, 29, 40, 143, 236, 310, 322,
459, 494, 518, 522
Wolfgang Amadeus Mozart, 19
wonder, 121, 124, 372, 406, 512,
538
wonderment, 118
word, 54, 55, 61, 62, 102, 104, 179,
218, 220, 221, 227, 228,
230, 241, 252, 261, 278,
311, 323, 362, 398, 399
wordplay, 371
work, 2, 11, 16, 31, 34, 36–38,
40–43, 46–49, 55, 56, 67,
69, 74, 76, 77, 82, 83, 98,
102, 111, 114, 122, 133,

134, 136, 139, 173–175,
180, 181, 183, 187,
189–191, 205, 237, 245,
253, 257, 261, 263, 264,
266, 267, 273–276, 278,
284, 285, 289, 290, 293,
296, 305, 306, 309, 311,
320, 322, 351, 356, 362,
364, 368, 410, 440, 444,
445, 453, 456, 457, 462,
468, 472, 474, 481, 495,
496, 498, 501, 506, 518,
522, 526, 534, 536, 544,
547, 557, 560, 565, 585,
595, 606, 607, 609, 611,
625, 628, 636, 644, 651,
655, 657
workflow, 180, 346, 498
working, 35, 46, 70, 81, 87, 99, 102,
103, 132, 163, 175, 184,
185, 187, 191, 194, 198,
205, 207, 219, 251, 257,
258, 277, 279, 298–300,
302, 303, 321, 339, 341,
358, 367, 393, 424, 435,
443, 445, 458–460, 467,
473, 475, 483, 497, 500,
502, 505, 506, 509, 512,
535, 556, 572, 582, 588,
613, 617, 630, 633, 645
workload, 134, 135
workout, 158, 552
workshop, 275, 302, 605
world, 1, 3, 5, 6, 10, 11, 14, 15, 21,
27, 29, 32, 33, 48, 49, 57,
61, 64, 66, 68–71, 73, 77,
78, 86, 89, 90, 96, 100,
101, 103, 104, 106, 108,
110, 112, 117–120, 122,

123, 129, 130, 132, 135,
137–139, 141, 143, 144,
152–162, 164, 167–173,
175, 177–179, 181, 186,
187, 194, 202–206, 208,
213–216, 218–220, 222,
224, 225, 230–233, 236,
238, 239, 241, 242, 244,
246, 249, 252–254, 260,
262, 264, 268, 284–286,
288, 289, 294, 296, 298,
300, 302, 303, 306,
308–311, 317–319, 321,
326, 327, 332, 333, 336,
337, 342, 343, 349, 352,
356, 357, 361, 362, 364,
369, 371, 372, 378, 383,
385, 386, 388, 389, 391,
393, 395, 401, 406, 417,
422, 424, 427, 429, 431,
433, 437, 438, 441, 443,
445–449, 452, 454, 457,
458, 466, 471, 473, 475,
476, 480–483, 485, 486,
489, 491, 496, 498, 499,
503, 511, 512, 517–520,
522, 525, 526, 528,
530–540, 544, 546, 549,
557, 559, 567, 570, 572,
575–578, 580, 581, 586,
587, 590, 594–596,
599–601, 604, 606–610,
612–614, 616–621,
623–625, 628, 629, 631,
638, 640, 641, 644,
649–651, 654, 655, 657,
659, 660
worth, 47, 108, 119, 136, 188, 301,
337, 353, 382, 468, 516,

539, 621
worthiness, 73, 74
writing, 162, 301
Wu-Tang Clan, 9

year, 224, 225, 242, 243
yield, 44
youth, 299, 633, 634, 639
Yung Pinch, 108
Yung Pinch's, 108

Zeds Dead, 6, 350, 421, 560
Zeds Dead's, 383, 385, 421, 560
zeitgeist, 570, 580, 581, 651–653,
        657
zest, 157, 159
zone, 35, 90, 157, 160, 164, 167,
        168, 174, 177, 183, 191,
        210, 258, 338, 432, 435,
        445, 455, 456, 474, 494,
        510, 512, 551

Milton Keynes UK
Ingram Content Group UK Ltd.
UKHW021501301024
450479UK00011B/275

9 781779 693624